W9-CHU-354

A QUICK GUIDE TO KEY TOPICS
BY PARAGRAPH NUMBER

THE
GREGG
REFERENCE
MANUAL

THE GREGG REFERENCE MANUAL

SIXTH EDITION

William A. Sabin
Publisher, Business Books
Professional and Reference Division
McGraw-Hill Book Company

GLENCOE

Macmillan/McGraw-Hill

GREGG DIVISION / McGRAW-HILL BOOK COMPANY

Lake Forest, Illinois
Columbus, Ohio
Mission Hills, California
Peoria, Illinois

Sponsoring Editors / **Roberta Moore, Marion B. Castellucci**
Editing Supervisor / **Elizabeth Huffman**
Design and Art Supervisor / Interior Design / **Caryl Valerie Spinka**
Production Supervisor / **S. Steven Canaris**

Cover Designer / **Richard Adelson**

Library of Congress Cataloging in Publication Data

Sabin, William A.
    The Gregg reference manual.

    Includes index.
    1. English language—Business English—Handbooks,
manuals, etc.   2. English language—Grammar—Handbooks,
manuals, etc.   3. English language—Transcription—
Handbooks, manuals, etc.   4. Typewriting—Handbooks,
manuals, etc.   5. Authorship—Handbooks, manuals, etc.
I. Title.
PE1479.B87S23   1985   653'.427   84-25061
ISBN 0-07-054399-2
ISBN 0-07-054403-4 (pbk.)
ISBN 0-07-054400-X (spiral)

THE GREGG REFERENCE MANUAL, Sixth Edition

Imprint 1990
Copyright © 1989 by the Glencoe Division of Macmillan/McGraw-
Hill Publishing Company

6 7 8 9 10 11 12 13 14 15 — 00 99 98 97 96 95 94 93 92 91 90

ISBN 0-07-054399-2

PREFACE

The Gregg Reference Manual is intended for anyone who writes, transcribes, or types. It presents the basic rules that apply in virtually every piece of writing, as well as the fine points that occur infrequently but cause trouble when they do. It offers an abundance of examples and illustrations so that you can quickly find a model on which to pattern a solution to a specific problem. It also provides the rationale underlying specific rules so that you can manipulate the principles of style with intelligence and taste.

Features of the New Edition. The sixth edition of *The Gregg Reference Manual* has been considerably expanded. (Even the size of the pages themselves is larger than in the preceding edition.) The objective of this expansion has been to ensure that users will find definitive answers to all the problems they are likely to encounter in written communications. In deciding what kinds of additional coverage to provide, I was guided by the following considerations:

1. Today's users typically inhabit two worlds—the business world and the academic—either as full-time students who are working to cover their expenses or as full-time workers who are going to school to upgrade their skills or train for a new career or enrich their personal lives. Therefore, in whatever written work they do, they are bound to encounter different requirements, different formats, different styles. The sixth edition of *The Gregg Reference Manual* acknowledges this situation by providing guidelines for academic reports, notes, and bibliographies wherever they tend to differ from what is done in business writing. (See, for example, ¶¶1413–1414, 1508*b*, 1534*c*.)

2. Word processors and computers have been integrated into today's offices and schools, bringing with them a new and often strange vocabulary. This new edition acknowledges the situation by providing a 14-page glossary of word processing terms (see Section 19) and by interpreting many of the common abbreviations and acronyms used in referring to computers (see ¶544). Word processors and computers have also brought with them some special style problems. For example, if the equipment you are using cannot produce superior figures easily, how do you handle footnote references? (See ¶¶1502*h*, 1523*b*.) How do you handle an attention line in conjunction with an inside address if you plan to use the inside address to generate the envelope address? (See ¶1345.) And what style should you use for names and addresses in a computerized mailing list if you plan to use that list for inside addresses in form letters? (See ¶¶1389*b*, 1390*b*.)

3. In the fourth and fifth editions of *The Gregg Reference Manual*, the primary attention was given to expanding the materials on grammar, style, usage, and business letters (Sections 1–11 and 13) to ensure full coverage of these key areas. (As a result, in the sixth edition these sections have chiefly required only an updating: the examples have been refreshed with contemporary terms and references, and the coverage has been refined and expanded wherever appropriate.) The real focus in the sixth edition has been on expanding the sections on techniques and procedures (Sections 12–16) and bringing them up to the same level of detailed coverage that the discussion of business letters has enjoyed. As a result, the following topics have been added or greatly enlarged:

   - **Machine Transcription.** New guidelines suggest how to process recorded dictation quickly and productively. (See ¶¶1225–1228.)

   - **Editing and Proofreading Techniques.** Detailed procedures and numerous examples show you what to look for and how to handle the problems you find. (See ¶¶1229–1232.)

- **Alphabetic Filing Rules.** Because of the frequency with which questions come up about alphabetic sequence, 25 rules of alphabetic filing are presented, following the style used in all Gregg training materials. In addition, because of the increasing use of the filing rules developed by ARMA (the Association of Records Managers and Administrators), the Gregg filing rules have been annotated to show where ARMA goes into greater detail or suggests another way of handling a specific situation. Thus users can have access to either the Gregg or the ARMA style as the occasion demands. (See ¶¶1237–1261.)

- **Memos and Social-Business Correspondence.** Coverage of these topics has been expanded from 2 pages in the last edition to 6 pages this time to provide detailed answers (with illustrations) to the many practical questions that arise in these areas. (See ¶¶1392–1395.)

- **Reports and Manuscripts.** Coverage has been expanded from 7 pages in the last edition to 26 pages this time to deal with all aspects of informal and formal reports, both business and academic. In addition, all-new material has been provided on preparing manuscripts for articles and for books. (See Section 14.)

- **Notes.** This topic, limited chiefly to footnotes in the last edition, has grown from 11 to 21 pages to cover the increasingly popular use of endnotes and textnotes, to present an academic as well as a business style, and to provide some additional patterns for constructing bibliographic reference notes. (See Section 15.)

- **Tables.** Coverage has been expanded from 6½ to 26 pages to deal with any situation likely to arise. (See Section 16.)

Available for use with *The Gregg Reference Manual* is a set of worksheets designed to build three critical editing skills. First, the *Worksheets for the Gregg Reference Manual* will familiarize you with the wide range of potential problems you are likely to encounter in any material that you write, transcribe, or type. Second, these worksheets will direct you to the key rules in each section of *The Gregg Reference Manual* so that later on, when you encounter similar problems in your own work, you will know where to look. Third, they will sharpen your ability to apply the rules correctly under many different circumstances. As in the previous edition, this set of worksheets begins with a 4-page survey of your editing skills at the outset and then, after you have completed a series of twenty-seven 2-page worksheets, you will encounter a parallel 4-page "final" survey so that you can see how much your skills have increased. As a new feature of this edition, four 2-page surveys have been interspersed at appropriate points within the sequence of worksheets to help you integrate the things you have been learning and to let you measure your progress.

An Overview of the Organization and the Coverage. This edition of *The Gregg Reference Manual* consists of 19 sections, organized as follows:

Part One (Sections 1–11) deals with grammar, usage, and the chief aspects of style—punctuation, capitalization, numbers, abbreviations, plurals and possessives, spelling, compound words, and word division.

Part Two (Sections 12–16) deals with techniques and procedures for producing all kinds of written communications—letters, memos, reports, manuscripts, and tables.

Part Three (Sections 17–19) provides three appendixes for fast reference: a listing of model forms of address, a glossary of grammatical terms, and a glossary of word processing terms.

The following comments provide a brief orientation to the manual and highlight features of each section that warrant special attention.

Section 1 (¶¶101–199) deals with the major marks of punctuation—the period, the question mark, the exclamation point, the comma, the semicolon, and the colon. As you scan Section 1, note ¶¶122–125, which provide an overview of commas used to *set off* and commas used to *separate*. Also note paragraphs such as ¶132, which provides an extensive list of model sentences.

Section 2 (¶¶201–299) deals with the other marks of punctuation—the dash, parentheses, quotation marks, the underscore, the apostrophe, ellipsis marks, the asterisk, the diagonal, and brackets. Of special note are the rules in ¶299, which indicate the spacing to be used before and after every mark of punctuation.

Section 3 (¶¶301–363) covers capitalization. Give particular attention to the introduction and the basic rules (¶¶301–310). If you grasp the function of capitalization, you will be better equipped to resolve capitalization problems on your own.

Section 4 (¶¶401–470) discusses number style. For an explanation of the concepts that underlie all aspects of number style, read the introduction and the basic rules (¶¶401–406). If you understand the functional difference between expressing numbers in figures and in words, you can solve many specific style questions without the manual.

Section 5 (¶¶501–549) deals with abbreviations. Study the basic rules (¶¶501–514), and note the new lists of symbols and computer abbreviations and acronyms given in ¶¶543–544.

Section 6 (¶¶601–651) covers plurals and possessives. Because of the frequency with which these forms occur, give special attention to the basic rules that govern their formation and usage.

Section 7 (¶¶701–720) provides a number of spelling guides that could help you reduce your dependence on the dictionary. For fast assistance on words that look alike or sound alike, consult ¶719, which provides a 13-page guide to these troublesome combinations. To avoid spelling errors, consult ¶720 for a 3-page list of words commonly misspelled.

Section 8 (¶¶801–839) deals with all kinds of compound words and provides guides as to whether they should be spaced, solid, or hyphenated. Note in particular ¶¶813–829 on compound adjectives.

Section 9 (¶¶901–922) discusses word division in terms of a few absolute rules and a number of preferred practices.

Section 10 (¶¶1001–1085) offers a compact survey of all the rules of grammar that you are likely to need. The coverage ranges from subject-verb agreement to proper sentence structure, with special attention given to problems involving verbs, pronouns, adjectives, adverbs, prepositions, and the use of negatives.

Section 11 (¶1101) deals with problems of usage. About 150 individual entries are provided for a wide range of troublesome words and phrases and are listed alphabetically for fast reference. Check the listing at the beginning of Section 11 to see at a glance which problems have been treated here.

Section 12 (¶¶1201–1261) provides a valuable set of guidelines on how to take dictation, how to transcribe (both from shorthand notes and from recorded dictation), how to edit and proofread, how to submit work for approval, and how to handle the problems of alphabetic filing (using either the standard Gregg rules or those developed by ARMA).

Section 13 (¶¶1301–1397) provides extensive styling notes on every element in a letter—from the letterhead to the postscript. It treats the preparation of envelopes and gives up-to-date instructions on how to handle addresses (including the nine-digit ZIP Code and the all-capital style for addresses). It also provides detailed guidelines on memos, social-business correspondence, and postcards.

Section 14 (¶¶1401–1436) provides detailed coverage on all aspects of reports (formal and informal, business and academic). It also provides valuable guidance on preparing manuscripts for articles and books.

Section 15 (¶¶1501–1536) describes the proper way to handle notes—footnotes, endnotes, and textnotes—and bibliographies in business and academic reports. See, in particular, ¶¶1508–1522, which offer a series of easy-to-follow patterns (expanded for this edition) on how to construct bibliographic reference notes.

Section 16 (¶¶1601–1644) covers virtually every problem you might encounter in executing tables effectively. Give special attention to ¶1601, which provides a comprehensive set of models for quick reference.

Section 17 (¶¶1701–1711) lists the correct forms of address and the appropriate salutations for individuals, couples, organizations, professionals, education officials, government officials and diplomats, members of the armed services, and religious dignitaries.

Section 18 (¶1801) provides an alphabetized glossary of grammatical terms. A listing at the beginning of the section will reveal at a glance which terms have been covered.

Section 19 (¶1901) presents an alphabetized glossary of word processing terms. A quick reading of this section can provide a useful introduction to (or brushup on) the new vocabulary of the office.

The foregoing notes are only a preliminary guide to what you can discover more effectively firsthand. As you make your own survey of the text, you will want to single out the key rules that deserve further study; these are the rules that deal with everyday situations, the rules you need to have at your command. You will also want to develop a passing acquaintance with the fine points of style. It is sufficient simply to know that such rules exist; then, when you need them, you will know where to find them. Finally, you will want to take note of special word lists, sentence patterns, and illustrations that could be useful to you later on. If you find out now what aids the manual provides, you will know what kind of help you can count on in the future. And what is more important, you will be able to find what you are looking for faster.

A Final Note. A book of this type cannot be put together without the help and support of many people. To my colleagues in McGraw-Hill, to my many good friends in business and office education, and to the countless teachers, students, and professionals who all helped me—by their questions and suggestions—to see what was missing and how things could be made better, I want to express a deep feeling of gratitude.

And to my family—to my mother, who gave me my first sense of what language could accomplish (and a good deal more); to Margaret, John, Kate, Chris, and Jim, to whom much has been entrusted and from whom I have gained much in return; and ultimately to my wife Marie, who has made the journey worth the struggle—my thanks and my love.

William A. Sabin

HOW TO LOOK THINGS UP

Suppose you were writing to someone in another department:

> I understand you are doing a confidential study of the Bronson matter. May I please get an advance copy of your report [At this point you hesitate. Should this sentence end with a period or a question mark?]

This is the kind of problem that continually comes up in any type of written communication. How do you find a fast answer to such questions? In this manual there are several ways to proceed.

Using the Index. The surest approach, perhaps, is to check the detailed index at the back of the manual (11 pages, with over 1700 entries). For example, any of the following entries will lead you to the right punctuation for the problem sentence above:

Periods, **101–109**	Question marks, **110–118**	Request, punctuation of, **103**
. . .	. . .	
at end of requests, **103**	at end of requests, **103, 113**	

In each entry the boldface number refers to the proper rule, ¶103. (If you look up ¶103, you will find that a question mark is the right punctuation for the sentence in question.)

In almost all of the index entries, references are made to specific rule numbers so that you can find what you are looking for fast. In a few cases, where a page reference will provide a more precise location (for example, when a rule runs on for several pages), a page number is given in lightface type. Suppose you were confronted with this problem:

> If you compare the performance records of Catano, Harris, and Williams, you won't find much difference (*between/among*) them.

The index will show the following entries:

> *among–between,* 223   **OR**   *between–among,* 223

The rule on page 223 indicates that *between* is correct in this situation.

Using a Fast-Skim Approach. Many users of reference manuals have little patience with detailed indexes. They would rather open the book and skim through the pages until they find what they are looking for. If you are the kind of person who prefers this approach, you will find the brief topical index on the inside front cover especially helpful, since it indicates the key paragraphs for each major topic. Moreover, at the start of each section you will find a detailed list of all the topics covered in that section. This list will help you quickly focus on the rule or rules that pertain to your problem. Extensive cross-references have also been provided throughout the manual so that you can quickly locate related rules that could prove helpful. Suppose the following problem came up:

> The only point still at issue is whether or not new *Federal* [or is it *federal?*] legislation is required.

The index on the inside front cover indicates that ¶¶301–363 deal with the topic of capitalization. A fast skim of the outline preceding ¶301 will turn up the entry *Names of Government Bodies* (¶¶325–330). If you turn to that set of rules, you will find in ¶328 that *federal* is the proper form.

Playing the Numbers. There is still a third way to find the answer to a specific problem—and this is an approach that will grow in appeal as you become familiar with the organization and the content of the manual. From a fast inspection of the rule numbers, you will observe that they all carry a section number as a prefix. Thus Section 3 (on capitalization) has a "300" series of rules—from 301 to 363; Section 4 (on number style) has a "400" series—from 401 to 470; and so on. Once you become familiar with the section numbers and the section titles, you can find your way around fairly quickly, without reference to either index, by using the section number tabs. For example, you are about to write the following sentence:

> *43* percent of the questionnaires have now been returned. [Or should it be "*Forty-three* percent of the questionnaires . . ."?]

If you know that matters of number style are treated in Section 4, you can quickly turn to the pages tabbed "4," where a fast skim of the outline of topics at the start of the section will lead you to the answer in ¶421. (*Forty-three percent* is the right answer in this instance.)

A familiarity with the section numbers and section titles can also save you time when you are using the index. If your index entry lists several different paragraph numbers, you can often anticipate what the paragraphs will deal with. For example, if you want to know whether to write *5 lb* or *5 lbs* on a purchase order, you might encounter the following entry in the index:

> Weights, **429–430, 535–538, 621**

If you know that Section 6 deals with plurals, you will try ¶621 first.

Looking Up Specific Words. Many of the problems that arise deal with specific words. For this reason the index provides as many entries for such words as space will permit. For example, in the following sentence, should *therefore* be set off by commas or not?

> It is(,) *therefore*(,) essential that operations be curtailed.

A check of the index will show the following entry:

> *therefore*, **122, 138–142**

A reading of the rules in ¶141 will indicate that no commas should be used in this sentence. If you ask the same question about another specific word and do not find it listed as a separate entry in the index, your best approach will be to check the index under "Comma" and investigate the most promising references or make a direct scan of the comma rules in Section 1 until you find the answer you are looking for.

If you are having difficulty with words that look alike and sound alike—*gibe* and *jibe* or *affect* and *effect*—turn directly to ¶719. For other troublesome words and phrases, consult ¶1101.

CONTENTS

Part 1□Grammar, Usage, and Style

The six brief essays that follow deal with a number of points of style that cause great difficulty for those who work with words. Out of this consideration of specific problems, these essays attempt to draw broader conclusions about the nature of style and the art of tailoring one's use of language to fit the needs of each situation.

Mastering Number Style:
One (or 1?) Approach

A number of years ago, while making a presentation on the subject of style, I asked the audience to select the preferable form in each of the following pairs of examples:

$87,525	**OR**	eighty-seven thousand five hundred and twenty-five dollars
$700 billion	**OR**	$700,000,000,000
4:30 p.m., January 19	**OR**	half after four o'clock, on the nineteenth of January

No one could see any use for the forms in the second column. Those in the first column were far easier to read and simpler to write and were clearly to be preferred in business writing. However, after some discussion, we tended to agree that Tiffany's had had the right idea in a recent ad, where beneath a picture of an elegant diamond necklace was the legend "Eighty-seven thousand five hundred and twenty-five dollars." Somehow, we felt, if they were going to charge that elegant a price, the least they could do was spell it out. Moreover, we tended to agree that a liberal in fiscal matters might readily dismiss the federal debt as "only $700 billion," whereas a fiscal conservative who wanted to emphasize the enormity of the amount might well have written "The federal debt now stands at $700,000,000,000" and thereby have forced upon us a sense of the magnitude of the amount by making us calculate it for ourselves. Finally, we agreed that we would much rather be married at "half after four o'clock, on the nineteenth of January" than at "4:30 p.m., January 19."*

These, admittedly, are extreme examples of occasions on which an unusual number style could be justified, but they tend to throw light on the more custom-

---

*One dissenter indicated that she simply wanted to get married and didn't much care how the invitations read.

ary style for expressing numbers and on the notion of style in general. At the very least, these examples suggest that style should not be thought of as a rigid set of rules but rather as a set of principles for adjusting one's means of expression to fit a particular set of circumstances. We express our style in clothes through a varied wardrobe that suits the needs not only of everyday situations but of formal and informal occasions as well. It is the impoverished person who meets every situation with the same set of clothes. By the same token, it is an impoverished writer who meets all situations with a rigid set of rules. The writer of the Tiffany ad, who chose words instead of figures to express an amount of money, in this instance had some true sense of how to vary style for best effect.

Manipulating principles of style for specific effect ought not to be a random, hit-or-miss exercise but should proceed from some coherent notion about style itself. In the case of numbers, an intelligent control of number style proceeds from an awareness of the difference in effect that results from using figures or words to express numbers.

Figures are big (like capital letters); when used in a sentence, they stand out clearly from the surrounding tissue of words. As a result, they are easier to grasp on first reading, and they are easier to locate for subsequent reference. Thus whenever quick comprehension and fast reference are important (and this is true of most business writing), figures are to be preferred to words.

But the very characteristics of figures that make them preferable to words can be disadvantageous in certain circumstances. Figures stand out so sharply against a background of words that they achieve a special prominence and obtain a special emphasis. Not all numbers warrant that kind of emphasis, however, and in such cases words are preferable to figures. Keep in mind, too, that figures have the conciseness and the informality of an abbreviation. Thus the more formal the occasion, the more likely one is to spell numbers out (as in the wedding announcement cited on page xiii).

Given these basic differences between using figures and using words, it is quite clear why figures are preferred in ordinary business letters. These are typically straightforward communications that pass between business firms and their suppliers or their customers, containing frequent references to price quotations, quantities, shipping dates, credit terms, and the like. Frequently, these numbers represent data that has to be extracted from the letter and processed in some way: they may have to be checked against other numbers or included in some computation or simply transferred to another document. The advantage of figures to words in these ordinary cases is so clear that the point does not need to be argued.

But there is another kind of business writing in which the writer is not typically dealing with the workaday transactions of the business. It may be a special promotion campaign with an air of elegance and formality; it may be a carefully constructed letter with special stylistic objectives in mind; or it may be a special report which involves community relations and will have a wider distribution than the normal technical business report. This kind of writing tends to occur more often at the executive level, and it tends to occur in the more creative departments of a business (such as sales promotion, advertising, public relations, and customer relations). In this kind of writing, numbers don't occur very frequently; when they do, they are usually expressed in words.

As a response to the different needs posed by these two kinds of writing, there are two basic number styles in use today. Both use figures and words but in different proportions. The *figure style* uses figures for all numbers above 10, whether exact or approximate; the *word style* spells out all numbers up through 100 and all numbers above 100 that can be expressed in one or two words (such as *twenty-five hundred*).

As a practical matter, your immediate job may require you to use only the figure style. However, your next job may call for the use of the word style. And if you are working and going to school at the same time (as more and more people are these days), you will probably find yourself following one style for office work and another for your academic work. Under these circumstances, if you grasp the basic difference between using words and figures to express numbers, you will be better able to decide how to proceed in specific situations without having to consult a style manual each time. In any case, keep the following ideas in mind:

1. There are no absolute rights and wrongs in number style—only varying sets of stylistic conventions that people follow in one set of circumstances or another. There are, however, effective differences in using words or figures, and you should take these differences into account.

2. Before deciding on which number style to follow for a given piece of writing, first determine the basic objective of the material. If the material is intended to communicate information as simply and as briefly as possible, use the *figure style*. If the material is of a formal nature or aspires to a certain level of literary elegance, use the *word style*.

3. Having decided on a basic style, *be consistent in context*. When related numbers occur together in the same context and according to the rules some should go in figures and some should go in words, treat these related numbers all the same way.

4. Treat an approximate number exactly the same way you would treat an exact number. If you would write *50 orders,* then you should also write *about 50 orders.* (If the figure 50 looks too emphatic to you when used in an approximation, the chances are that you should be using the word style—and not just for approximate numbers but throughout.)

5. In areas where the style could go either way (for example, *the 4th of June* vs. *the fourth of June* or *9 o'clock* vs. *nine o'clock*), decide in accordance with your basic style. Thus if you are following the figure style, you will automatically choose *the 4th of June* and *9 o'clock.*

6. In expressions involving ages, periods of time, and measurements, use figures whenever these numbers have technical significance or serve as measurements or deserve special emphasis; otherwise, use words. (For example, *you receive these benefits at 65, the note will be due in 3 months, the parcel weighs over 2 pounds;* but *my father will be sixty-five next week, that happened three months ago, I hope to lose another two pounds this week.*)

7. Use figures in dates (*June 6*) and in expressions of money (*$6*), except for reasons of formality or special effect (as in the wedding announcement or the Tiffany ad). Also use figures in percentages, proportions, ratios, scores, and with abbreviations and symbols.

8. Use words for numbers at the beginning of a sentence, for most ordinals (*the third time, the twentieth anniversary*), and for fractions standing alone (*one-third of our sales*).

All manuals of style (including this one) include many more than eight rules. They give exceptions and fine points beyond those just summarized. Yet for all practical purposes these eight rules—and the philosophy that underlies them—will cover almost every common situation. Just remember that the conventions of number style were meant to be applied, not as an absolute set of dogmas, but as a flexible set of principles that help to fit the form to the occasion. When manipulated with intelligence and taste, these principles of style can enhance and support your broader purposes in writing.

A Fresh Look at Capitalization

The rules on capitalization give most people fits. First of all, there are a seemingly endless number of rules to master; second, the authorities themselves don't agree on the rules; and third, the actual practices of writers often diverge from the contradictory recommendations of the authorities.

A frequent solution is to pretend that disagreements on capitalization style don't exist; instead, people are given one fixed set of rules to be applied under all circumstances. Yet all too many people never do remember the full complement of rules, and those they do remember they apply mechanically without comprehension. As a result, they never get to see that capitalization can be a powerful instrument of style if it is shrewdly and knowingly used.

To understand the basic function of capitalization, you should know that capitalization gives importance, emphasis, and distinction to everything it touches. That's why we capitalize the first word of every sentence—to signify emphatically that a new sentence has begun. That's why we capitalize proper nouns like *Marianne* and *California* and *April*—to indicate distinctively that these are the official names of particular people, places, or things. Moreover, when we take a word that normally occurs as a common noun and capitalize it, we are loading into that word the special significance that a proper noun possesses. The *fourth of July*, for example, is just another day in the year; when it signifies a national holiday, it becomes the *Fourth of July*. In exactly the same way, the *white house* that stands at 1600 Pennsylvania Avenue becomes the *White House* when we think of it, not as one of many white houses, but as the residence of the *President*, who is himself something special compared to the *president* of a business firm.

This process of giving special significance to a common noun and transforming it into a proper noun explains why we capitalize names coined from common nouns—for example, the *Windy City*, the *First Lady*, the *Sunflower State*, the *Stars and Stripes*, *Mother's Day*, and the *Industrial Revolution*. And it also explains why manufacturers who coin trade names try to register them whenever possible. As long as they can get legal protection for these names, they are entitled to capitalize them. The owners of such trade names as *Coke, Kleenex, Photostat, Dacron, Levi's,* and *Xerox* are likely to take legal action against anyone who uses such words generically. They are determined to protect their rights zealously because they don't want to lose the distinctive forcefulness that a capitalized noun possesses. In this respect they demonstrate an understanding of the function of capitalization that few of us can compete with.

Once it becomes clear that capitalization is a process of loading special significance into words, it's easier to understand why capitalization practices vary so widely. Individual writers will assign importance to words from their own vantage points. The closer they are to the term in question, the more inclined they will be to capitalize it. Thus it is quite possible that what is important to me (and therefore worthy of capitalization) may not be important to you and thus will not be capitalized.

One could cite any number of examples to prove the point. A retail merchant will take out full-page ads so that he can exclaim in print about his *Year-End Clearance Sale*. The rest of us can respect his right to capitalize the phrase, but we are under no obligation to share his enthusiasm for what is, after all, just another *year-end clearance sale*. In legal agreements, as another example, it's customary to load such terms as *buyer* and *seller* with the significance of proper nouns and thus write, "The *Buyer* agrees to pay the *Seller* . . ."; in all other contexts, however, this kind of emphasis would not be warranted.

When it is understood that it is appropriate to capitalize a given term in some contexts but not necessarily in all contexts, a lot of the agony about capitalization disappears. Instead of trying to decide whether *Federal Government* or *federal government* is correct, you should recognize that both forms are valid and that depending on the context and the importance you want to attach to the term, one form will be more appropriate to your purpose than another. If you are a federal employee, you are very likely to write *Federal Government* under all circumstances, out of respect for the organization that employs you. If you are not a government employee, you are more likely to write *federal government* under ordinary circumstances. If, however, you are writing to someone connected with the federal government or you are writing a report or document in which the federal government is strongly personified, you will probably choose the capitalized form.

By the same token, you need not agonize over the proper way to treat terms like *advertising department, finance committee,* and *board of directors.* These are well-established generic terms as well as the official names of actual units within an organization. Thus you are likely to capitalize these terms if they refer to units within your own organization, because you would be expected to assign a good deal of importance to such things. But you wouldn't have to capitalize these terms when referring to someone else's organization unless for reasons of courtesy or flattery you wanted to indicate that you considered that organization important. (For example, "I would like to apply for a job as copywriter in your Advertising Department.") Moreover, when writing to outsiders, you should keep in mind whether or not they would assign the same importance you do to units within your organization. In an interoffice memo you would no doubt write, "David Walsh has been appointed to the Board of Directors"; in a news release intended for a general audience, you would more likely write, "David Walsh has been appointed to the board of directors of the Wilmington Corporation."

This switch in form from one context to another will appear surprising only to those who assume that one form is intrinsically right and the other intrinsically wrong. Actually, there are many more familiar instances of this kind of flexibility. We normally write the names of seasons in lowercase (for example, *spring*), but when the season is meant to be personified, we switch to uppercase (*Spring*). The words *earth, sun,* and *moon* are normally expressed in lowercase, but when these terms are used in the same context with proper names like *Mars* and *Venus,* they also become capitalized. Or we write that we are taking courses in *history* and *art,* but once these terms become part of the official names of courses, we write *History 101* and *Art 5C.*

Once you come to view capitalization as a flexible instrument of style, you should be able to cope more easily with ambiguous or conflicting rules. For example, one of the most troublesome rules concerns whether or not to capitalize titles when they follow a person's name or are used in place of the name. According to many authorities, only the titles of "high-ranking" officials and dignitaries should be capitalized when they follow or replace a person's name. But how high is high? Where does one draw the line? You can easily become confused at this point because the authorities as well as individual writers have drawn the line at various places. So it helps to understand that the answer to how high is high will depend on where you stand in relation to the person named. At the international level, a lot of us would be willing to bestow initial caps on the *Queen of England,* the *Premier of France,* the *Pope,* the *Secretary General of the United Nations,* and people of similar eminence. At the national level in this country, many of us would agree on honoring with caps the *President,* the *Vice President,* Cabinet members (such as the *Attorney General* and the *Secretary of Defense*), the heads of federal agencies and bureaus (such as the *Director* or the *Commissioner*), but probably not lower-ranking officials in the national government. (However, if you worked in Washington and were closer to those lower-ranking people, you might very well draw the line so as to include at least some of them.) At the state level, we would probably all agree to honor the *Governor* and even the *Lieutenant Governor,* but most of us would probably refer to the *attorney general* of the state in lowercase (unless, of course, we worked for the state government or had dealings with the official in question, in which case we would write the *Attorney General*). Because most people who write style manuals are removed from the local levels of government, they rarely sanction the use of caps for the titles of local officials; but anyone who works for the local government or on the local newspaper or has direct dealings with these officials will assign to the titles of these officials a good deal more importance than the writers of style manuals typically do. Indeed, if I were writing to the mayor of my town or to someone in the mayor's office, I would refer to the *Mayor.* But if I discuss this official with you in writing, I would refer to the *mayor;* in this context it would be bestowing excessive importance on this person to capitalize the title.

What about titles of high-ranking officials in your own organization? They certainly are important to you, even if not to the outside world. Such titles are usually capped in formal minutes of a meeting or in formal documents (such as a company charter or a set of bylaws). In ordinary written communications, however, these titles are not—as a matter of taste—usually capitalized, for capitalization would confer an excessive importance on a person who is neither a public official nor a prominent dignitary. But those who insist on paying this gesture of respect and honor to their top executives have the right to do it if they want to. (And in some companies this gesture is demanded.)

In the final analysis, the important thing is for you to establish an appropriate capitalization style for a given context—and having established that style, to follow it consistently within that context, even though you might well adopt a different style in another context. Though others may disagree with your specific applications of the rules, no one can fault you if you have brought both sense and sensitivity to your use of capitalization.

The Comma Trauma

Consider the poor comma, a plodding workhorse in the fields of prose—exceedingly useful but like most workhorses overworked. Because it can do so many things, a number of writers dispense the comma to cure their ailing prose the way doctors dispense aspirin: according to this prescription, you take two at frequent intervals and hope the problem will go away. Other writers, having written, stand back to admire their handiwork as if it were a well-risen cake—and for the final touch they sprinkle commas down upon it like so much confectioner's sugar. And one writer I know, when pushed to desperation, will type several rows of commas at the bottom of her letter and urge you to insert them in the copy above wherever you think it appropriate.

It's too bad that commas induce a trauma in so many writers. Despite the seemingly endless set of rules that describe their varied powers, commas have only two basic functions: they either separate or set off. Separating requires only one comma; setting off requires two.

The separating functions of the comma, for the most part, are easy to spot and not hard to master. A separating comma is used:

1. To separate the two main clauses in a compound sentence when they are joined by *and, but, or,* or *nor.*

2. To separate three or more items in a series (*Tom, Dick, and Harry*)—unless all the items are joined by *and* or *or* (*Bob and Carol and Ted and Alice*).

3. To signify the omission of *and* between adjectives of equal rank (as in *a quiet, unassuming personality*).

4. To separate the digits of numbers into groups of thousands (*30,000*).

Writers get into trouble here mostly as a result of separating things that should not be separated—for example, a subject and a verb (*Bob, Carol, Ted, and Alice* decided to see a movie) or an adjective and a noun (*a quiet, unassuming personality*). Yet this is not where the comma trauma begins to set in.

The real crunch comes with the commas that set off. These are the commas that are intended to set off words, phrases, or clauses that (1) provide additional but nonessential information or (2) are out of their normal order in the sentence or (3) manage, in one way or another, to disrupt the flow of the sentence from subject to verb to object or complement. What makes it so difficult for people to use these commas correctly is that they have a hard time analyzing the difference between an expression used as an essential element in one context and as a nonessential element in another.

Consider the following example. I would venture that most people have been taught to punctuate the sentence exactly as it is given here:

It is, therefore, essential that we audit all accounts at once.

To be specific, they have probably been taught that *therefore* is always nonessential when it occurs within a sentence and that it must therefore always be set off by commas. What they probably have not been taught is that commas that set off (unlike commas that separate) usually signal the way a sentence should sound when spoken aloud. For example, if I were to read the foregoing sentence aloud the way it has been punctuated, I would pause slightly at the sign of the first comma and then let my voice drop on the word *therefore:*

IT IS, therefore, ESSENTIAL . . .

Now if this is the reading that is desired, then the use of commas around *therefore* is quite correct. Yet I would venture that most people would read the sentence this way:

It is THEREFORE essential . . .

letting the voice rise on *therefore* to give it the special emphasis it demands. If this is the desired reading, then commas would be altogether wrong in this sentence, for they would induce a "nonessential" inflection in the voice where none is wanted.

If people have been mechanically inserting commas around *therefore* and similar words where commas do not belong, it is because they have not been encouraged to listen to the way the sentences are supposed to sound. Certainly once you become aware of the differences in inflection and phrasing that accompany essential and nonessential elements, it becomes a lot easier for you to distinguish between them and to insert or omit commas accordingly. Given this kind of approach, sentences like the following pair are simple to cope with.

Please let me know *if I have remembered everything correctly.*

He said he would meet us at three, *if I remember correctly.*

Although it would be possible, by means of a structural analysis, to establish why the first *if* clause is essential and why the second is not, you would do well to be guided by the inflection implied in each sentence. In the first instance, the voice arcs as it bridges the gap between *Please let me know* and *if I have remembered everything correctly.* In the second instance, the inflectional arc embraces only the first part of the sentence, *He said he would meet us at three;* then comes a slight pause followed by the *if* clause, which is uttered in a much lower register, almost as if it were an afterthought.

As you gain confidence in your ability to detect the inflectional patterns characteristic of essential and nonessential expressions, you should have no difficulty in picking your way through a variety of constructions like these:

I must report, *nevertheless,* that his work is unsatisfactory.

I must *nevertheless* report that his work is unsatisfactory.

The location, *I must admit,* is quite attractive.

The location is one *I must admit* I find attractive.

There are, *of course,* other possible answers to the problem.

It is *of course* your prerogative to change your mind.

This awareness of inflectional patterns is especially helpful when it comes to coping with appositives, a frustrating area in which the use or omission of commas often seems illogical. When the appositive expression is truly nonessential, as in:

Ed Brown, *the president of Apex,* would like to meet you.

the customary pause and the characteristic drop in voice are there. And when the appositive expression is essential, as in phrases like *the year 1990* and *the term "recommend,"* you can hear the single inflectional arc that embraces each group of words in one closely knit unit. You can also hear the same continuous arc in the phrase *my wife Marie*. By all that is logical, the name *Marie* should be set off by commas because it is not needed to establish which of my wives I'm speaking about; unlike an Arabian sheik, I have only one wife. Yet according to today's standards, *my wife Marie* is considered good form. Although not essential to the meaning, the name *Marie* is treated as if it were essential because of what style manuals call "a very close relationship with the preceding words." Although it is difficult, if not impossible, to state in concrete terms what constitutes "a very close relationship," you can tell by the sound when it exists. There is a subtle but very real difference in the phrases *my sister Florence* and *my sister, Florence Stern*. Once the second name is added, there tends to be a slight pause after *sister* and the voice tends to drop while uttering the full name. Yet it is not safe to conclude that adding the second name accounts for the difference in the inflection, for when one speaks of *the composer John Cage* or *the author John Fowles*, one hears the same inflectional pattern as in *my wife Marie* or *the year 1990*. So in the case of appositives, it is wise to be wary of simple generalizations and to listen attentively in each case to the way the expression ought to sound.

In stressing, as I have, the significance of inflection and phrasing as a guide to the use of commas, I do not mean to suggest that one can punctuate by sound alone and can safely ignore structure and meaning. What I am suggesting is that in a number of cases, such as those I have cited, an awareness of the sound of sentences can help you grasp relationships that might otherwise be obscure.

There are many other problems involving the comma that should be discussed here, but someone else (Ogden Nash, perhaps) will have to take over . . .

And now if you'll excuse me comma
I must lie down and have my trauma . . . ,

The Plight of the Compound Adjective— Or, Where Have All the Hyphens Gone?

The hyphen, it grieves me to report, is in trouble. Indeed, unless concerted action is taken at once, the hyphen is likely to become as extinct as the apostrophe in *ladies aid*. The problem can be traced to two dangerous attitudes that are afoot these days. One is revolutionary in tone; its motto: "Compound adjectives, unite! You have nothing to lose but your hyphens." The other attitude reflects the view of the silent majority. These are the people who don't pretend to know how to cope with the "hyphen" mess; they just earnestly wish the whole problem would quickly disappear. It may now be too late to reverse the long-range trend. For the present, however, the hyphen exists—and anyone who expects to work with words at an acceptable level of proficiency needs to come to terms with the noble beast. Here, then, is a last-ditch effort to make sense out of an ever-changing and possibly fast-disappearing (but not-soon-to-be-forgotten) aspect of style.

As a general rule, the English language depends largely on word order to make the relationships between words clear. When word order alone is not sufficient to establish these relationships, we typically resort to punctuation. It is in this context that the hyphen has a service to offer. The function of the hyphen is to help the reader grasp clusters of words—or even parts of words—as a unit. When a word has to be divided at the end of a line, the hyphen signifies the connection between parts. Whenever two or more words function as a unit but cannot (for one reason or another) be written either as a solid word or as separate words, the hyphen clearly establishes the relationship between these words and prevents a lapse in comprehension.

If hyphens are typically required in compound adjectives, it is because there is something "abnormal" about the word order of such expressions. Other kinds of modifiers, by contrast, do not require hyphens. For example, if I write about "a *long, hard* winter," I am actually referring to a winter *that will be long and hard;* so I need a comma—not a hyphen—to establish the fact that *long* and *hard* modify *winter* independently. If I write about "a *long opening* paragraph," the word order makes it clear that *opening* modifies *paragraph* and that *long* modifies the two words together; so no punctuation is needed to establish the fact that I'm speaking about *"an opening paragraph that is long."*

However, if I write about "a *long-term* loan," an entirely different relationship is established between the elements in the modifier. I am not speaking of a *loan* that is *long* and *term*, nor am I referring to a *term loan* that is *long*. I am speaking about a loan "that is to run for a *long term* of years." The words *long-term* (unlike *long, hard* or *long opening*) have an internal relationship all their own; it is only as an integral unit that these two words can modify a noun. Thus a hyphen is inserted to establish this fact clearly.

For a better understanding of the internal relationship that exists between the elements in a compound adjective, one has to go back to its origins. A compound adjective is actually a compressed version of an adjective phrase or clause. For example, if I describe a product as carrying "a *money-back* guarantee," I am actually talking about "a guarantee *to give you your money back if you are not satisfied with the product.*" Or if I refer to "a *take-charge* kind of guy," I am really speaking of "the kind of guy *who always takes charge of any situation he finds himself in.*" One can easily see from these examples why compound adjectives are so popular, for these expressions are usually a good deal crisper and livelier than the phrases or clauses they represent. These examples give further evidence of why a hyphen is needed. In each case we have zeroed in on a couple of words, we have wrenched them out of context and out of their normal order in a descriptive phrase or clause, and we have inserted them before a noun as if they were an ordinary adjective—a role these two words were never originally designed to play. Deprived of all the other words that would clearly establish the relationship between them, these elements require a hyphen to hold them together.

The two factors of compression and dislocation are all the justification one needs to hyphenate a compound adjective. However, there are often additional clues to the need for a hyphen. In the process of becoming a compound adjective, the individual words frequently undergo a change in form: "a contract for *two years*" becomes "a *two-year* contract"; a blonde with *blue eyes*" becomes "a *blue-eyed* blonde." Sometimes the words are put in inverted order: "lands *owned* by the *government*" becomes "*government-owned* lands." Sometimes the elements undergo both a change in form *and* in word order: "an employee *who works hard*" becomes "a *hard-working* employee"; "bonds *exempt from taxation*" becomes "*tax-exempt* bonds." The change in form or the inversion in word order is an additional signal that you are in the presence of a compound adjective and ought to hyphenate it.

If the compound adjective is so simple to understand in theory, why is it so difficult to handle in practice? A good deal of the problem can be traced to that neat but now-discredited rule, "Hyphenate compound adjectives when they precede the noun but not when they follow the noun." It was indeed a very neat rule but not a very precise one. Let's take it apart and see why.

It is quite true that compound adjectives should be hyphenated when they occur *before* a noun—for the most part. There's the catch—"for the most part." The exceptions seem to occur in such a random, hit-and-miss, now-and-then, flip-a-coin, make-it-up-as-you-go-along fashion that one begins to lose respect for the rule. Yet there is a very definite pattern to the exceptions. Keep in mind that the hyphen serves to hold a cluster of words together as a unit. If, through some other means, these words make themselves clearly recognizable as a unit, the hyphen is superfluous and can be omitted. There are at least three such situations where a hyphen is unnecessary: when the compound modifier is a proper name, when it is a well-recognized foreign expression, and when it is a well-established compound noun serving as a compound adjective. Let's look at some samples.

If I speak of "a *Madison Avenue* agency," the capital *M* and *A* virtually guarantee that the expression will be quickly grasped as a unit. And if I talk about "a *bona fide* contract," the reader will recognize this Latin expression as a unit without the help of a hyphen. By the same token, terms like *social security, life insurance,* and *high school* are so well established as compound nouns that when they are used as adjectives, we immediately grasp such expressions as a unit, without the support of any punctuation.

If no hyphen is needed in "*social security* benefits," one may well ask why a hyphen is required in "*short-term* benefits." After all, words like *short term* and *long range* are adjective-noun combinations that closely resemble *social security, life insurance,* and *high school.* Why hyphenate some and not others? The reason is this: Words like *short term, long range,* and *high level* don't have any standing as compound nouns in their own right; they do not represent a concept or an institution (as terms like *social security* and *life insurance* do). Therefore, these words require a hyphen to hold them together when they occur before a noun.

Once you grasp the difference between *social security* and *short-term* as compound adjectives, you can use these two expressions as touchstones in deciding how to handle other adjective-noun combinations. With a principle like this in hand, you don't have to engage in profound analysis to resolve the "hyphen" problem. Consider a random list of examples such as these:

a *red letter* day	a *white collar* worker
a *civil service* test	a *real estate* agent
mass production techniques	*word processing* equipment
long distance calls	*high level* decisions

The expressions *civil service, mass production, real estate,* and *word processing* all resemble *social security,* since they stand for well-known concepts or institutions; therefore, as compound adjectives they can all be written without hyphens. However, *red-letter, long-distance, white-collar,* and *high-level* are much more like *short-term* and should have a hyphen.

So much for compound adjectives before the noun. When they occur *after* the noun, according to the traditional rule, they should not be hyphenated. Yet this traditional formulation is somewhat misleading. If we aren't supposed to hyphenate a "compound adjective" when it follows a noun, it's for the simple reason that the words in question no longer function as a compound adjective—they are playing a normal role in a normal order. It's one thing to use hyphens in the expression "an *up-to-date* report," for a prepositional phrase doesn't normally belong before a noun. However, if I said "This report is *up to date,*" there would be no more justification for hyphenating here than there would be if I said "This report is *in good shape.*" Both expressions—*in good shape* and *up to date*— are prepositional phrases playing a normal role in the predicate.

However, if the expression still exhibits an abnormal form or inverted word order in the predicate, it is still a compound adjective—and it must still be hyphenated. For example, whether I speak of "*tax-exempt* items" or say "these items are *tax-exempt,*" the hyphen must be inserted because regardless of where it appears—*before* or *after* the noun—the expression is a compressed version of the phrase "exempt from taxation."

There are at least four kinds of compound adjectives that must always be hyphenated *after* as well as *before* the noun (because of inverted word order or change of form). These compound adjectives consist of the following patterns:

noun + adjective (*duty-free*)
noun + participle (*interest-bearing*)
adjective + participle (*soft-spoken*)
adjective + noun + ed (*old-fashioned*)

Once you learn to recognize these four patterns, you can safely assume that any compound adjective that fits one of these patterns must always be hyphenated, no matter where it falls in a sentence.*

---

*There is only one worm in this rosy apple: some of the words that fit these patterns are now acceptably spelled as one word.

It does no good to pretend that compound adjectives are an easy thing to master. They aren't. And for that very reason writers and transcribers who have to cope with these expressions need more guidance than they get from a simple "hyphenate before but not after" kind of rule. In the final analysis, what becomes of the hyphen over the long run is of little consequence. What does matter is that we express ourselves with precision, verve, and grace. If the hyphen can help us toward that end, why not make use of it?

The Semicolon; and Other Myths

I n certain circles that I move in, the fastest way I know to start a quarrel is to attack the semicolon. If I knocked my friends' politics or sneered at their religious beliefs, they would simply smile. But attack their views on the semicolon and they reach for a bread knife. Why this particular mark of punctuation should excite such intense passion escapes me. The semicolon has always been a neurotic creature, continually undergoing an identity crisis. After all, it is half comma and half period, and from its name you would think it is half a colon. It is hardly any wonder, then, that a lot of people are half crazy trying to determine who the semicolon really is and what its mission in life is supposed to be.

In the course of this brief essay, I am going to explore three myths that have grown up over the years about the semicolon and about some other marks of punctuation.

Myth No. 1: If either clause in a compound sentence contains an internal comma, use a semicolon (not a comma) before the coordinating conjunction that connects the clauses. According to this line of reasoning, it is all right to use a comma in a compound sentence like this:

> The regional meeting in Salem has been canceled, but all other meetings will go on as scheduled.

However, if I use commas for a lesser purpose within either clause (for example, by inserting *Oregon* after *Salem* and setting it off with commas), then the comma before the conjunction must be upgraded to a semicolon.

> The regional meeting in Salem, Oregon, has been canceled; but all other meetings will go on as scheduled.

It is harsh, I concede, to dismiss this rule as a myth when it has been taught for years in various classes and various texts. But the unhappy fact is that outside those classes and those texts, almost no one punctuates that way anymore. The trouble with using a semicolon in such sentences is that it creates a break that is too strong for the occasion. It closes down the action of the sentence at a point where the writer would like it to keep on going. So contemporary writers see nothing wrong with using commas simultaneously to separate clauses and to perform lesser functions within the clauses—unless, of course, total confusion or misreading is likely to result. But in most cases it doesn't. In the following sentence, commas are used both *within* clauses and *between* clauses without any loss of clarity and also without any loss of verbal momentum.

> On March 16, 1989, I wrote to your credit manager, Mr. Lopez, but I have not yet heard from him.

This simultaneous use of commas within and between clauses may look offensive to anyone accustomed to the traditional rule. The fact remains that we have been using commas for both purposes in *complex* sentences all along, and it has never occasioned any comment.

> Although I wrote to your credit manager, Mr. Lopez, on March 16, 1989, I have not yet heard from him.

It should be clearly understood that the use of a semicolon before the conjunction in a compound sentence is not wrong. If you want a strong break at that point, the semicolon can and should be used. But you ought to know that the reason for using it is the special effect it creates—and not the presence of internal commas. For example:

> I have tried again and again to explain to George why the transaction had to be kept secret from him; but he won't believe me.

Myth No. 2: Always use a semicolon before an enumeration or an explanation introduced by *for example, namely,* or *that is.* In many cases this rule is quite true, but in other cases either a colon or a comma is better suited to the occasion. Let's look at some examples.

> There are several things you could do to save your business (?) namely, try to get a loan from the bank, find yourself a partner with good business judgment, or pray that your competitor goes out of business before you do.

If you put a semicolon before *namely*, you will close the action down just when the sentence is starting to get somewhere. Because the first part of the sentence creates an air of anticipation, because it implicitly promises to reveal several ways of saving the business, you need not a mark that closes the action down but one that supports the air of anticipation. Enter the colon.

The colon is one of the underrated stars in the firmament of punctuation. It would be more widely used, perhaps, if its sound effects were better understood. The colon is the mark of anticipation. It is a blare of trumpets before the grand entrance; it is the roll of drums before the dive off the 100-foot tower. It marks the end of the buildup and gets you ready for "the real thing." Thus:

> There are several things you can do to save your business: namely, try to get a loan . . .

Consider this example, however:

> Always express numbers in figures when they are accompanied by abbreviations; for example, *4 p.m., 8 ft.*

The first part of this sample sentence expresses a self-contained thought. If the sentence ended right there, the reader would not be left up in the air. The examples that follow are unexpected, unanticipated, added on almost as an afterthought. We're glad to have them, but they aren't anything we were counting on. The semicolon here is quite appropriate; it momentarily closes down the action of the sentence after the main point is expressed.

In other situations a comma may be the best mark to use before *namely, for example,* or *that is.* Consider this sentence as an example:

> Do not use quotation marks to enclose an *indirect quotation*, that is, a restatement of a person's exact words.

In this case, a semicolon would be inappropriate before *that is* because it would close off the action just as we were about to get a definition of a term within the main clause. Moreover, a colon would be inappropriate because it would imply that the sentence up to that point was a buildup for what follows—and that is not true in this case. Here all that is needed is a simple comma to preserve the close relationship between the term *indirect quotation* and the explanatory expression that follows it.

Myth No. 3: When a polite request is phrased as a question, end it with a period. This is another statement that does not, unfortunately, always hold true. In fact, once a period is used at the end of some requests, they no longer sound very polite. I once posted the following note in my home: "Will you please close the door." My children knew this was not really a polite request but a firm parental command. When they chose to ignore it, I amended the sign to read, "Will you please close the door!" (I was relying on the exclamation point to carry the full force of my exasperation.) That approach failed too, so I tried a new tack in diplomacy, amending the sign once again: "Will you please close the door?" My children now knew they had broken my spirit. They now sensed in the sign a pleading note, a petitioning tone, the begging of a favor. They also knew that now I was asking them a real yes-or-no question (or at least I was creating the illusion of asking). Then, in the paradoxical way that children have, once they knew they had the chance to say no, they began to answer my question with tacit affirmations, tugging the door after them on the way out or kicking it shut behind them on the way in.

My problems with my kids are, of course, my own, but learning how to express and punctuate polite requests tends to be a problem for all of us. Consider, for a moment, the wording of those three signs, alike in all respects except for the final mark of punctuation. The version that ends with a period is really a quiet but nonetheless firm demand. There is no element of a question in it at all. The voice rises in an arc and then flattens out at the end on a note of resolution. In the version that ends with an exclamation point, the voice rises in a higher arc and resounds with greater intensity and force of feeling, but it, too, comes down at the end—this time with something of a bang. In the final version, the one with the question mark, the voice starts on an upward curve and then trails off, still on an upward note. Three different readings of the same words, each with a different impact on the reader—all evoked by three different punctuation marks at the end.

Once you become sensitive to the effects produced by these marks of punctuation, handling polite requests becomes quite simple. All you have to do is say the sentence aloud and listen to the sound of your own voice. If you end the sentence with your voice on an upward note, you know that a question mark is the right punctuation to use. If your voice comes down at the end, you know that you need a period. (And if you really feel forceful about it, you probably want an exclamation point.)

If there is any potential danger in so simple a rule, it is this: we sometimes express our requests orally as flat assertions ("Will you please do this for me.") when, as a matter of good taste and good manners, we ought to be asking a question ("Will you please do this for me?").

Now it is true that in the normal course of events we all make demands on one another, and though we tack on a "Will you please" for the sake of politeness, these are still demands, not questions. As long as your reader is not likely to consider them presumptuous, it is appropriate to punctuate these demands with periods:

Will you please sign both copies of the contract and return the original to me.

May I suggest that you confirm the departure time for your flight before you leave for the airport.

Will you please give my best regards to your family.

As opposed to these routine demands, there is the kind of polite request that asks the reader for a special favor. Here, if you really want to be polite, you will punctuate your request as a question so as to give your reader the chance to say no.

May I please see you sometime next week?

May I please get an advance copy of the confidential report you are doing?

Will you please acknowledge all my correspondence for me while I'm away?

In these cases you are asking for things that the reader may be unable or unwilling to grant; therefore, you ought to pose these requests as questions. (If you try reading them as statements, you will observe how quickly they change into peremptory demands.) Suppose, however, that these requests were addressed to your subordinates. Under those conditions you would have the right to expect your reader to make the time to see you, to supply you with an advance copy of the confidential report, and to handle your mail for you; therefore, you would be justified in ending these sentences with periods. But even when you have this authority over your reader, you ought to consider the alternative of asking. The inspired public official who replaced the "Keep Off the Grass" signs with a simple "PLEASE?" understood people and how they like to be talked to. If a question mark will get faster results or establish a nicer tone, why not use it?

There are other myths that one could discuss, but these three are sufficient to permit me to make one central point. Mastery over the rules of punctuation depends to a considerable extent on cultivating a sensitivity to the way a sentence moves and the way it sounds.

Punctuating by ear has come to be frowned on—and with much justification—for it has come to mean punctuating solely by feeling, by instinct, by intuition, without much regard for (or knowledge of) the structure of the language and the function of punctuation. Yet the solution, it seems to me, is not to abandon the technique of punctuating by ear but to cultivate it, to develop in yourself a disciplined sense of the relationship between the sound and the structure and the mechanics of language. Many authorities on language, if pressed, have to concede that they often consider first whether a thing sounds right or looks right; only then do they utter a pronouncement as to why it is right. If they rely on their ears for this kind of assurance, then why shouldn't you provide yourself with the same skill?

Re Abbrevs.

Sensitive environmentalists will tell you that emissions from smokestacks and automobile exhaust pipes are not the only forms of pollution that are potentially deadly to human beings. All about us are forces of depersonalization that continually menace the human touches that have previously graced our lives. Most of us have become reconciled to being numerical entities on computer printouts. We have adjusted—many of us—to the loss of those elegant telephone exchanges (*PLaza 9, ASpinwall 7*).

But new forms of pollutants continually appear on the atmospheric scene. We are beginning to choke—some of us—on the fog of initials and abbreviations and "memorable" acronyms that are intended to identify worthwhile examples of human endeavor. One gem is *HURRAH* (*H*elp *U*s *R*each & *R*ehabilitate *A*merica's *H*andicapped), an instance where a dignified cause is demeaned by a fatuous label, a hollow cheer, an irrelevant salute. Perhaps in self-defense I ought to found a group called *HELP* (*H*elp *E*liminate *L*inguistic *P*ollution).

To put matters in perspective, it may help to think of abbreviations as belonging to the same class of objects as instant coffee, powdered eggs, and TV dinners. They don't take up much space and they're great when you're in a hurry, but they never have the taste of the real thing. Abbreviations are always appropriate in highly expedient documents (such as invoices, purchase orders, low-level interoffice memos, and routine correspondence), where the emphasis is on precise communication of data in the briefest possible space without concern for style or elegance of expression. But in other kinds of writing, where some attention is given to the *effect* to be made on the reader, a more formal style prevails—and under these circumstances only certain kinds of abbreviations are acceptable.

Some that are always acceptable, even in the most formal contexts, are those that precede or follow personal names (*Mr., Mrs., Jr., Sr., Ph.D., Esq.*), those that are part of an organization's legal name (*Inc., Ltd., Co.*), those used in expressions of time (*a.m., p.m., PST, EDT*), and a few miscellaneous expressions (such as *B.C.* and *A.D.*).

Those venerable Latin abbreviations *etc., i.e., e.g.,* and the like are usually acceptable, but in writing that aspires to a certain elegance or formality they ought to be replaced, not by the full Latin expressions, but rather by the English expressions *and so forth* (or *and the like*), *that is, for example,* or appropriate equivalents.

Organizations with long names are now commonly identified by their initials in all but the most formal writing—*IBM, AT&T, AFL-CIO, UNICEF, FBI, CBS.* Even the initials *U.S.* are now acceptable in all but the most formal writing when used in the names of federal agencies (such as the *U.S. Department of Labor*); however, using the initials by themselves (as in *throughout the U.S.*) is bad form.

Abbreviations of days of the week, of names of months, of geographic names, and of units of measure are appropriate only in business forms, in correspondence that is clearly expedient, and in tables where space is tight.

Although it may seem troublesome knowing *when* to abbreviate, it is often more troublesome knowing *how* to abbreviate. There are so many variations in style (involving the use of caps or small letters, the use or omission of periods, and the use or omission of internal space) that it is often difficult to find an authoritative source to follow. (*Webster's Ninth New Collegiate Dictionary,* for example, omits virtually all periods from its list of abbreviations, as if this were now the commonly accepted practice. Webster, of course, uses periods with many of the abbreviations that appear in the main text. See ¶503, note.) Here are a few safe guidelines:

1. An all-capital abbreviation made up of the initials of several words is normally written without periods and without internal space (for example, *RCA, UAW, BPOE, SEC, IQ*). The only major exceptions are geographic names (such as *U.S.A., U.S.S.R.*), academic degrees (such as *B.A., M.D.*), and a few odd expressions (such as *A.D., B.C.,* and *P.O.*).

2. A small-letter abbreviation that consists of the initials of several words is normally written *with* a period after each initial but *without* space after internal periods (for example, *a.m., e.g.*).

3. When an abbreviation can be styled in all caps (*COD, FOB*) or in small letters (*c.o.d., f.o.b.*), reserve the use of all caps for business forms and similar documents where the blatant look of the capitals will not matter.

4. When an abbreviation stands for several words and consists of more than initials, insert a period and a space after each element in the abbreviation (for example, *Lt. Col., op. cit.*). Academic degrees, however, are an exception: write them *with* the periods but *without* internal space (for example, *Ph.D., Ed.D., LL.B.*).

5. A person's initials are now usually written without periods and space (as in *JKF*) unless they are part of the full name (as in *J. F. Kennedy*).

So much, in brief, on abbreviations. Useful devices on many occasions, but—except for an *R.S.V.P.* delicately scripted in the lower left corner of a formal invitation—not very elegant.

THE
GREGG
REFERENCE
MANUAL

Punctuation: Major Marks

THE PERIOD

THE QUESTION MARK

THE EXCLAMATION POINT

THE COMMA

Punctuation marks are the mechanical means for making the meaning of a sentence easily understood. They indicate the proper relationships between words, phrases, and clauses when word order alone is not sufficient to make these relationships clear.

One important caution about punctuation. If you find it particularly hard to determine the appropriate punctuation for a sentence you have written, the chances are that the sentence is improperly constructed. To be on the safe side, recast your thought in a form you can handle with confidence. In any event, do not try to save a badly constructed sentence by means of punctuation.

Section 1 deals with the three marks of terminal punctuation (the period, the question mark, and the exclamation point) plus the three major marks of internal punctuation (the comma, the semicolon, and the colon). All other marks of punctuation are covered in Section 2.

THE PERIOD

AT THE END OF A STATEMENT OR COMMAND

101 Use a period to mark the end of a sentence that makes a statement or expresses a command.

> We are pleased to announce the promotion of Lynn Williams to executive vice president of Currier Inc.
>
> The board questions the need to acquire additional warehouse space.
>
> Make sure that Kate gets to the airport by 10 a.m.

102 Use a period to mark the end of an *elliptical* (condensed) expression that represents a complete statement or command. These elliptical expressions often occur as answers to questions or as transitional phrases.

> Yes.   No.   Of course.   Indeed.   By all means.
>
> Enough on that subject.   Now, to proceed to your next point.

NOTE: Do not confuse elliptical expressions with sentence fragments. An elliptical expression represents a complete sentence. A sentence fragment is a word, phrase, or clause that is incorrectly treated as a separate sentence when in fact it ought to be incorporated with adjacent words to make up a complete sentence.

> Great news! The shipment arrived yesterday. After we had waited for six weeks. (*Great news* is an elliptical expression; it represents a complete sentence, *I have great news*. *After we had waited for six weeks* is a sentence fragment, incorrectly treated as a sentence in its own right; this dependent clause should be linked with the main clause that precedes it.)
>
> **REVISED:** Great news! The shipment arrived yesterday, after we had waited for six weeks.

AT THE END OF A POLITE REQUEST OR COMMAND

103   **a.** Requests, suggestions, and commands are often phrased as questions out of politeness. Use a period to end this kind of sentence if you expect your reader to respond *by acting* rather than by giving you a yes-or-no answer.

> Will you please call us at once if we can be of further help.
>
> Would you please send all bills to my bank for payment while I'm out of the country.
>
> May I suggest that you put your request in writing and send it to Mr. Herzog for his approval.
>
> If you can't attend the meeting, could you please send someone else in your place.

b. If your reader might think your request presumptuous when presented as a statement, use a question mark instead. The question mark offers your reader a chance to say no to your request and helps to preserve the politeness of the situation.

> May I ask a favor of you? Could you spare fifteen minutes to tell my son about career opportunities in your company?

> Will you be able to have someone in your department help me on the Woonsocket project?

> Will you please handle the production reports for me while I'm away?

c. If you are not sure whether to use a question mark or a period, reword the sentence so that it is clearly a question or a statement; then punctuate accordingly. For example, the sentence directly above could be revised as follows:

> Would you be willing to handle the production reports for me while I'm away?

> I would appreciate your handling the production reports for me while I'm away.

AT THE END OF AN INDIRECT QUESTION

104 Use a period to mark the end of an indirect question. (See also ¶¶115–116.)

> Frank Wilcox has asked whether an exception can be made to our leave-of-absence policy.

> The only question she asked was when the report had to be on your desk.

> Why Janet Murray left the company so quickly has never been explained.

> We know what needs to be done; the question is how to pay for it.

WITH DECIMALS

105 Use a period (without space before or after it) to separate a whole number from a decimal fraction; for example, $5.50, 33.33 *percent*.

IN OUTLINES AND DISPLAYED LISTS

106 Use periods after numbers or letters that enumerate items in an outline or a displayed list—unless the numbers or letters are enclosed in parentheses. (See ¶¶107, 199c, 223, 1357c, 1424e for illustrations.)

107 Use periods after independent clauses, dependent clauses, or long phrases that are displayed on separate lines in a list. No periods are needed after short phrases unless the phrases are essential to the grammatical completeness of the statement introducing the list.

> Please get me year-end figures on:
>> a. Domestic sales revenues.
>> b. Total operating costs.
>> c. Net operating income.

> This snowblower offers features typically found on much more expensive models:
>> 1. Automatic clutch
>> 2. On-off switch
>> 3. Easy-swivel snow chute

WITH HEADINGS

108 **a.** Use a period after a *run-in* heading (one that begins a paragraph and is immediately followed by text matter on the same line) unless some other mark of punctuation, such as a question mark, is required.

b. Omit the period if the heading is *free-standing* (displayed on a line by itself). However, retain a question mark or an exclamation point with a free-standing head if the wording requires it.

TAX-SAVING TECHNIQUES

Tax Elimination or Reduction

    Nontaxable Income. Of the various types of nontaxable income, the most significant is the interest paid on municipal bonds. Investment in municipals has become one of the most popular ways to avoid . . .

NOTE: A period follows a run-in expression like *Table 6*, even though the heading as a whole is free-standing.

    Table 6.   Management Salary Ranges   Figure 2-4.   Departmental Staff Needs

❏ *For the treatment of headings in reports and manuscripts, see ¶1425; for the treatment of headings in tables, see ¶¶1612–1615.*

A FEW DON'TS

109   Don't use a period:

a. After letters used to designate persons or things (for example, *Manager A, Class B, Grade C, Brand X*). **EXCEPTION:** Use a period when the letter is the actual initial of a person's last name (for example, *Mr. A.* for *Mr. Adams*).

b. After contractions (for example, *o'clock;* see ¶505).

c. After ordinals expressed in figures (*1st, 2d, 3d, 4th*).

d. After roman numerals (for example, *Volume I, Henry Ford II*). **EXCEPTION:** Periods follow roman numerals in an outline. (See ¶223.)

❏ *Periods with abbreviations: see ¶¶506–510.*
❏ *Periods with dashes: see ¶¶213, 214a, 215a.*
❏ *Periods with parentheses: see ¶¶224c, 225a, 225c, 226c.*
❏ *Periods with quotation marks: see ¶¶247, 252, 253, 257, 258, 259.*
❏ *Three spaced periods (ellipsis marks): see ¶¶274–280, 291.*
❏ *Typewriter spacing with periods: see ¶299.*

THE QUESTION MARK

TO INDICATE DIRECT QUESTIONS

110   Use a question mark at the end of a direct question. (See ¶¶104, 115, 116 for the punctuation of indirect questions.)

    Will you be able to meet with us after 5 p.m.?

    Why not come in and see for yourself?

    Either way, how can we lose?

NOTE: Be sure to place the question mark at the *end* of the question.

    How do you account for this entry: "Paid to E. M. Johnson, $300"?

    (**NOT:** How do you account for this entry? "Paid to E. M. Johnson, $300.")

111   Use a question mark at the end of an *elliptical* (condensed) *question*, that is, a word or phrase that represents a complete question.

    Marion tells me that you are coming to the Bay Area. When? (The complete question is, "When are you coming?")

(Continued on page 6.)

NOTE: Punctuate complete and elliptical questions separately, according to your meaning.

> When will the job be finished? In a week or two? (**NOT:** When will the job be finished in a week or two?)

> Where shall we meet? At the airport? (As punctuated, the writer allows for the possibility of meeting elsewhere.)

> Where shall we meet at the airport? (As punctuated, the writer simply wants to pinpoint a more precise location within the airport.)

112   Use a question mark at the end of a sentence that is phrased like a statement but spoken with the rising intonation of a question.

> You expect me to believe this story?

> Now that he has all the facts, he still intends to proceed?

113   A request, suggestion, or command phrased as a question out of politeness may not require a question mark. (See ¶103.)

TO INDICATE QUESTIONS WITHIN SENTENCES

114   When a short direct question falls *within a sentence,* set the question off with commas and put a question mark at the end of the sentence. However, when a short direct question falls *at the end of a sentence,* use a comma before it and a question mark after.

> I can alter the terms of my will, *can't I,* whenever I wish?

> We aren't obligated to attend the meeting, *are we?*

115   When a direct question comes *at the end of a longer sentence,* it starts with a capital letter and is preceded by a comma or a colon. The question mark that ends the question also serves to mark the end of the sentence.

> The key question is, Whom *shall we* nominate for next year's election?

> This is the key question: Whom *shall we* nominate for next year's election? (Use a colon if the introductory matter is an independent clause.)

> **BUT:** We now come to the key question of whom *we shall* nominate for next year's election. (**An indirect question requires no special punctuation or capitalization.** See ¶116, note.)

> We now come to the key question of whom to nominate for next year's election.

116   When a direct question comes *at the beginning of a longer sentence,* it should be followed by a question mark (for emphasis) or simply a comma.

> How *can we* achieve these goals? is the next question. (Leave one space after a question mark within a sentence.)

> **OR:** How *can we* achieve these goals, is the next question.

> **BUT:** How *we can* achieve these goals is the next question. (Indirect question; no special punctuation is needed.)

NOTE: In the examples in ¶¶115–116, notice how a simple shift in word order converts a direct question to an indirect question. When the verb precedes the subject (*shall we, can we*), the question is direct. When the verb follows the subject (*we shall, we can*), the question is indirect.

117   A series of brief questions at the end of a sentence may be separated by commas or (for emphasis) by question marks. Do not capitalize the individual questions.

> Who will be responsible for drafting the proposal, obtaining comments from all the interested parties, and preparing the final version?

> **OR:** Who will be responsible for drafting the proposal? obtaining comments from all the interested parties? preparing the final version?

NOTE: Notice that these brief questions are all related to a common subject and predicate *(Who will be responsible for)*. Do not confuse this type of sentence pattern with a series of independent questions. Each independent question must start with a capital and end with a question mark.

> Before you accept the job offer, think about the following: Will this job give you experience relevant to your real career goal? Will it permit you to keep abreast of the latest technology? Will it pay you what you need?

Independent questions in a series are often elliptical (condensed) expressions. (See ¶111.)

> Has Walter's loan been approved? *When? By whom? For what amount?* (In other words: *When* was the loan approved? *By whom* was the loan approved? *For what amount* was the loan approved?)

> (**NOT:** Has Walter's loan been approved, when, by whom, and for what amount?)

TO EXPRESS DOUBT

118 A question mark enclosed in parentheses may be used to express doubt or uncertainty about a word or phrase within a sentence.

> He joined the firm after his graduation from Columbia Law School in 1968(?).

NOTE: When dates are already enclosed within parentheses, question marks may be inserted as necessary to indicate doubt.

> the explorer Verrazano (1485?–1528?)

❑ *Question marks with dashes: see ¶¶214b, 215a.*
❑ *Question marks with parentheses: see ¶¶224d, 225a, 225d, 226c.*
❑ *Question marks with quotation marks: see ¶¶249, 252, 254, 257, 258, 259.*
❑ *Typewriter spacing with question marks: see ¶299.*

THE EXCLAMATION POINT

The exclamation point is an "emotional" mark of punctuation that is most often found in advertising copy and sales correspondence. However, like the word *very,* it loses its force when overused. Therefore, avoid it wherever possible.

NOTE: If your typewriter does not have an exclamation point as a standard character, you can construct it by typing the apostrophe, backspacing once, and then typing the period.

TO EXPRESS STRONG FEELING

119 Use an exclamation point at the end of a sentence (or an elliptical expression that stands for a sentence) to indicate enthusiasm, surprise, disbelief, urgency, or strong feeling.

> Yes! We're selling our entire inventory at below our actual cost!

> No! I don't believe it!   How could you do it!   Incredible!

NOTE: The exclamation point may be enclosed in parentheses and placed directly after a word that the writer wants to emphasize.

> We won exclusive(!) distribution rights in the Western Hemisphere.

120 **a.** A single word may be followed by an exclamation point to express intense feeling. The sentence that follows it is punctuated as usual.

> Congratulations! Your summation at the trial was superb.

b. When such words are repeated for emphasis, an exclamation point follows each repetition.

Going! Going! Our bargains are almost gone!

c. When exclamations are mild, a comma or a period is sufficient.

Well, well, things could be worse.   No. I won't accept those conditions.

WITH *OH* AND *O*

121 The exclamation *oh* may be followed by either an exclamation point or a comma, depending on the emphasis desired. It is capitalized only when it starts a sentence. The capitalized *O*, the sign of direct address, is not usually followed by any punctuation.

Oh! I didn't expect that!   O Lord, help me!

Oh, what's the use?   O America, where are you headed?

☐ *Exclamation point with dashes: see ¶¶214b, 215a.*
☐ *Exclamation point with parentheses: see ¶¶224d, 225a, 225d, 226c.*
☐ *Exclamation point with quotation marks: see ¶¶249, 252, 254, 257, 258, 259.*
☐ *Typewriter spacing with exclamation points: see ¶299.*

THE COMMA

The comma has two primary functions: it *sets off* nonessential expressions that interrupt the flow of thought from subject to verb to object or complement, and it *separates* elements within a sentence to clarify their relationship to one another. It takes only a single comma to "separate," but it typically requires two commas to "set off."

The following rules (¶¶122–125) present an overview of the rules governing the use of the comma. For a more detailed treatment of the specific rules, see ¶¶126–175.

BASIC RULES FOR COMMAS THAT SET OFF

122 Use commas to set off *nonessential expressions*—words, phrases, and clauses that are not necessary for the meaning or the structural completeness of the sentence.

IMPORTANT NOTE: In many sentences you can tell whether an expression is nonessential or essential by trying to omit the expression. If you can leave it out without affecting the meaning or the structural completeness of the sentence, the expression is nonessential and should be set off by commas.

NONESSENTIAL: Let's get the advice of Harry Stern, *who has in-depth experience with all types of personal computers.*

ESSENTIAL: Let's get the advice of someone *who has in-depth experience with all types of personal computers.* (Without the *who* clause, the meaning of the sentence would be incomplete.)

NONESSENTIAL: There is, *no doubt,* a reasonable explanation for his behavior at the board meeting.

ESSENTIAL: There is *no doubt* about her honesty. (Without *no doubt* the structure of the sentence would be incomplete.)

However, in other sentences the only way you can tell whether an expression is nonessential or essential is by the way you would say it aloud. If your voice tends to *drop* as you utter the expression, it is nonessential; if your voice tends to *rise*, the expression is essential.

NONESSENTIAL: Finch and Helwig would prefer, *therefore,* to limit the term of the agreement to two years.

ESSENTIAL: Finch and Helwig would *therefore* prefer to limit the term of the agreement to two years.

❑ *For additional examples, see ¶141, note.*

a. **Interrupting Elements.** Use commas to set off words, phrases, and clauses when they break the flow of a sentence from subject to verb to object or complement. (See also ¶¶144–147.)

We can deliver the car on the day of your husband's birthday or, *if you wish,* on the Saturday before then. (When this sentence is read aloud, notice how the voice drops on the nonessential expression *if you wish.*)

They have sufficient assets, *don't they,* to cover these losses?

Let's take advantage of the special price and order, *say,* 200 reams this quarter instead of our usual quantity of 75.

Mary Cabrera, *rather than George Spengler,* has been appointed head of the Phoenix office.

BUT: Mary Cabrera has been appointed head of the Phoenix office *rather than George Spengler.* (The phrase is not set off when it does not interrupt.)

b. **Afterthoughts.** Use commas to set off words, phrases, or clauses loosely added onto the end of a sentence. (See also ¶144.)

Send us your check as soon as you can, *please.*

Grant promised to share expenses with us, *if I remember correctly.*

It is not too late to place an order, *is it?*

c. **Transitional Expressions and Independent Comments.** Use commas to set off transitional expressions (like *however, therefore, on the other hand*) and independent comments (like *obviously, in my opinion, of course*) when they interrupt the flow of the sentence. Do not set off these elements, however, when they are used to emphasize the meaning (the voice goes up in such cases). In the examples that follow, consider how the voice drops when the expression is nonessential and how it rises when the expression is essential. (See also ¶¶138–143.)

NONESSENTIAL: We are determined, *nevertheless,* to finish on schedule.

ESSENTIAL: We are *nevertheless* determined to finish on schedule.

NONESSENTIAL: It is, *of course,* your prerogative to change your mind. (Here the voice rises on *is* and drops on *of course.*)

ESSENTIAL: It is *of course* your prerogative to change your mind. (Here the voice rises on *of course.*)

d. **Descriptive Expressions.** When descriptive expressions *follow* the words they refer to and provide additional but nonessential information, use commas to set them off. (See also ¶¶148–153.)

NONESSENTIAL: His most recent article, "How to Make a Profit With High-Tech Investments," appeared in the June 1 issue of *Forbes.* (*His most recent* indicates which article is meant; the title gives additional but nonessential information.)

ESSENTIAL: The article "How to Make a Profit With High-Tech Investments" appeared in the June 1 issue of *Forbes.* (Here the title is essential to indicate which article.)

(Continued on page 10.)

NONESSENTIAL: Thank you for your letter of April 12, in which you questioned our discount terms. (The date indicates which letter; the *in which* clause gives additional information. See also ¶152.)

ESSENTIAL: Thank you for your letter in which you questioned our discount terms. (Here the *in which* clause is needed to indicate which letter is being referred to.)

e. Dates. Use commas to set off the year in complete dates (May 1, *1987, . . .*). (See also ¶¶154–155.)

f. Names. Use commas to set off abbreviations that follow a person's name (Julie Merkin, *CPA,* announces the opening . . .) and names of states or countries following city names (Rye, *New York,* will host . . .). In personal names and company names the trend is not to set off elements like *Jr., Sr., III, Inc.,* or *Ltd.* (for example, *Guy Tracy Jr.* and *Redd Inc.*); however, individual preferences should be respected when known. (See also ¶¶156–161.)

BASIC RULES FOR COMMAS THAT SEPARATE

123   Use a single comma:

a. To separate the two main clauses in a compound sentence when they are joined by *and, but, or,* or *nor.* (See also ¶¶126–129.)

We can't accept the marketing restrictions you proposed, *but* we think there is some basis for a mutually acceptable understanding.

b. To separate three or more items in a series—unless all the items are joined by *and* or *or.* (See also ¶¶162–167.)

It takes time, effort, *and* a good deal of money.

BUT: It takes time *and* effort *and* a good deal of money.

c. To separate two or more adjectives that both modify the same noun. (See also ¶¶168–171.)

We need to mount an *exciting, hard-hitting* ad campaign.

d. To separate the digits of numbers into groups of thousands. (See ¶461.)

Sales projections for the Southern Region next year range between $900,000 and $1,000,000.

e. To indicate the omission of key words or to clarify meaning when the word order is unusual. (See also ¶¶172–175.)

Half the purchase price is due on delivery of the goods; the balance, in three months. (The comma here signifies the omission of *is due.*)

What will happen, we don't know. (The comma separates the object, *What will happen,* from the subject, *we,* which follows.)

124   Use a single comma after *introductory elements*—items that begin a sentence and come before the subject and verb of the main clause.

Yes, we can deliver your new microprocessor by Wednesday. (Introductory word.)

Taking all the arguments into consideration, we have decided to modernize these facilities rather than close them down. (Introductory participial phrase.)

To determine the proper mix of ingredients for a particular situation, see the table on page 141. (Introductory infinitive phrase.)

Before we can make a final decision, we will need to run another cost-profit analysis. (Introductory dependent clause.)

a. Use a comma after an *introductory request or command*.

Look, we've been through tougher situations before.

You see, the previous campaigns never did pan out.

Please remember, all expense accounts must be on my desk by Friday.

BUT: *Please remember that* all . . . (With the addition of *that, please remember* becomes the main verb and is no longer an introductory element.)

b. Commas are not needed after *ordinary introductory adverbs* or *short introductory phrases* that answer such questions as:

WHEN:	tomorrow, yesterday, recently, early next week, in the morning, soon, in five years, in 1988
HOW OFTEN:	occasionally, often, frequently, once in a while
WHERE:	here, in this case, at the meeting
WHY:	for that reason, because of this situation

However, commas are used after introductory adverbs and phrases:

(1) When they function as *transitional expressions* (such as *well, therefore, however, for example, in the first place*), which provide a transition in meaning from the previous sentence.

(2) When they function as *independent comments* (such as *in my opinion, by all means, obviously, of course*), which express the writer's attitude toward the meaning of the sentence. (See also ¶¶138–143.)

In the morning things may look better. (Short prepositional phrase telling *when;* no comma needed.)

In the first place, they don't have sufficient capital. (Transitional expression; followed by comma.)

In my opinion, we ought to look for another candidate. (Independent comment; followed by comma.)

Recently we had a request for school enrollment trends. (Introductory adverb telling *when;* no comma needed.)

Consequently, we will have to cancel the agreement. (Transitional expression; followed by comma.)

Obviously, the request will have to be referred elsewhere. (Independent comment; followed by comma.)

NOTE: Many writers use commas after *all* introductory elements to avoid having to analyze each situation.

125 Separating commas are often improperly used in sentences. In the following examples the diagonal marks indicate points at which single commas *should not* be used.

a. Do not separate a subject and its verb.

The person she plans to hire for the job/ is Peter Crotty.

BUT: The person she plans to hire for the job, *I believe,* is Peter Crotty. (Use *two* commas to set off an interrupting expression.)

Whether profits can be improved this year/ depends on several key variables. (Noun clause as subject.)

BUT: *Anyone who contributes, contributes* to a most worthy cause. (In special cases like this, a comma may be required for clarity. See also ¶175*b*.)

b. Do not separate a verb and its object or complement.

The test mailing *has not produced/ the results* we were hoping for. (Verb and object.)

Rebecca Hingham *said/ that the research data would be on your desk by Monday morning.* (Noun clause as object.)

BUT: Rebecca Hingham *said, "The research data will be on your desk by Monday morning."* (A comma ordinarily follows a verb when the object is a direct quotation. See also ¶256.)

OR: The question we really need to address *is, Do we have a better solution to propose?* (A comma also follows a verb when the object or complement is a direct question. See also ¶115.)

Mrs. Paterra *will be/ the new director of marketing.* (Verb and complement.)

The equipment *is/ easy to operate, inexpensive to maintain, and built to give reliable service for many years.* (Verb and complement.)

c. Do not separate an adjective and a noun.

We need a person who is willing to put in long, *hard/ hours.* (Adjective and noun.)

d. Do not separate a noun and a prepositional phrase that follows.

The board of directors/ of the Fastex Corporation will announce its decision this Friday.

BUT: The board of directors, *of necessity,* must turn down the merger at this time. (Use *two* commas to set off an interrupting expression.)

e. Do not separate a coordinating conjunction (*and, but, or,* or *nor*) and the following word.

You can read it now *or/ when* you get home tonight.

BUT: You can read it now or, *if you prefer,* when you get home tonight. (Use *two* commas to set off an interrupting expression.)

f. Do not separate *two* items joined by a coordinating conjunction.

The letters on the Gray case/ and *those concerning Mr. Pendleton* should be shown to Mrs. Almquist. (Two subjects.)

I *have read the report/* and *find it well done.* (Two predicates. See also ¶127.)

We hope *that you will visit our store soon/* and *that you will find the styles you like.* (Two objects of the verb *hope.*)

He may go on to graduate school at *Stanford/* or *Harvard.* (Two objects of the preposition *at.*)

BUT: *Frank Albano will handle the tickets,* and *Edna Hoehn will be responsible for publicity.* (A comma separates two independent clauses joined by a coordinating conjunction. See ¶126.)

The following rules (¶¶126–137) deal with the punctuation of clauses and phrases in sentences.

WITH CLAUSES IN COMPOUND SENTENCES

126 **a.** When a compound sentence consists of *two* independent clauses joined by a coordinating conjunction (*and, but, or,* or *nor*), place a separating comma before the conjunction. (See ¶129.)

Mrs. Fenster noticed a small discrepancy in the figures, *and* on that basis she began to reanalyze the data.

BUT: Mrs. Fenster noticed a small discrepancy in the figures *and* on that basis she began to reanalyze the data. (See ¶127a–b.)

Show this proposal to Mr. Florio, *and* ask him for his reaction. (See ¶127c.)

Either we step up our promotion efforts, *or* we must be content with our existing share of the market.

Not only were we the developers of this process, *but* we were the first to apply it to the field of pollution control.

b. When a compound sentence consists of *three* or more independent clauses, punctuate this series of clauses like any other series. (See also ¶162.)

Bob can deal with the caterer, Nora can handle publicity, and Bev and I can take care of the rest.

127 Do not confuse a *compound sentence* with a simple sentence containing a *compound predicate*.

a. A *compound sentence* contains at least two independent clauses, and each clause contains a subject and a predicate.

Barbara just got her master's in economics, and *she is now looking for a job in corporate planning.*

b. A sentence may contain one subject with a *compound predicate*, that is, two predicates connected by a coordinating conjunction. In such sentences no comma separates the two predicates.

Barbara *just got her master's in economics* and *is now looking for a job in corporate planning.* (When *she* is omitted from the example in *a* above, the sentence is no longer a compound sentence. It is now a simple sentence with a compound predicate.)

Ogleby not only *wants a higher discount* but also *demands faster turnarounds on his orders.* (Compound predicate; no comma before *but.*)

BUT: *Ogleby not only wants a higher discount,* but *he also demands faster turnarounds on his orders.* (Compound sentence; comma before *but.*)

c. When one or both verbs are in the imperative and the subject is not expressed, treat the sentence as a compound sentence and use a comma between the clauses. (See ¶129.)

Call Ellen Chen sometime next week, and *ask* her if she will speak at our conference next fall.

Please look at the brochure I have enclosed, and then *get* back to me if you have additional questions.

You may not be able to get away right now, but *do plan* to stay with us whenever you find the time.

d. When nonessential elements precede the second part of a *compound predicate,* they are treated as interrupting expressions and are set off by two commas. When these same expressions precede the second clause of a *compound sentence,* they are treated as introductory expressions and are followed by one comma.

We can bill you on our customary terms or, *if you prefer,* on our new deferred payment plan. (Interrupting expression requires two commas.)

We can bill you on our customary terms, or *if you prefer,* we can offer you our new deferred payment plan. (Introductory expression requires one comma.)

(*Continued on page 14.*)

Frank Bruchman went into the boardroom and, *without consulting his notes,* proceeded to give the directors precise details about our financial situation. (Interrupting expression.)

Frank Bruchman went into the boardroom, and *without consulting his notes,* he proceeded to give the directors precise details about our financial situation. (Introductory expression.)

❑ *See also ¶¶131c, 136a, 142.*

128 Do not use a comma between two independent clauses that are not joined by a coordinating conjunction *(and, but, or,* or *nor).* This error of punctuation is known as a *comma splice* and produces a *run-on sentence.* Use a semicolon, a colon, or a dash (whichever is appropriate), or start a new sentence.

WRONG: Please review the payroll worksheets quickly, I need them back tomorrow.

RIGHT: Please review the payroll worksheets quickly; I need them back tomorrow.

OR: Please review the payroll worksheets quickly. I need them back tomorrow.

129 If the two clauses of a compound sentence are short, the comma may be omitted before the conjunction.

Their prices are low and their service is efficient.

Please initial these forms and return them by Monday.

WITH CLAUSES IN COMPLEX SENTENCES

A complex sentence contains one independent clause and one or more dependent clauses. *After, although, as, because, before, if, since, unless, when,* and *while* are among the words most frequently used to introduce dependent clauses. (See ¶132 for a longer list.)

130 Introductory Dependent Clauses

a. When a dependent clause *precedes* the independent clause, separate the clauses with a comma.

Before we can make a decision, we must have all the facts.

When you read the Weissberg study, look at Appendix 2 first.

If, however, they had watched their investments more closely, do you think they could have avoided bankruptcy?

After we have studied all aspects of the complaint, we will make a recommendation.

BUT: *Only after we have studied all aspects of the complaint* will we make a recommendation. (No comma follows the introductory clause when the word order in the main clause is abnormal. Compare the abnormal *will we make* here with the normal *we will make* in the example above.)

b. Be sure you can recognize an introductory dependent clause, even if some of the essential words are omitted from the clause. (Such constructions are known as *elliptical clauses.)*

Whenever possible, he leaves his office by six. (Whenever *it is* possible, . . .)

If so, I will call you tomorrow. (If *that is* so, . . .)

Should you be late, just call to let me know. (*If* you should be late, . . .)

c. Use a comma after an introductory clause when it serves as the *object* of a sentence (but not when it serves as the *subject*).

Whomever you nominate, I will support. (Introductory clause as object.)

Whomever you nominate will have my support. (Introductory clause as subject.)

That the department must be reorganized, I no longer question. (Introductory clause as object.)

That the department must be reorganized is no longer questioned. (Introductory clause as subject.)

d. Sentences like those illustrated in ¶130*a–c* are often introduced by an expression such as *he said that*, *she believes that*, or *they know that*. In such cases use the same punctuation as prescribed in *a–c*.

Liz believes that *before we can make a decision,* we must have all the facts. (A separating comma follows the dependent clause, just as if the sentence began with the word *Before*. No comma precedes the dependent clause because it is considered introductory, not interrupting.)

BUT: He said that, *as you may already know,* he was planning to take early retirement. (Two commas are needed to set off an interrupting dependent clause. See also ¶131*c*.)

Harry says that *whenever possible,* he leaves his office by six.

Everyone knows that *whomever you nominate* will have my support.

131 Dependent Clauses Elsewhere in the Sentence

When a dependent clause *follows* the main clause or *falls within* the main clause, commas are used or omitted depending on whether the dependent clause is essential (restrictive) or nonessential (nonrestrictive).

a. An *essential* clause is necessary to the meaning of the sentence. Because it *cannot be omitted*, it should not be set off by commas.

The person *who used to be Englund's operations manager* is now doing the same job for Jenniman Brothers. (Tells which person.)

The Pennington bid arrived *after we had made our decision.* (Tells when.)

Damato's suggestion *that we submit the issue to arbitration* may be the only sensible alternative. (Tells which of Damato's suggestions is meant.)

Mrs. Foy said *that she would send us an advance program.* (Tells what was said.)

b. A *nonessential* clause provides additional descriptive or explanatory detail. Because it *can be omitted* without changing the meaning of the sentence, it should be set off by commas.

George Pedersen, *who used to be Englund's operations manager,* is now doing the same job for Jenniman Brothers. (The name indicates which person; the *who* clause simply gives additional information.)

The Pennington bid arrived on Tuesday, *after we had made our decision.* (*Tuesday* tells when; the *after* clause simply adds information.)

Damato's latest suggestion, *that we submit the issue to arbitration,* may be the only sensible alternative. (*Latest* tells which suggestion is meant; the *that* clause is not essential.)

c. A dependent clause occurring within a sentence must always be set off by commas when it *interrupts* the flow of the sentence.

We can review the wording of the announcement over lunch or, *if your time is short,* over the phone.

Please tell us when you plan to be in town and, *if possible,* where you will be staying. (The complete dependent clause is *if it is possible.*)

Senator Hemphill, *when offered the chance to refute his opponent's charges,* said he would respond at a time of his own choosing.

Mrs. Kourakis is the type of person who, *when you need help badly,* will be the first to volunteer.

(Continued on page 16.)

If, *when you have weighed the alternatives,* you choose one of the models that cost over $500, we can arrange special credit terms for you.

BUT: He said that *if we choose one of the models that cost over $500,* his firm can arrange special credit terms for us. (See ¶130*d* for dependent clauses following *he said that, she knows that,* and similar expressions.)

132   The following list presents the words and phrases most commonly used to introduce dependent clauses. For most of these expressions two sentences are given: one containing an essential clause and one a nonessential clause. In a few cases only one type of clause is possible. If you cannot decide whether a clause is essential or nonessential (and therefore whether commas are required or not), compare it with the related sentences below.

After.   ESSENTIAL: The cablegram came *after you left last evening.* (Tells when.) NONESSENTIAL: The cablegram came this morning, *after the decision had been made.* (The phrase *this morning* clearly tells when; the *after* clause provides additional but nonessential information.)

All of which.   ALWAYS NONESSENTIAL: The rumors, *all of which were unfounded,* brought about his defeat in the last election.

Although, even though, and **though.**   ALWAYS NONESSENTIAL: She has typed her letter of resignation, *although I do not believe she will submit it.* (Clause of concession.)

As.   ESSENTIAL: The results of the mailing are *as you predicted they would be.* NONESSENTIAL: The results of the mailing are disappointing, *as you predicted they would be.* (See page 222 for a usage note on *as.*)

As . . . as.   ALWAYS ESSENTIAL: He talked *as* persuasively at the meeting *as* he did over the telephone.

As if and **as though.**   ESSENTIAL: She drove *as if* (or *as though*) *the road were a minefield.* (The *as if* clause tells how she drove.) NONESSENTIAL: She drove cautiously, *as if* (or *as though*) *the road were a minefield.* (The adverb *cautiously* tells how she drove; the *as if* clause provides additional but nonessential information.)

As soon as.   ESSENTIAL: We will fill your order *as soon as we receive new stock.* NONESSENTIAL: We will fill your order next week, *as soon as we receive new stock.*

At, by, for, in, and **to which.**   ESSENTIAL: I went to the floor *to which I had been directed.* NONESSENTIAL: I went to the tenth floor, *to which I had been directed.*

Because.   *Essential* or *nonessential,* depending on closeness of relation. ESSENTIAL: She left *because she had another appointment.* (Here the reason expressed by the *because* clause is essential to complete the meaning.) NONESSENTIAL: I need to have two copies of the final report by 5:30 tomorrow, *because I am leaving for Chicago on a 7:30 flight.* (Here the meaning of the main clause is complete; the reason expressed in the *because* clause offers additional but nonessential information.)

Before.   ESSENTIAL: The shipment was sent *before your letter was received.* NONESSENTIAL: The shipment was sent on Tuesday, *before your letter was received.* (*Tuesday* tells when the shipment was sent; the *before* clause provides additional but nonessential information.)

Even though.   See *Although.*

For.   ALWAYS NONESSENTIAL: He read the book, *for he was interested in psychology.* (A comma should always precede *for* as a conjunction to prevent misreading *for* as a preposition.)

If.   ESSENTIAL: Let us hear from you *if you are interested.* NONESSENTIAL: She promised to write from Toronto, *if I remember correctly.* (Clause added loosely.)

In order that.   *Essential* or *nonessential,* depending on closeness of relation. ESSENTIAL: Please notify your instructor promptly *in order that a makeup examination may be scheduled.* NONESSENTIAL: Please notify your instructor promptly if you will be unable to attend the examination on Friday, *in order that a makeup examination may be scheduled.*

No matter what (why, how, etc.**).** ALWAYS NONESSENTIAL: The order cannot be ready by Monday, *no matter what the store manager says.*

None of which. ALWAYS NONESSENTIAL: We received five boxes of samples, *none of which are in good condition.*

None of whom. ALWAYS NONESSENTIAL: We have interviewed ten applicants, *none of whom were satisfactory.*

Since. ESSENTIAL: We have taken no applications *since we received your memo.*
NONESSENTIAL: We are taking no more applications, *since our lists are now closed.* (Clause of reason.)

So ... as. ALWAYS ESSENTIAL: The second copy was not *so* clear *as* the first one.

So that. *Essential* or *nonessential*, depending on closeness of relation.
ESSENTIAL: Examine all shipments *so that any damage may be detected promptly.*
NONESSENTIAL: Examine all shipments as soon as they arrive, *so that any damage may be detected promptly.*

So ... that. ALWAYS ESSENTIAL: The costs ran *so* high *that we could not make a profit on the job.*

Some of whom. ALWAYS NONESSENTIAL: The agency has sent us five applicants, *some of whom seem promising.*

Than. ALWAYS ESSENTIAL: The employees seem to be more disturbed by the rumor *than they care to admit.*

That. When used as a relative pronoun, *that* refers to things; also to persons when a class or type is meant. ALWAYS ESSENTIAL: Enclosed is a picture of the plane *that Lynn now owns.* She is the kind of candidate *that I prefer.* (See also ¶1062.)

Though. See *Although.*

Unless. ESSENTIAL: This product line will be discontinued *unless customers begin to show an interest in it.*
NONESSENTIAL: I plan to work on the Aspen proposal all through the weekend, *unless Cindy comes into town.* (Clause added loosely as an afterthought.)

Until. ALWAYS ESSENTIAL: I will continue to work *until my children are out of school.*

When. ESSENTIAL: The changeover will be made *when Mr. Ruiz returns from his vacation.*
NONESSENTIAL: The changeover will be made next Monday, *when Mr. Ruiz returns from his vacation.* (*Monday* tells when; the *when* clause provides additional but nonessential information.)

Where. ESSENTIAL: I plan to visit the town *where I used to live.*
NONESSENTIAL: I plan to stop off in Detroit, *where I used to live.*

Whereas. ALWAYS NONESSENTIAL: The figures for last year cover urban areas only, *whereas those for this year include rural areas as well.* (Clause of contrast.)

Which. Used in referring to animals, things, and ideas. Always use *which* (instead of *that*) to introduce nonessential clauses: The bay, *which was full of small sailing craft,* was very rough. *Which* may also be used to introduce essential clauses. (See ¶1062b, note.)

While. ESSENTIAL: The union has decided not to strike *while negotiations are still going on.* (*While* meaning "during the time that.")
NONESSENTIAL: The workers at the Apex Company have struck, *while those at the Powers Company are still at work.* (*While* meaning "whereas.")

Who. ESSENTIAL: All students *who are members of the Backpackers Club* will be leaving for Maine on Friday.
NONESSENTIAL: John Behnke, *who is a member of the Backpackers Club,* will be leading a group on a weekend trip to Maine.

Whom. ESSENTIAL: This package is for the friend *whom I am visiting.*
NONESSENTIAL: This package is for my cousin Amy, *whom I am visiting.*

Whose. ESSENTIAL: The prize was awarded to the employee *whose suggestion yielded the greatest cost savings.*
NONESSENTIAL: The prize was awarded to Joyce Bruno, *whose suggestion yielded the greatest cost savings.*

WITH CLAUSES IN COMPOUND-COMPLEX SENTENCES

133 A compound-complex sentence typically consists of two independent clauses (joined by *and, but, or,* or *nor*) and one or more dependent clauses. To punctuate a sentence of this kind, first place a separating comma before the conjunction that joins the two main parts. Then consider each half of the sentence alone and provide additional punctuation as necessary.

> The computer terminals were not delivered until June 12, five weeks after the promised delivery date, and *when I wrote to complain to your sales manager,* it took another three weeks simply for him to acknowledge my letter. (No comma precedes *when* because the *when* clause is considered an introductory expression, not an interrupting expression. See also ¶127d.)
>
> Jeff Adler, the CEO of Marshfield & Duxbury, is eager to discuss a joint venture with my boss, *who is off on a six-week trip to the Far East,* but the earliest date I see open for such a meeting is Wednesday, October 20.

NOTE: If a misreading is likely or a stronger break is desired, use a semicolon rather than a comma to separate the two main clauses. (See ¶177.)

134 When a sentence starts with a dependent clause that applies to both independent clauses that follow, no comma separates the independent clauses. (A comma would make the introductory dependent clause seem to apply only to the first independent clause.)

> Before you start to look for venture capital, you need to prepare an analysis of the market *and* you must make a detailed set of financial projections. (The *before* clause applies equally to the two independent clauses that follow; hence no comma before *and.*)
>
> **BUT:** Before you start to look for venture capital, you need to prepare an analysis of the market, *but* don't think that's all there is to it. (The *before* clause applies only to the first independent clause; hence a comma is used before *but.*)

WITH PARTICIPIAL, INFINITIVE, AND PREPOSITIONAL PHRASES

135 Introductory Phrases

a. Use a comma after an *introductory participial phrase.*

> *Seizing the opportunity,* I presented an overview of our medium-range plans.
>
> *Established in 1905,* our company takes great pride in its reputation for high-quality products and excellent service.
>
> *Having checked the statements myself,* I feel confident that they are accurate.

NOTE: Watch out for phrases that look like introductory participial phrases but actually represent the subject of the sentence or part of the predicate. Do not put a comma after these elements.

> *Looking for examples of good acknowledgment letters in our files* has taken me longer than I had hoped. (Gerund phrase as subject.)
>
> **BUT:** *Looking for examples of good acknowledgment letters in our files,* I found four you can use. (Participial phrase used as an introductory element; the subject is *I.*)
>
> *Following Mrs. Fahnstock's speech* was a presentation by Ms. Paley. (With normal word order, the sentence would read, "A presentation by Ms. Paley was *following Mrs. Fahnstock's speech.*" The introductory phrase is actually part of the predicate.)
>
> **BUT:** *Following Mrs. Fahnstock's speech,* Ms. Paley made her presentation. (Participial phrase used as an introductory element; the subject is *Ms. Paley.*)

b. Use a comma after an *introductory infinitive phrase* unless the phrase is the subject of the sentence. (Infinitive phrases are introduced by the word *to* plus a verb.)

To get the best results from your dishwasher, follow the printed directions. (The subject *you* is understood.)

To have displayed the goods more effectively, he should have consulted a lighting specialist. (The subject is *he.*)

BUT: *To have displayed the goods more effectively* would have required a lighting specialist. (Infinitive phrase used as subject.)

c. As a general rule, use a comma after all *introductory prepositional phrases.* A comma may be omitted after a *short* prepositional phrase if (1) the phrase does not contain a verb form, (2) the phrase is not a transitional expression or an independent comment, or (3) there is no sacrifice in clarity or desired emphasis. (Many writers use a comma after all introductory prepositional phrases to avoid having to analyze each situation.)

In response to the many requests of our customers, we are opening a branch in Kenmore Square. (Comma required after a long phrase.)

On Monday morning the first mail delivery is always late. (No comma required after a short phrase.)

In 1984 our entire inventory was destroyed by fire. (No comma required after a short phrase.)

BUT: *In 1984,* 384 cases of potential lung infections were reported. (Comma required to separate two numbers. See ¶456.)

At the time you called, I was tied up in a meeting. (Comma required after a short phrase containing a verb form.)

In preparing your report, be sure to include last year's figures. (Comma required after a short phrase containing a verb form.)

In addition, a 6 percent city sales tax must be imposed on these orders. (Comma required after a short phrase used as a transitional expression. See ¶¶138a, 139.)

In my opinion, your ads are misleading as they now appear. (Comma required after short phrase used as an independent comment. See ¶¶138b, 139.)

CONFUSING: After all you have gone through a great deal.

CLEAR: *After all,* you have gone through a great deal. (Comma required after a short phrase to prevent misreading.)

In legal documents, amounts of money are often expressed both in words and figures. (Comma used to give desired emphasis to the introductory phrase.)

NOTE: Omit the comma after an introductory prepositional phrase if the word order in the rest of the sentence is inverted.

Out of an initial investment of $5000 came a stake in a bioengineering company that is currently worth over $2,500,000. (Normal word order: A stake in a bioengineering company that is currently worth over $2,500,000 came out of an initial investment of $5000.)

In an article I read in Time last week was an account of our company's decision to go public. (Omit the comma after the introductory phrase when the verb in the main clause immediately follows.)

BUT: *In an article I read in Time last week,* there was an account of our company's decision to go public.

136   Phrases at the Beginning of a Clause

a. When a participial, infinitive, or prepositional phrase occurs *at the beginning of a clause within the sentence,* insert or omit the comma following, just as if the phrase were an introductory element at the beginning of the sentence. (See ¶135.)

(Continued on page 20.)

I was invited to attend the monthly planning meeting last week, and *seizing the opportunity,* I presented an overview of our medium-range plans. (A separating comma follows the participial phrase just as if the sentence began with the word *Seizing.* No comma precedes the phrase because the phrase is considered introductory, not interrupting. See also ¶127*d*.)

The salesclerk explained that *to get the best results from your dishwasher,* you should follow the printed directions.

We would like to announce that *in response to the many requests of our customers,* we are opening a branch in Kenmore Square.

Last year we had a number of thefts, and *in 1984* our entire inventory was destroyed by fire. (No comma is needed after a short introductory prepositional phrase.)

b. If the phrase interrupts the flow of the sentence, set it off with two commas.

Pamela is the type of person who, *in the midst of disaster,* will always find something to laugh about.

If, *in the attempt to push matters to a resolution,* you offer that gang new terms, they will simply dig in their heels and refuse to bargain.

137   Phrases Elsewhere in the Sentence

When a participial, infinitive, or prepositional phrase occurs *at some point other than the beginning of a sentence* (see ¶135) *or the beginning of a clause* (see ¶136), commas are omitted or used depending on whether the phrase is essential or nonessential.

a. An *essential* participial, infinitive, or prepositional phrase is necessary to the meaning of the sentence and cannot be omitted. Therefore, do not use commas to set it off.

The catalog *scheduled for release in November* will have to be delayed until January. (Participial.)

The decision *to expand our export activities* has proved sound. (Infinitive.)

The search *for a new general manager* is still going on. (Prepositional.)

b. A *nonessential* participial, infinitive, or prepositional phrase provides additional information but is not needed to complete the meaning of the sentence. Set off such phrases with commas.

This new collection of essays, *written in the last two years before his death,* represents his most distinguished work. (Participial.)

I'd rather not attend her reception, *to be frank about it.* (Infinitive.)

Morale appears to be much better, *on the whole.* (Prepositional.)

c. A phrase occurring within a sentence must always be set off by commas when it *interrupts* the flow of the sentence.

The commission, *after hearing arguments on the proposed new tax rate structure,* will consider amendments to the tax law.

The company, *in its attempt to place more women in high-level management positions,* is undertaking a special recruitment program.

The following rules (¶¶138–161) deal with the various uses of commas to set off nonessential expressions. See also ¶¶201–202 and ¶¶218–219 for the use of dashes and parentheses to set off these expressions.

WITH TRANSITIONAL EXPRESSIONS AND
INDEPENDENT COMMENTS

138 **a.** Use commas to set off *transitional expressions.* These nonessential words and phrases are called *transitional* because they help the reader mentally relate the preceding thought with the idea now being introduced. They express the notion of:

ADDITION:	also, besides, furthermore, in addition, moreover, too (see ¶143), what is more
CONSEQUENCE:	accordingly, as a result, consequently, hence (see ¶139*b*), otherwise, so (see ¶179), then (see ¶139*b*), therefore, thus (see ¶139*b*)
SUMMARIZING:	after all, all in all, all things considered, briefly, by and large, in any case (event), in brief, in conclusion, in short, in summary, in the final analysis, in the long run, on balance, on the whole, to sum up
GENERALIZING:	as a rule, as usual, for the most part, generally (speaking), in general, ordinarily, usually
RESTATEMENT:	in essence, in other words, namely, that is, that is to say
CONTRAST AND COMPARISON:	by contrast, by the same token, conversely, instead, likewise, on one hand, on the contrary, on the other hand, rather, similarly, yet (see ¶179)
CONCESSION:	anyway, at any rate, be that as it may, even so, however, in any case (event), nevertheless, still, this fact notwithstanding
SEQUENCE:	afterward, at first, at the same time, finally, first, first of all, for now, for the time being, in conclusion, in the first place, in time, in turn, later on, meanwhile, next, second, then (see ¶139*b*), to begin with
DIVERSION:	by the by, by the way, incidentally
ILLUSTRATION:	for example, for instance, for one thing

b. Use commas to set off *independent comments,* that is, nonessential words or phrases that express the writer's attitude toward the meaning of the sentence. By means of these independent comments, the writer indicates that what he is about to say carries his wholehearted endorsement (*indeed, by all means*) or deserves only his lukewarm support (*apparently, presumably*) or hardly requires saying (*as you already know, clearly, obviously*) or represents only his personal views (*in my opinion, personally*) or arouses some emotion in him (*unfortunately, happily*) or presents his honest position (*frankly, actually, to tell the truth*). Such terms modify the meaning of the sentence as a whole rather than a particular word within the sentence.

AFFIRMATION:	by all means, indeed, of course, yes
DENIAL:	no
REGRET:	alas, unfortunately
PLEASURE:	fortunately, happily
QUALIFICATION:	ideally, if necessary, if possible, literally, strictly speaking, theoretically
PERSONAL VIEWPOINT:	according to her, as I see it, in my opinion, personally
ASSERTION OF CANDOR:	actually, frankly, in reality, to be honest, to say the least, to tell the truth
ASSERTION OF FACT:	as a matter of fact, as it happens, as you know, believe it or not, certainly, clearly, doubtless, in fact, naturally, needless to say, obviously, without doubt
WEAK ASSERTION:	apparently, perhaps, presumably

139 At the Beginning of a Sentence

a. When the words and phrases listed in ¶138*a*–*b* appear at the beginning of a sentence, they should be followed by a comma unless they are used as essential elements.

NONESSENTIAL: *After all,* you have done more for him than he had any right to expect.

ESSENTIAL: *After all* you have done for him, he has no right to expect more.

NONESSENTIAL: *However,* you look at the letter yourself and see whether you interpret it as I do.

ESSENTIAL: *However* you look at the letter, there is only one possible interpretation.

NONESSENTIAL: *Obviously,* the guest of honor was quite moved by the welcome she received.

ESSENTIAL: *Obviously* moved by the welcome she received, the guest of honor spoke with an emotion-choked voice. (Here *obviously* modifies *moved.* In the preceding sentence, *obviously* modifies the meaning of the sentence as a whole.)

b. When *hence, then,* or *thus* occurs at the beginning of a sentence, the comma following is omitted unless the connective requires special emphasis or a nonessential element occurs at that point.

Thus they thought it wise to get an outside consultant's opinion.

Then they decided to go back to their original plan.

BUT: *Then,* after they rejected the consultant's recommendation, they decided to go back to their original plan.

❏ *See also* ¶*142a, note.*

c. When an introductory transitional expression or independent comment is incorporated into the flow of the sentence without any intervening pause, the comma may be omitted.

Of course I can handle it.   *Perhaps* she was joking.

No doubt he meant well.   *Indeed* she was not.

140 At the End of a Sentence

Use one comma to set off a transitional expression or an independent comment at the end of a sentence. However, be sure to distinguish between nonessential and essential elements.

NONESSENTIAL: Philip goes to every employee reception, *of course.*

ESSENTIAL: Philip goes to every employee reception as a matter *of course.*

NONESSENTIAL: The deal is going to fall through, *in my opinion.*

ESSENTIAL: She doesn't rank very high *in my opinion.*

141 Within the Sentence

Use two commas to set off a transitional expression or an independent comment when it occurs as a nonessential element *within the sentence.*

I, *too,* was not expecting a six-month convalescence.

The doctors tell me, *however,* that I will regain full use of my left leg.

If, however, the expression is used as an essential element, omit the commas.

NONESSENTIAL: Let me say, *to begin with,* that I have always thought highly of him.

ESSENTIAL: If you want to improve your English, you ought *to begin with* a good review of grammar.

NOTE: In many sentences the only way you can tell whether an expression is nonessential or essential is by the way you say it. If your voice tends to *drop* as you utter the expression, it is nonessential and should be set off by commas.

> We concluded, *nevertheless,* that their offer was not serious.
>
> Millie understands, *certainly,* that the reassignment is only temporary.
>
> It is critical, *therefore,* that we rework all these cost estimates.

If your voice tends to *rise* as you utter the expression, it is essential and should not be set off by commas.

> We *nevertheless* concluded that their offer was not serious.
>
> Millie *certainly* understands that the reassignment is only temporary.
>
> It is *therefore* critical that we rework all these cost estimates.

If commas are inserted in the previous example, the entire reading of the sentence will be changed. The voice will rise on the word *is* and drop on *therefore.* (If this is the inflection intended, then commas around *therefore* are appropriate.)

> It is, *therefore,* critical that we rework all these cost estimates.

142   At the Beginning of a Clause

a. When a transitional expression or independent comment occurs *at the beginning of the second independent clause* in a compound sentence and is *preceded by a semicolon,* use one comma following the expression.

> I would love to work in a side trip to Vail; *however,* I don't think I can pull it off.
>
> My boss just approved the purchase order; *therefore,* let's confirm a delivery date.

NOTE: When *hence, then,* or *thus* appears at the beginning of an independent clause, the comma following is omitted unless the connective requires special emphasis or a nonessential element occurs at that point. (See also ¶139*b.*)

> Melt the butter over high heat; *then* add the egg.
>
> **BUT:** Melt the butter over high heat; *then,* when the foam begins to subside, add the egg.

❑ *For the use of a semicolon before a transitional expression, see ¶¶178–180.*

b. When the expression occurs *at the beginning of the second independent clause* in a compound sentence and is *preceded by a comma and a coordinating conjunction,* use one comma following the expression. (See also ¶127*d.*)

> The location of the plant was not easy to reach, and *to be honest about it,* I wasn't very taken with the people who interviewed me.
>
> The job seemed to have no future, and *to tell the truth,* the salary was pretty low.
>
> *In the first place,* I think the budget for the project is unrealistic, and *in the second place,* the deadlines are almost impossible to meet.

NOTE: If the expression is a simple adverb like *therefore* or *consequently,* the comma following the expression is usually omitted. (See also ¶180.)

> The matter must be resolved by Friday, and *therefore* our preliminary conference must be held no later than Thursday.
>
> All the general managers have been summoned to a three-day meeting at the home office, and *consequently* I have had to reschedule all my meetings for the week of May 6.

c. If the expression occurs *at the beginning of a dependent clause,* either treat the expression as nonessential (and set it off with two commas) or treat it as essential (and omit the commas).

(Continued on page 24.)

If, *moreover,* they do not meet the deadline, we have the right to cancel the contract.
If *indeed* they want to settle the dispute, why don't they agree to arbitration?
He is a man who, *in my opinion,* will make a fine marketing director.
She is a woman who *no doubt* knows how to run a department smoothly and effectively.
The situation is so serious that, *strictly speaking,* bankruptcy is the only solution.
The situation is so serious that *perhaps* bankruptcy may be the only solution.

143   With the Adverb *Too*

a. When the adverb *too* (in the sense of "also") occurs at the end of a clause or a
sentence, the comma preceding is omitted.

If you feel that way *too,* why don't we just drop all further negotiation?

They are after a bigger share of the market *too.*

b. When *too* (in the sense of "also") occurs elsewhere in the sentence, particularly between subject and verb, set if off with two commas.

You, *too,* could be in the Caribbean right now.

Then, *too,* there are the additional taxes to be considered.

c. When *too* is used as an adverb meaning "excessively," it is never set off with
commas.

The news is almost *too* good to be believed.

WITH INTERRUPTIONS AND AFTERTHOUGHTS

144   Use commas to set off words, phrases, or clauses that interrupt the flow of a
sentence or that are loosely added at the end as an afterthought.

She has received, *so I was told,* a letter of commendation from the mayor.

The exhibit contained only modern art, *if I remember correctly.*

Our lighting equipment, *you must admit,* is most inadequate.

His record is outstanding, *particularly in the field of electronics.*

This book is as well written as, *though less exciting than,* her other books.

This course of action is the wisest, *if not the most expedient,* one under the given
circumstances.

❏ *See also ¶¶131c, 136b, 137c.*

CAUTION: When enclosing an interrupting expression with two commas, be
sure the commas are inserted accurately.

WRONG: That is the best, *though not the cheapest method,* of rebuilding your garage.
RIGHT: That is the best, *though not the cheapest,* method of rebuilding your garage.

WRONG: Glen has a deep interest in, *as well as a great fondness,* for jazz.
RIGHT: Glen has a deep interest in, *as well as a great fondness for,* jazz.

WITH DIRECT ADDRESS

145   Names and titles used in direct address must be set off by commas.

We agree, *Mrs. Connolly,* that your order was badly handled.

No, *sir,* that is privileged information.

I count on your support, *Bob.*

WITH ADDITIONAL CONSIDERATIONS

146 A phrase introduced by *as well as, in addition to, besides, along with, including, accompanied by, together with, plus,* or a similar expression should be set off by commas when it falls between the subject and the verb.

> The trustees, *as well as the creditors,* approved the refinancing terms.

When the phrase occurs elsewhere in the sentence, commas may be omitted if the phrase is closely related to the preceding words.

> The refinancing terms have been approved by the trustees *as well as the creditors.*
>
> **BUT:** I attended the international monetary conference in Bermuda, *together with five associates from our Washington office.*

WITH CONTRASTING EXPRESSIONS

147 Contrasting expressions should be set off by commas. (Such expressions often begin with *but, not,* or *rather than.*)

> The Sanchezes are willing to sell, *but only on their terms.*
>
> He had changed his methods, *not his objectives,* we noticed.
>
> Paula, *rather than Al,* has been chosen for the job.

NOTE: When such phrases fit smoothly into the flow of the sentence, no commas are required.

> It was a busy *but enjoyable* trip.   They have chosen Paula *rather than Al.*

❑ *For the punctuation of balancing expressions, see ¶172c.*

The following rules (¶¶148–153) deal with descriptive expressions that immediately follow the words to which they refer. When nonessential, these expressions are set off by commas.

WITH IDENTIFYING, APPOSITIVE, OR EXPLANATORY EXPRESSIONS

148 Use commas to set off expressions that provide additional but *nonessential* information about a noun or pronoun immediately preceding. Such expressions serve to further identify or explain the word they refer to.

> Harriet McManus, *an independent real estate broker for the past ten years,* will be joining our agency on Tuesday, *October 1.* (Phrases such as those following *Harriet McManus* and *Tuesday* are appositives.)
>
> Acrophobia, *that is, the fear of great heights,* can now be successfully treated. (See also ¶¶181–183 for other punctuation with *that is, namely,* and *for example.*)
>
> His first book, *written while he was still in graduate school,* launched a successful writing career.
>
> Our first thought, *to run to the nearest exit,* would have resulted in panic.
>
> Ms. Ballantine, *who has been a copywriter for six years,* will be our new copy chief.
>
> Everyone in our family likes outdoor sports, *such as tennis and skiing.*

NOTE: In some cases other punctuation may be preferable in place of commas.

> **CONFUSING:** Mr. Newcombe, *my boss,* and I will discuss this problem next week. (Does *my boss* refer to Mr. Newcombe, or are there three people involved?)
>
> **CLEAR:** Mr. Newcombe (my boss) and I will be discussing this problem next week. (Use parentheses or dashes instead of commas when an appositive expression could be misread as a separate item in a series.)

(Continued on page 26.)

There are two factors to be considered, *sales and collections*. (A colon or a dash could be used in place of the comma. See ¶¶189, 201.)

BUT: There are three factors to be considered: sales, collections, and inventories. (When the explanatory expression consists of a series of *three* or more items and comes at the end of the sentence, use a colon or dash. See ¶¶189, 201.)

OR: These three factors—sales, collections, and inventories—should be considered. (When the explanatory series comes within the sentence, set it off with dashes or parentheses. See ¶¶183, 202, 219.)

149 When the expression is *essential* to the completeness of the sentence, do not set it off. (In the following examples, the expression is needed to identify which particular item is meant. If the expression were omitted, the sentence would be incomplete.)

The year *1988* marks the one hundredth anniversary of our company.

The word *liaison* is often misspelled.

The novelist *Anne Tyler* gave a reading last week from a work in progress.

The statement *"I don't remember"* was frequently heard in court yesterday.

The impulse *to get away from it all* is very common.

The notes *in green ink* were made by Mrs. Long.

The person *who takes over as general manager* will need everyone's support.

Everyone in our family likes *such* outdoor sports *as tennis and skiing.*

NOTE: Compare the following set of examples:

Her article *"Color and Design"* was published in June. (The title is essential; it identifies *which* article.)

Her latest article, *"Color and Design,"* was published in June. (Nonessential; the word *latest* already indicates which article.)

Her latest article *on color and design* was published in June. (Without commas, this means she had earlier articles on the same subject.)

Her latest article, *on color and design,* was published in June. (With commas, this means her earlier articles were on other subjects.)

150 A number of expressions are treated as essential simply because of a very close relationship with the preceding words. (If read aloud, the combined phrase sounds like one unit, without any intervening pause.)

After a while Gladys *herself* became disenchanted with the Washington scene.

We *legislators* need to provide adequate funds for retraining workers displaced by the new technology.

My wife Patricia has begun her own consulting business. (Strictly speaking, *Patricia* should be set off by commas, since the name is not needed to indicate *which* wife. However, commas are omitted in expressions like these because they are read as a unit.)

My brother Paul may join us as well.
BUT: My brother, *Paul Engstrom,* may join us.

The composer *Stephen Sondheim* has many Broadway hits to his credit.
BUT: My favorite composer, *Stephen Sondheim,* has many Broadway hits . . .

151 When *or* introduces a word or a phrase that identifies or explains the preceding word, set off the explanatory expression with commas.

Determine whether the clauses are coordinate, *or of equal rank.*

However, if *or* introduces an alternative thought, the expression is essential and should not be set off by commas.

Determine whether the clauses are coordinate *or noncoordinate.*

152 When a business letter is referred to by date, any related phrases or clauses that follow are usually nonessential.

> Thank you for your letter of February 27, *in which you questioned the balance on your account.* (The date is sufficient to identify which letter is meant; the *in which* clause simply provides additional but nonessential information.)

However, no comma is needed after the date if the following phrase is short and closely related.

> Thank you for your letter of February 27 *about the balance on your account.*

WITH RESIDENCE AND BUSINESS CONNECTIONS

153 Use commas to set off a *long phrase* denoting a person's residence or business connections.

> Gary Kendall, *of the Van Houten Corporation in Provo, Utah,* will be visiting us next week.
>
> Gary Kendall *of Provo, Utah,* will be visiting us next week. (Omit the comma before *of* to avoid too many breaks in a short phrase. The state name must always be set off by commas when it follows a city name.)
>
> Gary Kendall *of the Van Houten Corporation* will be visiting us next week. (Short phrase; no commas.)
>
> Gary Kendall *of Provo* will be visiting us next week. (Short phrase; no commas.)

The following rules (¶¶154–161) deal with the "nonessential" treatment of certain elements in dates, personal names, company names, and addresses. Because these elements cannot truly be called nonessential, the established tradition of setting them off with commas has in many cases begun to change.

IN DATES

154 Use two commas to set off the year when it follows the month and day.

> On July 1, *1990,* I hope to retire from my present job and start on a second career.
>
> The July 15, *1985,* issue of *Business Week* had a good write-up on compensation based on the concept of comparable worth.

NOTE: Some writers omit the comma following the year.

155 Omit the commas when only the month and year are given.

> In *August 1984* Glen and I dissolved our partnership and went our independent ways.
>
> An analysis of water filters appeared in the *February 1985* issue of *Consumer Reports.*

❑ *For additional examples involving dates, see ¶410.*

WITH *JR., SR.,* ETC.

156 Do not use commas to set off *Jr., Sr.,* or roman or arabic numerals following a person's name unless you know that the person in question prefers to do so.

> Kelsey R. Patterson Jr.   Benjamin Hart 2d
> Christopher M. Gorman Sr.   Anthony Jung III
>
> John Bond Jr.'s resignation will be announced tomorrow.

(Continued on page 28.)

NOTE: When a person prefers to use commas in his name, observe the following style:

> Peter Passaro, Jr. (Use one comma when the name is displayed on a line by itself.)
> Peter Passaro, Jr., director of . . . (Use two commas when other copy follows.)
> Peter Passaro, Jr.'s promotion . . . (Drop the second comma when a possessive ending is attached.)

157 Abbreviations like *Esq.* and those that stand for academic degrees or religious orders are set off by two commas when they follow a person's name.

> Address the letter to Helen E. Parsekian, *Esq.,* in New York.
> Roger Farrier, *LL.D.,* will address the Elizabethan Club on Wednesday.
> The Reverend James Hanley, *S.J.,* will serve as moderator of the panel.

158 When a personal name is given in inverted order, set off the inverted portion with commas.

> McCaughan, James W., Jr.

WITH *INC.* AND *LTD.*

159 Do not use commas to set off *Inc., Ltd.,* and similar expressions in a company name unless you know that a particular company prefers to do so. (See also ¶¶1328–1329.)

> Time Inc.   Field Hats, Ltd.

> Time *Inc.* has expanded its operations beyond magazine publishing.
> Field Hats, *Ltd.,* should be notified about this mistake.

NOTE: When commas are to be used in a company name, follow this style:

> McGraw-Hill, Inc. (Use one comma when the name is displayed on a line by itself.)
> McGraw-Hill, Inc., announces the publication of . . . (Use two commas when other copy follows.)
> McGraw-Hill, Inc.'s annual statement . . . (Drop the second comma after a possessive ending.)

❑ *For the use of commas with other parts of a company name, see ¶163.*

IN GEOGRAPHIC REFERENCES AND ADDRESSES

160 Use two commas to set off the name of a state, country, county, or the equivalent when it directly follows the name of a city.

> Four years ago I was transferred from Bartlesville, *Oklahoma,* to Kinshasa, *Zaire.*
> They are now living somewhere in Marin County, *California.*
> Our Pierre, *South Dakota,* office is the one nearest to you.
> **OR:** Our Pierre (South Dakota) office is the one nearest to you. (Parentheses are clearer than commas when a city-state expression serves as an adjective.)
> Washington, *D.C.'s* transportation system has improved greatly since I was last there. (Omit the second comma after a possessive ending.)

161 When expressing complete addresses, follow this style:

> **IN SENTENCES:** During the month of August you can send material directly to me at 402 Woodbury Road, Pasadena, CA 91104, or you can ask my secretary to forward it. (Note that a comma follows the ZIP Code but does not precede it.)
>
> **IN DISPLAYED BLOCKS:** 402 Woodbury Road
>   Pasadena, CA 91104

The following rules (¶¶162–175) deal with various uses of separating commas: to separate items in a series, to separate adjectives that precede a noun, and to clarify meaning in sentences with unusual word order or omitted words.

IN A SERIES

162 When three or more items are listed in a series and the last item is preceded by *and, or,* or *nor,* place a comma before the conjunction as well as between the other items. (See also ¶126*b*.)

> Study the rules for the use of the comma, the semicolon, *and* the colon.
>
> The consensus is that your report is well written, that your facts are accurate, *and* that your conclusions are sound.
>
> The show will appeal equally to women and men, adults and children, *and* sophisticates and innocents. (See page 221 for a usage note on *and* in Section 11.)

NOTE: If a nonessential element follows the conjunction (*and, or,* or *nor*) in a series, omit the comma before the conjunction to avoid excessive punctuation.

> We have invited Ben's business associates, his friends and, of course, his parents. (**RATHER THAN:** . . . his friends, and, of course, his parents.)

163 For a series in a company name, always follow the style preferred by the particular firm.

> Merrill Lynch Pierce Fenner & Smith Inc.   Peat, Marwick, Mitchell & Co.

If you do not have the company's letterhead or some other reliable resource at hand, follow the standard rule on commas in a series (¶162).

> Our primary supplier is *Ames, Koslow, Milke, and Company.*

NOTE: Do not use a comma before an ampersand (&) in a company name unless you know that a particular company prefers to do so.

> Aspinwall, Bromley, Carruthers & Dalgleish

164 When an expression such as *and so on* or *etc.* closes a series, use a comma before and after the expression (unless the expression falls at the end of a sentence).

> Our sale of suits, coats, hats, *and so on,* starts tomorrow.
>
> Tomorrow morning we will start our sale of suits, coats, hats, *etc.*

❑ *For a usage note on* etc., *see page 225.*

165 Do not insert a comma after the last item in a series unless the sentence structure demands a comma at that point.

> May 8, June 11, and July 14 are the dates for the next three hearings.
>
> May 8, June 11, and July 14, 1986, are the dates for the next three hearings. (The comma following the year is one of the pair that sets off the year. See ¶154.)

166 When *and, or,* or *nor* is used to connect all the items in a series, do not separate the items by commas. (See also ¶123*b*.)

> Copies of our recently published company history are being distributed to employees *and* stockholders *and* major customers.

167 If a series consists of only two items, do not separate the items with a comma. (See also ¶125*f*.)

> We can send the samples to you *by regular mail* or *by one of the express services.*

(Continued on page 30.)

NOTE: Use a comma, however, to separate two independent clauses joined by *and, but, or,* or *nor.* (See ¶126a.)

❑ *For the use of the semicolon in a series, see ¶¶184–185.*

WITH ADJECTIVES

168 When two consecutive adjectives modify the same noun, separate the adjectives with a comma.

Most people think of her as a *generous, outgoing* person. (A person who is *generous* and *outgoing.*)

NOTE: Do *not* use a comma between the adjectives if they are connected by *and, or,* or *nor.*

Most people think of her as a *generous* and *outgoing* person.

169 When two adjectives precede a noun, the first adjective may modify the combined idea of the second adjective plus the noun. In such cases do not separate the adjectives by a comma.

The estate is surrounded by an *old stone* wall. (A *stone* wall that is *old.*)

Ms. Klaussen is working on the *annual financial* statement. (A *financial* statement that is *annual.*)

TEST: To decide whether consecutive adjectives should be separated by a comma or not, try using them in a relative clause *after* the noun, with *and* inserted between them. If they read smoothly and sensibly in that position, they should be separated by a comma in their actual position.

We need an *intelligent, enterprising* person for the job. (One can speak of "a person who is *intelligent* and *enterprising*," so a comma is correct in the original wording.)

Throw out your *old winter* coat. (One cannot speak of "a coat that is *old* and *winter*," so no comma should be used in the actual sentence.)

170 When more than two adjectives precede a noun, insert a comma only between those adjectives where *and* could have been used.

an easy, relaxed, unruffled manner (an easy *and* relaxed *and* unruffled manner)

a competent, efficient legal secretary (a competent *and* efficient legal secretary)

the established American political system (*and* cannot be inserted between these three adjectives)

171 Do not use a comma between the final adjective in a series and the following noun.

I put in a long, hard, *demanding day* on Monday.

(**NOT:** I put in a long, hard, *demanding, day* on Monday.)

TO INDICATE OMITTED WORDS

172 a. **Omission of Repetitive Wording.** Use a comma to indicate the omission of repetitive wording in a compound sentence. (This use of the comma usually occurs when clauses are separated by semicolons.)

Employees aged 55 and over are eligible for a complete physical examination every year; those between 50 and 54, every two years; and those under 50, every three years.

NOTE: If the omitted words are clearly understood from the context, simpler punctuation may be used.

Employees aged 55 and over are eligible for a complete physical examination every year, those between 50 and 54 every two years, and those under 50 every three years.

b. **Omission of *That*.** In some sentences the omission of the conjunction *that* creates a definite break in the flow of the sentence. In such cases insert a comma to mark the break.

Remember, this offer is good only through May 31.

The problem is, not all of these assumptions may be correct.

The fact is, things are not working out as we had hoped.

Chances are, the deal will never come off.

NOTE: In sentences that are introduced by expressions such as *he said, she thinks, we feel,* or *they know,* the conjunction *that* is often omitted following the introductory expression. In such cases no comma is necessary because there is no break in the flow of the sentence.

I know you can do it.	She said she would handle all the arrangements.
They think our price is too high.	We believe we offer the best service in the area.

c. **Balancing Expressions.** Use a comma to separate the two parts of a balancing expression from which many words have been omitted.

First come, first served.	The more we give, the more they take.
First in, last out.	GIGO: garbage in, garbage out.
Here today, gone tomorrow.	The less I see of him, the better I like it.

NOTE: The phrase *The sooner the better* usually appears without a separating comma.

TO INDICATE UNUSUAL WORD ORDER

173   In some colloquial sentences, clauses or phrases occur out of normal order and connective words may be omitted. Use a comma to mark the resulting break in the flow of the sentence.

You must not miss the play, it was that good.
(**NORMAL ORDER:** The play was so good that you must not miss it.)

Why he took the money, I'll never understand.

That the shipment would be late, we were prepared to accept; that you would ship the wrong goods, we did not expect.

NOTE: In formal writing, these sentences should be recast in normal word order.

❏ *See also ¶135c, note.*

FOR SPECIAL EMPHASIS

174   Individual words may be set off by commas for special emphasis.

I have tried, *sincerely,* to understand your problems.

They contend, *unrealistically,* that we can cut back on staff and still generate the same amount of output.

NOTE: The use of commas in the examples above forces the reader to dwell momentarily on the word that has been set off in each case. Without this treatment *sincerely* and *unrealistically* would not receive this emphasis.

FOR CLARITY

175   a. Use a comma to prevent misreading.

As you know, nothing came of the meeting. (**NOT:** As you know nothing came of the meeting.)

To a liberal like Bill, Buckley seems hard to take.

Soon after, the committee disbanded without accomplishing its goal.

b. Sometimes, for clarity, it is necessary to separate even a subject and a verb.

All any insurance policy is, is a contract for services.

c. Use a comma to separate repeated words.

It was a *long, long* time ago.

That was a *very, very* old argument.

Well, well, we'll find a way.

Now, now, you don't expect me to believe that!

❑ *Commas with dashes: see ¶¶213, 215b.*
❑ *Commas with numbers: see ¶¶461–463.*
❑ *Commas with questions within sentences: see ¶¶114–117.*
❑ *Commas with parentheses: see ¶224a.*
❑ *Commas inside closing quotation marks: see ¶247.*
❑ *Commas at the end of quotations: see ¶¶253–255.*
❑ *Commas preceding quotations: see ¶256.*
❑ *Commas with quotations within a sentence: see ¶¶259–261.*
❑ *Commas to set off interruptions in quoted matter: see ¶¶262–263.*
❑ *Typewriter spacing with commas: see ¶299.*

THE SEMICOLON

BETWEEN INDEPENDENT CLAUSES—*AND, BUT, OR,* OR *NOR* OMITTED

176

a. When a coordinating conjunction (*and, but, or,* or *nor*) is omitted between two independent clauses, use a semicolon—not a comma—to separate the clauses. (See ¶187.)

Most of the stockholders favored the sale; the management and the employees did not.

(**NOT:** Most of the stockholders favored the sale, the management and the employees did not.)

b. If the clauses are not closely related, treat them as separate sentences.

WEAK: Thank you for your letter of September 8; your question has already been passed on to the manager of mail-order sales, and you should be hearing from Mrs. Livonia within three days.

BETTER: Thank you for your letter of September 8. Your question has already been passed on to the manager of mail-order sales, and you should be hearing from Mrs. Livonia within three days.

c. The omission of *but* between two independent clauses requires, strictly speaking, the use of a semicolon between the two clauses. However, in certain idiomatic constructions a comma is commonly used to preserve the flow of the sentence.

IDIOMATIC: The food was not only bad, the portions were minuscule.

FORMAL: Not only was the food bad, but the portions were minuscule.

BETWEEN INDEPENDENT CLAUSES—*AND, BUT, OR,* OR *NOR* INCLUDED

177

A comma is normally used to separate two independent clauses joined by a coordinating conjunction. However, under certain circumstances a semicolon is appropriate before the coordinating conjunction.

a. Use a semicolon in order to achieve a stronger break between clauses than a comma provides.

NORMAL BREAK: Many people are convinced that they could personally solve the problem if given the authority to do so, but no one will come forward with a clear-cut plan that we can evaluate in advance.

STRONG BREAK: Many people are convinced that they could personally solve the problem if given the authority to do so; but no one will come forward with a clear-cut plan that we can evaluate in advance.

b. Use a semicolon when one or both clauses have internal commas and a misreading might occur if a comma were also used to separate the clauses.

CONFUSING: I sent you an order for bond letterheads, onionskin paper, carbons, and envelopes, and shipping tags, cardboard cartons, stapler wire, and binding tape were sent to me instead.

CLEAR: I sent you an order for bond letterheads, onionskin paper, carbons, and envelopes; and shipping tags, cardboard cartons, stapler wire, and binding tape were sent to me instead.

c. If no misreading is likely, a comma is sufficient to separate the clauses, even though commas are also used within the clauses.

On June 8, 19—, I discussed this problem with your customer service manager, Betty Dugan, but your company has taken no further action.

All in all, we're satisfied with the job Bergquist Associates did, and in view of the tight deadlines they had to meet, we're pleased that they came through as well as they did.

❑ *For additional examples, see ¶133.*

WITH TRANSITIONAL EXPRESSIONS

178 When independent clauses are linked by transitional expressions (see a partial list below), use a semicolon between the clauses. (If the second clause is long or requires special emphasis, treat it as a separate sentence.)

accordingly	however	so (see ¶179)
besides	moreover	that is (see ¶181)
consequently	namely (see ¶181)	then (see ¶139*b*)
for example (see ¶181)	nevertheless	therefore
furthermore	on the contrary	thus
hence	otherwise	yet (see ¶179)

They have given us an oral okay to proceed; *however,* we're still waiting for written confirmation.

Our costs have started to level off; our sales, *moreover,* have continued to grow.

Let's give them another month; *then* we can pin them down on their progress.

NOTE: Use a comma after the transitional expression when it occurs at the start of the second clause. (See the first example above.) However, no comma is needed after *hence, then, thus, so,* and *yet* unless a pause is wanted at that point. (See the third example above.)

❑ *For the use of commas with transitional expressions, see ¶¶138–142.*

179 An independent clause introduced by *so* (in the sense of "therefore") or *yet* may be preceded by a comma or a semicolon. Use a comma if the two clauses are closely related and there is a smooth flow from the first clause to the second. Use a semicolon if the clauses are long and complicated or if the transition between clauses calls for a long pause or a strong break.

(*Continued on page 34.*)

Sales have been good, *yet* profits are low.

This report explains why production has slowed down; *yet* it does not indicate how to avoid future delays.

These sale-priced toasters are going fast, *so* don't delay if you want one.

We have been getting an excessive number of complaints during the last few months about our service; *so* I would like each of you to review the operations in your department and indicate what corrective measures you think ought to be taken.

180 If both a coordinating conjunction and a transitional expression occur at the start of the second clause, use a comma before the conjunction.

The site has a number of disadvantages, *and furthermore* the asking price is quite high. (See ¶142*b* and note.)

REMEMBER: A semicolon is needed to separate independent clauses, not so much because a transitional expression is present but because a coordinating conjunction is absent.

WITH *FOR EXAMPLE, THAT IS, NAMELY,* ETC.

181 Before an Independent Clause

a. In general, when two independent clauses are linked by a transitional expression such as *for example (e.g.), namely,* or *that is (i.e.),* use a semicolon before the expression and a comma afterward.

She is highly qualified for the job; *for example,* she has had ten years' experience as a research chemist.

b. If the first clause serves to anticipate the second clause and the full emphasis is to fall on the second clause, use a colon before the transitional expression.

Your proposal covers all but one point: *namely,* who is going to foot the bill?

c. For a stronger but less formal break between clauses, the semicolon or the colon may be replaced by a dash.

Hampton says he will help—*that is,* he will help if you ask him to.

182 At the End of a Sentence

When *for example, namely,* or *that is* introduces words, phrases, or a series of clauses *at the end of a sentence,* the punctuation preceding the expression may vary as follows:

a. If the first part of the sentence expresses the complete thought and the explanation seems to be added on as an afterthought, use a semicolon before the transitional expression.

Always use figures with abbreviations; *for example,* 6 m, 9 sq in, 4 p.m. (Here the earlier part of the sentence carries the main thought; the examples are a welcome but non-essential addition.)

b. If the first part of the sentence suggests that an important explanation or illustration will follow, use a colon before the transitional expression to throw emphasis on what *follows*.

My assistant has three important duties: *namely,* attending all meetings, writing the minutes, and sending out notices. (The word *three* anticipates the enumeration following *namely.* The colon suggests that what follows is the main thought of the sentence.)

NOTE: Use a comma before the transitional expression to throw emphasis on what *precedes*.

I checked these figures with three people, *namely, Alma, Andy, and Jim.* (This punctuation emphasizes *three people* rather than the specific names.)

c. If the expression introduces an appositive that explains a word or phrase immediately preceding, a comma should precede the transitional expression.

Do not use quotation marks to enclose an indirect quotation, *that is, a restatement of a person's exact words.* (Here again, a comma is used because what precedes the transitional expression is more important than what follows.)

d. The semicolon, the colon, and the comma in the examples above and on page 34 may be replaced by a dash or by parentheses. The dash provides a stronger but less formal break; the parentheses serve to subordinate the explanatory element.

183   Within a Sentence

When *for example, namely,* or *that is* introduces words, phrases, or clauses *within a sentence,* treat the entire construction as nonessential and set it off with commas, dashes, or parentheses. Dashes will give emphasis to the interrupting construction; parentheses will make the construction appear less important than the rest of the words in the sentence.

Many of the components, *for example, the motor,* are manufactured by outside suppliers.

Many of the components—*for example, the motor*—are manufactured by . . .

Many of the components (*for example, the motor*) are manufactured by . . .

NOTE: Commas can be used to set off the nonessential element so long as it contains no internal punctuation (other than the comma after the introductory expression). If the nonessential element is internally punctuated with several commas, set it off with either dashes or parentheses.

Many of the components—*for example, the motor, the batteries, and the cooling unit*—are manufactured by outside suppliers. (Use dashes for emphasis.)

OR: Many of the components (*for example, the motor, the batteries, and the cooling unit*) are manufactured by outside suppliers. (Use parentheses for subordination.)

IN A SERIES

184   Use a semicolon to separate items in a series if any of the items already contain commas.

The company will be represented on the Longwood Environmental Council next year by Martha Janowski, director of public affairs; Harris Mendel, vice president of manufacturing; and Daniel Santoya, director of environmental systems.

NOTE: As an alternative, the title following each name may be enclosed in parentheses. In that case, commas can be used to separate the items in the series.

The company will be represented on the Longwood Environmental Council next year by Martha Janowski (director of public affairs), Harris Mendel (vice president of manufacturing), and Daniel Santoya (director of environmental systems).

185   Avoid starting a sentence with a series punctuated with semicolons. Try to recast the sentence so that the series comes at the end.

AWKWARD: New offices in Framingham, Massachusetts; Rochester, Minnesota; Metairie, Louisiana; and Eugene, Oregon, will be opened by the middle of next year.

IMPROVED: By the middle of next year we will open new offices in Framingham, Massachusetts; Rochester, Minnesota; Metairie, Louisiana; and Eugene, Oregon.

WITH DEPENDENT CLAUSES

186   Use semicolons to separate a series of parallel dependent clauses if they are long or contain internal commas. (However, a simple series of dependent clauses

requires only commas, just like any other kind of series. For an example, see
¶162.)

> They promised that they would review the existing specifications, costs, and sales esti-
> mates for the project; that they would analyze Merkle's alternative figures; and that
> they would prepare a detailed comparison of the two proposals.

> If you have tried special clearance sales but have not raised the necessary cash; if you
> have tried to borrow the money and have not been able to find a lender; if you have
> offered to sell part of the business but have not been able to find a partner, then your
> only course of action is to go out of business.

❑ *Semicolons with dashes: see ¶¶213, 215c.*
❑ *Semicolons with parentheses: see ¶224a.*
❑ *Semicolons with quotation marks: see ¶248.*
❑ *Typewriter spacing with semicolons: see ¶299.*

THE COLON

BETWEEN INDEPENDENT CLAUSES

187   Use a colon between two independent clauses when the second clause explains
or illustrates the first clause and there is no coordinating conjunction or transitional expression linking the two clauses.

> I have a special fondness for the Maine coast: it reminds me of the many happy sum-
> mers we spent there when our children were still in school.

NOTE: The second clause that explains or illustrates the first clause may itself
consist of more than one independent clause.

> The job you have described sounds very attractive: the salary is good, and the opportu-
> nities for advancement seem excellent.

> **BUT:** The job you have described sounds very attractive; for example, the salary is good,
> and the opportunities for advancement seem excellent. (Use a semicolon when a transi-
> tional expression links the clauses.)

> The job you have described sounds very attractive; it is the kind of job I have been
> looking for. (Use a semicolon when the second clause does not explain the first clause.)

BEFORE LISTS AND ENUMERATIONS

188   Place a colon before such expressions as *for example, namely,* and *that is* when
they introduce words, phrases, or a series of clauses anticipated earlier in the
sentence.

> The company provides a number of benefits not commonly offered in this area: for
> example, free dental insurance, low-cost term insurance, and personal financial coun-
> seling services.

❑ *For additional examples, see ¶182b.*

189   When a clause contains an anticipatory expression (such as *the following, as
follows, thus,* and *these*) and directs attention to a series of explanatory words,
phrases, or clauses, use a colon between the clause and the series.

> *These* are some of the new features in this year's models: a fuel economy indicator, a
> new rear suspension, and a three-year limited warranty.

> The *following* staff members have been selected to attend the national sales conference
> in Honolulu:
>
> > Frances Berkowitz
> > Thomas Gomez
> > Thomas Miscina
> > Kelly Prendergast

190   Use a colon even if the anticipatory expression is only implied and not stated.

> The house has attractive features: cross ventilation in every room, a two-story living room, and two terraces.

191   Do not use a colon in the following cases:

a. If the anticipatory expression occurs near the beginning of a long sentence.

> We have set *the following* restrictions on the return of merchandise, because many customers have abused the privilege. Goods cannot be returned after five days, and price tags must not be removed.
>
> **BUT:** We have set *the following* restrictions on the return of merchandise: goods cannot be returned . . .

b. If the sentence containing the anticipatory expression is followed by another sentence.

> Campers will find that *the following* small items will add much to their enjoyment of the summer. These articles may be purchased from a store near the camp.
>
> | | |
> |---|---|
> | Flashlight | Hot-cold food bag |
> | Camera | Fishing gear |

c. If an explanatory series follows a preposition or a verb.

> The panel consists of Ms. Seidel, Mrs. Kitay, and Mr. Haddad.
> (**NOT:** The panel consists of: Ms. Seidel, Mrs. Kitay, and Mr. Haddad.)
>
> This set of china includes 12 dinner plates, 12 salad plates, and 12 cups and saucers.
> (**NOT:** This set of china includes: 12 dinner plates, 12 salad plates, and 12 cups and saucers.)
>
> **NOTE:** Retain the colon if the items in the series are listed on separate lines.
>
> This set of china includes:
>
> 12 dinner plates
> 12 salad plates
> 12 cups and saucers

IN EXPRESSIONS OF TIME AND PROPORTIONS

192   When hours and minutes are expressed in figures, separate them with a colon, as in the expression *8:25.* (No space precedes or follows this colon.)

193   A colon is used to represent the word *to* in proportions, as in the ratio *2:1.* (No space precedes or follows this colon.)

AFTER SALUTATIONS

194   In business letters, use a colon after the salutation (see also ¶1346). In social-business letters, use a comma (see also ¶1395*b*).

IN REFERENCES TO BOOKS OR PUBLICATIONS

195   Use a colon to separate the title and the subtitle of a book.

> William Least Heat Moon, in *Blue Highways: A Journey Into America,* has provided an extraordinary portrait of a country and its people.

CAPITALIZING AFTER A COLON

196   Do not capitalize after a colon if the material cannot stand alone as a sentence.

> All cash advances must be countersigned by me, with one exception: when the amount is less than $50. (Dependent clause following a colon.)
>
> Two courses are required: algebra and English. (Words following a colon.)

EXCEPTION: Capitalize the first word after the colon if it is a proper noun, a proper adjective, or the pronoun *I*.

> Two courses are required: English and algebra.

197   Do not capitalize the first word of an independent clause after a colon if the clause explains, illustrates, or amplifies the thought expressed in the first part of the sentence. (See ¶196, exception.)

> Essential and nonessential elements require altogether different punctuation: the latter should be set off by commas; the former should not.

198   Capitalize the first word of an independent clause after a colon if it requires special emphasis or is presented as a formal rule. (In such cases the independent clause expresses the main thought; the first part of the sentence usually functions only as an introduction.)

> Let me say this: If the company is to recover from its present difficulties, we must immediately devise an entirely new marketing strategy.
>
> Here is the key principle: Nonessential elements must be set off by commas; essential elements should not.

199   Also capitalize the first word after a colon under these circumstances:

a. When the material following the colon consists of two or more sentences.

> There are several drawbacks to this proposal: First, it will tie up a good deal of capital for the next five years. Second, the likelihood of a significant return on the investment has not been shown.

b. When the material following the colon is a quoted sentence.

> Frederick Fontina responded in this way: "We expect to win our case once all the facts are brought out in the trial." (See ¶256 for the use of a colon before a quoted sentence.)

c. When the material following the colon starts on a new line (for example, the body of a letter following the salutation or the individual items displayed on separate lines in a list).

> Dear John:
>
> I have read your latest draft, and I find it much improved. However, on page 4 I wish you would redo . . .

> Capitalize the first word of:
>
> a. Every sentence.
> b. Direct quotations.
> c. Salutations in letters.

d. When the material *preceding* the colon is a short introductory word such as *Note, Caution,* or *Wanted*.

> Note: All expense reports must be submitted no later than Friday.
>
> Remember: All equipment must be turned off before you leave.

❑ *Colons with dashes: see ¶¶213, 215c.*
❑ *Colons with parentheses: see ¶224a.*
❑ *Colons with quotation marks: see ¶¶248, 256.*
❑ *Typewriter spacing with colons: see ¶299.*

Punctuation:
Other Marks

2

THE UNDERSCORE

OTHER MARKS OF PUNCTUATION

SPACING WITH PUNCTUATION
MARKS (¶299)

THE DASH

Although the dash has a few specific functions of its own, it most often serves in place of the comma, the semicolon, the colon, or parentheses. When used as an alternative to these other marks, it creates a much more emphatic separation of words within a sentence. Because of its versatility, some writers are tempted to use a dash to punctuate almost any break within a sentence. However, this indiscriminate use of dashes destroys the special forcefulness that a dash can convey. So please use the dash sparingly—and then only for deliberate effect.

IN PLACE OF COMMAS

201 Use dashes in place of commas to set off a nonessential element that requires special emphasis.

At this year's annual banquet, the speakers—and the food—were superb.

Of all the color samples you sent me, there was only one I liked—taupe.

202   If a nonessential element already contains internal commas, use dashes in place of commas to set the element off. (If dashes provide too emphatic a break, use parentheses instead. See ¶¶183, 219.)

> Our entire inventory of Oriental rugs—including a fine selection of Sarouks, Kashans, and Bokharas—will be offered for sale at a 40 percent discount.

203   To give special emphasis to the second independent clause in a compound sentence, use a dash rather than a comma before the coordinating conjunction.

> The information I sent you is true—and you know it!

IN PLACE OF A SEMICOLON

204   For a stronger but less formal break, use a dash in place of a semicolon between closely related independent clauses.

> I do the work—he gets the credit!
>
> The job needs to be done—moreover, it needs to be done well.
>
> Wilson is totally unprepared for a promotion—for example, he still does not grasp the basic principles of good management.

IN PLACE OF A COLON

205   For a stronger but less formal break, use a dash in place of a colon to introduce explanatory words, phrases, or clauses.

> I need only a few items for my meeting with Kaster—namely, a copy of his letter of May 18, a copy of the contract under dispute, and a bottle of aspirin.
>
> My arrangement with Gina is a simple one—she handles sales and promotion, and I take care of production.

IN PLACE OF PARENTHESES

206   Use dashes instead of parentheses when you want to give the nonessential element strong emphasis. (See ¶¶183, 219.)

> Call Mike Habib—he's with Jax Electronics—and get his opinion.

TO INDICATE AN ABRUPT BREAK OR AN AFTERTHOUGHT

207   Use a dash to show an abrupt break in thought or to separate an afterthought from the main part of a sentence.

> I wish you would— Is there any point in telling you what I wish for you?
>
> We offer the best service in town—and the fastest!
>
> George Parrish's plane will be landing at O'Hare—or did he say Midway?

208   If a *question* or an *exclamation* breaks off abruptly before it has been completed, use a dash followed by a question mark or an exclamation point as appropriate. If the sentence is a *statement*, however, use a dash alone, followed by two spaces.

> Do you want to tell him or—? Suppose I wait to hear from you.
>
> If only— Yet there's no point in talking about what might have been.
> (**NOT:** If only—. Yet there's no point in talking about what might have been.)

❑ *For the use of ellipsis marks to indicate a break in thought, see ¶291b.*

TO SHOW HESITATION

209 Use a dash to indicate hesitation, faltering speech, or stammering.

> The work on the Patterson dam was begun—oh, I should say—well, about May 1—certainly no later than May 15.

TO EMPHASIZE SINGLE WORDS

210 Use dashes to set off single words that require special emphasis.

> Jogging—that's what he lives for.
>
> There is, of course, a secret ingredient in my pasta sauce—fennel.

WITH REPETITIONS AND RESTATEMENTS

211 Use dashes to set off and emphasize words that repeat or restate a previous thought.

> Next week—on Thursday at 10 a.m.—we will be making an important announcement at a press conference.
>
> Don't miss this opportunity—the opportunity of a lifetime!

BEFORE SUMMARIZING WORDS

212 Use a dash before such words as *these, they,* and *all* when these words stand as subjects summarizing a preceding list of details.

> Network television, magazines, and direct mail—*these* will be the big gainers in advertising revenues next year.
>
> India, Korea, and Australia—*all* are important new markets for us.
>
> **BUT:** India, Korea, and Australia are all important new markets for us. (No dash is used when the summarizing word is not the subject.)

PUNCTUATION PRECEDING AN OPENING DASH

213 Do not precede an opening dash with a comma, a semicolon, a colon, or a period (except a period following an abbreviation).

> Quality circles boost productivity—and they pay off in higher profits too.
> (**NOT:** Quality circles boost productivity,—and they pay off in higher profits too.)
>
> The catalog proofs arrived before 11 a.m.—just as you promised.

PUNCTUATION PRECEDING A CLOSING DASH

214 **a.** When a *statement* or a *command* is set off by dashes within a sentence, do not use a period before the closing dash (except a period following an abbreviation).

> Ernie Krauthoff—he used to have his own consulting firm—has gone back to his old job at Marker's.
>
> (**NOT:** Ernie Krauthoff—He used to have his own consulting firm.—has gone back to his old job at Marker's.)

b. When a *question* or an *exclamation* is set off by dashes within a sentence, use a question mark or an exclamation point before the closing dash.

> The representative of the Hitchcock Company—do you know her?—has called again for an appointment.
>
> The new sketches—I can't wait to show them to you!—should be ready by Monday.

NOTE: When a complete sentence is set off in dashes, do not capitalize the first word unless it is a proper noun, a proper adjective, the pronoun *I,* or the first word of a quoted sentence.

PUNCTUATION FOLLOWING A CLOSING DASH

215 When the sentence construction requires some mark of punctuation following a closing dash, either retain the dash or use the sentence punctuation—but do not use both marks together.

a. When a closing dash falls at the end of a sentence, it should be replaced by the punctuation needed to end the sentence—a period, a question mark, or an exclamation point. (See ¶208 for exceptions.)

Wheeler's Transport delivers the goods—on time!

(**NOT:** Wheeler's Transport delivers the goods—on time—!)

b. When a closing dash occurs at a point where the sentence requires a comma, retain the closing dash and omit the comma.

The situation has become critical—indeed dangerous—but no one seems to care. (Here the closing dash is retained, and the comma before the coordinating conjunction is omitted.)

If you feel you are qualified for the job—and you may very well be—you ought to take the employment test. (Here the closing dash is retained, and the comma that separates a dependent clause from an independent clause is omitted.)

Brophy said—and you can check with him yourself—"This office must be vacated by Friday." (Here the closing dash is retained, and the comma before the quotation is omitted.)

c. If a closing dash occurs at a point where the sentence requires a semicolon, a colon, or a closing parenthesis, drop the closing dash and use the required sentence punctuation.

Please try to get your sales projections to us by Wednesday—certainly by Friday at the latest; otherwise, they will be of no use to us in planning the budget.

Here is what Marsha had to say—or at least the gist of it: look for new opportunities for advancement, and prepare yourself for them.

You need a volunteer (for example, someone like Louis Morales—he's always cooperative) to play the part of the customer.

TYPING DASHES

216 The dash is constructed by striking the hyphen key *twice,* with no space before, between, or after the hyphens.

`Don't believe him--ever!`   **NOT:** `Don't believe him -- ever!`

BUT: `If I had only realized how the news would affect her--` (Two spaces follow a dash when a statement breaks off abruptly. See ¶208.)

217 Type a dash at the end of a line (rather than at the start of a new line).

`Next year our national sales conference is in Hawaii--`
`on Maui, I believe.`

NOT: `Next year our national sales conference is in Hawaii`
`    --on Maui, I believe.`

PARENTHESES

Parentheses and dashes serve many of the same functions, but they differ in one significant respect: parentheses can set off only nonessential elements, whereas dashes can set off essential and nonessential elements.

REMEMBER: In setting off elements, dashes emphasize; parentheses de-emphasize.

WITH EXPLANATORY MATTER

218 Use parentheses to enclose explanatory material that is independent of the main thought of the sentence. The material within parentheses may be a single word, a phrase, or even an entire sentence.

> We called him Mr. B. for so long that when I ran into him last week, I couldn't remember his last name (Bertolucci). (A single word.)
>
> By Friday (and sooner if at all possible) I will have an answer for you. (A phrase.)
>
> Our competitors (we consistently underprice them) can't understand how we do it. (A sentence.)

NOTE: Be sure that the parentheses enclose only what is truly parenthetical and not words essential to the construction of the sentence.

> **WRONG:** I merely said I was averse (not violently opposed *to*) your suggestion.
>
> **RIGHT:** I merely said I was averse (not violently opposed) *to* your suggestion.

219 Use parentheses to set off a nonessential element when dashes would be too emphatic and commas would be inappropriate or might prove confusing.

a. Parentheses are clearer than commas when a city-state expression occurs as an adjective.

> Sales are down in our Middletown (Connecticut) office.
>
> **BETTER THAN:** Sales are down in our Middletown, Connecticut, office.

b. Parentheses are clearer than commas when the nonessential element already contains commas.

> In three of our factories (Gary, Detroit, and Milwaukee) output is up.

WITH REFERENCES

220 Use parentheses to set off references and directions.

> When I last wrote to you (see my letter of July 8 attached), I enclosed photocopies of checks that you had endorsed and deposited.

When a reference falls *at the end of a sentence*, it may be treated as part of the sentence or as a separate sentence.

> This point is discussed at greater length in Chapter 7 (see pages 90–101).
>
> **OR:** This point is discussed at greater length in Chapter 7. (See pages 90–101.)

❏ *See also the note following ¶225d.*

WITH DATES

221 Use parentheses to enclose dates that accompany a person's name or an event.

> He claims that he can trace his family back to Charlemagne (742–814).
>
> The "Sin On" Bible (1716) got its name from an extraordinary typographical error: instead of counseling readers to "sin no more," it urged them to "sin on more."

WITH ENUMERATED ITEMS

222   a. **Within a Sentence.** Use parentheses to enclose numbers or letters that accompany enumerated items within a sentence.

> We need the following information to complete our record of Ms. Pavlick's experience: (1) the number of years she worked for your company, (2) a description of her duties, and (3) the number of promotions she received.

> **NOTE:** Letters are used to enumerate items within a sentence when the sentence itself is part of a *numbered* sequence.

> 3. Please include these items on your expense account: (*a*) the cost of your hotel room; (*b*) the cost of meals, including tips; and (*c*) the amount spent on transportation.

b. **In a Displayed List.** If the enumerated items appear on separate lines, the letters or numbers are usually followed only by periods. (See ¶223.)

223   Subdivisions in outlines are often enclosed in parentheses. It is sometimes necessary to use a single closing parenthesis to provide another level of subdivision.

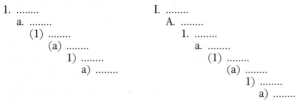

NOTE: At every level of an outline there should be at least two items. If an item is labeled *A,* there must be at least one more item labeled *B* at the same level.

PARENTHETICAL ITEMS WITHIN SENTENCES

224   If the item in parentheses falls *within a sentence:*

a. Make sure that any punctuation that comes after the item (such as a comma, a semicolon, a colon, or a dash) falls *outside* the closing parenthesis.

> Unless I hear from you within five working days (by May 3), I will turn this matter over to my attorney.

> I tried to reach you last Monday (I called just before noon); however, no one in your office knew where you were.

> For Jane there is only one goal right now (and you know it): getting that M.B.A.

> I saw your picture in a magazine last week (in *People,* I think)—and how I laughed when I saw who was standing next to you!

> **NOTE:** Do not insert a comma, a semicolon, a colon, or a dash *before* an opening parenthesis.

b. Do not capitalize the first word of the item in parentheses, even if the item is a complete sentence. **EXCEPTIONS:** Proper nouns, proper adjectives, the pronoun *I,* and the first word of a quoted sentence. (See examples in *c* and *d.*)

c. Do not use a period before the closing parenthesis except with an abbreviation.

> Plan to stay with us (we're only fifteen minutes from the airport) whenever you come to New Orleans.

> **NOT:** Plan to stay with us (We're only fifteen minutes from the airport.) whenever . . .

> Paul Melnick (Bascomb's new sales manager) wants to take you to lunch next week.

> At last week's hearing (I had to leave at 4 p.m.), was the relocation proposal presented?

d. Do not use a question mark or an exclamation point before the closing parenthesis unless it applies solely to the parenthetical item *and* the sentence ends with a different mark of punctuation.

At the coming meeting (will you be able to make it on the 19th?), let's plan to discuss next year's budget. (Question mark used in parentheses because the sentence ends with a period.)

May I still get tickets to the show (and may I bring a friend), or is it too late? (Question mark omitted in parentheses because the sentence ends with a question mark.)

NOT: May I still get tickets to the show (and may I bring a friend?), or is it too late?

PARENTHETICAL ITEMS AT THE END OF SENTENCES

225 If the item in parentheses is to be incorporated *at the end of a sentence:*

a. Place the punctuation needed to end the sentence *outside* the closing parenthesis.

Please return the payroll review sheets by Monday (October 8).

How can I reach Jan Weidner (she spoke at yesterday's seminar)?

What a prima donna I work with (you know the one I mean)!

b. Do not capitalize the first word of the item in parentheses, even if the item is a complete sentence. **EXCEPTIONS:** Proper nouns, proper adjectives, the pronoun *I*, and the first word of a quoted sentence. (See examples in *c* and *d.*)

c. Do not use a period before the closing parenthesis except with an abbreviation.

Our office is open late on Thursdays (until 9 p.m.).

Our office is open late on Thursdays (we're here until nine).
NOT: Our office is open late on Thursdays (We're here until nine.).

d. Do not use a question mark or an exclamation point before the closing parenthesis unless it applies solely to the parenthetical element *and* the sentence ends with a different mark of punctuation.

My new assistant is Bill Romero (didn't you meet him once before?).

Be sure to send the letter to Portland, Oregon (not Portland, Maine!).

Then he walked out and slammed the door (can you believe it?)!

Do you know Ellen Smyth (or is it Smythe)?
NOT: Do you know Ellen Smyth (or is it Smythe?)?

I'm through with the job (and I mean it)!
NOT: I'm through with the job (and I mean it!)!

NOTE: When a complete sentence occurs within parentheses at the end of another sentence, it may be incorporated into the sentence (as in the examples above) so long as it is fairly short and closely related. If the sentence in parentheses is long or requires special emphasis, it should be treated as a separate sentence (see ¶226).

PARENTHETICAL ITEMS AS SEPARATE SENTENCES

226 If the item in parentheses is to be treated as a *separate sentence:*

a. The preceding sentence should close with its own punctuation mark.

b. The item in parentheses should begin with a capital.

c. A period, a question mark, or an exclamation point (whichever is appropriate) should be placed *before* the closing parenthesis.

d. No other punctuation mark should follow the closing parenthesis.

> Then Steven Pelletier stood up and made a motion to replace the existing board of directors. (He does this at every stockholders' meeting.) However, this year . . .

> I was most impressed with the speech given by Helena Verdi. (Didn't you used to work with her?) She knew her subject, and perhaps more important, she knew her audience.

❏ *Parentheses around question marks: see ¶118.*
❏ *Parentheses around exclamation points: see ¶119, note.*
❏ *Parentheses around confirming figures: see ¶420.*
❏ *Parenthetical elements within parenthetical elements: see ¶297.*

QUOTATION MARKS

Quotation marks have three main functions: to indicate the use of someone else's exact words (see ¶¶227–234), to set off words and phrases for special emphasis (see ¶¶235–241), and to display the titles of literary and artistic works (see ¶¶242–244).

For guidance on how to position punctuation marks in relation to the closing quotation mark—*inside* or *outside*—see ¶¶247–251.

For more specific guidance on when to use punctuation with quoted matter and which punctuation to use, refer to the following paragraphs:

❏ *Quotations standing alone: see ¶252.*
❏ *Quotations at the beginning of a sentence: see ¶¶253–255.*
❏ *Quotations at the end of a sentence: see ¶¶256–258.*
❏ *Quotations within a sentence: see ¶¶259–261.*
❏ *Quotations with interrupting expressions: see ¶¶262–263.*
❏ *Quotations within quotations: see ¶¶245–246.*
❏ *Long quotations: see ¶¶264–265.*
❏ *Quoted letters: see ¶266.*
❏ *Quoted poetry: see ¶¶267–268.*
❏ *Quoted dialogues and conversations: see ¶¶269–270.*

WITH DIRECT QUOTATIONS

227 Use quotation marks to enclose a *direct quotation,* that is, the exact words of a speaker or a writer.

> When the final gavel sounded, Ferguson merely said, "Let's get out of here before someone reconsiders the verdict."

> When I asked Diana whether she liked the new format of the magazine, all she said was "No." (See ¶¶233, 256*a*.)

228 **a.** Do not use quotation marks for an *indirect quotation,* that is, a restatement or a rearrangement of a person's exact words. (An indirect quotation is often introduced by *that* or *whether* and usually differs from a direct quotation in person, verb tense, or word order.)

> **DIRECT QUOTATION:** Mrs. Knudsen asked her boss, "Am I still being considered for the transfer?"

> **INDIRECT QUOTATION:** Mrs. Knudsen asked her boss whether she was still being considered for the transfer.

> **DIRECT QUOTATION:** Her boss said, "You're still in the running, but don't expect a quick decision."

> **INDIRECT QUOTATION:** Her boss said that she was still in the running but should not expect a quick decision.

> **NOTE:** Sometimes *direct* quotations are introduced by *that.* See ¶¶256*f* and 272, note.

b. In some cases a person's exact words may be treated as either a direct or an indirect quotation, depending on the kind of emphasis desired.

The chairman himself said, "The staff should be told at once that the relocation rumors have no foundation." (The use of quotation marks emphasizes that these are the chairman's exact words.)

The chairman himself said the staff should be told at once that the relocation rumors have no foundation. (Without quotation marks, the emphasis falls on the message itself. The fact that the chairman used these exact words is not important.)

229 Do not use quotation marks to set off a *direct question* at the end of a sentence unless it is also a *direct quotation* of someone's exact words.

> **DIRECT QUESTION:** The question is, Who will pay for the restoration of the landmark?

> **DIRECT QUOTATION:** Mrs. Burchall then asked, "Who will pay for the restoration of the landmark?"

> **DIRECT QUOTATION:** Mrs. Burchall then replied, "The question is, Who will pay for the restoration of the landmark?"

230 When only a word or phrase is quoted from another source, be sure to place the quotation marks around only the words extracted from the original source and not around any rearrangement of those words.

Tanya said she would need "more help" in order to finish your report by this Friday. (Tanya's exact words were, "How can he expect me to finish his report by this Friday without more help?")

NOTE: When a quoted word or phrase comes at the end of a sentence, the period goes *inside* the closing quotation mark. See ¶247, particularly examples 2–4.

231 Be particularly sure not to include such words as *a* and *the* at the beginning of the quotation or *etc.* at the end unless these words were actually part of the original material.

Ben thought you did a "super" job on the packaging design. (Ben's exact words were, "Tell Bonnie I thought the job she did on the packaging design was super.")

Explain the decision any way you want, but tell George I said, "I'm truly sorry about the way things turned out," etc., etc.

232 When quoting a series of words or phrases in the exact sequence in which they originally appeared, use quotation marks before and after the complete series. However, if the series of quoted words or phrases did not appear in this sequence in the original, use quotation marks around each word or phrase.

According to Selma, the latest issue of the magazine looked "fresh, crisp, and appealing." (Selma's actual words were, "I think the new issue looks especially fresh, crisp, and appealing.")

BUT: Selma thinks the magazine looks "fresh" and "crisp." (**NOT:** "fresh and crisp.")

233 Do not quote the words *yes* and *no* unless you wish to emphasize that these were the exact words spoken.

Please answer the question yes or no.

Don't say no until you have heard all the terms of the proposal.

Once the firm's board of directors says yes, we can draft the contract.

When asked if he would accept a reassignment, Nick thought for a moment; then, without any trace of emotion, he said "Yes." (The quotation marks imply that Nick said precisely this much and no more. See ¶256a, note, for the use or omission of a comma in constructions like this.)

NOTE: When quoting these words, capitalize them if they represent a complete sentence.

> All she said was "No."
>
> I would have to answer that question by saying "Yes and no."
>
> **BUT:** That question requires something more than a yes-or-no answer.

234 Do not use quotation marks with well-known proverbs and sayings. They are not direct quotations.

> Sidney really believes that an apple a day keeps the doctor away.

FOR SPECIAL EMPHASIS

235 In nontechnical material, technical or trade terms should be enclosed in quotation marks when they are first introduced.

> Don't be alarmed if your editor tells you your book is "on the skids." It simply means that books are now stacked on pallets (skids) and ready for distribution.

236 **a.** Words used humorously or ironically may be enclosed in quotation marks. However, unless you are convinced your reader will otherwise miss the humor or the irony, omit the quotation marks.

> We were totally underwhelmed by his ideas on reorganizing the department.

b. A slang expression, the use of poor grammar, or a deliberate misspelling is enclosed in quotation marks to indicate that such usage is not part of the writer's normal way of speaking or writing.

> Now that his kids have run off to Europe with the college tuition money, Bob has stopped boasting about his close-knit "nucular" family. (The writer is mimicking Bob's habitual mispronunciation of *nuclear*.)
>
> As far as I'm concerned, Polly's version of what happened "ain't necessarily so."

c. Quotation marks are not needed for colloquial expressions.

> He cares less about the salary than he does about the *perks*—you know, chauffeured limousine, stock options, and all the rest of it. (*Perks* is short for perquisites, meaning "special privileges.")

237 Use quotation marks to enclose words and phrases that have been made to play an abnormal role in a sentence—for example, verb phrases made to function as adjectives.

> We were all impressed by her "can do" attitude. (*Can do* is a verb phrase used here as an adjective modifying *attitude*.)
>
> **OR:** We were all impressed by her can-do attitude. (A hyphen may also be used to hold together a phrase used as an adjective before a noun. See ¶828.)
>
> **BUT NOT:** We were all impressed by her "can-do" attitude. (Do not use both quotation marks and a hyphen for the same purpose.)
>
> Put that book on your "must read" list.
>
> **BUT:** You have to read that book; it's a must. (The word *must*, originally only a verb form, is now well established as a noun; therefore, it does not have to be enclosed in quotation marks.)

NOTE: Do not use quotation marks to enclose phrases that are taken from other parts of speech and are now well established as nouns; for example, *haves and have-nots, pros and cons, ins and outs.* (See also ¶626.)

> My predecessor left me a helpful list of dos and don'ts.
>
> This document will explain all the whys and wherefores.
>
> Give me an agreement without a lot of ands, ifs, and buts. (See also ¶285.)

238 **a.** Words and phrases introduced by such expressions as *marked, labeled, signed,* and *entitled* are enclosed in quotation marks.

> The carton was marked "Fragile."
>
> He received a message signed "A Friend."
>
> The article entitled "Write Your Senator" was in that issue.

> **NOTE:** Titles of complete published works following the expression *entitled* require underscoring rather than quotation marks. (See ¶289 for titles to be underscored; ¶¶242–244 for titles to be quoted.)

b. Words and phrases introduced by *so-called* require neither quotation marks nor underscoring. The expression *so-called* is sufficient to give special emphasis to the term that follows.

> The so-called orientation session struck Paula and me as more of an exercise in outright brainwashing.

239 A word referred to as a word may be enclosed in quotation marks but is now more commonly underscored. (See ¶285.)

240 When a word or an expression is formally defined, the word to be defined is usually underscored (italicized in print) and the definition is usually quoted so that the two elements may be easily distinguished. (See ¶286.)

241 The translation of a foreign expression is enclosed in quotation marks; the foreign word itself is underscored. (See ¶287.)

WITH TITLES OF LITERARY AND ARTISTIC WORKS

242 Use quotation marks around the titles that represent only *part* of a complete published work—for example, the titles of chapters, lessons, topics, sections, and parts within a book; the titles of articles and feature columns in newspapers and magazines; and the titles of essays, short poems, lectures, sermons, and conference themes. (Underscore titles of *complete* published works. See ¶289.)

> The heart of her argument can be found in Chapter 3, "The Failure of Traditional Therapy." You'll especially want to read the section entitled "Does Father Know Best?"
>
> An exciting article, "Can Cancer Now Be Cured?" appears in the magazine I'm enclosing. (See ¶¶260–261 for the use of commas with quoted titles.)
>
> The title of my speech for next month's luncheon will be "Reforming Our Local Tax Policy."
>
> **BUT:** At next month's luncheon I will be talking about reforming our local tax policy. (Do not enclose the words with quotation marks when they describe the topic rather than signify the exact title.)
>
> The theme of next month's workshop is "Imperatives for the Coming Decade—From the Ragged Edge to the Cutting Edge."

> **NOTE:** The titles *Preface, Contents, Appendix,* and *Index* are not quoted, even though they represent parts within a book. They are often capitalized, however, for special emphasis.

> All the supporting data is given in the Appendix. (Often capitalized when referring to another section within the same work.)
>
> **BUT:** You'll find that the most interesting part of his book is contained in the appendix. (Capitalization is not required when reference is made to a section within another work.)

243 Use quotation marks around the titles of *complete but unpublished* works, such as manuscripts, dissertations, and reports.

> I would like to get a copy of Sandor's study, "Criteria for Evaluating Staff Efficiency."

244 Use quotation marks around the titles of songs and other short musical compositions and around the titles of individual segments or programs that are part of a larger television or radio series. (Series titles are underscored.)

> Just once I would like to get through a company party without having to hear Reggie sing "Danny Boy."

> I understand that our company was briefly mentioned on the <u>Frontline</u> program entitled "Pentagon, Inc.," which was shown last Monday night.

QUOTATIONS WITHIN QUOTATIONS

245 A quotation within another quotation is enclosed in single quotation marks. On a typewriter or word processor, use the apostrophe key for a single quotation mark.

> Fowler then said, "We were all impressed by her 'can do' attitude."

246 If a quotation appears within the single-quoted matter, revert to double quotation marks for the inner portion.

> Mrs. DeVries then remarked, "I thought it a bit strange when Mr. Fowler said, 'Put these checks in an envelope marked "Personal Funds," and set them aside for me.'" (When single and double quotation marks occur together, do not insert any extra space between them in typewritten material.)

NOTE: For the positioning of punctuation in relation to a single quotation mark, see the following paragraphs:

- ❏ *For placement of periods and commas, see ¶247, note.*
- ❏ *For placement of semicolons and colons, see ¶248, note.*
- ❏ *For placement of question marks and exclamation points, see ¶249, note.*
- ❏ *For placement of dashes, see ¶250b.*

The following rules (¶¶247–251) indicate how to position punctuation marks in relation to the closing quotation mark—inside *or* outside.

WITH PERIODS AND COMMAS

247 Periods and commas always go *inside* the closing quotation mark. This is the preferred American style. (Some writers in this country follow the British style: Place the period *outside* when it punctuates the whole sentence, *inside* when it punctuates only the quoted matter. Place the comma *outside*, since it always punctuates the sentence, not the quoted matter.)

> Before the conference, Mr. Karras made a point of saying, "Let me do the talking."

> He wants to change "on or about May 1" to read "no later than May 1."

> The price tag on the leather sofa was clearly marked "Sold."

> Sign your name wherever you see an "X."

> "Let's go over the details again," she said.

> "The date stamp indicates that my copy arrived at 10:50 a.m.," he said.

> Their latest article, "Scanning the Future," will appear in next month's issue of *Inc.* magazine.

> "Witty," "clever," "amusing," and "hilarious" are only a few of the adjectives that are being applied to her new book.

> The package was labeled "Fragile," but that meant nothing to your delivery crew.

(Continued on page 52.)

NOTE: Periods and commas also go *inside* the single closing quotation mark.

> Mr. Poston said, "Please let me see all the orders marked 'Rush.'"
> "All he would say was 'I don't remember,'" answered the witness.

WITH SEMICOLONS AND COLONS

248 Semicolons and colons always go *outside* the closing quotation mark.

> Last Tuesday you said, "I will mail a check today"; however, it has not yet arrived.
> When the announcement of the changeover was made, my reaction was "Why?"; John's only reaction was "When?"
> Please send me the following items from the file labeled "In Process": the latest draft of the Berryman agreement and FASB Statement 33.

NOTE: Semicolons and colons also go *outside* the single quotation mark.

> Alice Arroyo called in from her country place to say, "Please send me the following items from the file labeled 'In Process': the latest draft of the Berryman agreement and FASB Statement 33."

WITH QUESTION MARKS AND EXCLAMATION POINTS

249 **a.** A question mark or an exclamation point goes *inside* the closing quotation mark when it applies only to the quoted material.

> His first question was, "How long have you worked here?" (Quoted question at the end of a statement.)
> Garland still ends every sales meeting by shouting, "Go get 'em!" (Quoted exclamation at the end of a statement.)

b. A question mark or an exclamation point goes *outside* the closing quotation mark when it applies to the entire sentence.

> When will she say, for a change, "You did a nice job on that"? (Quoted statement at the end of a question.)
> Stop telling me, "Don't worry"! (Quoted statement at the end of an exclamation.)

c. If the quoted material and the entire sentence each require the same mark of punctuation, use only one mark—the one that comes first. (See also ¶¶257–258.)

> Have you seen the advertisement that starts, "Why pay more?" (Quoted question at the end of a question.)
> Let's not panic and yell "Fire!" (Quoted exclamation at the end of an exclamation.)

NOTE: These same principles govern the placement of a question mark or an exclamation point in relation to a single quotation mark.

> What prompted her to say, "Be careful in handling documents marked 'Confidential'"? (Quoted phrase within a quoted statement within a question.)
> Dr. Marks asked, "Was the check marked 'Insufficient Funds'?" (Quoted phrase within a quoted question within a statement.)
> Miss Parsons then said, "How did you answer him when he asked you, 'How do you know?'" (Quoted question within a quoted question within a statement.)

WITH DASHES

250 **a.** A dash goes *inside* the closing quotation mark to indicate that the speaker's or writer's words have broken off abruptly.

> It was tragic to hear Tom say, "If he had only listened—"

b. A dash goes *outside* the closing quotation mark when the sentence breaks off abruptly *after* the quotation.

> If I hear one more word about "boosting productivity"—
>
> **BUT:** Mrs. Halliday said, "If I hear one more word about 'boosting productivity'—"

c. A closing dash goes *outside* the closing quotation mark when the quotation itself is part of a nonessential element being set off by a pair of dashes.

> Get the latest draft—it's the one with the notation "Let's go with this"—and take it to Miss Pomeroy for her approval.

WITH PARENTHESES

251 **a.** The closing parenthesis goes *inside* the closing quotation mark when the parenthetical element is part of the quotation.

> Wagner agreed to settle his account "by Friday (July 28)" when he last wrote us.

b. The closing parenthesis goes *outside* the closing quotation mark when the quotation is part of the parenthetical element.

> Joe Elliott (the one everyone calls "Harper's fair-haired boy") will probably get the job.

The following rules (¶¶252–270) indicate what punctuation to use with various kinds of quoted matter.

PUNCTUATING QUOTATIONS THAT STAND ALONE

252 When a quoted sentence stands alone, put the appropriate mark of terminal punctuation—a period, a question mark, or an exclamation point—*inside* the closing quotation mark.

> "I think we should switch suppliers at once."
>
> "Can you send us your comments within two weeks?"
>
> "I won't accept that kind of response!"

PUNCTUATING QUOTATIONS AT THE BEGINNING OF A SENTENCE

253 When a quoted *statement* occurs at the beginning of a sentence, omit the period before the closing quotation mark and use a comma instead.

> "I think we should switch suppliers at once," he said.
> (**NOT:** . . . at once.," he said.)

EXCEPTION: Retain the period if it accompanies an abbreviation.

> "I'm still planning to go on for an LL.B.," she said.

254 When a quoted *question* or *exclamation* occurs at the beginning of a sentence, retain the question mark or the exclamation point before the closing quotation mark and do *not* insert a comma.

> "Can you send us your comments within two weeks?" she asked.
> (**NOT:** . . . within two weeks?," she asked.)
>
> "I won't accept that kind of response!" I told him.
> (**NOT:** . . . that kind of response!," I told him.)

255 When a quoted *word* or *phrase* occurs at the beginning of a sentence, no punctuation should accompany the closing quotation mark unless required by the overall construction of the sentence.

"An utter bore" was the general reaction to yesterday's speaker.

"Managing Your Portfolio," the second chapter in the book, sets forth some guidelines I have never seen anywhere else. (The comma that follows the chapter title is the first of a pair needed to set off a nonessential expression.)

PUNCTUATING QUOTATIONS AT THE END OF A SENTENCE

256 **a.** When a quoted *statement, question,* or *exclamation* comes at the end of a sentence and is introduced by an expression such as *he said* or *she said,* a comma usually precedes the opening quotation mark.

Mr. Kelley said, "We'll close early on Friday."

In her letter Diana said, "I plan to arrive on Thursday at 6 p.m."

NOTE: If the quotation is quite short or is woven into the flow of the sentence, omit the comma.

All she said was "No." **OR:** All she said was, "No." (The comma creates a slight pause and throws greater emphasis on the quotation.)

Why does he keep saying "It won't work"?

b. Use a colon in place of a comma if the introductory expression is an independent clause.

Jerry would say only this: "I'll send you my new address once I'm settled."

Here is the key statement in his letter: "If my loan is approved, the deal is on."

c. Use a colon in place of a comma if the quotation contains more than one sentence.

Mr. Bowles then said: "If the legislation is passed by Congress, we have an excellent chance to compete effectively in international markets. However, if the legislation gets bottled up in committee, our competitive position will worsen."

d. Use a colon in place of a comma if the quotation is set off on separate lines as an extract. (See also ¶265.)

Sheila's letter said in part:

> I have always valued your assistance on our various projects. You have always acted as if you were actually part of our staff, with our best interests in mind . . .

e. Do not use either a comma or a colon before an indirect quotation.

Sheila said that she had always valued Bob's assistance on various projects.

f. Do not use either a comma or a colon when a direct quotation is introduced by *that* or is otherwise woven into the flow of the sentence.

In a previous letter to you, I noted that "you have always acted as if you were actually part of our staff, with our best interests in mind."

NOTE: The first word of the quotation is not capitalized in this case, even though it was capitalized in the original. Compare *you* here with *You* in the example in *d* above. (See ¶272 for the rule on capitalization.)

257 When a quoted *sentence* (a statement, a question, or an exclamation) falls at the end of a larger sentence, do not use double punctuation—that is, one mark to

end the quotation and another to end the sentence. Choose the stronger mark. (**REMEMBER:** *A question mark is stronger than a period; an exclamation point is stronger than a period or a question mark.*) If the same mark of punctuation is required for both the quotation and the sentence as a whole, use the first mark that occurs—the one within quotation marks.

Quoted Sentences at the End of a Statement

Bob said, "I can't wait to get back to work." (Not .".)

Mrs. Fahey asked, "How long have you been away?" (Not ?".)

Mr. Auden shouted, "We can't operate a business this way!" (Not !".)

Quoted Sentences at the End of a Question

Did you say, "I'll help out"? (Not ."?)

Why did Mary ask, "Will Joe be there?" (Not ?"?)

Who yelled "Watch out!" (Not !"?)

Quoted Sentences at the End of an Exclamation

How could you forget to follow up when you were specifically told, "Give this order special attention"! (Not ."!)

Stop saying "How should I know"! (Not ?"!)

How I'd like to walk into his office and say, "I quit!" (Not !"!)

NOTE: When a quoted sentence ends with an abbreviation, retain the abbreviation period, even though a question mark or an exclamation point follows as the terminal mark of punctuation.

The reporter asked, "When did you first hear about the sale of Modem Inc.?"

Didn't Larry tell Meg, "I'll help you with the tuition for your M.D."?

However, if a period is required as the terminal mark of punctuation, use only one period to mark the end of the abbreviation and the end of the sentence.

Gloria said, "You can call as early as 6:30 a.m." (Not .".)

❏ *For placement of periods, see ¶247; for placement of question marks and exclamation points, see ¶249.*

258 When a quoted *word* or *phrase* occurs at the end of a sentence, punctuate according to the appropriate pattern shown below. (**NOTE:** If the quoted word or phrase represents a complete sentence, follow the patterns shown in ¶257.)

Quoted Words and Phrases at the End of a Statement

He says he is willing to meet "at your convenience." (Not ".)

I thought her letter said she would arrive "at 10 p.m." (Not .".)

I've been meaning to read "Who Pays the Bill?" (Not ?".)

Critics have praised his latest article, "Freedom Now!" (Not !".)

Quoted Words and Phrases at the End of a Question

Why is he so concerned about my "convenience"?

Didn't she clearly state she would arrive "at 10 p.m."?

Have you had a chance to read "Who Pays the Bill?" (Not ?"?)

What did you think of the article "Freedom Now!"?

Quoted Words and Phrases at the End of an Exclamation

He couldn't care less about my "convenience"!

You're quite mistaken—she clearly said "at 10 a.m."!

Don't waste your time reading "Who Pays the Bill?"!

What a reaction he got with his article "Freedom Now!" (Not !"!)

PUNCTUATING QUOTATIONS WITHIN A SENTENCE

259 Do not use a comma before or after a quotation when it is woven into the flow of the sentence.

> Don't say "I can't do it" without trying.
>
> No considerate person would say "Why should I care?" under those circumstances.
>
> The audience shouted "Bravo!" and "Encore!" at the end of the concerto.

NOTE: In such cases do not use a period at the end of a quoted statement, but retain the question mark or the exclamation point at the end of a quoted question or exclamation (as illustrated in the examples above).

260 Do not set off a quotation that occurs within a sentence as an *essential* expression. (See ¶149.)

> The luxurious practice of booking passage between England and India on the basis of "Port Outward, Starboard Homeward" (so as to get a cabin on the cooler side of the ship) is said to be the origin of the word *posh.*
>
> The chapter entitled "Locating Sources of Venture Capital" will give you specific leads you can pursue.

261 When a quotation occurs within a sentence as a *nonessential* expression, use a comma before the opening quotation mark and before the closing quotation mark.

> His parting words, "I hardly know how to thank you," were sufficient.
>
> The next chapter, "The Role of Government," further clarifies the answer.

However, if the quoted matter requires a question mark or an exclamation point before the closing quotation mark, omit the comma at that point.

> The final chapter, "Where Do We Go From Here?" shows how much remains to be accomplished.
>
> Your last question, "How can we improve communications between departments?" can best be answered by you.

NOTE: As an alternative, use a pair of dashes or parentheses to set off the quoted matter.

> Your last question—"How can we improve communications between departments?"— can best be answered by you.

PUNCTUATING QUOTED SENTENCES WITH INTERRUPTING EXPRESSIONS

262 When a quoted sentence is *interrupted* by an expression such as *he asked* or *she said,* use a comma and a closing quotation mark before the interrupting expression and another comma after it. Then resume the quotation with an opening quotation mark and put the first word in small letters.

> "During the past month," the memo said in part, "we have received some welcome news from our overseas branches."

263 If the interrupting expression ends the sentence and the quotation continues in a new sentence, put a period after the interrupting expression and start the new sentence with an opening quotation mark and a capital letter.

> "Perhaps we should decline the invitation," he said. "It would be better not to go than to arrive late."

PUNCTUATING LONG QUOTATIONS

264   If a quotation consists of more than one sentence without any interrupting elements, use quotation marks only at the beginning and at the end of the quotation. Do not put quotation marks around each sentence within the quotation.

> Here is the full text of the release he gave to the media: "I have decided to withdraw from the upcoming election. I wish to thank my supporters for their enormous help. I am sorry to disappoint them."

265   A long quotation that will make four or more typewritten lines may be handled in one of the following ways:

a. The preferred style for displaying the quoted matter is to type it as a single-spaced extract. Indent the extract 5 spaces from each side margin, and leave 1 blank line above and below the extract. Do not enclose the quoted matter in quotation marks; the indention replaces the quotes. (See page 264 for an illustration.)

> **NOTE:** Ordinarily, start typing the quoted matter flush left on the shorter line length; however, if a paragraph indention was called for in the original, indent the first line 5 spaces. Indent the first line of any additional paragraphs 5 spaces also, but do not leave a blank line between indented paragraphs.

b. Type the quoted matter using the same line length and spacing as for the remainder of the material.

  (1) If the quoted matter consists of one paragraph only, place quotation marks at the beginning and end of the paragraph. Use the normal paragraph indention of 5 spaces.

  (2) If the quoted matter consists of two or more paragraphs, place a quotation mark *at the start* of each paragraph but at the end of only one paragraph—the last one.

  (3) Change double quotation marks within the quoted matter to single quotation marks, and vice versa. (See ¶¶245–246.)

> "When writing a letter that grants a request, you can follow this pattern:
>
> "First, express appreciation for the writer's interest in the company's product or service.
>
> "Next, give the exact information requested and, if possible, additional information that may be of interest.
>
> "Finally, express willingness to 'be of further help.'"

QUOTING LETTERS

266   Letters and other business documents that are to be quoted word for word may be handled in one of the following ways:

a. Type the material on a separate sheet of paper headed *COPY*. In this case no quotation marks are used.

b. Make a photocopy of the material. In this case neither the heading *COPY* nor quotation marks are used.

c. The material, if short, may be treated like a long quotation (see ¶265). If it is typed on a shorter line length, omit the quotation marks. If it is typed on the same line length as other material on the page, then type the opening quotation mark before the first word (in a letter, the date line); type the closing quotation mark after the last word (in a letter, the last word in the signature block).

QUOTING POETRY

267　When quoting a complete poem (or an extended portion of one) in a letter or a report, type it line for line, single-spaced (except for stanza breaks). If the line length is shorter than that of the normal text above and below the poem, no quotation marks are needed; the poem will stand out sufficiently as an extract. If, however, quotation marks are needed to indicate the special nature of the material, place a quotation mark at the beginning of each stanza and at the end of only the last stanza. (See also ¶284*b*.)

268　A short extract from a poem is sometimes woven right into a sentence or a paragraph. In such cases use quotation marks at the beginning and end of the extract and a diagonal line to indicate where each line would break in the original arrangement of the poem.

> As Alexander Pope put it, "A little learning is a dang'rous thing; / Drink deep, or taste not the Pierian spring . . . ." (Note that one space precedes and follows the diagonal.)

QUOTING DIALOGUES AND CONVERSATIONS

269　When quoting dialogues and conversations, start the remarks of each speaker as a new paragraph, no matter how brief.

> "Waiter, what was in that glass?"
>
> "Arsenic, sir."
>
> "*Arsenic.* I asked you to bring me absinthe."
>
> "I thought you said arsenic. I beg your pardon, sir."
>
> "Do you realize what you've done, you clumsy fool? I'm dying."
>
> "I am extremely sorry, sir."
>
> "I DISTINCTLY SAID ABSINTHE."
>
> "I realize that I owe you an apology, sir. I am extremely sorry."
>
> —Myles na Gopaleen

270　In plays and court testimony, where the name of the speaker is indicated, quotation marks are not needed.

> CECILY: Uncle Jack is sending you to Australia.
>
> ALGER: Australia! I'd sooner die.
>
> CECILY: Well, he said at dinner on Wednesday night that you would have to choose between this world, the next world, and Australia.
>
> ALGER: Oh, well! The accounts I have received of Australia and the next world are not particularly encouraging. This world is good enough for me, cousin Cecily.
>
> —Oscar Wilde

The following rules (¶¶271–284) cover a number of stylistic matters, such as how to capitalize in quoted matter (¶¶272–273), how to handle omissions in quoted matter (¶¶274–280), and how to handle insertions in quoted matter (¶¶281–283).

STYLE IN QUOTED MATTER

271 In copying quoted matter, follow the style of the extract exactly in punctuation, spelling, hyphenation, and number style. (See ¶282 for the use of [*sic*] to indicate errors in the original.)

CAPITALIZATION IN QUOTED MATTER

272 Ordinarily, capitalize the first word of every complete sentence in quotation marks.

> I overheard Ellis mutter, "Only a fool would make such a claim."

> Here is the key sentence in her memo: "Despite the understaffing in the department, everyone is expected to meet the goals established for the year."

NOTE: If the quoted sentence is preceded by *that* or is otherwise incorporated into the flow of a larger sentence, do not capitalize the first word (unless it is a proper noun, a proper adjective, or the pronoun *I*).

> I overheard Ellis mutter that "only a fool would make such a claim."

> In essence, she says that "despite the understaffing in the department, everyone is expected to meet the goals established for the year."

273 When quoting a word or phrase, do not capitalize the first word unless it meets *one* of these conditions:

a. It is a proper noun, a proper adjective, or the pronoun *I*.

> No one is terribly impressed by his "Irish temper."

b. It was capitalized in its original use.

> I watched her scrawl "Approved" and sign her name at the bottom of the proposal.

c. The quoted word or phrase occurs at the beginning of a sentence.

> "Outrageous" was the general reaction of the public to Maxon's attempt to duck the questions of the reporters. (Even if the expression was not capitalized in the original material, it is capitalized here to mark the start of the sentence.)

d. It represents a complete sentence.

> The Crawleys said "Perhaps"; the Calnans said "No way."

❑ *See ¶¶277–278 on capitalizing the first word of a quoted sentence fragment.*

OMISSIONS IN QUOTED MATTER

274 If one or more words are omitted *within a quoted sentence,* use ellipsis marks (three spaced periods, with one typewriter space before and after each period) to indicate the omission.

> "During the past twenty-five years . . . we have been witnessing a change in buying habits, particularly with respect to food."

NOTE: Omit any marks of internal punctuation (a comma, a semicolon, a colon, or a dash) on either side of the ellipsis marks unless they are required for the sake of clarity.

> **ORIGINAL VERSION:** "The objectives of the proposed bill are admirable, I will cheerfully concede; the tactics being used to gain support for the bill are not."

> **CONDENSED VERSION:** "The objectives of the proposed bill are admirable . . .; the tactics being used to gain support for the bill are not." (The comma preceding the omitted phrase is not needed; however, the semicolon following the omitted phrase must be retained for clarity.)

275   If one or more words are omitted *at the end of a quoted sentence,* use three spaced periods followed by the necessary terminal punctuation for the sentence as a whole.

> "Can anyone explain why . . . ?" (The original question read, "Can anyone explain why this was so?")

> "During the past twenty-five years, starting in the late 1950s, we have been witnessing a change in buying habits . . . .   Consumers have become more concerned with what's in the package rather than with the package itself." (The first three periods represent the omitted words "particularly with respect to food"; the fourth period marks the end of the sentence. Two typewriter spaces follow before the next sentence.)

NOTE: If the quotation is intended to trail off, use only three spaced periods at the end of the sentence. (See also ¶291*b*.)

> His reaction was, "If I had only known . . ."

276   If one or more sentences are omitted *between other sentences* within a long quotation, use three spaced periods *after* the terminal punctuation of the preceding sentence.

> "During the past twenty-five years, starting in the late 1950s, we have been witnessing a change in buying habits, particularly with respect to food. . . .   How far this pattern of change will extend cannot be estimated."

NOTE: There is no space between *food* and the first period because that period marks the end of a sentence. The remaining three periods signify the omission of one or more complete sentences. Two spaces follow before the next sentence.

277   If only a fragment of a sentence is quoted within another sentence, it is not necessary to signify the omission of words before or after the fragment.

> According to Robertson's report, there has been "a change in buying habits" during the past twenty-five years.

Moreover, if the fragment as given can be read as a complete sentence, capitalize the first word in the quoted fragment, even though this word was not capitalized in the original. (Compare *We* in the following example with *we* in the example in ¶276.)

> According to Robertson's report, "We have been witnessing a change in buying habits, particularly with respect to food."

278   If a displayed quotation starts in the middle of a sentence, use three spaced periods at the beginning of the quotation.

> According to Robertson's report, there has been

> > . . . a change in buying habits, particularly with respect to food. . . .   How far this pattern of change will extend cannot be estimated.

If the fragment, however, can be read as a complete sentence, capitalize the first word of the fragment and omit the ellipsis marks. (Compare *Starting* in the following example with *starting* in the example in ¶276.)

> According to Robertson's report:

> > Starting in the late 1950s, we have been witnessing a change in buying habits, particularly with respect to food.

279   When a long quotation starts with a complete sentence and ends with a complete sentence, do not use three spaced periods at the beginning or the end of the quotation unless you need to emphasize that the quotation has been extracted from a larger body of material.

280   If one or more paragraphs are omitted within a long quotation, indicate the omission by adding three spaced periods *after* the terminal punctuation that concludes the preceding paragraph.

INSERTIONS IN QUOTED MATTER

281   For clarity it is sometimes necessary to insert explanatory words or phrases within quoted matter. Enclose such insertions in brackets. (See also ¶¶296–298.)

> Miss Rawlings added, "At the time of the first lawsuit [1976], there was clear-cut evidence of an intent to defraud."

282   When the original wording contains a misspelling, a grammatical error, or a confusing expression of thought, insert the term *sic* (meaning "so" or "this is the way it was") in brackets to indicate that the error existed in the original material.

> As he wrote in his letter, "I would sooner go to jail then [*sic*] have to pay your bill." (The word *sic* is not underscored in typed material.)

283   For special emphasis, you may wish to underscore words that were not so treated in the original. In such cases insert a phrase like *emphasis added* in brackets at the end of the quotation or immediately after the underscored words.

> Upon cross-examination, she replied, "I never met Mr. Norman in my life, to the best of my recollection. [Emphasis added.]"

❑ *For simple interruptions such as* he said *or* she said, *see* ¶¶262–263.

TYPING QUOTATION MARKS

284   **a.** In a typed list, any opening quotation mark should align with the first letter of the other items.

> I urge you to read the following materials (which I am sending to you under separate cover):
>
> Federal Tax Policy by Joseph A. Pechman
> "Tax Policy and Capital Formation" by the Joint Committee on Taxation
> The Zero-Sum Society by Lester C. Thurow

   b. In poems, the opening quotation mark at the beginning of each stanza should clear the left margin so that the first letter of each line will be in alignment. (See also ¶267.)

> "So here I am, in the middle way . . .
> Trying to learn to use words, and every attempt
> Is a wholly new start, and a different kind of failure
> Because one has only learnt to get the better of words
> For the thing one no longer has to say, or the way in which
> One is no longer disposed to say it. And so each venture
> Is a new beginning, a raid on the inarticulate
> With shabby equipment always deteriorating. . . ."
>
>   —T. S. Eliot

THE UNDERSCORE

Underscoring in typewritten material is the counterpart of *italic type* in printed material.

FOR SPECIAL EMPHASIS

285 A word referred to as a word is usually underscored, but it may be enclosed in quotation marks instead. A word referred to as a word is often introduced by the expression *the term* or *the word*.

> The word quay is pronounced exactly the same as key.
>
> **ALSO:** The word "quay" is pronounced exactly the same as "key."

> If you used fewer compound sentences, you wouldn't have so many ands in your writing. (Only the root word is underscored, not the *s*.)

> **BUT:** She refused to sign the contract because she said it had too many ands, ifs, and buts. (No underscores are required for the phrase *ands, ifs, and buts* because the writer is not referring literally to these words as words. The phrase means "too many conditions and qualifications.")

286 In a formal definition the word to be defined is usually underscored and the definition quoted. In this way the two elements may be easily distinguished.

> The verb prevaricate (a polite way of saying "to lie") comes from the Latin word praevaricari, which means "to go zigzag, to walk crookedly."

NOTE: An informal definition does not require any special punctuation.

> A wainwright is a person who makes or repairs wagons.

287 Underscore foreign expressions that are not considered part of the English language. (Use quotation marks to set off translations of foreign expressions.)

> It's true, n'est-ce pas? (Meaning "isn't that so?")

NOTE: Once an expression of foreign origin has become established as part of the English language, underscoring is no longer necessary. (Most dictionaries offer guidance on this point.) Here are some frequently used expressions that no longer require underscoring or any other special display:

à la carte	de facto	non sequitur	quid pro quo
à la mode	et al.	ombudsman	rendezvous
a priori	etc.	op. cit.	repertoire
ad hoc	ex officio	per annum	résumé
ad infinitum	habeas corpus	per se	sine qua non
alma mater	ibid.	prima facie	sotto voce
alter ego	laissez-faire	prix fixe	status quo
bona fide	magnum opus	pro forma	tour de force
carte blanche	modus operandi	pro rata	vice versa
cul-de-sac	modus vivendi	pro tem	vis-à-vis

❏ *For the use of accents and other diacritical marks with foreign words, see ¶718.*

288 The *individual* names of ships, trains, airplanes, and spacecraft may be underscored for special display or written simply with initial caps.

> The S.S. Parlin will sail on Thursday.　　**OR:** The S.S. Parlin . . .

> **BUT:** I flew to Paris on a Concorde and came back on a DC-10. (No special display is needed for the names *Concorde* and *DC-10* because they identify classes of aircraft but are not the individual names of planes.)

WITH TITLES OF LITERARY AND ARTISTIC WORKS

289   Underscore titles of *complete* works that are published as separate items—for example, books, pamphlets, long poems, magazines, and newspapers. Also underscore titles of movies, plays, musicals, operas, television and radio series, long musical compositions, paintings, and pieces of sculpture.

> You will particularly enjoy a novel entitled <u>Dinner at the Homesick Restaurant</u>.
>
> Our ads in <u>The Wall Street Journal</u> have produced excellent results.
>
> Next Thursday we will go to hear one of John's favorite operas, <u>Der Rosenkavalier</u>.

NOTE: The titles of musical pieces that are identified by form (for example, symphony, concerto, sonata) or by key are neither underscored nor quoted. However, if a descriptive phrase accompanies this type of title, it is underscored if the work is long, quoted if the work is short.

> Beethoven's Sonata No. 18 in E Flat Minor, Op. 31, No. 3
>
> Tchaikovsky's Symphony No. 6 in B Flat Minor (the <u>Pathetique</u>)
>
> Chopin's Etude No. 12 (the "Revolutionary" Etude)

a.   Titles of complete works may be typed in all capitals as an alternative to underscoring.

> Every executive will find THE PRODUCTIVITY PRESCRIPTION a valuable guide.

NOTE: The use of all capitals is acceptable (1) in business correspondence where titles occur frequently (as in the correspondence of a publishing house) and (2) in advertising and sales promotion copy where the use of all capitals is intended to have an eye-catching effect. In other circumstances use underscoring.

b.   In typewritten material that is *to be set in type,* titles of complete works must be underscored. The underscoring indicates to the printer that the title should be set in italics.

> Every executive will find <u>The Productivity Prescription</u> a valuable guide.

c.   In titles of magazines, do not underscore or capitalize the word *magazine* unless it is part of the actual title.

> <u>Time</u> magazine   **BUT:** <u>The New York Times Magazine</u>

d.   In some cases the name of the publishing company is the same as the name of the publication. Underscore the name when it refers to *the publication* but not when it refers to *the company.*

> I saw her column in <u>Business Week</u>.
>
> **BUT:** I wrote to Business Week about a job.

❑   *For the use of quotation marks with titles of literary and artistic works, see ¶¶242–244; for the treatment of titles of sacred works, see ¶350.*

TYPING UNDERSCORES

290   Underscore as a unit whatever should be grasped as a unit—individual words, titles, phrases, or even whole sentences.

a.   When underscoring a unit consisting of two or more words, be sure to underscore the space between words.

> Have you read that extraordinary history of the fourteenth century, <u>A Distant Mirror</u>?
>
> **BUT:** Do you understand the meaning of terms like <u>ipso facto</u>, <u>sine qua non</u>, and <u>pro forma</u>? (Only the individual units are underscored, not the series as a whole.)

b. Do not underscore a mark of *sentence punctuation* that comes directly after the underscored matter. (However, underscore all punctuation marks that are an integral part of the underscored matter.)

> This week the Summertime Playhouse is presenting <u>Oklahoma!</u>, next week <u>Where's Charley?</u>, and the following week <u>My Fair Lady</u>.

c. Do not underscore a possessive or plural ending that is added on to an underscored word.

> the <u>Times</u>'s editorial   too many <u>and</u>s

OTHER MARKS OF PUNCTUATION

THE APOSTROPHE (')

The use of the apostrophe is covered in the following paragraphs:

- ❏ *As a single quotation mark, see ¶¶245–246.*
- ❏ *To indicate the omission of figures in dates, see ¶412.*
- ❏ *As a symbol for feet, see ¶¶432, 543.*
- ❏ *To form contractions, see ¶505.*
- ❏ *To form plurals of figures, letters, etc., see ¶¶623–626.*
- ❏ *To form possessives, see ¶¶627–651.*

ELLIPSIS MARKS (. . .)

291 **a.** Ellipsis marks (three spaced periods, with one typewriter space before and after each period) are often used, especially in advertising, to display individual items or to connect a series of loosely related phrases.

> The Inn at the End of the Road . . . where you may enjoy the epicure's choicest offerings . . . by reservation only . . . closed Tuesdays.

> Where can you match these services—
> . . . Free ticket delivery
> . . . Flight insurance
> . . . On-time departures

b. Ellipsis marks are also used to indicate that a sentence trails off before the end. The three spaced periods create an effect of uncertainty or suggest an abrupt suspension of thought. (No terminal punctuation is used with ellipsis marks in this kind of construction.)

> He could easily have saved the situation by . . .   But why talk about it?

- ❏ *For the use of ellipsis marks to indicate omissions in quoted matter, see ¶¶274–280.*

THE ASTERISK (*)

292 The asterisk may be used to refer the reader to a footnote placed at the bottom of a page or a table. (See ¶¶1502f, 1636c.)

a. When the asterisk and some other mark of punctuation occur together within a sentence, the asterisk *follows* the punctuation mark, with no intervening space. (See also ¶1502b and f.)

b. In the footnote itself, leave no space after the asterisk.

293 Asterisks are used to replace words that are considered unprintable.

> If the TV cameras had been present when Finney called Schultz a ***** (and about 50 other names as well), tonight's newscast would have contained the longest bleep in television history.

THE DIAGONAL (/)

294 The diagonal occurs (without space before or after) in certain abbreviations and expressions of time.

> B/L   bill of lading   km/h   kilometers per hour   c/o   care of
>
> Check the figures for fiscal year 1985/86.
>
> I'm concerned about their P/E ratio. (Referring to the price-to-earnings ratio of a company's stock.)

295 **a.** The diagonal is used to express alternatives.

> an either/or proposition
> meet on Monday and/or Tuesday (see ¶1101)

b. The diagonal may be used to indicate that a person or thing has two functions.

> the owner/manager   zoned for commercial/industrial activities
> our secretary/treasurer   planning to hold a dinner/dance

> **NOTE:** The use of a hyphen is preferred in such expressions. (See ¶806.)

c. The diagonal is also used in writing fractions (for example, 4/5) and in some code and serial numbers (for example, 2S/394756).

> ❏ *For the use of the diagonal when quoting poetry, see ¶268.*

BRACKETS ([ ])

296 A correction or an insertion in a quoted extract should be enclosed in brackets. (See also ¶¶281–283.)

> "If we all pull together, we can bring a new level of political leadership to this state. [Extended applause.] Please give me your support in this campaign."

297 When a parenthetical element falls within another parenthetical element, enclose the smaller element in brackets and the larger element in parentheses.

> Scalzo said on television yesterday that prices would begin to fall sharply. (However, in an article published in the *Times* [May 12, 19—], he was quoted as saying that prices would remain at their current levels for the foreseeable future.)

298 If brackets do not appear on your keyboard, either construct them (as shown in the illustration below) or leave a space at the point where each mark should appear and pen in the marks after you remove the paper from the machine.

> `"We returned to Salem /Massachusetts/ the following year."`

NOTE: If the term to be enclosed in brackets has to be underscored, do the underscoring on the machine and insert the brackets by hand.

> `Halliburton's press release stated, "If it hadn't been for a certain newspaper [ The Tribune ], we never would have lost the election."`
>
> (**RATHER THAN:** /The Tribune/ **OR** /The Tribune/)

SPACING WITH PUNCTUATION MARKS

299   Period

Two spaces *after* the end of a sentence.

One space *after* an abbreviation within a sentence. (See also ¶511.)

No space *after* a decimal point.

No space *after* when another mark of punctuation immediately follows the period (for example, a closing quotation mark, a closing parenthesis, or a comma following an "abbreviation" period).

Two spaces *after* a number or letter that indicates an enumeration.

Question Mark or Exclamation Point

Two spaces *after* the end of a sentence.

No space *after* when another mark of punctuation immediately follows (for example, a closing quotation mark, a closing parenthesis, or a closing dash).

Comma

No space *before*.

One space *after,* unless a closing quotation mark immediately follows the comma.

No space *after* commas within a number.

Semicolon

No space *before;* one space *after*.

Colon

No space *before*.

Two spaces *after* within a sentence.

No space *before* or *after* in expressions of time *(8:20 p.m.)* or proportions *(2:1)*.

Dash

No space *before, between,* or *after* two hyphens used to represent a dash.

Two spaces *after* a dash at the end of a statement that breaks off abruptly. (See ¶208.)

Opening Parenthesis or Bracket

One space *before* when parenthetic matter is within a sentence.

Two spaces *before* when parenthetic matter follows a sentence. In this case the parenthetic matter starts with a capital and closes with its own sentence punctuation. (See ¶¶226, 296.)

No space *after*.

Closing Parenthesis or Bracket

No space *before*.

One space *after* when parenthetic matter is within a sentence.

Two spaces *after* when parenthetic matter is itself a complete sentence and another sentence follows. (See ¶¶226, 296.)

No space *after* if another mark of punctuation immediately follows.

Opening Quotation Mark

Two spaces *before* when quoted matter starts a new sentence or follows a colon.

No space *before* when a dash or an opening parenthesis precedes.

One space *before* in all other cases.

No space *after*.

Closing Quotation Mark

No space *before*.

Two spaces *after* when quoted matter ends the sentence.

No space *after* when another mark of punctuation immediately follows (for example, a semicolon or a colon).

One space *after* in all other cases.

Single Quotation Mark

No space between single and double quotation marks. (See ¶246.)

Apostrophe (')

No space *before*, either within a word or at the end of a word.

One space *after* only if it is at the end of a word within a sentence.

Ellipsis Marks (. . .)

One space *before* and *after* each of the three periods within a sentence. (See ¶¶274–275.)

No space *before* when an *opening* quotation mark precedes the ellipsis marks.

No space *after* when a *closing* quotation mark follows the ellipsis marks. (See last example in ¶275.)

Two spaces *after* ellipsis marks that follow a period, question mark, or exclamation point at the end of a sentence. (See example in ¶276.)

Asterisk (*)

No space *before* an asterisk following a word or punctuation mark within a sentence or at the end of a sentence.

Two spaces *after* an asterisk at the end of a sentence.

One space *after* an asterisk following a word or punctuation mark within a sentence.

No space *after* an asterisk in a footnote. (See ¶292.)

Diagonal (/)

No space *before* or *after* a diagonal line. (See ¶268 for an exception in poetry.)

Capitalization

The function of capitalization is to give distinction, importance, and emphasis to words. Thus the first word of a sentence is capitalized to indicate distinctively and emphatically that a new sentence has begun. Moreover, proper nouns like *George, Chicago, Dun & Bradstreet, the Parthenon, January,* and *Friday* are capitalized to signify the special importance of these words as the official names of particular persons, places, and things. A number of words, however, may function either as proper nouns or as common nouns—for example, terms like *the board of directors* or *the company.* For words like these, capitalization practices vary widely, but the variation merely reflects the relative importance each writer assigns to the word in question.

Despite disagreements among authorities on specific rules, there is a growing consensus against overusing capitalization in business writing. When too many words stand out, none stand out. The current trend, then, is to use capitalization more sparingly—to give importance, distinction, or emphasis only when and where it is warranted.

The following rules of capitalization are written with ordinary situations in mind. If you work or study in a specialized field, you may find it necessary to follow a different style of capitalization.

BASIC RULES

FIRST WORDS

301 Capitalize the first word of:

a. Every sentence. (See ¶302 for exceptions.)

> Medium-range plans must be submitted within two weeks.
> Will you be able to pull everything together by then?
> The deadline we have been given is absolutely impossible!

b. An expression used as a sentence. (See also ¶¶102, 111, 119–120.)

So much for that.	Really?	No!
Enough said.	How come?	Unbelievable!

c. A quoted sentence. (See also ¶¶272–273.)

> Mrs. Eckstein herself said, "We surely have not heard the complete story."

d. An independent question within a sentence. (See also ¶¶115–117.)

> The question is, Whose version of the argument shall we believe?
>
> **BUT:** Have you approved the divisional sales forecasts? the expense projections? the requests for staff expansion? (See ¶117.)

e. Each item displayed in a list or an outline. (See also ¶¶107, 1357c, 1424e.)

> Here is a powerful problem-solving tool that will help you:
>
> · Become an effective leader.
> · Improve your relations with subordinates, peers, and superiors.
> · Cope with stressful situations on the job.

f. Each line in a poem. (Always follow the style of the poem itself, however.)

> From wrong to wrong the exasperated spirit
> Proceeds, unless restored by that refining fire
> Where you must move in measure, like a dancer.
> —T. S. Eliot

g. The salutation and the complimentary closing of a letter.

Dear Mrs. Pancetta: *Sincerely* yours,

302   **a.** When a sentence is set off by *dashes* or *parentheses* within another sentence, do not capitalize the first word following the opening dash or parenthesis unless it is a proper noun, a proper adjective, the pronoun *I*, or the first word of a quoted sentence. (See ¶¶214, 224–225 for examples.)

  b. Do not capitalize the first word of a sentence following a colon except under certain circumstances. (See ¶¶196–199.)

PROPER NOUNS

303   Capitalize every *proper noun,* that is, the official name of a particular person, place, or thing. Also capitalize the pronoun *I*.

Ronald W. Reagan	Wednesday, February 8
Baton Rouge, Louisiana	the Great Depression
Xerox Corporation	the Civil Rights Act of 1964
the Red Cross	the Japanese
the Export-Import Bank	Jupiter and Uranus
Johns Hopkins University	French Literature 212
the World Trade Center	Scotch tape
the Statue of Liberty	*Gone With the Wind*
the Center for Action on	the Department of Health and
Endangered Species	Human Services

NOTE: Prepositions (like *of, for,* and *on*) are not capitalized unless they have four or more letters (like *with* and *from*). (See also ¶360.) The articles *a* and *an* are not capitalized; the article *the* is capitalized only under special circumstances. (See ¶324.) Conjunctions (like *and* and *or*) are also not capitalized.

304   Capitalize adjectives derived from proper nouns.

Jefferson (n.), Jeffersonian (adj.)   America (n.), American (adj.)

EXCEPTIONS: Congress, congressional; the Senate, senatorial; the Constitution (U.S.), constitutional. (See also ¶306.)

305   Capitalize imaginative names and nicknames that designate particular persons, places, or things. (See ¶¶333–335 for imaginative place names; ¶344 for imaginative names of historical periods.)

the Founding Fathers	Benji
the First Lady	Boom Boom Mancini
the White House	Bloody Mary
the Oval Office	the Establishment
the Stars and Stripes	Big Brother
the Gopher State (Minnesota)	Down Under (Australia)

306   Some expressions that originally contained or consisted of proper nouns or adjectives are now considered common nouns and should not be capitalized. (See ¶309b.)

charley horse	napoleon	ampere	texas leaguer
plaster of paris	boycott	watt	arabic numbers
manila envelope	diesel	joule	roman numerals
bone china	macadam	kelvin	**BUT:** Roman laws

NOTE: Check an up-to-date dictionary to determine capitalization for words of this type.

COMMON NOUNS

307 A *common noun* names a class of things (for example, *books*), or it may refer indefinitely to one or more things within that class (*a book, several books*). Nouns used in this way are considered general terms of classification and are often modified by indefinite words such as *a, any, every,* or *some.* Do not capitalize nouns used as general terms of classification.

| a company | any corporation | every board of directors | some senators |

308 A common noun may also be used to name a *particular* person, place, or thing. Nouns used in this way are often modified by *the, this, these, that,* or *those,* or by possessive words such as *my, your, his, her, our,* or *their.* Do not capitalize a general term of classification, even though it refers to a particular person, place, or thing.

COMMON NOUN: our doctor	the hotel	the river
PROPER NOUN: Dr. Tsai	Hotel Algonquin	the Colorado River

309 **a.** Capitalize a common noun when it is part of a proper name but not when it is used alone in place of the full name. (See ¶310 for exceptions.)

Professor Perry	**BUT:** the professor
the Goodall Corporation	the corporation
the Easton Municipal Court	the court
Sunset Boulevard	the boulevard
the Clayton Antitrust Act	the act

NOTE: Also capitalize the plural form of a common noun in expressions such as *the Republican and the Democratic Parties, Main and Tenth Streets, the Missouri and Ohio Rivers,* and *the Atlantic and Pacific Oceans.*

b. In a number of compound nouns, the first element is a proper noun or adjective and the second element is a common noun. In such cases capitalize only the first element, since the compound as a whole is a common noun.

| Brownie points | a Ferris wheel | a Rhodes scholar | a Labrador retriever |

NOTE: Check an up-to-date dictionary for words of this type. After extensive usage, the proper noun or adjective may become a common noun and no longer require capitalization. (See ¶306.)

310 Some *short forms* (common-noun elements replacing the complete proper name) are capitalized when they are intended to carry the full significance of the complete proper name. It is in this area, however, that the danger of over-capitalizing most often occurs. Therefore, do not capitalize a short form unless it clearly warrants the importance, distinction, or emphasis that capitalization conveys. The following kinds of short forms are commonly capitalized:

PERSONAL TITLES: Capitalize titles replacing names of high-ranking national, state, and international officials (but not ordinarily local officials or company officers). (See ¶313.)

ORGANIZATIONAL NAMES: Do not capitalize short forms of company names except in formal or legal writing. (See ¶321.)

GOVERNMENTAL NAMES: Capitalize short forms of names of national and international bodies (but not ordinarily state or local bodies). (See ¶¶326–327, 334–335.)

PLACE NAMES: Capitalize only well-established short forms. (See ¶¶332, 335.)

NOTE: Do not use a short form to replace a full name unless the full name has been mentioned earlier or will be clearly understood from the context.

SPECIAL RULES

PERSONAL NAMES

311 **a.** Treat a person's name—in terms of capitalization, spelling, punctuation, and spacing—exactly as the person does.

Alice Mayer	Charles Burden Wilson
Alyce Meagher	L. Westcott Quinn
Steven J. Szczesny, Jr.	R. W. Ferrari
Stephen J. Chesney Jr.	Peter B. J. Hallman

❑ *For the treatment of initials such as* FDR, *see ¶516.*
❑ *For the use or omission of commas with terms such as* Jr., *see ¶156.*

b. Respect individual preferences in the spelling of personal names.

Ann Marie, Anne Marie, Anna Marie, Annemarie, Annamarie, Anne-Marie, AnneMarie

Macmillan, MacMillan, Mac Millan, Macmillen, MacMillen, MacMillin, McMillan, Mc Millan, McMillen, McMillin, McMillon

c. In names containing the prefix *O'*, always capitalize the *O* and the letter following the apostrophe; for example, *O'Brian* or *O'Brien.*

d. Watch for differences in capitalization and spacing in names containing prefixes like *d', da, de, del, della, di, du, l', la, le, van,* and *von.*

D'Amelio, d'Amelio, Damelio	deLaCruz, DeLacruz, Dela Cruz, DelaCruz
LaCoste, Lacoste, La Coste	VanDeVelde, Van DeVelde, vandeVelde, van deVelde

e. When a surname with an uncapitalized prefix stands alone (that is, without a first name, a title, or initials preceding it), capitalize the prefix to prevent a misreading.

Anthony de Luca	Mr. de Luca	A. R. de Luca

BUT: I hear that *De Luca* is leaving the company.

f. When names that contain prefixes are to be typed in all-capital letters, follow these principles: If there is no space after the prefix, capitalize only the initial letter of the prefix. If space follows the prefix, capitalize the entire prefix.

Normal Form	**All-Capital Form**
MacDonald	MacDONALD
BUT: Mac Donald	MAC DONALD

❑ *For plurals of personal names, see ¶¶615–616; for possessives of personal names, see ¶¶630–633.*

TITLES WITH PERSONAL NAMES

312 **a.** Capitalize all official titles of honor and respect when they *precede* personal names.

PERSONAL TITLES:

Mrs. Norma Washburn (see ¶517)	Miss Popkin
Ms. Terry Fiske	Mr. Benedict

EXECUTIVE TITLES:

President Julia McLeod	Vice President Saulnier

PROFESSIONAL TITLES:

Professor Henry Pelligrino	Dr. Khalil (see ¶517)

CIVIC TITLES:

Governor Samuel O. Bolling Ambassador Staedler

Mayor-elect Louis K. Uhl (see ¶317) ex-Senator Hausner (see ¶317)

MILITARY TITLES:

Colonel Perry L. Forrester Commander Comerford

RELIGIOUS TITLES:

the Reverend William F. Dowd Rabbi Gelfand

 b. Do not capitalize such titles when the personal name that follows is in apposition and is set off by commas.

Yesterday the *president*, Julia McLeod, revealed her plans to retire next June.

BUT: Yesterday *President* Julia McLeod revealed her plans to retire next June.

 c. Do not capitalize occupational titles (such as *author, surgeon, publisher*, and *lawyer*) preceding a name.

The reviews of *drama critic* Simon Ritchey have a life-or-death effect on every play that opens in town.

NOT: The reviews of *Drama Critic* Simon Ritchey . . .

NOTE: Occupational titles can be distinguished from official titles in that only official titles can be used with a last name alone. Since one would not address a person as "Author Mailer" or "Publisher Johnson," these are not official titles and should not be capitalized.

313 **a.** In general, do not capitalize titles of honor and respect when they *follow* a personal name or are used *in place of* a personal name.

Julia McLeod, *president* of McLeod Publications, has revealed her plans to retire next June. During her sixteen years as *president*, the company grew . . .

However, exceptions are made for important officials and dignitaries, as indicated in the following paragraphs.

 b. Retain the capitalization in titles of high-ranking national, state, and international officials when they *follow* or *replace* a specific personal name. Below are examples of titles that remain capitalized.

NATIONAL OFFICIALS: the *President*, the *Vice President*, Cabinet members (such as the *Secretary of State* and the *Attorney General*), the heads of government agencies and bureaus (such as the *Director* or the *Commissioner*), the *Chief Justice*, the *Ambassador*, the *Senator*, the *Representative*.

STATE OFFICIALS: the *Governor*, the *Lieutenant Governor*. (**BUT:** the *attorney general*, the *senator*.)

FOREIGN DIGNITARIES: the *Queen of England*, the *King*, the *Prime Minister*, the *Premier*.

INTERNATIONAL FIGURES: the *Pope*, the *Secretary General of the United Nations*.

NOTE: Some authorities now recommend that even these titles should not be capitalized.

 c. Titles of local governmental officials and those of lesser federal and state officials are not usually capitalized when they follow or replace a personal name. However, these titles are sometimes capitalized in writing intended for a limited readership (for example, in a local newspaper, in internal communications within an organization, or in correspondence coming from or directed to the official's office), where the person in question would be considered to have high rank by the intended reader.

(Continued on page 74.)

The *Mayor* promised only last fall to hold the city sales tax at its present level. (Excerpt from an editorial in a local newspaper.)

BUT: Francis Fahey, *mayor* of Coventry, Rhode Island, appeared before a House committee today. The *mayor* spoke forcefully about the need to maintain federal aid to . . . (Excerpt from a national news service release.)

I would like to request an appointment with the *Attorney General.* (In a letter sent to the state attorney general's office.)

BUT: I have written for an appointment with the *attorney general* and expect to hear from his office soon.

d. Titles of *company officials* (for example, the *president,* the *general manager*) should not be capitalized when they follow or replace a personal name. Exceptions are made in formal minutes of meetings and in rules and bylaws.

The *president* will visit thirteen countries in a tour of company installations abroad. (Normal style.)

The *Secretary's* minutes were read and approved. (In formal minutes.)

NOTE: Some companies choose to capitalize these titles in all their communications because of the great respect the officials command within the company. However, this practice confers excessive importance on people who are neither public officials nor eminent dignitaries, and it should be avoided.

e. In general, do not capitalize job titles when they stand alone. (**NOTE:** In procedures manuals and company memos and announcements, job titles are sometimes capitalized for special distinction and emphasis.)

Marion Conroy has been promoted to the position of *senior accountant* (**OR** *Senior Accountant*).

f. Titles *following* a personal name or *standing alone* are sometimes capitalized in formal citations and acknowledgments.

314 Do not capitalize titles used as general terms of classification. (See ¶307.)

a United States senator   every king
a state governor   any ambassador

EXCEPTION: Because of the special regard for the office of the President of the United States, this title is capitalized even when used as a general term of classification (for example, a *President,* every *President*).

315 Capitalize any title (even if not of high rank) when it is used in *direct address* (that is, quoted or unquoted speech made directly to another person).

DIRECT ADDRESS: Please tell me, *Doctor,* what risks are involved in this treatment.

INDIRECT ADDRESS: I asked the *doctor* what risks were involved in this treatment.

NOTE: In direct address, do not capitalize a term like *madam, miss,* or *sir* if it stands alone without a proper name following.

Isn't it true, *sir,* that the defendant offered you money for trade secrets?

316 In the *inside address* of a letter, in the *writer's identification block,* and on an *envelope,* capitalize all titles whether they precede or follow the name. (See ¶¶1322–1325, 1362–1368, and the illustrations on page 294.)

317 Do not capitalize *former, late, ex-,* or *-elect* when used with titles. (See ¶363 for the style in headings.)

the late President Truman ex-President Carter Mayor-elect Bawley

FAMILY TITLES

318 Capitalize words such as *mother, father, aunt,* and *uncle* when they stand alone or are followed by a personal name.

> Let me ask *Mother* and *Dad* if that date is open for them.
>
> We'll be glad to put up *Aunt Peg* and *Uncle Fred* when they come to visit.
>
> I hear that *Brother Bobby* has gone off the deep end again.
>
> Do you think *Grandmother Harvey* will be pleased when she hears the news?

319 Do not capitalize family titles when they are preceded by possessives (such as *my, your, his, her, our,* and *their*) and simply describe a family relationship.

> Let me ask my *mother* and *dad* if that date is open for them.
>
> Do you think your *brother* Bobby would like to meet my *sister* Fern?

NOTE: If the words *uncle, aunt,* or *cousin* form a unit when used together with a first name, capitalize these titles, even when they are preceded by a possessive.

> Frank wants us to meet his *Uncle John.* (Here *Uncle John* is a unit.)
>
> **BUT:** Frank wants us to meet his *uncle,* John Cunningham. (Here *uncle* simply describes a family relationship.)
>
> I hope you can meet my *Cousin May.* (The writer thinks of her as *Cousin May.*)
>
> **BUT:** I hope you can meet my *cousin* May. (Here the writer thinks of her as *May;* the word *cousin* merely indicates relationship.)

NAMES OF ORGANIZATIONS

320 Capitalize the names of companies, unions, associations, societies, independent committees and boards, schools, political parties, conventions, foundations, fraternities, sororities, clubs, and religious bodies. (Follow the style established by the organization itself, as shown in the letterhead or some other written communication from the organization.)

> BellSouth Corporation
> the Transport Workers Union of America
> the American Society for Training and Development
> the Committee for Economic Development
> the Financial Accounting Standards Board
>
> the Hopewell Chamber of Commerce
> the University of North Dakota
> the Democratic and Liberal Parties
> the Republican National Convention
> the Andrew W. Mellon Foundation
> the Overseas Press Club of America
> the United Fund
> St. Mark's United Methodist Church
> Parents Anonymous

❏ *For the treatment of articles (like* the*), prepositions (like* of *or* for*), and conjunctions (like* and*), see* ¶303, *note. For the capitalization of abbreviations and acronyms used as organizational names, see* ¶¶520, 522.

321 When the common-noun element is used in place of the full name (for example, *the company* in place of *the Andersen Hardware Company*), do not capitalize the short form unless special emphasis or distinction is required (as in legal documents, minutes of meetings, bylaws, and other formal communications, where the short form is intended to invoke the full authority of the organization). In most cases, however, capitalization is unnecessary because the short form is used only as a general term of classification (see ¶¶307–308).

> The *company,* in my opinion, has always made a conscientious effort to involve itself in community affairs. (As used here, *company* is a general term of classification.)
>
> **BUT:** On behalf of the *Company,* I am authorized to accept your bid. (Here the full authority of the company is implied; hence the capital *C.*)

(Continued on page 76.)

Mr. Weinstock has just returned from a visit to Haverford College. He reports that the *college* is planning a new fund-raising campaign.

BUT: The *College* hopes to raise an additional $10,000,000 this year to finance the construction of the new media resource center. (Announcement in the alumni bulletin.)

NOTE: Do not capitalize the short form if it is modified by a word other than *the*. In constructions such as *our company, this company,* and *every company,* the noun is clearly a general term of classification. (See also ¶308.)

322 Common organizational terms such as *advertising department, manufacturing division, finance committee,* and *board of directors* are ordinarily capitalized when they are the actual names of units within the writer's own organization. These terms are not capitalized when they refer to some other organization unless the writer has reason to give these terms special importance or distinction.

The *Board of Directors* will meet next Thursday at 2:30. (From a company memo.)

BUT: Julia Perez has been elected to the *board of directors* of the Kensington Trade Corporation. (From a news release intended for a general audience.)

The *Finance Committee* will meet all week to review next year's budget. (Style used by insiders.)

BUT: Gilligan says his company can give us no encouragement until its *finance committee* has reviewed our proposal. (Style normally used by outsiders.)

The *Advertising Department* will unveil the fall campaign this Friday. (Style used by insiders.)

The *advertising department* of Black & London will unveil its fall campaign this Friday. (Style used by outsiders.)

NOTE: Do not capitalize these organizational terms when they are modified by a word other than *the*. Constructions such as *this credit department, their credit department, every credit department, your credit department,* and *our credit department* are terms of general classification and should not be capitalized. (See also ¶321, note.)

Black & London always seems to have a lot of turnover in *its advertising department.*

We don't have as much turnover in *our advertising department* as you may think. (Some insiders prefer to write "our Advertising Department" because of the special importance they attach to their own organizational structure.)

I would like to apply for the position of copywriter that is currently open in *your advertising department.* (Some outsiders might write "your Advertising Department" if they wanted to flatter the reader by giving special importance to the reader's organizational structure.)

323 Capitalize such nouns as *marketing, advertising,* or *promotion* when they are used alone to designate a department within an organization.

Paul Havlicek in *Corporate Communications* is the person to talk with.

I want to get a reaction from our people in *Marketing* first.

BUT: I want to talk to our *marketing* people first. (Here *marketing* is simply a descriptive adjective.)

324 Capitalize the word *the* preceding the name of an organization only when it is part of the legal name of the organization.

The Associated Press	The New York Times (see ¶289d)
The Conference Board	The Wall Street Journal

a. Even when part of the organizational name, *the* is often uncapitalized except in legal or formal contexts where it is important to give the full legal name.

b. Do not capitalize *the* when the name is used as a modifier or is abbreviated.

the Associated Press report	the AP	works for the Times

NAMES OF GOVERNMENT BODIES

325 Capitalize the names of countries and international organizations as well as national, state, county, and city bodies and their subdivisions.

the British Commonwealth	the Utah Tax Commission
the Federal Republic of Germany	the Ohio Legislature
the United Nations	the Court of Appeals of the State of
the Reagan Administration	Wisconsin (see ¶303, note)
the Cabinet	the New York State Board of Education
the Ninety-ninth Congress	the Fairfax County Shade Tree Commission
(see ¶363)	the Boston City Council
the House of Representatives	the Legal Services Corporation

❑ *For city and state names, see ¶¶334–335.*

326 Capitalize short forms of names of national and international bodies and their major divisions.

the House (referring to the House of Representatives)

the Department (referring to the Department of Justice, the State Department, the Department of the Treasury, etc.)

the Bureau (referring to the Bureau of the Budget, the Federal Bureau of Investigation, the Bureau of the Census, etc.)

the Court (referring to the United States Supreme Court, the International Court of Justice, etc.)

As a rule, do not capitalize short forms of names of state or local governmental groups except when special circumstances warrant emphasis or distinction. (See ¶327.)

327 Common terms such as *police department, board of education,* and *county court* need not be capitalized (even when referring to a specific body), since they are terms of general classification. However, such terms should be capitalized when the writer intends to refer to the organization in all of its official dignity.

The *Police Department* has announced the promotion of Robert Boyarsky to the rank of sergeant. (The short form is capitalized here because it is intended to have the full force of the complete name, the *Cranfield Police Department.*)

BUT: The Cranfield *police department* sponsors a youth athletic program that we could well copy. (No capitalization is used here because the writer is referring to the department in general terms and not by its official name.)

NOTE: Do not capitalize the short form if it is not actually derived from the complete name. For example, do not capitalize the short form *police department* if the full name is *Department of Public Safety.*

328 Capitalize *federal* only when it is part of the official name of a federal agency, a federal act, or some other proper noun.

the *Federal* Reserve Board   the *Federal* Insurance Contributions Act

BUT: . . . subject to *federal,* state, and local laws.

329 The terms *federal government* and *government* (referring specifically to the United States government) are now commonly written in small letters because they are considered terms of general classification. In government documents and correspondence, and in other communications where these terms are intended to have the force of an official name, they are capitalized.

330 Capitalize the words *union* and *commonwealth* only when they refer to a specific government.

Wilkins has lectured on the topic in almost every state in the *Union.*

NAMES OF PLACES

331 Capitalize the names of places, such as streets, buildings, parks, monuments, rivers, oceans, and mountains. Do not capitalize short forms used in place of the full name. (See ¶332 for a few exceptions.)

Montgomery Street **BUT:**	the street	Bighorn Mountain **BUT:**	the mountain
Sears Tower	the tower	Shoshone Falls	the falls
Stone Mountain Park	the park	the Washington	the monument
Sacramento River	the river	Monument	
Lake Pontchartrain	the lake	Logan Airport	the airport
Colony Surf Hotel	the hotel	the Fogg Art Museum	the museum
Rittenhouse Square	the square	Verrazano Bridge	the bridge
Riverside Drive	the drive	Lincoln Park Zoo	the zoo

❑ *For plural expressions like* the Atlantic and Pacific Oceans, *see ¶309a, note. For the treatment of prepositions and conjunctions in proper names, see ¶303, note.*

332 A few short forms are capitalized because of clear association with one place.

the Coast (the West Coast)	the Hill (Capitol Hill)
the Continent (Europe)	the Canal (the Panama Canal)
the Channel (English Channel)	the Village (Greenwich Village)

333 Capitalize imaginative names that designate specific places.

the Bay Area (San Francisco)	the Right Bank (in Paris)
the Loop (in Chicago)	the Twin Cities (Minneapolis and St. Paul)
the Big Apple (New York)	the City of Brotherly Love (Philadelphia)
the Sunbelt	the Beehive State (Utah)
Back Bay (in Boston)	the French Quarter (in New Orleans)

334 Capitalize the word *city* only when it is part of the corporate name of the city or part of an imaginative name.

Kansas City	the Windy City (Chicago)
BUT: the city of San Francisco	the Eternal City (Rome)

335 Capitalize *state* only when it follows the name of a state or is part of an imaginative name.

New York *State* is also called the Empire *State*.

The *state* of Alaska is the largest in the Union.

Washington *State* entered the Union in 1889, the forty-second *state* to do so.

The *state* of Arizona is also known as the Grand Canyon *State*.

After a two-year assignment overseas, we returned to the *States*. (Meaning the United States.)

NOTE: Do not capitalize *state* even when used in place of the actual state name.

He is an employee of the *state*. (People working for the state government, however, might write *State*.)

336 Capitalize *the* only when it is a part of the official name of a place.

The Dalles	The Hague
BUT: the Bronx	the Netherlands

337 Capitalize the words *upper* and *lower* only when they are part of an actual place name or a well-established imaginative name.

Upper Montclair	Lower Waterford
Upper Peninsula	Lower California
Upper West Side	Lower East Side

POINTS OF THE COMPASS

338   Capitalize *north, south, east, west,* and derivative words when they designate definite regions or are an integral part of a proper name.

in the North	the Far North	the North Pole
down South	the Deep South	the South Side
out West	the Middle West	the West Coast
back East	the Near East	the Eastern Seaboard
		OR: the East Coast

Do not capitalize these words when they merely indicate direction or general location.

> Many textile plants have moved from the *Northeast* and relocated in the *South.* (Region.)

> They maintain a villa in the *south* of France. (General location.)

> Go *west* on Route 517 and then *south* on I-95. (Direction.)

> John is coming back *East* after three years on the *West Coast.* (Region.)
> **BUT:** The *west coast* of the United States borders on the Pacific. (Referring only to the shoreline, not the region.)

> Most of our customers live on the *East Side.* (Definite locality.)
> **BUT:** Most of our customers live on the *east side* of town. (General location.)

339   Capitalize such words as *Northerner, Southerner,* and *Midwesterner.*

340   Capitalize such words as *northern, southern, eastern,* and *western* when these words pertain to the people in a region and to their political, social, or cultural activities. Do not capitalize these words, however, when they merely indicate general location or refer to the geography or climate of the region.

Eastern bankers	**BUT:** the eastern half of Pennsylvania
Southern hospitality	southern temperatures
Western civilization	westerly winds
the Northern vote	a northern winter

> The *Northern* states did not vote as they were expected to. (Political activities.)
> **BUT:** The drought is expected to continue in the *northern* states. (Climate.)

> My sales territory takes in most of the *southeastern* states. (General location.)

NOTE: When terms like *western region* and *southern district* are used to name organizational units within a company, capitalize them.

> The *Western Region* (referring to a part of the national sales staff) reports that sales are 12 percent over budget for the first six months this year.

341   When words like *northern, southern, eastern,* and *western* precede a place name, they are not ordinarily capitalized because they merely indicate general location within a region. However, when these words are actually part of the place name, they must be capitalized. (Check an atlas or the geographic listings in a dictionary when in doubt.)

Preceding a Place Name	Part of a Place Name
northern New Jersey	**BUT:** Northern Ireland
western Massachusetts	Western Australia

NOTE: Within certain regions it is not uncommon for many who live there to capitalize the adjective because of the special importance they attach to the regional designation. Thus people who live in southern California may prefer to write *Southern California.*

DAYS OF THE WEEK, MONTHS, HOLIDAYS, SEASONS, EVENTS, PERIODS

342 Capitalize names of days, months, holidays, and religious days.

Tuesday	Ash Wednesday
February	Good Friday
New Year's Eve	Passover
Mother's Day	Rosh Hashanah
Veterans Day (no apostrophe)	Yom Kippur
Martin Luther King Day	Ramadan

343 Do not capitalize the names of the seasons unless they are personified.

We hold our regional sales conferences during the *fall* and *winter*, but our national conference always takes place early in the *spring*.

BUT: Summer was dead and Autumn was expiring,
And infant Winter laughed upon the land . . .
—Percy Bysshe Shelley

344 **a.** Capitalize the names of historical events and imaginative names given to historical periods.

the Boston Tea Party	the Renaissance
the American Revolution	the Reformation
World War II	Prohibition
Fire Prevention Week	the Great Depression

b. References to cultural *ages* are usually capitalized. However, contemporary references are not usually capitalized unless they appear together with a capitalized reference.

the Bronze Age	**BUT:**	the space age
the Dark Ages		the atomic age
the Middle Ages		the nuclear age

The course spans the development of civilization from the *Stone Age* to the *Space Age*.

c. References to cultural *eras* are usually capitalized, but references to cultural periods are usually not.

the Christian Era	**BUT:**	the romantic period
the Victorian Era		the colonial period

345 Do not capitalize the names of decades and centuries.

during the fifties	in the twenty-first century
in the nineteen-eighties	during the nineteen hundreds

NOTE: Decades are capitalized, however, in special expressions.

the Gay Nineties	the Roaring Twenties

ACTS, LAWS, BILLS, TREATIES

346 **a.** Capitalize formal titles of acts, laws, bills, and treaties, but do not capitalize common-noun elements that stand alone in place of the full name.

the Airline Deregulation Act		the act
Public Law 480		the law
the Treaty of Versailles		the treaty
the First Amendment		the amendment
the Constitution of the United States	**BUT:**	the Constitution

b. Do not capitalize generic or informal references to existing or pending legislation except for proper nouns and adjectives.

environmental protection laws   the Bradley-Gephardt tax proposals

PROGRAMS, MOVEMENTS, CONCEPTS

347 a. Do not capitalize the names of programs, movements, or concepts when used as general terms.

social security benefits (**BUT:** the Social Security Administration)
medicare payments (**BUT:** the Medicare Act)
the civil rights movement
women's lib
existentialism and rationalism

b. Capitalize proper nouns and adjectives that are part of such terms.

the Socratic method   Boolean algebra
Keynesian economics   Marxist-Leninist theories

c. Capitalize imaginative names given to programs and movements.

the New Deal   the New Frontier
the Great Society   the War on Poverty

d. Capitalize terms like *democrat, socialist,* and *communist* when they signify formal membership in a political party but not when they merely signify belief in a certain philosophy.

a lifelong *democrat* (refers to a person who believes in the principles of democracy)

a lifelong *Democrat* (refers to a person who consistently votes for candidates of the Democratic Party)

independent voters   leftists
the right wing   fascist tendencies

RACES, PEOPLES, LANGUAGES

348 Capitalize the names of races, peoples, tribes, and languages.

| Caucasians | Afro-Americans | the Sioux | **BUT:** the blacks |
| the Chinese | Hispanics | Mandarin Chinese | the whites |

RELIGIOUS REFERENCES

349 a. Capitalize all references to a supreme being.

| God | the Supreme Being | the Almighty | Allah |
| the Lord | the Messiah | the Holy Spirit | Yahweh |

b. Capitalize personal pronouns referring to a supreme being when they stand alone, without an antecedent nearby.

Offer thanks unto *Him.*   **BUT:** Ask the Lord for *his* blessing.

c. Capitalize references to persons revered as divine.

| the Apostles | Buddha | John the Baptist |
| the Blessed Virgin | the Prophet | Saint Peter (see ¶518e) |

(Continued on page 82.)

d. Capitalize the names of religions, their members, and their buildings.

Reform Judaism	Mormons	Saint Mark's Episcopal Church
Zen Buddhism	Methodists	Temple Beth Sholom

the Roman Catholic *Church* (meaning the institution as a whole)
BUT: the Roman Catholic *church* on Wyoming Avenue (an indefinite reference to a specific building)

e. Capitalize references to religious events. (See also ¶342.)

the Creation	the Exodus	the Crucifixion
the Flood	the Second Coming	the Resurrection

f. In general, do not capitalize references to specific religious observances and services.

bar mitzvah	baptism	**BUT:** the Eucharist
seder	christening	the Mass

350 Capitalize (but do not quote or underscore) references to works regarded as sacred.

the King James Bible	the Koran	the Ten Commandments
(**BUT:** biblical sources)	the Talmud	the Sermon on the Mount
the Revised Standard	the Torah	Psalms 23 and 24
Version	the Our Father	Kaddish
the Old Testament	the Lord's Prayer	Hail Mary
the Book of Genesis	Hebrews 13:8	the Apostles' Creed

CELESTIAL BODIES

351 Capitalize the names of planets (*Jupiter, Mars*), stars (*Polaris, the North Star*), and constellations (*the Big Dipper, the Milky Way*). However, do not capitalize the words *sun, moon,* and *earth* unless they are used in connection with the capitalized names of other planets or stars.

With the weather we've been having, we haven't seen much of the *sun*.

We have gone to the ends of the *earth* to assemble this collection of jewelry.

Compare the orbits of *Mars, Venus,* and *Earth*.

COURSE TITLES, SUBJECTS, ACADEMIC DEGREES

352 Capitalize the names of specific course titles. However, do not capitalize names of subjects or areas of study (except for any proper nouns or adjectives in such names).

American History 201 meets on Tuesdays and Thursdays. (Course title.)

Harriet has decided to major in *American history*. (Area of study.)

353 Do not capitalize academic degrees used as general terms of classification (for example, *a bachelor of arts degree, working on her master's*). However, capitalize a degree used after a person's name (*Claire Hurwitz, Doctor of Philosophy*).

354 In references to academic years, do not capitalize the words *freshman, sophomore, junior,* and *senior*. In references to elementary and high school grade levels, capitalize the word *grade* when a number follows but not when a number precedes.

All incoming *freshmen* must register by September 4.

Harriet spent her *junior* year in Germany.

Our oldest child is in *Grade 6*, our second child is in the *third grade*, and our youngest is in kindergarten.

COMMERCIAL PRODUCTS

355 Capitalize trademarks, brand names, proprietary names, names of commercial products, and market grades. The common noun following the name of a product should not ordinarily be capitalized; however, manufacturers and advertisers often capitalize such words in the names of their own products to give them special emphasis.

> Ivory soap   Hotpoint dishwasher   Choice lamb (market grade)

356 Capitalize all trademarks except those that have become clearly established as common nouns. To be safe, check an up-to-date dictionary or consult the United States Trademark Association (6 East 45 Street, New York, NY 10017).

Coca-Cola, Coke	Teflon	Dacron	Dictaphone
Pyrex	TelePrompTer	Teletype	Frigidaire
Photostat	Xerox	Windbreaker	Kleenex
Band-Aid	Jeep	Levi's	Realtor

> **BUT:** nylon, cellophane, mimeograph, dry ice, aspirin

ADVERTISING MATERIAL

357 Words ordinarily written in small letters may be capitalized in advertising copy for special emphasis. (This style is inappropriate in all other kinds of written communication.)

> Save money now during our *Year-End Clearance Sale*.
>
> It's the event *Luxury Lovers* have been waiting for . . . from Whitehall's!

LEGAL CORRESPONDENCE

358 In legal documents many words that ordinarily would be written in small letters are written with initial capitals or all capitals—for example, references to parties, the name of the document, special provisions, and sometimes spelled-out amounts of money (see ¶420*b*).

> THIS AGREEMENT, made this 31st day of January 1987 . . .
> . . . hereinafter called the SELLER . . .
> WHEREAS the Seller has this day agreed . . .
> WITNESS the signatures . . .

NOUNS WITH NUMBERS OR LETTERS

359 Capitalize a noun followed by a number or a letter that indicates sequence. **EXCEPTIONS:** Do not capitalize the nouns *line, note, page, paragraph, size,* and *verse.*

Act I	Class 4	Lesson 20	Policy 394857
Appendix A	Column 1	line 4	Room 501
Article 2	Diagram 4	Model B671-4	Section 1
Book III	Exercise 8	note 1	size 10
Bulletin T-119	Exhibit A	page 158	Table 7
Car 8171	Figure 9	paragraph 2a	Track 2
Chapter V	Flight 626	Part Three	Unit 2
Chart 3	Illustration 19	Plate XV	verse 3
Check 181	Invoice 270487	Platform 3	Volume II

> For a more detailed discussion of this argument, see *Chapters 5–6.*

> **NOTE:** It is often unnecessary to use *No.* before the number. (See ¶455*a.*)

> Purchase Order 4713 (**RATHER THAN:** Purchase Order *No.* 4713)

TITLES OF LITERARY AND ARTISTIC WORKS; HEADINGS

360 In titles of literary and artistic works and in displayed headings, capitalize all words with *four or more* letters. Also capitalize words with fewer than four letters except:

ARTICLES: *the, a, an*

SHORT CONJUNCTIONS: *and, as, but, if, or, nor*

SHORT PREPOSITIONS: *at, by, for, in, of, off, on, out, to, up*

How to Succeed in Business Without Really Trying

"Redevelopment Proposal Is Not Expected to Be Approved"

NOTE: Even articles, short conjunctions, and short prepositions should be capitalized under the following circumstances:

a. Capitalize the first and last word of a title.

"A Home to Be Proud Of"

CAUTION: Do not capitalize *the* at the beginning of a title unless it is actually part of the title.

For further details check the *Encyclopaedia Britannica*.

This clipping is from *The New York Times*.

b. Capitalize the first word following a dash or colon in a title.

Abraham Lincoln—The Early Years

The Treaty of Versailles: A Reexamination

c. Capitalize short words like *in, out, off,* and *up* in titles when they serve as adverbs rather than as prepositions. (These words may occur as adverbs in verb phrases or in hyphenated compounds derived from verb phrases.)

"IBM Chalks *Up* Record Earnings for the Year"

"LeClaire Is Runner-*Up* in Election" (see also ¶363)

BUT: "Sailing *up* the Mississippi"

d. Capitalize short prepositions like *in* and *up* when used together with prepositions having four or more letters.

"Sailing *Up* and *Down* the Mississippi"

"Happenings *In* and *Around* Town"

❑ *For the capitalization of* Preface, Contents, Appendix, *and* Index, *see ¶242, note; for the use of all capitals with titles, see ¶289a.*

361 Do not capitalize a book title when it is incorporated into a sentence as a descriptive phrase.

In his book on *economics* Samuelson points out that . . .

BUT: In his book *Economics* Samuelson points out that . . .

AWARDS AND MEDALS

362 Capitalize the names of awards and medals.

Pulitzer Prize winners	the Congressional Medal of Honor
the Nobel Prize	the Distinguished Service Medal
Oscars and Emmys	the Purple Heart

HYPHENATED WORDS

363 *Within a sentence,* capitalize only those elements of a hyphenated word that are proper nouns or proper adjectives. *At the beginning of a sentence,* capitalize the first element in the hyphenated word but not other elements unless they are proper nouns or adjectives. *In a heading or title,* capitalize all the elements except articles, short prepositions, and short conjunctions (see ¶360).

Within Sentences	Beginning Sentences	In Headings
up-to-date	Up-to-date	Up-to-Date
Spanish-American	Spanish-American	Spanish-American
English-speaking	English-speaking	English-Speaking
mid-September	Mid-September	Mid-September
ex-President Carter	Ex-President Carter	Ex-President Carter
Senator-elect Murray	Senator-elect Murray	Senator-Elect Murray
self-confidence	Self-confidence	Self-Confidence
de-emphasize	De-emphasize	De-Emphasize
follow-up	Follow-up	Follow-Up (see ¶360c)
Ninety-ninth Congress	Ninety-ninth Congress	Ninety-Ninth Congress
one-sixth	One-sixth	One-Sixth
post-World War II	Post-World War II	Post-World War II

❑ *Capitalization of questions within sentences: see ¶¶115, 117.*
❑ *Capitalization after a colon: see ¶¶196–199.*
❑ *Capitalization after an opening dash: see ¶214, note.*
❑ *Capitalization after an opening parenthesis: see ¶¶224–226.*
❑ *Capitalization after an opening quotation mark: see ¶¶272–273.*
❑ *Capitalization of abbreviations: see ¶514.*

Numbers

There is a significant difference between using figures and using words to express numbers. Figures are big (like capital letters) and compact and informal (like abbreviations); when used in a sentence, they stand out clearly from the surrounding words. By contrast, numbers expressed in words are unemphatic and formal; they do not stand out in a sentence. It is this functional difference between figures and words that underlies all aspects of number style.

BASIC RULES

The rules for expressing numbers would be quite simple if writers would all agree to express numbers entirely in figures or entirely in words. But in actual practice the exclusive use of figures is considered appropriate only in tables and statistical matter, whereas the exclusive use of words to express numbers is found only in ultraformal documents (such as proclamations and social invitations). In writing that is neither ultraformal nor ultratechnical, most style manuals call for the use of both figures and words in varying proportions. Although authorities do not agree on details, there are two sets of basic rules in wide use: the *figure style* (which uses figures for most numbers above 10) and the *word style* (which uses figures for most numbers above 100). Unless you deal with a very limited type of business correspondence, you should be familiar with both styles and be prepared to use each appropriately as the situation demands.

FIGURE STYLE

The figure style is most commonly used in ordinary business correspondence (dealing with sales, production, finance, advertising, and other routine commercial matters). It is also used in journalistic and technical material and in academic work of a technical or statistical nature. In writing of this kind most numbers represent significant quantities or measurements that should stand out for emphasis or quick comprehension.

401   Spell out numbers from 1 through 10; use figures for numbers above 10. This rule applies to both exact and approximate numbers.

> I would like *ten* copies of this article, but I need only *two* or *three* right away.
>
> At the convention we got over 75 requests for a copy of your report.
>
> We expect about 30 to 35 employees to sign up for the graphic arts course.
>
> The advertising is deliberately pitched at the *40-plus* age group.
>
> My letter in last Sunday's paper apparently provoked over 25 letters and some *60-odd* phone calls.
>
> One bookstore chain has already ordered 2500 copies. (See ¶461 on the omission of commas in four-digit figures.)
>
> The exhibition drew more than *12,000* people in the first month.

a. Use all figures—even for the numbers 1 through 10 (as in this sentence)— when they have technical significance or need to stand out for quick comprehension. This all-figure style is used in tables, in statistical matter, and in expressions of dates (*May 3*), money (*$6*), clock time (*4 p.m.*), proportions and ratios (*a 10-to-1 shot*), percentages (*8 percent*), and scores (*3 to 1*). This style is also used with abbreviations and symbols (*12 cm, 8°F*), with numbers referred to as numbers (*think of a number from 1 to 10*), with highway designations (*U.S. Route 1, I-80*), and with technical or emphatic references to age (*a clinical study of 5-year-olds*), periods of time (*a 6-month loan*), and measurements (*parcels over 3 pounds*).

(Continued on page 88.)

b. In isolated cases spell out a number above 10 in order to de-emphasize the number or make it seem indefinite. (See ¶¶465–467 for rules on how to express numbers in words.)

He could give you *a thousand and one* reasons for his decision.

I have *a hundred* things to do today. (In this context *100 things* would seem too precise, too exact.)

NOTE: Also use words for numbers at the beginning of a sentence, for most ordinals (*our twenty-fifth anniversary*), for fractions (*one-third of our sales*), and for nontechnical or nonemphatic references to age (*my son just turned twelve*), periods of time (*twenty years ago*), and measurements (*I need to lose another thirty pounds*).

402 Use the same style to express *related* numbers above and below 10. (If any of the numbers are above 10, put them all in figures.)

We used to have *two* dogs, *one* cat, and *one* rabbit.
BUT: We now have 5 dogs, 11 cats, and 1 rabbit. (The rabbit is male.)

Our *four* sons consumed a total of 18 hamburgers, 5 large bottles of Coke, 12 apples, and about 2000 cookies—all at *one* sitting. (Figures are used for all the related items of food; the other numbers—*four* and *one*—are spelled out, since they are not related and are not over 10.)

403 For fast comprehension, numbers in the *millions* or higher may be expressed as follows:

21 million (in place of 21,000,000)   14½ million (in place of 14,500,000)
3 billion (in place of 3,000,000,000)   2.4 billion (in place of 2,400,000,000)

Bindel & Boggs is placing an order for 2.4 *million* barrels of oil.
BUT: Bindel & Boggs is placing a 2.4-*million-barrel* order. (See ¶817.)

a. This style may be used only when the amount consists of a whole number with nothing more than a simple fraction or decimal following. A number such as 4,832,067 must be written all in figures.

b. Treat related numbers alike.

Last year we sold 21,557,000 items; this year, nearly 23,000,000. (**NOT:** 23 million.)

❑ *For examples involving money, see ¶416.*

WORD STYLE

The word style of numbers is used in high-level executive correspondence (see ¶¶1394–1395) and in nontechnical material, where the writing is of a more formal or literary nature and the use of figures would give numbers an undesired emphasis and obtrusiveness. Here are the basic rules for the word style.

404 Spell out all numbers, whether exact or approximate, that can be expressed in one or two words. (A hyphenated compound number like *twenty-one* or *twenty-nine* counts as one word.) In effect, spell out all numbers from 1 through 100 and all round numbers above 100 that require no more than two words (such as *sixty-two thousand* or *forty-five million*).

Mr. Ryan received *twenty-three* letters praising his talk at the Rotary Club.

Last year more than *twelve million* people attended the art exhibition our company sponsored.

Some *sixty-odd* people have called to volunteer their services.

Over *two hundred* people attended the reception for Helen and Frank Russo.

BUT: Over 250 people attended the reception. (Use figures when more than two words are required.)

NOTE: In writing of an ultraformal nature—proclamations, social invitations, and many legal documents—even a number that requires more than two words is spelled out. However, as a matter of practicality the word style ordinarily uses figures when more than two words are required.

❑ *For rules on how to express numbers in words, see ¶¶465–467.*

405 Express related numbers the same way, even though some are above 100 and some below. If any are in figures, put all in figures.

> We sent out *three hundred* invitations and have already received over *one hundred* acceptances.

> **BUT:** We sent out *300* invitations and have already received *125* acceptances.
> (**NOT:** three hundred . . . 125.)

406 Numbers in the millions or higher *that require more than two words when spelled out* may be expressed as follows:

> 231 million (in place of 231,000,000)
> 9¾ billion (in place of 9,750,000,000)
> 671.4 million (in place of 671,400,000)

Even a two-word number such as *sixty-two million* should be expressed as *62 million* when it is related to a number such as *231 million* (which cannot be spelled in two words). Moreover, it should be expressed as *62,000,000* when it is related to a number such as *231,163,520.*

SPECIAL RULES

The preceding rules on figure style (¶¶401–403) and word style (¶¶404–406) are basic guidelines that govern in the absence of more specific principles. The following rules cover those situations which require special handling (for example, expressions of dates and money). In a number of cases where either figures or words are acceptable, your choice will depend on whether you are striving for emphasis or formality.

DATES

These rules apply to dates in sentences. See ¶1314 for date lines in business correspondence.

407 When the day *precedes* the month or *stands alone*, express it either in ordinal figures (*1st, 2d, 3d, 4th,* etc.) or in ordinal words (the *first,* the *twelfth,* the *twenty-eighth*).

> **FOR EMPHASIS:** The sales conference runs from the *2d* of August through the *5th.*

> **FOR FORMALITY:** We leave for Europe on the *third* of June and don't return until the *twenty-fifth.*

408 When the day *follows* the month, express it in cardinal figures (*1, 2, 3,* etc.).

> on March 6 (**NOT:** March *6th* **OR** March *sixth*)

409 **a.** Express complete dates in month-day-year sequence.

> March 6, 1989

> **NOTE:** In United States military correspondence and in letters from foreign countries, the complete date is expressed in day-month-year sequence.

> 6 March 1989

b. The form *3/6/89* (representing a *month*-day-year sequence) is acceptable on business forms and in informal letters and memos. Avoid this form, however, if there is any chance your reader could misinterpret it as a *day*-month-year sequence.

c. Avoid the following forms: *March 6th, 1989; Mar. 6, 1989; the 6th of March, 1989; the sixth of March, 1989.*

410 Note the current use of commas and other punctuation with expressions of dates.

On *August 13, 1984,* my husband and I received the bank loan that permitted us to start our own restaurant. (Two commas set off the year following the month and day.)

We set a formal opening date of *November 15, 1984;* we actually opened on *March 18, 1985* (because of the flash fire that virtually destroyed the restaurant and forced us to start from scratch). (Note that the second comma is omitted when some other punctuation mark—in this case a semicolon and an opening parenthesis—is required at that point.)

Sales for *February 1984* hit an all-time low. (Omit commas around the year when it follows the month alone.)

BUT: Once we introduced our new product line in *September 1985,* it was clear that we were finally on the road to a strong recovery. (The comma following *1985* is needed to separate an introductory dependent clause from the rest of the sentence, not because of the date.)

The *August 1984* issue of *The Atlantic* carries an excerpt from Brenda's forthcoming book. (No commas are used when the month and year serve as an adjective.)

BUT: The *August 6, 1984,* issue of *Newsweek* broke the story. (Use two commas to set off the year when a complete date serves as an adjective. See ¶154.)

In *1985* we opened six branch offices in the Southwest. (No comma follows the year in a short introductory phrase.)

On *February 28* the board will decide whether to sell off its holdings in Oregon real estate. (No comma follows the month and day in a short introductory phrase.)

BUT: On *February 28,* 27 managers from the Cincinnati plant will leave on a tour of Asian manufacturing facilities. (Insert a comma when another figure immediately follows. See ¶456.)

Yesterday, *April 3,* I spoke to a group of exporters in Los Angeles. Two days from now, *April 6,* I will speak to a similar group in San Francisco. Then on Wednesday, *April 11,* I will be speaking at an international trade fair in Honolulu. (Set off a month-day expression when it serves as an appositive. See ¶148.)

❑ *For the use or omission of a comma when a date is followed by a related phrase or clause, see ¶152.*

411 In formal legal documents, formal invitations, and proclamations, spell out the day and the year. A number of styles may be used:

May twenty-first	nineteen hundred and eighty-nine
the twenty-first of May	one thousand nine hundred and eighty-nine
this twenty-first day of May	in the year of our Lord one thousand nine hundred and eighty-nine

412 Class graduation years and well-known years in history may appear in abbreviated form.

the class of '88	the winter of '85

❑ *For the expression of centuries and decades, see ¶¶438–439; for dates in a sequence, see ¶¶458–460.*

MONEY

413   **a.** Use figures to express exact or approximate amounts of money.

$7	about $1500	over $5,000,000 a year	a $50 bill
$13.50	nearly $50,000	a $5,000,000-a-year account	$350 worth

b. When amounts of money from different countries are referred to in the same context, the unit of currency in each case usually appears as an abbreviation or symbol (or both) directly preceding the numerical amount.

US$10,000	(refers to 10,000 U.S. dollars)
Can$10,000	(refers to 10,000 Canadian dollars)
Mex$10,000	(refers to 10,000 Mexican pesos)
DM10,000	(refers to 10,000 West German deutsche marks)
£10,000	(refers to 10,000 British pounds)
¥10,000	(refers to 10,000 Japanese yen)

NOTE: To form the symbol for the British pound on the keyboard, type a capital *L* over a small *f*. To form the symbol for the Japanese yen, type a capital Y over an equal sign (=). The results will appear as follows:

   £   ¥

c. An isolated, nonemphatic reference to money may be spelled out.

two hundred dollars	a half-dollar
nearly a thousand dollars	half a million dollars
a twenty-dollar bill	five thousand dollars' worth (note
a million-dollar beach house	the apostrophe with *dollars*)

414   Spell out indefinite amounts of money.

    a few million dollars   many thousands of dollars

415   It is not necessary to add a decimal point or zeros to a *whole* dollar amount when it occurs in a sentence.

    I am enclosing a check for *$125* as payment in full.

    This model costs $12.50; that one costs *$10*.

In a column, however, if any amount contains cents, add a decimal point and two zeros to all *whole* dollar amounts to maintain a uniform appearance.

    $150.50
      25.00
       8.05
    $183.55

416   Money in round amounts of a million or more may be expressed partially in words. (The style given in the first column is preferred.)

$12 million	**OR**	12 million dollars		
$10½ million	**OR**	10½ million dollars		
$10.5 million	**OR**	10.5 million dollars		
$6¼ billion	**OR**	6¼ billion dollars	**OR**	$6250 million
$6.25 billion	**OR**	6.25 billion dollars	**OR**	6250 million dollars

a. This style may be used only when the amount consists of a whole number with nothing more than a simple fraction or decimal following. Write an amount like *$10,235,000* entirely in figures.

b. Express related amounts the same way.

    from $500,000 to $1,000,000 (**NOT:** from $500,000 to $1 million)

c. Repeat the word *million* (*billion,* etc.) with each figure to avoid misunderstanding.

$5 million to $10 million (**NOT:** $5 to $10 million)

417 Fractional expressions of large amounts of money should be either completely spelled out or converted to an all-figure style.

one-quarter of a million dollars **OR** $250,000
(**BUT NOT:** ¼ of a million dollars **OR** $¼ million)

a half-billion dollars **OR** $500,000,000
(**BUT NOT:** ½ billion dollars **OR** $½ billion)

418 a. For amounts under a dollar, ordinarily use figures and the word *cents*.

I am sure that customers will not pay more than *50 cents* for this item.

This machine can be fixed with *80 cents'* worth of parts. (Note the apostrophe with *cents*.)

These *75-cent* tokens can be used on the bus or the subway.

NOTE: An isolated, nonemphatic reference to cents may be spelled out.

I wouldn't give *two cents* for that car.

b. Do not use the style $.75 in sentences except when related amounts require a dollar sign.

It will cost you *$4.84* a copy to do the company manual: *$.86* for the paper, *$1.54* for the printing, and *$2.44* for the special binder.

c. The cent sign (¢) may be used in technical and statistical matter.

The price of finished steel, approximately *6.5¢* a pound in 1967, now runs around *25¢* a pound; aluminum ingots, averaging *25¢* a pound in 1967, now sell for *47¢* a pound.

419 When using the dollar sign or the cent sign with a price range or a series of amounts, use the sign with each amount.

$5,000 to $10,000 $10 million to $20 million
10¢ to 20¢   (**BUT NOT:** $10 to $20 million)

These three properties are valued at $32,900, $54,500, and $87,000, respectively.

If the term *dollars* or *cents* is to be spelled out, use it only with the final amount.

10 to 20 cents   10 million to 20 million dollars (see ¶416c)

420 In legal documents, amounts of money are often expressed first in words and then, within parentheses, in figures. (See also ¶¶465–467.)

One Hundred Dollars ($100)   **OR**   One Hundred (100) Dollars
BUT NOT: One Hundred ($100) Dollars

Three Thousand One Hundred and 50/100 Dollars ($3100.50)

a. When spelling out amounts of money, omit the *and* between hundreds and tens of dollars if *and* is used before the fraction representing cents.

Six Hundred Thirty-two and 75/100 Dollars
(**NOT:** Six Hundred *and* Thirty-two and 75/100 Dollars)

NOTE: In whole dollar amounts, the use of *and* between hundreds and tens of dollars is optional.

Six Hundred Thirty-two Dollars   **OR**   Six Hundred and Thirty-two Dollars

b. The capitalization of spelled-out amounts may vary. Sometimes the first letter of each main word is capitalized (as in the examples in ¶420a); sometimes only the first letter of the first word is capitalized (as on checks); sometimes the entire amount is given all in capitals.

The following rules (¶¶421–428) cover situations in which numbers are usually spelled out: at the beginning of sentences and in expressions using indefinite numbers, ordinal numbers, and fractions.

AT THE BEGINNING OF A SENTENCE

421 Spell out a number that begins a sentence, as well as any related numbers.

> *Thirty-four* former students of Dr. Helen VanVleck came from all parts of the country to honor their professor on the occasion of her retirement.
>
> *Eight hundred* people have already signed the recall petition.
>
> *Forty* to *fifty* percent of the people polled on different occasions expressed disapproval of the mayor's performance in office.
>
> (**NOT:** *Forty* to *50* percent . . .)

422 If the number requires more than two words when spelled out or if figures are preferable for emphasis or quick reference, reword the sentence.

> The company sent out *298* copies of its consumer guidelines last month.
> (**NOT:** *Two hundred and ninety-eight* copies of its consumer guidelines were sent out by the company last month.)
>
> We had a good year in *1984*.
> (**NOT:** *Nineteen hundred eighty-four* **OR** *1984* was a good year for us.)
>
> Our mining operations provide *60* to *70* percent of our revenues.
> (**NOT:** *Sixty* to *seventy* percent of our revenues come from our mining operations.)

INDEFINITE NUMBERS AND AMOUNTS

423 Spell out indefinite numbers and amounts.

> several hundred investors
> a few thousand acres
> a multimillion-dollar sale
> a man in his late forties
>
> hundreds of inquiries
> thousands of readers
> many millions of dollars
> a roll of fifties and twenties

❑ *For approximate numbers, see ¶401 (figure style) and ¶404 (word style).*

ORDINAL NUMBERS

424 In general, spell out all ordinal numbers (*first, second, third,* etc.) that can be expressed in one or two words. (A hyphenated number like *twenty-first* counts as one word.)

> in the twenty-first century
> twentieth-century art (see ¶817)
> on the forty-eighth floor
> on my fifty-fifth birthday
> the Fourteenth Ward
> the two millionth visitor to
> EPCOT
>
> the firm's one hundredth anniversary
> (**BUT:** the firm's 125th anniversary)
> the Ninety-ninth Congress (in text)
> the Ninety-Ninth Congress (in headings and titles; see ¶363)
> the 101st Congress
> the Eighteenth Amendment

❑ *For the rule on how to express ordinal numbers in words, see ¶465; for the distinction between ordinals and fractions, see ¶427d.*

425 Use figures for ordinals in certain expressions of dates (see ¶¶407–409), in numbered street names above 10 (see ¶1333*b*), and for special emphasis.

In Advertising Copy

Come to our 25*th* Anniversary Sale! (Figures for emphasis.)

Come to our *Twenty-fifth* Anniversary Sale! (Words for formality.)

In Ordinary Correspondence

Watkins & Glenn is having a *twenty-fifth* anniversary sale.

NOTE: Ordinal figures are expressed as follows: *1st, 2d* or *2nd, 3d* or *3rd, 4th, 5th, 6th*, etc. Do not use an "abbreviation" period following an ordinal figure.

❑ *For the use of* 2d *in preference to* 2nd, *see* ¶503.

426 Use arabic or roman numerals for ordinals that follow a name.

James A. Wilson 3d   **OR**   James A. Wilson III
C. Roy Post 4th   C. Roy Post IV

❑ *For the use or omission of commas with numerals, see* ¶156.

FRACTIONS

427 Fractions Standing Alone

a. Ordinarily, spell out a fraction that stands alone (that is, without a whole number preceding). Use figures, however, if the spelled-out form is long and awkward or if the fraction is used in a technical measurement or some type of computation.

one-half the audience (see ¶427*c*)   three-fourths of the profits
a two-thirds majority   nine-tenths of a mile away

3/4-yard lengths (**BETTER THAN:** three-quarter-yard lengths)

5/32 inch (**BETTER THAN:** five thirty-seconds of an inch)

multiply by 2/5

This recipe calls for only *a quarter pound* of butter.

He came back *a half hour* later (**OR** *half an hour* later).

I'll take *a half dozen* (**OR** *half a dozen*).

BUT: I'll take *a half-dozen* eggs (**OR** *half-a-dozen* eggs). (Hyphenate *half dozen* or *half a dozen* when this phrase is used as a compound modifier before a noun.)

b. When a fraction is spelled out, the numerator and the denominator should be connected by a hyphen unless either element already contains a hyphen.

five-eighths   thirteen thirty-seconds
thirteen-sixteenths   twenty-seven sixty-fourths

c. In constructions involving the balanced phrases *one half . . . the other half*, do not hyphenate *one half*.

One half of the shipment was damaged beyond use; *the other half* was salvageable.

d. Distinguish between large spelled-out fractions (which are hyphenated) and large spelled-out ordinals (which are not).

The difference is less than *one-hundredth* of 1 percent. (Hyphenated fraction referring to 1/100.)

BUT: This year the company will be celebrating the *one hundredth* anniversary of its founding. (Unhyphenated ordinal referring to 100th.)

e. Fractions expressed in figures should not be followed by endings like *sts, ds, nds,* or *ths* or by an *of* phrase.

3/200 (**NOT:** 3/200ths)   9/64 inch (**NOT:** 9/64ths of an inch)

If a sentence requires the use of an *of* phrase following the fraction, spell the fraction out.

three-quarters of an hour (**NOT:** 3/4 of an hour)

428   Fractions in Mixed Numbers

a. A mixed number (a whole number plus a fraction) is written in figures except at the beginning of a sentence.

Retail sales are now 3½ times what they were in 1967.

Two and a quarter (**OR** *Two and one-quarter*) inches of rain fell over the weekend. (Note the use of *and* between the whole number and the fraction.)

b. When constructing fractions that do not appear on the keyboard, use the diagonal (/). Separate a whole number from a fraction by means of a space (not with a hyphen).

I can remember when an *8 5/8* percent mortgage seemed high. (**NOT:** 8-5/8.)

c. In the same sentence, do not mix constructed fractions (7/8, 5/16) with those that appear on the keyboard (½, ¼).

The rate on prime commercial paper has dropped from *11 1/2* percent a year ago to *8 3/4* percent today. (**NOT:** 11½ . . . 8 3/4.)

NOTE: To simplify typing, convert constructed fractions (and simpler ones used in the same context) to a decimal form whenever feasible.

The rate on prime commercial paper has dropped from *11.5* percent a year ago to *8.75* percent today.

The following rules (¶¶429–442) deal with measurements and with expressions of age and time (elements that often function as measurements). When these elements have technical or statistical significance, they are expressed in figures; otherwise, they are expressed in words.

MEASUREMENTS

429   Most measurements have a technical significance and should be expressed in figures (even from 1 through 10) for emphasis or quick comprehension. However, spell out an isolated measurement that lacks technical significance.

A higher rate is charged on parcels over *2 kilograms.*
BUT: I'm afraid I've gained another *two kilograms* this week.

Add *1 quart* of sugar for each *4 quarts* of strawberries.
BUT: Last weekend we picked *four quarts* of strawberries from our own patch.

There is no charge for delivery within a *30-mile* radius of Chicago.
BUT: It's only a *thirty-mile* drive up to our summer place.

NOTE: Dimensions, sizes, and actual temperature readings are always expressed in figures.

I'm looking for a *4- by 6-foot* Oriental rug for my reception room. (See also ¶432.)

Please send me a half-dozen blue oxford shirts, size *17½/33.*

The thermometer now stands at *32,* a drop of five degrees in the past two hours.

BUT: The temperature has been in the low *thirties* (**OR** *30s*) all week. (An indefinite reference to the temperature may be spelled out or expressed in figures.)

430 When a measurement consists of several elements, do not use commas to separate the elements. The measurement is considered a single unit. (See also ¶817.)

> The package weighed *8 pounds 11 ounces.*
> The punch bowl holds *4 quarts 1 pint.*
> Hal is *6 feet 8 inches* tall in his stocking feet.

NOTE: If this type of measurement is used as a compound modifier before a noun, use hyphens to connect all the elements as a single unit.

> a *6-foot-8-inch* man

431 The unit of measurement may be abbreviated (for example, *12 ft*) or expressed as a symbol (for example, *12'*) in technical material or in tables. If either an abbreviation or a symbol is used, the number must be expressed as a figure.

> ❏ *For the style of abbreviations for units of measure, see ¶¶535–538.*
> ❏ *For the use of figures with abbreviations and symbols, see ¶¶453–454.*

432 Dimensions may be expressed as follows:

GENERAL USAGE:	a room 15 by 30 feet	a 15- by 30-foot room
TECHNICAL USAGE:	{ a room 15 × 30 ft	a 15- × 30-ft room
	a room 15' × 30'	a 15' × 30' room
GENERAL USAGE:	a room 5 by 10 meters	a 5- by 10-meter room
TECHNICAL USAGE:	a room 5 × 10 m	a 5- × 10-m room
GENERAL USAGE:	15 feet 6 inches by 30 feet 9 inches	
TECHNICAL USAGE:	15 ft 6 in × 30 ft 9 in **OR** 15' 6" × 30' 9"	

AGES AND ANNIVERSARIES

433 Express ages in figures (including 1 through 10) when they are used as significant statistics or as technical measurements.

> Ethel Kassarian, *38,* has been promoted to director of marketing services.
> The attached printout projects the amount of the monthly retirement benefit payable to you *at the age of 65.* (Avoid the abrupt construction *at age 65.*)
> A computer literacy program is being offered in the schools to all *8- and 9-year-olds.* (See ¶829.)
> This insurance policy is specially tailored for people in the *50-plus* age group.
> You cannot disregard the job application of a person *aged 58.* (**NOT:** age 58.)

NOTE: When age is expressed in years, months, and days, do not use commas to separate the elements; they make up a single unit.

> On January 1 she will be *19 years 4 months and 17 days old.* (The *and* linking months and days may be omitted.)

434 Spell out ages in nontechnical references and in formal writing.

> My son is *three years old,* and my daughter is *two.*
> Shirley is in her early *forties;* her husband is in his *mid-sixties.*
> Have you ever tried keeping a group of *five-year-olds* happy and under control at the same time?

435 Spell out ordinals in references to birthdays and anniversaries except where special emphasis or more than two words are required. (See also ¶¶424–425.)

> on my thirtieth birthday
> our twenty-fifth anniversary
> the company's 135th anniversary

PERIODS OF TIME

436 Use figures (even from 1 through 10) to express periods of time when they are used as technical measurements or significant statistics (as in discounts, interest rates, and credit terms).

  a 35-hour workweek   a note due in 6 months   a 30-year mortgage

437 Spell out nontechnical references to periods of time unless the number requires more than two words.

a twenty-minute wait	in twenty-four months	three hundred years ago
eight hours later	in the last thirty years	**BUT:** 350 years ago
twelve days from now	forty-odd years ago	two thousand years ago

438 Centuries may be expressed as follows:

  the 1900s   **OR:** the nineteen hundreds
  the twenty-first century   twentieth-century literature

439 Decades may be expressed as follows:

  the 1980s   **OR**   the nineteen-eighties   **OR**   the eighties   **OR**   the '80s
  the mid-1960s   **OR**   the mid-sixties   **OR**   the mid-'60s
  during the years 1980-1990   **OR**   from 1980 to 1990 (see ¶459)
  OR   between 1980 and 1990

NOTE: Decades are not capitalized except in special expressions such as *the Gay Nineties, the Roaring Twenties.*

CLOCK TIME

440 With *a.m., p.m., Noon,* and *Midnight*

a. Always use figures with *a.m.* or *p.m.*

  We take off at *8:45 a.m.*   The bus is due at *2 p.m.*

  By *8 p.m.*, CST, the first election returns should be in.

  OR: By *8 p.m.* (CST) the first election returns should be in.

b. Type the abbreviations *a.m.* and *p.m.* in small letters without spaces. (In printed matter they usually appear in small capitals: A.M., P.M.)

c. For time "on the hour," zeros are not needed to denote minutes.

  Our store is open from 9:30 a.m. to *6 p.m.* (**NOT:** 6:00 p.m.)

  We always close from *12 noon* to 1:30 p.m.

  You can buy your tickets between *9* and *10 a.m.*

In tables, however, when some entries are given in hours and minutes, add a colon and two zeros to exact hours to maintain a uniform appearance. (See also ¶442 for the use of zeros.)

Arr.	Dep.
8:45	9:10
9:00	9:25
9:50	10:00

d. Do not use *a.m.* or *p.m.* unless figures are used.

  this morning (**NOT:** this a.m.)   tomorrow afternoon (**NOT:** tomorrow p.m.)

e. Do not use *a.m.* or *p.m.* with *o'clock.*

  6 o'clock   **OR**   6 p.m.   ten o'clock   **OR**   10 a.m.
  (**NOT:**   6 p.m. o'clock)   (**NOT:**   10 a.m. o'clock)

  NOTE: The expression *o'clock* is more formal than *a.m.* or *p.m.*

f. Do not use *a.m.* or *p.m.* with the expressions *in the morning, in the afternoon, in the evening,* and *at night.* The abbreviations themselves already convey one of these meanings.

> at 9 p.m.   **OR**   at nine in the evening   (**NOT:** at 9 p.m. in the evening)

g. Use a colon (without space before or after) to separate hours from minutes (as in *3:22*).

h. The times *noon* and *midnight* may be expressed in words alone. However, use the forms *12 noon* and *12 midnight* when these times are given with other times expressed in figures.

> Dinner is served in the main dining room until *midnight.*
>
> **BUT:** Dinner is served from *6 p.m.* until *12 midnight.*

441 **With *O'Clock***

a. With *o'clock* use figures for emphasis or words for formality.

> 3 o'clock (for emphasis)   three o'clock (for formality)

b. To express hours and minutes with *o'clock,* use this style:

> half past four o'clock   **OR**   half after four o'clock
> (**BUT NOT:** four-thirty o'clock)

c. Expressions of time containing *o'clock* may be reinforced by such phrases as *in the morning, in the afternoon,* and the like.

> 10 o'clock at night   seven o'clock in the morning

For quick comprehension, the forms *10 p.m.* and *7 a.m.* are preferable.

442 **Without *a.m., p.m.,* or *O'Clock***

When expressing time without *a.m., p.m.,* or *o'clock,* either spell the time out or—for quick comprehension—convert the expression to an all-figure style.

> arrive at eight   **OR**   arrive at 8:00   (**NOT:** at 8)
> five after six   **OR**   6:05
> a quarter past ten   **OR**   10:15
> twenty of four   **OR**   3:40
> a quarter to five   **OR**   a quarter of five   **OR**   4:45
> half past nine   **OR**   nine-thirty   **OR**   9:30
> nine forty-two   **OR**   9:42

NOTE: A hyphen is used between hours and minutes (*seven-thirty*) but not if the minutes must be hyphenated (*seven thirty-five*).

The following rules (¶¶443–455) deal with situations in which numbers are always expressed in figures.

DECIMALS

443 Always write decimals in figures. Never insert commas in the decimal part of a number.

> 665.3184368 (no comma in decimal part of the number)
> 58,919.23785 (comma used in whole part of the number)

❏ *For the metric style of writing decimals, see ¶461b.*

444   When a decimal stands alone (without a whole number preceding the decimal point), insert a zero before the decimal point. (Reason: The zero keeps the reader from overlooking the decimal point.)

　　　0.55 inch　　　　0.08 gram　　　**EXCEPTIONS:** a Colt .45; a .36 caliber revolver

445   Ordinarily, drop the zero at the end of a decimal (for example, write 2.787 rather than 2.7870). However, retain the zero (*a*) if you wish to emphasize that the decimal is an exact number or (*b*) if the decimal has been rounded off from a longer figure. In a column of numbers add zeros to the end of a decimal in order to make the number as long as other numbers in the column.

446   Do not begin a sentence with a decimal figure.

　　　The temperature at 8 a.m. was 63.7.　　　(**NOT:** 63.7 was the temperature at 8 a.m.)

PERCENTAGES

447   Express percentages in figures, and spell out the word *percent*. (See ¶¶421–422 for percentages at the beginning of a sentence.)

　　　Carpenter Industries has increased its prices by only 3 *percent* this year.

　　　My client had been expecting at least a 25 *percent* discount from you. (**NOT:** a 25-percent discount.)

　　　Our terms are 2 *percent* 10 days, net 30 days. (These credit terms may be abbreviated as 2/10, *n*/30 on invoices and other business forms.)

NOTE: The % symbol may be used in tables, on business forms, and in statistical or technical matter.

448   **a.** Fractional percentages *under 1 percent* may be expressed as follows:

　　　one-half of 1 percent　**OR**　0.5 percent

　　　NOTE: The zero before the decimal point in *0.5 percent* prevents misreading the amount as 5 *percent*.

　　　b. Fractional percentages *over 1 percent* should be expressed in figures.

　　　7½ percent　**OR**　7.5 percent　　　9¼ percent　**OR**　9.25 percent

449   In a range or series of percentages, the word *percent* follows the last figure only. If the symbol % is used, it must follow each figure (see ¶447, note).

　　　Price reductions range from *20 to 50 percent*. (**BUT:** from 20% to 50%.)

　　　We give discounts of *10, 20, and 30 percent*. (**BUT:** 10%, 20%, and 30%.)

　　　❏ *For the use of % in a column of figures, see ¶1629; for the use of* percent *and* percent-age, *see page 232.*

RATIOS AND PROPORTIONS

450   As a rule, write ratios and proportions in figures.

　　　a proportion of 5 to 1　**OR**　a 5-to-1 ratio　**OR**　a 5:1 ratio
　　　the odds are 100 to 1　**OR**　a 100-to-1 shot
　　　7 parts benzene to 3 parts water

NOTE: A nontechnical reference to a ratio or a proportion may be spelled out.

　　　a *fifty-fifty* chance of success　**OR**　a 50-50 chance of success

SCORES AND VOTING RESULTS

451 Use figures (even for 1 through 10) to express scores and voting results.

a score of 85 on the test
New York 8, Chicago 6

a vote of 17 to 6
BUT: a 17-6 vote

NUMBERS REFERRED TO AS NUMBERS

452 Always use figures to express numbers referred to as numbers.

pick a number from 1 to 10
the number 7 is considered lucky

divide by 16
multiply by ⅞

FIGURES WITH ABBREVIATIONS AND SYMBOLS

453 Always use figures with abbreviations and symbols.

$50	10:15 a.m.	43%	2 in **OR** 2″	FY1987 (see ¶1616c)
65¢	6 p.m.	No. 631	I-95	200 km (see ¶537)

454 If a symbol is used in a range of numbers, it should be repeated with each number. A full word or an abbreviation used in place of the symbol is given only with the last number.

20°–30°C **BUT:** 20 to 30 degrees Celsius (see ¶537, note)
5½″ × 8″   5½ by 8 inches **OR** 5½ × 8 in
9′ × 12′   9 by 12 feet **OR** 9 × 12 ft
30%–40%   30 to 40 percent
50¢–60¢   50 to 60 cents
$70–$80   seventy to eighty dollars

NOTE: A symbol should also be repeated when used with a series of numbers.

discounts of 5%, 10%, and 15% **BUT:** discounts of 5, 10, and 15 percent

NO. OR # WITH FIGURES

455 If the term *number* precedes a figure, express it as an abbreviation (singular: *No.;* plural: *Nos.*). At the beginning of a sentence, however, spell out *Number* to prevent misreading.

Our check covers the following invoices: *Nos.* 8592, 8653, and 8654.

Number 82175 has been assigned to your new policy.

a. If an identifying noun precedes the figure (such as *Invoice, Check, Room, Box,* or the like), the abbreviation *No.* is usually unnecessary.

Our check covers *Invoices* 8592, 8653, and 8654.

EXCEPTIONS: License No. HLM 744; Social Security No. 169-35-8142; Patent No. 953,461

b. The symbol # may be used on business forms (such as invoices) and in technical matter.

❑ *For the capitalization of nouns preceding figures, see ¶359.*

The following rules (¶¶456–470) deal with two technical aspects of style: treating numbers that are adjacent or in a sequence and expressing numbers in figures, words, or roman numerals.

ADJACENT NUMBERS

456 When two numbers come together in a sentence and both are in figures or both are in words, separate them with a comma.

> In *1984, 78* percent of our field representatives exceeded their sales goal.
>
> Although the meeting was scheduled for *two, ten* of the participants did not show up until two-thirty.
>
> On page *192, 25* problems are provided for review purposes.
>
> On Account *53512, $125.40* is the balance outstanding.
>
> On May *8, 18* customers called to complain about missing assembly instructions.

NOTE: No comma is necessary when one number is in figures and the other is in words.

> On May *9 seven* customers called to complain.

457 When two numbers come together and one is part of a compound modifier (see ¶817), express one of the numbers in figures and the other in words. As a rule, spell the first number unless the second number would make a significantly shorter word.

> two 8-room houses   **BUT:** 500 four-page leaflets
> sixty $5 bills   150 five-dollar bills

NUMBERS IN A SEQUENCE

458 Use commas to separate numbers that do not represent a continuous sequence.

> on pages 18, 20, and 28   data for the years 1982, 1986, and 1988

459 **a.** A hyphen may be used in place of the word *to* to link two figures that represent a continuous sequence. (Do not leave any space before or after the hyphen.)

> on pages 18–28   in Articles I–III
> during the week of May 15–21   during the years 1975–1985

b. Do not use the hyphen if the sequence is introduced by the word *from* or *between.*

> from 1975 to 1988   between 1977 and 1984
> (**NOT:** from 1975–1988)   (**NOT:** between 1977–1984)

460 **a.** In a continuous sequence of figures connected by a hyphen, the second figure may be expressed in abbreviated form. This style is used for sequences of page numbers or years when they occur quite frequently. (In isolated cases, do not abbreviate.)

> 1970–85 (**OR** 1970–1985)   pages 110–12 (**OR** pages 110–112)
> 1901–2 (**OR** 1901–1902)   pages 101–2 (**OR** pages 101–102)

b. Do not abbreviate the second number when the first number ends in two zeros.

> 1900–1985   pages 100–101

c. Do not abbreviate the second number when it starts with different digits.

> 1890–1902   pages 998–1004

d. Do not abbreviate the second number when it is under 100.

> 46–48 A.D. (see ¶1101)   pages 46–48

EXPRESSING NUMBERS IN FIGURES

461   **a.** When numbers run to five or more figures, use commas to separate thousands, hundreds of thousands, millions, etc., in whole numbers.

     12,375   147,300 $11,275,478   4,300,000,000   **BUT:** 70,650.37248

     NOTE: Many writers omit the comma in four-digit numbers unless these numbers occur together with larger numbers that require commas.

     3500 **OR** 3,500 $2000 **OR** $2,000

   b. In metric quantities use a space (not a comma) to separate digits into groups of three. Separate whole numbers and decimal fractions, counting from the decimal point.

     12 945 181 (**RATHER THAN:** 12,945,181)   0.594 31 (**RATHER THAN:** 0.59431)

     NOTE: When a four-digit number is used as a metric quantity, do not leave a space unless the number is used in a column with larger numbers.

     5181 **OR** 5 181   0.3725 **OR** 0.372 5

462   Do not use commas in year numbers, page numbers, house or building numbers, room numbers, ZIP Code numbers, telephone numbers, heat units, and decimal parts of numbers.

     1986   8760 Sunset Drive   New York, New York 10021   1500°C
     page 1246   Room 1804   (212) 555-2174   13,664.9999

463   Serial numbers (for example, invoice, style, model, or lot numbers) are usually written without commas. However, some serial numbers are written with hyphens, spaces, or other devices. In all cases follow the style of the source.

     Invoice 38162   **BUT:** Social Security No. 152-22-8285
     Model G-43348   License No. SO14 785 053
     Lot 75/23512   Patent No. 222,341

     ❏ *For the capitalization of nouns before numbers, see ¶359; for the use of* No., *see ¶455.*

464   To form the plurals of figures, add *s*.

     in the 1990s   temperatures in the 80s

EXPRESSING NUMBERS IN WORDS

465   When expressing numbers in words, hyphenate all compound numbers between *21* and *99* (or *21st* and *99th*), whether they stand alone or are part of a number over 100.

     twenty-one   twenty-one hundred
     twenty-first   twenty-one hundredth

     seven hundred and twenty-five (*and* may be omitted)

     five thousand seven hundred and twenty-five (no commas)

   Do not hyphenate other words in a spelled-out number over 100.

     one hundred   nineteen hundred
     two thousand   three hundred thousand
     four million   six hundred million
     twenty-three billion   fifty-eight trillion

     ❏ *For the capitalization of hyphenated numbers, see ¶363.*

466 When there are two ways to express a number in words, choose the simpler form. For example, use the form *fifteen hundred* rather than *one thousand five hundred*. (The longer form is rarely used except in formal expressions of dates. See ¶411 for examples.)

467 To form the plurals of spelled-out numbers, add *s* or *es*. (For numbers ending in *y*, change the *y* to *i* before *es*.)

ones	twos	threes	six*es*	twenty-fives
thirds	sixths	eighths	twen*ties*	thirty-seconds

❏ *For spelled-out dates, see ¶411; for spelled-out amounts of money, see ¶¶413c, 414, 417, 418, 420; for spelled-out fractions, see ¶¶427–428.*

EXPRESSING NUMBERS IN ROMAN NUMERALS

468 Roman numerals are used chiefly for the important divisions of literary and legislative material, for main topics in outlines, in dates on public buildings, and in proper names.

Chapter VI	World Wars I and II	Part IX	King Edward VII
Volume III	MCMLXXXVIII (1988)	Roy Ward II	Pope John XXIII

NOTE: Pages in the front section of a book or a formal report (such as the preface and table of contents) are usually numbered in small roman numerals: *iii, iv, v,* etc. Other pages are numbered in arabic numerals: *1, 2, 3,* etc.

469 To form roman numerals, consult the following table.

1	I	19	XIX	300	CCC	1800	MDCCC
2	II	20	XX	400	CD	1900	MCM
3	III	21	XXI	500	D	2000	MM
4	IV	24	XXIV	600	DC	3000	MMM
5	V	25	XXV	700	DCC	4000	M$\overline{\text{V}}$
6	VI	29	XXIX	800	DCCC	5000	$\overline{\text{V}}$
7	VII	30	XXX	900	CM	6000	$\overline{\text{V}}$M
8	VIII	40	XL	1000	M	7000	$\overline{\text{V}}$MM
9	IX	50	L	1100	MC	8000	$\overline{\text{V}}$MMM
10	X	60	LX	1200	MCC	9000	M$\overline{\text{X}}$
11	XI	70	LXX	1300	MCCC	10,000	$\overline{\text{X}}$
12	XII	80	LXXX	1400	MCD	50,000	$\overline{\text{L}}$
13	XIII	90	XC	1500	MD	100,000	$\overline{\text{C}}$
14	XIV	100	C	1600	MDC	500,000	$\overline{\text{D}}$
15	XV	200	CC	1700	MDCC	1,000,000	$\overline{\text{M}}$

NOTE: A dash drawn or typed over any roman numeral indicates that the original value of the numeral is to be multiplied by 1000.

EXPRESSING THOUSANDS AND MILLIONS IN ABBREVIATED FORM

470 In technical and informal contexts and in material where space is tight (for example, newspaper headlines and classified advertisements), numbers in the thousands or millions may be expressed as follows:

	Roman Style		**Metric Style**	
38,000	38M		38K	(short for *kilo,* a metric prefix signifying thousands)
3,500,000	3.5$\overline{\text{M}}$	(rarely used)	3.5M	(short for *mega,* a metric prefix signifying millions)

❏ *Division at the end of a line: see ¶915.*
❏ *House, street, and ZIP Code numbers: see ¶¶1332–1333, 1339, 1341c.*

Abbreviations

BASIC RULES

WHEN TO USE ABBREVIATIONS

501 An abbreviation is a shortened form of a word or phrase used primarily to save space. Abbreviations occur most frequently in technical writing, statistical matter, tables, and notes.

502 In business writing, abbreviations are appropriate in "expedient" documents (such as business forms, catalogs, and routine memos and letters between business offices), where the emphasis is on communicating data in the briefest form. In other kinds of writing, where a more formal style is appropriate, use abbreviations sparingly. When in doubt, spell it out.

a. Some abbreviations are always acceptable, even in the most formal contexts: those that precede or follow personal names (such as *Mr., Ms., Mrs., Jr., Sr., Esq., Ph.D., S.J.*); those that are part of an organization's legal name (such as *Co., Inc., Ltd.*); those used in expressions of time (such as *a.m., p.m., CST, EDT*); and a few miscellaneous expressions (such as *A.D.* and *B.C.*).

b. Organizations with long names are now commonly identified by their initials in all but the most formal writing (for example, *YMCA, NAACP, IBM, SEC*).

c. Days of the week, names of the months, geographic names, and units of measure should be abbreviated only on business forms, in "expedient" correspondence, and in tables and lists where space is tight.

503 Consult a dictionary or an authoritative reference work for the acceptable forms of abbreviations. When a term may be abbreviated in several ways, choose the form that is shortest without sacrifice of clarity.

continued:	Use *cont.* rather than *contd.*
2 pounds:	Use 2 *lb* rather than 2 *lbs* (see ¶621).
Enclosures 2:	Use *Enc.* 2 rather than *Encs.* 2 or *Encl.* 2.
second, third:	Use *2d, 3d* rather than *2nd, 3rd* (see also ¶425, note).

NOTE: *Webster's Ninth New Collegiate Dictionary,* the basic authority for all spelling in this manual, shows virtually every abbreviation without any periods, even though in actual practice many abbreviations are still written with periods.* Thus, for example, unless your Latin is very good, you may not realize that in the expression *et al.,* the word *et* is a full word (meaning "and") and requires no period, whereas *al.* is short for *alii* (meaning "others") and does require a period. Under these circumstances, for specific abbreviations not shown in this manual, you will need to consult another up-to-date dictionary.

The forms shown here reflect the spellings found in Webster, but the punctuation is based on observations of actual practice and is consistent with the style recommended by other authorities.

504 Be consistent within the same material: do not abbreviate a term in some sentences and spell it out in other sentences. Moreover, having selected one form of an abbreviation (say, *c.o.d.*), do not use a different style (*COD*) elsewhere in the same material.

NOTE: When using an abbreviation that may not be familiar to the reader, spell out the full term along with the abbreviation when it is first used.

At the end of *fiscal year (FY)* 1985, we showed a profit of $1.2 million; at the end of FY1986, however, we showed a loss of $1.8 million.

---

*It is interesting to note that Webster itself uses periods with certain abbreviations (for example, *masc., fem., neut., fr., prob., lit.,* and *ca.*) when they occur functionally within the main text of the dictionary, even though these same abbreviations are given *without* periods in the section on abbreviations at the back of the dictionary.

505 Given a choice between an abbreviation and a contraction, choose the abbreviation. It not only looks better but is easier to type.

cont. (**RATHER THAN:** cont'd)	govt. (**RATHER THAN:** gov't)
dept. (**RATHER THAN:** dep't)	mfg. (**RATHER THAN:** m'f'g)

NOTE: When a word or phrase is shortened by contraction, an apostrophe is inserted at the exact point where letters are omitted and no period follows the contraction except at the end of a sentence. (**EXAMPLES:** *let's, ham 'n' eggs, doesn't, sou'wester.*) As a rule, contractions are used only in informal writing or in tabular matter where space is limited. However, contractions of verb phrases (such as *can't* and *shouldn't*) are commonly used in business letters where the writer is striving for an easy, colloquial tone. In formal writing, contractions are not used (except for *o'clock*, which is considered a more formal way to express time than *a.m.* or *p.m.*).

PUNCTUATION AND SPACING WITH ABBREVIATIONS

506 The abbreviation of a single word requires a period at the end.

Mrs.	Jr.	Corp.	pp.	Wed.
misc.	Esq.	Inc.	Nos.	Oct.

NOTE: Units of measurement are now commonly written without periods. (See ¶¶535*a*, 538*a*.)

507 Almost all small-letter abbreviations made up of single initials require a period after each initial but no space after each internal period.

a.m.	i.e.	f.o.b.	**BUT:** rpm	mpg
p.m.	e.g.	e.o.m.	ips	mph

❏ *For the omission of periods with abbreviations of units of measure, see ¶535a.*

508 All-capital abbreviations made up of single initials normally require no periods and no internal space.

TWA	AMA	AICPA	IRS	TLC
MIT	UAW	NFL	UN	UFO

EXCEPTIONS: Retain the periods in abbreviations of geographic names (such as *U.S.A., U.S.S.R.*), academic degrees (such as *B.A., M.S.*), and a few miscellaneous expressions (such as *A.D., B.C., P.O.,* and *V.P.*).

509 If an abbreviation stands for two or more words and consists of more than single initials, insert a period and a space after each element in the abbreviation.

N. Mex.	Lt. Col.	Rt. Rev.	loc. cit.	nol. pros.

EXCEPTIONS: Academic abbreviations, such as *Ph.D., Ed.D., LL.B.,* and *Litt.D.,* are written with periods but no spaces. Units of measurement such as *sq ft* and *cu cm* are written with spaces but no periods. In isolated cases an abbreviation consisting of more than single initials is written without periods or spaces; for example, *PCjr* (referring to IBM's small personal computer).

510 A number of shortened forms of words are not abbreviations and should not be followed by periods.

ad	condo	info	memo	typo
auto	co-op	lab	photo	before the 2d
caps	exam	math	stereo	after the 5th

❏ *See also ¶524, note.*

511 *One space* should follow an abbreviation within a sentence unless another mark of punctuation follows immediately.

> You ought to talk to your CPA about that problem.
>
> I expect to finish work on my Ph.D. dissertation in six months.
>
> Dr. Wilkins works in Washington, D.C., but his home is in Bethesda.
>
> Please call tomorrow afternoon (before 5:30 p.m.).
>
> Get PRV's approval before you send the letter. (See ¶¶638–639 for possessive forms of abbreviations.)

512 *Two spaces* should follow an abbreviation at the end of a sentence that makes a statement. If the abbreviation ends with a period, that period also serves to mark the end of the sentence. If the abbreviation ends without a period, insert one to mark the end of the sentence and then leave two spaces.

> Helen has just returned from a trip to the U.S.S.R.   Next year . . .
>
> We're flying out on American and coming back on TWA.   If you . . .

513 *No space* should follow an abbreviation at the end of a question or an exclamation. The question mark or the exclamation point should come directly after the abbreviation.

> Did you see Jack Hainey being interviewed last night on CBS?
>
> Because of bad weather our flight didn't get in until 4 a.m.!

CAPITALIZATION

514 Most abbreviations use the same capitalization as the full words for which they stand.

Mon.	Monday	a.m.	ante meridiem
Btu	British thermal unit	D.C.	District of Columbia

> **EXCEPTIONS:** CST   Central standard time   A.D.   anno Domini

❑ *For abbreviations with two forms (for example, COD or c.o.d.), see ¶542.*

The following rules (¶¶515–549) offer guidance on specific types of abbreviations.

SPECIAL RULES

PERSONAL NAMES AND INITIALS

515 Use periods with abbreviations of first or middle names but not with nicknames.

Thos.	Jas.	Jos.	Wm.	Robt.	Saml.	Benj.	Edw.
Tom	Jim	Joe	Bill	Bob	Sam	Ben	Ed

NOTE: Do not abbreviate first and middle names unless (1) you are preparing a list or table where space is tight or (2) a person uses such abbreviations in his or her legal name. (See also ¶1322, note.)

516 **a.** Initials in a person's name should each be followed by a period and one space.

> John T. Noonan   Mr. L. Bradford Anders
> J. T. Noonan & Co.   L. B. Anders Inc. (see also ¶159)

b. When personal initials stand alone, type them preferably without periods or space. If periods are used, omit the internal space.

JTN **OR** J.T.N.

c. For names with prefixes, initials are formed as follows:

JDM (for John D. MacDonald)   FGO (for Frances G. O'Brien)

NOTE: If you know that an individual prefers some other form (for example, *FGO'B* rather than *FGO*), respect that preference.

d. Do not use a period when the initial is only a letter used in place of a real name. (See also ¶109*a*.)

I have selected three case studies involving a Ms. A, a Mr. B, and a Miss C. (Here the letters are used in place of real names, but they are not abbreviations of those names.)

BUT: Call Mrs. *G.* when you get a chance. (Here *G.* is an initial representing an actual name like *Galanos*.)

ABBREVIATIONS WITH PERSONAL NAMES

517   a. Always abbreviate the following titles when they are used with personal names:

SINGULAR: { Mrs. (for Mistress)   Ms.   Mr.   Dr.
                 { Mme. (for Madame)

PLURAL: Mmes. **OR** Mesdames   Mses. **OR** Mss.   Messrs.   Drs.

Mr. and *Mrs.* Pollo both speak highly of *Dr.* Fry.

Ms. Harriet Porter will serve as a consultant to the Finance Committee.

NOTE: The abbreviation *Ms.* is used (1) when a woman has indicated that she prefers this title, (2) when a woman's marital status is unknown, or (3) when a woman's marital status is considered not relevant to the situation. (See also ¶¶618, 1322*b*, 1366*a*.)

❑ *For the proper use of the singular and plural forms of these titles, see ¶¶618–619; for the use of* Dr. *with degrees, see ¶519c.*

b. The titles *Miss* and *Misses* are not abbreviations and should not be followed by periods.

c. In general, spell out all other titles used with personal names.

Vice President Howard Morse   Professor Harriman
Mayor Wilma Washington   Father Hennelly

d. Long military, religious, and honorable titles are spelled out in formal situations but may be abbreviated in informal situations as long as the surname is accompanied by a first name or initials.

Formal   **Informal**
Brigadier General Percy J. Cobb   Brig. Gen. P. J. Cobb
Lieutenant Governor Nancy Pulaski   Lt. Gov. Nancy Pulaski

(**BUT NOT:** Brig. Gen. Cobb, Lt. Gov. Pulaski)

NOTE: Do not abbreviate *Reverend* or *Honorable* when these words are preceded by *the*.

Formal   **Informal**
the Reverend William R. Bullock   Rev. W. R. Bullock
the Honorable Sarah T. McCormack   Hon. Sarah T. McCormack

❑ *For the treatment of titles in addresses, see ¶¶1322–1323; for the treatment of titles in salutations, see ¶¶1347–1350.*

518   **a.** Always abbreviate *Jr.*, *Sr.*, and *Esq.* when they follow personal names.

     b. The forms *Jr.* and *Sr.* should be used only with a full name or initials, but not with a surname alone. A title like *Mr.* or *Dr.* may precede the name.

       Mr. Henry J. Boardman *Jr.*   **OR**   Mr. H. J. Boardman *Jr.*

       (**BUT NOT:** Mr. Boardman Jr.)

     ❏ *For the use or omission of commas with* Jr. *and* Sr., *see* ¶156.

     c. The form *Esq.* should also be used only with a full name or initials, but no title should precede the name.

       George W. LaBarr, *Esq.*   **NOT:** Mr. George W. LaBarr, Esq.

       NOTE: In the United States the form *Esq.* is used primarily by lawyers. Although by derivation the title applies strictly to males, it is now common practice for women who are lawyers to use the title as well.

     d. The terms *2d* or *II* and *3d* or *III* following personal names are not abbreviations and should not be used with periods.

     e. When the word *Saint* is part of a person's name, follow that person's preference for abbreviating or spelling out the word.

       Yves Saint-Laurent   Ruth St. Denis
       Camille Saint-Saëns   St. John Perse

       NOTE: When used with the name of a person revered as holy, the word *Saint* is usually spelled out, but it may be abbreviated in informal contexts and in lists and tables where space is tight.

       Saint Martin   Saint Thérèse
       Saint Francis   Saint Catherine

     ❏ *For the treatment of* Saint *in place names, see* ¶529b.

ACADEMIC DEGREES, RELIGIOUS ORDERS, AND PROFESSIONAL DESIGNATIONS

519   **a.** Abbreviations of academic degrees and religious orders require a period after each element in the abbreviation but no internal space.

       B.S.   Ph.D.   LL.B.   B.Ch.E.   M.D.   S.J.
       M.B.A.   Ed.D.   Litt.D.   B.Arch.   R.N.   O.S.B.

     b. The term *M.B.A.* is now commonly written without periods when it is used to signify an executive with a certain type of training rather than the degree itself.

       We have just hired two Stanford *MBAs* and one from Harvard.

       BUT: After I get my *M.B.A.*, I plan to go on to law school.

     c. When academic degrees follow a person's name, do not use such titles as *Dr.*, *Mr.*, *Ms.*, *Miss*, or *Mrs.* before the name.

       Dr. Helen Garcia   **OR**   Helen Garcia, M.D. (**BUT NOT:** Dr. Helen Garcia, M.D.)

       However, other titles may precede the name as long as they do not convey the same meaning as the degree that follows.

       Professor George Perrier, Ph.D.   the Reverend John Day, D.D.
       President Grace Dillard, L.H.D.   **OR:** the Reverend Dr. John Day
       Dean Marion Konopka, J.S.D.   (**BUT NOT:** the Reverend Dr. John Day, D.D.)

     ❏ *See also* ¶¶1324c, 1324d, 1364a.

d. Academic degrees standing alone may be abbreviated except in very formal writing.

I am now completing my *Ph.D.* thesis.
She received her *M.A.* degree last year.
OR . . . her *master of arts* degree last year. (See also ¶353.)

e. Professional designations such as *CPA* (certified public accountant), *CPS* (certified professional secretary), *CFP* (certified financial planner), *CLU* (chartered life underwriter), and *FACS* (fellow of the American College of Surgeons) are commonly written *without* periods when they are used alone but *with* periods when they are used with academic degrees.

Anthony Filippo, CPA   **BUT:** Anthony Filippo, B.S., M.B.A., C.P.A.
Ruth L. Morris, CLU   Ruth L. Morris, B.A., C.L.U.

NAMES OF ORGANIZATIONS

520   Names of well-known business organizations, labor unions, societies, and associations (trade, professional, charitable, and fraternal) are often abbreviated except in the most formal writing. When these abbreviations consist of all-capital initials, they are typed without periods or spaces.

CDC	Control Data Corporation
AFL-CIO	American Federation of Labor and Congress of Industrial Organizations
ILGWU	International Ladies' Garment Workers' Union
ASCAP	American Society of Composers, Authors, and Publishers
NAACP	National Association for the Advancement of Colored People
NYSE	New York Stock Exchange
NAM	National Association of Manufacturers
NIMH	National Institute of Mental Health
YMCA	Young Men's Christian Association
IOOF	Independent Order of Odd Fellows

521   The following terms are often abbreviated in the names of business organizations. However, follow the individual company's preference for abbreviating or spelling out.

Mfg.	Manufacturing	Co.	Company	Inc.	Incorporated
Mfrs.	Manufacturers	Corp.	Corporation	Ltd.	Limited
Bro.	Brother	Cie	Company (from the French *Compagnie*)		
Bros.	Brothers	N.V.	Limited (from the Dutch *Naamloze Vennootschap*)		

ACRONYMS

522   **a.** An acronym—for example, *NOW*—is a shortened form derived from the initial letters of the words that make up the complete form. Thus *NOW* is derived from *National Organization for Women*. Like all-capital abbreviations such as *IBM* and *NAM*, acronyms are usually written in all capitals and without periods; however, unlike those abbreviations, which are pronounced letter by letter, acronyms are pronounced like words. Because they have been deliberately coined to replace the longer expressions they represent, acronyms are appropriate for use on all occasions.

UNESCO	United Nations Educational, Scientific, and Cultural Organization
PERT	program evaluation and review technique
ZIP (Code)	Zone Improvement Plan
PUSH	People United to Save Humanity
SALT	strategic arms limitation talks
CARE	Cooperative for American Relief to Everywhere
CORE	Congress of Racial Equality

OPEC	Organization of Petroleum Exporting Countries
EPCOT	Experimental Prototype Community of Tomorrow
STEP	School to Employment Program
FONZ	Friends of the National Zoo
HOPE	Help Obese People Everywhere

NOTE: In a few cases acronyms derived from initial letters are written entirely in small letters without periods.

scuba	self-contained underwater breathing apparatus
laser	light amplification by stimulated emission of radiation

b. Some coined names use more than the first letters of the words they represent. Such names are usually written with only the first letter capitalized.

Nabisco	National Biscuit Company
Delmarva	an East Coast peninsula made up of Delaware and parts of Maryland and Virginia
radar	radio detecting and ranging
sonar	sound navigation ranging
modem	modulator and demodulator

NAMES OF BROADCASTING STATIONS AND SYSTEMS

523   The names of radio and television broadcasting stations and the abbreviated names of broadcasting systems are written in capitals without periods and without spaces.

Norfolk:	WAVY—TV (Channel 10—NBC)
Omaha:	KOIL—AM
San Antonio:	KISS—FM
Pittsburgh:	WEEP—AM
New Orleans:	WAIL—FM

According to *ABC* and *CBS* news reports, the earthquake registered 6.8 on the Richter scale.

NAMES OF GOVERNMENT AND INTERNATIONAL AGENCIES

524   The names of well-known government and international agencies are often abbreviated. They are written without periods or spaces.

FNMA	the Federal National Mortgage Association (often referred to as "Fannie Mae," the result of trying to sound out the initials *FNMA*)
HUD	the Department of Housing and Urban Development
GAO	the General Accounting Office
EEOC	the Equal Employment Opportunity Commission
SBA	the Small Business Administration
WHO	the World Health Organization

NOTE: Expressions such as *the Fed* (for the Federal Reserve Board) and *the Ex-Im Bank* (for the U.S. Export-Import Bank) involve shortened forms rather than true abbreviations and thus are written without periods.

525   The name *United States* is usually abbreviated when it is part of the name of a government agency. When used as an adjective, the name is often abbreviated, though not in formal usage. When used as a noun, the name is spelled out.

U.S. Employment Service	**OR**	USES
U.S. Department of Agriculture		USDA
U.S. Air Force		USAF
the United States government		the U.S. government
United States foreign policy		U.S. foreign policy

throughout the United States (**NOT:** throughout the U.S.)

GEOGRAPHIC NAMES

526   Do not abbreviate geographic names except in tables, business forms, and "expedient" correspondence (see ¶502). **EXCEPTION:** Because of its great length, the name *Union of Soviet Socialist Republics* is often replaced by the abbreviation *U.S.S.R.*

527   When abbreviating state names *in addresses,* use the two-letter abbreviations (without periods) shown in ¶1341. *In all other situations,* use the following abbreviations (with periods and spacing as shown).

Alabama	Ala.	Missouri	Mo.
Alaska	—	Montana	Mont.
Arizona	Ariz.	Nebraska	Nebr.
Arkansas	Ark.	Nevada	Nev.
California	Calif.	New Hampshire	N.H.
Canal Zone	C.Z.	New Jersey	N.J.
Colorado	Colo.	New Mexico	N. Mex.
Connecticut	Conn.	New York	N.Y.
Delaware	Del.	North Carolina	N.C.
District of		North Dakota	N. Dak.
Columbia	D.C.	Ohio	—
Florida	Fla.	Oklahoma	Okla.
Georgia	Ga.	Oregon	Oreg.
Guam	—	Pennsylvania	Pa.
Hawaii	—	Puerto Rico	P.R.
Idaho	—	Rhode Island	R.I.
Illinois	Ill.	South Carolina	S.C.
Indiana	Ind.	South Dakota	S. Dak.
Iowa	—	Tennessee	Tenn.
Kansas	Kans.	Texas	Tex.
Kentucky	Ky.	Utah	—
Louisiana	La.	Vermont	Vt.
Maine	—	Virgin Islands	V.I.
Maryland	Md.	Virginia	Va.
Massachusetts	Mass.	Washington	Wash.
Michigan	Mich.	West Virginia	W. Va.
Minnesota	Minn.	Wisconsin	Wis.
Mississippi	Miss.	Wyoming	Wyo.

NOTE: Alaska, Guam, Hawaii, Idaho, Iowa, Maine, Ohio, and Utah are not abbreviated.

528   Geographic abbreviations made up of single initials require a period after each initial but *no* space after each internal period.

U.K.	United Kingdom	B.W.I.	British West Indies
N.S.W.	New South Wales	U.A.E.	United Arab Emirates

If the geographic abbreviation contains more than single initials, space once after each internal period.

    N. Mex.   N. Dak.   W. Va.   W. Aust.

529   **a.** In place names do not abbreviate *Fort, Mount, Point,* or *Port* except in tables and lists where space is tight.

Fort Wayne	Point Pleasant
Fort Myers	Point Pelee
Mount Pleasant	Port Arthur
Mount Rainier	Port Ludlow

b. In U.S. place names abbreviate *Saint.* For other place names involving *Saint,* follow the style shown in an authoritative dictionary or gazetteer.

St. Louis, Missouri	St. Lawrence River
St. Paul, Minnesota	St. Charles Avenue
St. Petersburg, Florida	St. Patrick's Cathedral
St. Thomas, U.S. Virgin Islands	St. Regis–Sheraton Hotel

❑ *For the abbreviation or the spelling out of names of streets, cities, states, and countries, see also ¶¶1334–1337, 1340–1341, 1343–1344.*

COMPASS POINTS

530 **a.** Spell out compass points used as ordinary nouns and adjectives.

The company has large landholdings in the *Southwest.*

We purchased a lot at the *southwest* corner of Green and Union Streets.

❑ *For the capitalization of compass points, see ¶¶338–341.*

b. Spell out compass points included in street names except in lists and tables where space is tight. (See also ¶1334.)

143 South Mountain Avenue   1232 East Franklin Street

531 **a.** Abbreviate compass points without periods when they are used *following* a street name to indicate the section of the city. (See also ¶1335.)

1330 South Bay Boulevard, SW

b. In technical material (especially pertaining to real estate and legal or nautical matters) abbreviate compass points without periods.

N   north   NE   northeast   NNE   north-northeast

DAYS AND MONTHS

532 Do not abbreviate names of days of the week and months of the year except in tables or lists where space is limited. In such cases the following abbreviations may be used:

Sun.	Thurs., Thu.	Jan.	May	Sept., Sep.
Mon.	Fri.	Feb.	June, Jun.	Oct.
Tues., Tue.	Sat.	Mar.	July, Jul.	Nov.
Wed.		Apr.	Aug.	Dec.

NOTE: When space is extremely tight, the following one- and two-letter abbreviations may be used.

Su   M   Tu   W   Th   F   Sa   Ja   F   Mr   Ap   My   Je
Jl   Au   S   O   N   D

TIME AND TIME ZONES

533 Use the abbreviations *a.m.* and *p.m.* in expressions of time (see ¶440). Small letters are preferred for these abbreviations. For more formal expressions of time, use *o'clock* (see ¶441).

534 **a.** The standard time zones are abbreviated as follows:

EST (Eastern standard time)	MST (Mountain standard time)
CST (Central standard time)	PST (Pacific standard time)

b. When daylight saving time is in effect, the following forms are used:

DST (daylight saving time)   **OR**   EDT (Eastern daylight time)
CDT (Central daylight time)
MDT (Mountain daylight time)
PDT (Pacific daylight time)

❏ *See ¶440a for examples.*

CUSTOMARY MEASUREMENTS

535   Abbreviate units of measure when they occur frequently, as in technical and scientific work, on invoices and other business forms, and in tables.

a. Units of measure are now commonly abbreviated without periods.

yd (yard, yards)   oz (ounce, ounces)   rpm (revolutions per minute)
ft (foot, feet)   gal (gallon, gallons)   mpg (miles per gallon)
mi (mile, miles)   lb (pound, pounds)   mph (miles per hour)

NOTE: Even the abbreviation *in* (for inch or inches) may be written without a period so long as it is not likely to be confused with the preposition *in*.

8 in   **OR**   8 in.   **BUT:**   8 sq in   8 ft 2 in

b. In a set of simple dimensions or a range of numbers, an abbreviation is given only with the last number; a symbol is repeated with each number.

a room 10 × 15 ft   35° to 45°F
BUT: a room 10′ × 15′   **OR:** 35°–45°F

NOTE: In a set of complex dimensions, where more than one unit of measure is involved, repeat the abbreviations with each number for clarity.

a room 10 ft 6 in × 19 ft 10 in   **OR**   a room 10′ 6″ × 19′ 10″ (see ¶432)

536   In nontechnical writing, spell out units of measure.

a 20-gallon container   8½ by 11 inches
a 150-acre estate   an 8½- by 11-inch book (see ¶817)

METRIC MEASUREMENTS

The following rules of style are based on the *Metric Editorial Guide*, published in January 1978 by the American National Metric Council (Washington, D.C.). For a full listing of metric terms, consult a dictionary.

537   The most common metric measurements are derived from three basic units and several prefixes indicating multiples or fractions of a unit, as shown below. The abbreviations for these terms are given in parentheses.

Basic Units

meter   (m)   One meter is 10 percent longer than a yard (39.37 inches).
gram   (g)   A thousand grams (a *kilogram*) is 10 percent heavier than 2 pounds (2.2 pounds).
liter   (L)   A liter is about 5 percent bigger than a quart (1.057 quarts).

Prefixes Indicating Fractions

deci   (d)   1/10   A *decimeter* (dm) equals 1/10 meter.
centi   (c)   1/100   A *centigram* (cg) equals 1/100 gram.
milli   (m)   1/1000   A *milliliter* (mL) equals 1/1000 liter.

Prefixes Indicating Multiples

deka   (da)   10   A *dekameter* (dam) equals 10 meters (about 11 yards).
hecto   (h)   100   A *hectogram* (hg) equals 100 grams (about 3½ ounces).
kilo   (k)   1000   A *kilometer* (km) equals 1000 meters (about 5/8 mile).

NOTE: Temperatures are expressed in terms of degrees on the Celsius scale (abbreviated *C*).

Water freezes at 0°C (32°F) and boils at 100°C (212°F).

With a temperature of 37°C (98.6°F), you can't be very sick.

The temperature here on the island stays between 20° and 30°C (68° and 86°F).

❏ *For the use of spaces in figures expressing metric quantities, see ¶461b.*

538 Metric units of measurement, like the customary units of measurement described in ¶535, are abbreviated in technical and scientific work, on business forms, and in tables. In nontechnical writing, metric units are ordinarily spelled out, but some expressions typically appear in abbreviated form (for example, *35-mm film*).

a. Abbreviations of metric units of measurement are written without periods except at the end of a sentence.

100-mm cigarettes (10 centimeters or about 4 inches)
a 30-cm width (about 12 inches or 1 foot)
an office 5 × 3 m (about 5.5 yards by 3.3 yards)
a 1000-km trip (620 miles)
weighs 100 kg (about 220 pounds)
50 to 75 kg (about 110 to 165 pounds)
feels like 10°C weather (50°F weather)

NOTE: In abbreviations of expressions like *kilometers per hour*, a diagonal is used to express *per*.

an 80 km/h speed limit (50 miles per hour)

b. Metric abbreviations are the same for the singular and the plural.

1 kg (1 kilogram)   5 kg (5 kilograms)

c. When expressing temperatures, leave no space between the number and the degree symbol or between the degree symbol and the abbreviation for Celsius.

14°C (**NOT:** 14° C)

d. In printed material, metric measurements for area and volume are usually expressed with raised numbers.

m^2 square meter cm^3 cubic centimeter

In typewritten material, these measurements may be expressed as shown above or in another form (to avoid typing raised numbers).

sq m   square meter   cu cm   cubic centimeter

NOTE: In typewritten material that uses raised numbers for footnote references, use the forms *sq m* and *cu cm* to avoid the possibility of confusion.

CHEMICAL AND MATHEMATICAL EXPRESSIONS

539 Do not use a period after the symbols that represent chemical elements and formulas.

K (potassium) H_2O (water)   NaCl (sodium chloride—table salt)

540 Do not use a period after such mathematical abbreviations as *log* (for *logarithm*) and *tan* (for *tangent*).

BUSINESS EXPRESSIONS

541   A number of terms are commonly abbreviated on business forms, in tables, and in routine business correspondence.

acct.	account	e.o.m. **OR**	end of month (see ¶542)
addl.	additional	EOM	
agt.	agent	Esq.	Esquire
a.k.a.	also known as	ETA	estimated time of arrival
amt.	amount	F	Fahrenheit (temperature)
AP	accounts payable	f.a.s. **OR**	free alongside ship
approx.	approximately	FAS	(see ¶542)
AR	accounts receivable	f.b.o. **OR**	for the benefit of
ASAP	as soon as possible	FBO	(see ¶542)
Assn.	Association	FIFO	first in, first out
assoc.	associate(s)	f.o.b. **OR**	free on board (see ¶542)
asst.	assistant	FOB	
att.	attachment	ft	foot, feet
Attn.	Attention	ft-tn	foot-ton(s)
avg.	average	fwd.	forward
bal.	balance	FY	fiscal year (see ¶504)
bbl	barrel(s)	FYI	for your information
bl	bale(s)	g	gram(s) (see ¶537)
B/L **OR**	bill of lading	gal	gallon(s)
BL		GM	general manager
bldg.	building	gr.	gross
B/S **OR**	bill of sale	gr. wt.	gross weight
BS		hdlg.	handling
bu	bushel(s)	HP **OR** hp	horsepower
C	100; Celsius (temperature)	HQ **OR**	headquarters
CEO	chief executive officer	hdqrs.	
CFO	chief financial officer	hr	hour(s)
cg	centigram(s)	in **OR** in.	inch(es) (see ¶535a, note)
chg.	charge	Inc.	Incorporated
c.i.f. **OR**	cost, insurance, and	incl.	including, inclusive
CIF	freight (see ¶542)	ins.	insurance
cm	centimeter(s)	intl.	international
Co.	Company	inv.	invoice
c/o	care of	ips	inches per second
c.o.d. **OR**	cash (or collect) on	kg	kilogram(s)
COD	delivery (see ¶542)	km	kilometer(s)
cont.	continued	km/h	kilometers per hour
COO	chief operating officer	L	liter(s) (see ¶537)
Corp.	Corporation	l., ll.	line, lines
CPA	certified public accountant	lb	pound(s)
	(see ¶519e)	l.c.l. **OR**	less-than-carload lot
cr.	credit	LCL	(see ¶542)
ctn.	carton	LIFO	last in, first out
cwt.	hundredweight	Ltd.	Limited
d.b.a. **OR**	doing business as	m	meter(s) (see ¶537)
DBA	(see ¶542)	M	1000
dept.	department	max.	maximum
dis.	discount	mdse.	merchandise
dist.	district	mfg.	manufacturing
distr.	distributor, distribution,	mfr.	manufacturer
	distributed	mg	milligram(s)
div.	division	mgr.	manager
doz.	dozen	min	minute(s)
dr.	debit	min.	minimum
dstn.	destination	misc.	miscellaneous
dtd.	dated	mL	milliliter(s)
ea.	each	mm	millimeter(s)

mo	month(s)		pt.	part, point(s), port
MO	mail order, money order		qr	quire(s)
mpg	miles per gallon		qt	quart(s)
mph	miles per hour		qtr.	quarter(ly)
n/30	net in 30 days		qty.	quantity
NA	not applicable, not available		recd.	received
n.d.	no date		reg.	registered
No., Nos.	number(s) (see ¶455)		req.	requisition
nt. wt.	net weight		ret.	retired
opt.	optional		rev.	revised
OS	out of stock		rm	ream(s)
OTC	over the counter		rpm	revolutions per minute
oz	ounce(s)		/S/	signed (before a copied
p., pp.	page, pages			signature)
P.C.	professional corporation		SASE	self-addressed, stamped
pd.	paid			envelope
P.E.	professional engineer		sec	second(s)
PERT	program evaluation and		sec.	secretary
	review technique		shtg.	shortage
pkg.	package(s)		SO	shipping order
PO	purchase order		std.	standard
P.O.	post office		stge.	storage
p.o.e. **OR**	port of entry (see ¶542)		stmt.	statement
POE			treas.	treasury, treasurer
PP	parcel post		V.P.	vice president
ppd.	postpaid, prepaid (post-		vs.	versus (v. in legal
	age paid in advance)			citations)
pr.	pair(s)		whsle.	wholesale
PS, PS.	postscript		wt.	weight
pstg.	postage		yd	yard(s)
pt	pint(s)		yr	year(s)

542 A few common business abbreviations listed in ¶541 are frequently typed in small letters (with periods) when they occur within sentences but are typed in all-capital letters (without periods) when they appear on business forms.

c.i.f.	**OR**	CIF	e.o.m.	**OR**	EOM	l.c.l.	**OR**	LCL
c.o.d.	**OR**	COD	f.o.b.	**OR**	FOB	p.o.e.	**OR**	POE

SYMBOLS

543 A number of symbols are commonly used on business forms, in tables and statistical matter, and in informal business communications.

@	at	#	number (before a figure)
&	and	#	pounds (after a figure)
%	percent	′	feet
$	dollar(s)	″	inches; ditto
¢	cent(s)	¶	paragraph
°	degree(s)	§	section
=	equals	×	by, multiplied by

a. Leave 1 space before and after the following symbols:

@	order 200 @ $49.95	=	if $a = 7$ and $b = 9$
&	Kaye & Elman Inc.	×	a room 12 × 18 ft

BUT: R&D at AT&T (no extra space in all-cap abbreviations)

b. Do not leave any space between a figure and one of the following symbols:

%	a 65% sales increase	#	use 50# paper for the job
¢	about 30¢ a pound	′	a 9′ × 12′ Oriental carpet
°	reduce heat to 350°	″	an 8½″ × 11″ sheet of paper

c. Do not leave any space after these symbols when they are followed by a figure:

$	in the $250–$500 range	¶	as explained in ¶1218
#	reorder #4659 and #4691	§	will be covered in §14.26

COMPUTER ABBREVIATIONS AND ACRONYMS

544 The following list presents some of the abbreviations and acronyms commonly used in references to computers and office automation.

ADC	analog to digital converter
ALGOL	algorithmic language
ALU	arithmetic and logic unit
APL	a programming language
BASIC	Beginner's All-Purpose Symbolic Instruction Code
BCD	binary-coded decimal
BIOS	basic input/output system
bit	contraction of binary digit
CAD	computer-aided design
CAI	computer-aided instruction
CAM	computer-aided manufacturing
CCP	console command processor
CMOS	complementary metal-oxide semiconductor
COBOL	common business-oriented language
CP/M	Control Program for Microprocessors
CPU	central processing unit
CRT	cathode-ray tube
FORTRAN	formula translation
IC	integrated circuit
I/O	input/output
K	kilobyte
LSI	large-scale integration
PL/1	programming language/1
RAM	random-access memory
ROM	read-only memory
RPG	report program generator
TTL	transistor-transistor logic

❑ *For a glossary of word processing terms, see Section 19.*

FOREIGN EXPRESSIONS

545 Many foreign expressions contain short words, some of which are abbreviations and some of which are not. Use periods only with abbreviations.

ad hoc	(meaning "for a particular purpose")
ad val.	(*ad valorem*, meaning "according to the value")
c. **OR** ca.	(*circa*, meaning "approximately")
cf.	(*confer*, meaning "compare")
e.g.	(*exempli gratia*, meaning "for example")
et al.	(*et alii*, meaning "and other people")
etc.	(*et cetera*, meaning "and other things," "and so forth")
ibid.	(*ibidem*, meaning "in the same place")
idem	(meaning "the same")
i.e.	(*id est*, meaning "that is")
infra	(meaning "below")
inst.	(*instans*, meaning "the current month")
loc. cit.	(*loco citato*, meaning "in the place cited")
M.O.	(*modus operandi*, meaning "the way in which something is done")
N.B.	(*nota bene*, meaning "note well")
nol. pros.	(*nolle prosequi*, meaning "to be unwilling to prosecute")
non seq.	(*non sequitur*, meaning "it does not follow")
op. cit.	(*opere citato*, meaning "in the work cited")

pro tem.	(*pro tempore*, meaning "for the time being")
prox.	(*proximo*, meaning "in the next month")
Q.E.D.	(*quod erat demonstrandum*, meaning "which was to be demonstrated")
q.v.	(*quod vide*, meaning "which see")
re **OR** in re	(meaning "in the matter of," "concerning")
R.S.V.P. **OR** R.s.v.p.	(*Répondez s'il vous plaît*, meaning "please reply")
supra	(meaning "above")
ult.	(*ultimo*, meaning "in the last month")
viz.	(*videlicet*, meaning "namely")

MISCELLANEOUS EXPRESSIONS

546   The following list of expressions presents common abbreviations acceptable in general (but not formal) usage.

AV	audiovisual	a list of AV materials
CAT	clear-air turbulence	a plane crash caused by CAT
CB	citizens band	called in on her CB radio
CD	certificate of deposit	investing in 9.5% CDs
ESP	extrasensory perception	their sales manager must have ESP
GNP	gross national product	the GNP for the fourth quarter
ID	identification data	show your ID card
IQ	intelligence quotient	take an IQ test
PA	public address	a problem with our PA system
PR	public relations	need to work on your PR campaign
R&D	research and development	need a bigger R&D budget
SRO	standing room only	an SRO audience at our presentation
TLC	tender, loving care	give this customer some TLC
TV	television	watch for it on TV
UFO	unidentified flying object	took off like a UFO
VCR	videocassette recorder	play this tape on your VCR
VIP	very important person	treat these dealers like VIPs

547   Do not use periods with capitalized letters that are not abbreviations. (See also ¶109*a*.)

IOU	Brand X	SOS	T-shirt	I beam	X ray

548   The abbreviation *OK* is written without periods. In sentences, the forms *okay*, *okayed*, and *okaying* look better than *OK*, *OK'd*, and *OK'ing*, but the latter forms may be used.

549   The dictionary recognizes *x* as a verb; however, *cross out*, *crossed out*, and *crossing out* look better than *x out*, *x-ed out*, and *x-ing out*.

❑ *Plurals of abbreviations: see* ¶¶620–624.
❑ *Possessives of abbreviations: see* ¶¶638–639.

Plurals and Possessives

FORMING PLURALS

FORMING POSSESSIVES

FORMING PLURALS

When you are uncertain about the plural form of a word, consult the dictionary. If no plural is shown, form the plural according to the rules in ¶¶601–605.

BASIC RULE

601   Plurals are regularly formed by adding *s* to the singular form.

flight	flights	idea	ideas
chance	chances	committee	committees
prism	prisms	taxi	taxis
quota	quotas	menu	menus

NOTE: A few words have the same form in the plural as in the singular. See ¶¶603, 1013, 1016, 1017.

NOUNS ENDING IN *S, X, CH, SH,* OR *Z*

602   When the singular form ends in *s, x, ch, sh,* or *z,* the plural is formed by adding *es* to the singular.

bias	biases	tax	taxes
lens	lenses	sketch	sketches
business	businesses	wish	wishes
process	processes	quartz	quartzes

603   Singular nouns ending in silent *s* do not change their forms in the plural.

one corps	two corps	one chassis	two chassis

NOUNS ENDING IN *Y*

604   When a singular noun ends in *y* preceded by a *consonant*, the plural is formed by changing the *y* to *i* and adding *es* to the singular.

copy	copies	liability	liabilities
policy	policies	commodity	commodities

605   When a singular noun ends in *y* preceded by a *vowel*, the plural is formed by adding *s* to the singular.

delay	delays		guy	guys
attorney	attorneys	**BUT:** soliloquy	soliloquies
boy	boys		colloquy	colloquies

NOUNS ENDING IN *O*

606   Singular nouns ending in *o* preceded by a *vowel* form their plurals by adding *s* to the singular.

stereo	stereos	tattoo	tattoos
ratio	ratios	duo	duos

607   Singular nouns ending in *o* preceded by a *consonant* form their plurals in different ways.

a. Some nouns in this category simply add *s.*

hairdo	hairdos	memo	memos
photo	photos	dynamo	dynamos
auto	autos	two	twos

b. Some add *es*.

potato	potatoes		hero	heroes
tomato	tomatoes		veto	vetoes

c. Some have two plural forms. (The preferred form is given first.)

cargo	cargoes, cargos		zero	zeros, zeroes
no	noes, nos		ghetto	ghettos, ghettoes

d. Singular musical terms ending in *o* form their plurals by simply adding *s*.

soprano	sopranos		piano	pianos
alto	altos		cello	cellos
basso	bassos		banjo	banjos

❏ *For foreign nouns ending in* o, *see ¶614.*

NOUNS ENDING IN *F, FE,* OR *FF*

608 **a.** Most singular nouns that end in *f*, *fe*, or *ff* form their plurals by adding *s* to the singular form.

belief	beliefs		safe	safes
proof	proofs		tariff	tariffs

b. Some commonly used nouns in this category form their plurals by changing the *f* or *fe* to *ve* and adding *s*.

half	halves		shelf	shelves
wife	wives		knife	knives
leaf	leaves		life	lives

c. A few of these nouns have two plural forms. (The preferred form is given first.)

scarf	scarves, scarfs		dwarf	dwarfs, dwarves

NOUNS WITH IRREGULAR PLURALS

609 The plurals of some nouns are formed by a change of letters within.

wom*a*n	wom*e*n		f*oo*t	f*ee*t
m*ou*se	m*i*ce		g*oo*se	g*ee*se

610 A few plurals end in *en* or *ren*.

ox	oxen		child	children
brother	brethren (*an alternative plural to* brothers)			

COMPOUND NOUNS

611 When a compound noun is a *solid* word, pluralize the final element in the compound as if it stood alone.

print*out*	print*outs*		birth*day*	birth*days*
flash*back*	flash*backs*		photo*copy*	photo*copies*
wine*glass*	wine*glasses*		grand*child*	grand*children*
hat*box*	hat*boxes*		foot*hold*	foot*holds*
eye*lash*	eye*lashes*		fore*foot*	fore*feet*
straw*berry*	straw*berries*		tooth*brush*	tooth*brushes*
book*shelf*	book*shelves*		mouse*trap*	mouse*traps*

EXCEPTION: *passer*by   *passers*by

612   The plurals of *hyphenated* or *spaced* compounds are formed by pluralizing the chief element of the compound.

father-in-law	*fathers*-in-law
senator-elect	*senators*-elect
looker-on	*lookers*-on
runner-up	*runners*-up
bill of lading	*bills* of lading
editor in chief	*editors* in chief
letter of credit	*letters* of credit
leave of absence	*leaves* of absence
account payable	*accounts* payable
deputy *chief* of staff	deputy *chiefs* of staff
lieutenant *general*	lieutenant *generals*

EXCEPTION: time-*out*   time-*outs*

a. When a hyphenated compound does not contain a noun as one of its elements, simply pluralize the final element.

go-*between*	go-*betweens*
hang-*up*	hang-*ups*
also-*ran*	also-*rans*
come-*on*	come-*ons*
tie-*in*	tie-*ins*
hand-me-*down*	hand-me-*downs*
get-*together*	get-*togethers*
show-*off*	show-*offs*
fade-*out*	fade-*outs*
has-*been*	has-*beens*
boo-*boo*	boo-*boos*

b. Some of these compounds have two recognized plural forms. (The first plural form shown below is preferred because it adds the plural sign to the chief element of the compound.)

court-martial	*courts*-martial, court-*martials*
notary public	*notaries* public, notary *publics*
attorney general	*attorneys* general, attorney *generals*

613   The plurals of compounds ending in *ful* are formed by adding *s*.

armful	armfuls
cupful	cupfuls
handful	handfuls
teaspoonful	teaspoonfuls

Compare the difference in meaning in these phrases:

six *cupfuls* of sugar (a quantity of sugar that would fill one cup six times)

six *cups full* of sugar (six separate cups, each filled with sugar)

FOREIGN NOUNS

614   Many nouns of foreign origin retain their foreign plurals, others have been given English plurals, and still others have two plurals—an English and a foreign one. When two plural forms exist, one may be preferred to the other or there may be differences in meaning that govern the use of each. Consult your dictionary to be sure of the plural forms and the meanings attached to them.

❏ *For agreement of foreign-plural subjects with verbs, see ¶1018.*

(Continued on page 124.)

WORDS ENDING IN *US*

Singular	English Plural	Foreign Plural
alumnus		alumni
apparatus	apparatuses*	apparatus
census	censuses	
focus	focuses*	foci
nucleus	nucleuses	nuclei*
opus	opuses	opera*
prospectus	prospectuses	
radius	radiuses	radii*
status	statuses	
stimulus		stimuli
syllabus	syllabuses	syllabi*
terminus	terminuses	termini*

WORDS ENDING IN *A*

Singular	English Plural	Foreign Plural
agenda	agendas	
alumna		alumnae
antenna	antennas (of radios)	antennae (of insects)
formula	formulas*	formulae
minutia		minutiae
stigma	stigmas	stigmata*
vertebra	vertebras	vertebrae*

WORDS ENDING IN *UM*

Singular	English Plural	Foreign Plural
addendum		addenda
bacterium		bacteria
curriculum	curriculums*	curricula†
datum	datums	data* (see ¶1018)
erratum		errata
maximum	maximums*	maxima†
medium	mediums	media (for advertising and communication)
memorandum	memorandums*	memoranda
millennium	millenniums*	millennia†
minimum	minimums*	minima†
referendum	referendums*	referenda†
stadium	stadiums*	stadia†
stratum		strata
symposium	symposiums*	symposia†
ultimatum	ultimatums*	ultimata

WORDS ENDING IN *O*

Singular	English Plural	Foreign Plural
graffito		graffiti
libretto	librettos*	libretti
tempo	tempos	tempi (in music)
virtuoso	virtuosos*	virtuosi

WORDS ENDING IN *ON*

Singular	English Plural	Foreign Plural
automaton	automatons*	automata
criterion	criterions	criteria*
phenomenon	phenomenons	phenomena*

*Preferred form.   †Webster shows these forms first.

WORDS ENDING IN *IX* OR *EX*

Singular	English Plural	Foreign Plural
appendix	appendixes*	appendices
index	indexes (of books)	indices (math symbols)
matrix	matrixes	matrices*
vertex	vertexes	vertices*
vortex	vortexes	vortices*

WORDS ENDING IN *IS*

Singular	English Plural	Foreign Plural
analysis		analyses
axis		axes
basis		bases
crisis		crises
diagnosis		diagnoses
ellipsis		ellipses
emphasis		emphases
hypothesis		hypotheses
parenthesis		parentheses
synopsis		synopses
synthesis		syntheses
thesis		theses

WORDS ENDING IN *EAU*

Singular	English Plural	Foreign Plural
bureau	bureaus*	bureaux
plateau	plateaus*	plateaux
tableau	tableaus	tableaux*
trousseau	trousseaus	trousseaux*

NOTE: The *x* ending for these foreign plurals is pronounced like *z*.

PROPER NAMES

615   **a.** Most *surnames* are pluralized by the addition of *s*.

Mr. and Mrs. Brinton	the Brintons
Mr. and Mrs. Romano	the Romanos

b. When a surname ends in *s*, *x*, *ch*, *sh*, or *z*, add *es* to form the plural.

Mr. and Mrs. Banks	the Bankses
Mr. and Mrs. Van Ness	the Van Nesses
Mr. and Mrs. Maddox	the Maddoxes
Mr. and Mrs. March	the Marches
Mr. and Mrs. Welsh	the Welshes
Mr. and Mrs. Katz	the Katzes
Mr. and Mrs. Jones	the Joneses
Mr. and Mrs. James	the Jameses
Mr. and Mrs. Barnes	the Barneses

NOTE: Omit the *es* if it makes the plural surname awkward to pronounce.

the Hodges (**NOT:** Hodgeses)	the Hastings (**NOT:** Hastingses)

c. Never change the original spelling of a surname when forming the plural. Simply add *s* or *es*, according to *a* and *b* above.

Mr. and Mrs. McCarthy	the McCarthys (**NOT:** McCarthies)
Mr. and Mrs. Wolf	the Wolfs (**NOT:** Wolves)
Mr. and Mrs. Martino	the Martinos (**NOT:** Martinoes)
Mr. and Mrs. Goodman	the Goodmans (**NOT:** Goodmen)

d. When a surname is followed by *Jr., Sr.,* or a number like *2d* or *II*, the plural can be formed two ways:

ORDINARY USAGE: the Roy Van Allen *Jrs.*   the Ellsworth Hadley *3ds*
FORMAL USAGE: the Roy Van *Allens* Jr.   the Ellsworth *Hadleys* 3d

616   To form the plurals of *first names*, add *s* or *es* but do not change the original spellings.

Marie	Maries	Douglas	Douglases	Timothy	Timothys
Ralph	Ralphs	Dolores	Doloreses	Beatrix	Beatrixes
Waldo	Waldos	Gladys	Gladyses	Fritz	Fritzes

617   To form the plural of other proper names, add *s* or *es* but do not change the original spelling.

the Norwegians   the Dakotas   Februarys
three Texans   the two Kansas Citys (**NOT:** Cities)   Marches

EXCEPTIONS:
the Alleghenies (for Allegheny Mountains)   the Rockies (for Rocky Mountains)

PERSONAL TITLES

618   The plural of *Mr.* is *Messrs.;* the plural of *Ms.* is *Mses.* or *Mss.;* the plural of *Mrs.* or *Mme.* is *Mmes.;* the plural of *Miss* is *Misses* (no period follows). However, the use of plural titles normally occurs only in formal situations. In ordinary usage, simply retain the singular form and repeat it with each name.

Formal Usage	**Ordinary Usage**
Messrs. Rae and Tate	Mr. Rae and Mr. Tate
Mmes. (**OR** Mesdames) Byrd and Clyde	Mrs. Byrd and Mrs. Clyde
Misses Russo and Dupree	Miss Russo and Miss Dupree
Mses. (**OR** Mss.) Lai and Cohen	Ms. Lai and Ms. Cohen

619   When personal titles apply to two or more people with the same surname, the plural may be formed in two ways: (*a*) pluralize only the title (formal usage); (*b*) pluralize only the surname (ordinary usage).

Formal Usage	**Ordinary Usage**
the Messrs. Steele	the Mr. Steeles
the Mmes. (**OR** Mesdames) Bergeret	the Mrs. Bergerets
the Misses Conroy	the Miss Conroys
the Mses. (**OR** Mss.) Purdy	the Ms. Purdys

ABBREVIATIONS, LETTERS, NUMBERS, AND WORDS

620   Form the plurals of most abbreviations by adding *s* to the singular.

bldg.	bldgs.	No.	Nos.
vol.	vols.	Dr.	Drs.
par.	pars.	Bro.	Bros.

621   **a.** The abbreviations of many customary units of weight and measure, however, are the same in both the singular and plural.

oz (ounce **OR** ounces)   ft (foot **OR** feet)
deg (degree **OR** degrees)   in (inch **OR** inches)
bbl (barrel **OR** barrels)   mi (mile **OR** miles)

NOTE: For a number of these abbreviations, two plural forms have been widely used: for example, *lb* or *lbs* (meaning "pounds"), *yd* or *yds* (meaning "yards"), *qt* or *qts* (meaning "quarts"). However, the trend is toward using *lb, yd,* and *qt* to signify the plural.

b. The abbreviations of metric units of weight and measure are the same in both the singular and plural. (See also ¶¶537–538.)

km (kilometer **OR** kilometers)   cg (centigram **OR** centigrams)
mL (milliliter **OR** milliliters)   dam (dekameter **OR** dekameters)

❏ *For the omission of periods with abbreviations of measurements, see ¶¶535a, 538a.*

622 The plurals of a few single-letter abbreviations (such as *p.* for *page* and *f.* for *the following page*) consist of the same letter doubled.

p. 64 (page 64)   l. 23 (line 23)
pp. 64–72 (pages 64 through 72)   ll. 23–24 (lines 23 through 24)

pp. 291 f. (page 291 and the following page)   n. 3 (note 3)
pp. 291 ff. (page 291 and the following pages)   nn. 3–4 (notes 3 and 4)

623 Capital letters and abbreviations ending with capital letters are pluralized by adding *s* alone.

three Rs   CEOs   V.P.s
four Cs   IQs   M.D.s
five VIPs   PTAs   M.B.A.s
six CPUs   YWCAs   Ph.D.s

NOTE: Some authorities still sanction the use of an apostrophe before the *s* (for example, *four C's, PTA's*). However, the apostrophe is functionally unnecessary except where confusion might otherwise result.

three A's   too many I's   two U's on his report card

624 For the sake of clarity, uncapitalized letters and uncapitalized abbreviations with internal periods are pluralized by adding an apostrophe plus *s*.

dotting the *i*'s   *p*'s and *q*'s   counting the c.o.d.'s

625 Numbers expressed in figures are pluralized by the addition of *s* alone. (See, however, ¶623, note.)

in the 1980s   sort the W-2s   temperature in the low 20s

Numbers expressed in words are pluralized by the addition of *s* or *es*.

ones   twos   threes   sixes   twenties   twenty-fives

626 **a.** When words taken from other parts of speech are used as nouns, they are usually pluralized by the addition of *s* or *es*.

ands, ifs, and buts   pros and cons
dos and don'ts   whys and wherefores
yeses and noes   yeas and nays
the haves and the have-nots   the ins and outs
this year's hopefuls   ups and downs

b. If the pluralized form is unfamiliar or is likely to be misread, use an apostrophe plus *s* to form the plural.

which's and that's   or's and nor's

c. If the singular form already contains an apostrophe, simply add *s* to form the plural.

ain'ts   mustn'ts   don'ts   ma'ams

❏ *For the underscoring of words referred to as words, see ¶¶285, 290c.*

FORMING POSSESSIVES

POSSESSION VERSUS DESCRIPTION

627   A noun ending in the sound of *s* is usually in the possessive form if it is followed immediately by another noun. (An apostrophe alone or an apostrophe plus *s* is the sign of the possessive. See ¶¶630–640.)

> the *company's* profits (meaning the profits *of the company*)
> *Hodgkins'* product line (meaning the product line *of the Hodgkins Company*)
> *Faulkner's* novels (meaning the novels *written by Faulkner*)
> *McTavish's* property (meaning the property *belonging to McTavish*)
> the *patient's* medicine (meaning the medicine *intended for the patient*)
> a two *weeks'* vacation (meaning a vacation *for* or *lasting two weeks*)

To be sure that the possessive form should be used, try substituting an *of* phrase or a similar pattern as in the examples above. If the substitution works, the possessive form is correct.

628   Do not mistake a descriptive form ending in *s* for a possessive form.

> sales effort (*sales* describes the kind of effort)
> savings account (*savings* describes the kind of account)
> news release (*news* describes the type of press release)
> earnings record (*earnings* describes the type of record)

❑ *For descriptive and possessive forms in organizational names, see ¶640.*

629   In a number of cases, only a slight difference in wording distinguishes a descriptive phrase from a possessive phrase.

Descriptive	**Possessive**
a six-month leave of absence	a six months' leave of absence
the California climate	California's climate
the Burgess account	Burgess's account
the Crosby children	the Crosbys' children
	OR: Mr. and Mrs. Crosby's children

SINGULAR NOUNS

630   To form the possessive of a singular noun *not* ending in an *s* sound, add an apostrophe plus *s* to the noun.

> my lawyer's advice   Illinois's highways
> Gloria's career   Arkansas's mountains
> Mr. and Mrs. Goodwin's party   Des Moines's mayor
> Maine's coastline   the corps's leadership

631   To form the possessive of a singular noun that ends in an *s* sound, be guided by the way you pronounce the word.

a. If a new syllable is formed in the pronunciation of the possessive, add an apostrophe plus *s*.

> your boss's approval   Mr. and Mrs. Morris's plane tickets
> the witness's reply   Miss Knox's decision
> Congress's intention   Ms. Lopez's application
> the church's location (see ¶646)   Mr. Marsh's office
> Paris's boulevards   Dallas's business district
> St. Louis's airport   Phoenix's suburbs

b. If the addition of an extra syllable would make a word ending in an *s* sound hard to pronounce, add the apostrophe only.

Mrs. Phillips' request	Jesus' parables
Mr. Hastings' proposal	Moses' flight from Egypt
the Burroughs' condominium	Athens' ruins
Los Angeles' freeways	New Orleans' restaurants
for goodness' sake (see ¶646)	for convenience' sake

NOTE: Individual differences in pronunciation will affect the way some of these plurals are written. For example, if you pronounce the possessive form of *Perkins* as two syllables, you will write *Mr. Perkins' kindness;* if you pronounce the possessive of *Perkins* as three syllables, you will write *Mr. Perkins's kindness.* The important thing is to listen to your own pronunciation. When you hear yourself pronounce the possessive of *boss* as two syllables (*boss's*) and the possessive of *witness* as three (*witness's*), you will not be tempted to write *your boss' approval* or *the witness' reply.*

c. In forming the possessive of any noun ending in *s* (for example, *Mr. Hodges*), always place the apostrophe at the end of the original word, never within it.

Mr. Hodges' message (**NOT:** Mr. Hodge's message)

PLURAL NOUNS

632   For a *regular* plural noun (one that ends in *s*), add only an apostrophe to form the plural possessive. (See ¶¶639–640 for the use of the apostrophe in organizational names.)

investors' objectives	attorneys' fees
the witnesses' contradictions	the agencies' conflicting rules
the United States' policy	the Gaineses' legal residence

NOTE: Since the singular and plural possessives for the same word usually sound exactly alike, pay particularly close attention to the meaning in order to determine whether the noun in question is singular or plural.

An *investor's* objectives should largely define investment strategy.
BUT: *Investors'* objectives are often not clearly defined.

We will need a ride to Mr. and Mrs. *Gaines's* party.
BUT: We will need a ride to the *Gaineses'* party.

633   For an *irregular* plural noun (one that does not end in *s*), add an apostrophe plus *s* to form the plural possessive.

women's coats	children's toys

IMPORTANT NOTE: To avoid mistakes in forming the possessive of plural nouns, form the plural first; then apply the rule in ¶632 or ¶633, whichever fits.

Singular	Plural	Plural Possessive
boy	boys (regular)	boys'
boss	bosses (regular)	bosses'
Mr. and Mrs. Fox	the Foxes (regular)	the Foxes'
child	children (irregular)	children's
alumnus	alumni (irregular)	alumni's
mother-in-law	mothers-in-law (irregular)	mothers-in-law's

COMPOUND NOUNS

634   To form the *singular* possessive of a compound noun (whether solid, spaced, or hyphenated), add an apostrophe plus *s* to the last element of the compound.

my son-in-law's job prospects	my stockbroker's advice
the secretary-treasurer's report	the notary public's seal

635 To form the *plural* possessive of a compound noun, first form the plural.

a. If the plural form ends in *s*, add only an apostrophe.

Singular	Plural	Plural Possessive
stockholder	stockholders	stockholders'
vice president	vice presidents	vice presidents'
clerk-typist	clerk-typists	clerk-typists'
salesclerk	salesclerks	salesclerks'

b. If the plural form does not end in *s*, add an apostrophe plus *s*.

Singular	Plural	Plural Possessive
editor in chief	editors in chief	editors in chief's
brother-in-law	brothers-in-law	brothers-in-law's

NOTE: To avoid the awkwardness of a plural possessive such as *editors in chief's* or *brothers-in-law's*, rephrase the sentence.

AWKWARD: We may have to invite my three *sisters-in-law's* parents too.
BETTER: We may have to invite the parents of my three *sisters-in-law* too.

AWKWARD: Mr. Ahmed's statement agrees with both *attorneys general's* views.
BETTER: Mr. Ahmed's statement agrees with the views of both *attorneys general.*

PRONOUNS

636 The possessive forms of *personal pronouns* and of the relative pronoun *who* do not require the apostrophe. These pronouns have their own possessive forms.

I: my, mine	she: her, hers	they: their, theirs
you: your, yours	it: its	who: whose
he: his	we: our, ours	

My copy of the letter arrived last week, so she should have received *hers* by now. (**NOT:** her's.)

Each unit comes carefully packed in *its* own carton. (**NOT:** it's.)

The two products look so much alike that it's (it is) hard to tell *ours* from *theirs*. (**NOT:** our's from their's.)

CAUTION: Do not confuse personal possessive pronouns with similarly spelled contractions. (See ¶1056*e* for examples.)

637 Some *indefinite pronouns* have regular possessive forms.

one's choice	the other's claim	anybody's guess
anyone else's job	the others' claim	no one's responsibility
one another's time	each other's claim	someone's chance

For those indefinite pronouns that do not have possessive forms, use an *of* phrase.

Although the children in this group seem very much alike, the needs *of each* are different. (**NOT:** each's needs.)

ABBREVIATIONS

638 To form the singular possessive of an abbreviation, add an apostrophe plus *s*. To form the plural possessive, add an *s* plus an apostrophe to the singular form. (See also ¶639.)

Singular	Plural
Mr. C.'s opinion	the M.D.s' diagnoses
the FCC's ruling	the Ph.D.s' theses
the CPA's audit	the CPAs' meeting

PERSONAL AND ORGANIZATIONAL NAMES; TITLES

639 To form the possessive of a personal or organizational name that ends with an abbreviation, a number, or a prepositional phrase, add an apostrophe plus *s* at the end of the complete name.

the Winger Co.'s new plant	McGraw-Hill, Inc.'s dividends
the Knights of Columbus's drive	David Weild II's retirement
United Bank of Arizona's loan rates	Walter Frick Jr.'s campaign

NOTE: If *no* extra *s* sound is created when you pronounce the possessive form, add only an apostrophe.

the Gerald Curry Jrs.' yacht

❏ *For the treatment of possessive forms when terms like* Jr. *and* Inc. *are set off by commas, see* ¶¶*156 and 159.*

640 Many organizational names and titles contain words that could be construed as either possessive or descriptive terms.

a. As a rule, use an apostrophe if the term is a singular possessive noun or an irregular plural noun.

McCall's	*Harper's Bazaar*	*Women's Wear Daily*	Children's Hospital

b. Do not use an apostrophe if the term is a regular plural.

American Bankers Association	Chemical Workers Union
Government Employees Insurance Company	Investors Trust Company

c. In all cases follow the organization's preference when known.

Investor's Management Services, Inc.	*Ladies' Home Journal*
International Ladies' Garment Workers' Union	*Reader's Digest*
Boys' Clubs of America	*Barron's*

d. When adding the sign of the possessive to a phrase that must be underscored, do not extend the underscore beneath the possessive ending.

<u>Gone With the Wind</u>'s main characters   <u>The Wind in the Willows</u>' author

NOUNS IN APPOSITION

641 Sometimes a noun that ordinarily would be in the possessive is followed by an *appositive,* a closely linked explanatory word or phrase. In such cases add the sign of the possessive to the appositive only.

Rockport, *Massachusetts'* attraction for artists goes back many decades. (Note that the comma that normally follows an appositive is omitted after a possessive ending.)

You will faint when you see Paul *the plumber's* bill. (If the noun and the appositive are closely linked as a unit, even the first comma is omitted. See also ¶150.)

NOTE: To avoid an awkward construction, use an *of* phrase instead.

You will need to get the signature *of Mr. Bartel*, the executor.
(**BETTER THAN:** You will need to get Mr. Bartel, *the executor's* signature.)

SEPARATE AND JOINT POSSESSION

642 To indicate separate possession, add the sign of the possessive to the name of each individual.

the buyer's and the seller's signatures   the Joneses' and the Browns' houses

NOTE: The repetition of *the* with each name emphasizes separate ownership.

643   To indicate joint (or common) ownership, add the sign of the possessive to the *final* name alone. However, if one of the owners is identified by a pronoun, make each name and pronoun possessive.

> Karen and Brian's ski lodge   **BUT:** Karen's and my ski lodge
> the Barneses and Terrys' property line

POSSESSIVES STANDING ALONE

644   Sometimes the noun that the possessive modifies is merely understood.

> Ask for it at your *grocer's* [store].
>
> Wear your oldest shirt and *Levi's* [jeans]. (The trademark *Levi's* is a singular possessive form.)
>
> We have been invited to dinner at the *Furnesses'* [house].
>
> **BUT:** We always enjoy an evening with the *Furnesses*. (The people themselves are referred to; hence no possessive.)

NOTE: The possessive form must be used in the following construction in order to keep the comparison parallel.

> This year's product line is pulling better than *last year's* [product line].
>
> **NOT:** This year's product line is pulling better than *last year*. (Incorrectly compares *product line* with *last year*.)

INANIMATE POSSESSIVES

645   As a rule, nouns referring to inanimate things should not be in the possessive. Use an *of* phrase instead.

> the bottom of the barrel (**NOT:** the barrel's bottom)
> the wording of the agreement (**NOT:** the agreement's wording)
> the lower level of the terminal (**NOT:** the terminal's lower level)

646   In many common expressions that refer to time and measurements, however, and in phrases implying personification, the possessive form has come to be accepted usage. (See also ¶817a, note.)

> | | | |
> |---|---|---|
> | one day's notice | a dollar's worth | a stone's throw |
> | an hour's work | several dollars' worth | for heaven's sake |
> | two years' progress | at arm's length | for conscience' sake |
> | the company's assets | New Year's resolutions | (see ¶631b) |
> | the sun's rays | this morning's news | the earth's atmosphere |

NOTE: Be sure to distinguish possessive expressions like those above from similar wording where no possessive relation is involved.

> two weeks' salary   **BUT:** two weeks ago, two weeks later, two weeks overdue
>
> I bought *five dollars' worth* of chocolate truffles.
>
> **BUT:** I found *five dollars lying* on the sidewalk.

POSSESSIVES PRECEDING VERBAL NOUNS

647   When a noun or a pronoun modifies a *gerund* (the *ing* form of a verb used as a noun), the noun or pronoun should be in the possessive form.

> What was the point of *our* asking any further questions? (**NOT:** of us asking.)
>
> He wanted to be reassured about his *children's* being given a ride home. (This sentence is grammatically correct but stylistically awkward.)
>
> **BETTER:** He wanted to be reassured that his children would be given a ride home.

NOTE: Not every noun or pronoun preceding the *ing* form of a verb should be in the possessive form. Compare the following pairs of examples:

I heard *you* singing at the party. (Here the emphasis is on *you*, the object of *heard*; *singing* is a participle that modifies *you*.)

I liked *your* singing at the party. (Here the emphasis is on *singing*, a gerund that is the object of *liked*; the pronoun *your* is in the possessive form because it modifies *singing*.)

Our success in this venture depends on *Allen* acting as the coordinator. (This suggests that the success depends on Allen himself rather than on the role he is playing. Even if Allen's role should change, success seems likely as long as he is associated with the project in some way.)

Our success in this venture depends on *Allen's* acting as the coordinator. (This puts the emphasis squarely on Allen's acting in a certain role. If he ceases to function as the coordinator, the venture may not succeed.)

POSSESSIVES IN *OF* PHRASES

648   The object of the preposition *of* should not ordinarily be in the possessive form, since the *of* phrase as a whole expresses possession. However, possessives are used in a few idiomatic expressions.

Tony and Fiona are good friends of *ours* as well as our *children's*.

Did you know that Polly and Fred are neighbors of the *Joneses'*?

Bobby Busoni is a business associate of *Gordon's*.

NOTE: Avoid adding the sign of the possessive to an *of* phrase.

AWKWARD: A *friend of mine's house* burned down last night.
BETTER: The *house of a friend of mine* burned down last night.

AWKWARD: One *of my friends' son* has been named a Rhodes scholar. (**NOT:** One of my friend's son.)
BETTER: The *son of one of my friends* has been named a Rhodes scholar.

POSSESSIVES MODIFYING POSSESSIVES

649   Avoid attaching a possessive form to another possessive. Change the wording if possible.

AWKWARD: I have not yet seen the *utility company's lawyer's* petition.
BETTER: I have not yet seen the petition of the *utility company's lawyer*.

POSSESSIVES IN HOLIDAYS

650   Possessives in names of holidays are usually singular.

Mother's Day	Lincoln's Birthday	**BUT:** April Fools' Day
New Year's Eve	Valentine's Day	Presidents' Day
Martin Luther King's Birthday	St. Patrick's Day	Veterans Day

MISCELLANEOUS EXPRESSIONS

651   A number of common expressions contain possessive forms. Most of these involve singular possessives.

collector's items	seller's market	cat's cradle
traveler's checks	baker's dozen	mare's nest
writer's cramp	mariner's compass	rabbit's foot
tailor's chalk	dog's life	

BUT: proofreaders' marks, lovers' lane, bakers' yeast

Spelling

SPELLING GUIDES

WORDS THAT SOUND OR LOOK ALIKE (¶719)

TROUBLESOME WORDS (¶720)

In matters of spelling, the most important rule is this: *When in doubt, consult the dictionary.* The next most important rule: *Try to master the principles of spelling so as to avoid frequent trips to the dictionary.*

Section 7 offers three kinds of assistance: ¶¶701–718 present the basic guidelines for correct spelling; ¶719 provides a 13-page list of look-alike and sound-alike words for review and fast reference; ¶720 presents a list of troublesome words—those that are frequently misspelled or that frequently send writers to their dictionaries.

NOTE: The 1983 printing of *Webster's Ninth New Collegiate Dictionary* and *Webster's Third New International Dictionary* (both published by Merriam-Webster, Springfield, Massachusetts) serve as the authority for the spelling in this manual. Whenever two spellings are allowable, only the first form is usually given here.

SPELLING GUIDES

WHEN A FINAL CONSONANT IS DOUBLED

701 When a word of one syllable ends in a single consonant (ba*g*) preceded by a single vowel (b*a*g), double the final consonant before a suffix beginning with a vowel (bagg*age*) or before the suffix *y* (bagg*y*). (Compare ¶703.)

rub	rub*b*ed	swim	swim*m*er	slip	slip*p*age
glad	glad*d*en	skin	skin*n*y	star	star*r*ing
beg	beg*g*ar	clan	clan*n*ish	bet	bet*t*or

EXCEPTIONS:

yes	yeses	dew	dewy	fix	fixed
bus	buses	bow	bowed	box	boxy

NOTE: When a one-syllable word ends in *y* preceded by a single vowel, do not double the *y* before a suffix beginning with a vowel. (See ¶711.)

pay	payee	joy	joyous	toy	toying
key	keyed	boy	boyish	buy	buyer

702 When a word of more than one syllable ends in a single consonant (refe*r*) preceded by a single vowel (ref*e*r) and the accent falls on the last syllable of the root word (re*fer*), double the final consonant before a suffix beginning with a vowel (referr*ed*). (Compare ¶704.)

forbid	forbid*d*en	begin	begin*n*ing	infer	infer*r*ed
unclog	unclog*g*ed	unzip	unzip*p*ed	occur	occur*r*ing
control	control*l*er	concur	concur*r*ent	regret	regret*t*able

EXCEPTIONS:

display	displaying	obey	obeyed	enjoy enjoyable (see ¶711)

NOTE: If the accent *shifts* to the first syllable of a word when a suffix beginning with a vowel is added, do not double the final consonant.

refer	referred	prefer	preferred	transfer	transferred
BUT: reference		**BUT:** preferable		**BUT:** transferee	

WHEN A FINAL CONSONANT IS NOT DOUBLED

703 When a word of one syllable ends in a single consonant (ba*d*) preceded by a single vowel (b*a*d), *do not* double the final consonant before a suffix beginning with a *consonant* (bad*ly*).

glad	glad*ness*	star	star*dom*	play	play*ful*
ten	ten*fold*	wit	wit*less*	joy	joy*fully*
ship	ship*ment*	flag	flag*ship*	boy	boy*hood*

704 When a word of more than one syllable ends in a single consonant (benefi*t*) preceded by a single vowel (benef*i*t) and the accent *does not* fall on the last syllable of the root word (be*ne*fit), *do not* double the final consonant before a suffix beginning with a vowel (benefit*ed*).

catalog	cataloged, cataloging	differ	differed, different
total	totaled, totaling	credit	credited, creditor
cancel	canceled, canceling	profit	profited, profiting
	(**BUT:** cancellation)	benefit	benefited, benefiting
diagram	diagramed, diagraming	borrow	borrowed, borrowing
worship	worshiped, worshiper	index	indexed, indexing

EXCEPTIONS:

program	programmed, programming	kidnap	kidnapped, kidnapping
format	formatted, formatting	handicap	handicapped, handicapping
overstep	overstepped, overstepping	outfit	outfitted, outfitting

705 When a word of one or more syllables ends in a single consonant (clou*d*, repea*t*) preceded by more than one vowel (cl*ou*d, rep*ea*t), *do not* double the final consonant before any suffix, whether it begins with a consonant (cloud*less*) or a vowel (repeat*ing*).

gain	gain*ful*	bias	bias*ed*	wool	wool*en*
haul	haul*ing*	chief	chief*ly*		(**BUT:** wool*ly*)
dream	dream*y*	riot	riot*ous*	loud	loud*ness*
cheer	cheer*y*	broad	broad*ly*	equal	equal*ed*
deceit	deceit*ful*	poet	poet*ic*	duel	duel*ing*
feud	feud*al*	toil	toil*some*	buoy	buoy*ant*

EXCEPTIONS:

equip	equipped, equipping (**BUT:** equipment)	quit	quitting
quiz	quizzed, quizzing, quizzical		

706 When a word of one or more syllables ends with more than one consonant (wor*k*, deta*ch*), *do not* double the final consonant before any suffix (work*day*, detach*ed*).

comb	comb*ing*	back	back*ward*	shirr	shirr*ing*
hand	hand*y*	curl	curl*y*	mass	mass*ive*
self	self*ish*	warm	warm*ly*	slant	slant*wise*
swing	swing*ing*	return	return*ed*	jinx	jinx*ed*
wish	wish*ful*	harp	harp*ing*	blitz	blitz*ing*

NOTE: Words ending in *ll* usually retain both consonants before a suffix. However, when adding the suffix *ly,* drop one *l* from the root word. When adding the suffix *less* or *like,* insert a hyphen between the root and the suffix to avoid three *l*'s in a row.

skill	skillful	full	fully	hull	hull-less
install	installment	dull	dully	shell	shell-like

FINAL SILENT *E*

707 **a.** Words ending in silent *e* usually *drop* the *e* before a suffix beginning with a vowel.

sale	sal*able*	sense	sens*ible*	propose	propos*ition*
move	mov*able*	argue	argu*ing*	sincere	sincer*ity*
store	stor*age*	issue	issu*ing*	execute	execut*ive*
arrive	arriv*al*	blue	blu*ish*	desire	desir*ous*
accuse	accus*ation*	true	tru*ism*	use	us*ual*

EXCEPTIONS:

agree	agreeing	mile	mileage	dye	dyeing
see	seeing	acre	acreage	hoe	hoeing

b. Words ending in silent *e* usually *drop* the *e* before the suffix *y*.

ease	easy	ice	icy	edge	edgy
chance	chancy	bounce	bouncy	range	rangy

EXCEPTIONS:

cage	cagey	dice	dicey	price	pricey

c. Words ending in *ce* or *ge* usually *retain* the *e* before a suffix beginning with *a* or *o*.

enforce	enforce*able*	service	service*able*	change	change*able*
notice	notice*able*	advantage	advantage*ous*	knowledge	knowledge*able*
peace	peace*able*	courage	courage*ous*	manage	manage*able*
replace	replace*able*	outrage	outrage*ous*	marriage	marriage*able*

EXCEPTIONS:

pledge	pledgor	mortgage	mortgagor

NOTE: Before suffixes beginning with *i*, the *e* is usually dropped.

force	forc*ible*	college	colleg*ial*	age	ag*ing*
reduce	reduc*ible*	finance	financ*ial*	enforce	enforc*ing*

EXCEPTIONS:

singe	singeing	tinge	tingeing	age	ageism

708 Words ending in silent *e* usually *retain* the *e* before a suffix beginning with a consonant.

hope	hope*ful*	manage	manage*ment*	trouble	trouble*some*
care	care*less*	like	like*ness*	nine	ninet*y*
sincere	sincere*ly*	flame	flame*proof*	subtle	subt*l*et*y*

EXCEPTIONS:

wise	wisdom	gentle	gently	subtle	subtly
awe	awful	whole	wholly	nine	ninth
true	truly	judge	judgment	acknowledge	acknowledgment

709 Words ending in *ie* change the *ie* to *y* before adding *ing*.

die	dying	tie	tying	lie	lying (**BUT:** liar)

WHEN FINAL *Y* IS CHANGED TO *I*

710 Words ending in *y* preceded by a consonant change the *y* to *i* before any suffix except one beginning with *i*.

vary	vari*able*	easy	easi*er*	accompany	accompani*ment*
custody	custod*ial*	heavy	heavi*est*	happy	happi*ness*
Italy	Ital*ian*	fifty	fifti*eth*	fallacy	fallaci*ous*
defy	defi*ant*	fancy	fanci*ful*	**BUT:** dry	dry*ly*
carry	carri*ed*	likely	likeli*hood*	shy	shy*ly*
fly	fli*er*	ordinary	ordinari*ly*	country	country*wide*
try	try*ing*	lobby	lobby*ist*	**BUT:** academy	academ*ic*
thirty	thirty*ish*	Kennedy	Kennedy*ite*	economy	econom*ist*

711 Words ending in *y* preceded by a vowel usually retain the *y* before any suffix.

okay	okay*ed*	convey	convey*ance*	employ	employ*able*
clay	clay*ey*	obey	obey*ing*	joy	joy*ful*
display	display*ing*	survey	survey*or*	buy	buy*er*

EXCEPTIONS:

pay	paid	day	daily	gay	gaily
lay	laid	say	said	slay	slain

EI AND *IE* WORDS

712 Put *i* before *e*   Or when sounded like *a*
Except after *c*   As in *neighbor* and *weigh*.

I Before E

believe	brief	field	niece	**BUT:** either	height
relieve	chief	wield	piece	neither	leisure
belief	thief	yield	anxiety	seize	foreign
relief	friend	view	variety	weird	forfeit

After C

deceive	receive	conceive	perceive	**BUT:** ancient	species
deceit	receipt	conceit	ceiling	science	financier

Sounded Like A

freight	their	eight	vein
weight	heir	sleigh	skein

WORDS ENDING IN *ABLE* AND *IBLE*

713 **a.** The ending *able* is more commonly used.

admirable	dependable	likable	probable	salable
advisable	doable	movable	reasonable	transferable
changeable	knowledgeable	payable	receivable	valuable

❑ *See ¶707 on dropping or retaining silent* e *before the ending.*

b. However, a number of frequently used words end in *ible*.

compatible	eligible	irrepressible	possible	susceptible
convertible	feasible	irresistible	responsible	terrible
credible	flexible	legible	sensible	visible

WORDS ENDING IN *ANT/ANCE* AND *ENT/ENCE*

714 Words ending in *ant, ance, ent,* and *ence* follow no clear-cut pattern. Therefore, consult a dictionary when in doubt.

exist*ent*	persist*ent*	defend*ant*	descend*ant*	occurr*ence*
insist*ent*	resist*ant*	depend*ent*	transcend*ent*	recurr*ence*
assist*ance*	mainten*ance*	relev*ance*	surveill*ance*	intelli*gence*

WORDS ENDING IN *IZE, ISE,* AND *YZE*

715 **a.** Most words end in *ize*.

apologize	characterize	economize	prize	summarize
authorize	criticize	emphasize	realize	vandalize

b. A number of common words end in *ise*.

advertise	compromise	enterprise	improvise	supervise
advise	devise	exercise	merchandise	surprise
arise	disguise	franchise	revise	televise

c. Only a few words end with *yze*.

analyze	paralyze	catalyze

WORDS ENDING IN *CEDE, CEED,* AND *SEDE*

716 **a.** Only *one* word ends in *sede: supersede.*

b. Only *three* words end in *ceed: exceed, proceed, succeed.* (Note, however, that derivatives of these three words are spelled with only one *e: excess, procedure, success.*)

c. All other words ending with the syllable pronounced "seed" are spelled *cede: precede, secede, recede, concede, accede, intercede.*

WORDS ENDING IN *C*

717 Words ending in *c* usually take the letter *k* before a suffix so as to preserve the hard sound of the *c*.

mimic	mimicked, mimicking (**BUT:** mimicry)
panic	panicked, panicking, panicky
picnic	picnicked, picnicking, picnicker
shellac	shellacked, shellacking
traffic	trafficked, trafficking

BUT: arc   arced, arcing

WORDS WITH DIACRITICAL MARKS

718 Many French words are now considered part of the English language and therefore do not require underscoring (see ¶287). Nevertheless, some (but not all) of these words retain diacritical marks from their original French form.

a. Acute Accent. An acute accent (´) over the letter *e* (*é*) signifies that the letter is to be pronounced "ay" (as in *may*). Moreover, it signifies that at the end of a word the letter *é* is to be pronounced as a separate syllable.

attaché	éclair	passé
blasé	élan	risqué
café	entrée	sauté
canapé	exposé	soufflé
cliché	fiancé (m.)	touché
communiqué	fiancée (f.)	**BUT:** matinee
consommé	naiveté	melee
détente	née	puree

NOTE: A few words call for two acute accents:

résumé	protégé	décolleté

b. Grave Accent. A few expressions taken from the French retain a grave accent (`).

à la carte	vis-à-vis	pièce de résistance
à la mode	pied-à-terre	cause célèbre

c. The Circumflex. A few phrases derived from the French still retain a circumflex (^).

maître d'hôtel	raison d'être	pâté
table d'hôte	tête-à-tête	bête noire

WORDS THAT SOUND ALIKE OR LOOK ALIKE

719 The following list contains two types of words: (*a*) words that are pronounced *exactly alike*, though spelled differently (and for which the shorthand outlines are therefore identical); and (*b*) words that look and sound *somewhat alike* (and for which the shorthand outlines may be very nearly the same).

NOTE: An open square (□) marks the start of each group of similar words.

□ **accede**	to comply with; to give consent		□ **adapt**	to adjust	
exceed	to surpass		**adept**	proficient	
			adopt	to choose	
□ **accent**	stress in speech or writing		□ **addenda**	(see *agenda*)	
ascent	act of rising		□ **addition**	something added	
assent	consent		**edition**	one version of a printed work	
□ **accept**	to take; to receive		□ **adherence**	attachment	
except	(v.) to exclude; (prep.) excluding		**adherents**	followers	
□ **access**	admittance		□ **adverse**	hostile, unfavorable	
excess	surplus		**averse**	disinclined	
□ **ad**	short for *advertisement*		□ **advice**	(n.) information; recommendation	
add	to join		**advise**	(v.) to recommend; to give counsel	

☐ **affect**	to influence; to change; to assume (see ¶1101)
effect	(n.) result; impression; (v.) to bring about
☐ **agenda**	list of things to be done
addenda	additional items
☐ **aid**	(n.) a form of help; (v.) to help
aide	an assistant
☐ **ail**	to be in ill health
ale	a drink much like beer
☐ **air**	atmosphere
heir	one who inherits
☐ **aisle**	(see *isle*)
☐ **allowed**	permitted
aloud	audibly
☐ **allusion**	an indirect reference
illusion	an unreal vision; misapprehension
delusion	a false belief
elusion	adroit escape
☐ **almost**	nearly (see ¶1101)
all most	all very much
☐ **already**	previously (see ¶1101)
all ready	all prepared
☐ **altar**	part of a church
alter	to change
☐ **alternate**	(n.) substitute; (v.) to take turns
alternative	(n.) one of several things from which to choose
☐ **altogether**	entirely (see ¶1101)
all together	everyone in a group
☐ **always**	at all times (see ¶1101)
all ways	all means or methods
☐ **annual**	yearly
annul	to cancel
☐ **ante-**	a prefix meaning "before"
anti-	a prefix meaning "against"
☐ **antecedence**	priority
antecedents	preceding things; ancestors
☐ **anyone**	anybody (see ¶1010)
any one	any one person in a group

☐ **anyway**	in any case (see ¶1101)
any way	any method
☐ **apportion**	(see *portion*)
☐ **appraise**	to set a value on (see ¶1101)
apprise	to inform
☐ **arc**	something arched or curved
ark	a ship; a place of protection and safety
☐ **are**	(see *hour*)
☐ **area**	surface; extent
aria	a melody
arrears	that which is due but unpaid
☐ **arrange**	to put in order
arraign	to call into court
☐ **ascent**	(see *accent*)
☐ **assay**	to test, as an ore or a chemical
essay	(n.) a treatise; (v.) to attempt
☐ **assent**	(see *accent*)
☐ **assistance**	help
assistants	those who help
☐ **assure**	(see *ensure*)
☐ **ate**	past tense of *eat*
eight	a number
☐ **attain**	to gain, to achieve
attend	to be present at
☐ **attendance**	presence
attendants	escorts; followers; companions; associates
☐ **aught**	(see *ought*)
☐ **averse**	(see *adverse*)
☐ **awhile**	(adv.) for a short time (see ¶1101)
a while	(phrase) a short period of time
☐ **bail**	(n.) security; the handle of a pail; (v.) to dip water
bale	a bundle
☐ **bare**	(adj.) naked; empty; (v.) to expose
bear	(n.) an animal; (v.) to carry; to endure; to produce
☐ **base**	(n.) foundation; (adj.) mean
bass	lower notes in music; a fish

☐ **bases**	plural of *base* and of *basis*
basis	foundation
☐ **bazaar**	(see *bizarre*)
☐ **beat**	(n.) throb; tempo; (v.) to strike
beet	a vegetable
☐ **berry**	a fruit
bury	to submerge; to cover over
☐ **berth**	a bed
birth	being born
☐ **beside**	by the side of; separate from (see ¶1101)
besides	in addition to; also
☐ **biannual**	occurring twice a year
biennial	occurring once in two years
☐ **bibliography**	list of writings pertaining to a given subject or author
biography	written history of a person's life
☐ **billed**	charged
build	to construct
☐ **birth**	(see *berth*)
☐ **bizarre**	fantastic, extravagantly odd
bazaar	a place for selling goods
☐ **blew**	past tense of *blow*
blue	a color
☐ **block**	(n.) a solid piece of material; (v.) to obstruct
bloc	an interest group pursuing certain political or economic goals
☐ **board**	a piece of wood; an organized group; meals
bored	penetrated; wearied
☐ **boarder**	one who pays for meals and often for lodging as well
border	edge
☐ **bolder**	more daring
boulder	a large rock
☐ **born**	brought into life
borne	carried; endured
☐ **boy**	a male child
buoy	a float

☐ **brake**	(n.) a retarding device; (v.) to retard
break	(n.) an opening; a fracture; (v.) to shatter; to divide
☐ **bread**	food
bred	brought up
☐ **breath**	respiration
breathe	(v.) to inhale and exhale
breadth	width
☐ **bridal**	concerning the bride or the wedding
bridle	(n.) means of controlling a horse; (v.) to take offense
☐ **broach**	to open; to introduce
brooch	ornamental clasp
☐ **build**	(see *billed*)
☐ **bullion**	uncoined gold or silver
bouillon	broth
☐ **buoy**	(see *boy*)
☐ **bury**	(see *berry*)
☐ **cache**	(see *cash*)
☐ **calendar**	a record of time
calender	a machine used in finishing paper and cloth
colander	a strainer
☐ **callous**	(adj.) hardened
callus	(n.) a hardened surface
☐ **cannot**	usual form (meaning "to be unable")
can not	two words in the phrase *can not only* (meaning "to be able")
☐ **canvas**	(n.) a coarse cloth
canvass	(v.) to solicit
☐ **capital**	(n.) city serving as the seat of government; a principal sum of money; a large-sized letter; (adj.) chief; foremost; punishable by death
capitol	the building in which a state legislative body meets
Capitol	the building in which the U.S. Congress meets

☐ **carton**	a pasteboard box	☐ **command**	(n.) an order; (v.) to order
cartoon	a caricature		
☐ **cash**	ready money	**commend**	to praise; to entrust
cache	a hiding place	☐ **commence**	(v.) to begin
☐ **casual**	incidental	**comments**	(n.) remarks
causal	causing	☐ **complement**	something that completes
☐ **cease**	to stop	**compliment**	(n.) a flattering speech; (v.) to praise
seize	to grasp		
☐ **cede**	to grant; to give up		
seed	that from which anything is grown	☐ **comprehensible**	understandable
		comprehensive	extensive
☐ **ceiling**	top of a room; any overhanging area	☐ **confidant**	a friend; an adviser (feminine form: *confidante*)
sealing	closing		
☐ **cell**	(see *sell*)	**confident**	sure; positive
☐ **cellar**	(see *seller*)	☐ **confidently**	certainly; positively
☐ **census**	statistics of population	**confidentially**	privately
senses	mental faculties	☐ **conscience**	(n.) the sense of right and wrong
☐ **cent**	(see *scent*)	**conscious**	(adj.) cognizant; sensible; aware
☐ **cereal**	any grain food		
serial	arranged in a series	☐ **conservation**	preservation
☐ **cession**	a yielding up	**conversation**	a talk
session	the sitting of a court or other body	☐ **consul**	(see *council*)
		☐ **consular**	(see *councillor*)
☐ **choose**	to select	☐ **continual**	occurring steadily but with occasional breaks
chose	did choose (past tense of *choose*)		
chews	masticates	**continuous**	uninterrupted; unbroken
☐ **chord**	combination of musical tones	☐ **cooperation**	the art of working together
cord	string or rope	**corporation**	a form of business organization
☐ **chute**	(see *shoot*)		
☐ **cite**	(v.) to quote; to summon	☐ **cord**	(see *chord*)
sight	a view; vision	☐ **core**	the central part; the heart
site	a place	**corps**	a group of persons with a common activity
☐ **click**	a slight sharp noise		
clique	an exclusive group		
cliché	a trite phrase	☐ **correspondence**	letters
☐ **climatic**	referring to climate	**correspondents**	those who write letters; journalists
climactic	referring to a climax		
☐ **clothes**	garments	**corespondents**	parties in divorce suits
cloths	fabrics		
close	(n.) the end; (v.) to shut	☐ **costume**	dress
		custom	habit
☐ **coarse**	rough; common	☐ **council**	an assembly
course	direction; action; a way; part of a meal	**counsel**	(n.) an attorney; advice; (v.) to give advice
☐ **colander**	(see *calendar*)		
☐ **collision**	a clashing	**consul**	a foreign representative
collusion	a scheme to defraud		
☐ **coma**	an unconscious state	☐ **councillor**	a member of a council
		counselor	one who advises
comma	a mark of punctuation	**consular**	(adj.) of a consul

☐ **course**	(see *coarse*)		☐ **detract** **distract**	to take away from to divert the attention of
☐ **courtesy** **curtesy**	a favor; politeness a husband's life interest in the lands of his deceased wife		☐ **device** **devise**	(n.) a contrivance (v.) to plan; to convey real estate by will
curtsy	a gesture of respect		☐ **dew**	(see *do*)
☐ **credible** **creditable**	believable meritorious, deserving of praise		☐ **diary**	(see *dairy*)
credulous	ready to believe		☐ **die**	(n.) mold; (v.) to cease living
☐ **critic**	one who makes judgments		**dye**	(n.) that which changes the color of; (v.) to change the color of
critique	(n.) a critical assessment; (v.) to judge; to criticize		☐ **differ**	(see *defer*)
☐ **cue** **queue**	a hint a line of people		☐ **difference**	(see *deference*)
☐ **currant** **current**	a berry (adj.) belonging to the present; (n.) a flow of water or electricity		☐ **disapprove** **disprove**	to withhold approval to prove the falsity of
☐ **custom**	(see *costume*)		☐ **disassemble** **dissemble**	to take apart to disguise; to feign
☐ **dairy**	source of milk products		☐ **disburse** **disperse**	to pay out to scatter
diary	daily record		☐ **discreet** **discrete**	prudent distinct; separate
☐ **deceased** **diseased**	dead sick		☐ **diseased**	(see *deceased*)
☐ **decent** **descent** **dissent**	proper; right going down disagreement		☐ **disinterested** **uninterested**	unbiased; impartial bored; unconcerned
☐ **decree** **degree**	a law a grade; a step		☐ **disposition**	(see *deposition*)
☐ **deduce** **deduct**	to infer to subtract		☐ **disprove**	(see *disapprove*)
☐ **defer** **differ**	to put off to disagree		☐ **dissemble**	(see *disassemble*)
☐ **deference**	respect, regard for another's wishes		☐ **dissent**	(see *decent*)
difference	dissimilarity; controversy		☐ **dissolute**	(see *desolate*)
☐ **delusion**	(see *allusion*)		☐ **distract**	(see *detract*)
☐ **deposition**	a formal written statement		☐ **divers**	various or sundry; plural of *diver*
disposition	temper; disposal		**diverse**	different
☐ **depraved** **deprived**	morally debased taken away from		☐ **do** **due** **dew**	to perform owing moisture
☐ **deprecate** **depreciate**	to disapprove to lessen in estimated value		☐ **done** **dun**	finished a demand for payment
☐ **desert**	(n.) barren land; a deserved reward; (v.) to abandon		☐ **dose** **doze**	a measured quantity to sleep lightly
dessert	the last course of a meal		☐ **dual** **duel**	double a combat
☐ **desolate** **dissolute**	lonely; sad loose in morals		☐ **due**	(see *do*)
			☐ **dye**	(see *die*)
			☐ **dying** **dyeing**	near death changing the color of

7

☐ **edition**	(see *addition*)
☐ **effect**	(see *affect*)
☐ **eight**	(see *ate*)
☐ **elapse**	(see *lapse*)
☐ **elicit**	to draw forth
illicit	unlawful
☐ **eligible**	fitted; qualified
illegible	unreadable
☐ **elusion**	(see *allusion*)
☐ **elusive**	baffling; hard to catch
illusive	misleading; unreal
☐ **emerge**	to rise out of
immerge	to plunge into
☐ **emigrate**	to go away from a country
immigrate	to come into a country
☐ **eminent**	well-known; prominent
imminent	threatening; impending
emanate	to originate from; to come out of
☐ **en route**	(see *root*)
☐ **ensure**	to make certain
insure	to protect against loss
assure	to give confidence to someone
☐ **envelop**	(v.) to cover; to wrap
envelope	(n.) a wrapper for a letter
☐ **equable**	even; tranquil
equitable	just; right
☐ **erasable**	capable of being erased
irascible	quick-tempered
☐ **especially**	to an exceptional degree
specially	particularly, as opposed to generally
☐ **essay**	(see *assay*)
☐ **everyday**	daily (see ¶1101)
every day	each day
☐ **everyone**	each one (see ¶1010)
every one	each one in a group
☐ **ewe**	(see *you*)
☐ **exalt**	to glorify
exult	to be joyful
☐ **exceed**	(see *accede*)
☐ **except**	(see *accept*)
☐ **excess**	(see *access*)

☐ **expand**	to increase in size
expend	to spend
☐ **expansive**	capable of being extended
expensive	costly
☐ **expatiate**	to enlarge on
expiate	to atone for
☐ **explicit**	easily understood
implicit	unquestioning
☐ **extant**	still existing
extent	measure
☐ **exult**	(see *exalt*)
☐ **facet**	aspect
faucet	a tap
☐ **facetious**	witty
factitious	artificial
fictitious	imaginary
☐ **facilitate**	to make easy
felicitate	to congratulate
☐ **facility**	ease
felicity	joy
☐ **faint**	(adj.) dim, weak; (v.) to pass out
feint	a trick; a deceptive move
☐ **fair**	(adj.) favorable; just; (n.) an exhibit
fare	(n.) cost of travel; food; (v.) to go forth
☐ **farther**	at a greater distance, referring to *actual* distance (see ¶1101)
further	to a greater extent or degree, referring to *figurative* distance; moreover; in addition
☐ **faucet**	(see *facet*)
☐ **faze**	to disturb
phase	a stage in development
☐ **feet**	plural of *foot*
feat	an act of skill or strength
☐ **fictitious**	(see *facetious*)
☐ **finale**	the end
finally	at the end
finely	in a fine manner
☐ **fineness**	delicacy
finesse	tact
☐ **fir**	a tree
fur	skin of an animal
☐ **fiscal**	(see *physical*)
☐ **flair**	aptitude
flare	a light; a signal

☐ **flaunt** to display showily
flout to treat with contempt

☐ **flew** did fly
flue a chimney
flu short for *influenza*

☐ **flounder** to move clumsily
founder to collapse; to sink

☐ **flour** ground meal
flower blossom

☐ **for** a preposition
fore first; preceding; the front
four numeral

☐ **forbear** to bear with
forebear an ancestor

☐ **forgo** to relinquish; to let pass
forego to go before

☐ **formally** in a formal manner
formerly before

☐ **fort** a fortified place
forte (n.) area where one excels; (adv.) loud (musical direction)

☐ **forth** away; forward
fourth next after third

☐ **forward** ahead
foreword preface

☐ **foul** unfavorable; unclean
fowl a bird

☐ **founder** (see *flounder*)

☐ **four** (see *for*)

☐ **fur** (see *fir*)

☐ **further** (see *farther*)

☐ **genius** talent
genus a classification in botany or zoology

☐ **gibe** (n.) a sarcastic remark; (v.) to scoff at
jibe to agree

☐ **grate** (n.) a frame of bars (as in a fireplace); (v.) to scrape; to irritate
great large; magnificent

☐ **guessed** past tense of *guess*
guest visitor

☐ **hail** (n.) a shower of icy pellets; (v.) to call out to
hale (adj.) healthy; (v.) to compel to go

☐ **hall** a corridor
haul to drag

☐ **heal** to cure
heel part of the foot or a shoe

☐ **healthful** promoting health (e.g., a *healthful* food)
healthy being in good health (e.g., a *healthy* person)

☐ **hear** to perceive by ear
here in this place

☐ **heard** past tense of *hear*
herd a group of animals

☐ **heir** (see *air*)

☐ **higher** at a greater height
hire to employ; to use someone's services

☐ **holy** sacred
holey full of holes
wholly entirely
holly a tree

☐ **hour** sixty minutes
our belonging to us
are a form of *to be* (as in *we are, you are, they are*)

☐ **human** pertaining to humanity
humane kindly

☐ **hypercritical** overcritical
hypocritical pretending virtue

☐ **ideal** a standard of perfection
idle unoccupied; without worth
idol object of worship
idyll a description of rural life

☐ **illegible** (see *eligible*)

☐ **illicit** (see *elicit*)

☐ **illusion** (see *allusion*)

☐ **illusive** (see *elusive*)

☐ **imitate** to resemble; to mimic
intimate (adj.) innermost; familiar; (v.) to hint; to make known

☐ **immerge** (see *emerge*)

☐ **immigrate** (see *emigrate*)

☐ **imminent** (see *eminent*)

☐ **implicit** (see *explicit*)

☐ **imply** to suggest (see ¶1101)
infer to deduce; to guess; to conclude

☐ **inane**	senseless
insane	of unsound mind
☐ **incidence**	range of occurrence
incidents	occurrences; happenings
☐ **incinerate**	to burn
insinuate	to imply
☐ **incite**	(v.) to arouse
insight	(n.) understanding
☐ **indict**	to charge with a crime
indite	to compose; to write
☐ **indifferent**	without interest
in different	in other (see ¶1101)
☐ **indigenous**	native
indigent	needy
indignant	angry
☐ **indirect**	not direct
in direct	*in* (preposition) + *direct* (adjective) (see ¶1101)
☐ **infer**	(see *imply*)
☐ **ingenious**	clever
ingenuous	naive
☐ **insane**	(see *inane*)
☐ **insight**	(see *incite*)
☐ **insinuate**	(see *incinerate*)
☐ **insoluble**	incapable of being dissolved
insolvable	not explainable
insolvent	pertaining to a person unable to pay his debts
☐ **instants**	short periods of time
instance	an example
☐ **insure**	(see *ensure*)
☐ **intelligent**	possessed of understanding
intelligible	understandable
☐ **intense**	acute; strong
intents	aims
☐ **interstate**	between states
intrastate	within one state
☐ **intimate**	(see *imitate*)
☐ **into, in to**	(see ¶1101)
☐ **irascible**	(see *erasable*)
☐ **isle**	island
aisle	passage between rows
☐ **its**	possessive form of *it*
it's	contraction of *it is* or *it has* (see ¶1056e)
☐ **jibe**	(see *gibe*)
☐ **key**	a means of gaining entrance or understanding
quay	a wharf (also pronounced *key*)
☐ **knew**	understood
new	fresh, novel
☐ **know**	to understand
no	not any
☐ **lapse**	to become void
elapse	to pass
relapse	to slip back into a former condition
☐ **last**	final (see ¶1101)
latest	most recent
☐ **later**	more recent; after a time
latter	second in a series of two
☐ **lath**	a strip of wood
lathe	a wood-turning machine
☐ **lay**	to place (see ¶1101)
lie	(n.) a falsehood; (v.) to recline; to tell an untruth
lye	a strong alkaline solution
☐ **lead**	(n.) heavy metal; (v.) to guide
led	guided (past tense of *to lead*)
☐ **lean**	(adj.) thin; (v.) to incline
lien	a legal claim
☐ **leased**	rented
least	smallest
☐ **legislator**	a lawmaker
legislature	a body of lawmakers
☐ **lend**	to allow the use of temporarily
loan	(n.) something lent; (v.) to lend
lone	solitary
☐ **lessee**	a tenant
lesser	of smaller size
lessor	one who gives a lease
☐ **lessen**	(v.) to make smaller
lesson	(n.) an exercise assigned for study
☐ **levee**	embankment of a river
levy	(n.) an amount collected by levying; (v.) to raise a collection of money

7

☐ **liable**	responsible	☐ **mien**	(see *mean*)
libel	defamatory statement	☐ **miner**	a worker in a mine
☐ **lie**	(see *lay*)	**minor**	(adj.) lesser, as in size, extent, or importance; (n.) a person who is under legal age
☐ **lien**	(see *lean*)		
☐ **lightening**	making lighter		
lightning	accompaniment of thunder	☐ **mist**	haze
lighting	illumination	**missed**	failed to do
☐ **loan, lone**	(see *lend*)	☐ **mite**	a tiny particle
☐ **loath**	(adj.) reluctant	**might**	(n.) force; (v.) past tense of *may*
loathe	(v.) to detest		
☐ **local**	pertaining to a particular place	☐ **mood**	disposition
locale	a particular place	**mode**	fashion; method
☐ **loose**	(adj.) not bound; (v.) to release	☐ **moral**	virtuous
		morale	spirit
lose	(v.) to suffer the loss of; to part with unintentionally	☐ **morality**	virtue
		mortality	death rate
		☐ **morning**	before noon
loss	something lost	**mourning**	grief
☐ **lye**	(see *lay*)	☐ **munificent**	(see *magnificent*)
☐ **made**	constructed	☐ **naught**	(see *ought*)
maid	a servant	☐ **new**	(see *knew*)
☐ **magnificent**	having splendor	☐ **no**	(see *know*)
munificent	unusually generous	☐ **nobody**	no one
☐ **mail**	correspondence	**no body**	no group (see ¶1101)
male	masculine		
☐ **main**	(adj.) chief; (n.) a conduit	☐ **none**	not one (see ¶1013)
		no one	nobody (see ¶1010)
mane	long hair on the neck of certain animals	☐ **oculist**	an ophthalmologist or an optometrist
		ophthalmologist	a doctor who treats eyes
☐ **manner**	a way of acting (as in "to the manner born")	**optician**	one who makes or sells eyeglasses
manor	an estate	**optometrist**	one who measures vision
☐ **marital**	pertaining to marriage	☐ **official**	authorized
martial	military	**officious**	overbold in offering services
marshal	(n.) an official; (v.) to arrange	☐ **one**	a single thing
		won	did win
☐ **maybe**	perhaps	☐ **ordinance**	a local law
may be	*two words* (see ¶1101)	**ordnance**	arms; munitions
		☐ **ought**	should
☐ **mean**	(adj.) unpleasant; (n.) the midpoint; (v.) to intend	**aught**	anything, all
		naught	nothing, zero
mien	appearance	☐ **our**	(see *hour*)
☐ **meat**	flesh of animals	☐ **overdo**	to do too much
meet	to join	**overdue**	past due
mete	to measure	☐ **packed**	crowded
☐ **medal**	a badge of honor	**pact**	an agreement
meddle	to interfere	☐ **pail**	a bucket
metal	a mineral	**pale**	(adj.) light-colored; (n.) an enclosure
mettle	courage; spirit		

□ **pain**	suffering	□ **perspective**	a view in correct proportion
pane	window glass	**prospective**	anticipated
□ **pair**	two of a kind	□ **peruse**	to read
pare	to peel	**pursue**	to chase
pear	a fruit	□ **petition**	(see *partition*)
□ **parameter**	a quantity with an assigned value; a constant	□ **phase**	(see *faze*)
		□ **physic**	a medicine
perimeter	the outer boundary	**physique**	bodily structure
□ **partition**	division	**psychic**	(adj.) pertaining to the mind or spirit; (n.) a medium
petition	prayer; a formal written request		
□ **partly**	in part	□ **physical**	relating to the body
partially	to some degree	**fiscal**	pertaining to finance
□ **past**	(n.) time gone by; (adj., adv., or prep.) gone by	□ **piece**	(see *peace*)
		□ **pier**	(see *peer*)
passed	moved along; transferred (past tense of *pass*)	□ **pique, piqué**	(see *peak*)
		□ **plain**	(adj.) undecorated; (n.) prairie land
□ **patience**	composure; endurance	**plane**	(n.) a level surface; (v.) to make level
patients	sick persons		
□ **peace**	calmness	□ **plaintiff**	party in a lawsuit
piece	a portion	**plaintive**	mournful
□ **peak**	the top	□ **pleas**	plural of *plea*
peek	to look slyly at	**please**	to be agreeable
pique	(n.) resentment; (v.) to offend; to arouse	□ **pole**	a long, slender piece of wood or metal
piqué	cotton fabric	**poll**	(n.) the casting of votes by a body of persons; (v.) to register the votes of
□ **peal**	to ring out		
peel	(n.) the rind; (v.) to strip off		
□ **pear**	(see *pair*)	□ **poor**	(adj.) inadequate; (n.) the needy
□ **pedal**	(adj.) pertaining to the foot; (n.) a treadle	**pore**	to study; to gaze intently
		pour	to flow
peddle	to hawk; to sell	□ **populace**	the common people; the masses
□ **peek**	(see *peak*)	**populous**	thickly settled
□ **peer**	(n.) one of equal rank; a nobleman; (v.) to look steadily	□ **portend**	(see *pretend*)
		□ **portion**	a part
		proportion	a ratio of parts
pier	a wharf	**apportion**	to allot
□ **perfect**	without fault	□ **practicable**	workable; feasible
prefect	an official	**practical**	useful
□ **perimeter**	(see *parameter*)	□ **pray**	to beseech
□ **perpetrate**	to be guilty of	**prey**	a captured victim
perpetuate	to make perpetual	□ **precede**	to go before
□ **perquisite**	privilege	**proceed**	to advance
prerequisite	a preliminary requirement	□ **precedence**	priority
		precedents	established rules
□ **persecute**	to oppress	□ **prefect**	(see *perfect*)
prosecute	to sue	□ **preposition**	a part of speech
□ **personal**	private	**proposition**	an offer
personnel	the staff		

☐ **prerequisite** (see *perquisite*)

☐ **prescribe** to designate
proscribe to outlaw

☐ **presence** bearing; being present

presents gifts

☐ **presentiment** a foreboding
presentment a proposal

☐ **pretend** to make believe
portend to foreshadow

☐ **principal** (adj.) chief; leading; (n.) a capital sum of money that draws interest; chief official of a school

principle a general truth; a rule

☐ **proceed** (see *precede*)

☐ **profit** gain
prophet one who forecasts

☐ **prophecy** a prediction
prophesy to foretell

☐ **propose** to suggest
purpose intention

☐ **proposition** (see *preposition*)

☐ **proscribe** (see *prescribe*)

☐ **prosecute** (see *persecute*)

☐ **prospective** (see *perspective*)

☐ **psychic** (see *physic*)

☐ **purpose** (see *propose*)

☐ **pursue** (see *peruse*)

☐ **quay** (see *key*)

☐ **queue** (see *cue*)

☐ **quiet** calm; not noisy
quite entirely; wholly
quit to stop

☐ **rain** falling water
rein part of a bridle; a curb
reign (n.) the term of a ruler's power; (v.) to rule

☐ **raise** to lift something (see ¶1101)
raze to destroy
rays beams

☐ **rap** to knock
wrap (n.) a garment; (v.) to enclose

☐ **read** to perform the act of reading
reed a plant; a musical instrument
red a color

☐ **real** actual
reel (n.) a spool; a dance; (v.) to whirl

☐ **reality** actuality
realty real estate

☐ **receipt** an acknowledgment of a thing received

recipe a formula for mixing ingredients

☐ **recent** late
resent (v.) to feel hurt by

☐ **reference** that which refers to something
reverence profound respect

☐ **reign, rein** (see *rain*)

☐ **relapse** (see *lapse*)

☐ **residence** a house
residents persons who reside in a place

☐ **respectably** in a manner worthy of respect

respectfully in a courteous manner

respectively in the order indicated

☐ **right** (adj.) correct; (n.) a privilege
rite a ceremony
wright a worker, a maker (used as a combining form, as in *playwright*)

write to inscribe

☐ **role** a part in a play
roll (n.) a list; a type of bread; (v.) to revolve

☐ **root** (n.) underground part of a plant; (v.) to implant firmly
route (n.) an established course of travel; (v.) to send by a certain route
en route on or along the way
rout (n.) confused flight; (v.) to defeat

☐ **rote** repetition
wrote did write

☐ **sail** (n.) part of a ship's rigging; (v.) to travel by water
sale the act of selling

☐ **scene** a setting; an exhibition of strong feeling
seen past participle of *to see*

7

WORDS THAT SOUND ALIKE OR LOOK ALIKE 149

□ scent   odor
sent   did send
cent   penny
sense   meaning

□ sealing   (see *ceiling*)

□ seam   a line of junction
seem   to appear

□ seed   (see *cede*)

□ seize   (see *cease*)

□ sell   to transfer for a price
cell   a small compartment

□ seller   one who sells
cellar   an underground room

□ sense, sent   (see *scent*)

□ senses   (see *census*)

□ serge   a kind of cloth
surge   (n.) a billow; (v.) to rise suddenly

□ serial   (see *cereal*)

□ serve   to help (see ¶1101)
service   to keep in good repair

□ session   (see *cession*)

□ sew   (see *so*)

□ shear   to cut; to trim
sheer   transparent; unqualified

□ shoot   to fire
chute   a slide

□ shown   displayed; revealed; past participle of *show*
shone   gave off light; did shine

□ sight, site   (see *cite*)

□ simple   plain, uncomplicated
simplistic   oversimplified; falsely simple

□ sleight   dexterity, as in "sleight of hand"
slight   (adj.) slender; scanty; (v.) to make light of

□ so   therefore
sew   to stitch
sow   to scatter seed

□ soar   (see *sore*)

□ soared   did fly
sword   weapon

□ sole   one and only
soul   the immortal spirit

□ soluble   having the ability to dissolve in a liquid
solvable   capable of being solved or explained

□ some   a part of
sum   a total

□ someone   somebody (see ¶1010)
some one   some person in a group

□ sometime   at some unspecified time (see ¶1101)
some time   a period of time
sometimes   now and then

□ son   male child
sun   the earth's source of light and heat

□ sore   painful
soar   to fly

□ soul   (see *sole*)

□ sow   (see *so*)

□ spacious   having ample room
specious   outwardly correct but inwardly false

□ specially   (see *especially*)

□ staid   grave; sedate
stayed   past tense and past participle of *to stay*

□ stair   a step
stare   to look at

□ stake   (n.) a pointed stick; the prize in a contest; (v.) to wager
steak   a slice of meat or fish

□ stationary   fixed
stationery   writing materials

□ statue   a carved or molded figure
stature   height
statute   a law

□ steal   to take unlawfully
steel   a form of iron

□ straight   not crooked; directly
strait   a water passageway; (plural) a distressing situation

□ suit   (n.) a legal action; clothing; (v.) to please
suite   a group of things forming a unit
sweet   having an agreeable taste; pleasing

□ sum   (see *some*)

7

☐ **sun** (see *son*)

☐ **superintendence** management
superintendents supervisors

☐ **surge** (see *serge*)

☐ **sweet** (see *suite*)

☐ **sword** (see *soared*)

☐ **tack** (n.) direction; (v.) to change direction (see ¶1101)

tact considerate way of behaving so as to avoid offending others

☐ **tail** the end
tale a story

☐ **tare** allowance for weight

tear (n.) a rent; a secretion from the eye; (v.) to rip

tier a row or layer

☐ **taught** did teach
taut tight; tense

☐ **team** a group
teem to abound

☐ **tenant** one who rents property

tenet a principle

☐ **than** conjunction of comparison

then (adv.) at that time

☐ **their** belonging to them (see ¶1056*e*)
there in that place
they're contraction of *they are*

☐ **theirs** possessive form of *they*, used without a following noun (see ¶1056*e*)

there's contraction of *there is* or *there has*

☐ **therefor** for that thing
therefore consequently

☐ **throes** a painful struggle
throws hurls; flings

☐ **through** by means of; from beginning to end; because of

threw did throw
thorough carried through to completion

☐ **tier** (see *tare*)

☐ **to** (prep.) toward
too (adv.) more than enough; also
two one plus one

☐ **tortuous** winding; twisty; devious
torturous cruelly painful

☐ **track** a trail
tract a treatise; a piece of land

☐ **trial** examination; an experiment; hardship
trail a path

☐ **undo** to open; to render ineffective
undue improper; excessive

☐ **uninterested** (see *disinterested*)

☐ **urban** pertaining to the city
urbane polished; suave

☐ **vain** proud; conceited; futile
vane a weathercock
vein a blood vessel; a bed of mineral materials

☐ **vale** a valley
veil a concealing cover or cloth

☐ **vendee** purchaser
vendor seller

☐ **veracious** truthful
voracious greedy

☐ **veracity** truthfulness
voracity ravenousness; greediness

☐ **vice** wickedness; a prefix used with nouns to designate titles of office (see ¶808*b*)
vise a clamp

☐ **waist** part of the body; a garment
waste (n.) needless destruction; useless consumption; (v.) to expend uselessly

☐ **wait** to stay
weight quantity of heaviness

☐ **waive** (v.) to give up
wave (n.) a billow; a gesture; (v.) to swing back and forth

☐ **waiver** the giving up of a claim
waver to hesitate

☐ **want** (n.) a need; (v.) to lack; to desire
wont a custom (pronounced like *want*)
won't contraction of *will not*

□ **ware** goods
wear to have on
were form of *to be*
where at the place in which

□ **wave** (see *waive*)

□ **way** direction; distance; manner
weigh to find the weight of

□ **weak** not strong
week period of seven days

□ **weather** (n.) state of the atmosphere; (v.) to come through safely
whether if (see ¶1101)

□ **weight** (see *wait*)

□ **whoever** anyone who
who ever *two words* (see ¶1101)

□ **wholly** (see *holy*)

□ **whose** possessive of *who*
who's contraction of *who is* (see ¶1063)

□ **won** (see *one*)

□ **wont, won't** (see *want*)

□ **wood** lumber
would an auxiliary verb form (as in *they would like some*)

□ **wrap** (see *rap*)

□ **wright, write** (see *right*)

□ **wrote** (see *rote*)

□ **yoke** a crosspiece that holds two things together; an oppressive constraint
yolk the yellow part of an egg

□ **you** second-person pronoun
yew an evergreen tree or bush
ewe a female sheep

□ **your** referring to *you* (see ¶1056*e*)
you're contraction of *you are*

TROUBLESOME WORDS

720   The following list presents a selection of those words that business writers often misspell or stop and puzzle over. In some cases the difficulty results from the inability to apply an established rule; for such words, references to the rules are given. In many other instances, however, errors result from the peculiar spelling of the words themselves; in such cases the only remedy is to master the correct spelling of such words on an individual basis.

NOTE: For troublesome words that sound alike or look alike, see ¶719. For troublesome compound words, see Section 8.

absence
accidentally (see ¶1101)
accommodate
accompanying
achievement
acknowledgment (see ¶708)
acquaintance
acquiesce
acquire
acquisition
across
adjacent
advantageous (see ¶707)
aegis
affidavit
aggressive
aging (see ¶707)
aisle
Albuquerque
alignment
all right (see ¶1101)
alleged
already (see ¶1101)

amateur
amortize (see ¶715)
analogous
analysis
analyze (see ¶715)
anomalous
answer
appall
apparatus
apparently
appreciable
approximate
arbitrary
architect
argument (see ¶708)
assistance (see ¶714)
attorney
autumn
auxiliary
bachelor
bankruptcy
basically
beginning (see ¶702)

believe (see ¶712)
beneficiary
benefited (see ¶704)
Berkeley (California)
biased (see ¶705)
boundary
breakfast
brochure
buoyant
buses (see ¶701)
business
busy
calendar
calorie
campaign
canceled (see ¶704)
cancellation (see ¶704)
candor
Caribbean
carriage
catalog
category
cemetery
census
chaise longue
changeable (see ¶707)
chronological
Cincinnati
coincidence
collateral
colonel
colossal
column
commitment
committee
comparison
concede (see ¶716)
connoisseur
conscience
conscientious
conscious
consensus
consistent
continuous
controversy
convenience
criticism
debt
debtor
deductible
defendant (see ¶714)
defense
deficit
definite
dependent (see ¶714)
Des Moines
descendant (see ¶714)
describe
detrimental
develop
development
dignitary
dilemma
disappoint

disastrous
dissatisfied
dissimilar
doctrinaire
dossier
double
ecstasy
eighth
either
eligible
eliminate
embarrass
emphasize
empty
entrepreneur
enumerate
environment
escrow
exaggerate
exceed (see ¶716)
excellent
exercise
exhaustible
exhibition
exhilarate
existence (see ¶714)
exonerate
exorbitant
experience
extension
extraordinary
eyeing
facsimile
familiar
fantasy
fascinating
February
fiery
financier
fluorescent
forbade
foreign (see ¶712)
foresee
forfeit
forty
fourteen
fourth
fulfill
gauge
glamorous
glamour
government
grammar
grateful
gray
grievous
gruesome (see ¶708)
guarantee
guardian
harass
height (see ¶712)
hemorrhage
heterogeneous
hindrance

hors d'oeuvre
hygiene
hypocrisy
impasse
inasmuch as
incidentally
indispensable
innocuous
innovation
innuendo
inoculate
insistence (see ¶714)
interfering
interim
intern
irrelevant (see ¶714)
itinerary
jeopardy
judgment (see ¶708)
labeled (see ¶704)
laboratory
ledger
leisure
liable
liaison
library
license
lien
lieutenant
lightning
likable (see ¶707)
liquefy
lose
maintenance
maneuver
marriage
medieval
mediocre
memento
mileage (see ¶707)
milieu
millennium
millionaire
miniature
minuscule
minutiae (see ¶614)
misapprehension
miscellaneous
mischievous
misspell
mortgage
motor
movable
necessary
negotiate
neither (see ¶712)
nickel
ninety
ninth
noticeable (see ¶707)
nuclear
obsolescent
occasionally
occurrence (see ¶702)

offense
offered (see ¶704)
omelet
omission
oneself
ophthalmology
opinion
pamphlet
panicky (see ¶717)
parallel
partially
pastime
patience
permissible (see ¶713)
perseverance
persistent
persuade
phase
phenomenal
phony
physician
picnicking (see ¶717)
Pittsburgh
plagiarism
plausible (see ¶713)
possessions
practically
practice
prairie
preceding (see ¶716)
preferable (see ¶702)
prerogative
presumptuous
pretense
privilege
procedure (see ¶716)
proceed (see ¶716)
programmed (see ¶704)
prohibition
promissory
pronunciation
psychiatric
psychological
publicly
pursue
quantity
questionnaire
queue
rarefy
receipt
receive (see ¶712)
recipient
recommend
recruit
reference (see ¶702)
regrettable (see ¶702)
reinforce
relevant (see ¶714)
renaissance
renowned
rescind
resistance (see ¶714)
restaurant
résumé (see ¶718)

retroactive
rhapsody
rhetorical
rhyme
rhythm
rhythmic
sacrilegious
salable (see ¶707)
San Francisco
satellite
schedule
scissors
seize (see ¶712)
separate
sergeant
siege (see ¶712)
similar
simultaneous
sincerely (see ¶708)
sizable (see ¶707)
skeptic
skiing
skillful
souvenir
specimen
sponsor
stratagem
strength
subpoena
subtlety
subtly
suing
summary
superintendent
supersede (see ¶716)
surgeon
surprise
surreptitious

surveillance (see ¶714)
susceptible
tariff
taxiing
technique
temperament
temperature
tempt
theater
their (see ¶712)
theory
thoroughly
threshold
through
totaled (see ¶704)
tragedy
transferred (see ¶702)
traveler (see ¶704)
unctuous
unforgettable (see ¶702)
unique
unmanageable (see ¶707)
unwieldy (see ¶712)
usage (see ¶707)
vacillate
vegetable
victim
volume
warehouse
Wednesday
weird (see ¶712)
whether
whiskey
wholly
wield (see ¶712)
woeful
woolly (see ¶705)
yield (see ¶712)

Compound Words

Some compound words are written as solid words, some are written as separate words, and some are hyphenated. As in other areas of style, authorities do not agree on the rules. Moreover, style is continually changing: many words that used to be hyphenated are now written solid or as separate words. The only complete guide is an up-to-date dictionary. However, a careful reading of the following rules will save you many a trip to the dictionary.

NOTE: The spellings in this section agree with those in the 1983 printing of *Webster's Ninth New Collegiate Dictionary* and *Webster's Third New International Dictionary* (published by Merriam-Webster, Springfield, Massachusetts) unless otherwise indicated.

COMPOUND NOUNS

801 Compound nouns follow no regular pattern. Some are written solid, some are spaced, and some are hyphenated.

checklist	check mark	check-in	airmail	air mile
closeout	close shave	close-up	bankroll	bank note
courtyard	court order	court-martial	bookstore	book review
crossroad	cross section	cross-reference	bylaw	by-product
eyewitness	eye shadow	eye-opener	daytime	day student
foothold	foot brake	foot-pound	handbook	hand truck
goodwill	good sense	good-bye	hometown	home port
halftime	half hour	half-truth	linecut	line printer
lifeline	life raft	life-style	masterpiece	master plan
lightweight	light bulb	light-year	paperwork	paper clip
moneylender	money order	money-maker	salespeople	sales tax
nightlife	night court	night-light	schoolteacher	school board
showdown	show biz	show-off	sickbed	sick pay
timetable	time sheet	time-saver	standby	stand-in
trademark	trade name	trade-off	workday	work load

NOTE: To be sure of the spelling of a compound noun, check a dictionary. If the noun is not listed, treat the components as separate words. For the spelling of compounds in company names, check letterheads for possible variations. (Compare, for example, *Eastern Airlines* with *Delta Air Lines*.)

802 Some solid and hyphenated compound nouns closely resemble verb phrases. Be sure, however, to treat the elements in a verb phrase as separate words.

Nouns	Verb Phrases
a *breakdown* in communications	when communications *break down*
a thorough *follow-up* of the report	to *follow up* the report thoroughly
operate a *drive-in*	*drive in* to your dealer's
a high school *dropout*	don't *drop out* of high school
at the time of *takeoff*	planes cannot *take off* or land
when they give us a *go-ahead*	we can *go ahead* with the plan
come to a *standstill*	we can't *stand still*
let's have a *run-through*	let's *run through* the plan
plan a *get-together*	plan to *get together*
they have the *know-how*	they *know how* to handle it
expect a *turnaround* in sales	once our sales *turn around*
we have to make a *getaway*	we have to *get away*
to attempt a *takeover* of their firm	to attempt to *take over* their firm
I was a *standby* on Flight 968A	we can't *stand by* and do nothing
Paul's speech was merely a *put-on*	your requisition was *put on* hold
devise an alternative plan as a *fallback*	we can always *fall back* on Plan B
serve as a *go-between* in the dispute	this note should *go between* the two tables on page 5

803 **a. *Up* Words.** Compound nouns ending in *up* are either solid or hyphenated. For example:

backup	linkup	call-up	mock-up
breakup	makeup	close-up	runner-up
brushup	markup	flare-up	shake-up
buildup	pileup	follow-up	start-up
checkup	setup	foul-up	tie-up
cleanup	slipup	hang-up	touch-up
getup	warmup*	lead-up	wrap-up
letup	windup	mix-up	write-up

b. *Down* Words. Most compound nouns ending in *down* are solid. For example:

breakdown	lowdown	shakedown	**BUT:** put-down
comedown	markdown	showdown	sit-down
countdown	rubdown	slowdown	step-down
crackdown	rundown	sundown	write-down

c. *In* Words. Compound nouns ending in *in* are typically hyphenated. For example:

break-in	listener-in	sit-in	trade-in
cave-in	run-in	stand-in	walk-in
check-in	shoo-in	teach-in	weigh-in
drive-in	shut-in	tie-in	write-in

d. *Out* Words. Most compound nouns ending in *out* are solid. For example:

blackout	hangout	shakeout	**BUT:** diner-out
breakout	holdout	standout	fade-out
closeout	layout	tryout	falling-out
fallout	printout	washout	shoot-out
handout	sellout	workout	time-out

e. *On* Words. Compound nouns ending in *on* are typically hyphenated. For example:

carryings-on	goings-on	lookers-on	run-on
come-on	hangers-on	put-on	slip-on

f. *Off* Words. Compound nouns ending in *off* are either solid or hyphenated. For example:

checkoff	payoff	drop-off	send-off
cutoff	runoff	goof-off	show-off
falloff	shutoff	lift-off	spin-off
knockoff	takeoff	rake-off	trade-off
layoff	turnoff	rip-off	write-off

g. *Over* Words. Most compound nouns ending in *over* are solid. For example:

carryover	holdover	slipover	takeover
changeover	layover	spillover	turnover
crossover	leftover	stopover	**BUT:** going-over
hangover	pushover	strikeover	once-over

h. *Back* Words. Compound nouns ending in *back* are typically solid. For example:

callback	fallback	pullback	snapback
comeback	kickback	rollback	throwback
drawback	playback	setback	tieback

---

*Webster shows this as a hyphenated word, but it frequently appears as a solid word in business.

i. *Away* Words. These compounds are typically solid. For example:

breakaway	hideaway	runaway	straightaway
getaway	layaway	stowaway	throwaway

j. Compounds Ending in *About*, *Around*, and *By*. These compounds are typically solid. For example:

knockabout	runabout	runaround	passersby
layabout	turnabout	turnaround	standbys

k. Compounds Ending in *Between*, *Through*, and *Together*. These compounds are typically hyphenated. For example:

go-between	follow-through	walk-through	get-together
in-between	run-through	**BUT:** breakthrough	

804 a. Hyphenate a compound noun that lacks a noun as one of its elements.

the also-rans	know-it-alls	a set-to
a cure-all	hand-me-downs	a lean-to
a go-getter	a pick-me-up	a talking-to
a has-been	a shoot-'em-up	the well-to-do
the have-nots	do-it-yourselfers	give-and-take
the higher-ups	a good-for-nothing	a five-and-ten
know-how	a ne'er-do-well	half-and-half
a look-alike	a merry-go-round	on the up-and-up
make-believe	a free-for-all	**BUT:** ups and downs
say-so	the be-all and end-all	wear and tear

b. Words coined from repeated syllables or rhyming syllables are typically hyphenated. Other coined words may be hyphenated or solid.

boo-boo	hurly-burly	one-upmanship
goody-goody	nitty-gritty	stick-to-itiveness
no-no	razzle-dazzle	comeuppance
yo-yo	walkie-talkie	whodunit

c. Many compound nouns that end with a prepositional phrase are hyphenated.

ambassador-at-large	lady-in-waiting	**BUT:** bill of lading
attorney-at-law	man-about-town	editor in chief
brother-in-law	right-of-way	line of credit
jack-of-all-trades	stock-in-trade	power of attorney
Johnny-on-the-spot	theater-in-the-round	rule of thumb

805 Treat a compound noun like *problem solving* as two words unless your dictionary specifically shows it as solid or hyphenated. (Most words of this pattern are not shown in a dictionary. However, the solid and hyphenated examples below have been taken from the 1983 printing of *Webster's Ninth New Collegiate Dictionary*.)

data processing	brainstorming	clock-watching
decision making	housewarming	foot-dragging
problem solving	lawmaking	job-hopping
profit sharing	logrolling	soul-searching
skill building	safekeeping	time-sharing

❑ *For words like* air conditioning, *which are derived from hyphenated infinitives like* air-condition, *see ¶812.*

806 Hyphenate two nouns when they signify that one person or one thing has two functions.

actor-director	dinner-dance	secretary-treasurer
clerk-typist	lawyer-diplomat	wheeler-dealer

807   Compound nouns that have a single letter as their first element are either hyphenated or written as two words.

A-frame	I beam	c-mitosis
H-bomb	T square	f-number
T-shirt	V neck	x-axis
U-turn	X ray	y-coordinate

NOTE: The term X *ray* (which is written as two words when used as a noun) is hyphenated when used as a verb or an adjective. (See also ¶815*a*.)

808   Do not hyphenate civil, military, and naval titles of two or more words.

Chief of Police Potenza	Attorney General Leibowitz
General Manager Werner	Rear Admiral Byrd

a. Hyphenate compound titles containing *ex* and *elect*.

ex-President Carter   Vice President-elect Jordan

NOTE: Also use a hyphen when *ex* is attached to a noun (for example, *ex-wife, ex-convict*), but omit the hyphen in Latin phrases (for example, *ex officio, ex cathedra*).

❏ *For the capitalization of titles with* ex *and* elect, *see* ¶¶317 *and* 363; *for the correct usage of* ex, *see the entry for* Ex–former *in* ¶1101.

b. The hyphen is being dropped from titles containing *vice*. It is still customary in *vice-chancellor* and *vice-consul*, but it is gone from *vice president* and *vice admiral*.

Vice-Chancellor Safran   Vice President Bush   Vice Admiral Bissell

809   Compound nouns containing *man* or *men* as an element have traditionally been used generically to refer to males and females alike.

not for the average *layman*	the history of *mankind*
of concern to all *businessmen*	reduce the number of *man-hours*
write your *congressman*	a new supply of *manpower*

a. The *generic* use of such terms has been criticized on the grounds that the masculine bias of these terms makes them unsuitable for reference to women as well as men. The following list suggests appropriate alternatives:

In Place of the Generic Term	Use
businessmen	business owners, business executives, business managers, business people
salesmen	sales representatives, salespersons, salesclerks, sales staff, sales force
foremen	supervisors
policemen	police officers
mailmen	mail carriers
congressmen	members of Congress, representatives
mankind	people, humanity, the human race, human beings
man-hours	worker-hours
manpower	work force, human energy

b. When naming a job or role, avoid the use of compound terms ending in *man* or *woman* unless the term refers to a specific person whose gender is known.

There are ten candidates seeking election to the City *Council*. (**NOT:** . . . seeking election as city *councilmen*.)

BUT: *Councilwoman* Walters and *Councilman* Holtz will study the proposal.

Write to your *representative in Congress.* (**NOT:** Write to your *congressman.*)

BUT: I was very much impressed by *Congresswoman* Patricia Schroeder of Colorado.

Who will be appointed as *head* of the committee? **OR** Who will be appointed to *chair* the committee? (**NOT:** . . . appointed *chairman* of the committee?)

BUT: Robert Haas has been appointed *chairman* of the committee.

NOTE: Words like *chairperson* and *spokesperson* have been coined as a means of avoiding the generic use of masculine compound nouns. Personal taste or institutional policy will dictate whether to use these terms or not.

810　Terms like *doctor, lawyer,* and *nurse* are generic—that is, they apply equally to women and men. Therefore, do not use compound nouns like *woman lawyer* and *male nurse* unless there is a legitimate reason for making a distinction according to gender.

Next Wednesday there will be a seminar on the problems facing *women lawyers* in the courtroom.

❑ *Capitalization of hyphenated compound nouns: see ¶363.*
❑ *Plurals of compound nouns: see ¶¶611–613.*
❑ *Possessives of compound nouns: see ¶¶634–635.*

COMPOUND VERBS

811　**a.** Compound verbs are usually hyphenated or solid.

to air-condition	to off-load	to backstop	to moonlight
to baby-sit	to pinch-hit	to bulldoze	to pinpoint
to blue-pencil	to rubber-stamp	to buttonhole	to proofread
to deep-six	to short-circuit	to downgrade	to shortchange
to double-space	to soft-pedal	to hamstring	to sidetrack
to dry-clean	to speed-read	to handpick	to troubleshoot
to field-test	to spot-check	to highlight	to waterproof
to Indian-wrestle	to window-shop	to mastermind	to whitewash

NOTE: If you try to check the spelling of a compound verb in a dictionary and do not find the verb listed, hyphenate the components.

b. Do not hyphenate verb-adverb combinations such as *make up, slow down, tie in.* (See ¶802 for examples.)

812　**a.** If the infinitive form of a compound verb contains a hyphen, retain the hyphen in the other forms of the verb. (See ¶812*b* for one exception.)

Would you like to *air-condition* your entire house?
The theater was not *air-conditioned.*
We need an *air-conditioning* expert to advise us.

You need to *double-space* all these reports.
Please *double-space* this letter.
This material should not be *double-spaced.*
BUT: Leave a *double space* between paragraphs. (No hyphen in *double space* as a compound noun.)

b. The gerund derived from a hyphenated compound verb requires no hyphen unless it is followed by an object.

(Continued on page 162.)

Dry cleaning is the best way to clean this garment.
BUT: *Dry-cleaning* this *sweater* will not remove the spot.

Air conditioning is no longer as expensive as it used to be.
BUT: In *air-conditioning* an *office,* you must take more than space into account.

Spot checking is all we have time for.
BUT: In *spot-checking* the *data,* I found some disturbing errors.

COMPOUND ADJECTIVES

No aspect of style causes greater difficulty than compound adjectives. When a compound adjective is shown hyphenated in the dictionary, you can safely assume only that the expression is hyphenated when it occurs directly *before* a noun. When the same combination of words falls elsewhere in the sentence, the use or omission of hyphens depends on how the words are used.

For the basic rules, see ¶¶813–815. For detailed comments, see the following paragraphs:

❑ *Adjective + noun (as in* short-term *note): see ¶816.*
❑ *Compound with number or letter (as in* 40-hour *week): see ¶817.*
❑ *Compound noun (as in* high school *graduate): see ¶818.*
❑ *Proper name (as in* Madison Avenue *agencies): see ¶819.*
❑ *Noun + adjective (as in* tax-free *imports): see ¶820.*
❑ *Noun + participle (as in* time-consuming *details): see ¶821.*
❑ *Adjective + participle (as in* nice-looking *layout): see ¶822.*
❑ *Adjective + noun + ed (as in* quick-witted *girl): see ¶823.*
❑ *Adverb + participle (as in* privately owned *stock): see ¶824a.*
❑ *Adverb + participle (as in* well-known *facts): see ¶824b.*
❑ *Adverb + adjective (as in* very exciting *test results): see ¶825.*
❑ *Participle + adverb (as in* warmed-over *ideas): see ¶826.*
❑ *Adjective + adjective (as in* black leather *notebook): see ¶827.*
❑ *Phrasal compound (as in* up-to-date *accounts): see ¶828.*

NOTE: If you try to check the spelling of a compound adjective in a dictionary and do not find it listed, match up the components with one of the patterns shown above and follow the standard style for that pattern.

BASIC RULES

813   A compound adjective consists of two or more words that function as a unit and express a single thought. These one-thought modifiers are derived from (and take the place of) adjective phrases and clauses. In the following examples the left column shows the original phrase or clause; the right column shows the compound adjective.

Adjective Phrase or Clause	Compound Adjective
imports *that are free of duty*	*duty-free* imports
a woman *who speaks quietly*	a *quiet-spoken* woman
an actor *who is well known*	a *well-known* actor
a conference *held at a high level*	a *high-level* conference
a building *ten stories high*	a *ten-story* building
a report *that is up to date*	an *up-to-date* report
an article *that is as long as a book*	a *book-length* article

NOTE: In the process of becoming compound adjectives, the adjective phrases and clauses are usually reduced to a few essential words. In addition, these words frequently undergo a change in form (for example, *ten stories high* becomes *ten-story*); sometimes they are put in inverted order (for example, *free of duty* becomes *duty-free*); sometimes they are simply extracted from the phrase or clause without any change in form (for example, *well-known, high-level*).

814 Hyphenate the elements of a compound adjective that occurs *before* a noun. (**REASON:** The words that make up the compound adjective are not in their normal order or a normal form and require hyphens to hold them together.)

> an *old-fashioned* dress (a dress *of an old fashion*)
> a *$10,000-a-year* salary (a salary *of $10,000 a year*)
> *long-range* plans (plans *projected over a long range of time*)
> *machine-readable* copy (copy *readable by a machine*)
> an *eye-catching* display (a display *that catches the eye*)
> a *high-ranking* official (an official *who ranks high in the organization*)
> *same-day* service (service *completed the same day you bring the item in*)

EXCEPTIONS: A number of compounds like *real estate* and *high school* do not need hyphens when used as adjectives before a noun. (See ¶818.)

815 **a.** When these expressions occur *elsewhere in the sentence*, drop the hyphen if the individual words occur in a normal order and in a normal form. (In such cases the expression no longer functions as a compound adjective.)

Before the Noun	Elsewhere in Sentence
an *X-ray* treatment	It can be treated by *X ray*. (Object of preposition.)
an *up-to-date* report	Please bring the report *up to date*. (Prepositional phrase.)
a *high-level* decision	The decision must be made at a *high level*. (Object of preposition.)
a *never-to-be-forgotten* book	That book is *never to be forgotten*. (Adverb + infinitive phrase.)
an *off-the-record* comment	This comment is *off the record*. (Prepositional phrase.)

b. When these expressions occur elsewhere in the sentences *but are in an inverted word order or an altered form*, retain the hyphen.

Before the Noun	Elsewhere in Sentence
a *tax-exempt* purchase	The purchase was *tax-exempt*. **BUT:** The purchase was *exempt from taxes*.
government-owned lands	These lands are *government-owned*. **BUT:** These lands are *owned by the government*.
a *friendly-looking* salesclerk	That salesclerk is *friendly-looking*. **BUT:** That salesclerk *looks friendly*.
high-priced goods	These goods are *high-priced*. **BUT:** These goods carry a *high price*.

NOTE: The following kinds of compound adjectives almost always need to be hyphenated:

- ❏ *Noun + adjective (for example, tax-exempt): see ¶820.*
- ❏ *Noun + participle (for example, government-owned): see ¶821.*
- ❏ *Adjective + participle (for example, friendly-looking): see ¶822.*
- ❏ *Adjective + noun + ed (for example, high-priced): see ¶823.*

ADJECTIVE + NOUN (see also ¶¶817–819)

816 **a.** Hyphenate this combination of elements *before* a noun. Do not hyphenate these elements when they play a normal function *elsewhere in the sentence* (for example, as the object of a preposition or of a verb). However, if the expression continues to function as a compound adjective, retain the hyphen.

(Continued on page 164.)

Before the Noun	Elsewhere in Sentence
high-speed printers	These printers run at *high speed*. (Object of preposition.)
random-access memory	This computer permits *random access* to the stored data. (Object of verb.)
red-carpet treatment	They plan to roll out the *red carpet*. (Object of infinitive.)
a *closed-door* discussion	The discussion was held behind *closed doors*. (Object of preposition.)
a *long-term* investment in bonds	This investment in bonds runs for a *long term*. (Object of preposition.)
	BUT: This investment in bonds is *long-term*. (Compound adjective.)
a *part-time* job	This job is *part-time*. (Compound adjective.)
	I work *part-time*. (Compound adverb.)
	I travel *part of the time*. (Normal adverbial phrase.)

NOTE: Combinations involving comparative or superlative adjectives plus nouns follow the same pattern.

Before the Noun	Elsewhere in Sentence
a *larger-size* shirt	He wears a *larger size*. (Object of verb.)
the *finest-quality* goods	These goods are of the *finest quality*. (Object of preposition.)

b. A few compound adjectives in this category are now written solid—for example, *a commonsense solution, a freshwater pond, a surefire success*.

COMPOUND WITH NUMBER OR LETTER

817 **a.** When a number and a noun form a one-thought modifier *before* a noun (as in *six-story building*), make the noun singular and hyphenate the expression. When the expression has a normal form and a normal function *elsewhere in the sentence*, do not hyphenate it.

Before the Noun	Elsewhere in Sentence
a *one-way* street	a street that runs only *one way*
a *first-person* account	a story written in the *first person*
a *first-rate* job	a job that deserves the *first* (or highest) *rating*
	BUT: a job that is *first-rate*
a *two-piece* suit	a suit consisting of *two pieces*
a *three-ring* circus	a circus with *three rings*
a *four-color* illustration	an illustration printed in *four colors*
a *5-liter* container	a container that holds *5 liters*
an *8-foot* ceiling	a ceiling *8 feet* above the floor
a *20-year* mortgage	a mortgage running for *20 years*
twentieth-century art	art of the *twentieth century*
a *50-cent* fee	a fee of *50 cents*
an *$85-a-month* charge	a charge of *$85 a month*
a *100-meter* sprint	a sprint of *100 meters*
an *8½- by 11-inch* book (see ¶829)	a book *8½ by 11 inches*
a *55-mile-an-hour* speed limit	a speed limit of *55 miles an hour*
a *2-million-ton* shipment of steel	a shipment of *2 million tons* of steel
a *10-inch-thick* panel	a panel *10 inches thick*
a *7-foot-2-inch* basketball player	a basketball player *7 feet 2 inches* tall (see ¶430)
24-hour-a-day, 7-day-a-week service	service *24 hours a day, 7 days a week*

EXCEPTIONS: a *15 percent* increase, a *$4 million* profit, a *secondhand* car

NOTE: A hyphenated compound adjective and an unhyphenated possessive expression often provide *alternative* ways of expressing the same thought. Do not use both styles together.

a *one-year* extension **OR** a *one year's* extension (**BUT NOT:** a one-year's extension)

a *two-week* vacation **OR** a *two weeks'* vacation (**BUT NOT:** a two-weeks' vacation)

b. Hyphenate compound adjectives involving a number and the word *odd* or *plus*.

The embezzlement occurred some *twenty-odd* years ago.

I now simply give my age as *forty-plus*.

c. Compound adjectives involving two numbers (as in ratios and scores) are expressed as follows:

a *50-50* (**OR** *fifty-fifty*) chance a *1000-to-1* possibility
20/20 (**OR** *twenty-twenty*) vision a *3-to-1* ratio **OR** a *3:1* ratio
an *18-7* victory over the Giants **BUT:** a ratio of *3 to 1*

❏ *See also ¶¶450–451.*

d. Other compound expressions involving a number or letter are expressed as follows:

our *number-one** (**OR** *No. 1*) priority a grade of *A plus* (**OR** *A+*)
BUT: our goal is to be *number one* **BUT:** consistently does *A-plus* (**OR** *A+*) work

Title IX provisions a passing mark of *D minus* (**OR** *D−*)
Class A materials **BUT:** a *D-minus* (**OR** *D−*) student

COMPOUND NOUN

818 **a.** A number of adjective-noun combinations (such as *real estate*) and noun-noun combinations (such as *life insurance*) are actually well-established compound nouns serving as adjectives. Unlike *short-term, low-risk,* and the other examples in ¶816, these expressions refer to well-known concepts or institutions. Because they are easily grasped as a unit, they *do not* require a hyphen.

accounts payable records *life insurance* policy *public relations* adviser
civil service examination *mass production* techniques *real estate* agent
high school diploma *money market* funds *social security* tax
income tax return *nuclear energy* plan *word processing* center

EXCEPTION: a *mail-order* business

NOTE: When dictionaries and style manuals do not provide guidance on a specific adjective-noun combination, consider whether the expression resembles a well-known compound like *social security* or whether it is more like *short-term*. Then space the combination or hyphenate it accordingly.

b. When a noun-noun combination involves two words of relatively equal rank, hyphenate the combination.

the *price-earnings* ratio the *space-time* continuum an *air-sea* search
takeoff-landing procedure *labor-management* relations a *sand-gravel* mixture

PROPER NAME

819 **a.** Do not hyphenate the elements in a proper name used as an adjective.

a *Supreme Court* decision a *Rodeo Drive* location
a *Saks Fifth Avenue* store the *Republican Party* platform

---

*Webster does not hyphenate *number-one* before a noun.

b. When two or more distinct proper names are combined to form a one-thought modifier, use a hyphen to connect the elements.

a *German-American* restaurant

the *New York-Chicago-Los Angeles* flight (no hyphens within *New York* and *Los Angeles*)

the cuisine is *German-American*

BUT: the flight to New York, Chicago, and Los Angeles

NOTE: If one of the elements already contains a hyphen, use a dash (two hyphens) to connect the two proper names.

the *Winston-Salem--Atlanta* bus trip

NOUN + ADJECTIVE

820 **a.** When a compound adjective consists of a noun plus an adjective, hyphenate this combination whether it appears before or after the noun. (See ¶815*b*.)

accident-prone	ice-cold	sky-high
age-old	letter-perfect	tax-exempt
bone-dry	machine-readable	tone-deaf
capital-intensive	paper-thin	top-heavy
color-blind	pitch-dark	user-friendly
cost-effective	scot-free	year-round

You are trying to solve an *age-old* problem.

She wants everything to be *letter-perfect*.

We import these *water-repellent* fabrics *duty-free*.

b. A few words in this category are now written solid. For example:

-wide: worldwide, nationwide, countrywide, statewide, countywide, citywide, communitywide, industrywide, companywide, storewide

-proof: waterproof, fireproof, shatterproof, weatherproof

-worthy: airworthy, seaworthy, praiseworthy, newsworthy, trustworthy

-sick: homesick, airsick, carsick, heartsick

-long: daylong, nightlong, yearlong, lifelong, agelong

NOUN + PARTICIPLE

821 **a.** When a compound adjective consists of a noun plus a participle, hyphenate this combination whether it appears before or after the noun. (See ¶815*b*.)

awe-inspiring	law-abiding	market-tested
eye-catching	mind-blowing	panic-stricken
habit-forming	computer-aided	pear-shaped
hair-raising	custom-made	smoke-filled
interest-bearing	jet-propelled	tax-sheltered

Computer-aided design (CAD) is one of the technological breakthroughs of this decade.

The layout of the catalog cover is *eye-catching*.

Buying *custom-made* suits can easily become *habit-forming*.

b. When an open compound noun is combined with a participle to form a one-thought modifier, insert a hyphen only before the participle.

U.S. *government-owned* lands
a *Labor Department-sponsored* conference
a *Pulitzer Prize-winning* play

health care-related expenditures
solar energy-oriented research
property tax-based revenues

c. A few words in this category are now written solid. For example:

hand-:   handmade, handpicked, handwoven, handwritten

heart-:   heartbreaking, heartbroken, heartfelt, heartrending, heartwarming

home-:   homebound, homegrown, homemade, homespun

time-:   timesaving, timeserving, timeworn
      BUT: time-consuming, time-honored, time-sharing, time-tested

ADJECTIVE + PARTICIPLE (see also ¶824b)

822   **a.** When a compound adjective consists of an adjective plus a participle, hyphenate this combination whether it appears before or after the noun. (See ¶815b.)

smooth-talking	high-ranking	half-baked
soft-spoken	friendly-looking (see ¶824a)	half-cocked
odd-sounding	sweet-smelling	half-tempted

EXCEPTIONS: easygoing, halfhearted

I'm *half-tempted* to apply for the Singapore opening myself.

He is a *smooth-talking* operator who never delivers what he promises.

Betty was anything but *soft-spoken* in arguing against the new procedures.

b. Retain the hyphen even when a comparative or superlative adjective is combined with a participle—for example, *nicer-looking, best-looking, oddest-sounding, better-tasting.*

As the *highest-ranking* official present, Mrs. Egan took charge of the meeting.

This year's brochure is *better-looking* than last year's.

ADJECTIVE + NOUN + *ED*

823   **a.** When a compound adjective consists of an adjective plus a noun plus *ed*, hyphenate this combination whether it appears before or after the noun. (See ¶815b.)

broad-minded	high-handed	good-natured
quick-tempered	light-fingered	double-spaced (see ¶812)
green-eyed	flat-footed	high-priced
snub-nosed	full-bodied	middle-aged
sharp-tongued	thin-skinned	old-fashioned
tight-lipped	red-blooded	short-lived (pronounced "līvd")
dog-eared	long-winded	three-sided
two-faced	quick-witted	pint-sized (see ¶823d)

Our success was *short-lived:* the business folded after six months.

These symptoms commonly occur in *middle-aged* executives.

I'm too *old-fashioned* to be that *broad-minded.*

b. Retain the hyphen when a comparative or superlative adjective is combined with a noun plus *ed*—for example, *smaller-sized, highest-priced, best-natured.*

Our *higher-priced* articles sold well this year.

These goods are *higher-priced* than the samples you showed me.

Fred is the *longest-winded* speaker I ever heard.

Fred's speech was the *longest-winded* I ever heard.

c. Some words in this category are now written solid. For example:

-headed: bareheaded, clearheaded, hardheaded, hotheaded, levelheaded
BUT: bald-headed, light-headed

-hearted: bighearted, coldhearted, heavyhearted, openhearted, tenderhearted, warmhearted, wholehearted
BUT: good-hearted, single-hearted

-mouthed: closemouthed, openmouthed, widemouthed, bigmouthed, loudmouthed
BUT: tight-mouthed

-fisted: hardfisted, tightfisted, closefisted
BUT: two-fisted

-sighted: nearsighted, shortsighted, farsighted
BUT: clear-sighted, sharp-sighted

d. Compound adjectives such as *pint-sized, pocket-sized, life-sized, full-sized, king-sized,* and *twin-sized* may also be written without the final *d*.

ADVERB + PARTICIPLE (see also ¶825)

824　**a.** Do not hyphenate an adverb-participle combination if the adverb ends in *ly*.

a *poorly constructed* house　　　　a *privately owned* corporation
a *highly valued* employee　　　　a *newly created* staff

NOTE: Hyphenate adjectives ending in *ly* when they are used with participles. (See ¶822.)

a *friendly-sounding* voice　　　　a *motherly-looking* woman

❑ *To distinguish between adjectives and adverbs ending in* ly, *see* ¶1069.

b. Other adverb-participle compounds are hyphenated *before* the noun. When these same combinations occur in the predicate, drop the hyphen if the participle is part of the verb.

Before the Noun	Elsewhere in Sentence
a *well-known* consultant	This consultant *is* well *known*.
much-needed reforms	These reforms *were* much *needed*.
the *above-mentioned* facts	These facts *were mentioned* above.
the *ever-changing* tides	The tides *are* ever *changing*.
a *long-remembered* tribute	Today's tribute *will be* long *remembered*.

However, if the participle does not become part of the verb and continues to function with the adverb as a one-thought modifier in the predicate, retain the hyphen.

Before the Noun	Elsewhere in Sentence
a *well-behaved* child	The child is *well-behaved*.
a decision with *far-reaching* implications	The implications are *far-reaching*.
a *clear-cut* position	Their position was *clear-cut*.

NOTE: You couldn't say, "The child is behaved" or "The implications are reaching" or "Their position was cut." Since the participle is not part of the verb, it must be treated as part of a compound adjective. Compare the use of *fast-moving* in the following examples.

Before the Noun	Elsewhere in Sentence
a *fast-moving* narrative	The narrative is *fast-moving*.
	BUT: The narrative *is* fast *moving* toward a climax.

c. Hyphenated adverb-participle combinations like those in *b* retain the hyphen even when the adverb is in the comparative or superlative.

a *better-known* brand   the *hardest-working* secretary
the *best-behaved* child   a *faster-moving* stock clerk

d. A few words in this category are now written solid. For example:

-going: ongoing, thoroughgoing

far-: farfetched
   BUT: far-reaching

free-: freestanding, freewheeling
   BUT: free-floating, free-spoken, free-swinging

wide-: widespread
   BUT: wide-spreading, wide-ranging

ADVERB + ADJECTIVE

825 **a.** A number of adverb-adjective combinations closely resemble the adverb-participle combinations described in ¶824. However, since an adverb normally modifies an adjective, do not use a hyphen to connect these words.

a *not too interesting* report   a *very moving* story
a *rather irritating* delay   feeling *extremely tired*

b. Do not hyphenate comparative and superlative forms where the adverbs *more, most, less,* and *least* are combined with an adjective.

a *more determined* person   a *less complicated* transaction
the *most exciting* event   the *least interesting* lecture

PARTICIPLE + ADVERB

826 Hyphenate a participle-adverb combination *before* the noun but not when it occurs elsewhere in the sentence.

Before the Noun	Elsewhere in Sentence
filled-in forms	These forms should be *filled in.*
worn-out equipment	The equipment was *worn out.*
a *tuned-up* engine	The engine has been *tuned up.*
a *scaled-down* proposal	The proposal must be *scaled down.*
a *turned-on* look	The customers are *turned on.*
a *cooling-off* period	Don't negotiate without *cooling off* first.
unheard-of bargains	These bargains were *unheard of.*
warmed-over ideas	He gave us stale ideas that were *warmed over* for the occasion.

❑ *See also the examples in ¶828.*

ADJECTIVE + ADJECTIVE

827 **a.** Do not hyphenate independent adjectives preceding a noun.

a *distinguished public* orator (*public* modifies *orator; distinguished* modifies *public orator*)

a *long* and *tiring* trip (*long* and *tiring* each modify *trip*)

a *warm, enthusiastic* reception (*warm* and *enthusiastic* each modify *reception;* a comma marks the omission of *and*)

❑ *For the use of commas with adjectives, see ¶¶168–171.*

b. In a few special cases two adjectives joined by *and* are hyphenated because they function as one-thought modifiers. These, however, are rare exceptions to the rule stated in *a*.

a *cut-and-dried* presentation
a *hard-and-fast* rule
a *high-and-mighty* attitude

an *open-and-shut* case
an *out-and-out* lie
an *up-and-coming* lawyer

Henry views the matter in *black-and-white* terms. (A one-thought modifier.)

BUT: Sue wore a *black and white* dress to the party. (Two independent adjectives.)

c. Hyphenate two adjectives that express the dual nature of the thing that they refer to.

a *true-false* test

a *compound-complex* sentence

d. Hyphenate repeated or rhyming words used before a noun.

a *go-go* attitude
a *rah-rah* spirit

an *artsy-craftsy* boutique
a *fancy-schmancy* wedding

e. Hyphenate expressions such as *blue-black, green-gray,* and *red-hot* before and after a noun. However, do not hyphenate expressions such as *bluish green, dark gray,* or *bright red* (where the first word clearly modifies the second).

Always use *blue-black* ink in this office.

Her dress was *bluish green.*

PHRASAL COMPOUND

828   **a.** Hyphenate phrases used as compound adjectives *before* a noun. Do not hyphenate such phrases when they occur normally elsewhere in the sentence.

Before the Noun	Elsewhere in Sentence
up-to-date expense figures	The expense figures are *up to date.*
behind-the-scenes negotiations	Negotiations were going on *behind the scenes.*
on-the-job training	I got my training *on the job.*
an *in-depth* analysis	Bergin has analyzed the subject *in depth.*
over-the-counter stocks	These stocks are sold *over the counter.*
run-on sentences	Please fix the sentences that *run on.*
break-even point	At what point will we *break even?*
a *would-be* expert	Roy hoped he *would be* accepted as an expert.
a *pay-as-you-go* plan	This plan lets you *pay as you go.*
step-by-step directions	These directions lead you *step by step.*
a *door-to-door* campaign	We went from *door to door* seeking votes.
a *change-of-address* notice	This notice shows his *change of address.*
a *word-for-word* account	I got the full story *word for word.*
a *yes-or-no* answer	Please answer the question *yes or no.*
a *life-and-death* matter	It is a matter of *life and death.*
stop-and-go traffic	All we did was *stop and go* for two hours.
an *eight-year-old* boy	That boy is only *eight years old.*
a *$150,000-a-year* fee	Our legal fees run about *$150,000 a year.*
straight-from-the-shoulder talk	I spoke *straight from the shoulder.*
a *well-thought-of* strategy	The strategy was *well thought of.*
a *well-thought-out* plan	The plan was *well thought out.*
a *much-talked-about* party	Your party was *much talked about.*

BUT: in the *not too distant* future (see ¶825a)

b. As a rule, do not hyphenate foreign phrases used as adjectives before a noun. (See also ¶287.)

an *ad hoc* committee	a *bona fide* transaction	a *pro rata* assessment
an *à la carte* menu	an *ex officio* member	a *per diem* fee

EXCEPTIONS: an *ad-lib* speech, a *laissez-faire* economic policy

c. When a compound modifier consists of two or more hyphenated phrases, separate the phrases with a comma.

a *penny-wise, pound-foolish* approach to handling money
a *knock-down, drag-out* fight over ownership of the company
the *first-in, first-out* method of accounting
a *first-come, first-served* policy of seating
a *chin-up, back-straight, stomach-in* posture
an *on-again, off-again* wedding

SUSPENDING HYPHEN

829 **a.** When a series of hyphenated adjectives has a common basic element and this element is shown only with the last term, insert a "suspending" hyphen after each of the incomplete adjectives to indicate a relationship with the last term.

long- and *short-term* securities   *10-* and *20-year* bonds   *8½- by 11-inch* paper

b. Space once after each suspending hyphen unless a comma is required at that point.

a *six- to eight-week* delay   a *10- to 12-hour* trip   *3-, 5-, and 8-gallon* buckets

PREFIXES AND SUFFIXES

830 **a.** In general, do not use a hyphen to set off a prefix at the beginning of a word or a suffix at the end of a word. (See ¶808*a* for two exceptions: *ex-* and *-elect.*)

*after*taste	*mini*bike	chang*eable*
*ambi*dextrous	*mis*spell	patron*age*
*ante*date	*mono*syllable	free*dom*
*anti*trust	*multi*purpose	six*fold*
*audio*visual	*non*essential	meaning*ful*
*bi*weekly	*off*beat	cable*gram*
*by*line (**BUT:** by-product)	*out*run	photo*graph*
*circum*locution	*over*confident	convert*ible*
*co*author	*para*medical	misspell*ing*
*counter*balance	*poly*syllabic	fifty*ish*
*de*centralize	*post*test	thank*less*†
*extra*legal	*pre*requisite	book*let*
*fore*front	*pro*active	child*like*†
*hyper*sensitive	*pseudo*scientific	induce*ment*
*hypo*critical	*re*organize	upper*most*
*il*legal	*retro*active	happi*ness*
*im*material	*semi*annual	computer*nik*
*in*defensible	*sub*division	fire*proof*
*infra*structure	*super*natural	censor*ship*
*inter*office	*supra*natural	hand*some*
*intra*mural	*trans*continental	home*stead*
*intro*version	*ultra*conservative	back*ward*
*macro*economics	*un*accustomed	nation*wide* (see ¶820*b*)
*micro*processor	*under*current	edge*wise*
*mid*stream*	*up*shot	trust*worthy*

---

*A hyphen normally follows *mid* in an expression of age or time (as in *mid-sixties*). See ¶¶434, 439.
†If, in the addition of these suffixes, three *l*'s occur in succession, use a hyphen; for example, *bell-like*, *shell-less*.

b. Whenever necessary, use a hyphen to prevent one word from being mistaken for another; for example, *co-op/coop, re-cover/recover, un-ionized/unionized.* (See also ¶832, 834.)

831 When the prefix ends with *a* or *i* and the base word begins with the same letter, use a hyphen after the prefix to prevent misreading.

ultra-active	anti-intellectual	semi-independent
intra-abdominal	anti-inflationary	semi-indirect

832 When the prefix ends with *e* or *o* and the base word begins with the same letter, the hyphen is almost always omitted.

coordinate	reeducate	preeminent	de-emphasize
cooperate	reelect	preemployment	de-escalate
BUT: co-op	reemphasize	preempt	
co-opt	reemploy	preexisting	
co-owner	reenforce	**BUT:** pre-engineered	

NOTE: In a few cases a hyphen follows *co,* even though the base word begins with a letter other than *o.*

co-anchor	**BUT:** coauthor	copartner	cosigner
co-edition	cochair	copilot	cosponsor
	codefendant	coproducer	costar
	coeditor	copublisher	coworker

833 Use a hyphen after *self* when it serves as a prefix.

self-addressed	self-evident	self-study
self-confidence	self-importance	self-supporting

Omit the hyphen when *self* serves as the base word and is followed by a suffix.

selfdom	selfhood	selfness
selfish	selfless	selfsame

834 As a rule, the prefix *re* (meaning "again") should not be followed by a hyphen. A few words require the hyphen so that they can be distinguished from other words with the same spelling but a different meaning.

to *re-collect* the slips	to *recollect* the mistake
to *re-cover* a chair	to *recover* from an illness
to *re-form* the class	to *reform* a sinner
to *re-lease* the apartment	to *release* the hostage
she *re-marked* the ticket	as he *remarked* to me
to *re-press* the jacket	to *repress* one's emotions
to *re-sort* the cards	to *resort* to violence

835 When a prefix is added to a word that begins with a capital, use a hyphen after the prefix.

anti-American	mid-January	pre-Revolutionary War days
non-Asiatic	trans-Canadian	post-World War II period

BUT: transatlantic, transpacific, the Midwest

836 Always hyphenate family terms involving the prefix *great* or the suffix *in-law,* but treat terms involving *step* and *grand* solid.

my great-grandfather	my grandmother	your brother-in-law
their great-aunt	his grandchild	my stepdaughter

837   Avoid feminine suffixes like *ess, ette,* and *trix.*

> She has an established reputation as an *author* and a *poet.* (**NOT:** *authoress* and *poetess.*)

> If you have any questions, ask your *flight attendant.* (**NOT:** *steward* or *stewardess.*)

NOTE: A few terms with feminine suffixes are still widely used; for example, *actress, waitress, hostess, heroine,* and *fiancée.*

838   Use a hyphen after *quasi* when an adjective follows.

> quasi-judicial   quasi-public
> quasi-legislative   **BUT:** quasi corporation

SOMETIMES ONE WORD, SOMETIMES TWO WORDS

839   A number of common words may be written either as one solid word or as two separate words, depending on the meaning. See individual entries listed alphabetically in ¶1101 (unless otherwise indicated) for the following words:

Almost–all most	Into–in to (see *In*)
Already–all ready	Maybe–may be
Altogether–all together	Nobody–no body
Always–all ways	None–no one (see ¶1013)
Anyone–any one (see ¶1010, note)	Onto–on to (see *On*)
Anytime–any time	Someday–some day
Anyway–any way	Someone–some one (see
Awhile–a while	¶1010, note)
Everyday–every day	Sometime–sometimes–
Everyone–every one (see ¶1010, note)	some time
Indifferent–in different	Upon–up on (see *On*)
Indirect–in direct	Whoever–who ever

❏ *Hyphens in spelled-out numbers: see ¶465.*
❏ *Hyphens in spelled-out dates: see ¶411.*
❏ *Hyphens in spelled-out amounts of money: see ¶420.*
❏ *Hyphens in spelled-out fractions: see ¶427.*
❏ *Hyphens in numbers representing a continuous sequence: see ¶459.*

Word Division

Basic Rules (¶¶901–906)
Preferred Practices (¶¶907–918)
Breaks Within Word Groups (¶¶919–920)
Guides to Correct Syllabication (¶¶921–922)

Whenever possible, avoid dividing a word at the end of a line. Word divisions are unattractive, and they may slow down or even confuse the reader. When word division is unavoidable, try to divide at a point that will least disrupt the reader's grasp of the word.

The rules that follow are intended for those who use a typewriter or a word processor. (Typesetters may take greater liberties.) The rules fall into two categories: (1) those that must never be violated (see ¶¶901–906) and (2) those that should be followed whenever space permits a choice (see ¶¶907–920).

NOTE: The 1983 printing of *Webster's Ninth New Collegiate Dictionary* (published by Merriam-Webster, Springfield, Massachusetts) is the authority for the word divisions shown in this manual.

BASIC RULES

901   Divide words only between syllables. Whenever you are unsure of the syllabication of a word, consult a dictionary. (See also ¶¶921–922 for some guides to correct syllabication.)

NOTE: Some syllable breaks shown in the dictionary are not acceptable in typewritten or keyboarded material as points of word division. See ¶¶903–904.

902   Do not divide one-syllable words. Even when *ed* is added to some words, they still remain one-syllable words and cannot be divided.

stressed	through	spring	hour
planned	thoughts	straight	rhythm

903 Do not set off a one-letter syllable at the beginning or the end of a word.

> amaze (**NOT:** a- maze)   media (**NOT:** medi- a)
> ideal (**NOT:** i- deal)   lucky (**NOT:** luck- y)

NOTE: So as to discourage word division at the beginning or end of a word, some dictionaries no longer mark one-letter syllables at these points.

904 Do not divide a word unless you can leave a syllable of at least three characters (the last of which is the hyphen) on the upper line and you can carry a syllable of at least three characters (the last may be a punctuation mark) to the next line.

> *ad*- mit   *de*- ter   *un*- der   *in*- ert
> do- *ing*   re- *new*   set- *up,*   happi- *ly.*

NOTE: Whenever possible, avoid dividing any word with fewer than six letters.

905 Do not divide abbreviations.

> ILGWU   UNICEF   AMVETS   ASCAP
> irreg.   approx.   assoc.   introd.

NOTE: An abbreviation like *AFL-CIO* may be divided after the hyphen.

906 Do not divide contractions.

> haven't   shouldn't   mustn't   o'clock

PREFERRED PRACTICES

While it is acceptable to divide a word at any syllable break shown in the dictionary, it is often better to divide at some points than at others in order to obtain a more intelligible grouping of syllables. The following rules indicate preferred practices whenever you have sufficient space left in the line to permit a choice.

907 Divide a solid compound word between the elements of the compound.

> eye- witness   time- saving   grand- father   master- piece

908 Divide a hyphenated compound word at the point of the hyphen.

> self- confidence   father- in-law   cross- reference   senator- elect

909 Divide a word *after* a prefix (rather than within the prefix).

Preferred		Acceptable	
....	intro-	....	in-
duce	inter-	troduce	in-
national ...	super-	ternational	su-
sonic	circum-	personic	cir-
stances	ambi-	cumstances ...	am-
dextrous		bidextrous	

However, avoid divisions like the following, which can easily confuse a reader.

Confusing		Better	
....	inter-	....	in-
rogate	super-	terrogate	su-
lative	circum-	perlative	cir-
ference ...	ambi-	cumference ...	am-
tious	hyper-	bitious	hy-
bole	extra-	perbole	ex-
neous		traneous	

910 Divide a word *before* a suffix (rather than within the suffix).

> appli- cable (**RATHER THAN:** applica- ble)
> comprehen- sible (**RATHER THAN:** comprehensi- ble)

911 When a word has both a prefix and a suffix, choose the division point that groups the syllables more intelligibly.

> replace- ment (**RATHER THAN:** re- placement)

The same principle applies when a word contains a suffix added on to a suffix. Choose the division point that produces the better grouping.

> helpless- ness (**RATHER THAN:** help- lessness)

912 Whenever you have a choice, divide after a prefix or before a suffix (rather than within the root word).

> over- active (**RATHER THAN:** overac- tive)
> success- ful (**RATHER THAN:** suc- cessful)

NOTE: Avoid divisions that could confuse a reader.

> re- address (**RATHER THAN:** read- dress)
> re- allocate (**RATHER THAN:** real- locate)
> re- apportion (**RATHER THAN:** reap- portion)
> re- arrange (**RATHER THAN:** rear- range)
> re- invest (**RATHER THAN:** rein- vest)
> re- settle (**RATHER THAN:** reset- tle)
> co- insure (**RATHER THAN:** coin- sure)
> co- operate (**RATHER THAN:** coop- erate)

913 When a one-letter syllable occurs within the root of a word, divide *after* it (rather than before it).

impera- tive	pene- trate	simi- lar	congratu- late
nega- tive	reme- dies	apolo- gize	salu- tary

914 When two separately sounded vowels come together in a word, divide between them.

recre- ation	compli- ance	pro- active	influ- ential
athe- istic	experi- ence	po- etic	issu- ing
courte- ous	patri- otic	situ- ated	continu- ous

NOTE: Do not divide between two vowels when they are used together to represent one sound.

quaint	es- teemed	char- treuse	en- croach
clause	per- ceive	pa- tience	ap- point
breach	sur- geon	por- tion	an- nounce

915 When necessary, an extremely long number can be divided after a comma; for example, 24,358,- 692,000. Try to leave at least four digits on the line above and at least six digits on the line below, but always divide after a comma.

916 Try not to end more than two consecutive lines in hyphens.

917 Try not to divide at the end of the first line or at the end of the last full line in a paragraph.

918 Do not divide the last word on a page.

BREAKS WITHIN WORD GROUPS

919   Try to keep together certain kinds of word groups that need to be read together—
for example, page and number, month and day, month and year, title and surname, surname and abbreviation (or number), number and abbreviation, or
number and unit of measure.

page 203	September 1989	Paula Schein, J.D.	10:30 a.m.
April 29	Mrs. Connolly	Adam Hagerty Jr.	465 miles

920   When necessary, longer word groups may be broken as follows:

a. *Dates* may be broken between the day and year.

.... November 14,   **NOT:** .... November
1989 ....   14, 1989 ....

b. *Street addresses* may be broken between the name of the street and *Street,
Avenue,* or the like. If the street name consists of two or more words, the break
may come between words in the street name.

.... 1024 Westervelt   **NOT:** 1024
Boulevard ....   Westervelt Boulevard ....
.... 617 North   **NOT:** 617
Fullerton Street ....   North Fullerton Street ....

c. *Names of places* may be broken between the city and the state or between the
state and the ZIP Code. If the city or state name consists of two or more words,
the break may come between words in the city or state name.

.... Portland,   **OR:** .... Portland, Oregon
Oregon 97229, ...   97229, ...
.... Grand   **OR:** .... Grand Forks, North
Rapids, MI 49505, ...   Dakota, ...

d. *Names of persons* may be broken between the given name (including middle
initial if given) and surname.

.... Mildred R.   **NOT:** .... Mildred
Palumbo ....   R. Palumbo ....

NOTE: If it is absolutely necessary, a person's name may be divided. Follow
the same principles given for dividing ordinary words.

Samuel- son	Eisen- hower
Lind- quist	Spil- lane (see ¶922*c*)
Cala- brese	**BUT:** Spell- man (see ¶922*a*)

e. *Names preceded by long titles* may be broken between the title and the name
(preferably) or between words in the title.

.... Assistant Commissioner   **OR:** .... Assistant
Roy N. Frawley ....   Commissioner Roy N. Frawley ....

f. *A numbered or lettered enumeration* may be broken before (but not directly
after) any number or letter.

.... these points: · **NOT:** .... these points: (1)
(1) All cards should ....   All cards should ....

g. *A sentence with a dash in it* may be broken after the dash.

.... Early next year—   **NOT:** .... Early next year
say, in March—let's ....   —say, in March—let's ....

GUIDES TO CORRECT SYLLABICATION

921 Syllabication is generally based on pronunciation rather than on roots and derivations. Careful pronunciation will often aid you in determining the correct syllabication of a word.

knowl- edge (**NOT:** know- ledge)   prod- uct (**NOT:** pro- duct)
chil- dren (**NOT:** child- ren)   ser- vice (**NOT:** serv- ice)

Note how syllabication changes as pronunciation changes.

Verbs	**Nouns**
pre- sent (to make a gift)	pres- ent (a gift)
re- cord (to make an official copy)	rec- ord (an official copy)
pro- ject (to throw forward)	proj- ect (an undertaking)

922 The following paragraphs offer some guides to syllabication. You are not obliged to divide a word at the points named, but you can safely do so without checking a dictionary.

a. If a word ends in double consonants *before* a suffix is added, you can safely divide *after* the double consonants (so long as the suffix creates an extra syllable).

sell- ers   bless- ing   staff- ing   buzz- ers
BUT: filled, distressed

b. If a final consonant of the base word is doubled *because* a suffix is added, you can safely divide *between* the double consonants (so long as the suffix creates an extra syllable).

ship- ping   omit- ted   begin- ner   refer- ral
BUT: shipped, referred

c. When double consonants appear elsewhere *within* the base word (but not as the final consonants), you can safely divide between them.

bub- bling	dif- fer	recom- mend	cur- rent
suc- cess	strug- gle	con- nect	neces- sary
mid- dle	mil- lion	sup- pose	bet- ter

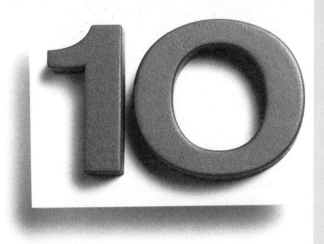

Grammar

Infinitives (¶¶1044–1046)
Sequence of Tenses (¶1047)
Omitting Parts of Verbs (¶1048)
Troublesome Verbs

PRONOUNS

Agreement With Antecedents: Basic Rules (¶1049)
Agreement With Common-Gender Antecedents (¶¶1050–1052)
Agreement With Indefinite-Pronoun Antecedents (¶1053)
Personal Pronouns (¶¶1054–1059)
   Nominative Forms of Personal Pronouns (¶1054)
   Objective Forms of Personal Pronouns (¶1055)
   Possessive Forms of Personal Pronouns (¶1056)
Compound Personal Pronouns (¶1060)
Interrogative and Relative Pronouns (¶¶1061–1063)
   Who *and* Whom; Whoever *and* Whomever (¶1061)
   Who, Which, *and* That (¶1062)
   Whose *and* Who's (¶1063)
Pronouns With *To Be* (¶1064)
Troublesome Pronouns

ADJECTIVES AND ADVERBS (¶¶1065–1073)

NEGATIVES (¶¶1074–1076)

PREPOSITIONS

Words Requiring Certain Prepositions (¶1077)
Superfluous Prepositions (¶1078)
Necessary Prepositions (¶1079)
Prepositions at the End of Sentences (¶1080)
Troublesome Prepositions

SENTENCE STRUCTURE

Parallel Structure (¶1081)
Dangling Constructions (¶¶1082–1085)

SUBJECTS AND VERBS

BASIC RULE OF AGREEMENT

1001 **a.** A verb must agree with its subject in number and person.

I am eager to get back to work. (First person singular subject *I* with first person singular verb *am*.)

You alone *have understood* the full dimensions of the problem. (Second person singular subject *you* with second person plural verb *have understood*. See note below.)

He is coming to stay with us for a week. (Third person singular subject *he* with third person singular verb *is coming*.)

She does intend to call you this week. (Third person singular subject *she* with third person singular verb *does intend*.)

It seems odd that *Farmer hasn't followed up* on our last conversation. (Third person singular subjects *it* and *Farmer* with third person singular verbs *seems* and *hasn't followed up*.)

We were delighted to read about your promotion. (First person plural subject *we* with first person plural verb *were*.)

You both *have been* a great help to us. (Second person plural subject *you* with second person plural verb *have been*.)

They are convinced that the *Parkinsons are* worth millions. (Third person plural subjects *they* and *Parkinsons* with third person plural verbs *are convinced* and *are*.)

Your *order* for six computer terminals *was shipped* last Friday. (Third person singular subject *order* with third person singular verb *was shipped*.)

All our *efforts* to save the business *have been* unsuccessful. (Third person plural subject *efforts* with third person plural verb *have been*.)

NOTE: A plural verb is always required after *you*, even when *you* is singular, referring to only one person.

You do enjoy your work, *don't you?*

b. Although *s* or *es* added to a *noun* indicates the plural form, *s* or *es* added to a verb indicates the third person singular. (See ¶1035.)

Singular	**Plural**
The price *seems* reasonable.	The prices *seem* reasonable
The tax *applies* to everyone.	The taxes *apply* to everyone.

SUBJECTS JOINED BY *AND*

1002 **a.** If the subject consists of two or more words connected by *and* or by *both . . . and*, the subject is plural and requires a plural verb.

Ms. Rizzo and *Mr. Bruce have received* promotions.

Both the *collection* and the *delivery* of mail *are* to be curtailed. (The repetition of *the* with the second subject emphasizes that two different items are meant.)

The *general managers* and the *controllers are attending* a three-day meeting in Chicago this week.

The *director of marketing* and the *product managers are reviewing* the advertising budgets for next year.

The *sales projections* and the *cost estimate do not have* to be revised.

b. Use a singular verb when two or more subjects connected by *and* refer to the same person or thing. (See also ¶1028*a*, fourth example.)

Our *secretary and treasurer is* Frances Eisenberg. (One person.)

Corned beef and cabbage was his favorite dish. (One dish.)

c. Use a singular verb when two or more subjects connected by *and* are preceded by *each, every, many a,* or *many an.* (See also ¶1009*b.*)

Every jacket, suit, and topcoat *is marked* for reduction.

Many a woman and man *has responded* to our plea for funds.

SUBJECTS JOINED BY *OR* OR SIMILAR CONNECTIVES

1003 If the subject consists of two or more *singular* words connected by *or, either . . . or, neither . . . nor,* or *not only . . . but also,* the subject is singular and requires a singular verb.

Either *July* or *August is* a good time for the sales conference.

Neither the *Credit Department* nor the *Accounting Department has* the file.

Not only a cost-profit *analysis* but also a marketing *plan needs* to be developed.

1004 If the subject consists of two or more *plural* words connected by *or, either . . . or, neither . . . nor,* or *not only . . . but also,* the subject is plural and requires a plural verb.

Neither the regional *managers* nor the *salesclerks have* the data you want.

Not only the *dealers* but also the *retailers are* unhappy about our new pricing policy.

1005 If the subject is made up of both singular and plural words connected by *or, either . . . or, neither . . . nor,* or *not only . . . but also,* the verb agrees with the nearer part of the subject. Since sentences with singular and plural subjects usually sound better with plural verbs, try to locate the plural subject closer to the verb whenever this can be done without sacrificing the emphasis desired.

Either *Miss Hertig* or her *assistants have* the data. (The verb *have* agrees with the nearer subject, *assistants.*)

Neither the *buyers* nor the *sales manager is* in favor of the system. (The verb *is* agrees with the nearer subject, *sales manager.*)

BETTER: Neither the *sales manager* nor the *buyers are* in favor of the system. (The sentence reads better with the plural verb *are.* The subjects *sales manager* and *buyers* have been rearranged without changing the emphasis.)

Not only the *teachers* but also the *superintendent is* in favor of the plan. (The verb *is* agrees with the nearer subject, *superintendent.* With the use of *not only . . . but also,* the emphasis falls on the subject following *but also.*)

Not only the *superintendent* but also the *teachers are* in favor of the plan. (When the sentence is rearranged, the nearer subject *teachers* requires the plural verb *are.* However, the emphasis has now changed.)

Not only my *colleagues* but I *am* in favor of the plan. (The first person verb *am* agrees with the nearer subject *I.* Rearranging this sentence will change the emphasis.)

NOTE: When the subjects reflect different grammatical persons (first, second, or third), the verb should agree in person as well as number with the nearer subject. If the resulting construction seems awkward, reword as necessary.

ACCEPTABLE: Neither you nor *I am* in a position to pay Ben's legal fees.

BETTER: Neither *one* of us *is* in a position to pay Ben's legal fees. (See ¶1009*a.*)

ACCEPTABLE: Neither you nor *she has* the time to take on the Fuller case.

ACCEPTABLE: Neither she nor *you have* the time to take on the Fuller case.

BETTER: *She* and *you are* each too busy to take on the Fuller case. (See ¶1009*c.*)

❑ *For* neither *. . . nor constructions following* there is, there are, there were, *or* there was, *see the last four examples in ¶1028a; for examples of subject-verb-pronoun agreement in these constructions, see also ¶1049c.*

INTERVENING PHRASES AND CLAUSES

1006 a. When establishing agreement between subject and verb, disregard intervening phrases and clauses.

The *purchase order* for new supplies *has not been found*. (Disregard *for new supplies*. *Purchase order* is the subject and takes the singular verb *has not been found*.)

The *prices* shown in our catalog *do not include* sales tax.

Only *one* of the items that I ordered *has been delivered*. (See also ¶1008.)

Her *experience* with banks and brokerage houses *gives* her excellent qualifications for the position.

A key *factor*, the company's assets, *is not being given* sufficient weight in the analysis. (The subject *factor*, not the intervening appositive, determines that the verb should be singular in this case.)

BUT: The company's *assets*, a key factor, *are not being given* sufficient weight in the analysis.

NOTE: When certain indefinite pronouns (*all, none, any, some, more, most*) and certain fractional expressions (for example, *one-half of, a part of, a percentage of*) are used as subjects, you may have to look at an intervening phrase or clause to determine whether the verb should be singular or plural. See ¶¶1013, 1025 for examples.

b. When a sentence has both a positive and a negative subject, make the verb agree with the positive subject and regard the negative subject as an intervening element.

Profit and not sales *is* the thing to keep your eye on. (The verb *is* agrees with the positive subject *profit*. Consider *and not sales* an intervening phrase rather than the second part of a plural subject.)

The *design* of the container, not the contents, *determines* what the consumer's initial reaction to the product will be.

The *members* of the Executive Committee and not the president *wield* the real power in the corporation.

It *is* not the president but the *members* of the Executive Committee who *wield* the real power in the corporation. (In the main clause the verb *is* agrees with the subject *it*; the verb *wield* in the *who* clause is plural to agree with the positive subject *members*.)

BUT: It is the *president* and not the members of the Executive Committee who *wields* the real power in the corporation. (In this sentence the positive subject is *president*, a singular noun; therefore, the verb *wields* in the *who* clause must also be singular.)

1007 The number of the verb is not affected by the insertion between subject and verb of phrases beginning with such expressions as:

with	as well as	plus	without
along with	in addition to	besides	except
together with	accompanied by	including	rather than

If the subject is singular, use a singular verb; if the subject is plural, use a plural verb.

Mrs. Swenson, together with her husband and daughter, *is going* to Arizona.

This *study*, as well as many earlier reports, *shows* that the disease can be arrested if detected in time.

The sales *reports*, including the summary, *were sent* to you last week.

No one except you and me *knows* the full story. (See ¶1010.)

10

ONE OF . . .

1008 **a.** Use a singular verb after a phrase beginning with *one of* or *one of the;* the singular verb agrees with the subject *one*. (Disregard any plural that follows *of* or *of the*.)

One of the sales journals *has been lost.*

One of the reasons for so many absences *is* poor motivation.

One of us *has* to take the responsibility.

One of you *is* to be nominated for the office.

b. The phrases *one of those who* and *one of the things that* are followed by plural verbs because the verbs refer to *those* or *things* (rather than to *one*).

She is one of *those* who *favor* increasing the staff. (In other words, of *those* who *favor* increasing the staff, she is one. *Favor* is plural to agree with *those*.)

He is one of our *employees* who *are* never late. (Of our *employees* who *are* never late, he is one.)

I ordered one of the new *copiers* that *were advertised* in *Business Week*. (Of the new *copiers* that *were advertised* in *Business Week,* I ordered one.)

EXCEPTION: When the words *the only* precede such phrases, the meaning is singular and a singular verb is required. Note that both words, *the* and *only*, are required to produce a singular meaning.

John is *the only one* of the staff members who *is going* to be transferred. (Of the staff members, John is *the only one* who *is going* to be transferred. Here the singular verb *is* is required to agree with *one*.)

BUT: John is only one of the *staff members* who *are going* to be transferred. (Of the *staff members* who *are going* to be transferred, John is only one.)

INDEFINITE PRONOUNS ALWAYS SINGULAR

1009 **a.** The words *each, every, either, neither, one, another,* and *much* are always singular. When they are used as subjects or as adjectives modifying subjects, a singular verb is required.

Each has a clear-cut set of responsibilities.

Each employee is responsible for maintaining an orderly work station.

Neither one of the applicants *is* eligible. (**OR:** *Neither applicant is* eligible.) (See ¶¶1003–1005 for the use of *either . . . or* and *neither . . . nor*.)

One shipment *has* already gone out; *another is* to leave the warehouse tomorrow morning.

Much remains to be done. (**OR:** *Much work remains* to be done.)

b. When *each, every, many a,* or *many an* precedes two or more subjects joined by *and*, the verb should be singular.

Every customer and supplier *has been notified*. (See ¶1002c for other examples.)

c. When *each* follows a plural subject, keep the verb plural. In that position, *each* has no effect on the number of the verb. To test the correctness of such sentences, mentally omit *each*.

The *members* each *feel* their responsibility.

They each *have* high expectations.

Twelve each of these items *are required*.

1010 The following compound pronouns are always singular and require a singular verb:

anybody	everybody	somebody	nobody
anything	everything	something	nothing
anyone	everyone	someone	no one
OR any one	**OR** every one	**OR** some one	

Everyone is required to register in order to vote.

Something tells me I'm wrong.

NOTE: Spell *anyone, everyone,* and *someone* as two words when these pronouns are followed by an *of* phrase or are used to mean "one of a number of things."

Every one of us (each person in the group) *likes* to be appreciated.

BUT: *Everyone* (everybody) *likes* to be appreciated.

1011 Use a singular verb when two compound pronouns joined by *and* are used as subjects.

Anyone and *everyone is entitled* to a fair hearing.

INDEFINITE PRONOUNS ALWAYS PLURAL

1012 The words *both, few, many, others,* and *several* are always plural. When they are used as subjects or as adjectives modifying subjects, a plural verb is required.

Several members *were invited;* the *others were overlooked.*

Both books *are* out of print.

Many were asked, but *few were* able to answer.

INDEFINITE PRONOUNS SINGULAR OR PLURAL

1013 *All, none, any, some, more,* and *most* may be singular or plural, depending on the noun that they refer to. (The noun often occurs in an *of* phrase that follows immediately.)

All the manuscript *has been finished.*   *All* the reports *have been handed* in.

Some was acceptable. (Meaning some of the manuscript.)

Some were acceptable. (Meaning some of the reports.)

Is there *any* (money) left?   *Are* there *any* (bills) to be paid?

Do any of you *know* John Ferguson well? (*Any* is plural because it refers to the plural *you;* hence the plural verb *do know.*)

Does any one of you *know* John Ferguson well? (*Any* is singular because it refers to the singular *one;* hence the singular verb *does know.*)

More than one customer *has complained* about that item. (*More* refers to the singular noun *customer;* hence the singular verb *has complained.*)

More than five customers *have complained* . . . (*More* refers to the plural noun *customers;* hence the plural verb *have complained.*)

Most of the stock *has been sold,* but *more* of these suits *are* due.

Some of the material *seems* too high-priced.

Some of the items *seem* too high-priced.

None of the merchandise *was stolen.*

None of the packages *were* properly *wrapped.*

None were injured. (Meaning none of the passengers.)

(Continued on page 186.)

NOTE: In formal usage, *none* is still considered a singular pronoun. In general usage, however, *none* is considered singular or plural, depending on the number of the noun to which it refers. *No one* or *not one* is often used in place of *none* to stress the singular idea.

> *Not one* of the associates *has* a good word to say about the managing partner.

NOUNS ENDING IN *S*

1014 Some nouns appear to be plural but are actually singular. When used as subjects, these nouns require singular verbs.

news *(no plural)*	measles *(no plural)*
lens *(plural:* lenses)	summons *(plural:* summonses)

> The *news* from overseas *is* very discouraging.

> The *lens has* to be reground.

1015 A number of nouns are always considered plural, even though they each refer to a single thing. As subjects, they require plural verbs.

assets	earnings	leavings	proceeds	savings
belongings	goods	odds	quarters	thanks
credentials	grounds	premises	riches	winnings

> The *premises are* now available for inspection.

> My *earnings* this year *are* not what I had counted on.

NOTE: The following nouns are considered plural unless preceded by the term *a pair of*.

glasses	scissors	pliers	pants	trousers

> The *scissors need* sharpening. (**BUT:** A *pair* of scissors *has been taken*.)

1016 A few nouns (not all of which end in *s*) have the same form in the plural as in the singular. When used as subjects, these nouns take singular or plural verbs according to the meaning.

series	means	chassis	headquarters	deer
species	gross	corps	sheep	moose

> The *series* of concerts planned for the spring *looks* very enticing. (One series.)

> Three *series* of tickets *are going* to be issued. (Three series.)

> One *means* of breaking the impasse *is* to offer more money.

> Other *means* of solving the problem *have* not *come* to mind.

> *Headquarters is* not pleased with the performance of the Northeastern Region. (Referring to top management or central authority.)

> The Pesco Corporation *headquarters are located* at the intersection of Routes 80 and 287. (Referring to the offices of top management.)

NOUNS ENDING IN *ICS*

1017 Many nouns ending in *ics* (such as *economics, ethics, politics,* and *statistics*) take singular or plural verbs, depending on how they are used. When they refer to a body of knowledge or a course of study, they are *singular*. When they refer to qualities or activities, they are *plural*.

> *Economics* (a course of study) *is* a prerequisite for advanced business courses.

> The *economics* (the economic aspects) of his plan *are* not very sound.

> *Statistics is* the one course I needed my wife's help in.

> The *statistics indicate* that the market for this product line is shrinking at a rapid rate.

NOUNS WITH FOREIGN PLURALS

1018 Watch for nouns with foreign-plural endings (see ¶614). Such plural nouns, when used as subjects, require plural verbs.

> No *criteria have been established*. (**BUT:** No *criterion has been established*.)
>
> *Parentheses are required* around such references. (**BUT:** The closing *parenthesis was omitted*.)
>
> The *media* through which we reach our clients *are* quality magazines and radio broadcasts. (**BUT:** The *medium* we find most effective *is* television.)

NOTE: The noun *data* (which is plural in form) is commonly followed by a singular verb.

> The *data* obtained after two months of experimentation *is* now *being analyzed*.
>
> **BUT:** The *data* assembled by six researchers *are* now *being compared*. (When the term *data* implies several distinct sets of information, use a plural verb.)

COLLECTIVE NOUNS

1019 The following rules govern the form of verb to be used when the subject is a collective noun. (A *collective noun* is a word that is singular in form but represents a group of persons, animals, or things; for example, *army, audience, board, cabinet, class, committee, company, corporation, council, department, faculty, firm, group, jury, majority, minority, public, school, society*.)

a. If the group is thought of as acting as a unit, the verb should be singular.

> The *Board of Directors meets* Friday.   The *firm is* one of the oldest in the field.
>
> The *committee has agreed* to submit *its* report on Monday. (The pronoun *its* is also singular to agree with *committee*.)

b. If the members of the group are thought of as acting separately, the verb should be plural.

> The *committee are* not in agreement on the action *they* should take. (The verb *are* and the pronoun *they* are plural to agree with the plural *committee*.)

NOTE: The use of a collective noun with a plural verb often produces an awkward sentence. Whenever possible, recast the sentence by inserting a phrase like *the members of* before the collective noun.

> The *members* of the committee *are* not in agreement on the action *they* should take.

c. In a number of constructions, the choice of a singular or plural verb often depends on whether you wish to emphasize the group as a unit or as a collection of individuals. However, once the choice has been made, treat the collective noun consistently within the same context. If the resulting sentence sounds awkward, recast it as necessary.

> I hope your *family is* well. (Emphasizes the family as a whole.)
>
> **OR:** I hope your *family are* all well. (Emphasizes the individuals in the family.)
>
> **SMOOTHER:** I hope all the *members* of your family *are* well.
>
> **OR:** I hope *everyone* in your family *is* well.
>
> The *couple was married* (**OR** *were married*) last Saturday.
>
> **OR:** *Bob and Pauline were married* last Saturday.
>
> The *couple have moved* into *their* new house. (More idiomatic than: "The *couple has moved* into *its* new house.")
>
> **OR:** The *Goodwins have moved* into *their* new house.

NOTE: The expression *a couple of* is plural in meaning.

> A *couple* of customers *have* already *reported* the error in our ad.

COMPANY NAMES

1020 Company names may be treated as either singular or plural. Ordinarily, treat the name as singular unless you wish to emphasize the individuals who make up the firm; in that case, use the plural. Once a choice has been made, treat the term consistently within the same context.

> Brooks & Rice *has lost its* lease. *It is* now *looking* for a new location.
>
> **OR:** Brooks & Rice *have lost their* lease. *They are* now *looking* for . . .
>
> (**BUT NOT:** Brooks & Rice *has lost its* lease. *They are* now *looking* for . . .)

NOTE: If the company is referred to as *they* or *who,* use a plural verb with the company name. If the company is referred to as *it* or *which,* use a singular verb.

GEOGRAPHIC NAMES

1021 Geographic names that are plural in form are treated as *singular* if they refer to only one thing.

> The *Netherlands is* the first stop on my itinerary.
>
> The *United States has undertaken* a new foreign aid program.
>
> **BUT:** These *United States are bound* together by a common heritage of political and religious liberty.

TITLES OF PUBLICATIONS

1022 The title of a book or magazine is considered singular, even though it is plural in form.

> <u>Better Homes and Gardens</u> *has* a handsome spread on the Furlong estate.
>
> <u>Consumer Reports</u> *is publishing* an update on automobile insurance costs.

THE NUMBER; A NUMBER

1023 The expression *the number* has a singular meaning and requires a singular verb; *a number* has a plural meaning and requires a plural verb.

> *The number* of branch offices *has increased* by an annual average of 9 percent.
>
> *A number* of our branch offices *are* now *located* in suburban malls rather than in the central business district.

EXPRESSIONS OF TIME, MONEY, AND QUANTITIES

1024 When subjects expressing periods of time, amounts of money, or quantities represent *a total amount,* use singular verbs. When these subjects represent *a number of individual units,* use plural verbs.

> *Three months is* too long a time to wait.
>
> **BUT:** *Three months have passed* since our last exchange of letters.
>
> That *$10,000 was* an inheritance from my uncle.
>
> **BUT:** *Thousands* of dollars *have* already *been spent* on the project.
>
> *Ten acres is considered* a small piece of property in this area.
>
> **BUT:** *Ten acres were plowed* last spring.
>
> Everybody knows that 2 *and* 2 *equals* 4, that 4 *plus 1 is* 5, and that 5 *times 5 comes to* 25.

FRACTIONAL EXPRESSIONS

1025 When the subject is an expression such as *one-half of, two-thirds of, a part of, a majority of, a percentage of, a portion of,* or *the rest of*:

a. Use a *singular verb* if a *singular noun* follows *of* or is implied.

Three-fourths of the *mailing list has been checked.*

Part of our Norfolk *operation is being closed down.*

A *majority* of *2000 signifies* a landslide in this town. (The noun *2000* is considered singular because it is a total amount. See ¶1024.)

A large *percentage* of the *material has* to be retyped.

b. Use a *plural verb* when a *plural noun* follows *of* or is implied.

Two-thirds of our *customers live* in the suburbs.

Part of the *walls are* to be papered.

A *majority* of our *employees have contributed* to the United Way fund drive.

A large *percentage* of our *students work* part-time.

NOTE: In the following example, the word *half* is a condensed version of *one-half of.*

Over *half* the *staff have signed up* for the additional benefits. (A collective noun such as *staff,* though singular in form, takes a plural verb when it is plural in meaning.)

PHRASES AND CLAUSES AS SUBJECTS

1026 When a phrase or clause serves as the subject, the verb should be singular.

Analyzing financial reports takes all my time these days.

Whether the decision was right or not is no longer important.

That they will accept the offer is far from certain.

Whomever you support is likely to be elected.

EXCEPTION: Clauses beginning with *what* may be singular or plural according to the meaning.

What we need *is* a new *statement* of policy. (The *what* clause refers to *statement;* hence the verb is singular.)

What we need *are* some *guidelines* on personal time off. (Here the *what* clause refers to *guidelines;* hence the verb is plural.)

SUBJECTS IN INVERTED SENTENCES

1027 In sentences in which the verb precedes the subject, make sure that the subject and verb agree.

On the results of this survey *depend the extent* and the *type* of campaign we shall wage.

Attached *are* two *copies* of the January mailing piece.

What *were* your *reasons* for resigning?

What *is* the *likelihood* of our persuading you to stay?

Where *are* the *reviews* of the Carter book?
NOT: Where *is* (**OR** Where's) the *reviews* of the Carter book?

What *is* missing from the report *is* the *rationale* for the decision.

What *appear* to be problems *are* often *opportunities.*

10

1028 **a.** In a sentence beginning with *there is, there are, here is, here are,* or similar constructions, the real subject follows the verb. Use *is* when the real subject is singular, *are* when it is plural.

There *is* a vast *difference* between the two plans.

There *are* a great many *angles* to this problem.

Here *are* a *catalog* and an *order blank.* (See ¶¶1002*a,* 1028*b.*)

Here *is* an old *friend* and former *partner* of mine. (The subject, *friend and partner,* is singular because only one person is referred to. See ¶1002*b.*)

There *is many an investor* who now *wishes* he had bought our stock when it was only $5 a share. (See ¶1002*c.*)

There *is* a *branch office* or an *agency* representing us in every major city in the country. (See ¶1003.)

There *is* not only a *state tax* of 5 percent but also a *city tax* of 2.5 percent. (See ¶1003.)

There *is* the *cost* of your own time in addition to the substantial outlay for materials that must be figured in. (See ¶1007.)

There *is more* than one *way* to solve the problem. (See also ¶1013.)

There *are more* than five *candidates* running for mayor.

There *are* a *number* of problems to be resolved. (See also ¶1023.)

Here *is* the *number* of orders received since Monday.

Here *is ten dollars* as a contribution. (See also ¶1024.)

Here *are ten* silver *dollars* for your collection.

There *is* neither a *hospital* nor a *clinic* on the island. (See ¶1003 for two singular subjects joined by *neither . . . nor.*)

There *are* neither *motel rooms* nor *condominiums* available for rent this late in the season. (See ¶1004 for two plural subjects joined by *neither . . . nor.*)

There *were* neither *tennis courts* nor a *swimming pool* in the hotel where we finally found a room. (*Were* agrees with the nearer subject, *tennis courts.* See also ¶1005 for singular and plural subjects joined by *neither . . . nor.*)

There *was* neither central *air conditioning* nor *fans* for any of the rooms in the hotel. (*Was* agrees with the nearer subject, *air conditioning.* See also ¶1005.)

b. When the subject consists of a series of singular nouns—or a series of nouns, the first of which is singular—*there is* or *here is* usually sounds more idiomatic (despite the fact that the subject is plural) than *there are* or *here are.* If you do not feel comfortable in handling this idiomatic construction, change the wording as necessary.

In the higher-priced model there *is* automatic number *alignment,* automatic right-margin *justification,* and proportional *spacing.* (In this construction, *there is* is understood to be repeated before the second and third subjects.)

OR: In the higher-priced model there *are* the following *features:* automatic number alignment, automatic right-margin justification, and proportional spacing. (In this version *are* agrees with the plural subject *features;* the three subjects in the sentence above are now simply appositives modifying *features.*)

Within a mile of the airport there *is* a full-service *hotel* and three *motels.*

OR: Within a mile of the airport there *is* a full-service hotel *plus* (**OR** *in addition to* **OR** *as well as*) three motels. (By changing the connective from *and* to *plus* or a similar connective, you are left with a singular subject, *hotel,* that calls for the singular verb *is.*)

OR: Within a mile of the airport there *are* three *motels* and a full-service *hotel.* (When the first subject in the series is plural, the verb *are* not only is grammatically correct but also sounds natural.)

SUBJECTS AND PREDICATE COMPLEMENTS

1029 Sentences containing a linking verb (such as *become* or some form of *to be*) sometimes have a plural subject and a singular complement or a singular subject and a plural complement. In such cases make sure that the verb agrees with the *subject* (and not with the complement).

> *Bicycles are* the only product we make.
>
> The key *issue is* higher wages.
>
> *One* of the things we have to keep track of *is* entertainment expenses. (Use *is* to agree with *one*, the subject.)
>
> *It is* they who are at fault. (Use *is* to agree with *it*, the subject.)

NOTE: Do not confuse the last two examples with the *inverted* sentences shown in ¶1028. In a sentence beginning with *here is* or *there is*, the subject *follows* the linking verb. In a sentence beginning with *it is* or *one . . . is*, the subject *precedes* the linking verb.

VERBS

This section deals with the correct use of verb tenses and other verb forms. For the rules on agreement of verbs with subjects, see ¶¶1001–1029.

PRINCIPAL PARTS

1030 The principal parts of a verb are the four simple forms upon which all tenses and other modifications of the verb are based.

a. In most verbs, the past and the past participle are formed simply by adding *d* or *ed* to the present form; the present participle is formed by adding *ing* to the present.

Present	Past	Past Participle	Present Participle	
fill	filled	filled	filling	
need	needed	needed	needing	
taxi	taxied	taxied	taxiing	
drop	dropped	dropped	dropping	(see ¶701)
occur	occurred	occurred	occurring	(see ¶702)
offer	offered	offered	offering	(see ¶704)
argue	argued	argued	arguing	(see ¶707)
die	died	died	dying	(see ¶709)
try	tried	tried	trying	(see ¶710)
obey	obeyed	obeyed	obeying	(see ¶711)

b. Many frequently used verbs, however, have principal parts that are irregularly formed.

Present	Past	Past Participle	Present Participle	
choose	chose	chosen	choosing	
do	did	done	doing	
forget	forgot	forgotten **OR** forgot	forgetting	
see	saw	seen	seeing	
write	wrote	written	writing	
lay	laid	laid	laying	(see ¶1101)
lie	lay	lain	lying	(see ¶1101)

NOTE: The dictionary shows the principal parts for all *irregular* verbs. If you are in doubt about any form, consult the dictionary. If the principal parts are not shown, the verb is regular (see ¶1030*a* above).

c. The past participle and the present participle, if used as a part of a verb phrase, must *always* be used with one or more auxiliary verbs. The most common auxiliary verbs are:

is	was	can	do	has	have	might	shall	will
are	were	could	did	had	may	must	should	would

VERB TENSES

1031 The first principal part of the verb (the *present tense*) is used:

a. To express *present time*.

We *fill* all orders promptly.   She *does* what is expected of her.

b. To make a statement that is *true at all times*.

Water *seeks* its own level.

c. With *shall* or *will* to express *future time*.

We *will order* (**OR** *shall order*) new stock next week. (For the use of these auxiliary verbs in the future tense, see the entry for *Shall-will* in ¶1101.)

❏ *For the third person singular form of the present tense, see ¶1035.*

1032 The second principal part of the verb (the *past tense*) is used to express *past time*. (No auxiliary verb is used with this form.)

We *filled* the order yesterday.   She *did* what was expected of her.

NOTE: Do not use a past participle form to express the past tense.

He *drank* his coffee. (**NOT:** He *drunk* his coffee.)

I *saw* it. (**NOT:** I *seen* it.)

They *began* it together. (**NOT:** They *begun* it together.)

He was the one who *did* it. (**NOT:** He was the one who *done* it.)

1033 The third principal part of the verb (the *past participle*) is used:

a. To form the *present perfect tense*. This tense indicates action that was started in the past and has recently been completed or is continuing up to the present time. It consists of the verb *have* or *has* plus the past participle.

We *have filled* the orders. (**NOT:** We *have filled* the orders yesterday.)

She *has done* what was expected of her.

The consumer movement *has become* an articulate force in today's business world.

b. To form the *past perfect tense*. This tense indicates action that was completed *before another past action*. It consists of the verb *had* plus the past participle.

We *had filled* the orders before we saw your letter.

She *had done* the job before we arrived.

c. To form the *future perfect tense*. This tense indicates action that will be completed *before a certain time in the future*. It consists of the verb *shall have* or *will have* plus the past participle.

We *will have filled* the orders by that time. (See ¶1101 for the use of *shall* and *will*.)

She *will have finished* the job by next Friday.

NOTE: Be careful not to use a past tense form (the second principal part) in place of a past participle.

> I have *broken* the racket. (**NOT:** I have *broke* the racket.)
> The dress has *shrunk*. (**NOT:** The dress has *shrank*.)
> Prices have *risen* again. (**NOT:** Prices have *rose* again.)
> He has *worn* his shoes out. (**NOT:** He has *wore* his shoes out.)

1034 The fourth principal part of the verb (the *present participle*) is used:

a. To form the *present progressive tense*. This tense indicates action still in progress. It consists of the verb *am, is,* or *are* plus the present participle.

> We *are filling* all orders as fast as we can.
> She *is doing* all that can be expected of her.

b. To form the *past progressive tense*. This tense indicates action in progress sometime in the past. It consists of the verb *was* or *were* plus the present participle.

> We *were waiting* for new stock at the time your order came in.
> She *was doing* a good job when I last checked her work.

c. To form the *future progressive tense*. This tense indicates action that will be in progress in the future. It consists of the verb *shall be* or *will be* plus the present participle.

> We *will be working* overtime for the next two weeks. (See ¶1101 for the use of *shall* and *will*.)
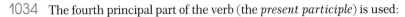
> They *will be receiving* additional stock throughout the next two weeks.

d. To form the *present perfect progressive,* the *past perfect progressive,* and the *future perfect progressive tenses*. These tenses are exactly like the simple perfect tenses (see ¶1033) except that the progressive element suggests continuous action. These tenses consist of the verbs *has been, have been, had been, shall have been,* and *will have been* plus the present participle. Compare the following examples with those in ¶1033.

> We *have been filling* these orders with Model 212A instead of 212. (Present perfect progressive.)
> We *had been filling* these orders with Model 212A until we saw your directive. (Past perfect progressive.)
> By next Friday we *will have been working* overtime for two straight weeks. (Future perfect progressive.)

1035 The first principal part of the verb undergoes a change in form to express the third person singular in the present tense.

a. Most verbs simply add *s* in the third person singular.

he feels	**BUT:** I feel, you feel, we feel, they feel
she thinks	I think, you think, we think, they think
it looks	I look, you look, we look, they look

b. Verbs ending in *s, x, z, sh, ch,* or *o* add *es*.

he misses	he wishes
she fixes	she watches
it buzzes	it goes

c. Verbs ending in a vowel plus *y* add *s;* those ending in a consonant plus *y* change *y* to *i* and add *es.*

say: he says	employ: she employs	try: it tries
convey: she conveys	buy: he buys	apply: she applies

d. Verbs ending in *i* simply add *s.*

taxi: he taxis   ski: she skis

e. The verb *to be* is irregular since *be,* the first principal part, is not used in the present tense.

I am	we are
you are	you are
he, she, it is	they are

f. A few verbs remain unchanged in the third person singular.

he may	she can	it will
he might	she could	it would

❏ *See the entry for* Don't *in* ¶1101.

PASSIVE FORMS

1036 The passive forms of a verb consist of some part of the auxiliary verb *to be* plus the past participle of the main verb.

it is intended (present passive of *intend*)
we were expected (past passive of *expect*)
they will be audited (future passive of *audit*)
she has been notified (present perfect passive of *notify*)
you had been told (past perfect passive of *tell*)
he will have been given (future perfect passive of *give*)

1037 A *passive* verb directs the action toward the subject. An *active* verb directs the action toward an object.

ACTIVE: Melanie (subject) will lead (verb) the discussion (object).

PASSIVE: The discussion (subject) will be led (verb) by Melanie.

❏ *For additional examples, see the entry for* Voice *in the Glossary, page 396.*

a. The passive form of a verb is appropriate (1) when you want to emphasize the *receiver* of the action (by making it the subject) or (2) when the *doer* of the action is not important or is deliberately not mentioned.

I was seriously injured as a result of your negligence. (Emphasizes *I*, the receiver of the action. **RATHER THAN:** Your negligence seriously injured me.)

This proposal is based on a careful analysis of all available research studies. (Emphasizes the basis for the proposal; the person who drafted the proposal is not important.)

Unfortunately, the decision was made without consulting any of the board members. (Emphasizes how the decision was made and deliberately omits the name of the person responsible.)

b. In all other cases use active verb forms to achieve a simpler and more vigorous style. Except in those circumstances cited in *a* above, passive verb forms typically produce awkward or stilted sentences.

WEAK PASSIVES: It *has been decided* by the Personnel Committee that full pay *should be given* to you for the period of your hospitalization.

STRONG ACTIVES: The Personnel Committee *has decided* that you *should receive* full pay for the period of your hospitalization.

VERBS FOLLOWING CLAUSES OF NECESSITY, DEMAND, ETC.

1038 Sentences that express *necessity, demand, strong request, urging,* or *resolution* in the main clause require a *subjunctive* verb in the dependent clause that follows.

a. If the verb in the dependent clause requires the use of the verb *to be,* use the form *be* with all three persons (not *am, is,* or *are*).

NECESSITY: It is necessary (**OR** important **OR** essential) that these questions *be answered* at once. (**NOT:** are answered.)

DEMAND: I insist that I *be allowed* to present a minority report at the next board meeting. (**NOT:** am allowed.)

REQUEST: They have asked that you *be notified* at once if matters do not proceed according to plan. (**NOT:** are notified.)

URGING: We urged (**OR** suggested) that he *be given* a second chance to prove himself in the job. (**NOT:** is given.)

RESOLUTION: The committee has resolved (**OR** decided **OR** ruled) that the decision *be deferred* until the next meeting. (**NOT:** is deferred.)

b. If the verb in the dependent clause is a verb other than *be,* use the ordinary *present tense* form for all three persons. However, do not add *s* for the third person singular.

NECESSITY: It is essential that he *arrive* on time. (**NOT:** arrives.)

DEMAND: They insist that he *do* the work over. (**NOT:** does.)

REQUEST: They have asked that she *remain* on the committee until the end of the year. (**NOT:** remains.)

URGING: I suggested that she *type* the material triple-spaced to allow room for some very heavy editing. (**NOT:** types.)

RESOLUTION: They have resolved that Fred *represent* them. (**NOT:** represents.)

❏ *See the entry for* Mood, subjunctive *in the Glossary, page 391.*

VERBS FOLLOWING *WISH* CLAUSES

1039 Sentences that start with *I wish, she wishes,* and so on, require a subjunctive verb in the dependent clause that follows.

a. To express *present* time in the dependent clause, put the verb in the *past tense.*

I wish I *knew* how to proceed.

I wish I *could attend.*

NOTE: If the verb is *to be,* use *were* for all three persons.

I wish I *were going* to the reception. (**NOT:** was going.)

I wish he *were going* with me.

b. To express *past* time in the dependent clause, put the verb in the *past perfect tense.*

I wish that she *had invited* me.

I wish that I *had been* there.

I wish that I *could have attended.*

c. To express *future* time in the dependent clause, use the auxiliary verb *would* instead of *will.*

I wish he *would arrive* on time.

VERBS IN *IF* CLAUSES

1040   When an *if* clause states a condition that is *highly improbable, doubtful,* or *contrary to fact,* the verb in the *if* clause requires special treatment, like that described in ¶1039: *to express present time, use the past tense; to express past time, use the past perfect tense.* (In the following examples note the relationship of tenses between the dependent clause and the main clause.)

If I *knew* the answer (but I don't), I *would* not *ask* you.

If I *had known* the answer (but I didn't), I *would* not *have asked* you.

If I *were* you (but I am not), I *would take* the job.

If I *had been* in your shoes (but I wasn't), I *would have taken* the job.

If he *were invited* (but he isn't), he *would be* glad to go.

If he *had been invited* (but he wasn't), he *would have been* glad to go.

NOTE: Do not use *would have* for *had* in an *if* clause. See the entry for *Would have* in ¶1101.

1041   When an *if* clause states a condition that is *possible* or *likely,* the verb in the *if* clause requires no special treatment. *To express present time, use the present tense; to express past time, use the past tense.* Compare the following pairs of examples. Those labeled "Probable" reflect the verb forms described here in ¶1041. Those labeled "Improbable" reflect the verb forms described in ¶1040.

PROBABLE: If I *leave* this job (and I may do so), I *will take* a teaching position.

IMPROBABLE: If I *left* this job (but I probably won't), I *would take* a teaching position.

PROBABLE: If I *go* to San Francisco (and I may), I *will want* you to go with me.

IMPROBABLE: If I *were going* to San Francisco (but I probably won't), I *would want* you to go with me.

PROBABLE: If she *was* in the office yesterday (and she may have been), I *did* not *see* her.

IMPROBABLE: If she *had been* in the office yesterday (but she wasn't), I *would have seen* her.

VERBS IN *AS IF* OR *AS THOUGH* CLAUSES

1042   When an *as if* or *as though* clause expresses a condition *contrary to fact,* the verb in the clause requires special treatment, like that described in ¶1040.

She acts as if she *were* the only person who mattered. (But she isn't.)

He talks as if he *knew* the facts of the situation. (But he doesn't.)

You act as if you *hadn't* a care in the world. (But you have.)

1043   *As if* or *as though* clauses are now often used to express a condition that is *highly probable.* In such cases do not give the verb special treatment. *Use the present tense to express present time, the future tense to express future time, and the past tense to express past time.*

It looks as if it *will* rain. (**OR:** It looks as if it *is going* to rain.)

She acted as if she *planned* to look for another job.

INFINITIVES

1044   An infinitive is the form of the verb preceded by *to* (for example, *to write, to do, to be*). When two or more infinitives are used in a parallel construction, the word *to* may be omitted after the first infinitive unless special emphasis is desired.

Ask Ruth Gonzales *to sign* both copies of the contract, *return* the original to us, and *keep* the other copy for her own files. (*Return* and *keep* are infinitives without *to*.)

I would like you *to explain* the job to Harry, *to give* him help if he needs it, and *to see* that the job is done properly. (For emphasis, *to* is used with all three infinitives— *explain, give,* and *see*.)

NOTE: The word *to* is usually dropped when the infinitive follows such verbs as *see, hear, feel, let, help,* and *need.*

Will you please help me *prepare* the report? (**RATHER THAN:** help me *to prepare* the report?)

You need not *return* the clipping. (**OR:** You do not need *to return* the clipping.)

1045 Infinitives have two main tense forms: the present infinitive and the perfect infinitive.

a. The perfect infinitive is used to express action that has been completed before the time of the main verb.

I *am sorry to have caused* you so much trouble last week. (The act of causing trouble was completed before the act of expressing regret; therefore, the perfect infinitive is used.)

b. The present infinitive is used in all other cases.

I planned *to leave* early. (**NOT:** *to have left.* The act of leaving could not have been completed before the act of planning; therefore, the present infinitive is used.)

1046 *Splitting an infinitive* (that is, inserting an adverb between *to* and the verb) should be avoided because (*a*) it typically produces an awkward construction and (*b*) the adverb usually functions more effectively in another location.

WEAK: It was impossible to *even* see a foot ahead.
BETTER: It was impossible to see *even* a foot ahead.

WEAK: He always tries to *carefully* do the work.
BETTER: He always tries to do the work *carefully.*

However, split the infinitive when alternative locations of the adverb produce an awkward or weakly constructed sentence.

a. Before splitting an infinitive, first try to place the adverb *after the object* of the infinitive. In many instances the adverb functions most effectively in that location.

You ought *to review* these plans *thoroughly.*
(**BETTER THAN:** You ought to thoroughly review these plans.)
I need *to make* the decision *quickly.*
(**BETTER THAN:** I need to quickly make the decision.)

b. If step *a* does not produce an effective sentence, try to locate the adverb directly *before* or directly *after* the infinitive. In some cases the adverb functions effectively in this position; in other cases the resulting sentence is awkward.

CONFUSING: I want you *to supervise* the work that is to be done *personally.* (When the object of the infinitive is long or involved, it is difficult to place the adverb after the object without creating confusion. Here *personally* seems to modify *to be done* when in fact it should modify *to supervise.*)

AWKWARD: I want you to supervise *personally* the work that is to be done.

GOOD: I want you *personally* to supervise the work that is to be done.

c. If steps *a* and *b* fail to produce an effective sentence, try splitting the infinitive. If a good sentence results, keep it; if not, try rewording the sentence.

CONFUSING: I want you *to consider* Jenkins' proposal to handle all our deliveries *carefully*. (When *carefully* is located after the complete object, it no longer clearly refers to *to consider*.)

AWKWARD: I want you *carefully* to consider Jenkins' proposal to handle all our deliveries.

AWKWARD: I want you to consider *carefully* Jenkins' proposal to handle all our deliveries.

GOOD: I want you to *carefully* consider Jenkins' proposal to handle all our deliveries.

d. When an infinitive consists of *to be* plus a past participle of another verb, inserting an adverb before the past participle is not considered splitting an infinitive.

These plans need to be *thoroughly* reviewed.

Time appears to be *fast* running out.

NOTE: Nevertheless, in many such sentences the adverb may be located to better advantage elsewhere in the sentence.

❏ *For dangling infinitive phrases, see also ¶1082b.*

SEQUENCE OF TENSES

1047 When the verb in the main clause is in the past tense, the verb in a subordinate *that* clause should also express past time. Compare the tenses in the following pairs of examples:

She *says* (present) that she *is* now *working* (present) for CBS.
She *said* (past) that she *was* now *working* (past) for CBS.

He *says* (present) that he *has seen* (present perfect) your résumé.
He *said* (past) that he *had seen* (past perfect) your résumé.

I *think* (present) that he *will see* (future) you tomorrow.
I *thought* (past) that he *would see* (past form of *will see*) you tomorrow.

EXCEPTION: The verb in the subordinate clause should remain in the present tense if it expresses a general truth.

Our legal adviser *pointed out* (past) that all persons under 18 *are* (present) legally considered minors. (General truth.)

OMITTING PARTS OF VERBS

1048 When compound verbs in the same sentence share a common element, that element does not need to be repeated.

We *have* received your letter and forwarded it to our St. Louis office. (The auxiliary verb *have* is shared by the two main verbs, *received* and *forwarded*.)

We can and will *achieve* these goals. (The main verb *achieve* is shared by the two auxiliary verbs, *can* and *will*.)

However, do not omit any element when different parts of the main verb are required.

WRONG: I never have and I never will forget what you have done for me.
RIGHT: I never have *forgotten* and I never will *forget* . . .

WRONG: We have and still are asking for an accounting of the assets.
RIGHT: We have *asked* and still are *asking* for . . .

TROUBLESOME VERBS

❏ *See individual entries listed alphabetically in ¶1101 for the following verbs:*

Affect–effect	Ensure–insure–assure	Maybe–may be
Appraise–apprise	Enthused over	Of–have
Appreciate	Graduated–was graduated	Raise–rise
Bring–take	Help	Serve–service
Come–go	Imply–infer	Set–sit
Come and	Lay–lie	Shall–will
Comprise–Compose	Learn–teach	Should–would
Done	Leave–let	Try and
Don't	May–can (might–would)	Would have

PRONOUNS

AGREEMENT WITH ANTECEDENTS: BASIC RULES

1049 **a.** A pronoun must agree with its *antecedent* (the word for which the pronoun stands) in number, gender, and person.

I must stand by *my* client, just as *you* must stand by *yours*.

Frank said that *he* could do the job alone.

Alice wants to know whether *her* proposal has been approved.

The *company* has not decided whether to change *its* policy on vacations. (See ¶¶1019–1020.)

The company's *auditors* will issue *their* report tomorrow.

The *Vanderveers* are giving a party at *their* house.

The *grand jury* has completed *its* investigation. (See ¶1019 for collective nouns.)

Why not have *each witness* write *his* or *her* version of the accident? (See ¶1053 for indefinite pronouns as antecedents.)

It is *I* who *am* at fault. (*Who* agrees in person and number with the antecedent *I;* the verb *am* also agrees with *I.*)

It is *they* who *are* behind schedule.

It is *you* who *are* to blame. (*Who* refers to *you;* hence the verb *are* is plural to agree with *you.* See also ¶1001*a*, note.)

BUT: You are the *person* who *is* to blame. (Here *who* refers to *person;* hence the verb *is* is singular to agree with *person.*)

b. Use a plural pronoun when the antecedent consists of two nouns joined by *and.*

Harry and *I* think *we* can handle the assignment.

Can *Mary* and *you* give us *your* decision by Monday?

Sonia and *Dave* say *they* will attend.

The *Montaignes* and the *Reillys* have sent *their* regrets.

c. Use a singular pronoun when the antecedent consists of two *singular* nouns joined by *or* or *nor.* Use a plural pronoun when the antecedent consists of two *plural* nouns joined by *or* or *nor.* (See also ¶¶1003–1005.)

Either *Will* or *Ed* will have to give up *his* office. (**NOT:** their.)

Neither *Joan* nor *Helen* wants to do *her* share. (**NOT:** their.)

Either the *Kopecks* or the *Henleys* will bring *their* videocassette recorder.

(Continued on page 200.)

NOTE: When *or* or *nor* joins a singular noun and a plural noun, a pronoun that refers to this construction should agree in number with the nearer noun. However, a strict application of this rule can lead to problems in sentence structure and meaning. Therefore, always try to make this kind of construction plural by locating the plural subject nearer the verb.

> Neither Mr. Wing nor his *employees have* reached *their* goal. (The plural pronoun *their* is used to agree with the nearer noun, *employees;* the verb *have* is also in the plural.)

> **NOT:** Neither the employees nor Mr. *Wing has* reached *his* goal. (The sentence follows the rule—*his* agrees with Mr. *Wing*, the nearer noun, and the verb *has* is singular; however, the meaning of the sentence has been distorted.)

AGREEMENT WITH COMMON-GENDER ANTECEDENTS

1050 Nouns that apply both to males and females have a *common* gender.

parent	manager	professor	boss	writer
child	doctor	instructor	supervisor	speaker
customer	lawyer	student	employee	listener

When a singular noun of common gender serves as a *definite* antecedent (one that names a specific person whose gender is known), use the pronoun *he* or *she* as appropriate.

> My *boss* (previously identified as Robert Hecht) prefers to open *his* own mail.

> Ask your *doctor* (known to be a woman) to sign *her* name on the attached forms.

1051 When a singular noun of common gender serves as an *indefinite* antecedent (*a doctor, any doctor, every doctor*) or as a *generic* antecedent (*the doctor,* meaning "doctors in general"), the traditional practice has been to use *he* as a generic pronoun applying equally to males and females.

> The *writer* should include a table of contents with *his* manuscript.

When an indefinite or generic antecedent names an occupation or a role in which women predominate (for example, *the teacher, the secretary, the nurse*), the traditional practice has been to use *she* as a generic pronoun.

> A *secretary* needs to organize *her* work and set priorities each day.

1052 The traditional use of *he* and *she* as generic pronouns (described in ¶1051 above) has been under attack for over a decade. Critics feel that the masculine bias in the word *he* makes it unsuitable as a pronoun that applies equally to women and men. Moreover, they feel that the generic use of *she* serves to reinforce stereotyped notions about women's occupations or roles. The ideal solution would be a new generic pronoun without masculine or feminine connotations. However, until such a pronoun has been devised and accepted into common usage, here are a number of alternatives to the generic use of *he* or *she*.

a. Use *he or she, his or her,* or *him or her.* (This solution works well in isolated cases but can be clumsy if repeated frequently in the same context.)

> An *instructor* should offer *his or her* students challenging projects.

> (**RATHER THAN:** An instructor should offer *his* students . . .)

b. Change the wording from singular to plural.

> *Parents* of teenage children often *wonder* where *they* went wrong.

> (**RATHER THAN:** The *parent* of a teenage child often *wonders* where *he or she* went wrong.)

c. Reword to avoid the generic pronoun.

When a customer calls, be sure to ask for a phone number.

(**RATHER THAN:** . . . ask *him or her* to leave *his or her* phone number.)

A secretary tries to anticipate the needs of the boss.

(**RATHER THAN:** . . . the needs of *his or her* boss.)

d. If the application of these various alternatives produces wordiness or an unacceptable shift in meaning or emphasis, use the generic *he* or the generic *she* as described in ¶1051. The generic use of these pronouns continues to be acceptable. However, sensitive writers will try, whenever possible, to avoid it.

AGREEMENT WITH INDEFINITE-PRONOUN ANTECEDENTS

1053 **a.** Use a singular pronoun when the antecedent is a singular indefinite pronoun. The following indefinite pronouns are always singular:

anyone	everyone	someone	no one
anybody	everybody	somebody	nobody
anything	everything	something	nothing
each	every	either	one
each one	many a	neither	another

Every company has *its* own vacation policy. (**NOT:** their.)

Neither one of the campaigns did as well as *it* was supposed to. (**NOT:** they were.)

NOTE: These singular indefinite pronouns often call for the generic use of *he* or *she* (see ¶¶1051–1052). In the following sentences *he* and *she* are correctly used as generic pronouns. However, alternative wording is shown, wherever possible, to suggest how the generic *he* or *she* can be avoided.

Everyone should submit *his* expense account by Friday.

BETTER: All staff *members* should submit *their* expense accounts by Friday.

OR: *Everyone* should submit *his or her* expense account by Friday.

If *anyone* should ask for me, tell *him* that I won't return until Monday.

BETTER: If anyone should ask for me, say that I won't return . . .

While the conference is in session, does *every secretary* know how *she* is to handle *her* boss's correspondence?

BETTER: . . . do *all the secretaries* know how *they* are to handle *their bosses'* correspondence?

Nobody could have helped *himself* in a situation like that.

❑ *For agreement of these indefinite pronouns with verbs, see ¶¶1009–1011; for possessive forms of these pronouns, see ¶637.*

b. Use a plural pronoun when the antecedent is a plural indefinite pronoun. The following indefinite pronouns are always plural:

many	few	several	others	both

Many customers prefer to help *themselves; others* usually like to have someone to wait on *them*.

A *few* of the secretaries have not yet taken *their* vacations.

Several sales representatives made *their* annual goals in nine months.

Both managers have said that *they* want to be considered for Mr. Hall's job when he retires next year.

❑ *For agreement of these indefinite pronouns with verbs, see ¶1012.*

c. The following indefinite pronouns may be singular or plural, depending on the noun they refer to.

all   none   any   some   more   most

When these words are used as antecedents, determine whether they are singular or plural. Then make the pronouns that refer to them agree in number.

Some employees have not yet had *their* annual physical checkup. (*Some* refers to *employees* and is plural; *some* is the antecedent of *their*.)

Some of the manuscript has been typed, but *it* has not been proofread. (*Some* refers to *manuscript* and is singular; *some* is the antecedent of *it* in the second clause.)

❑ *For agreement of these indefinite pronouns with verbs, see ¶1013.*

d. Since indefinite pronouns express the third person, pronouns referring to these antecedents should also be in the third person (*he, she, it, they*).

If *anyone* wants a salary advance, *he* or *she* should apply for it in writing.

(**NOT:** If *anyone* wants a salary advance, *you* should apply for it in writing.)

If the indefinite pronoun is modified so that it strongly expresses the first or second person, the personal pronoun must also agree in number. Compare the following examples:

Most parents want *their* children to go to college. (Third person.)

Most of us want *our* children to go to college. (First person.)

A *few* have missed *their* deadlines. (Third person.)

A *few* of you have missed *your* deadlines. (Second person.)

Each employee knows how much *he* or *she* ought to contribute. (Third person.)

BUT: *Each* of us knows how much *he* or *she* ought to contribute. (Third person. In this sentence, *of us* does not shift the meaning to the first person; the emphasis is on what the individual contributes, not on what *we* contribute.)

IMPORTANT NOTE: **Pronouns take different forms, not only to indicate a difference in person *(I, you, he)*, number *(he, they)*, and gender *(he, she)* but also to indicate a difference in case *(nominative, possessive, objective)*. Although a pronoun must agree with its antecedent in person, number, and gender, it does *not* necessarily agree with its antecedent in case. The case of a pronoun depends on its own relation to the other words in the sentence. The rules in ¶¶1054–1064 indicate how to choose the right case for pronouns.**

PERSONAL PRONOUNS

1054 Nominative Forms of Personal Pronouns
Use *I, we, you, he, she, it, they:*

a. When the pronoun is the subject of a verb.

I wrote to Eileen McIntyre, but *she* hasn't answered.

Debbie and *I* can handle the job ourselves. (**NOT:** Debbie and me.)

Either *he* or *I* can work late tonight. (**NOT:** him or me.)

NOTE: In sentences like the last two above, try each subject alone with the verb. You would not say "Me can handle the job" or "Him can work late tonight." Therefore, *I* and *he* must be used.

b. When the pronoun appears in the predicate after some form of the verb *to be* (*am, is, are, was, were*) or after a verb phrase containing some form of *to be* (see the list below). Pronouns that follow these verb forms should be in the nominative.

shall (**OR** will) be	have (**OR** has) been
should (**OR** would) be	had been
shall (**OR** will) have been	may (**OR** might) be
should (**OR** would) have been	may (**OR** might) have been
can (**OR** could) be	must (**OR** ought to) be
could have been	must have (**OR** ought to have) been

It could have been *they*.	Was it *he* or *she* who phoned?
It is *I*.	This is *she*.

NOTE: Sentences like "It is me" and "This is her" are acceptable in colloquial speech but should not be used in writing. Moreover, a sentence like "It could have been they," while grammatically correct, would be better if reworded in idiomatic English: "They could have been the ones."

❑ *For special rules governing pronouns with the infinitive* to be, *see* ¶1064.

1055 Objective Forms of Personal Pronouns
Use *me, us, you, him, her, it, them*:

a. When the pronoun is the direct or indirect object of a verb.

Larry gave Maris and *us* tickets for the opening.

They invited my husband and *me* for the weekend.

NOTE: When *my husband and* is mentally omitted, the objective form *me* is clearly the correct pronoun ("They invited *me* for the weekend").

b. When the pronoun is the object of a preposition.

This is for *you* and *her*.

No one knows except *you* and *me*. (**NOT:** except you and I.)

Between *you* and *me*, that decision is unfair. (**NOT:** between you and I.)

EXCEPTION: He is a friend of *mine* (*yours, his, hers, ours, theirs*). (See ¶648.)

c. When the pronoun is the subject or object of an infinitive. (See ¶1064.)

The department head asked *him* to resign. (*Him* is the subject of *to resign*.)

Did you ask Janet to call *me*? (*Me* is the object of *to call*.)

1056 Possessive Forms of Personal Pronouns

a. Most personal pronouns have two possessive forms:

my	your	his	her	its	our	their
mine	yours	....	hers	...	ours	theirs

b. Use *my, your, his, her, its, our,* or *their* when the possessive pronoun immediately precedes the noun it modifies.

That is *my* book.   It was *their* choice.   George is *her* neighbor.

c. Use *mine, yours, his, hers, its, ours,* or *theirs* when the possessive pronoun stands apart from the noun it refers to.

That book is *mine*.   The choice was *theirs*.   George is a neighbor of *hers*.

NOTE: Do not insert an apostrophe before the final *s* in possessive pronouns.

d. A pronoun that modifies a *gerund* (a verbal noun ending in *ing*) should be in the possessive. (See ¶647.)

I appreciated *your* shipping the order so promptly.

e. Do not confuse certain possessive pronouns with contractions and other phrases that sound like the possessive pronouns.

its (possessive)	it's (it is **OR** it has)
their (possessive)	they're (they are **OR** there are)
theirs (possessive)	there's (there is **OR** there has)
your (possessive)	you're (you are)

As a test for the correct form, try to substitute *it is* (or *it has, they are, there are, there is, there has,* or *you are,* whichever is appropriate). If the substitution does not make sense, use the corresponding possessive form.

The firm must protect *its* assets. ("Protect it is assets" makes no sense.)

BUT: *It's* time to take stock of our achievements.

Their investing in high-tech stocks was a shrewd idea.

BUT: *They're* investing in high-tech stocks.

Their complaints have proved to be unfounded.

BUT: *There are* complaints that have proved to be unfounded.

Theirs no longer works; that's why they borrow ours.

BUT: *There's* no use expecting him to change.

Your thinking is sound, but we lack the funds to underwrite your proposal.

BUT: *You're* thinking of applying for a transfer, I understand.

❏ *For other possessive pronouns, see also ¶¶636–637.*

1057 When a pronoun follows *than* or *as* in a comparison, determine the correct form of the pronoun by mentally supplying any missing words.

She types better than *I*. (Than *I do.*)

I like you better than *him*. (Than *I like him.*)

Joe is not as talented as *she*. (As talented as *she is.*)

1058 When a pronoun is used to identify a noun or another pronoun, it is either nominative or objective, depending on how the antecedent is used.

The committee has asked *us*, Ruth and *me*, to present the report. (Since *us* is objective, the identifying pronoun *me* is also objective.)

The explanation was for the *newcomers*, Marie and *me*. (Was for *me*.)

The exceptions were the *newcomers*, Marie and *I*. (Exception was *I*.)

Let's *you* and *me* go to the convention. (*Let's* is a contraction for *let us*. Since *us* is the objective form, the explanatory pronouns *you* and *me* are also objective.)

NOTE: In sentences like the following, mentally omit the noun (*employees*) to determine the correct form.

The company wants *us* employees to work on Saturdays. (The company wants *us* to work on Saturdays.

We employees need to confer. (*We* need to confer.)

1059 Some writers consistently use *we* instead of *I* to avoid a seeming overemphasis on themselves. However, it is preferable to use *we* only when you are speaking on behalf of an organization you represent and to use *I* when speaking for yourself alone.

We shall prepare the necessary forms as soon as you send *us* a signed release. (This writer is speaking on behalf of the firm.)

It is *my* opinion that this patient may be discharged at once. (This writer is speaking only for himself. Under these circumstances it would sound pompous to say, "It is *our* opinion.")

COMPOUND PERSONAL PRONOUNS

1060 The *self-* or *selves*-ending pronouns (*myself, yourself, himself, herself, itself, our-selves, yourselves, themselves*) should be used:

a. To direct the action expressed by the verb back to the subject.

She found *herself* the only one in favor of the move.

We have satisfied *ourselves* as to the wisdom of the action.

We think that *they* have insured *themselves* against a possible loss.

b. To emphasize a noun or pronoun already expressed.

The *trainees themselves* arranged the program.

I myself am bewildered.

I will write her *myself*.

NOTE: Do not use a compound personal pronoun unless the noun or pronoun to which it refers is expressed in the same sentence.

The tickets are for the Wrights and *me*. (**NOT:** myself.)

Henry and *I* can distribute all the mail. (**NOT:** Henry and myself.)

INTERROGATIVE AND RELATIVE PRONOUNS

1061 *Who* and *Whom; Whoever* and *Whomever*

a. These pronouns are both *interrogative* pronouns (used in asking questions) and *relative* pronouns (used to refer to a noun in the main clause).

Who is going? (Interrogative.)

Mr. Sears is the one *who* is going. (Relative, referring to *one*.)

To *whom* shall I deliver the message? (Interrogative.)

Ms. DeAngelis, *whom* I have never met, is in charge of the program. (Relative, referring to *Ms. DeAngelis*.)

b. These pronouns may be either singular or plural in meaning.

Who is talking? (Singular.) *Whom* do you prefer for this job? (Singular.)

Who are to be selected? (Plural.) *Whom* do you prefer for these jobs? (Plural.)

c. *Who* (or *whoever*) is the nominative form. Use *who* whenever *he, she, they, I,* or *we* could be substituted in the *who* clause. If in doubt, mentally rearrange the clause as is done in parentheses after each of the following examples. (See also ¶1054*b*.)

Who is at the door? (*She* is at the door.)

Who sang the duet with you? (*He* sang.)

Who shall we say referred us? (We shall say *he* referred us.)

Who did they say was chosen? (They did say *she* was chosen.)

(Continued on page 206.)

Who could it have been? (It could have been *he*.)

The matter of <u>who should pay</u> was not decided. (*He* should pay.)

Everybody wants to know <u>who you think should be appointed</u>. (You think *she* should be appointed.)

<u>Whoever wins the primary</u> will win the election. (*She* wins the primary.)

We will select <u>whoever meets our minimum qualifications</u>. (*He* meets our minimum qualifications.)

I will speak to <u>whoever answers the phone</u>. (*He* answers the phone.)

Please write at once to <u>whoever you think can supply the information desired</u>. (You think *she* can supply the information desired.)

Gloria is the one <u>who can best do the job</u>. (*She* can best do the job.)

James is the one <u>who we expect will win</u>. (We expect *he* will win.)

Please vote for the member <u>who you believe has done the most for the firm</u>. (You believe *he* has done the most for the firm.)

We have referred your claim to our attorney, <u>who we are sure will reply soon</u>. (We are sure *she* will reply soon.)

We have sent this order blank to all <u>who we have reason to believe are interested in our book</u>. (We have reason to believe *they* are interested in our book.)

d. *Whom* (or *whomever*) is the objective form. Use *whom* whenever *him, her, them, me,* or *us* could be substituted as the object of the verb or as the object of a preposition in the *whom* clause.

Whom did you see today? (You did see *her* today.)

To *whom* were you talking? (You were talking to *him*.)

Whom were you talking about? (You were talking about *him*.)

Whom did you say you wanted to see? (You did say you wanted to see *her*.)

It depends on <u>whom they mean</u>. (They mean *him*.)

The question of <u>whom we should charge</u> is at issue. (We should charge *her*.)

<u>Whomever you designate</u> will get the promotion. (You designate *him*.)

I will hire <u>whomever I can find</u>. (I can find *her*.)

I will speak to <u>whomever you suggest</u>. (You suggest *her*.)

I will give the job to <u>whomever you think you can safely recommend</u>. (You think you can safely recommend *him*.)

BUT: I will give the job to <u>whoever you think can be safely recommended</u>. (You think *he* can be safely recommended.)

I need a cashier <u>whom I can trust</u>. (I can trust *her*.)

The man to <u>whom I was referring</u> is Ed Meissen. (I was referring to *him*.)

The person <u>whom I was thinking of</u> doesn't have all those qualifications. (I was thinking of *her*.)

The person <u>whom we invited to address the committee</u> cannot attend. (We invited *him* to address the committee.)

Jo Olsen is the nominee <u>whom they plan to support</u>. (They plan to support *her*.)

Steve Koval is the person <u>whom we all thought the committee would nominate</u>. (We all thought the committee would nominate *him*.)

Elaine Gerrity, <u>whom I considered to be their most promising representative</u>, resigned this month. (I considered *her* to be their most promising representative.)

1062 *Who, Which,* and *That*

a. *Who* and *that* are used when referring to persons. Select *who* when the individual person or the individuality of a group is meant and *that* when a class, species, or type is meant.

She is the only one of my students *who* can speak French fluently.

He is the kind of student *that* should take advanced math.

b. *Which* and *that* are used when referring to places, objects, and animals. *Which* is always used to introduce nonessential clauses, and *that* is ordinarily used to introduce essential clauses.

Laura's report on personnel benefits, *which* I sent you last week, should be of some help. (*Which* introduces a nonessential clause.)

The report *that* I sent you last week should be of some help. (*That* introduces an essential clause.)

NOTE: Many writers now use either *which* or *that* to introduce an essential clause. Indeed, *which* is to be preferred to *that* (1) when there are two or more parallel essential clauses in the same sentence, (2) when *that* has already been used in the sentence, or (3) when the essential clause is introduced by an expression such as *this . . . which, that . . . which, these . . . which,* or *those . . . which.*

Vivian is taking courses *which* will earn her a higher salary rating in her current job and *which* will qualify her for a number of higher-level jobs.

That is a movie *which* you must not miss.

We need to reinforce *those* ideas *which* were presented in earlier chapters.

1063 *Whose* and *Who's*

Do not confuse *whose* (the possessive form of *who*) with *who's* (a contraction meaning "who is" or "who has").

Whose house is it? (It is *his.*)

Who's the owner of that house? (*She* is.)

PRONOUNS WITH *TO BE*

1064 a. If a pronoun is the subject of *to be*, use the *objective* form.

I want *her* to be successful.   I expected *them* to be late.

Whom do you consider to be the more expert driver? (You do consider *whom* to be the more expert driver?)

b. If *to be* has a subject and is followed by a pronoun, put that pronoun in the *objective* case.

They mistook the *visitors* to be *us.* (*Visitors,* the subject of *to be,* is in the objective; therefore, the predicate pronoun following *to be* is objective, *us.*)

They took *her* to be *me.*

Whom do you take *him* to be? (You do take *him* to be *whom*?)

c. If *to be* has *no* subject and is followed by a pronoun, put that pronoun in the *nominative* case.

The *caller* was thought to be *I.* (*I* agrees with the subject of the sentence, *caller.*)

The *Macauleys* were thought to be *we.*

Who was *he* thought to be? (*He* was thought to be *who*?)

NOTE: The examples above are all grammatically correct, but they also sound quite awkward. Whenever possible, use more idiomatic wording. For example, the three sentences above could be recast as follows:

They thought I was the one who called.

The Macauleys were mistaken for us.

What did they think his name was?

TROUBLESOME PRONOUNS

❑ *See the paragraphs indicated for each of the following pronouns. Entries listed in ¶1101 are in alphabetic order.*

All of
  (see ¶1101)
Anyone–any one
  (see ¶1010, note)
Between you and me
  (see ¶1055*b*)
Both–each
  (see ¶1101)
Both alike
  (see ¶1101)

Each other–one another
  (see ¶1101)
Everyone–every one
  (see ¶1010, note)
Most
  (see ¶1101)
Nobody–no body
  (see ¶1101)
None–no one
  (see ¶1013)

Someone–some one
  (see ¶1010, note)
That–which–who
  (see ¶1062)
These sort–these kind
  (see ¶1101)
Who–whom
  (see ¶1061)
Whoever–who ever
  (see ¶1061)

ADJECTIVES AND ADVERBS

For definitions of the terms *adjective* and *adverb*, see the appropriate entries in the Glossary (¶1801, page 387).

1065 Only an adverb can modify an adjective.

> Packard's will give you a *really* good buy. (**NOT:** real good.)

1066 When the word following a verb refers to the *action of the verb,* use an *adverb.*

> He *reads slowly,* but he *talks rapidly.*
>
> She *entered* the room *briskly.*
>
> We guarantee *to ship* the goods *promptly.*
>
> They *were injured badly* in the accident.

TEST: If *in a . . . manner* can be substituted for the *ly*-ending word, choose the adverb.

> *Read* the directions *carefully* (in a careful manner).

1067 When the word following a verb describes the *subject* of the sentence, use an *adjective* (not an adverb). Verbs of the *senses (feel, look, sound, taste, smell)* and *linking* verbs (the various forms of *be, seem, appear, become*) are followed in most cases by adjectives. A few other verbs (such as *grow, prove, get, keep, remain,* and *turn*) are sometimes followed by adjectives.

> I feel *bad* (**NOT** badly).
> She looked *happy.*
> Your voice sounded *strong.*
> He seemed (**OR** appeared) *shy.*
> They became *famous.*
>
> He has grown *tall.*
> The work proved *hard.*
> I got *lucky.*
> Let's all keep (**OR** remain) *calm.*
> The weather has turned *cold.*

TEST: If *is, are, was, were,* or some other form of *be* can be substituted for the verb, choose the adjective.

> He *looks happy.*   He *is happy.*

NOTE: In the following group of examples, verbs of the senses and linking verbs are used as verbs of action (¶1066). Since the modifier refers to the action of the verb (and does not describe the subject), the modifier must be an adverb.

> She *looked suspiciously* at the visitor in the reception room.
>
> He *felt carefully* along the ledge for the key.
>
> That tree *has grown quickly.*
>
> He *appeared quietly* in the doorway.

1068   Several of the most frequently used adverbs have two forms.

close, closely	fair, fairly	loud, loudly	short, shortly
deep, deeply	hard, hardly	quick, quickly	slow, slowly
direct, directly	late, lately	right, rightly	wide, widely

10

a. In a number of cases the two forms have different meanings.

Ship the goods *direct*. (Meaning "straight," "without detour.")

They were *directly* responsible. (Meaning "without any intervention.")

They arrived *late*.　　　　　　　The truck stopped *short*.

I haven't seen her *lately*.　　　　You will hear from us *shortly*.

You've been working too *hard*.　　Turn *right* at the first traffic light.

I could *hardly* hear him.　　　　　I don't *rightly* remember.

b. In some cases the choice is largely a matter of idiom. Some verbs take the *ly* form; others take the short form.

dig deep	go slow	open wide	come close	play fair
wound deeply	proceed slowly	travel widely	watch closely	treat fairly

c. In still other cases the choice is simply one of formality. The *ly* forms are more formal.

sell cheap　**OR**　sell cheaply　　　　talk loud　**OR**　talk loudly

1069   **a.** Although the *ly* ending usually signifies an adverb, a few adjectives also end in *ly*—for example, *costly, orderly, timely, motherly, fatherly, friendly, neighborly, worldly, earthly, lively, lovely, lonely*.

Let's look for a less *costly* solution.

Her offer to help you was intended as a *friendly* gesture.

b. A few common *ly*-ending words are used both as adjectives and adverbs—for example, *early, only, daily, weekly, monthly, yearly*.

I always go to bed at an *early* hour. (Adjective.)

The explosion *occurred early* in the day. (Adverb.)

1070   Words such as *up, in, out, on,* and *off*—commonly recognized as prepositions—also function as adverbs, especially in verb phrases where these words are needed to complete the meaning of the verb.

	Used as Adverbs	Used as Prepositions
up:	to look *up* the definition	to jog *up* the hill
in:	to trade *in* your old car	to see *in the dark*
out:	to phase *out* operations	to look *out the window*
on:	to put *on* a performance	to act *on the stage*
off:	to write *off* our losses	to drive *off the road*

NOTE: When used in headings and titles as *adverbs*, these short words are capitalized; when used as *prepositions*, they are not. (See ¶360c–d.)

1071   Problems of Comparison

a. Form the comparative degree of *one-syllable* adjectives and adverbs by adding *er* to the positive form. Form the superlative degree by adding *est*. (See e on the next page for a few exceptions.)

thin: thinner, thinnest　　　　　　soon: sooner, soonest

b. Form the comparative degree of *two-syllable* adjectives and adverbs either by adding *er* to the positive form or by inserting either *more* or *less* before the positive form. Form the superlative degree by adding *est* in some cases or by inserting *most* or *least* before the positive form.

happy: happier, more (**OR** less) happy   often: oftener, more (**OR** less) often
likely: likeliest, most (**OR** least) likely   highly: highest, most (**OR** least) highly

NOTE: If the positive form ends in a consonant plus *y* (for example, *happy, likely*), change the *y* to *i* before adding *er* or *est*. Some *ly*-ending words drop the *ly* in the comparative and superlative (for example, *highly, higher, highest; deeply, deeper, deepest*).

c. Form the comparative degree of adjectives and adverbs containing *three or more syllables* by inserting *more* or *less* before the positive form. Form the superlative degree by inserting *most* or *least* before the positive form.

competent: more competent   adventurous: less adventurous
acceptable: most acceptable   carefully: least carefully

d. Avoid double comparisons.

cheaper (**NOT:** more cheaper)   unkindest (**NOT:** most unkindest)

e. A few adjectives and adverbs have irregular comparisons. For example:

Positive	Comparative	Superlative
good or well (see ¶1101)	better	best
bad or ill	worse	worst
far	farther, further (see ¶719)	farthest, furthest
late	later, latter (see ¶719)	latest, last
little	littler, less, lesser	littlest, least
many, much	more	most

f. Some adjectives and adverbs, from their very meanings, do not logically admit comparison. (Examples: *square, round, unique, completely, universally, correct, perfect, always, never, dead.*) Nevertheless, a number of these words may be modified by *more, less, nearly, hardly,* and similar adverbs to suggest an approach to the absolute.

Next year we hope to do a *more complete* study.

He is looking for a *more universally* acceptable solution.

Handicraft of this caliber is *virtually unique* these days.

g. When referring to *two* persons, places, or things, use the comparative form; when referring to *more than two*, use the superlative form.

That is the *finer* piece of linen. (Only two pieces are involved; hence the comparative.)

This is the *finest* piece of linen I could find. (Many pieces are involved; hence the superlative.)

Of the two positions open, you have chosen the *more* promising.

Of the three positions open, you have chosen the *most* promising.

That is the *more* efficient of the two methods.

This is the *most* efficient method that could be devised.

I like Evelyn's plan *better* than Joe's or Betty's. (Although three things are involved in this comparison, they are being compared two at a time; hence the comparative.)

h. When comparing a person or a thing *within* the group to which it belongs, use the superlative. When comparing a person or a thing with individual members of the group, use the comparative and the words *other* or *else*.

10

Susan is the *most* conscientious employee on the staff.

Susan is *more* conscientious than any *other* employee on the staff. (Without the word *other*, the sentence would imply that Susan is not on the staff.)

Los Angeles is the *largest* city in California.

Los Angeles is *larger* than any *other* city in California. (Without *other*, the sentence would imply that Los Angeles is not in California.)

Bert's proposal was the *best* of all that were presented to the committee.

Bert's proposal was *better* than anyone *else's*. (**NOT:** anyone's.)

i. Be sure to compare like things. (See also ¶644, note.)

This year's output is lower than last year's. (In other words, "This year's *output* is lower than last year's *output*.")

NOT: This year's output is lower than last year. (Incorrectly compares *this year's output* with *last year*.)

1072 The adverbs *only, nearly, almost, ever, scarcely, merely, too,* and *also* should be placed as close to the word modified—usually before—as possible. Putting the adverb in the wrong position may change the entire meaning of the sentence.

Our list of depositors numbers *almost* 50,000. (**NOT:** almost numbers.)

Only the Board of Directors can nominate the three new officers. (Cannot be nominated by anyone else.)

The Board of Directors can *only* nominate the three officers. (They cannot elect.)

The Board of Directors can nominate *only* the three officers. (They cannot nominate anyone else.)

Only Robert liked her. (No one else liked her.)

Robert *only* liked her. (Robert did not love her.)

Robert liked *only* her. (Robert liked no one else.)

1073 Do not use an adverb to express a meaning already contained in the verb.

assemble (**NOT:** assemble together)	finish (**NOT:** finish up or off)
begin (**NOT:** first begin)	follow (**NOT:** follow after)
cancel (**NOT:** cancel out)	refer (**NOT:** refer back)
continue (**NOT:** continue on)	repeat (**NOT:** repeat again)
convert (**NOT:** convert over)	return (**NOT:** return back)
cooperate (**NOT:** cooperate together)	revert (**NOT:** revert back)

TROUBLESOME ADJECTIVES AND ADVERBS

❑ *For the following adjectives and adverbs, see individual entries listed alphabetically in* ¶1101.

A–an	Ex–former	More important–
Accidentally	Farther–further	more importantly
All right	Fewer–less	Only
Almost–all most	First–firstly, etc.	Real–really
Already–all ready	Flammable–inflammable	Said
Altogether–all	Former–first	Same
together	Good–well	Scarcely
Always–all ways	Hardly	Someday–some day
Anxious–eager	Healthy–healthful	Sometime–
Anytime–any time	Hopefully	sometimes–some time
Anyway–any way	Incidentally	Sure–surely
Awhile–a while	Indifferent–in different	This here
Bad–badly	Indirect–in direct	Unique
Different–differently	Last–latest	Up
Equally as good	Latter–last	Very
Everyday–every day	Maybe–may be	Wise

NEGATIVES

1074 To express a negative idea in a simple sentence, use only one negative expression in the sentence. (A *double negative*—two negative expressions in the same sentence—gives a *positive* meaning.)

> We can sit by and do *nothing*.
>
> We can*not* sit by and do *nothing*. (The *not* and *nothing* create a double negative; the sentence now has a positive meaning: "We ought to do something.")
>
> Jim is *un*aware of the facts. (Here the negative element is the prefix *un*.)
>
> Jim is *not un*aware of the facts. (With the double negative, the sentence means "Jim *is* aware of the facts.")

NOTE: A double negative is not wrong in itself. As the examples above indicate, a double negative may offer a more effective way of expressing a *positive thought* than a straightforward positive construction would. However, a double negative *is* wrong if the sentence is intended to have a negative meaning. Remember that two negatives make a positive.

1075 A negative expression gives a negative meaning to the *clause* in which it appears. In a simple sentence, where there is only one clause, the negative expression affects the entire sentence (see ¶1074). In a sentence where there are two or more clauses, a negative expression affects only the clause in which it appears. Therefore, each clause may safely contain one negative expression. A double negative results when there are two negative expressions within the *same* clause.

> If Mr. Bogosian can*not* lower his price, there is *no* point in continuing the negotiations. (The *if* clause contains the negative *not;* the main clause contains the negative *no*. Each clause has its own negative meaning.)
>
> I have *not* met Halliday, and I have *no* desire to meet him.
>
> **OR:** I have *not* met Halliday, *nor* do I have *any* desire to meet him. (When the negative conjunction *nor* replaces *and*, the adjective *no* changes to *any* so as to avoid a double negative.)
>
> We have *never* permitted, *nor* will we permit, any lowering of our standards. (Here the second clause interrupts the first clause. If written out in full, the sentence would read, "We have *never* permitted any lowering of our standards, *nor* will we permit any lowering of our standards.")

NOTE: A second negative expression may be used in a clause to repeat or intensify the first negative expression. This construction is not a double negative.

> *No*, I did *not* make that statement.
>
> He would *never, never* do a thing like that.

1076 To preserve the *negative* meaning of a clause, follow these basic principles:

a. If the clause has a *negative verb* (a verb modified by *not* or *never*), do not use any additional negative expressions, such as *nor, neither . . . nor, no, none, no one*, or *nothing*. Instead, use corresponding positive expressions such as *or, either . . . or, any, anyone*, or *anything*.

> I have *not* invited *anyone*. (**WRONG:** I have *not* invited *no one*.)
>
> She does *not* want *any*. (**WRONG:** She does *not* want *none*.)
>
> Mary did *not* have *anything* to do. (**WRONG:** Mary did *not* have *nothing* to do.)
>
> I can*not* find *either* the letter *or* the envelope. (**WRONG:** I can*not* find *neither* the letter *nor* the envelope.)
>
> He did *not* say whether he would mail the money to us *or* whether he would bring it himself. (**WRONG:** He did *not* say whether he would mail the money to us *nor* whether he would bring it himself.)

b. If a clause contains any one of the following expressions—*no, no one, none, nothing,* or *neither . . . nor* (this counts as one expression)—make sure that the verb and all other words are *positive.*

I see *nothing* wrong with *either* proposal. (**NOT:** neither proposal.)

Neither Paul Gutowski *nor* Yvonne Christopher *can* handle the meeting for me next Thursday. (**NOT:** cannot.)

c. The word *nor* may be used alone as a conjunction (see the third and fourth examples in ¶1075) or together with *neither.* Do not use *nor* in the same clause with any other negative; use *or* instead.

There are *neither* pens *nor* pencils in the stockroom.
BUT: There are *no* pens *or* pencils in the stockroom. (**WRONG:** *no* pens *nor* pencils.)

There are *no* clear-cut rights *or* wrongs in the situation. (**WRONG:** *no . . .* rights *nor* wrongs.)

Francine has *not* called *or* written us for some time. (**WRONG:** *not* called *nor* written.)

Never try to argue *or* debate with Larry. (**WRONG:** *Never . . .* argue *nor* debate.)

❏ *For* Hardly, Only, *and* Scarcely, *which have a negative meaning, see individual entries in ¶1101.*

PREPOSITIONS

WORDS REQUIRING CERTAIN PREPOSITIONS

1077 Usage requires that certain words be followed by certain prepositions. Some of the most frequently used combinations are listed below.

account for something or someone: I find it hard to *account for* his behavior.

account to someone: You will have to *account to* Anne Cuneo for the loss of the key.

agree on or **upon** (reach an understanding): We cannot *agree on* the price.

agree to (accept another person's plan): Will you *agree to* their terms?

agree with (concur with a person or an idea): I *agree with* your objectives.

angry at or **about** something: He was *angry about* the total disorder of the office.

angry with someone: You have every right to be *angry with* me.

apply for a position: You ought to *apply for* Harry's job, now that he has left.

apply to someone or something: You must *apply* yourself *to* the job in order to master it. I am thinking of *applying to* the Field Engineering Company.

argue about something: We *argued about* the terms of the contract.

argue with a person: It doesn't pay to *argue with* Bremer.

compare to (assert a likeness): She *compared* my writing *to* E. B. White's. (She said I wrote like E. B. White.)

compare with (analyze for similarities and differences): When she *compared* my writing *with* E. B. White's, she said that I had a similar kind of humor but that my sentences lacked the clean and easy flow of White's material.

conform to (preferred to *with*): These blueprints do not *conform to* the original plans.

consists in (exists in): Happiness largely *consists in* knowing what it is that will make you happy.

consists of (is made up of): Their new formula for a wage settlement *consists of* the same old terms expressed in different language.

(Continued on page 214.)

convenient for (suitable): What time will be most *convenient for* you?

convenient to (near at hand): Our plant is *convenient to* all transportation facilities in the area.

correspond to (agree with): The shipment does not *correspond to* the sample.

correspond with (exchange letters with): It may be better to see him in person than to *correspond with* him.

differ about (something): We *differed about* means but not about objectives.

differ from (something else): This job *differs* very little *from* the one that I used to have.

differ with (someone): I *differ with* you over the consequences of our plan.

different from: This product is *different from* the one I normally use.

different than: I view the matter in a *different* way *than* you do. (Although *from* is normally preferred, *than* is acceptable in order to avoid sentences like "I view the matter in a different way from the way in which you do.")

identical with (not *to*): This $180 suit is *identical with* one advertised for $235 at other stores.

independent of (not *from*): He wants to be *independent of* his family's money.

interested in: We are *interested in* discussing the matter further with you at the conference in July.

retroactive to (not *from*): This salary adjustment is *retroactive to* May 1.

speak to (tell something to): You must *speak to* them about their frequent absences.

speak with (discuss with): It was good to *speak with* you yesterday.

SUPERFLUOUS PREPOSITIONS

1078 Omit prepositions that add nothing to the meaning—as in the following examples. (See also the entry for *All of* in ¶1101.)

Where is she [at]?

Where did that paper go [to]?

The new applicant seems to be [of] about sixteen years of age.

She could not help [from] laughing.

His house is opposite [to] hers.

The chair is too near [to] the desk.

Why don't we meet at about one o'clock? (Omit either *at* or *about*.)

The carton fell off [of] the truck.

The strike is now over [with].

NECESSARY PREPOSITIONS

1079 Conversely, do not omit essential prepositions.

I bought a couple *of* books. (**NOT:** I bought a couple books.)

Of what use is this gadget? (**NOT:** What use is this gadget?)

We don't sell that type *of* filter. (**NOT:** We don't sell that type filter.)

You seem to have a great interest *in,* as well as a deep respect *for,* fine antiques. (**NOT:** You seem to have a great interest, as well as a deep respect *for,* fine antiques.)

She frequently appears in movies, *in* plays, and on television. (**NOT:** in movies, plays, and on television.)

NOTE: The preposition *of* is understood in expressions such as *what color cloth* and *what size shoes.*

PREPOSITIONS AT THE END OF SENTENCES

1080 Whether or not a sentence should end with a preposition depends on the emphasis and effect desired.

INFORMAL: I wish I knew which magazine her article appeared *in*.

FORMAL: I wish I knew the magazine *in which* her article appeared.

STILTED: It is difficult to know *about* what you are thinking.

NATURAL: It is difficult to know what you are thinking *about*.

Short questions frequently end with prepositions.

How many can I count *on*?   What is this good *for*?

What is this made *of*?   We need tools to work *with*.

TROUBLESOME PREPOSITIONS

❑ *For the following prepositions, see individual entries listed alphabetically in ¶1101.*

At about	From–off	Off
Beside–besides	In–into–in to	On–onto–on to
Between–among	In regards to	On–upon–up on
Due to–because of–	Indifferent–in different	Opposite
on account of	Indirect–in direct	Per–a
Except	Like–as, as if	Toward–towards
	Of–have	

SENTENCE STRUCTURE

PARALLEL STRUCTURE

1081 Express parallel ideas in parallel form.

a. Adjectives should be paralleled by adjectives, nouns by nouns, infinitives by infinitives, subordinate clauses by subordinate clauses, etc.

WRONG: Your new sales training program was *stimulating* and a *challenge*. (Adjective and noun.)

RIGHT: Your new sales training program was *stimulating* and *challenging*. (Two adjectives.)

WRONG: The sales representatives have already started *using* the new techniques and *to produce* higher sales. (Participial phrase and infinitive phrase.)

RIGHT: The sales representatives have already started *using* the new techniques and *producing* higher sales. (Two participial phrases.)

RIGHT: The sales representatives have already started *to use* the new techniques and *produce* higher sales. (Two infinitive phrases.)

WRONG: This desk copier is *easy* to operate, *efficient*, and *it is relatively inexpensive*. (Two adjectives and a clause.)

RIGHT: This desk copier is *easy* to operate, *efficient*, and relatively *inexpensive*. (Three adjectives.)

NOTE: Parallelism is especially important in displayed enumerations.

POOR: This article will discuss:

      1. How to deal with corporate politics.
      2. Coping with stressful situations.
      3. What the role of the manager should be in the outside community.

(Continued on page 216.)

BETTER: This article will discuss:

    1. *Ways* to deal with corporate politics.
    2. *Techniques* of coping with stressful situations.
    3. The *role* of the manager in the outside community.

OR: This article will tell managers how to:

    1. Deal with corporate politics.
    2. Cope with stressful situations.
    3. Function in the outside community.

b. Correlative conjunctions (*both . . . and, either . . . or, neither . . . nor, not only . . . but also, whether . . . or,* etc.) should be followed by elements in parallel form.

WRONG: Kevin is not only gifted as a painter but also as a sculptor.

RIGHT: Kevin is gifted not only *as a painter* but also *as a sculptor.*

WRONG: We are flying both to Chicago and San Francisco.

RIGHT: We are flying to both *Chicago* and *San Francisco.*

RIGHT: We are flying both *to Chicago* and *to San Francisco.*

WRONG: He would neither apologize nor would he promise to reform.

RIGHT: He would neither *apologize* nor *promise to reform.*

RIGHT: He would not apologize, nor would he promise to reform.

DANGLING CONSTRUCTIONS

1082 When a sentence begins with a participial phrase, an infinitive phrase, a gerund phrase, or an elliptical clause (one in which essential words are missing), make sure that the phrase or clause logically agrees with the subject of the sentence; otherwise, the construction will "dangle." To correct a dangling construction, make the subject of the sentence the doer of the action expressed by the opening phrase or clause. If that is not feasible, use an entirely different construction.

a. Participial Phrases

WRONG: Having studied your cost estimates, a few *questions* occur to me. (As worded, this version implies that the *questions* have studied the cost estimates.)

RIGHT: Having studied your cost estimates, I would like to ask you a few questions. (As corrected, the person who studied the cost estimates is now the subject of the sentence and is the one asking the questions.)

WRONG: Putting the matter of costs aside, the *matter* of production delays remains to be discussed.

RIGHT: Putting the matter of costs aside, *we* must still discuss the matter of production delays.

NOTE: A few words ending in *ing* (such as *concerning, considering, pending,* and *regarding*) have now become established as prepositions. Therefore, when they introduce phrases at the start of a sentence, it is not essential that they refer to the subject of the sentence.

Considering how long the lawsuit has dragged on, it might have been wiser not to sue.

b. Infinitive Phrases

WRONG: To appreciate the full significance of Fox's latest letter, all the previous correspondence should be read.

RIGHT: To appreciate the full significance of Fox's latest letter, you should read all the previous correspondence.

WRONG: To obtain this free booklet, the coupon should be mailed at once.

RIGHT: To obtain this free booklet, mail the coupon at once.

c. Prepositional-Gerund Phrases

WRONG: In passing your store windows, many handsome displays caught my eye.

RIGHT: In passing your store windows, I noticed many handsome displays.

WRONG: By installing a computerized temperature control system, a substantial saving in fuel costs was achieved.

RIGHT: By installing a computerized temperature control system, we achieved a substantial saving in fuel costs.

WRONG: In analyzing these specifications, several errors have been found.

RIGHT: In analyzing these specifications, I have found several errors.

d. Elliptical Clauses

WRONG: If ordered before May 1, a 5 percent discount will be allowed on these goods.

RIGHT: If ordered before May 1, these goods will be sold at a 5 percent discount.

WRONG: When four years old, my family moved to Omaha.

RIGHT: When I was four years old, my family moved to Omaha.

e. Absolute Phrases

Absolute phrases (typically involving passive participles) are not considered to "dangle," even though they come at the beginning of a sentence and do not refer to the subject. Such constructions, though grammatically correct, are usually awkward and should be avoided.

WEAK: The speeches having been concluded, we proceeded to take a vote.

BETTER: After the speeches were concluded, we proceeded to take a vote.

1083 When verbal phrases and elliptical clauses fall elsewhere in the sentence, be alert for illogical or confusing relationships. Adjust the wording as necessary.

WRONG: I saw two truck drivers get into a fistfight while jogging down the street.

RIGHT: While jogging down the street, I saw two truck drivers get into a fistfight.

1084 A prepositional phrase will dangle at the beginning of a sentence if it leads the reader to expect a certain word as the subject and then another word is used instead.

WRONG: As head of the program committee, we think you should make immediate arrangements for another speaker. (The head of the committee is *you*, not *we*.)

RIGHT: We think that as head of the program committee you should make immediate arrangements for another speaker.

1085 A verbal phrase will dangle at the end of a sentence if it refers to the meaning of the main clause as a whole rather than to the doer of the action.

WRONG: Our sales have been steadily declining for the past six months, thus creating a sharp drop in profits. (As worded, the sentence makes it appear that *our sales*, by themselves, have created the drop in profits. Actually, it is *the fact* that our sales have been declining which has created the drop in profits.)

RIGHT: The steady decline in our sales for the past six months has created a sharp drop in profits.

RIGHT: Our sales have been steadily declining for the past six months. As a result, we have experienced a sharp drop in profits.

Usage

A–An
A–Of
Accidentally
A.D.–B.C.
Affect–Effect
Age–Aged–At the Age of
All of
All Right
Almost–All Most
Already–All Ready
Altogether–All Together
Always–All Ways
Amount–Number
And
And Etc.
And/Or
Anxious–Eager
Anyone–Any One
Anytime–Any Time
Anyway–Any Way
Appraise–Apprise
Appreciate
As
As . . . as–Not so . . . as
At About
Awhile–A While
Bad–Badly
Balance
Being That
Beside–Besides
Between–Among
Between You and Me
Both–Each

Both Alike–Equal–Together
Bring–Take
But . . . However
But What
Cannot Help But
Class
Come–Go
Come and
Comprise–Compose
Data
Different–Differently
Different From–Different Than
Done
Don't (Do Not)
Doubt That–Doubt Whether
Due to–Because of–On Account of
Each Other–One Another
Ensure–Insure–Assure
Enthused Over
Equally as Good
Etc.
Everyday–Every Day
Everyone–Every One
Ex–Former
Except
Farther–Further
Fewer–Less
First–Firstly, etc.
Flammable–Inflammable
Former–First
From–Off
Good–Well
Graduated–Was Graduated

Hardly
Healthy–Healthful
Help
Hopefully
If–Whether
Imply–Infer
In–Into–In to
In Regards to
Incidentally
Indifferent–In Different
Indirect–In Direct
Individual–Party–Person–People
Irregardless
Is Where–Is When
Its–It's
Kind
Kind of–Sort of
Kind of a
Last–Latest
Latter–Last
Lay–Lie
Learn–Teach
Leave–Let
Like–As, As if
Literally
May–Can (Might–Could)
Maybe–May Be
Media
More Important–More Importantly
Most
Nobody–No Body
None–No One
Of–Have
Off
On–Onto–On to
On–Upon–Up on
Only
Opposite
Per–A

Percent–Percentage
Plus
Raise–Rise
Real–Really
Reason Is Because
Retroactive to
Said
Same
Scarcely
Serve–Service
Set–Sit
Shall–Will
Should–Would
So–So That
Someday–Some Day
Someone–Some One
Sometime–Sometimes–Some Time
Sort
Such as . . . etc.
Sure–Surely
Sure and
Tack–Tact
Than–Then
That–Which–Who
These Sort–These Kind
This Here
Toward–Towards
Try and
Type
Unique
Up
Very
Ways
Where–That
Who–Which–That
Who–Whom
Whoever–Who Ever
Wise
Would Have

11

1101　The following words and phrases are often used incorrectly.

A–an.　In choosing *a* or *an,* consider the sound (not the spelling) of the following word. Use the article *a* before all *consonant* sounds, including sounded *h,* long *u,* and *o* with the sound of *w* (as in *one*).

a day	a home	a unit	a youthful spirit	a one-week delay
a week	a house	a union	a euphoric feeling	a 60-day note
a year	a hotel	a uniform	a European trip	a CPA

Use *an* before all *vowel* sounds except long *u* and before words beginning with silent *h.*

an asset	an outcome	an heir	an X ray (pronounced "ex ray")
an essay	an upsurge	an hour	an f.o.b. order (pronounced "ef oh bee")
an input	an eyesore	an honor	an 8-hour day

NOTE:　In speech, both *a historic occasion* and *an historic occasion* are correct, depending on whether the *h* is sounded or left silent. In writing, *a historic occasion* is the form more commonly used.

A–of.　Do not use *a* in place of *of.*

What sort *of* turnout did you have at your seminar?
(**NOT:** What sort *a* turnout did you have at your seminar?)

The weather has been kind *of* cool for this time of year.
(**NOT:** The weather has been *kinda* cool for this time of year.)

❑ *See* Kind of–sort of *and* Kind of a.

A–per.　See *Per–a.*

Accidentally.　Note that this word ends in *ally.* (The form *accidently* is incorrect.)

A.D.–B.C.　*A.D.* (abbreviation of *anno Domini,* Latin for "in the year of our Lord") and *B.C.* ("before Christ") are written in all capitals, with a period following each letter.

150 B.C.　　465 A.D. (ordinary usage)　**OR**　A.D. 465 (formal usage)

NOTE:　Do not use a comma to separate *B.C.* or *A.D.* from the year.

Affect–effect.　*Affect* is normally used as a verb meaning "to influence, change, assume." *Effect* can be either a verb meaning "to bring about" or a noun meaning "result, impression."

The court's decision in this case will not *affect* (change) the established precedent.

She *affects* (assumes) an unsophisticated manner.

It is essential that we *effect* (bring about) an immediate improvement in sales.

It will be months before we can assess the full *effect* (result) of the new law.

NOTE:　In psychology, *affect* is used as a noun meaning "feeling, emotion," and the related adjective *affective* means "emotional." Because of the limited context in which these terms are likely to be used with these meanings, it should be easy to distinguish them from *effect* as a noun and the related adjective *effective.*

We need to analyze the *effects* (results) of this new marketing strategy.

We need to analyze the *affects* (emotions) produced by this encounter.

Which of these techniques are *effective* (capable of producing the desired results)?

Let's deal with the *affective* (emotional) factors first.

Age–aged–at the age of

I interviewed a man *aged* 52 for the job. (**NOT:** a man age 52.)

You can collect these benefits *at the age of* 62. (**NOT:** at age 62.)

All of. *Of* is not necessary after *all* unless the following word is a pronoun.

> *All* the staff members belong to the softball team. (**ALSO:** All of the staff members . . .)
> *All of* us belong to the softball team.

All right. Like *all wrong*, the expression *all right* should be spelled as two words. (While some dictionaries list *alright* without comment, this spelling is not generally accepted as correct.)

Almost–all most. See also *Most*.

> The plane was *almost* (nearly) three hours late.
> We are *all most* pleased (all very much pleased) with the new schedule.

Already–all ready

> The order had *already* (previously) been shipped.
> The order is *all ready* (all prepared) to be shipped.

Altogether–all together

> He is *altogether* (entirely) too lazy to be a success.
> The papers are *all together* (all in a group) on your secretary's desk.

Always–all ways

> She has *always* (at all times) done good work.
> We have tried in *all ways* (by all methods) to keep our employees satisfied.

Among–between. See *Between–among*.

Amount–number. Use *amount* for things in bulk, as in "a large amount of lumber." Use *number* for individual items, as in "a large number of inquiries."

And. Retain *and* before the last item in a series, even though that last item consists of two words joined by *and*.

> We need to increase our expense budgets for advertising, staff training, *and* research and development.
> (**NOT:** We need to increase our expense budgets for advertising, staff training, research and development.)

And etc. Never use *and* before *etc*. (See *Etc.*)

And/or. This is a legalistic term and should be avoided in ordinary writing.

Anxious–eager. Both *anxious* and *eager* mean "desirous," but *anxious* also implies fear or concern.

> I'm *anxious* to hear whether we won the bid or not.
> I'm *eager* (**NOT** anxious) to hear about your new house.

Anyone–any one. See ¶1010, note.

Anytime–any time

> Come see us *anytime* you are in town. (One word meaning "whenever.")
> Did you have dealings with Crosby at *any time* in the past? (Two words after a preposition such as *at*.)

Anyway–any way

> *Anyway* (in any case), we can't spare him now.
> If we can help in *any way* (by any method), please phone.

Appraise–apprise

> We would like to *appraise* (set a value on) Mrs. Ellsworth's estate.
> I will *apprise* (inform) you of any new developments.

11

Appreciate. When used with the meaning "to be thankful for," the verb *appreciate* requires an object.

> **NOT:** We would appreciate if you could give us your decision by May 1.
>
> **BUT:** We would appreciate *it* if you could give us your decision by May 1. (Pronoun as object.)
>
> **OR:** We would appreciate *your* (**NOT** you) *giving us your decision by May 1.* (Noun clause as object. See ¶647 on the use of *your* before *giving.*)
>
> I will appreciate *whatever you can do for us.* (Relative clause as object.)
>
> We will always appreciate the *help* you gave us. (Noun as object.)

As. Do not use for *that* or *whether.*

> I do not know *whether* (**NOT** as) I can go.

Use *because, since,* or *for* rather than *as* in clauses of reason.

> I cannot attend the meeting in Omaha, *because* (**NOT** as) I will be out on the West Coast that day.

As−as if. See *Like−as, as if.*

As . . . as−not so . . . as. The term *as . . . as* is now commonly used in both positive and negative comparisons. Some writers, however, prefer to use *not so . . . as* for negative comparisons.

> Bob is every bit *as* bright *as* his older sister. (Positive comparison.)
>
> It is *not as* important *as* you think. **OR:** . . . *not so* important *as* you think. (Negative comparison.)

Assure. See *Ensure−insure−assure.*

At about. Use either *at* or *about,* but not both words together. For example, "Plan to arrive *at* ten" **OR** "Plan to arrive *about* ten." (**BUT NOT:** Plan to arrive *at about* ten.)

Awhile−a while. One word as an adverb; two words as a noun.

> You may have to wait *awhile.* (Adverb.)
>
> You may have to wait for *a while.* (Noun; object of *for.*)
>
> I ran into him *a while* back.

Bad−badly. Use the adjective *bad* (not the adverb *badly*) after the verb *feel* or *look.* (See ¶1067.)

> I feel *bad* (**NOT** badly) about the mistake.
>
> **BUT:** He was hurt *badly* in the accident.

Balance. Do not use *balance* to mean "rest" or "remainder" except in a financial or accounting sense.

> I plan to use the *rest* of my vacation time next February.
>
> (**NOT:** I plan to use the *balance* of my vacation time next February.)
>
> **BUT:** The *balance* of the loan falls due at the end of this quarter.

B.C.−A.D. See *A.D.−B.C.*

Because. See *Reason is because.*

Because of. See *Due to−because of−on account of.*

Being that. Do not use for *since* or *because.*

> *Because* I arrived late, I could not get a seat.
>
> (**NOT:** *Being that* I arrived late, I could not get a seat.)

Beside–besides

I sat *beside* (next to) Mr. Parrish's father at the meeting.

Besides (in addition), we need your support of the measure.

Between–among. Ordinarily, use *between* when referring to *two* persons or things and *among* when referring to *more than* two persons or things.

The territory is divided evenly *between* the two sales representatives.

The profits are to be evenly divided *among* the three partners.

Use *between* with more than two persons or things when they are being considered in pairs as well as in a group.

There are distinct differences *between* New York, Chicago, and Dallas.

In packing china, be sure to place paper *between* the plates. (**NOT:** between *each* of the plates.)

The memo says something different when you read *between* the lines.

Between you and me (not *I*). See ¶1055*b*.

Both–each. *Both* means "the two considered together." *Each* refers to the individual members of a group considered separately.

Both designs are acceptable.   The designs are *each* acceptable.

Each sister complained about the other.

(**NOT:** *Both* sisters complained about the other.)

Both alike–equal–together. *Both* is unnecessary when used with *alike*, *equal*, or *together*.

These ink-jet printers are *alike*. (**NOT:** both alike.)

These tape systems are *equal* in cost. (**NOT:** both equal.)

We will travel *together* to the Far East. (**NOT:** both travel together.)

Bring–take. *Bring* indicates motion toward the speaker. *Take* indicates motion away from the speaker.

Please *bring* the research data with you when you next come to the office.

Please *take* the enclosed letter to Farley when you go to see him.

You may *take* my copy with you if you will *bring* it back by Friday.

❑ *See note under* Come–go.

But . . . however. Use one or the other.

We had hoped to see the show, *but* we couldn't get tickets.

OR: We had hoped to see the show; *however*, we couldn't get tickets.

(**BUT NOT:** . . . *but* we couldn't get tickets, *however*.)

But what. Use *that*.

I do not doubt *that* (**NOT** but what) he will be elected.

Can–could. See *May–can (might–could)*.

Cannot help but. This expression is a confusion of two others, namely, *can but* and *cannot help*.

I *can but* try. (**BETTER:** I *can only* try.)

I *cannot help* feeling sorry for her. (**NOT:** cannot help but feel.)

Class. See *Kind*.

Come–go. The choice between verbs depends on the location of the speaker. *Come* indicates motion *toward; go,* motion *away from.* (See also *Bring–take.*)

> When Bellotti *comes* back, I will *go* to the airport to meet him.
>
> *A secretary speaking over the phone to a customer:* Will it be convenient for you to *come* to our office tomorrow?
>
> *Anyone outside the office speaking:* Will it be convenient for you to *go* to their office tomorrow?

NOTE: When writing about your travel plans to a person at your destination, adopt that person's point of view and use *come.*

> *Midwesterner to Californian:* I am *coming* to California during the week of the 11th. I will *bring* the plans with me if they are ready.

However, if you are telling your travel plans to someone who is *not* at your destination, observe the regular distinction between *come* and *go.*

> *Midwesterner to Midwesterner:* I am *going* to California during the week of the 11th. I will *take* the plans with me if they are ready.

Come and. In formal writing use *come to* instead of the colloquial *come and.*

> Come *to* see me. (**NOT:** Come *and* see me.)

Comprise–compose. *Comprise* means "to include, contain, consist of"; *compose* means "to make up." The parts *compose* (make up) the whole; the whole *comprises* (includes) the parts; the whole *is composed of* (**NOT** is comprised of) the parts.

> The parent corporation *comprises* (consists of) three major divisions.
>
> Three major divisions *compose* (make up) the parent corporation.
>
> The parent corporation *is composed of* (is made up of) three major divisions.

Data. See ¶1018, note.

Different–differently. When the meaning is "in a different manner," use the adverb *differently.*

> I wish we had done it *differently.*
>
> It came out *differently* than we expected. (See ¶1077.)

After linking verbs and verbs of the senses, the adjective *different* is correct. (See ¶1067.)

> That music sounds completely *different.*
>
> He seems (appears) *different* since his promotion.
>
> Don't believe anything *different.* (Meaning "anything that is different.")

Different from–different than. See ¶1077.

Done. Do not say "I *done* it." Say "I *did* it." (See also ¶1032, note.)

Don't (do not). Do not use *don't* with *he, she,* or *it;* use *doesn't.*

> He *doesn't* talk easily.   **BUT:** I *don't* think so.
>
> She *doesn't* need any help.   They *don't* want any help.
>
> It *doesn't* seem right to penalize them.   We *don't* understand.

Doubt that–doubt whether. Use *doubt that* in negative statements and in questions. Use *doubt whether* in all other cases. (See also *If–whether.*)

> We do not *doubt that* she is capable. (Negative statement.)
>
> Does anyone *doubt that* the check was mailed? (Question.)
>
> I *doubt whether* I can go.

Due to–because of–on account of. *Due to* introduces an adjective phrase and should modify nouns. It is normally used only after some form of the verb *to be* (*is, are, was, were*, etc.)

Her success is *due to* talent and hard work. (*Due to* modifies *success*.)

Because of and *on account of* introduce adverbial phrases and should modify verbs.

He resigned *because of* ill health. (*Because of* modifies *resigned*.)

(**NOT:** He resigned *due to* ill health.)

Each–both. See *Both–each*.

11

Each other–one another. Use *each other* to refer to two persons or things; *one another* for more than two.

The two partners had great respect for *each other's* abilities.

The four winners congratulated *one another*.

Eager–anxious. See *Anxious–eager*.

Effect–affect. See *Affect–effect*.

Ensure–insure–assure. *Ensure* means "to make certain." *Insure* means "to protect against loss." *Assure* means "to give someone confidence"; the object of this verb should always refer to a person.

I want to *ensure* (make certain) that nothing can go wrong tomorrow.

I want to *assure* you (give you confidence) that nothing will go wrong.

I want to *insure* this necklace (protect it against loss) for $5000.

Enthused over. Use *was* or *were enthusiastic about* instead.

The sales staff *was enthusiastic about* (**NOT** enthused over) next year's styles.

Equal. See *Both alike–equal–together*.

Equally as good. Use either *equally good* or *just as good*.

This model is newer, but that one is *equally good*. (**NOT:** equally as good.)

Those are *just as good* as these. (**NOT:** equally as good.)

Etc. This abbreviation of *et cetera* means "and other things." Therefore, do not use *and* before it. A comma both precedes and follows *etc.* (see ¶164). In formal writing, avoid the use of *etc.;* use a phrase such as *and the like* or *and so on* instead.

NOTE: Do not use *etc.* or an equivalent expression at the end of a series introduced by *such as*. The term *such as* implies that only a few selected examples will be given; therefore, it is unnecessary to add *etc.* or *and so on*, which suggests that further examples could be given.

As part of its employee educational program, the company offers courses in report writing, business correspondence, grammar and style, *and so on*.

OR: . . . the company offers courses *such as* report writing, business correspondence, and grammar and style.

(**BUT NOT:** . . . the company offers courses *such as* report writing, business correspondence, grammar and style, *and so on*.)

Everyday–every day

You'll soon master the *everyday* (ordinary or daily) routine of the job.

He has called *every day* (each day) this week.

Everyone–every one. See ¶1010, note.

Ex–former. Use *ex-* with a title to designate the person who *immediately* preceded the current titleholder in that position; use *former* with a title to designate an earlier titleholder.

> Charles Feldman is the *ex-president* of the Harrisburg Chamber of Commerce. (Held office immediately before the current president.)
>
> **BUT:** . . . is a *former* president of the Harrisburg Chamber of Commerce. (Held office sometime before the current president and that person's immediate predecessor.)

Except. When *except* is a preposition, be sure to use the objective form of a pronoun that follows. (See also ¶1055*b*.)

> Everyone has been transferred *except* Jean and *me*. (**NOT:** except Jean and I.)

Farther–further. *Farther* refers to actual distance; *further* refers to figurative distance and means "to a greater degree" or "to a greater extent."

> The drive from the airport to Boone was *farther* (in actual distance) than we expected.
>
> Let's plan to discuss the proposal *further* (to a greater extent).

Fewer–less. *Fewer* refers to number and is used with *plural* nouns. *Less* refers to degree or amount and is used with *singular* nouns.

> *Fewer* accidents (a smaller number) were reported than was expected.
>
> *Less* effort (a smaller degree) was put forth by the organizers, and thus *fewer* people (a smaller number) attended.

NOTE: The expression *less than* (rather than *fewer than*) precedes plural nouns referring to periods of time, amounts of money, and quantities.

> less than ten years ago   **BUT:** fewer than 60 people
>
> *Less than* five years ago our sales were under $1 million a year.

First–firstly, etc. In enumerations use the forms *first, second, third* (**NOT** firstly, secondly, thirdly).

Flammable–inflammable. Both terms mean "easily ignitable, highly combustible." However, since some readers may misinterpret *inflammable* to mean "*non*flammable," use *flammable* as the clearer of the two alternatives.

Former–ex. See *Ex–former*.

Former–first. *Former* refers to the first of two persons or things. When more than two are mentioned, use *first*. (See also *Latter–last*.)

> This item is available in wool and in Dacron, but I prefer the *former*.
>
> This item is available in wool, in Dacron, and in Orlon, but I prefer the *first*.

From–off. Use *from* (**NOT** off) with persons.

> I got the answer I needed *from* Margaret. (**NOT:** off Margaret.)

Go–come. See *Come–go*.

Good–well. *Good* is an adjective. *Well* may be used as an adverb or (with reference to health) as an adjective.

> Marie got *good* grades in school. (Adjective.)
>
> I will do the job as *well* as I can. (Adverb.)
>
> He admits he does not feel *well* today. (Adjective.)
>
> The security guards look *good* in their new uniforms. (Adjective.)

NOTE: *To feel well* means "to be in good health." *To feel good* means "to be in good spirits."

Graduated – was graduated. Both forms are acceptable. However, use *from* after either expression.

> My daughter *graduated from* MIT last year.
>
> (**NOT:** My daughter *graduated* MIT last year.)

Hardly. *Hardly* is negative in meaning. Therefore, do not use another negative with it.

> You *could hardly* (**NOT** couldn't hardly) expect him to agree.

Have – of. See *Of – have*.

Healthy – healthful. People are *healthy;* a climate or food is *healthful*.

> You ought to move to a more *healthful* (**NOT** healthier) climate.

Help. Do not use *from* after the verb *help*. For example, "I couldn't *help* (**NOT** help from) telling her she was wrong."

Hopefully. Although the subject of much controversy, the use of *hopefully* at the beginning of a sentence is no different from the use of *obviously, certainly, fortunately, actually, apparently,* and similar words functioning as "independent comments" (see ¶138*b*). These adverbs express the writer's attitude toward what he is about to say; as such they modify the meaning of the sentence as a whole rather than a particular word.

> *Hopefully,* the worst is over and we will soon see a strong upturn in sales and profits.

However. See *But . . . however*.

If – whether. *If* is often used colloquially for *whether* in such sentences as "He doesn't know *whether* he will be able to leave tomorrow." In written material use *whether*, particularly in such expressions as *see whether, learn whether, know whether,* and *doubt whether*. Also use *whether* when the expression *or not* follows or is implied.

> Find out *whether* (**NOT** if) this format is acceptable *or not*.

Imply – infer. *Imply* means "to suggest"; you imply something by *your own* words or actions.

> Verna *implied* (suggested) that we would not be invited.

Infer means "to assume, to deduce, to arrive at a conclusion"; you infer something from *another person's* words or actions.

> I *inferred* (assumed) from Verna's remarks that we would not be invited.

In – into – in to

> The correspondence is *in* the file. (*In* implies position within.)
>
> He walked *into* the outer office. (*Into* implies entry or change of form.)
>
> All sales reports are to be sent *in to* the sales manager. (*In* is an adverb in the verb phrase *are to be sent in; to* is a simple preposition.)
>
> Mr. Boehme came *in to* see me. (*In* is part of the verb phrase *came in; to* is part of the infinitive *to see*.)

In regards to. Substitute *in regard to, with regard to, regarding,* or *as regards*.

Incidentally. Note that this word ends in *ally*. Never spell the word *incidently*.

Indifferent – in different

> She was *indifferent* (not caring one way or the other) to the offer.
>
> He liked our idea, but he wanted it expressed *in different* (in other) words.

Indirect–in direct

Indirect (not direct) lighting will enhance the appearance of this room.

This order is *in direct* (the preposition *in* plus the adjective *direct*) conflict with the policy of this company.

Individual–party–person–people. Use *individual* to refer to someone whom you wish to distinguish from a larger group of people.

We wish to honor those *individuals* who had the courage to speak out against an unjust situation at a time when popular opinion was defending the status quo.

Use *party* only to refer to someone involved in some type of legal proceeding.

All the *parties* to the original agreement will have to sign the attached amendment.

Use *person* to refer to a human being in all other contexts.

Can you please tell me the name of the *person* in charge of your credit department?

If reference is made to more than one person, the term *people* usually sounds more natural than the plural form *persons*. In any event, always use *people* when referring to a large group.

If you like, I can send you a list of all the *people* in our corporation who will be attending this year's national convention.

Inflammable–flammable. See *Flammable–inflammable*.

Insure. See *Ensure–insure–assure*.

Irregardless. Use *regardless*.

Is where–is when. Do not use these phrases to introduce definitions.

A dilemma is a situation in which you have to choose between equally unsatisfactory alternatives.

(**NOT:** A dilemma *is where* you have to choose between equally unsatisfactory alternatives.)

However, these phrases may be correctly used in other situations.

The Ritz-Carlton *is where* the dinner-dance will be held this year.

Two o'clock *is when* the meeting is scheduled to begin.

Its–it's. See ¶1056e.

Kind. *Kind* is singular; therefore, write *this kind, that kind, these kinds, those kinds* (**BUT NOT** *these kind, those kind*). The same distinctions hold for *class, type*, and *sort*.

Kind of–sort of. These phrases are sometimes followed by an adjective (for example, *kind of sorry, sort of baffled*). Use this kind of expression only in informal writing. In more formal situations, use *rather* or *somewhat* (*rather sorry, somewhat baffled*).

I was *somewhat* (**NOT** kind of, sort of) surprised.

She seemed *rather* (**NOT** kind of, sort of) tired.

NOTE: When *kind of* or *sort of* is followed by a noun, the expression is appropriate in all kinds of situations.

What *sort of business* is Vern Forbes in?

❑ *See A–of and* Kind of a.

Kind of a. The *a* is unnecessary. For example, "That *kind of* (**NOT** kind of a) material is very expensive."

Last–latest. *Last* means "after all others"; *latest,* "most recent."

> Mr. Lin's *last* act before leaving was to recommend Ms. Roth's promotion.
>
> Attached is the *latest* report we have received from the Southern Region.

Latter–last. *Latter* refers to the second of two persons or things mentioned. When more than two are mentioned, use *last.* (See also *Former–first.*)

> July and August are good vacation months, but the *latter* is more popular.
>
> June, July, and August are good vacation months, but the *last* is the most popular.

Lay–lie. *Lay* (principal parts: *lay, laid, laid, laying*) means "to put" or "to place." This verb requires an object to complete its meaning.

> Please *lay* the *boxes* on the pallets with extreme care.
>
> I *laid* the *message* right on your desk.
>
> I *had laid* two other *notes* there yesterday.
>
> He *is* always *laying* the *blame* on his assistants. (Putting the blame.)
>
> The dress *was laid* in the box. (A passive construction implying that someone *laid* the dress in the box.)

Lie (principal parts: *lie, lay, lain, lying*) means "to recline, rest, or stay" or "to take a position of rest." It refers to a person or thing as either assuming or being in a reclining position. This verb cannot take an object.

> Now he *lies* in bed most of the day.
>
> The mountains *lay* before us as we proceeded west.
>
> This letter *has lain* unanswered for two weeks.
>
> Today's mail *is lying* on the receptionist's desk.

TEST: In deciding whether to use *lie* or *lay* in a sentence, substitute the word *place, placed,* or *placing* (as appropriate) for the word in question. If the substitute fits, the corresponding form of *lay* is correct. If it doesn't, use the appropriate form of *lie.*

> I will (*lie* or *lay?*) down now. (You could not say, "I will *place* down now." Therefore, write "I will *lie* down now.")
>
> I (*laid* or *lay?*) the pad on his desk. ("I *placed* the pad on his desk" works. Therefore, write "I *laid* the pad.")
>
> I (*laid* or *lay?*) awake many nights. ("I *placed* awake" doesn't work. Write "I *lay* awake.")
>
> These files have (*laid* or *lain?*) untouched for some time. ("These files have *placed* untouched" doesn't work. Write "These files have *lain* untouched.")
>
> He has been (*laying* or *lying?*) down on the job. ("He has been *placing* down on the job" doesn't work. Write "He has been *lying* down.")

NOTE: When the verb *lie* means "to tell a falsehood," it has regularly formed principal parts (*lie, lied, lied, lying*) and is seldom confused with the verbs just described.

Learn–teach. *Learn* (principal parts: *learn, learned, learned, learning*) means "to acquire knowledge." *Teach* (principal parts: *teach, taught, taught, teaching*) means "to impart knowledge to others."

> I *learned* from a master teacher.   A first-rate instructor *taught* me how.
>
> (**NOT:** I *was learned* by a master teacher.)   I was *taught* by a first-rate instructor.

Leave–let. *Leave* (principal parts: *leave, left, left, leaving*) means "to move away, abandon, or depart." *Let* (principal parts: *let, let, let, letting*) means "to permit or allow." **TEST:** In deciding whether to use *let* or *leave,* try substituting the appropriate form of *permit.* If *permit* fits, use *let;* if not, use *leave.*

(Continued on page 230.)

I now *leave* you to your own devices. (Abandon you.)

Mr. Morales *left* on the morning train. (Departed.)

Let me see the last page. (Permit me to see.)

Leave me alone. **OR:** *Let* me alone. (Either is acceptable.)

Less–fewer. See *Fewer–less*.

Like–as, as if. *Like* is correctly used as a preposition. Although *like* is also widely used as a conjunction in colloquial speech, use *as* or *as if* in written material.

We need to hire another person *like* you.

Kate, *like* her predecessor, will have to cope with the problem.

Mary looks *like* her mother.

Mary looks *as* (**NOT** like) her mother did at the same age.

It looks *like* snow.

It looks *as if* (**NOT** like) it will snow.

As (**NOT** Like) I told you earlier, we will not reorder for six months.

Literally. This adverb means "actually, truly." Do not use it in the sense of "almost" to modify a phrase describing an exaggerated or unreal situation.

NOT: When Jensen got the bill for all the "minor changes" made at the last minute, he *literally* hit the ceiling. (Omit the word *literally* unless Jensen actually exploded out of his chair and hit the ceiling headfirst.)

May–can (might–could). *May* and *might* imply permission or possibility; *can* and *could*, ability or power.

You *may* send them a dozen cans of paint on trial. (Permission.)

The report *may* be true. (Possibility.)

Can he present a workable plan? (Has he the ability?)

Miss Kovacs said I *might* (permission) have the time off if I *could* (had the power to) finish my work in time.

Maybe–may be. *Maybe* is an adverb; *may be* is a verb.

If we don't receive a letter from them today, *maybe* (an adverb meaning "perhaps") we should call.

Mr. Boston *may be* (a verb) out of town next week.

Media. *Media*, referring to various channels of communication and advertising, is a plural noun. *Medium* is the singular. (See ¶1018.)

More important–more importantly. *More important* is often used as a short form for "what is more important," especially at the beginning of a sentence. *More importantly* means "in a more important manner."

More important, we need to establish a line of credit very quickly. (What is more important.)

The incident was treated *more importantly* than it deserved. (In a more important manner.)

Most. Do not use for *almost*. For example, "*Almost all* the money is gone" **OR** "*Most* of the money is gone." (**BUT NOT:** *Most all* of the money is gone.)

Nobody–no body

There was *nobody* (no person) at the information desk when I arrived.

No body (no group) of employees is more cooperative than yours.

NOTE: Spell *no body* as two words when it is followed by *of*. (See also ¶1010.)

None–no one. See ¶1013.

Not so . . . as. See *As . . . as—not so . . . as.*

Number. See *Amount—number.*

Of–a. See *A–of.*

Of–have. Do not use *of* instead of *have* in verb forms. The correct forms are *could have, would have, should have, might have, may have, must have, ought to have,* etc.

> What *could have* happened? (**NOT:** What could *of* happened?)

Off. Do not use *off of* or *off from* in place of *off.* (See also ¶1078.)

> The papers fell *off* the desk. (**NOT:** off of the desk.)

Off–from. See *From–off.*

On–onto–on to

> It's dangerous to drive *on* the highway shoulder. (*On* implies position or movement over.)
>
> He lost control of the car and drove *onto* the sidewalk. (*Onto* implies movement toward and then over.)
>
> Let's go *on to* the next problem. (*On* is an adverb in the verb phrase *go on; to* is a preposition.)
>
> She then went *on to* tell about her experiences in Asia. (*On* is part of the verb phrase *went on; to* is part of the infinitive *to tell.*)

On–upon–up on

> His statements were based *on* (**OR** *upon*) experimental data. (*On* and *upon* are interchangeable.)
>
> Please follow *up on* the Updegraff case. (*Up* is part of the verb phrase *follow up; on* is a preposition.)

On account of. See *Due to—because of—on account of.*

One another–each other. See *Each other—one another.*

Only. The adverb *only* is negative in meaning. Therefore, do not use another negative with it unless you want a positive meaning. (See ¶1072 for the placement of *only* in a sentence.)

> I use this letterhead *only* for foreign correspondence. (I do not use this letterhead for anything else.)
>
> **BUT:** I do not use this letterhead *only* for foreign correspondence. (I use it for a number of other things as well.)

Opposite. When used as a noun, *opposite* is followed by *of.*

> Her opinion is the *opposite of* mine.

In other uses, *opposite* is followed by *to* or *from* or by neither.

> Her opinion is *opposite to* (**OR** *from*) mine.
>
> She lives *opposite* the school.

Party. See *Individual–party–person–people.*

Per–a. *Per,* a Latin word, is often used to mean "by the," as in 28 *miles per gallon (mpg)* or 55 *miles per hour (mph)*. Whenever possible, substitute *a* or *an;* for example, *at the rate of $8 an hour, 75 cents a liter.* Do *not* use *per* in the sense of "according to" or "in accordance with."

> We are sending you samples *as you requested.* (**NOT:** per your request.)

Percent–percentage. In ordinary usage *percent* should always be accompanied by a number; for example, *20 percent, 0.5 percent, 150 percent.* Similarly, in a table a column of figures representing percentages may be headed *Percent of Total* or something comparable. Otherwise, use the term *percentage.*

> A large *percentage* of the calls we got yesterday came from customers who misread our ad. (**NOT:** A large *percent* of the calls . . .)
>
> What *percentage* of our subscribers are in the 30–49 age group? (See also ¶1025.)

NOTE: In the percentage formula used in mathematics (base × rate = amount), the rate is called a *percent* and the amount is called a *percentage.* Thus you might be asked to calculate the *percentage* if a sales tax of 6 percent (the rate) was applied to a purchase of $50 (the base). By the same token, you might be asked to calculate the *percent* (the rate) if you knew that a tax of $5 (the amount, or percentage) had been paid on an order of $200. Outside of this special context, *percent* and *percentage* should be used as noted above.

Person–people. See *Individual–party–person–people.*

Plus. This word can be correctly used as a noun, an adjective, or a preposition. However, do not use it as a conjunction (with the sense of "and").

> Your presence at the hearing was a real *plus* for our cause. (*Plus* used correctly as a noun.)
>
> The decision to offer a 10 percent discount on all orders received by June 1 was a *plus* factor in the success of the campaign. (*Plus* used correctly as an adjective.)
>
> Your willingness to innovate *plus* your patient perspective on profits has permitted this company to grow at an astonishing rate. (*Plus* used correctly as a preposition. Note that a *plus* phrase following the subject of a sentence does not affect the number of the verb. See ¶1007.)
>
> **BUT NOT:** You have always been willing to innovate, *plus* you have been patient about the profits to be derived from the innovations. (Do not use *plus* as a conjunction; use *and* instead.)

Raise–rise. *Raise* (principal parts: *raise, raised, raised, raising*) means "to cause to lift" or "to lift something." This verb requires an object to complete its meaning.

> Mr. Pinelli *raises* a good *question.*
>
> Most growers *have raised* the *price* of coffee.
>
> We *are raising money* for the United Fund.
>
> Our rent *has been raised.* (A passive construction implying that someone *has raised* the rent.)

Rise (principal parts: *rise, rose, risen, rising*) means "to ascend," "to move upward by itself," or "to get up." This verb cannot be used with an object.

> We will have to *rise* to the demands of the occasion.
>
> The sun *rose* at 6:25 this morning.
>
> The river *has risen* to flood level.
>
> The temperature *has been rising* all day.

TEST: Remember, you cannot "rise" anything.

Real–really. *Real* is an adjective; *really,* an adverb. Do not use *real* to modify another adjective; use *very* or *really.*

> One taste will tell you that these cookies were made with *real* butter. (Adjective.)
>
> To be honest, we were *really* expecting a lower price from you this year. (Adverb.)
>
> **BUT:** It was *very* nice to see you and your family again. (**NOT:** real nice.)

Reason is because. Substitute *reason is that.* For example, "The *reason* for such low sales *is that* (**NOT** because) prices are too high."

Retroactive to (NOT from)

> These improvements in benefits under the company dental plan will be *retroactive to* July 1. (See also ¶1077.)

Said. The use of *said* in a phrase like "the *said* document" is appropriate only in legal writing. In normal usage write "the document referred to above." (In many cases the document being referred to will be clear to the reader without the additional explanation.)

Same. Do not use *same* to refer to a previously mentioned thing.

> We are now processing your order and will have *it* ready for you Monday.
>
> (**NOT:** We are now processing your order and will have *same* ready for you Monday.)

Scarcely. The adverb *scarcely* is negative in meaning. Therefore, do not use another negative with it. (See ¶1072 for the placement of *scarcely*.)

> I *scarcely* recognized (**NOT** didn't scarcely recognize) you.

Serve–service. Things can be *serviced*, but people are *served*.

> We take great pride in the way we *serve* (**NOT** service) our clients.
>
> For a small additional charge we will *service* the equipment for a full year.

Set–sit. *Set* (principal parts: *set, set, set, setting*) means "to place something somewhere." In this sense, *set* requires an object to complete its meaning. **REMEMBER:** You cannot "sit" anything.

> It's important to *set* down your *recollections* while they are still fresh.
>
> I must have dropped my wallet when I *set* my *suitcase* down.
>
> I *have set* my *alarm* for six in the morning.
>
> The crew *was setting* the *stage* for the evening performance.
>
> The date *was set* some time ago. (A passive construction implying that someone *set* the date.)

NOTE: *Set* has a few other meanings in which the verb does *not* require an object, but these meanings are seldom confused with *sit*.

> They *set* out on the trip in high spirits.
>
> The sun *set* at 5:34 p.m. Wednesday.
>
> Allow a full hour for the mixture to *set*.

Sit (principal parts: *sit, sat, sat, sitting*) means "to be in a position of rest" or "to be seated." This verb cannot be used with an object.

> So here we *sit*, waiting for a decision from top management.
>
> I *sat* next to Ebbetsen at the board meeting.
>
> They *had sat* on the plane a full hour before the flight was canceled.
>
> They *will be sitting* in the orchestra.

Shall–will. The auxiliary verb *shall* has largely given way to the verb *will* in all but the most formal writing and speech. The following rules reflect both ordinary and formal usage:

a. To express simple future time:

(1) In *ordinary* circumstances use *will* with all three persons.

> *I* (**OR** *we*) *will* be glad to help you plan the program.
>
> *You will* want to study these recommendations before the meeting.
>
> *He* (**OR** *she, it, they*) *will* arrive tomorrow morning.

(Continued on page 234.)

(2) In *formal* circumstances use *shall* with the first person (*I, we*) and *will* with the second and third persons (*you, he, she, it, they*).

I (**OR** *we*) *shall* be glad to answer all inquiries promptly.

You will meet the McGinnesses at the reception this evening.

They (**OR** *he, she*) *will* not find the trip too tiring.

b. To indicate *determination, promise, desire, choice,* or *threat:*

(1) In *ordinary* circumstances use *will* with all three persons.

(2) In *formal* circumstances use *will* for the first person (*I, we*) and *shall* for the second and third persons (*you, he, she, it, they*).

In spite of the risk, *I will* go where I please. (Determination.)

We will not be coerced. (Determination.)

They shall not interfere with my department. (Determination.)

I will send my check by the end of the week. (Promise.)

We will report you to the authorities if this is true. (Threat.)

You shall regret your answer. (Threat.)

He shall study, or *he shall* leave college. (Threat.)

c. To indicate *willingness* (to be willing, to be agreeable to) in both *ordinary* and *formal* circumstances, use *will* with all persons.

Yes, *I will* meet you at six o'clock.

Should–would. *Should* and *would* follow the same rules as *shall* and *will* (see preceding entry) in expressions of future time, determination, and willingness. The distinctions concerning ordinary and formal usage also apply here.

ORDINARY: I *would* like to hear from you. **ORDINARY:** We *would* be glad to see her.
FORMAL: I *should* like to hear from you. **FORMAL:** We *should* be glad to see her.

ORDINARY: I *would* be pleased to serve on that committee.
FORMAL: I *should* be pleased to serve on that committee.

a. Always use *should* in all persons to indicate "ought to."

I *should* study tonight.

You *should* report his dishonesty to the manager.

He *should* pay his debts.

b. Always use *would* in all persons to indicate customary action.

Every day I *would* swim half a mile.

They *would* only say, "No comment."

She *would* practice day after day.

c. Use *should* in all three persons to express a condition in an *if* clause.

If I *should* win the prize, I will share it with you.

If you *should* miss the train, please call me collect.

d. Use *would* in all three persons to express willingness in an *if* clause.

If he *would* apply himself, he could win top honors easily.

If you *would* delay your decision, I could offer you more attractive terms.

So–so that. *So* as a conjunction means "therefore"; *so that* means "in order that."

The work is now finished, *so* you can all go home. (See also ¶179.)

Please finish what you are doing *so that* we can all go home.

Someday–some day

Please set up a meeting with Al and Jerry *someday* next week.

BUT: Please set up a meeting with Al and Jerry *for some day* next week. (Two words when used as the object of a preposition such as *for*.)

Someone–some one.   See ¶1010, note.

Sometime–sometimes–some time

The order will be shipped *sometime* (at some unspecified time) next week.

Sometimes (now and then) reports are misleading.

It took me *some time* (a period of time) to complete the job.

I saw him *some time* ago.

Sort.   See *Kind.*

Sort of–kind of.   See *Kind of–sort of.*

Such as . . . etc.   See *Etc.*

Sure–surely.   *Sure* is an adjective, *surely* an adverb.

I am *sure* that I did not make that mistake. (Adjective.)

You can *surely* count on our help. (Adverb.)

Do not use *sure* as an adverb; use *surely* or *very*.

I was *very* glad to be of help. (**NOT:** sure glad.)

Sure and.   In formal writing use *sure to* in place of the colloquial *sure and*.

Be *sure to* give my best regards to the Meltzers.

(**NOT:** Be *sure and* give my best regards to the Meltzers.)

Tack–tact.   Use *tack* (not *tact*) in the expression *to take a different tack* (meaning "to move in a different direction"). *Tact* means "a considerate way of behaving so as to avoid offending others."

We may have to take a different *tack* in our negotiations with Firebridge.

Please use a great deal of *tact* when you reply to Korbman's letter.

Take–bring.   See *Bring–take.*

Teach–learn.   See *Learn–teach.*

Than–then.   *Than* is a conjunction introducing a subordinate clause of comparison. *Then* is an adverb meaning "at that time" or "next."

The compulsory retirement age is higher now *than* it was *then*.

They *then* asserted that they could handle the account better *than* we. (See ¶1057 for the case of pronouns following *than*.)

NOTE: Remember that *then* (like *when*) refers to time.

That–where.   See *Where–that.*

That–which–who.   See ¶1062.

These sort–these kind.   Incorrect; the correct forms are *this* sort, *this* kind. (See also *Kind*.)

This here.   Do not use for *this;* for example, "*this* (**NOT** this here) typewriter."

Together.   See *Both alike–equal–together.*

Toward–towards.   *Toward* is more common, but both forms are correct.

Try and.   In written material use *try to* rather than the colloquial *try and*. For example, "Please *try to* be here on time." (**NOT:** try and be here.)

Type. See *Kind.*

Unique. Do not use *unique* in the sense of "unusual." A unique thing is one of a kind. (See ¶1071*f.*)

Up. Many verbs (for example, *end, rest, lift, connect, join, hurry, settle, burn, drink, eat*) contain the idea of "up"; therefore, the adverb *up* is unnecessary. In the following sentences, *up* should be omitted.

The electrician will connect (up) the fan.   Can you help me lift (up) this case?

Let's divide (up) the sandwiches.   I will call him (up) tomorrow.

Upon–up on. See *On–upon–up on.*

Very. This adverb can be used to modify an adjective, another adverb, a present participle, or a "descriptive" past participle.

We are *very happy* with the outcome. (Modifying an adjective.)

This finish dries *very quickly.* (Modifying an adverb.)

It was a *very disappointing* showing. (Modifying a present participle.)

I was *very pleased* with the pictures. (Modifying a descriptive past participle.)

When the past participle expresses action rather than description, insert an adverb like *much* after *very.*

They are *very much opposed* to your plan. (*Opposed* is part of the complete verb *are opposed* and expresses action rather than description.)

Ways. Do not use for *way* in referring to distance. For example, "I live a short *way* (**NOT** ways) from here."

Well–good. See *Good–well.*

Where–that. Do not use *where* in place of *that.*

I saw in yesterday's paper *that* Schuster's had changed its mind about closing its midtown store.

(**NOT:** I saw in yesterday's paper *where* Schuster's had changed its mind about closing its midtown store.)

Whether–if. See *If–whether.*

Who–which–that. See ¶1062.

Who–whom. See ¶1061.

Whoever–who ever

Whoever (anyone who) is elected secretary should write that letter at once.

Who ever made such a statement? (*Ever* is an adverb.)

Will–shall. See *Shall–will.*

Wise. Avoid the temptation to coin new words by attaching the suffix *wise* to various nouns. (Stylewise, it's considered bad form.)

NOT: *Costwise,* we're already 20 percent over budget.

BUT: We're already 20 percent over budget on costs.

NOT: *Sizewise,* what comes after extra large? Gross? (Even when used in a conscious attempt at humor, the approach leaves much to be desired. Once again, avoid the temptation.)

Would–should. See *Should–would.*

Would have. Do not use for *had* in a clause beginning with *if.* For example, "If you *had* (**NOT** would have) come early, you could have seen him."

Guidelines on Dictation, Transcription, Editing, Proofreading, and Filing

TAKING DICTATION

1201   Start each day's dictation on a new notebook page.

1202   Write the date in longhand in the lower left corner of each notebook page that you use during the day; for example, *Jan. 11, 1989.*

1203   Use a ballpoint pen with the type of point that allows you the greatest writing fluency. Have several pens at hand for emergency use, and keep a red-ink pen handy for making special notations.

1204   Number the notes for each letter, starting with *1* each day. If the dictator hands you a letter or other material related to the dictation, number it to correspond to your notes. This will speed the identification of background material as you transcribe.

1205   Use circled letters to indicate insertions in the notes. For example, write Ⓐ at the point in the notes where the first insertion is to be made; then key the notes for the insertion in the same way, Ⓐ. If the dictator customarily makes many such changes during dictation, keep one notebook column free for writing these changes.

1206 Write the following in longhand:

a. The addressee's name, unless you are familiar with the correct spelling or can easily confirm it; for example, *ec welford*.

b. Street names, unless you know or can easily confirm the spelling.

c. Any unusual words or trade names.

1207 Underscore in your notes as follows:

a. Draw one line under words that are to be underscored in typewritten material.

b. Draw two lines under words that are to be typed in all-capital letters.

1208 Use a distinctive mark, such as a double line, to indicate the end of the notes for each dictated item.

1209 Leave a few blank lines between items of dictation so that you will have space to write any special instructions the dictator may give you—for example, *Transcribe first*.

1210 Mark the notes for top-priority items "Rush" (using a colored pen).

1211 Flag rush dictation by folding back the corner of the notebook page so that it projects beyond the edge of the cover.

1212 To turn notebook pages easily, use your "nonwriting" hand to keep the book steady, and with the thumb of that hand move the page gradually upward as you approach the bottom of the page.

1213 Watch for subdivisions of thought as you are taking dictation, and paragraph accordingly.

1214 Do not interrupt unless the dictator is so far ahead of you that you are losing the meaning of the dictation. Check doubtful words or sentences immediately after the dictator has finished the individual item of dictation. Read back the sentence containing the questioned word. If you are uncertain about an entire sentence, read back the sentence immediately preceding the one in question and as much of the one in question as you can.

NOTE: If you are getting too far behind, call out the last three words you are on. This simple procedure alerts the dictator that you are behind, and it also indicates exactly where you are in your note taking. The dictator will pick up your cue, go back to the words you repeated, and begin dictating again from that point.

TRANSCRIBING FROM SHORTHAND

1215 Check to see which items, if any, are to receive priority treatment. (See ¶¶1210–1211.)

1216 Check for special instructions from the dictator before you begin to transcribe (see ¶1209). Always make at least one copy of each item you transcribe.

1217 Confirm spelling, numbers, and other key details before you start transcribing.

1218 Transcribe directly from your notes. Develop the ability to read ahead as you transcribe in order to foresee such special problems as errors in grammar, incomplete sentences, and changes in the dictation (see ¶1205).

1219   If possible, do not make a paragraph more than eight to ten lines long. Also avoid dividing the letter into a great many very short (two- or three-line) paragraphs.

1220   Consider the advantages of displaying numbered or lettered items instead of running them together in a paragraph. (See ¶1357c, note.)

1221   Before you remove each page from the typewriter or print out the document, review the material for possible errors. (See ¶¶1229–1232 for techniques of editing and proofreading.)

1222   Cancel the transcribed notes with a diagonal line.

1223   Check your notebook at the end of each day to be sure that you have transcribed all your notes. If any are left, then the next day give them priority over all new dictation except for rush dictation (which should always be transcribed first).

1224   Keep a rubber band around the notebook at the last page transcribed so that you will know immediately where to resume transcribing or writing.

TRANSCRIBING FROM RECORDED DICTATION

1225   When you are transcribing from recorded dictation, the first decision you must make is whether to aim for finished work the first time around or whether to prepare drafts for review and possible revision. If the dictated material is straightforward and the dictator is not given to a great deal of mind changing (either while dictating or when reviewing the "finished" transcript), then it is more efficient to aim for finished work. However, if the material is complicated or if the dictator is likely to alter the wording, then it makes sense to prepare drafts.

NOTE: If you are doing a draft, insert the word *DRAFT* and the date in the upper left corner. For safety, keep a copy of the draft while the original is being reviewed by the dictator.

1226   By means of index slips, program disks, or electronic cuing (depending on the equipment being used), the dictator can indicate where each recorded item ends (and thereby permit the transcriber to guess at the length of each item). In the same way, the dictator can indicate where he or she has given special directions or made changes in the material previously dictated. If the dictator makes use of this type of device, then before you begin to transcribe:

   a. Try to gauge how long each dictated item will be when transcribed. In that way you can decide what line length, margins, and spacing to use so as to hold each item to one page if at all possible and still execute the material attractively in the space available.

   ❏ *For guidelines on line length, margins, and spacing, see ¶¶1304–1308 for letters, ¶¶1392–1393 for memos, and ¶¶1406–1410, 1424 for reports.*

   b. Scan the recorded dictation for any special directions or corrections given by the dictator. These could significantly affect the wording of the material or the order in which you transcribe the individual items.

   NOTE: If the dictator does not make use of this type of device, you may have to use a standard format with respect to line length, margins, and spacing unless you are using a word processor and can format the document later. Without advance warning about special directions or corrections elsewhere in the recorded material, you may find it necessary to present your transcripts as drafts, even if your objective was to produce final work the first time.

1227 As you transcribe from the recorded dictation:

a. Try to listen for a complete clause or at least a complete phrase. In that way you can grasp individual words in context, and you will know, for example, whether to type *there, their,* or *they're* when you hear the sound that could signify any of these words.

❏ *For an extensive list of words that sound alike, see ¶719.*

b. Listen for changes in the dictator's voice as well as for pauses. If the voice drops on a word or phrase within a sentence, that could be a cue that commas (or perhaps parentheses) are needed to set off a nonessential element (see ¶141, note). Moreover, the dictator's voice should indicate when you have come to the end of a complete thought. However, listen ahead to the next few words. You may simply have come to the end of the main clause in a larger sentence, and thus you may need to insert a comma (or perhaps a semicolon or colon or even a dash) instead of the customary period. And when you do come to the end of a sentence, the dictator's voice will usually suggest whether to end with a question mark (the voice goes up), a period (the voice comes down), or an exclamation point (the voice comes down hard).

NOTE: Review the examples in Sections 1 and 2, and even say them out loud so that you can become more sensitive to the voice changes, pauses, and connective words that suggest certain types of punctuation.

c. Listen also for the changes in thought and the long pauses that typically signify the start of new paragraphs. (See ¶1219.)

1228 Before you remove each page from the typewriter or print out the document, review the material for errors (see ¶¶1229–1232). Since you do not have an original version in writing to proofread your copy against, you must be especially attentive to the possibility that a word may have been omitted or misinterpreted (for example, *then* for *than*).

NOTE: As a rule, it is not feasible to play back the dictation as you read the page. However, if you spot a possible error or omission that you cannot resolve by reading the transcript, you should listen again to the recorded material or ask the dictator (whichever is simpler and faster).

EDITING AND PROOFREADING TECHNIQUES

1229 **a.** *Proofreading* is the process by which you confirm that the copy you are looking at faithfully reproduces the original material in the intended form. If the copy deviates in any way from the original, you have to mark it for correction, and once the corrections are made, you have to proofread the altered material to ensure that everything is now as it should be.

NOTE: Ordinarily, one person can handle the task of comparing the copy against the original and noting any necessary corrections. However, if the material is complex or involves many statistics or formulas, it is wise for two people to share the proofreading function—one (known as the *copyholder*) to read the original material aloud and also indicate the intended punctuation, capitalization, and paragraphing, as well as other significant details of style and format, while the other person examines the copy closely to ensure that everything appears as it ought to.

b. *Editing* is the process by which you examine material on its own terms (either in its original form or at a later stage): you question the material on the grounds of accuracy, clarity, coherence, and effectiveness; when you encounter problems, you resolve the ones you are equipped (and authorized) to handle, and you refer the other problems to the author of the original material.

c. If you were to encounter a set of figures as a proofreader, your responsibility—strictly speaking—would be only to ensure that the figures on the copy agreed with the corresponding figures in the original. However, as an editor, you might well question whether the figures in the original were correct as given or even the best figures that might be supplied. By the same token, if you were to examine running text as a proofreader, your responsibility would be only to confirm that the copy agreed with the original in wording and in stylistic intent. However, as an editor, you might question—and change—the wording, the format, and the style in the interests of accuracy, clarity, coherence, and effectiveness.

d. Many people function simultaneously as editors and proofreaders without realizing that they are operating at two different levels—one essentially *mechanical* (checking for similarities and differences) and the other essentially *analytical* and *judgmental* (looking for problems and solving them). Ideally, editing should be done on the original material so that all problems of substance, grammar, style, and form are resolved before a copy is executed in "final form." However, it would be a mistake to read the final copy merely as a mechanical proofreader, assuming that the original is perfect and that you need only to look for places where the copy deviates from the original. On the chance that problems may have gone undetected in the earlier editing, you need to read the final copy in that challenging, questioning way that distinguishes editing from simple proofreading. Depending on your experience and the length and complexity of the material at hand, you may be able to edit and proofread at the same time or you may need to make several readings, focusing each time on different things. The following paragraphs will suggest the kinds of things you should be looking for when you edit and proofread.

1230 When *proofreading* a document, be especially watchful for the following types of mistakes:

a. Repeated words (or parts of words), especially at the end of one line and the beginning of the next.

```
What are the chances of your        I have been awaiting some indi-
your coming to see us some-         indication of a willingness to
time this summer?                   compromise.

I can help you in the event         We are looking forward to the
in the event you have more          to the reception you are plan-
work than you can handle.           ning for the Lockwoods.
```

b. Substitutions and omissions, especially those that change meanings in a significant way.

```
Original Material                   Erroneous Copy
The courts have clearly ruled       The courts have clearly ruled
that this kind of transaction       that this kind of transaction
is now legal.                       is not legal.

In my opinion, there is no          In my opinion, there is
reason to suspect Fred.             reason to suspect Fred.

I hereby agree to pay you           I hereby agree to pay you
$87.50 in full settlement           $8750 in full settlement
of your claim.                      of your claim.

He is quite proud of his flat       He is quite proud of his fat
stomach.                            stomach.
```

(Continued on page 242.)

```
I'll gladly give you the job        I'll gladly give you the job
if you'll do it in a week and       if you'll reduce your price
if you'll reduce your price         by $200.
by $200.
```

c. Errors in copying key data.

	Original Material	Erroneous Copy
NAMES:	Katharine Ann Jorgensen	Katherine Anne Jorgenson
TITLES:	Ms. Margaret A. Kelly	Mrs. Margaret A. Kelly
ADDRESSES:	1640 Vauxhall Road Union, NJ 07083	140 Vauxhall Road Union, NH 07803
DATES:	October 13, 1986	October 31, 1987
PHONE NOS.:	(419) 555-1551	(418) 555-1515
AMOUNTS OF MONEY:	$83,454,000,000	$38,454,000
DECIMALS:	sales fell 5.2 percent	sales fell 52 percent
CLOCK TIME:	arrive at 4:15 p.m.	arrive at 4:51 p.m.
PERIODS OF TIME:	boil for 2 minutes	boil for 20 minutes

d. Transpositions in letters, numbers, and words as well as other typographical errors (such as strikeovers, floating capitals, and faint letters).

Original Material	Erroneous Copy
I'll buy two boats this May.	I'll buy tow boats this May.
a process of trial and error	a process of trail and error
Let's form a committee to re-view our pricing policy.	Let's from a committee to re-biew our pricing policy.
We'll need 82 binders for the seminar beginning July 12.	We'll need 28 binders for the seminar beginning July 21.
How can we thank you all for your thoughtfulness?	How can we thank you for all your thoughtfulness?

e. Errors in spacing and inconsistencies in format (for example, indenting some paragraphs but not others, leaving too little or too much space between words or after punctuation, improperly aligning or centering lines).

Original Material	Erroneous Copy
Dear Mrs. Neilson:	Dear Mrs. Neilson:
Thank you for your letter of April 24. Let me try to answer each of the questions you raised.	Thankyou for your letter of April 24. Let me try to answer each of the questions you raised.
First, we do not sell the components separately; they only come packaged as a set.	First,we do not sell the components separately; they only come pack aged as a set.

NOTE: As a final step in proofreading, check the appearance of the document. Have the corrections been neatly made and properly aligned? Are there any smudges or marks that need to be cleaned up? Does each page as a whole look attractive? Apply standards that are appropriate for the occasion. Documents prepared for higher management and for clients or customers of your organization should meet the highest standards of appearance. On the other hand, manuscripts, drafts, and even rush memos to coworkers can be sent forward with minor corrections neatly inserted by hand. Naturally, if you have access to word processing equipment, you should be able to input the corrections and quickly obtain a clean (and correct) page.

1231 When *editing* a document—either in its original form or in its final form—consider the material in light of the following factors.

❏ *For an explanation of the* proofreaders' marks *used to indicate the necessary corrections in the following examples, see* ¶1232.

a. Check for errors in *spelling* (see Section 7). Give special attention to compound words (see Section 8) and those with plural and possessive endings (see Section 6). Keep an up-to-date dictionary or a wordbook like *20,000 Words* at hand.

```
We had a similar break down in communications last May when a

high=level executive failed to inform us that the corporations

attornies had advised against it's proceding with merger neg-

gotiations.
```

NOTE: When the material is in its final form, also confirm the correctness of all word divisions. (See Section 9.)

b. Make sure that every necessary mark of *punctuation* is correctly inserted. (See Sections 1 and 2.)

```
How do you account for the fact that whenever we are about to

launch a new product the company cuts our marketing dollars
```

c. Inspect the material for possible errors in *capitalization, number,* and *abbreviation style.* (See Sections 3, 4, and 5.)

```
Please be sure to attend the Managers' meeting scheduled for

june 4th at three p. m.  There will be 5 or 6 announcements of

special interest.
```

d. Correct any errors in *grammar* or *usage.* (See Sections 10 and 11.)

```
Everyone of the sales representatives have made less calls in

the past six months then they did in the previous six-month

period.
```

e. Look for problems in *organization* and *writing style.* The material could be entirely correct in terms of grammar, style, and usage and still contain clumsy sentences, a weak organization, and a tone that is not appropriate for the occasion.

f. Be on the lookout for *inconsistencies* in the document. Resolve any problems that you can, and refer the rest to the person who wrote the original material.

When I met with you, Harry Mills, ⟨and Paula Fierro⟩ on May 8, we agreed that . . .

Ed: Wasn't Paula at the 5/8 meeting?

I think that as a next move you ought to ⟨fill Paula Fierro in⟩ on what happened at our May 8 meeting and get her thoughts about how we ought to proceed.

g. Look at the document as a whole and consider whether it is likely to accomplish its *objective*. If the document is intended to persuade readers to accept a recommendation that they currently tend to oppose, has the writer anticipated their objections and dealt with them? Or has the writer ignored the existence of such objections and thereby created the need for a follow-up document—or, worse, made it likely that the readers' negative leanings will harden into a flat rejection of the writer's recommendations?

PROOFREADERS' MARK	DRAFT	FINAL COPY
ss [Single-space	ss [I have heard / he is leaving.	I have heard he is leaving.
ds [Double-space	ds [When will you / have a decision?	When will you / have a decision?
+1ℓ# Insert 1 line space	Percent of Change / +1ℓ# 16.25	Percent of Change / 16.25
−1ℓ# Delete (remove) 1 line space	Northeastern / −1ℓ# regional sales	Northeastern / regional sales
Delete space	to̲gether	together
# Insert space	It may be	It may not be
Move as shown	it is ⟨not⟩ true	it is true
Transpose	believable	believable
	⟨is it⟩ so	it is so
O Spell out	② years ago	two years ago
	16 Elm ⟨St.⟩	16 Elm Street
∧ Insert a word	How much it?	How much is it?
Delete a word	it may not be true	it may be true
∧ or ∧ Insert a letter	tempe̲rature	temperature
Delete a letter and close up	commitment to buy	commitment to buy
Add on to a word	a real good day	a really good day
or / Change a letter	this supersedes	this supersedes
or — Change a word	and if you won't	but if you can't

NOTE: If you are editing material you yourself have written, consider all the points noted in ¶1231*a–g*. However, if you are editing material written by someone else, the extent of your editing will depend on your experience and your relationship with the writer. If you are on your first job and working for a literate boss, determine whether your boss has any special preferences with regard to matters of style. (What may look like an error to you could be an acceptable practice that you are not familiar with.) On the other hand, a boss who does not pretend to grasp the technical points of style will no doubt welcome your editing for such things as spelling, punctuation, capitalization, grammar, usage, and inconsistencies (see ¶1231*a–d, f*). How much your boss—or anyone else for that matter—will appreciate your comments about the organization, writing style, and effectiveness of the material (see ¶1231*e, g*) will depend not only on your relationship with the writer but also on the tact with which you make your comments. Do not assume that because you have a close relationship with the writer, you can speak bluntly. Indeed, the closer the relationship, the more tact you may need to exercise.

1232 Whether you are editing or proofreading, use the proofreaders' marks shown on page 244 and below to indicate the corrections that need to be made. Minor variations in the way these marks are formed are unimportant as long as the marks clearly indicate what corrections have to be made.

PROOFREADERS' MARK	DRAFT	FINAL COPY
···· Stet (don't delete)	I was ~~very~~ glad	I was very glad
/ Lowercase a letter (make it a small letter)	Federal Government	federal government
≡ Capitalize	Janet L. greyston	Janet L. Greyston
∨ Raise above the line	in her new book*	in her new book*
∧ Drop below the line	H2SO4	H_2SO_4
⊙ Insert a period	Mr Henry Grenada	Mr. Henry Grenada
⌃ Insert a comma	a large old house	a large, old house
⌄ Insert an apostrophe	my childrens car	my children's car
⌄⌄ Insert quotation marks	he wants a loan	he wants a "loan"
= Insert a hyphen	a first rate job	a first-rate job
	ask the coowner	ask the co-owner
OR ⊥/M Insert a dash or change a hyphen to a dash	Success at last! Here it is cash!	Success—at last! Here it is—cash!
___ Insert underscore	an issue of <u>Time</u>	an issue of <u>Time</u>
Delete underscore	a very long day	a very long day
( ) Insert parentheses	left today(May 3)	left today (May 3)
¶ Start a new paragraph	¶ If that is so	If that is so
⊐2 Indent 2 spaces	Net investment in tangible assets	Net investment in tangible assets
⊐ Move to the right	$38,367,000	$38,367,000
⊏ Move to the left	Anyone can win!	Anyone can win!
= Align horizontally	Bob Muller TO:	TO: Bob Muller
‖ Align vertically	‖Jon Peters Ellen March	Jon Peters Ellen March

SUBMITTING YOUR WORK

1233 Submit finished work and drafts in batches for your boss's review, approval, and (when appropriate) signature or initials. The size and timing of the batches will depend on your boss's schedule as well as the schedule for mail pickups.

NOTE: Present each top-priority item as soon as you complete it.

1234 Present each item unfolded, and attach any materials that are supposed to accompany the item when it is forwarded to the intended recipient. Also provide any related documents or drafts that your boss may need to refer to when reviewing the item.

1235 If the item is a letter that will be sent in a letter-size envelope, clip the envelope to the unfolded letter. If your boss's preference is to review the address on the envelope, place the top of the unfolded letter (plus any enclosures) under the flap of the envelope with the address side of the envelope facing up. If your boss does not wish to review the envelope, clip it to the underside of the letter.

NOTE: If copies of the letter also have to be signed, assemble each copy in the same way you arranged the original letter. Place these copies under the original when presenting them to the boss.

1236 Staple the file copy on top of the letter or other material to which it is related.

RULES FOR ALPHABETIC FILING

According to the Association of Records Managers and Administrators (ARMA), there are three types of alphabetic filing: (1) letter by letter (in which spaces between words are disregarded); (2) word by word; and (3) unit by unit (in which every word, abbreviation, and initial is considered a separate unit). ARMA has found that the unit-by-unit method is the easiest for training purposes.*

The 25 rules that follow reflect the unit-by-unit method and embody the filing principles incorporated in all Gregg texts and training materials. The rules of unit-by-unit alphabetizing vary to some extent from one authority to another, and actual practices vary to a far greater extent from one organization to another. While space limitations make it impossible to compare the Gregg filing rules with those of all the other major sources, the following paragraphs do indicate those few places where ARMA's rules differ from Gregg's. Moreover, the following paragraphs take note of ARMA recommendations that can prove very helpful as you apply these filing rules.

1237 Rule 1: Alphabetic Order

a. Alphabetize names by comparing the first units of the names letter by letter.

NAME	UNIT 1	UNIT 2	UNIT 3
Alphanumerics	Alphanumerics		
Butterfield	Butterfield		
Eagleton	Eagleton		
Eaton	Eaton		
Eberhardt	Eberhardt		
Eberhart	Eberhart		

---

*Rules for Alphabetic Filing, Association of Records Managers and Administrators, Inc., Prairie Village, Kans., 1972.

b. Consider second units only when the first units are identical.

NAME	UNIT 1	UNIT 2	UNIT 3
Fairbanks Enterprises	Fairbanks	Enterprises	
Fairbanks Industries	Fairbanks	Industries	

c. Consider third units only when both the first and second units are identical, and so on.

Gold Star Company	Gold	Star	Company
Gold Star Corporation	Gold	Star	Corporation

NOTE: If two names are identical, distinguish them on the basis of geographic location. See Rule 18 (¶1254).

1238 Rule 2: Nothing Comes Before Something

a. A name consisting of a single letter comes before a name consisting of a word that begins with the same letter.

H	H
Hancock	Hancock

b. A name consisting of one word comes before a name that consists of the same word plus one or more other words.

Harley	Harley	
Harley House	Harley	House

c. A name consisting of two or more words comes before a name that consists of the same two or more words plus another word, and so on.

Harrington Park	Harrington	Park	
Harrington Park Foods	Harrington	Park	Foods

The following rules (¶¶1239–1244) deal with the names of individuals.

1239 Rule 3: Last Name First

Treat each part of the name of an individual as a separate unit, and consider the units in this order: last name, first name or initial, middle name or initial (if any).

Jacobs	Jacobs		
L. Jacobs	Jacobs	L.	
L. Mitchell Jacobs	Jacobs	L.	Mitchell
Stephen Jacobson	Jacobson	Stephen	
Stephen B. Jacobson	Jacobson	Stephen	B.
Steven A. Jacobson	Jacobson	Steven	A.
B. Jacoby	Jacoby	B.	
B. T. Jacoby	Jacoby	B.	T.
Bruce Jacoby	Jacoby	Bruce	
Bruce E. Jacoby	Jacoby	Bruce	E.

NOTE: ARMA recommends that when you are dealing with a foreign name and cannot distinguish the surname from the first name, you should consider each part of the name in the order in which it is written. Naturally, whenever you can make the distinction, consider the last name first.

NAME	UNIT 1	UNIT 2	UNIT 3
Kwong Kow Ng	Kwong	Kow	Ng
Ng Kwong Cheung	Ng	Kwong	Cheung
Philip Ng	Ng	Philip	

1240 Rule 4: Prefixes

a. Consider a prefix (such as *Mc* in *McDonald*) as part of the name, not as a separate unit. Ignore variations in spacing, punctuation, or capitalization in names that contain prefixes (for example, *d', D', Da, de, De, Del, Dela, Des, Di, Du, Fitz, La, Le, M', Mac, O', St., Van, Van de, Van der, Von,* and *Von der*).

A. Serafino Delacruz	Delacruz	A.	Serafino
Anna C. deLaCruz	deLaCruz	Anna	C.
Michael B. DeLacruz	DeLacruz	Michael	B.
Victor P. DeLaCruz	DeLaCruz	Victor	P.
LaVerne F. Delano	Delano	LaVerne	F.
Pierre Des Trempes	Des Trempes	Pierre	
Brian K. De Voto	De Voto	Brian	K.

b. Consider the prefixes *M', Mac,* and *Mc* exactly as they are spelled.

Marilyn R. Mack	Mack	Marilyn	R.
Francis X. MacKay	MacKay	Francis	X.
Irene J. Mackay	Mackay	Irene	J.
Timothy F. Madison	Madison	Timothy	F.
Patrick J. McHale	McHale	Patrick	J.
Andrew W. Mead	Mead	Andrew	W.

c. Alphabetize the prefix *St.* as though it were spelled out—*Saint.*

George R. Sahady	Sahady	George	R.
Kyle N. St. Clair	Saint Clair	Kyle	N.
Peter St. Claire	Saint Claire	Peter	
Jeffrey T. Sakowitz	Sakowitz	Jeffrey	T.

NOTE: ARMA observes that when a file contains a large number of names all beginning with the same prefix, the trend is to treat the prefix as if it were a separate letter group. Since the prefixes *M', Mac,* and *Mc* are considered variants of a common prefix, all the names beginning with these forms would be grouped together in alphabetic order and placed before the regular sequence of names beginning with *M.*

1241 Rule 5: Hyphenated Individual Names

Consider the hyphenated part of a name as one unit. Ignore the hyphen.

S. T. Laverty-Powell	Laverty-Powell	S.	T.
Jean V. Tillery-Hall	Tillery-Hall	Jean	V.
Jean-Pierre Vigneau	Vigneau	Jean-Pierre	
Ann-Marie Woodward	Woodward	Ann-Marie	

a. Ignore a title used with the last name plus one or more parts of an individual's name, but consider a title as the first unit if it is used with only one part of an individual's name.

NAME	UNIT 1	UNIT 2	UNIT 3
Dr. Nelson P. Hatch	Hatch	Nelson	P.
Senator Wilma O. Norton	Norton	Wilma	O.
Prince Andrew	Prince	Andrew	
Saint Elizabeth*	Saint	Elizabeth	

*Note that *Saint* as a title is considered a separate unit, whereas *Saint* as a prefix in a personal name is considered only part of a unit. (See ¶1240c for examples of *Saint* used as a prefix.)

b. Consider the title *Mrs.* as a unit if a woman uses her husband's name and you do not know her first name. Treat *Mrs.* as it is spelled.

Colonel Harry Mouton	Mouton	Harry	
Mrs. Harry Mouton (whose own first name is not known)	Mouton	Harry	Mrs.
Mrs. Peter J. Nearing (whose own first name is known to be *June*)	Nearing	June*	
Mr. Peter J. Nearing	Nearing	Peter	J.

*When a married woman's name is treated in this way, provide a cross-reference to her husband's name. (In this case the cross-reference would read *Nearing, Peter J., Mrs.*)

NOTE: ARMA recommends that courtesy titles (*Mr., Miss, Mrs., Ms.*) not be considered as units unless they are needed to distinguish persons with identical names. If used, these titles are treated as the last unit and alphabetized in their abbreviated form.

Miss Leslie Warner	Warner	Leslie	(Miss)
Mr. Leslie Warner	Warner	Leslie	(Mr.)
Mrs. Leslie Warner	Warner	Leslie	(Mrs.)
Ms. Leslie Warner	Warner	Leslie	(Ms.)

By contrast, the Gregg style recommends that courtesy titles not be used to distinguish individuals with identical names (except as noted in *b* above). Rather, they should be distinguished on the basis of their geographic location. See Rule 18 (¶1254).

Ignore a seniority term (such as *Sr., Jr., II, 2d, III,* or *3d*), a professional or academic degree (such as *CPA, M.D.,* or *Ph.D.*), or any other designation following a name.

Foster R. Jamison*	Jamison	Foster	R.
Foster R. Jamison Jr.*	Jamison	Foster	R.
Foster R. Jamison III*	Jamison	Foster	R.
Jo-Anne D. Jensen, M.D.	Jensen	Jo-Anne	D.

*These three names are considered identical for filing purposes and must be distinguished on the basis of geographic location. See Rule 18 (¶1254).

NOTE: By contrast, ARMA considers *Sr., Jr., II, 2d, III,* and *3d* as units under all circumstances; *Sr.* and *Jr.* are alphabetized in their abbreviated form, and the numeric designations are sequenced in numeric order.

(Continued on page 250.)

NAME	UNIT 1	UNIT 2	UNIT 3
Edgar Kent	Kent	Edgar	
Edgar Kent Jr.	Kent	Edgar	Jr.
Edgar Kent Sr.	Kent	Edgar	Sr.
Edgar Kent 3d	Kent	Edgar	3d
Edgar Kent 4th	Kent	Edgar	4th

However, ARMA recommends ignoring degrees unless they are needed to distinguish individuals with identical names.

Ralph Arrington, LL.D.	Arrington	Ralph	(LL.D.)
Ralph Arrington, M.D.	Arrington	Ralph	(M.D.)
Ralph Arrington, Ph.D.	Arrington	Ralph	(Ph.D.)

1244 Rule 8: Abbreviated Names and Nicknames

Consider any abbreviated part of a name (such as *Wm.* for *William*) as if written in full. (For the purposes of this rule, initials standing for a first or middle name are not considered abbreviations.) Consider a name such as *Al* or *Kate* only if it is the person's true name or if the true name is not known.

Chas. E. Kassily	Kassily	Charles	E.
William (Skip) Leaden	Leaden	William	
Billy Joe Marker	Marker	Billy	Joe
J. D. Parkinson	Parkinson	J.	D.

NOTE: ARMA wisely observes that in certain areas, where it is common to find initials and nicknames used in place of given names, you need to exercise caution before converting these forms to full names. Moreover, ARMA notes that when an individual is known by a nickname alone, without a surname, you should consider each word in the nickname as a unit (except for *the*).

Big Al	Big	Al	
The Fat Lady	Fat	Lady	
Handy Joe Bob	Handy	Joe	Bob
Mad Man Marko	Mad	Man	Marko

The following rules (¶¶1245–1254) deal with organizational names.

1245 Rule 9: First Word First

a. Treat each word in the name of an organization as a separate unit, and consider the units in the same order as they are written.

NAME	UNIT 1	UNIT 2	UNIT 3	UNIT 4
American Data Communications	American	Data	Communications	
American Data Processing Corporation	American	Data	Processing	Corporation
Computer Enterprises	Computer	Enterprises		
Computer Systems Incorporated	Computer	Systems	Incorporated	

b. When the name of an organization includes the last name of an individual plus one or more parts of that person's full name, transpose only the parts of the personal name. See Rule 3 (¶1239).

NAME	UNIT 1	UNIT 2	UNIT 3	UNIT 4
Frank Balcom Construction Company	Balcom	Frank	Construction	Company
M. Clausen Optical Supplies	Clausen	M.	Optical	Supplies
Mark Clausen Interior Design	Clausen	Mark	Interior	Design
Mary G. Clausen Associates	Clausen	Mary	G.	Associates

NOTE: ARMA observes that some names of this type (for example, *John Hancock Mutual Life Insurance Company, Fred Astaire Dance Studios, Thomas Cook Travel*) are so well established that reversing the elements of the personal name could cause confusion. ARMA recommends that you consider such names in the order in which they are written and that you provide cross-references as necessary.

c. Consider a title in an organization's name as a unit. Treat abbreviated titles as though they were written in full, except for *Mr., Mrs.,* and *Ms.*

Captain Ahab Expeditions	Captain	Ahab	Expeditions	
Capt. Jack Seafood	Captain	Jack	Seafood	
Ma Blake Food Shops	Ma	Blake	Food	Shops
Miss Celeste Sportswear	Miss	Celeste	Sportswear	
Mother Goose Nurseries	Mother	Goose	Nurseries	
Mr. George Limousine Service	Mr.	George	Limousine	Service
Mrs. Ellis Bakeries	Mrs.	Ellis	Bakeries	
Princess Diana Gowns	Princess	Diana	Gowns	
Queen Anne Antique Shop	Queen	Anne	Antique	Shop

1246 Rule 10: Articles, Conjunctions, and Prepositions

Ignore an article (*a, an, the*), a conjunction (such as *and* or *&*), or a preposition (such as *for, in,* or *of*) in the name of an organization unless it is a distinctive part of the name.

The Lodge at Pebble Beach	Lodge	Pebble	Beach	
Top of the Triangle	Top	Triangle		
Trout & Ries Advertising	Trout	Ries	Advertising	
Ulwick and Shuster Enterprises	Ulwick	Shuster	Enterprises	

NOTE: In the following examples, certain prepositions are used distinctively.

In Plant Catering Corporation	In	Plant	Catering	Corporation
Off the Wall Racquet Club	Off	Wall	Racquet	Club
Out of Town News Distributors	Out	Town	News	Distributors
Over the Rainbow Gifts	Over	Rainbow	Gifts	
Up in the Air Tours	Up	Air	Tours	

1247 Rule 11: Abbreviations

a. Treat an abbreviation in an organization's name as if it were spelled out.

NAME	UNIT 1	UNIT 2	UNIT 3	UNIT 4
Smyly Grain Corp.	Smyly	Grain	Corporation	
Smyly Industries Inc.	Smyly	Industries	Incorporated	
Smyth Data Systems Co.	Smyth	Data	Systems	Company
Smythe Datafax Ltd.	Smythe	Datafax	Limited	

b. When a company name contains a person's initials plus a surname, do not treat those initials as abbreviations—that is, do not spell out the full names, even if you know what the initials stand for. However, transpose the elements in the person's name, as indicated in Rule 9 (¶1245*b*).

L. L. Bean Inc.	Bean	L.	L.	Incorporated
J. C. Hamill Corp.	Hamill	J.	C.	Corporation

NOTE: Although many organizations are commonly referred to by a set of initials, ARMA recommends that these corporate "nicknames" be changed to the official corporate name for filing purposes.

PBS	Public	Broadcasting	System	
YWCA	Young	Women's	Christian	Association

However, many people who recognize an organization by its initials do not know or cannot recall what the initials stand for. Moreover, they may not know when a company abandons its original name and adopts the initials as its formal name. For these reasons it may be safer to treat such initials under Rule 12 and provide cross-references as necessary.

1248 Rule 12: Single Letters

Treat single letters that are not abbreviations as separate units, whether separated by spaces or not. Consider single letters that are hyphenated as one unit.

A D S	A	D	S	
ADS Reports	A	D	S	Reports
A & D Terminals Inc.	A	D	Terminals	Incorporated
A–Z Rental System	A–Z	Rental	System	
Triple A Auto Parts	Triple	A	Auto	Parts
Triple A Realty Trust	Triple	A	Realty	Trust
WTOP (*a radio station*)	W	T	O	P
W Z Industries	W	Z	Industries	
W. Y. Young (*man's name*)	Young	W.	Y.	

1249 Rule 13: Hyphenated Organization Names

Consider hyphenated parts of an organization's name as one unit.

Mitchell Brothers Associates	Mitchell	Brothers	Associates
Mitchell-Brothers Financial Consultants	Mitchell-Brothers	Financial	Consultants
Mitchener Urban-Suburban Properties	Mitchener	Urban-Suburban	Properties

a. Consider as one unit a part of an organization's name that may be written as one word, as two words, or with a hyphen. (Ignore variations in spacing, punctuation, and capitalization.)

NAME	UNIT 1	UNIT 2	UNIT 3	UNIT 4
American Airlines	American	Airlines		
Delta Air Lines	Delta	Air Lines		
River View Country Club	River View	Country	Club	
Riverview Estates	Riverview	Estates		
River-View Gardens	River-View	Gardens		
Superior Millwork Co.	Superior	Millwork	Company	
Supreme Mill Work Co.	Supreme	Mill Work	Company	

b. This rule applies to words with phonetic spellings and to coined words consisting of prefixes, suffixes, and other combining forms. Treat all such words as one unit.

Aerospace Research Inc.	Aerospace	Research	Incorporated	
Aero Space Systems	Aero Space	Systems		
Aero-Space Unlimited	Aero-Space	Unlimited		
Paychex Inc.	Paychex	Incorporated		
Pay-Fone Systems Inc.	Pay-Fone	Systems	Incorporated	
Pay-O-Matic Corp.	Pay-O-Matic	Corporation		

NOTE: ARMA holds that combining forms which are now recognized as words by themselves should be considered separate units. Thus, instead of treating *Aerospace* as one unit (as shown in *b* above), ARMA would treat this term as two words, whether the original form is solid, spaced, or hyphenated.

c. Consider a compound compass point (for example, *Southeastern, Northwestern*) as one unit, even when the term is spaced or hyphenated.

Northeast Chemical Co.	Northeast	Chemical	Company	
North East Condominium Corp.	North East	Condominium	Corporation	
North-East Medical Labs	North-East	Medical	Labs	

NOTE: By contrast, ARMA recommends that each element in a compound compass point be treated as a separate unit, whether the original form is solid, spaced, or hyphenated.

Ignore the apostrophe and consider all letters in a possessive or a contraction as if they were written solid.

Curtis Imports	Curtis	Imports		
Curtis's Art Gallery	Curtis's	Art	Gallery	
Curtiss Courier Service	Curtiss	Courier	Service	
Curtis's Marine Supplies	Curtis's	Marine	Supplies	
Oleander's Window Displays	Oleander's	Window	Displays	
O'Leary's Camera Shop	O'Leary's	Camera	Shop	
What's Your Beef Restaurant	What's	Your	Beef	Restaurant

Consider a figure in the name of an organization as though it were written in words, and treat it as one unit. Express the number in as few words as possible. (For example, treat *1420* as *fourteen hundred twenty,* not *one thousand four hundred twenty.*) If the number is already given in words, accept the form in which it is expressed and treat the form as one unit.

NAME	UNIT 1	UNIT 2	UNIT 3	UNIT 4
Twelve Eighteen Realty Co.*	Twelve Eighteen	Realty	Company	
1200 Corp.	Twelve hundred	Corporation		
1218 Rentals*	Twelve hundred eighteen	Rentals		
1270 Cabaret	Twelve hundred seventy	Cabaret		
1265 Associates	Twelve hundred sixty-five	Associates		
Twentieth Century Press	Twentieth	Century	Press	
20th Century Travel Inc.	Twentieth	Century	Travel	Incorporated
Twenty-Eight Benbow Studios	Twenty-Eight	Benbow	Studios	
Twenty-five Hundred Club	Twenty-five Hundred	Club		
210th St. Assn.	Two hundred tenth	Street	Association	
Tyson's Route 23 Farm	Tyson's	Route	Twenty-three	Farm

*When converting *1218* to words, *twelve hundred eighteen* is the preferred form. However, if the number is already expressed in words some other way, accept the form and alphabetize it accordingly.

NOTE: By contrast, ARMA treats numbers quite differently. All names that start with *a number expressed as a figure* are to be sequenced in numeric order and placed as a group before the complete alphabetic file. All names that start with *a number expressed in words* are to be filed alphabetically. ARMA considers each word in the number as a separate unit. (A hyphenated word counts as one unit.) Note the difference when the examples given above are arranged according to the ARMA rules.

20th Century Travel Inc.	20	Century	Travel	Incorporated
210th St. Assn.	210	Street	Association	
1200 Corp.	1200	Corporation		
1218 Rentals	1218	Rentals		
1265 Associates	1265	Associates		
1270 Cabaret	1270	Cabaret		
A&A Leasing Corporation	A	A	Leasing	Corporation

Twelve Eighteen Realty Co.	Twelve	Eighteen	Realty	Company
Twentieth Century Press	Twentieth	Century	Press	
Twenty-Eight Benbow Studios	Twenty-Eight	Benbow	Studios	
Twenty-five Hundred Club	Twenty-five	Hundred	Club	
Tyson's Route 23 Farm	Tyson's	Route	23	Farm

NOTE: If a number appears *as a figure* elsewhere in the name, ARMA says that the name should appear immediately before the first similar name without a figure. If a number appears *spelled out* elsewhere in the name, ARMA says you should consider each word whether solid or hyphenated as a separate unit.

NAME	UNIT 1	UNIT 2	UNIT 3	UNIT 4
Parker 3-Hour Cleaners	Parker	3	Hour	Cleaners
The Parker 200 Club	Parker	200	Club	
Parker House	Parker	House		
Parker's One-Hour Photos	Parker's	One	Hour	Photos
Parker's One-Stop Shop	Parker's	One	Stop	Shop
Parker's Twenty-first Street Salon	Parker's	Twenty-first	Street	Salon

1253 Rule 17: Parts of Geographic Names

Consider each part of a geographic name as a separate unit. However, treat hyphenated parts of a geographic name as one unit.

St. Louis Packaging Inc.	Saint	Louis	Packaging	Incorporated
San Jose Graphics	San	Jose	Graphics	
South Carolina Paper Co.	South	Carolina	Paper	Company
U.S. Media Consultants	United	States	Media	Consultants
Wilkes-Barre Office Supplies Co.	Wilkes-Barre	Office	Supplies	Company

1254 Rule 18: Addresses

When two names are identical, alphabetize them according to their addresses.

a. First alphabetize by city or town.
b. If the city or town names are the same, consider the state. (For example, *Charleston, South Carolina,* comes before *Charleston, West Virginia.*)
c. If both the city or town and the state are identical, alphabetize by street name. (If the street name is a number, treat it as if it were spelled out.)
d. If the street names are also the same, alphabetize by direction if it is part of the address (for example, *north, south, northwest, southwest*).
e. If all these units of the addresses are identical, consider the house or building numbers by arranging them in numeric order from lowest to highest.

NAME	UNIT 1	UNIT 2	UNIT 3	UNIT 4	UNIT 5
McDonald's Durango, Colorado	McDonald's	Durango			
McDonald's Springfield, Missouri	McDonald's	Springfield	Missouri		
McDonald's Springfield, Ohio	McDonald's	Springfield	Ohio		
McDonald's 17th Street Tallahassee, Florida	McDonald's	Tallahassee	Seventeenth	Street	
McDonald's Spence Avenue, East Tallahassee, Florida	McDonald's	Tallahassee	Spence	Avenue	East
McDonald's Spence Avenue, West Tallahassee, Florida	McDonald's	Tallahassee	Spence	Avenue	West
McDonald's 23 Tangier Street Tallahassee, Florida	McDonald's	Tallahassee	Tangier	Street	23
McDonald's 870 Tangier Street Tallahassee, Florida	McDonald's	Tallahassee	Tangier	Street	870

The following rules (¶¶1255–1261) deal with special situations.

1255 Rule 19: Banks and Other Financial Institutions

Consider each part of the name of a bank or other financial institution in the same order as it is written.

NAME	UNIT 1	UNIT 2	UNIT 3	UNIT 4
Alameda First National Bank	Alameda	First	National	Bank
Bank of the West	Bank	West		
Cathay Bank of Los Angeles	Cathay	Bank	Los	Angeles
Farmers & Merchants Bank	Farmers	Merchants	Bank	
Mid-State Bank and Trust Co.	Mid-State	Bank	Trust	Company
Santa Clara State Bank	Santa	Clara	State	Bank

1256 Rule 20: Hotels and Motels

Consider each part of the name of a hotel or motel in the same order as it is written. If the word *Hotel* or *Motel* appears at the beginning of the name, consider the distinctive part of the name first.

Holiday Inn at the Embarcadero	Holiday	Inn	Embarcadero
Hotel Inter-Continental	Inter-Continental	Hotel	
Hotel Parker Meridien	Parker	Meridien	Hotel
Royal Motor Hotel	Royal	Motor	Hotel

1257 Rule 21: Hospitals and Religious Institutions

Consider each part of the name of a hospital or a religious institution in the same order as it is written. However, transpose the elements of a personal name that appear in the name of the institution.

Sidney Farber Cancer Institute	Farber	Sidney	Cancer	Institute
Lahey Clinic Medical Center	Lahey	Clinic	Medical	Center
Massachusetts Eye & Ear Infirmary	Massachusetts	Eye	Ear	Infirmary
New England Baptist Hospital	New	England	Baptist	Hospital
Newton-Wellesley Hospital	Newton-Wellesley	Hospital		
Beth Eden Baptist Church	Beth	Eden	Baptist	Church
First Congregational Church of Braintree	First	Congregational	Church	Braintree
Lutheran Church of the South Shore	Lutheran	Church	South	Shore
Saint Mary of the Assumption Church	Saint	Mary	Assumption	Church
Temple Shalom of Newton	Temple	Shalom	Newton	

a. Consider each part of the name of a university, college, high school, elementary school, or library in the same order as it is written. If a word like *University* or *College* appears at the beginning of the name, consider the distinctive parts of the name first.

NAME	UNIT 1	UNIT 2	UNIT 3	UNIT 4	UNIT 5
Cambridge Institute for Computer Programming	Cambridge	Institute	Computer	Programming	
Carnegie-Mellon University	Carnegie-Mellon	University			
LaGuardia Community College	LaGuardia	Community	College		
University of North Carolina at Chapel Hill	North	Carolina	Chapel	Hill	University
High School of the Sacred Heart	Sacred	Heart	High	School	
College of Saint Elizabeth	Saint	Elizabeth	College		
Walla Walla Community College	Walla	Walla	Community	College	
Washington and Lee University	Washington	Lee	University		
College of William and Mary	William	Mary	College		

b. Transpose the elements of a personal name that appear in the name of the institution.

Bernard M. Baruch College	Baruch	Bernard	M.	College	
John F. Kennedy Presidential Library	Kennedy	John	F.	Presidential	Library

NOTE: As in the case of certain company names like *John Hancock* (see ¶1245*b*, note), certain names of educational institutions (for example, *Sarah Lawrence College*) are so well established that transposing the elements could cause confusion. In such cases consider these names in the order in which they are written and provide cross-references as necessary. As a test, think of how these institutions are typically referred to. Most people speak of the *Kennedy Library* and *Baruch College,* so it would be natural for them to look up information under the surname. However, most people speak of *Sarah Lawrence,* so it is doubtful they would look up information under the name of *Lawrence.* (ARMA takes a slightly different position on this point: it sanctions the transposing of personal names when they appear in the names of *schools* but not when they appear in the names of *libraries.*)

For any organization that is part of the federal government, consider *United States Government* as the first three units. Then consider the name of the department, and finally the name of the bureau, division, commission, board, or other subdivision. (**REMEMBER:** For the following examples, the first three units are *United States Government.*)

(Continued on page 258.)

NAME	UNIT 4	UNIT 5	UNIT 6	UNIT 7	UNIT 8
U.S. Department of Commerce, Economic Development Administration	Commerce	Department	Economic	Development	Administration
U.S. Department of Labor, Bureau of Labor Statistics	Labor	Department	Labor	Statistics	Bureau
U.S. Department of the Treasury, Comptroller of the Currency	Treasury	Department	Comptroller	Currency	

NOTE: When you encounter the names of some federal agencies, they may not contain the initials *U.S.* or the department name (as in the examples above). As a result, it may not be obvious that you are dealing with a federal agency. In such cases you will have to consult a directory or some other reference work to determine the status of the agency. In this way you can confirm that the Customs Service is part of the U.S. Department of the Treasury, whereas Passport Services comes under the U.S. Department of State.

1260 Rule 24: State and Local Government Names

For any organization (except an educational institution) that is part of a state, county, city, or town government, first consider the distinctive name, followed by the word *state, county, city,* or *town* or by some other appropriate classification (whether or not the classifying term appears in the name as written). Then consider the name of the department, bureau, division, board, or other subdivision.

NAME	UNIT 1	UNIT 2	UNIT 3	UNIT 4	UNIT 5
Ohio Division of Consumer Protection	Ohio	State	Consumer	Protection	Division
Public Works Commission, City of Somerville	Somerville	City	Public	Works	Commission
Registry of Deeds, Suffolk County	Suffolk	County	Deeds	Registry	
Wisconsin State Bureau of Purchasing and Service	Wisconsin	State	Purchasing	Service	Bureau

1261 Rule 25: Foreign Government Names

For an organization that pertains to a foreign government, first consider the distinctive name of the country, followed by the word *Dominion, Republic,* or *Kingdom* or by some other appropriate classification. Then consider the name of the department, bureau, or other subdivision.

Dominion of Canada Department of State	Canada	Dominion	State	Department	
Federal Republic of Germany (West Germany), Ministry of Trade	Germany	Federal	Republic	Trade	Ministry

Letters and Memos

Section 13 provides guidelines for setting up letters and memos. These guidelines are not intended as inflexible rules; they can—and should—be modified to fit specific occasions as good sense and good taste require.

PARTS OF LETTERS

1301 A business letter has the following parts:

	Standard	Optional
Heading:	Letterhead or return address (¶¶1311–1313) Date line (¶1314)	Personal or confidential notation (¶1315) Reference notations (¶1316)
Opening:	Inside address (¶¶1317–1344) Salutation (¶¶1346–1351)	Attention line (¶1345)
Body:	Message (¶¶1354–1357)	Subject line (¶¶1352–1353)
Closing:	Complimentary closing (¶¶1358–1360) Writer's identification (¶¶1362–1369) Reference initials (¶¶1370–1372)	Company signature (¶1361) Enclosure notation (¶¶1373–1374) Mailing notation (¶1375) Copy notation (¶¶1376–1380) Postscript (¶1381)

❑ *Each of these parts is illustrated in the model letters on pages 262–265.*

1302 A business letter is usually arranged in one of the following styles:

a. **Modified-Block Style—Standard Format.** The date line, the complimentary closing, and the writer's identification all begin at center. All other lines begin at the left margin. This is the style most commonly used. (See page 262 for an illustration.)

b. **Modified-Block Style—With Indented Paragraphs.** This is exactly the same as the standard format described in ¶1302*a* except for one additional feature: the first line of each paragraph is indented 5 spaces. (See page 263 for an illustration.)

c. **Block Style.** All lines typically begin at the left margin. Nothing is indented except for displayed quotations, tables, and similar material. (See page 264 for an illustration.)

d. **Simplified Style.** As in the block style, all lines begin at the left margin. However, the simplified style has these additional features: the salutation is replaced by an all-capital subject line, the complimentary closing is omitted, the writer's identification is typed in all-capital letters on one line, and open punctuation (see ¶1309*b*) is always used. (See page 265 for an illustration.)

STATIONERY SIZES

1303 The following table lists the sizes of stationery most commonly found in current use, as well as the related metric sizes of stationery that might be introduced in the next decade.

Customary Sizes	**Metric Sizes**
Standard: 8½″ × 11″	A4: 210 × 297 mm (approx. 8¼″ × 11¾″)
Baronial: 5½″ × 8½″	A5: 148 × 210 mm (approx. 5⅞″ × 8¼″)
Monarch: 7¼″ × 10½″	(No metric equivalent)

LETTER PLACEMENT

1304 Top Margin

a. **Printed Stationery.** Place the date (the first element to be typed) on the third line below the printed letterhead, or position it somewhere between line 12 and line 15.

b. **Unprinted Stationery.** The top margin on the first page of a letter depends on whether you type a *letterhead* address for a standard business letter or a *return* address for a personal-business letter. (See ¶¶1312–1313 for positioning instructions.)

c. **Continuation Pages.** The top margin on each continuation page of a letter is 6 lines (1 inch or 25 mm). These pages are always typed on unprinted stationery (even if the first page is done on a printed letterhead). (See also ¶¶1382–1387.)

1305 Side Margins

a. The side margins will depend on the kind of stationery you are using and the size of the type—pica or elite.

NOTE: To identify *pica* type (also called 10-pitch type) or *elite* type (12-pitch type), type a series of periods and compare them with the ones below.

PICA: · · · · · · · · · ·   10 strokes to 1 inch (25 mm)

ELITE: · · · · · · · · · · · ·   12 strokes to 1 inch (25 mm)

(*Continued on page 266.*)

MODIFIED-BLOCK STYLE—STANDARD FORMAT

HEADING

OPENING

BODY

CLOSING

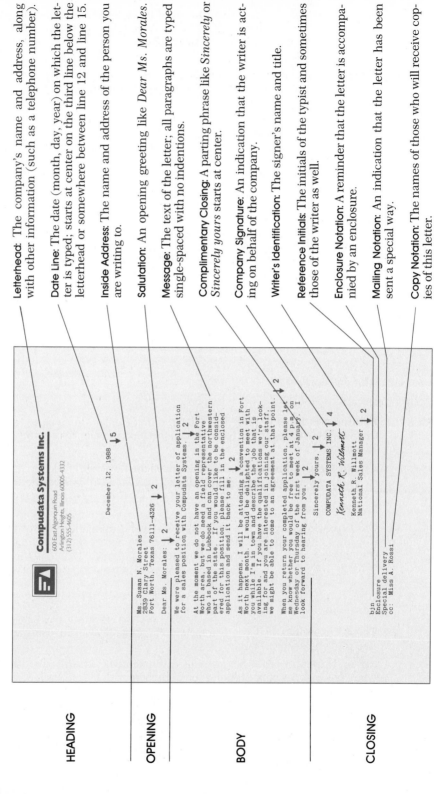

Compudata Systems Inc.
600 East Algonquin Road
Arlington Heights, Illinois 60005-4332
(312) 555-4605

December 12, 1988 ➜5

Ms. Susan N. Morales
2839 Clary Street
Fort Worth, Texas 76111-4326 ➜2

Dear Ms. Morales: ➜2

We were pleased to receive your letter of application
for a sales position with Compudata Systems. ➜2

At the moment we do not have an opening in the Fort
Worth area, but we do need a field representative
who is based in Lubbock and can cover the northwestern
part of the state. If you would like to be considered for this position, please fill in the enclosed
application and send it back to me. ➜2

As it happens, I will be attending a convention in Fort
Worth next month. I would be delighted to meet with
you while I'm in town and describe the job that is
available. If you have the qualifications we're looking for and you are interested in joining our staff,
we might be able to come to an agreement at that point. ➜2

When you return your completed application, please let
me know whether you would be free to meet at 4 p.m. on
Wednesday or Thursday of the first week of January. I
look forward to hearing from you. ➜2

Sincerely yours, ➜2

COMPUDATA SYSTEMS INC. ➜4

Kenneth R. Wilmott

Kenneth R. Wilmott
National Sales Manager ➜2

bjn
Enclosure
Special delivery
cc: Miss A. Rossi

Letterhead: The company's name and address, along with other information (such as a telephone number).

Date Line: The date (month, day, year) on which the letter is typed; starts at center on the third line below the letterhead or somewhere between line 12 and line 15.

Inside Address: The name and address of the person you are writing to.

Salutation: An opening greeting like *Dear Ms. Morales.*

Message: The text of the letter; all paragraphs are typed single-spaced with no indentions.

Complimentary Closing: A parting phrase like *Sincerely* or *Sincerely yours* starts at center.

Company Signature: An indication that the writer is acting on behalf of the company.

Writer's Identification: The signer's name and title.

Reference Initials: The initials of the typist and sometimes those of the writer as well.

Enclosure Notation: A reminder that the letter is accompanied by an enclosure.

Mailing Notation: An indication that the letter has been sent a special way.

Copy Notation: The names of those who will receive copies of this letter.

HEADING

OPENING

BODY

CLOSING

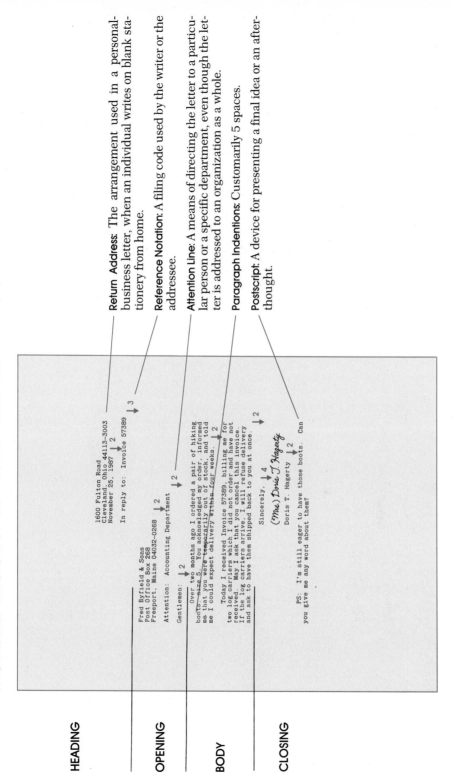

```
                                          1600 Fulton Road
                                          Cleveland, Ohio 44113-3003
                                          November 25, 1987

                                          In reply to: Invoice 57389

Fred Byfield & Sons
Post Office Box 2683
Freeport, Maine 04032-0268

Attention: Accounting Department

Gentlemen:

     Over two months ago I ordered a pair of hiking
boots—size 5.  You acknowledged my order, informed
me that you were temporarily out of stock, and told
me I could expect delivery within four weeks.

     Today I received Invoice 57389, billing me for
two log carriers which I did not order and have not
received.  May I ask that you cancel this invoice.
If the log carriers arrive, I will refuse delivery
and ask to have them shipped back to you at once.

                                          Sincerely,

                                          (Mrs.) Doris T. Hagerty

                                          Doris T. Hagerty

     PS: I'm still eager to have those boots.  Can
you give me any word about them?
```

Return Address: The arrangement used in a personal-business letter, when an individual writes on blank stationery from home.

Reference Notation: A filing code used by the writer or the addressee.

Attention Line: A means of directing the letter to a particular person or a specific department, even though the letter is addressed to an organization as a whole.

Paragraph Indentions: Customarily 5 spaces.

Postscript: A device for presenting a final idea or an afterthought.

BLOCK STYLE

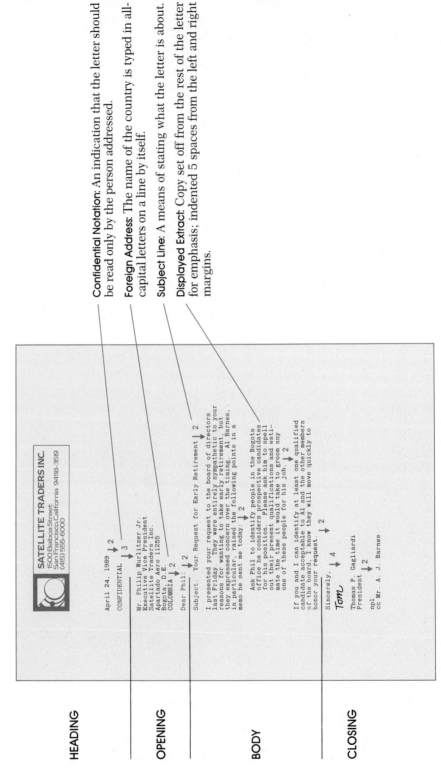

HEADING

OPENING

BODY

CLOSING

SATELLITE TRADERS INC.
1500 Balboa Street
San Francisco, California 94118-3519
(415) 555-6000

April 24, 1989 ↓ 2

CONFIDENTIAL ↓ 3

Mr. Philip Wurlitzer Jr.
Executive Vice President
Satellite Traders Inc.
Apartado Aero 11255
Bogota, D.E.
COLOMBIA ↓ 2

Dear Phil: ↓ 2

Subject: Your Request for Early Retirement ↓ 2

I presented your request to the board of directors
last Friday. They were entirely sympathetic to your
reasons for wanting to take early retirement, but
they expressed concern over the timing. Al Barnes,
in particular, raised the following points in a
memo he sent me today: ↓ 2

   Ask Phil to identify people in the Bogota
   office he considers prospective candidates
   for his position. Please ask him to spell
   out their present qualifications and estimate the time it would take to groom any
   one of these people for his job. ↓ 2

If you and I can identify at least one qualified
candidate acceptable to Al and the other members
of the board, I know they will move quickly to
honor your request. ↓ 2

Sincerely, ↓ 4

Tom

Thomas P. Gagliardi
President ↓ 2

npl
cc Mr. A. J. Barnes

Confidential Notation: An indication that the letter should be read only by the person addressed.

Foreign Address: The name of the country is typed in all-capital letters on a line by itself.

Subject Line: A means of stating what the letter is about.

Displayed Extract: Copy set off from the rest of the letter for emphasis; indented 5 spaces from the left and right margins.

SIMPLIFIED STYLE

HEADING

OPENING

BODY

CLOSING

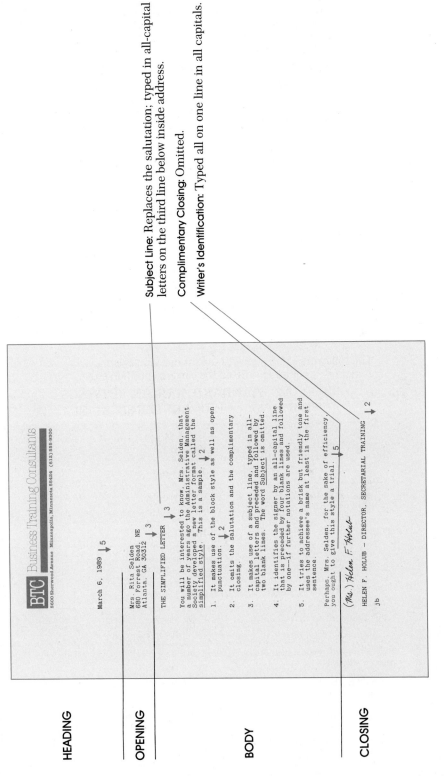

BTC Business Training Consultants
5600 Sherwood Avenue Minneapolis, Minnesota 55424 (612) 555-9300

March 6, 1989 ↓5

Mrs. Rita Selden
680 Forrest Road, NE
Atlanta, GA 30312 ↓3

THE SIMPLIFIED LETTER ↓3

You will be interested to know, Mrs. Selden, that
a number of years ago the Administrative Management
Society developed a new letter format called the
simplified style. This is a sample. ↓2

1. It makes use of the block style as well as open
   punctuation. ↓2

2. It omits the salutation and the complimentary
   closing.

3. It makes use of a subject line typed in all-
   capital letters and preceded and followed by
   two blank lines. The word Subject is omitted.

4. It identifies the signer by an all-capital line
   that is preceded by four blank lines and followed
   by one—if further notations are used.

5. It tries to achieve a brisk but friendly tone and
   uses the addressee's name at least in the first
   sentence.

Perhaps, Mrs. Selden, for the sake of efficiency,
you ought to give this style a trial. ↓5

(Mrs.) Helen F. Holub

HELEN F. HOLUB – DIRECTOR, SECRETARIAL TRAINING ↓2

jb

Subject Line: Replaces the salutation; typed in all-capital
letters on the third line below inside address.

Complimentary Closing: Omitted.

Writer's Identification: Typed all on one line in all capitals.

265

b. The following table shows standard margin settings to be used when the left edge of your stationery is positioned at zero on the carriage-position scale. (In this case your stationery is centered at 42 if you are using *pica* type or at 51 if you are using *elite* type.)

Table 13-1. STANDARD MARGIN SETTINGS WITH STATIONERY STARTING AT ZERO

STATIONERY	LINE LENGTH	MARGIN SETTINGS*
4-Inch Line		
Baronial and A5	Pica: 40 spaces Elite: 50 spaces	22–62 26–76
5-Inch Line		
Standard, A4, and Monarch	Pica: 50 spaces Elite: 60 spaces	17–67 21–81
6-Inch Line		
Standard and A4	Pica: 60 spaces Elite: 70 spaces	12–72 16–86

*Some writers add 5 spaces to the right margin setting in order to avoid making frequent use of the margin release key.

c. The following table shows standard margin settings to be used when your stationery is centered at 50 on the carriage-position scale.

Table 13-2. STANDARD MARGIN SETTINGS WITH STATIONERY CENTERED AT 50

STATIONERY	LINE LENGTH	MARGIN SETTINGS*
4-Inch Line		
Baronial and A5	Pica: 40 spaces Elite: 50 spaces	30–70 25–75
5-Inch Line		
Standard, A4, and Monarch	Pica: 50 spaces Elite: 60 spaces	25–75 20–80
6-Inch Line		
Standard and A4	Pica: 60 spaces Elite: 70 spaces	20–80 15–85

*Some writers add 5 spaces to the right margin setting in order to avoid making frequent use of the margin release key.

NOTE: If you are using a typewriter, follow this procedure to center your stationery at 50:

(1) Position the carriage or carrier so that the printing-point indicator is at 50 on the carriage-position scale.
(2) Crease a sheet of paper in half lengthwise; then unfold the sheet and insert it into the typewriter.

(3) Using the paper release, loosen the paper and slide it right or left until the crease is at the center of the printing-point indicator. Then reset the paper release to its original position.

(4) Set the paper guide at the left edge of the paper.

(5) Make a note of the point at which the paper guide appears on the carriage-position scale. Then, when using this size of stationery in the future, simply set the paper guide at the established point, and the paper will be automatically centered at 50.

d. Traditionally, business writers using standard (8½″ × 11″) stationery have set their margins for a 5-inch line for most letters; they have reserved the 6-inch line for very long letters. Now, however, an increasing number of writers are using a 6-inch line for most letters (the same line length used for reports and manuscripts).

1306 Bottom Margin

a. Leave a bottom margin of at least 6 lines (1 inch or 25 mm).

b. If the letter is continuing onto a second page, the bottom margin on the first page can be increased up to 12 lines (2 inches or 50 mm).

❑ *For guidelines on carrying a letter over from one page to the next, see ¶¶1382–1387.*

1307 Lengthening a Short Letter

To *spread* a short letter (under 75 words or about 8 lines of text) over one page, use any combination of the following techniques:

a. Lower the first line of typing by as many as 5 lines.

b. Allow 5 to 8 blank lines between the date and the inside address.

c. Use 1½ blank lines before and after the salutation, between the paragraphs, between the message and the complimentary closing, and between the complimentary closing and the company name.

d. Allow 4 to 6 blank lines for the signature.

e. Place the signer's name and title on separate lines.

f. Lower the reference initials 1 or 2 lines.

g. On standard, A4, and monarch stationery, use a 4-inch line length. (See the tables in ¶1305*b–c* for the appropriate margin settings.)

h. Type the inside address and the message double-spaced, but indent the first line of each paragraph.

1308 Shortening a Long Letter

To *condense* a long letter (over 225 words or 23 lines of text), use any combination of the following techniques:

a. On a page of printed stationery, type the date on the third line below the printed letterhead. On a page of blank stationery that calls for a letterhead (see ¶1312), type the letterhead single-spaced (rather than double-spaced), starting on line 7. On a page of blank stationery that calls for a return address (see ¶1313), leave a top margin of only 6 blank lines (rather than the 9 to 12 blank lines noted in ¶1313*d*).

b. Reduce the space between the date and the inside address to 2 or 3 blank lines (instead of the customary 4).

c. Reduce the space for the handwritten signature from 3 blank lines to 2.

d. Raise the reference initials 1 or 2 lines.

e. On standard and A4 stationery, use a 6-inch line length. (See the tables in ¶1305*b*–*c* for the appropriate margin settings.)

PUNCTUATION PATTERNS

1309 The message in a business letter is always punctuated with normal punctuation (see Sections 1 and 2). The other parts may be punctuated according to one of the following patterns:

a. **Standard (Mixed) Pattern.** A colon is used after the salutation and a comma after the complimentary closing. (This is the style most commonly used.)

b. **Open Pattern.** No punctuation is used at the end of any line outside the body of the letter unless that line ends with an abbreviation.

c. **Close (Full) Pattern.** Each line outside the body of the letter ends with a comma or a period. (This style is now rarely used.)

❑ *For an illustration of all three patterns, see page 269.*

SPACING

1310 Ordinarily, type all letters single-spaced. (For the use of double spacing in very short letters, see ¶1307*h*.)

The following rules (¶¶1311–1316) deal with the *heading* of a letter. The heading must always include two elements: a letterhead or a return address (¶¶1311–1313) and a date line (¶1314). It may also include a personal or confidential notation (¶1315) and reference notations (¶1316). The model letters on pages 262–265 show the relative position of these elements in the heading.

LETTERHEAD OR RETURN ADDRESS

1311 Printed Letterhead

The first page of a standard business letter is customarily written on stationery with a *printed letterhead* containing at least these elements: company name, street address or post office box number, and city, state, and ZIP Code. Most printed letterheads also show area code and telephone number. Some also provide a special address for cable messages as well as special phone numbers for the transmission of information by means of teletypewriter (telex) or telecopying equipment.

❑ *For the use of the nine-digit ZIP Code, see ¶1339, note.*

COLE, STEELE & BACKUS

1800 Avenue of the Stars   Los Angeles, California 90067-4201
Telephone: (213) 555-4345   Telex: ITT 424282
Telecopier: (213) 555-4265   Cable: COSTEBA

May 3, 1988

Mr. Bernard Kraus Jr.
Purchasing Agent
The Bergen Press Inc.
313 North Street
San Jose, CA 95113

Dear Mr. Kraus:

Sincerely,

HUDSON COMPANY

Lee Brower

Lee Brower
Sales Manager

mr
Enclosure
cc: Ms. Loo

May 3, 1988

Mr. Bernard Kraus Jr.
Purchasing Agent
The Bergen Press Inc.
313 North Street
San Jose, CA 95113

Dear Mr. Kraus

Sincerely

HUDSON COMPANY

Lee Brower

Lee Brower
Sales Manager

mr
Enclosure
cc: Ms. Loo

May 3, 1988

Mr. Bernard Kraus Jr.,
Purchasing Agent,
The Bergen Press Inc..
313 North Street,
San Jose, CA 95113.

Dear Mr. Kraus:

Sincerely,

HUDSON COMPANY,

Lee Brower

Lee Brower.
Sales Manager.

mr.
Enclosure.
cc: Ms. Loo.

1312 Typewritten Letterhead

If you are using plain paper and are writing a standard business letter on behalf of an organization, create a *typewritten letterhead* as shown below. Center the following information in four double-spaced lines, beginning on the seventh line from the top of the page: (1) the company name; (2) the street address or post office box number; (3) the city, state, and ZIP Code; (4) the telephone area code and number. (The date then follows on the third line below.)

```
                    ↓7
            TURPIN AND KELLY INC.
                             ↓2
            250 Mulberry Street
                             ↓2
        New York, New York 10012–4105
                                   ↓2
            (212) 555–3600
                          ↓3

                    September 28, 1988
```

1313 Return Address

If you are using plain paper for a *personal-business letter* (one you write as an individual from your home), type a *return address*.

a. Give the following information on three or more single-spaced lines: (1) the street address; (2) the city, state, and ZIP Code; (3) the phone number (if you want the addressee to have it); and (4) the date (see ¶1314).

```
212 West 22 Street, Apt. 2B    OR    Apartment 2B
New York, NY 10011–2706              212 West 22 Street
(212) 555–9097                       New York, NY 10011–2706
January 24, 1989                     (212) 555–9097
                                     January 24, 1989
```

b. For the *modified-block* letter style, start each line of the return address at the center of the page. (You may also position the return address so that the longest line ends at the right margin, but this format will require more time to execute.)

c. For the *block* and *simplified* styles, start each line at the left margin.

d. Leave a top margin of 1½ to 2 inches (9 to 12 blank lines).

DATE LINE

1314 a. The date line consists of the *name of the month* (written in full—never abbreviated or represented by figures), the *day* (written in figures and followed by a comma), and the *complete year*.

December 28, 1989 (**NOT** Dec. 28, 1989 **OR** December 28th, 1989)

NOTE: Do not use the style *12/28/89* or *'89* in the date line of a business letter.

b. Some writers write the date line in this order: day, month, year. This is the style typically used in military correspondence and letters from abroad.

28 December 1989

c. When using letterhead stationery (printed or typewritten), position the date line on the third line below the letterhead or somewhere between line 12 and line 15.

NOTE: For the *modified-block* letter style, you may position the date line as follows: (1) start it at the center of the page (preferred style); (2) position it so that it ends at the right margin; or (3) type it in some other position that is attractive in relation to the letterhead design (so long as it still stands out). For the *block* and the *simplified* styles, always start the date at the left margin.

d. When using a return address, position the date as shown in ¶1313.

PERSONAL OR CONFIDENTIAL NOTATION

1315 If a letter is of a personal or confidential nature, provide the appropriate notation on the second line below the date, at the *left* margin. Type the notation in all-capital letters or in capital and small letters that are underscored.

PERSONAL **OR** <u>Personal</u>   CONFIDENTIAL **OR** <u>Confidential</u>

REFERENCE NOTATIONS

1316 **a.** Printed letterheads for large organizations sometimes contain a line in the upper right corner that reads *When replying, refer to:* or something similar. When using this kind of letterhead, type the appropriate reference number or filing code 2 spaces after the colon. Align the number or code at the bottom with the printed words.

NOTE: If the guide words *When replying, refer to:* are not printed on the stationery but are desired, type them on the second line below the date (or on the second line below any notation that follows the date). Start typing at the same point as the date.

When replying, refer to: ALG–341

b. When you are replying to a letter that contains a reference number or when you want to emphasize the fact that your letter concerns an insurance policy, an order, or a similar document, type a reference notation on the second line below the date (or on the second line below any notation that follows the date). Start typing at the same point as the date.

In reply to: G241 782 935   Refer to: Policy 234844

c. When there are two reference notations to be given, type your own reference notation first (as indicated in *a* above). Then type the addressee's reference notation on the second line below.

When replying, refer to: F–17865
                                              ↓ 2
Your reference: GAR–X–7

NOTE: Some writers prefer to give the addressee's reference notation in a subject line. (See ¶1353*d.*)

The following rules (¶¶1317–1351) deal with the opening of a letter. The opening typically includes two elements: the inside address (¶¶1317–1344) and the salutation (¶¶1346–1351). It may also include an attention line (¶1345).

INSIDE ADDRESS

1317 Letters to an Individual

a. The inside address should include the following information: (1) the name of the person to whom you are writing; (2) the street address, the post office box number, or the rural route number; and (3) the city, state, and ZIP Code.

```
Dr. Margaret P. Vanden Heuvel        Mr. Albert W. Clemons Jr.
615 University Boulevard, NE         Meads Creek Road, R.R. 2
Albuquerque, NM 87106-4553          Painted Post, NY 14870
```

❏ *For the placement of the inside address, see ¶1319a; for the use of the nine-digit ZIP Code, see ¶1339, note.*

b. If the person lives in an apartment building, give the apartment number after the street address or on the line above.

```
Miss Susan H. Ellington              Mrs. Lorraine Martineau
Apartment 10G                        6834 Creston Road, Apt. 4D
3864 South Kettering Boulevard       Edina, MN 55435
Dayton, Ohio 45439-2017
```

c. Sometimes the address for a person living in a small town consists only of (1) the name and (2) the city, state, and ZIP Code. In this case type the address on two lines. (Do not separate the city from the state to make three lines.)

```
Mrs. Marie S. Allen
Thompson, ND 58278-9998
```

1318 Letters to an Organization

a. The inside address should include the following information: (1) the name of the business or organization, (2) a street address or a post office box number, and (3) the city, state, and ZIP Code. Whenever possible, address the letter to a specific person in the organization and include that person's job title and department (if known). If you do not have the name of a specific person, use a title instead (for example, *Director of Marketing* or *Advertising Manager*).

```
Mr. Arthur L. Quintero               Director of Research
National Sales Manager               Stanton Chemical Company
Paragon Industries                   Post Office Box 21431
211 North Ervay Street               Chattanooga, TN 37421-0431
Dallas, Texas 75201
```

b. When a room number or a suite number is included in the inside address, the following arrangements are acceptable:

```
Ms. Alice G. Alvarez                 James W. Chiverton, M.D.
Woodruff Construction Company        Suite 1200
416 12th Street, Room 12            1111 West Mockingbird Lane
Columbus, Georgia 31901-2528        Dallas, Texas 75247


Mr. Raymond Kermian                  Miss Pauline Leggett
Contemporary Tours Inc.              Steele & Leggett
Room 304, Tower Building             503 Hanna Building
2506 Willowbrook Parkway             1422 Euclid Avenue
Indianapolis, IN 46205              Cleveland, OH 44115-1901
```

1319   **a.** Whether a letter is going to an individual's home or to an organization, the inside address customarily begins on the *fifth* line below the date. If a notation falls between the date and the inside address (see ¶¶1315–1316), start the inside address on the *third* line below the notation.

> **NOTE:** In social-business correspondence (see ¶¶1394–1395), the inside address is typed at the bottom of the letter, aligned at the left margin and starting on the fifth line below the writer's signature or title (whichever comes last). In a purely personal letter, no inside address is given at all.

  b. Single-space the inside address, and align each line at the left. (If the message in a very short letter is to be double-spaced, double-space the inside address as well.)

1320   **a.** If a letter is addressed to two or more people at different addresses, the individual address blocks may be typed one under the other (with 1 blank line between) or attractively positioned side by side. If the inside address blocks take up too much space at the opening of the letter, they may be typed at the end of the letter, starting on the second line below the final notation at the left or, if there are no notations, on the fifth line below the signature block.

  b. If a letter is addressed to two or more people at the same address, list each name on a separate line. Do not show a position title for each person unless it is short and can go on the same line as the name. Moreover, omit the names of departments unless the persons are in the same department. In effect, type only those parts of the address that are common to the people named at the start. (On the respective envelopes for each individual, give the full address for that individual and omit all reference to others named in the inside address.)

```
Dr. Paul J. Rogers
Mr. James A. Dawes
Research Department
Sloan and Hewitt Advertising
700 North Harding Avenue
Chicago, Illinois 60624-1002
```

The following rules (¶¶1321–1344) provide additional details concerning the parts of inside addresses. See also Section 17 for special forms of address used for individuals, couples, organizations, professional people, education officials, government officials, diplomats, military personnel, and religious dignitaries.

NAME OF PERSON AND TITLE

1321   When writing the name of a person in an inside address or elsewhere in the letter, be sure to follow that person's preferences in the spelling, capitalization, punctuation, and spacing of the name. (See ¶311.)

NOTE: Do not abbreviate or use initials unless the person to whom you are writing uses an abbreviation or initials. For example, do not write *Wm. B. Sachs* or *W. B. Sachs* if the person to whom you are writing used *William B. Sachs* in his correspondence.

1322   In general, use a title before the name of a person in an inside address. (See ¶517 for appropriate abbreviations of such titles.)

  a. If the person has no special title (such as *Dr., Professor,* or *The Honorable*), use the courtesy title *Mr., Miss, Mrs.,* or *Ms.* (See also ¶1701.)

b. In selecting *Miss, Mrs.,* or *Ms.,* always respect the individual woman's preference. If her preference is unknown, use the title *Ms.* or omit the courtesy title altogether. (See also ¶1701*b*–*c*.)

NOTE: Follow the same practice in the salutation. (See ¶1349.)

c. If you do not know whether the person addressed is a man or a woman, do not use any courtesy title. (See also ¶1701*d*.) Follow the same practice in the salutation. (See ¶1349.)

NOTE: People who use initials in place of their first and middle names or who have ambiguous names (like *Marion, Leslie, Hilary,* and *Lee*) should always use a courtesy title when they sign their letters so that others may be spared the confusion over which title to use. (See also ¶¶1365–1366.)

1323 **a.** A letter to a husband and wife is customarily addressed in this form:

Mr. and Mrs. Harold D. Bennisch (**NOT:** Mr. & Mrs.)

b. If the husband has a special title such as *Dr.* or *Professor,* the couple is addressed as follows:

Dr. and Mrs. Thomas P. Geiger

c. If both husband and wife or the wife alone has a special title, list the names on separate lines.

Dean Walter O. Goetz   Dr. Eleanor V. McCormack
Professor Helen F. Goetz   Mr. Joseph L. McCormack

d. When these special titles are irrelevant to the occasion, use *Mr. and Mrs.*

Mr. and Mrs. Joseph L. McCormack

❏ *For other forms of address to use for couples in special circumstances, see ¶1702.*

1324 **a.** When *Jr., Sr.,* or a roman numeral such as *III* is typed after a name, omit the comma before *Jr., Sr.,* or the roman numeral unless you know that the person addressed prefers the use of a comma. (See also ¶156.)

b. Do not use a title before a name if the term *Esq.* follows the name. (See also ¶¶518*c,* 1704*a*.)

Rita A. Henry, Esq. (**NOT:** Ms. Rita A. Henry, Esq.)

NOTE: A comma separates the last name from the term *Esq.*

c. As a rule, do not use an academic degree with a person's name in an inside address. However, doctors of medicine and divinity often prefer the use of the degree after their names (rather than the title *Dr.* before). (See also ¶1704*b*.)

NOTE: If an academic degree does follow the person's name, separate it from the last name with a comma. Also omit the titles *Dr., Miss, Mr., Mrs.,* and *Ms.* before the name. Another title (for example, *Professor, The Reverend, Captain, Dean*) may be used before the name as long as it does not convey the same meaning as the degree that follows. (See ¶519*c*.)

Reva C. Calhoun, M.D.   The Reverend Ernest G. Wyzanski, D.D.

d. Abbreviations of religious orders, such as *S.J.* and *S.N.D.,* are typed after names and preceded by a comma. An appropriate title should precede the name, even though the abbreviation follows the name; for example, *The Reverend John DeMaio, O.P.* (See also ¶1709.)

1325 **a.** A title of position, such as *Vice President* or *Sales Manager*, should be included in an inside address whenever possible. Ordinarily, type it on the line following the name; if the title runs on to a second line, indent the turnover 2 spaces. Capitalize the first letter of every word in the title except (1) prepositions (like *of* and *for*) and conjunctions (like *and*) under four letters and (2) the articles *the, a,* and *an* when they appear *within* the title.

```
Mrs. Martha Hansen              Mr. Ralph Nielsen
Executive Vice President        Vice President and
                                  General Manager

Mr. Harry F. Benjamin           Ms. Evangeline S. Palmer
Chairman of the Board           Director of In-Service Training
```

NOTE: In the last example above, *In* is capitalized because it is the first element in a compound adjective (rather than a pure preposition as in *Editor in Chief*).

b. If the title is very short, it may be typed on the same line as the person's name in order to balance the length of the lines in the address; in this case the title should be preceded by a comma. As an alternative, a very short title may be typed on the same line as the name of the person's organization (or the name of the department or division within the organization); in this case the title should be followed by a comma.

```
Mr. J. C. Lee, President        Dr. Antoinette H. Marcantonio
Merchants National Bank         President, Haines & Company
```

IN CARE OF . . .

1326 Sometimes a letter cannot be sent to the addressee's home or place of business; it must be directed instead to a third person who will see that the letter reaches the addressee. In such cases use an "in care of" notation as shown below.

```
Professor Eleanor Marschak      OR  Professor Eleanor Marschak
In care of Henry Wardwell, Esq.     c/o Henry Wardwell, Esq.
```

NAME OF ORGANIZATION

1327 Ordinarily, type the organization's name on a line by itself. If the name of a division or a department is needed in the address, it should precede the organization name on a line by itself.

```
Ms. Laura J. Kidd
Assistant Vice President
Department of Corporate Planning
Holstein, Brooks & Co.
```

NOTE: A very short title may be typed on the same line as the name of the organization. (See ¶1325*b*.)

1328 When writing the name of an organization in an inside address, always follow the organization's style for spelling, punctuation, capitalization, spacing, and abbreviations. The letterhead on incoming correspondence is the best source for this information. Note the variations in style in these names.

(*Continued on page 276.*)

Time Inc.	BankAmerica Corp.
Newsweek, Inc.	Rogers Cablesystem Inc.
AMF Incorporated	USLife Corp.
Parker Pen Co.	U S West, Inc.
PepsiCo	Merrill Lynch Pierce Fenner & Smith Inc.
The Singer Company	Peat, Marwick, Mitchell & Co.
Engelhard Corp.	Gulf + Western Industries
Horizon Bancorp	Shearson/Lehman Brothers
Technicon Corporation	Ply*Gem Industries
Frye & Smith Ltd.	Ex-Cell-O Corporation
Fujitsu, Ltd.	La-Z-Boy Chair Co.
Canadian Pacific Limited	Fisher - Price Toys
INCO LTD	Prudential-Bache Securities, Inc.

NOTE: If the name is long and requires more than one line, indent any turnover line 2 spaces. (See ¶1329*e* for examples.)

1329 If you do not have some way of determining the official form of a company name, follow these rules:

a. Spell out the word *and*. Do not use an ampersand (&).

Haber, Curtis, and Hall Inc.   Acme Lead and Tin Company

b. Write *Inc.* for *Incorporated* and *Ltd.* for *Limited.* Do not use a comma before the abbreviation.

c. As a rule, spell out *Company* or *Corporation;* if the name is extremely long, however, use the abbreviation *Co.* or *Corp.*

d. Do not use the word *the* at the beginning of a name unless you are sure it is part of the official name; for example, *The Wall Street Journal* (see *e* below).

e. Capitalize the first letter of every word except (1) prepositions (like *of* and *for*) and conjunctions (like *and*) under four letters and (2) the articles *the, a,* and *an* when they appear *within* the organization's name.

```
Department of Health and        American Society for the
  Human Services                  Prevention of Cruelty
200 Independence Avenue, SW       to Animals
Washington, DC 20201-0001       441 East 92 Street
                                New York, New York 10028
```

NOTE: In the following example note that the article *the* is capitalized because it comes at the start of the organization's official name. Note also that the name of the newspaper is not underscored because it refers to the organization rather than to a piece of reading matter (see also ¶289*d*).

```
The Wall Street Journal
22 Cortlandt Street
New York, New York 10007
```

❏ *For the use or omission of apostrophes in company names, see ¶640.*

BUILDING NAME

1330 If the name of a building is included in the inside address, type it on a line by itself immediately above the street address. A room number or a suite number should accompany the building name.

```
Room 118, Acuff Building        858 Park Square Building
904 Bob Wallace Avenue, SW      31 St. James Avenue
Huntsville, AL 35801            Boston, MA 02116-4255
```

❏ *For additional examples, see ¶1318b.*

STREET ADDRESS

1331 Always type the street address on a line by itself, immediately preceding the city, state, and ZIP Code. (See ¶¶1317–1318 for examples.)

1332 Use figures for house and building numbers. Do not include the abbreviation *No.* or the symbol # before such numbers. **EXCEPTION:** For clarity, use the word *One* instead of the figure *1* in a house or building number; for example, *One Park Avenue.*

1333 Numbers used as street names are written as follows:

a. Spell out the numbers 1 through 10; for example, *177 Second Avenue.*

b. Use figures for numbers over 10; for example, *27 East 22 Street* or *27 East 22d Street.* The ordinal sign *st, d,* or *th* may be omitted so long as a word such as *East* or *West* separates the street number from the building number. If no such word intervenes, use the ordinal sign for clarity; for example, *144 65th Street.*

1334 When a compass point (for example, *East, West, Southeast, Northwest*) appears *before* a street name, do not abbreviate it except in a very long street address when space is tight.

    330 West 42 Street   3210 Northwest Grand Avenue

1335 When a compass point appears *after* a street name, follow the local style that predominates. In the absence of a local style, follow these guidelines:

a. Abbreviate compound directions (*NE, NW, SE, SW*) that represent a section of the city. Do not use a period with these abbreviations (see ¶531*a*), and insert a comma before them.

    817 Peachtree Street, NE   120 112th Street, NW

b. Spell out *North, South, East,* and *West* following a street name, and omit the comma. (In such cases these compass points are typically an integral part of the street name rather than a designation of a section of the city.)

    10 Park Avenue South   2049 Century Park East

1336 Use the word *and,* not an ampersand (&), in a street address; for example, *Tenth and Market Streets.* However, avoid the use of such "intersection" addresses if a house or building number plus a single street name is available.

1337 Avoid abbreviating such words as *Street* and *Avenue* in inside addresses. (It may be necessary to abbreviate in envelope addresses. See ¶1390.)

❏ *For apartment and room numbers with street addresses, see ¶¶1317b, 1318b, 1330.*

BOX NUMBER

1338 **a.** A post office box number may be used in place of the street address.

    Post Office Box 1518 **OR** P.O. Box 1518 **OR** Box 1518

b. A station name, if needed, should follow the post office box number (and a comma) on the same line. If very long, the station name may go on the line below.

```
Box 76984, Sanford Station      P.O. Box 11215
Los Angeles, CA 90076-0984      Linda Vista Station
                                San Diego, CA 92111
```

c. Some companies show both a street address and a post office box number in their mailing address. Whatever information appears in the line immediately preceding the city, state, and ZIP Code determines where the mail will be delivered.

```
Henson Supply Corp.
315 South Water Street  ───── The mail will be delivered to this address.
Post Office Box 181   ◄───
Hartford, CT 06101-0181 ◄─── Be sure that the ZIP Code refers in this case
                             to the post office in the line above (and not to
                             the street address).
```

CITY, STATE, AND ZIP CODE

1339 The city, state, and ZIP Code must always be typed on one line, immediately following the street address. Type the name of the city (followed by a comma and 1 space), the state (followed by 1 space but no comma), and the ZIP Code.

```
Denver, Colorado 80217  OR  Denver, CO 80217-9999
```

NOTE: The U.S. Postal Service has now introduced the nine-digit ZIP Code (consisting in each case of the original five digits followed immediately by a hyphen and another four digits). The use of the additional four digits is voluntary, but as an inducement the Postal Service is offering discounts on postage fees. To qualify for a discount, mailers must submit a minimum of 250 *first-class* letters or postcards at one time; moreover, the envelope addresses must be readable by electronic (OCR) equipment (see ¶¶1389–1390). Because of these restrictions, many high-volume mailers are still weighing the costs of converting and maintaining their lists against the savings to be realized from the discount in fees. Therefore, the use of the nine-digit ZIP Code is likely to be spotty for the next few years.

1340 When writing the name of a city in an inside address:

a. Never use an abbreviation (for example, *Chic.* for *Chicago*).

b. Never abbreviate the words *Fort, Mount, Point,* or *Port*. Write the name of the city in full; for example, *Fort Dodge, Mount Vernon, Point Pleasant, Port Huron.* (See also ¶529*a.*)

c. Abbreviate the word *Saint* in the names of American cities; for example, *St. Louis, St. Paul, St. Petersburg.* (See also ¶529*b.*)

NOTE: It may be necessary, for reasons of space, to abbreviate city names in envelope addresses. (See ¶1390*a.*)

1341 **a.** In an address, spell out the name of the state or use a two-letter abbreviation of the state name (as shown in the chart on page 279).

NOTE: The two-letter abbreviations (for example, *AL* for *Alabama*) were created by the U.S. Postal Service and should be used only with ZIP Codes in addresses. The more traditional abbreviations of state names (for example, *Ala.* for *Alabama*) should be used in other situations where abbreviations are appropriate. (See ¶¶526–527.)

b. When using the two-letter state abbreviations, type them in capital letters, with no periods after or space between the letters.

c. When giving an address in a sentence, insert a comma after the street address and after the city. Leave 1 space between the state and the ZIP Code. Insert a comma after the ZIP Code unless a stronger mark of punctuation is required at that point.

My address next month will be 501 South 71 Court, Miami, Florida 33144-2728, but mail sent to my office will reach me just as easily.

Alabama	AL	Missouri	MO
Alaska	AK	Montana	MT
Arizona	AZ	Nebraska	NE
Arkansas	AR	Nevada	NV
California	CA	New Hampshire	NH
Canal Zone	CZ	New Jersey	NJ
Colorado	CO	New Mexico	NM
Connecticut	CT	New York	NY
Delaware	DE	North Carolina	NC
District		North Dakota	ND
of Columbia	DC	Ohio	OH
Florida	FL	Oklahoma	OK
Georgia	GA	Oregon	OR
Guam	GU	Pennsylvania	PA
Hawaii	HI	Puerto Rico	PR
Idaho	ID	Rhode Island	RI
Illinois	IL	South Carolina	SC
Indiana	IN	South Dakota	SD
Iowa	IA	Tennessee	TN
Kansas	KS	Texas	TX
Kentucky	KY	Utah	UT
Louisiana	LA	Vermont	VT
Maine	ME	Virgin Islands	VI
Maryland	MD	Virginia	VA
Massachusetts	MA	Washington	WA
Michigan	MI	West Virginia	WV
Minnesota	MN	Wisconsin	WI
Mississippi	MS	Wyoming	WY

1342 Omit the name of the county or area (such as *Long Island*) in an address. However, the name of a community, subdivision, or real estate development may be included, so long as it comes before the lines containing the mail delivery address.

```
Ms. Janet G. Arnold          NOT: Ms. Janet G. Arnold
Muir Meadows                       1039 Erica Road
1039 Erica Road                    Muir Meadows
Mill Valley, CA 94941-3748         Mill Valley, CA 94941-3748
```

1343 In a Canadian address, you may spell out or abbreviate the name of the province or territory.

Alberta	AB	Nova Scotia	NS
British Columbia	BC	Ontario	ON
Labrador	LB	Prince Edward Island	PE
Manitoba	MB	Quebec	PQ
New Brunswick	NB	Saskatchewan	SK
Newfoundland	NF	Yukon Territory	YT
Northwest Territories	NT		

NOTE: The following formats are used for mail going to Canada. (The format on the left is preferred for envelopes.)

```
876 Wolfe Avenue             OR: 876 Wolfe Avenue
Moose Jaw, Saskatchewan          Moose Jaw, Saskatchewan
CANADA                           CANADA S6H 1J6
S6H 1J6
```

1344 In other foreign addresses, type the name of the country on a separate line in all-capital letters. Do not abbreviate the name of the country. **EXCEPTION:** *U.S.S.R.* (*Union of Soviet Socialist Republics*).

```
Graf-Adolf Strasse 100        Rua Tabapua, 1105
Dusseldorf 4000               Caixa Postal 20689
GERMANY                       Itaim-Bibi, Sao Paulo, S.P.
                              BRAZIL
```

ATTENTION LINE

1345 **a.** When a letter is addressed directly to a company, an attention line is often used to route the letter to a particular person (by name or title) or to a particular department. For example:

```
Shelton & Warren Industries   Carrolton Labs
6710 Squibb Road              1970 Briarwood Court
Mission, Kansas 66202-3223    Atlanta, GA 30329

Attention:  Mr. John Ellery   ATTENTION:  SALES MANAGER
```

NOTE: This form of address emphasizes the fact that the letter deals with a business matter (rather than a personal matter) and may be handled by another person or department than the one named in the attention line. However, it is simpler to type the name of the person or department above the company name and omit the attention line. A letter without a personal or confidential notation will be presumed to deal with company business and will be handled by others in the absence of the person named in the address.

b. The attention line should be typed on the second line below the inside address, starting at the left margin.

c. The attention line may be typed in capital and small letters or in all-capital letters.

d. The word *Attention* should not be abbreviated. Use a colon after *Attention*.

e. The attention line is now customarily typed without any underscoring. However, if extra emphasis is desired, the complete line may be underscored.

❏ *For the salutation to use with an attention line, see ¶1351.*

NOTE: If you are using word processing equipment and plan to generate the envelope address by repeating the inside address as typed, you should insert the attention line in the inside address—between the name of the addressee and the street address or box number. While this treatment gives much less emphasis to the attention line than the format described above, it does eliminate the need to add the attention line on the envelope by hand. (See also ¶¶1389*m*, 1390*h*.)

```
Shelton & Warren Industries   Carrolton Labs
Attention:  Mr. John Ellery   Attention:  Sales Manager
6710 Squibb Road              1970 Briarwood Court
Mission, Kansas 66202-3223    Atlanta, GA 30329
```

SALUTATION

1346 Type the salutation, beginning at the left margin, on the second line below the attention line (if used) or on the second line below the inside address. Follow the salutation with a colon unless you are using open punctuation (see ¶1309) or you are typing a social-business letter (see ¶1395*b*). Omit the salutation if you are using the simplified style, and replace it with a subject line. (See ¶1352.)

NOTE: Be sure that the spelling of the name in the salutation matches the spelling in the inside address.

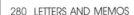

1347 Abbreviate only the titles *Mr., Ms., Mrs., Messrs.,* and *Dr.* All other titles, such as *Professor* and *Father,* should be written out. (See Section 17 for titles used by officials, dignitaries, and military personnel.)

1348 Capitalize the first word as well as any nouns and titles in the salutation; for example, *Dear Sir, My dear Mrs. Brand, Right Reverend and dear Sir.*

1349 The following are commonly used forms of salutation. (See also Section 17.)

To One Person (Name, Gender, and Courtesy Title Preference Known)
Dear Mr. Smith: Dear Ms. Simpson:
Dear Mrs. Gray: Dear Miss Wells:

To One Person (Name Known, Gender Unknown)
Dear Marion Parker: Dear R. V. Moore:

To One Person (Name Unknown, Gender Known)
Dear Madam: **OR**   Madam: (more formal)
Dear Sir: **OR**   Sir: (more formal)

To One Person (Name and Gender Unknown)
Dear Sir or Madam: **OR**   Sir or Madam: (more formal)
OR   Dear Madam or Sir: **OR**   Madam or Sir: (more formal)

To One Woman (Courtesy Title Preference Unknown)
Dear Ms. Malloy: **OR**   Dear Ruth Malloy: (see ¶1322*b*)

To Two or More Men
Dear Mr. Gelb and Mr. Harris: **OR**   Gentlemen:
OR   Dear Messrs. Gelb and Harris:

To Two or More Women
Dear Mrs. Allen, Ms. Ott, and Miss Day:
Dear Mrs. Jordan and Mrs. Kent: (see ¶618)
OR Dear Mesdames Jordan and Kent:
Dear Ms. Scott and Ms. Gomez: (see ¶618)
OR   Dear Mses. (**OR** Mss.) Scott and Gomez:
Dear Miss Winger and Miss Rossi: (see ¶618)
OR   Dear Misses Winger and Rossi:

To a Woman and a Man
Dear Ms. Kent and Mr. Winston: Dear Mrs. Kay and Mr. Fox:
Dear Mr. Fong and Miss Landis: Dear Mr. and Mrs. Green:

To Several Persons
Dear Mr. Anderson, Mrs. Brodsky, Ms. Carmino, Mr. Dellums, and Miss Eustace:
Dear Friends (Colleagues, Members, *or some other suitable collective term*):

To an Organization Composed Entirely of Men
Gentlemen:

To an Organization Composed Entirely of Women
Mesdames: **OR**   Ladies:

To an Organization Composed of Men and Women
See ¶1350.

NOTE: For greater formality, some writers use *My dear* in place of *Dear*.

1350 For an organization composed of both men and women, the salutation most commonly used is *Gentlemen:*

```
United Services Corporation
100 Kendall Parkway
Somerset, NJ 08873

Gentlemen:
```

However, this generic use of *Gentlemen* has come under attack, on the grounds that the masculine bias of the term makes it unsuitable for reference to a group that includes women as well as men.

a. One alternative is to use *Ladies and Gentlemen* or *Gentlemen and Ladies* in place of *Gentlemen* alone.

b. A second alternative is to address the letter, not to the organization as a whole, but to the head of the organization—by name and title if known, otherwise by title alone. Then the salutation would appear as shown below.

```
Mr. James V. Quillan          President
President                     (OR Chief Executive Officer)
United Services Corporation   United Services Corporation
100 Kendall Parkway           100 Kendall Parkway
Somerset, NJ 08873            Somerset, NJ 08873

Dear Mr. Quillan:             Dear Sir or Madam:
```

c. A third alternative is to use the name of the organization in the salutation; for example, *Dear United Services Corporation.* This approach is acceptable in routine or informal letters but should not be used in formal circumstances.

❏ *See also ¶1703c.*

d. Use the simplified letter style and omit the salutation.

1351 When an attention line is used (see ¶1345), the letter is considered to be addressed to the organization rather than to the person named in the attention line. Therefore, use one of the organizational salutations shown in ¶¶1349 and 1350. (Whenever possible, omit the attention line and address the letter directly to an individual in the organization—either by name or by title.)

The following rules (¶¶1352–1357) deal with the *body* of a letter. The body contains the text of the letter–in other words, the message (see ¶¶1354–1357). The body may also begin with a subject line (see ¶¶1352–1353), which briefly identifies the main idea in the message.

SUBJECT LINE

1352 In the *simplified letter style*, a subject line is used in place of the salutation. Start the subject line on the third line below the inside address. Begin at the left margin and type the subject line in all-capital letters. Do not use a term like *Subject:* to introduce the subject line. (See page 265.)

1353 In *other letter styles:*

 a. The subject line (if used) appears between the salutation and the body of the letter, with 1 blank line above and below. (See the illustration on page 264.)

 b. Ordinarily, the subject line starts at the left margin, but it may be centered for special emphasis. In a letter with indented paragraphs, the subject line may also be indented the same number of spaces.

 c. Type the subject line either in capital and small letters or in all-capital letters. The subject line is now customarily typed without underscoring, but for special emphasis the complete subject line may be underscored. The term *Subject:* or *In re:* or *Re:* usually precedes the actual subject but may be omitted.

```
Subject:  Introductory Offer to New        SUBJECT:  MORAN LEASE
Subscribers and Renewal Offer to
Present Subscribers                        In re:  Moran Lease
```

 d. When replying to a letter that carries a "refer to" notation, you may put the desired reference number or filing code in a subject line or below the date line. (See ¶1316.)

```
Refer to:  Policy 668485
```

MESSAGE

1354 Begin the text of the letter—the message—on the second line below the subject line, if used, or on the second line below the salutation.

1355 Use single spacing, and leave 1 blank line between paragraphs. (Very short letters may be double-spaced or lengthened by means of other techniques. See ¶1307.)

1356 **a.** Ordinarily, start each paragraph at the left margin. However, indent the first line of each paragraph 5 spaces if:

  (1) You are using the modified-block style with indented paragraphs. (See the illustration on page 263.)

  (2) You are typing the letter double-spaced.

  NOTE: Some writers use more than a 5-space indention for special effect.

 b. If a letter takes two or more pages, do not divide a paragraph with only two or three lines at the bottom of a page. Always leave at least two lines of the paragraph at the foot of one page and carry over at least two lines to the top of the next page. (See ¶¶1382–1387 on continuation pages.)

1357 **a.** **Quoted Material.** If a quotation will make four or more typewritten lines, type it as a single-spaced extract. Indent the extract 5 spaces from each side margin, and leave 1 blank line above and below the extract. (See page 264 for an illustration.) If the quoted matter represents the start of an indented paragraph in the original, indent the first word an additional 5 spaces.

  ❑ *For different ways of handling a long quotation, see ¶265.*

 b. **Tables.** When a table occurs in the text of a letter, center it between the left and right margins. Try to indent the table at least 5 spaces from each side margin. (If the table is very wide, reduce the normal 6 spaces between columns to as few as 2 spaces to prevent the table from extending beyond the width of the text.) Leave 1 to 3 blank lines above and below the table to set it off from the rest of the text. (See Section 16 for a full discussion on how to plan and execute tables.)

c. **Items in a List.** Type the list single-spaced with 1 blank line above and below the list as a whole. Either type the list on the full width of the letter, or indent the list 5 spaces from each side margin. If any item in the list requires more than one line, leave a blank line between all items in the list. If an item continues on to a second line, align the turnover with the first word in the line above.

```
When your analysis is ready to be distributed for the first
round of comments, I suggest you send it to the following
people inside the company:
                          ↓ 2
        Angela Lawless, director of information systems
        Thomas Podgorski, manager of corporate planning
        Herschel Farmer, vice president of finance
                                              ↓ 2
In addition, you may want to get reactions from two trust-
worthy consultants we have called on in the past:
                                            ↓ 2
        Dr. Harriet E. Fenster, professor of computer
        science at Michigan State University
                                        ↓ 2
        Wilson G. Witherspoon, president of Witherspoon
        Associates in Princeton, New Jersey
                                      ↓ 2
I can give you mailing addresses for these consultants if you
decide to get in touch with them.
```

NOTE: If the items each begin with a number or letter, type a period after the number or letter and leave 2 spaces before typing the text that follows. Align the numbers or letters on the period. If an item continues on to the second line, indent the turnover so that it aligns with the first word in the line above.

```
When I review the situation as you described it in your letter
of June 24, it seems to me that you have only two alternatives:
                                                            ↓ 2
1.  Agree to pay the additional amount that Henning now demands
    before he will start construction.
                                      ↓ 2
2.  Drop Henning and start the search all over again to find a
    firm qualified to handle a project of this size and this
    complexity.
              ↓ 2
As painful as it may be, you may find it easier to start looking
for a new contractor than to have to deal with new demands from
Henning once he is a quarter of the way through the job.
```

The following rules (¶¶1358–1381) deal with the *closing* of a letter. The closing typically includes a complimentary-closing phrase (¶¶1358–1360), the writer's name and title (¶¶1362–1369), and reference initials (¶¶1370–1372). It may also include a company signature line (¶1361), an enclosure notation (¶¶1373–1374), a mailing notation (¶1375), a copy notation (¶¶1376–1380), and a postscript (¶1381).

COMPLIMENTARY CLOSING

1358　Type the complimentary closing on the second line below the last line of the body of the letter. Ordinarily, start the closing at center. In a block-style letter, start the closing at the left margin. In a simplified letter, omit the closing.

1359　Capitalize only the first word of a complimentary closing. Place a comma at the end of the line (except when open punctuation is used).

1360　a. The following complimentary closings are commonly used:

PERSONAL IN TONE:	Sincerely,	Sincerely yours,
	Cordially,	Cordially yours,
MORE FORMAL IN TONE:	Very truly yours,	Very cordially yours,
	Very sincerely yours,	Respectfully yours,

　　b. An informal closing phrase may be typed in the complimentary closing position in place of one of the more conventional closings shown above. If the wording represents an adverbial phrase (one that tells *how* or *in what manner*—for example, *With all best wishes* or *With warmest regards*), follow the closing with a comma. If the wording represents a complete sentence (for example, *See you in New Orleans*), follow the closing with a period. In each case the comma and the period may be replaced with stronger punctuation as appropriate—that is, a question mark, an exclamation point, or a dash.

　　c. If both a complimentary closing and an informal closing phrase are used, type the complimentary closing in its regular position, and type the informal phrase at the end of the last paragraph or as a separate paragraph with the appropriate terminal punctuation.

　　d. Once a pattern of personal or informal closings is begun, it should not be discontinued without good reason. Otherwise, if a later letter returns to a more formal closing, the person addressed may wonder what has happened to the established relationship.

COMPANY SIGNATURE

1361　A company signature may be used to emphasize the fact that a letter represents the views of the company as a whole (and not merely the individual who has written it). If included, the company signature should be typed in all capitals on the second line below the complimentary closing. Begin the company signature at the same point as the complimentary closing.

```
Very truly yours,↓2
HASKINS & COHEN INC.
```

WRITER'S NAME AND TITLE

1362　a. Ordinarily, type the writer's name on the fourth line below the company signature, if used, or on the fourth line below the complimentary closing.

NOTE: If the letter is running short, you can leave up to 6 blank lines for the signature. If the letter is running long, you can reduce the signature space to 2 blank lines. (See also ¶¶1307–1308.)

b. Start typing at the same point as the company signature or the complimentary closing. **EXCEPTION:** In the simplified letter style, type the writer's name and title on the *fifth* line below the body, in all-capital letters starting at the left margin. (See ¶1363.)

c. Although some writers prefer to give only their title and department name in the signature block, a typewritten signature should also be included so that the copies will clearly show who sent the letter. If the writer prefers to omit the name from the signature block, then it should be spelled out in the reference initials. (See ¶1370*a*, *d*.)

d. Top-level executives usually have special stationery with their name and title imprinted along with other elements of the letterhead. In such cases supply a typewritten signature but omit the title.

1363 Arrange the writer's name, title, and department to achieve good visual balance. If a title takes two or more lines, block all the lines at the left.

```
Janice Mahoney, Manager        Ernest L. Welhoelter
Data Processing Division       Head, Sales Department

Charles Saunders               Franklin Browning
Assistant Manager              Vice President and
Credit Department              General Manager

CHARLES SAUNDERS — ASSISTANT MANAGER, CREDIT DEPARTMENT (simplified
style)
```

❏ *For guidance on capitalizing in signature blocks, see ¶1325a.*

1364 A person who has a special title should observe the following style in the signature block.

a. A person who wants to be addressed as *Dr.* should use an appropriate academic degree after his or her name (not *Dr.* before it).

Jane Bishop, M.D.   Morris Finley, D.D.   Nancy Buckwalter, Ph.D.

b. A person who wishes to be addressed by a title of academic or military rank (*Dean, Professor, Major*) should type this title *after* the name or on the next line, not before it.

Helene C. Powell   Joseph F. Corey
Dean of Students   Major, USAF

(**NOT:** Dean Helene C. Powell)   (**NOT:** Major Joseph F. Corey)

c. In cases where a title of address cannot be placed after a surname or cannot be inferred from the initials of an academic degree, then it may precede the name.

Rev. Joseph W. Dowd   Mother Ellen Marie O'Brien

1365 Ordinarily, a man should not include *Mr.* in his signature. However, if he has a name that could also be a woman's name (*Kay, Adrian, Beverly, Lynn*) or if he uses initials in place of a first and middle name (*J. G. Eberle*), he should use *Mr.* in either his handwritten or his typewritten signature when writing to people who do not know him. If given in the handwritten signature, *Mr.* should be enclosed in parentheses. If given in the typewritten signature, *Mr.* should appear without parentheses.

Sincerely,   Sincerely,

(Mr.) Lynn Treadway   *Lynn Treadway*

Lynn Treadway   Mr. Lynn Treadway

1366 A woman should include a courtesy title (*Ms.*, *Miss*, or *Mrs.*) in her signature unless she is called by a special title (see ¶1364). If she gives her name without any title at all, the reader of the letter is put in the awkward position of having to decide which title to use in a letter of reply.

NOTE: The courtesy title is enclosed in parentheses when it appears in the hand-written signature but not when it appears in the typewritten signature.

a. A woman who does not want to indicate whether she is married or single should use *Ms.* in either her handwritten or her typewritten signature.

Sincerely yours,   Sincerely yours,

(Ms.) Constance G. Booth   *Constance G. Booth*

Constance G. Booth   Ms. Constance G. Booth

b. A single woman who wants to indicate that she is a single woman should include *Miss* in either her handwritten or her typewritten signature.

Cordially,   Cordially,

(Miss) Margaret L. Galloway   *Margaret L. Galloway*

Margaret L. Galloway   Miss Margaret L. Galloway

c. A married woman who retains her unmarried name for career purposes may use either *Ms.* or *Miss*, as illustrated in *a* and *b* above.

d. A married woman or a widow who prefers to be addressed as *Mrs.* has many variations to choose from. The following examples show the possible styles for a woman whose maiden name was Nancy O. Ross and whose husband's name is John A. Wells.

Cordially yours,   Cordially yours,

(Mrs.) Nancy O. Wells   *Nancy O. Wells*

Nancy O. Wells   Mrs. Nancy O. Wells

Cordially yours,   Cordially yours,

(Mrs.) Nancy R. Wells   *Nancy R. Wells*

Nancy R. Wells   Mrs. Nancy R. Wells

Cordially yours,   Cordially yours,

(Mrs.) Nancy Ross Wells   *Nancy Ross Wells*

Nancy Ross Wells   Mrs. Nancy Ross Wells

Cordially yours,   Cordially yours,

(Mrs.) Nancy O. Ross-Wells   *Nancy O. Ross-Wells*

Nancy O. Ross—Wells   Mrs. Nancy O. Ross—Wells

NOTE: Giving the husband's name in the typewritten signature (as in the example below) is a style often used for social purposes. It should not be used in business.

Cordially yours,

Nancy O. Wells

Mrs. John A. Wells

e. A divorced woman who has resumed her maiden name may use *Ms.* or *Miss* in any of the styles shown in *a* and *b* on page 287. If she retains her ex-husband's surname, she may use *Ms.* or *Mrs.* in any of the styles shown in *a* and *d* on page 287. (**EXCEPTION:** The style that uses the husband's name in the type-written signature would be inappropriate for a divorcée.)

1367 A secretary who signs a letter at the boss's request customarily signs the boss's name and adds his or her initials. However, if the boss prefers, the secretary may sign the letter in his or her own name.

Sincerely yours,   Sincerely yours,

Robert H. Benedict   *Dorothy Kozinski*
        DK

Robert H. Benedict   Ms. Dorothy Kozinski
Production Manager   Secretary to Mr. Benedict

1368 If the person who signs for another is not actually the secretary, either of the following forms may be used:

Sincerely yours,   Sincerely yours,

(Miss) Alice R. Brentano   *Robert H. Benedict*
                                            ARB

For Robert H. Benedict   Robert H. Benedict
Production Manager   Production Manager

1369 When two people have to sign a letter, arrange the two signature blocks side by side or one beneath the other.

a. If they are placed side by side, start the first signature block at the left margin and the second block at center. If this arrangement is used, the complimentary closing should also begin at the left margin. (This arrangement is appropriate for all letter styles.)

b. If the signature blocks are positioned one beneath the other, start typing the second block on the fourth line below the end of the first block, aligned at the left. Ordinarily, begin typing at center; however, in a block-style or simplified letter, begin typing at the left margin.

REFERENCE INITIALS

1370 a. Type the initials of the typist alone (or those of the writer and the typist) at the left margin, on the second line below the writer's name and title. If the writer's name is typed in the signature block, the writer's initials are unnecessary here. However, if the writer wants his or her initials used, they should precede the initials of the typist.

b. Type the initials either in capital letters or in small letters. When giving two sets of initials, type them both the same way for speed and simplicity. To further simplify the typing, use a *colon* to separate two sets of all-cap initials and a *diagonal* to separate two sets of small-letter initials.

TYPIST ONLY:	GDL	**OR**	gdl
WRITER AND TYPIST:	DMD:MHS	**OR**	dmd/mhs

c. Include *Jr.* or *Sr.* with initials only if father and son work in the same office; for example, *EJMJr:FWL.* (However, it would be simpler to omit the writer's initials and make sure the writer's full name is typed in the signature block.)

❏ *For initials with names like* McFarland *and* O'Leary, *see ¶516c.*

d. If the writer's name is not typed in the signature line, type the writer's initials and surname before the initials of the typist; for example, *BSDixon/rp.*

NOTE: Assuming that the writer's name is given in the signature block, the simplest and most unobtrusive way to provide the necessary information here is to give the typist's initials alone in small letters.

1371 When the letter is written by someone other than the person who signs it, this fact may be indicated by showing the writer's and the typist's initials (not the signer's and the typist's).

> Sincerely yours, ↓4
>
> *Herbert Heymann*
>
> Herbert Heymann
> President ↓2
>
> pbr/jbp

1372 Do not include reference initials in a personal-business letter (see ¶1313 and the illustration on page 263) or a social-business letter (see ¶¶1394–1395 and the illustration on page 303).

ENCLOSURE NOTATION

1373 **a.** If one or more items are to be included in the envelope with the letter, indicate that fact by typing the word *Enclosure* (or an appropriate alternative) at the left margin, on the line below the reference initials.

NOTE: Before sending the letter, make sure that the number of enclosures shown in the enclosure notation agrees with the number cited in the body of the letter and also with the number of items actually enclosed.

b. The styles illustrated below are commonly used.

Enclosure	2 Enclosures	Enclosures:
Enc.	2 Enc. (see ¶503)	1. Check for $500
1 Enc.	Enc. 2	2. Invoice A37512
1 Enclosure	Enclosures 2	
Check enclosed	Enclosures (2)	

c. Some writers use the term *Attachment* or *Att.*

1374 If material is to be sent separately instead of being enclosed with the letter, indicate this fact by typing *Separate cover* or *Under separate cover* on the line below the enclosure notation (if any) or on the line directly below the reference initials. The following styles may be used:

Separate cover 1	Under separate cover:
	1. Annual report
	2. Product catalog
	3. Price list

MAILING NOTATION

1375   If a letter is to be delivered in a special way, type an appropriate notation on the line below the enclosure notation (if used) or on the line below the reference initials.

```
crj                HWM:FH                 tpg/wwc
Enc. 2             By Federal Express     Enclosures 4
Certified          cc Mr. Fry             By messenger
```

COPY NOTATION

1376   **a.** A copy notation lets the addressee know that one or more other persons will be sent a copy of the letter. The initials *cc* (for *carbon copy*) are still the ones most commonly used to introduce this notation, even when the copy has been made by some other process (like photocopying).

     NOTE: Some writers prefer to use a single *c* or the phrase *Copies to:* (or *Copy to:*) in place of *cc.*

     b. Type *cc* at the left margin, on the line below the mailing notation, the enclosure notation, or the reference initials, whichever comes last. If several persons are to receive copies, list the names according to the rank of the persons or in alphabetic order.

```
AMH:HT             mfn                    lbw/ncy
Enclosure          Enc. 4                 cc Contract File
Registered         cc Mrs. A. C. Case        Houston Office
cc Ms. Hoey           Mr. R. G. Flynn        Sales Department
```

     c. Type the initials *cc* with or without a colon following. When there are two or more names to be listed, type *cc* only with the first name. Align all the other names with the start of the first name.

```
cc:  Ms. Abernathy     OR    cc Ms. Abernathy
     Mrs. Bernardo           Mrs. Bernardo
     Mr. Cohen               Mr. Cohen
```

1377   When first names or initials are given along with last names, personal titles (*Mr., Miss, Mrs.,* and *Ms.*) may be omitted except in formal letters. Moreover, do not use personal titles if nicknames are given with last names.

```
cc James Diaz          cc J. Diaz          cc Jim Diaz
   Kenneth Eustis         K. Eustis           Ken Eustis
   Margaret Falmouth      M. Falmouth         Peggy Falmouth
```

1378   If the addressee is not intended to know that one or more other persons are being sent a copy of the letter, use a *blind copy notation*. First remove the original letter and any copies on which the *bcc* notation is not to appear. Then on each of the remaining copies, type a *bcc* notation in the upper left corner (starting at the left margin on the seventh line from the top). As an alternative, type the *bcc* notation on the second line below the last item in the letter (whether reference initials, an enclosure notation, a mailing notation, a *cc* notation, or a postscript). The file copy should show all the *bcc* notations, even though the individual copies do not.

     NOTE: The form of a blind copy notation should follow the form of the copy notation. If you have used *cc* or *c,* then use *bcc* or *bc* accordingly. If you have used *Copies to:* for the copy notation, use *Blind copies to:* for a blind copy notation.

1379   When a letter carries both an enclosure notation and a *cc* notation, it is assumed that the enclosures accompany only the original letter. If a copy of the enclosures is also to accompany a copy of the letter, this fact may be indicated as follows:

```
cc:     Mr. D. R. Wellak      (received only the letter)
cc/enc: Mr. J. Baldwin        (received the letter and the enclosures)
        Mrs. G. Conger        (received the letter and the enclosures)
```

1380   A copy is not usually signed unless the letter is addressed to several people and the copy is intended for one of the people named in the salutation. However, a check mark is usually made on each copy next to the name of the person or department for whom that copy is intended.

```
cc Ms. A. M. Starr ✓      cc Ms. A. M. Starr
   Mr. H. W. Fried           Mr. H. W. Fried ✓
```

NOTE: When an unsigned copy is likely to strike the recipient as cold and impersonal, it is appropriate for the writer to add a brief handwritten note at the bottom of the copy and sign or initial it.

POSTSCRIPT

1381   **a.** A postscript can be effectively used to express an idea that has been deliberately withheld from the body of a letter; stating this idea at the very end gives it strong emphasis. A postscript may also be used to express an afterthought; however, if the afterthought contains something central to the meaning of the letter, the reader may conclude that the letter was badly organized.

b. When a postscript is used:

(1) Start the postscript on the second line below the *cc* notation (or whatever was typed last). If the paragraphs are indented, indent the first line of the postscript (see page 263); otherwise, begin it at the left margin.

(2) Type *PS:* or *PS.* before the first word of the postscript, or omit the abbreviation altogether. (If *PS* is used, leave 2 spaces between the colon or period and the first word.)

(3) Use *PPS:* or *PPS.* (or no abbreviation at all) at the beginning of an additional postscript, and treat this postscript as a separate paragraph.

```
PS:  Instead of dashing for the airport as soon as the meeting
is over, why don't you have dinner and spend the night with us
and then go back on Saturday morning?

PPS:  Better yet, why don't you bring Joyce with you and plan
to stay for the whole weekend?
```

CONTINUATION PAGES

1382   Use plain paper of the same quality as the letterhead (but never a letterhead) for the second and each succeeding page of a long letter.

1383   Use the same left and right margins that you used on the first page.

1384   On the seventh line from the top of the page, type a continuation-page heading consisting of the following: the name of the addressee, the page number, and the date. Either of the following styles is acceptable:

```
  ↓ 7
Mrs. Laura R. Austin          2          September 30, 1987
                                                         ↓ 3

      ↓ 7
OR: Mrs. Laura R. Austin
    Page 2
    September 30, 1987
                      ↓ 3
```

1385   **a.** On the third line below the last line of the continuation-page heading, resume typing the body of the letter.

     b. Do not divide a paragraph that contains only two or three lines. For a paragraph of four or more lines, always leave at least two lines of the paragraph at the bottom of the previous page. Carry over at least two lines to the continuation page.

     c. Never use a continuation page to type only the closing section of a business letter. (The complimentary closing should always be preceded by at least two lines of the message.)

1386 Try to leave a uniform margin of 6 to 12 lines at the foot of each page of a letter (except the last page, which may run short).

1387 Do not divide the last word on a page.

ADDRESSING ENVELOPES

1388 The following table indicates which envelopes may be used, depending on the size of the stationery and the way in which it is folded (see ¶1391).

STATIONERY	FOLD	ENVELOPE
Standard (8½″ × 11″)	In thirds	No. 10 (9½″ × 4⅛″)
	In half, then in thirds	No. 6¾ (6½″ × 3⅝″)
Monarch (7¼″ × 10½″)	In thirds	No. 7 (7½″ × 3⅞″)
Baronial (5½″ × 8½″)	In thirds	No. 6¾ (6½″ × 3⅝″)
	In half	No. 5⅜ (5¹⁵⁄₁₆″ × 4⅝″)
A4 (210 × 297 mm) (approx. 8¼″ × 11¾″)	In thirds	DL (220 × 110 mm)
	In half, then in thirds	C7/6 (162 × 81 mm)
	In half, then in half	C6 (162 × 114 mm)
A5 (148 × 210 mm) (approx. 5⅞″ × 8¼″)	In thirds	C7/6 (162 × 81 mm)
	In half	C6 (162 × 114 mm)

NOTE: If you are using stationery and envelopes other than those shown above, keep in mind the Postal Service's standards for envelope size and thickness in order to qualify for automated processing:

Minimum size: 3½″ × 5″	Minimum thickness: ⁷⁄₁₀₀₀″
Maximum size: 6⅛″ × 11½″	Maximum thickness: ¼″

Envelopes smaller than 3½″ × 5″ are not mailable unless they are more than ¼″ thick. A postage surcharge is applied to envelopes that are larger or thicker.

1389 Typing an Address

When typing an address on an envelope:

a. Always use single spacing, and block each line at the left.

   ❑ *See the examples on page 294. For specific details on the handling of elements within the address block, see ¶¶1317–1344.*

b. Capitalize the first letter of every word except prepositions (like *of* and *for*), conjunctions (like *and*), and articles *(the, a, an)* used within a name or title.

> **NOTE:** The U.S. Postal Service has issued several brochures indicating that the use of all-capital letters "is preferred but not required" and that punctuation (such as periods with abbreviations and the comma between city and state) is not needed. Keep in mind that this style was devised primarily for the benefit of high-volume mailers, who must contend with space limitations for the address blocks they generate by computer or other automated equipment. (See ¶1390.) The traditional style (which uses capital and small letters plus punctuation as appropriate) is the style still universally seen on envelopes that are individually typed. Moreover, the Postal Service's OCRs (optical character readers) are programmed to read the traditional style of address as well as the all-cap style.

c. Type the city, state, and ZIP Code on the last line. If space limitations make it impossible for the ZIP Code to fit on the same line, the ZIP Code may be typed on the line directly below, blocked at the left.

d. Leave 1 space between the state name and the ZIP Code.

> **NOTE:** The U.S. Postal Service generally recommends either 1 or 2 spaces. However, it is significant that when advising mailers on how to limit the number of strokes in the city-state-ZIP Code line, the ZIP Code directory allows only 1 space between state and ZIP Code. (See ¶1390*a*, note.)

e. The state name may be spelled out or given as a two-letter abbreviation. (See ¶1341.)

f. The next-to-last line in the address block should contain a street address or post office box number. (See ¶1338*c*.)

```
Elvera Agresta, M.D.            Mr. Christopher Schreiber
218 Oregon Pioneer's Building   Director of Manufacturing
320 Southwest Stark Street      Colby Electronics Inc.
Portland, Oregon 97204-2628     P.O. Box 6524
                                Raleigh, NC 27628
```

g. When using a large envelope (No. 10 or DL), start the address on line 14 about 4 inches (40 pica spaces, 48 elite spaces) from the left edge. When using a small envelope (No. 7, 6¾, 5⅜, C6, or C7/6) or a postcard, start the address on line 12 about 2 inches (20 pica spaces, 24 elite spaces) from the left edge.

> **NOTE:** For OCR processing there should be a minimum margin of 1 inch at the left and right of the mailing address block. Therefore, decrease the left margins given above (4 inches for large envelopes, 2 inches for small) if necessary to keep extremely wide address blocks from intruding into the 1-inch right margin.

h. When using a window envelope, position the address block on the material to be inserted so that there will be a minimum clearance of ⅛ inch (and preferably ¼ inch) between the edges of the window and all four sides of the address block, no matter how much the inserted material shifts around inside the envelope. (See also ¶1391*e*.)

i. To facilitate OCR processing under any circumstances, make sure that the line containing the city, state, and ZIP Code starts no higher than 2¼ inches from the bottom edge, falls no lower than ⅝ inch from the bottom edge, and comes no closer than 1 inch from either the left or the right edge. Moreover, make sure that the lines in the address block are parallel to the bottom edge of the envelope and that there is good contrast between the typed address and the color of the envelope. In addition, do not use a script or italic typeface. The type should be clear and sharp; the characters should not touch or overlap.

j. When the envelope contains a printed return address for a company or an organization, type the name of the writer on the line above the return address. If all the lines in the printed return address are blocked at the left, align the writer's name at the left (as in the second illustration below). However, if all the lines in the printed return address are centered on the longest line, center the writer's name accordingly.

k. If a printed return address does not appear on the envelope, type a return address in the upper left corner, beginning on line 3 about a half inch (5 pica spaces, 6 elite spaces) in from the left edge. The return address should contain the following information, arranged on separate lines: (1) the name of the writer; (2) the name of the company (if appropriate); (3) a street address or post office box number; and (4) the city, state, and ZIP Code. (See the first illustration below.)

l. A notation such as *Personal, Confidential, Please Forward,* or *Hold for Arrival* goes below the return address. It should begin on line 9 or on the third line below the return address, whichever is lower. Begin each main word with a capital letter, and use underscoring. The notation should align at the left with the return address.

NOTE: Do not allow any notations or graphics to fall alongside or below the area established for the mailing address (see *i* on page 293). Copy placed in these locations will interfere with OCR processing.

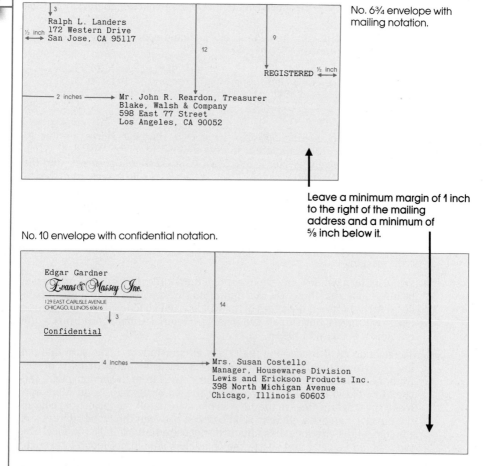

No. 6¾ envelope with mailing notation.

Leave a minimum margin of 1 inch to the right of the mailing address and a minimum of ⅝ inch below it.

No. 10 envelope with confidential notation.

m. If an attention line was used within the letter itself, it should appear on the envelope as well. The attention line may be treated exactly like a personal or confidential notation, as described in *l*, or it may be typed within the address block—between the name of the addressee and the street address or post office box number.

❑ *See ¶1345a, note, on avoiding the use of attention lines.*

n. If a special mailing procedure is used, type the appropriate notation (such as *SPECIAL DELIVERY* or *REGISTERED*) in all-capital letters in the upper right corner of the envelope. Type the notation on line 9 or on the third line below the bottom edge of the stamp, whichever is lower. The notation should end about a half inch (5 pica spaces, 6 elite spaces) from the right margin.

o. Make sure that the spelling of the name and address on the envelope agrees with the spelling shown in the inside address (and with the spelling shown on your records or the incoming document).

❑ *For letters being sent to two or more people at the same address, see ¶1320b.*

1390 Preparing an Address for Imprinting

When preparing an address that will be imprinted by means of an address plate or computerized equipment:

a. Keep in mind the maximum number of strokes you can get in any one line (typically, 26 to 28 strokes). Therefore, if necessary to save space, use abbreviations freely and omit punctuation.

NOTE: To help keep the line length down, the U.S. Postal Service has provided three special sets of abbreviations: one for state names; another for long names of cities, towns, and places; a third for names of streets and roads and general terms like *University* or *Institute*. By means of these abbreviations (see the ZIP Code directory), it is possible to limit the last line of any domestic address to 27 strokes: 13 for the city, 1 for the space between city and state, 2 for the state, 1 for the space between the state and the ZIP Code, 5 for the basic ZIP Code, 1 for the hyphen, and 4 for the additional four digits. For example:

```
Pass-a-Grill Beach, Florida 33741-9999     (38 strokes)
12345678901234567890123456789012345678
PAS-A-GRL BCH FL 33741-9999               (27 strokes)
```

b. Type the lines in all-capital letters, single-spaced and blocked at the left.

```
MR HENRY T POLING JR
CAMPING ENTERPRISES INC
412 HIGH ST ROOM 980
WASHINGTON DC 20017
```

❑ *See ¶1389b, note.*

NOTE: If your organization maintains its mailing lists on tapes or disks and uses these to generate inside addresses in business letters (as well as address blocks on envelopes), the all-cap, no-punctuation style designed for the envelope will look inappropriate inside the letter. In such cases use the traditional style described in ¶1389. You will then have a format that looks attractive as an inside address and that is also OCR-readable when used on an envelope. This approach is quite acceptable to the U.S. Postal Service.

c. Type the city, state, and ZIP Code on the last line. If space limitations make it impossible for the ZIP Code to fit on the same line, the ZIP Code may be typed on the line directly below, blocked at the left.

d. Leave 1 space between the state name and the ZIP Code. (The U.S. Postal Service generally recommends either 1 or 2 spaces. See ¶1389*d*, note.)

e. The state name is customarily given as a two-letter abbreviation.

f. The next-to-last line in the address block should contain a street address or post office box number. (See ¶1338*c*.)

g. If a room number or a suite number is part of the address, it should appear immediately after the street address on the same line. (See examples in *b* and *h*.) When it is impossible to fit this information on the same line as the street address, it may go on the line above but never on the line below. (See examples in ¶¶1317*b*, 1318*b*.)

h. If an attention line is to be included in the address, it should appear on the line between the name of the addressee and the street address or post office box number. If a serial number of some kind (for example, an account number or a file reference number) is required, enter it on the line above the name of the addressee.

```
H 048469 1078 AT5
BROCK & WILSON CORP
ATTN MRS M R TURKEVICH
79 WALL ST SUITE 1212
NEW YORK NY 10005-4101
```

i. To facilitate OCR processing, make sure that the line containing the city, state, and ZIP Code starts no higher than 2¼ inches from the bottom edge, falls no lower than ⅝ inch from the bottom edge, and comes no closer than 1 inch from either the left or the right edge. Do not allow any notations or graphics to fall alongside or below the area established for the mailing address. Moreover, make sure that the lines in the address block are parallel to the bottom edge of the envelope and that there is good contrast between the typed address and the color of the envelope. In addition, do not use a script or italic typeface. The type should be clear and sharp, and the characters should not touch or overlap.

FOLDING AND INSERTING LETTERS

1391 The following paragraphs describe several methods for folding letters and inserting them into envelopes. See the table in ¶1388 to determine which method is appropriate for the stationery and envelope you are using.

a. To fold a letter in thirds:

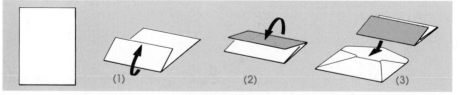

(1)   (2)   (3)

(1) Bring the bottom third of the letter up and make a crease.
(2) Fold the top of the letter down to within ⅜ inch (10 mm) of the crease you made in step 1. Then make the second crease.
(3) The creased edge you made in step 2 should go into the envelope first.

NOTE: Use this method for 8½″ × 11″ stationery with a No. 10 envelope; 7¼″ × 10½″ stationery with a No. 7 envelope; 5½″ × 8½″ stationery with a No. 6¾ envelope; A4 stationery with a DL envelope; A5 stationery with a C7/6 envelope. (See also ¶1388.)

b. To fold a letter in half and then in thirds:

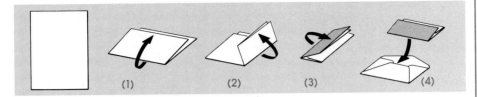

(1)　(2)　(3)　(4)

(1) Bring the bottom edge to within ⅜ inch (10 mm) of the top edge and make a crease.

(2) Fold from the right edge, making the fold a little less than one-third the width of the sheet before you crease it.

(3) Fold from the left edge, bringing it to within ⅜ inch (10 mm) of the crease you made in step 2 before you crease the sheet again.

(4) Insert the left creased edge into the envelope first. This will leave the crease you made in step 2 near the flap of the envelope.

NOTE: Use this method for 8½″ × 11″ stationery with a No. 6¾ envelope; also for A4 stationery with a C7/6 envelope. (See also ¶1388.)

c. To fold a letter in half:

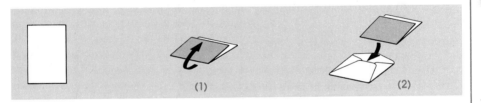

(1)　(2)

(1) Bring the bottom edge to within ⅜ inch (10 mm) of the top edge and make a crease.

(2) Insert the creased edge into the envelope first.

NOTE: Use this method for 5½″ × 8½″ stationery with a No. 5⅜ envelope; also for A5 stationery with a C6 envelope. (See also ¶1388.)

d. To fold a letter in half and then in half again:

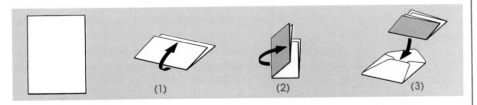

(1)　(2)　(3)

(1) Bring the bottom edge to within ⅜ inch (10 mm) of the top edge and make a crease.

(2) Bring the left edge to within ⅜ inch (10 mm) of the right edge and make a crease.

(3) Insert the left creased edge into the envelope first.

NOTE: Use this method for A4 stationery with a C6 envelope. (See also ¶1388.)

e. To fold a letter for insertion into a window envelope:

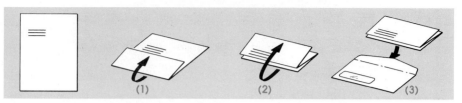

(1)   (2)   (3)

(1) Bring the bottom third of the letter up and make a crease.

(2) Fold the top of the letter *back* to the crease you made in step 1. (The inside address should now be facing you.)

(3) Insert the letter with the inside address toward the *front* of the envelope. The inside address should now be fully readable through the window of the envelope. There should be at least ⅛ inch (and preferably ¼ inch) between all four sides of the address and the edges of the window, no matter how much the letter slides around in the envelope.

MEMOS

An interoffice memorandum is intended to expedite the exchange of written messages within an organization. For that reason many organizations provide printed forms that simplify and standardize the treatment of key information (such as the names of the writer and the addressee, the subject of the memo, and the date). Depending on the circumstances, a memo may be as terse as a telegram, as impersonal as a formal announcement, or as warm and casual as a personal note.

1392 When typing a memo on a *printed form:*

a. Set the left margin stop at a point 2 spaces after the longest guide word in the left half of the printed heading—for example, after *Subject* in the illustration on page 299.

NOTE: Some writers prefer to set the left margin stop at the point where the printed guide words begin. In this case it is necessary to set a tab stop 2 spaces after the longest guide word in the left half of the printed heading.

b. Set a tab stop 2 spaces after the longest guide word in the right half of the printed heading—for example, after *Floor and Ext.* (floor number and telephone extension) in the illustration on page 299.

c. Set the right margin stop so as to leave a right margin approximately equal to the left margin.

d. Type in the appropriate information after each printed guide word, using capital and small letters. The typewritten fill-ins should block at the left and align at the bottom with the printed guide words.

NOTE: If you are sending the memo to someone within your own department (or to someone elsewhere in the company with whom you have a close working relationship), you can omit the fill-ins after the guide words *Dept.* and *Floor and Ext.*

e. After the guide words *To* and *From,* the names of the addressee and the writer are usually given without personal titles (*Mr., Miss, Mrs., Ms.*). Indeed, when you are doing a memo to someone within your immediate unit, the use of initials or simply a first name may suffice. In short, the way you treat these names will depend on the relative formality or informality of the occasion.

Interoffice Memorandum

To: Bernard O'Kelly

Dept: Special Sales

Floor: 4

Subject: Test Marketing Arrangements

Tab

From: Janet R. Wiley

Dept: Software Products

Floor and Ext: 7/3825

Date: April 7, 1987

Dear Bernie:

Let me try to summarize the outcome of our excellent meeting last Friday, in which we discussed how your group might sell our product lines to the markets you serve.

1. Steve Kubat, the chief product manager for my group, will provide you with product descriptions, catalog sheets, ad mats, and current price lists. If you need additional information, just call Steve (or me in his absence) and we'll be glad to help in any way that we can.

2. We will pay you an 18 percent commission on all orders you generate for our products. Please forward a copy of these orders to Steve, who will arrange to have the commission credited to your account.

3. We very much appreciate your offer to give us three hours at your week-long sales meeting next month to present our products to your field staff. Just tell us when and where to show up, and we'll be there.

4. We have agreed to give this new arrangement a six-month test to see (a) how much additional sales revenue you and your people can produce with our products and (b) what effect, if any, this special marketing effort will have on your sales of other products. At the end of the test period, we will analyze the results and decide whether to con-tinue the arrangement, modify it in some way, or abandon it altogether.

I don't think we'll be abandoning it, Bernie. In fact, I feel quite con-fident that this new arrangement is going to produce significant gains in sales and profits for both of us. I look forward to working with you to make it all happen.

Jan

JRW

imm
cc Steve Kubat
   Pat Rosario

f. If the memo is being sent to more than one person in another department, it may be possible to fit two or three names in the space following *To*.

To: Hal Parker, Meryl Crawford, Mike Monagle	From:
Dept: Profit Planning	Dept:

g. If fill-ins are omitted following such guide words as *Dept.* and *Floor* because the memo is going to two or more people in different departments and on different floors, you may list the names of the addressees vertically as long as you leave at least 1 blank line before the next fill-in.

(Continued on page 300.)

```
To:      Louise Landes
         Fred Mendoza
Dept.:   Jim Norton
         Ruth O'Hare
Floor:   Neil Sundstrom

Subject: Revised Overhead Rates
```

h. If it is not possible to fit the names of the addressees in the heading of the memo, then after the guide word *To*, type *Distribution* or *See distribution below* or something similar. Then on the third line below the reference initials or the enclosure notation (whichever comes last), type <u>*Distribution:*</u>. (Use capital and small letters, and underscore the word for special emphasis.) Leave 1 blank line, and then list the names of the individuals who are to receive a copy of the memo. Arrange the names either by rank or in alphabetic order, and type them blocked at the left margin. (If space is tight, the names may be arranged in two or more columns.)

NOTE: For purposes of actual distribution, simply place a check mark next to one of the listed names to indicate who is to receive that particular copy. (The illustration on page 301 shows the copy of a memo intended for V. Jellinek.)

i. Begin typing the body of the memo on the third line below the last fill-in line in the heading.

NOTE: An interoffice memo ordinarily does not require a salutation, especially if the memo is an impersonal announcement being sent to a number of people or the staff at large. However, when a memo is directed to one person, many writers use a salutation—such as *Dear Andy:* or *Andy:* alone—to keep the memo from seeming cold or impersonal. (If a salutation is used, begin typing the body of the memo on the second line below.)

j. Use single spacing, and either block or indent the paragraphs.

k. Type the writer's name or initials on the second line below the last line of the message, beginning at the tab stop you set in step *b*. Add the writer's title (if desired) on the following line.

NOTE: Although memos do not require a signature, many writers prefer to sign or initial their memos. In such cases type the writer's name or initials on the *fourth* line below the end of the message.

l. Type the reference initials (see ¶1370) on the second line below the writer's name, initials, or title; block them at the left margin.

m. Type an enclosure notation, if needed, on the line below the reference initials, beginning at the left margin. (See ¶1373.)

n. Type a copy notation, if needed, on the line below the enclosure notation, if used, or on the line below the reference initials. As an alternative, the copy notation may be typed one line below and aligned with the name of the person(s) to whom the memo is addressed. Use the same style for the copy notation as in a letter. (See ¶¶1376–1380.) If the addressee of the memo is not intended to know that a copy of the memo is being sent to one or more other persons, use a blind copy notation. (See ¶1378.)

o. If the memo continues beyond the first page, type a continuation heading on a fresh sheet of paper. (Use the same style as shown in ¶1384 for a letter.) Then continue typing the message on the third line below the last line of the continuation-page heading. (See ¶1385 for additional details on continuing the message from one page to another.)

Interoffice Memorandum

To: Distribution

Dept:

Floor:

Subject: Car Rentals

From: Stanley W. Venner

Dept: Accounting

Floor and Ext: 3 - x2291

Date: May 10, 1988

     We have just been informed that car rental rates will be increased by $1 to $2 a day, effective July 1.

     This daily rate increase can be more than offset if you refill the gasoline tank before returning your rental car to the local agency. According to our latest information, the car rental companies are charging an average of 32 percent more per gallon than gas stations in the same area. Therefore, you can help us achieve substantial savings and keep expenses down by remembering to fill up the gas tank before turning your rental car in.

                      SWV

jmb

Distribution:

  G. Bonardi
  D. Catlin
  S. Folger
√V. Jellinek
  E. Kasendorf
  P. Legrande
  T. Pacheco
  F. Sullivan
  J. Trotter
  W. Zysk

1393 When typing a memo on *plain paper* or *letterhead stationery:*

  a. Set your left and right margins for a 6-inch line. (See ¶1305*b*–*c*.)

  b. Type the heading *MEMORANDUM* in all-capital letters. On plain paper, center the heading on line 7 (leaving a 1-inch margin at the top). On letterhead stationery, center the heading on the third line below the letterhead.

  c. On the third line below the heading *MEMORANDUM*, start typing the guide words (*DATE:, TO:, FROM:,* and *SUBJECT:*, plus any others you wish to add) double-spaced and blocked at the left margin. Use all-capital letters, and follow each guide word with a colon.

d. Type all the entries that follow the guide words so that they block at the left, 2 spaces after the longest guide word (plus colon). If *SUBJECT:* is the longest guide word, you can set a tab stop 10 spaces in from the left margin and achieve the proper vertical alignment.

e. Begin typing the rest of the memo on the third line below the final guide word.

f. Type the writer's name or initials on the second line below the last line of the message, beginning at center.

❏ *For other guidelines to observe when typing the memo, see ¶1392d–o.*

```
                                    ↓7
                                MEMORANDUM
                                         ↓3

   DATE:      February 9, 1987
                                ↓2
   TO:        Joanne Malik, Forrest Talbot, Lee Wriston
                                                      ↓2
   FROM:      Sally Klein
                          ↓2
   SUBJECT:   Convention Invitation
                                   ↓3

   We have just been invited to make a one-hour presentation on catalog
   marketing at the annual convention of the International Marketing
   Institute.  The convention will be held on November 12-15 at the
   Camelback Inn in Scottsdale, Arizona.  I don't have all the details
   we need in order to start planning the presentation, but I would like
   you to block out these dates on your calendar now so as to avoid any
   schedule conflicts later on.
                                ↓2
   This invitation represents an excellent opportunity for us to show the
   profession some of the exciting things we have done in the past few
   years, and it could bring us a number of new clients next year.  Let's
   give it our best shot.
                          ↓2
   As soon as I receive more information from the program coordinator,
   I'll set up a luncheon at which we can decide how best to proceed.
                                                                     ↓2

                          SK
                             ↓2

   jam
```

SOCIAL-BUSINESS CORRESPONDENCE

1394 Social-business correspondence refers to the following types of letters:

a. Executive correspondence addressed to high-level executives, officials, and dignitaries. Unlike ordinary business correspondence (which deals with sales, production, finance, advertising, and other routine commercial matters), these letters deal with such topics as corporate policy and issues of social responsibility, and they are written in a more formal style.

b. Letters expressing praise, concern, or condolence to someone within or outside the organization. The occasion that prompts the letter could be exceptional performance on the job or in the community, an employment anniversary, the death or serious illness of a family member, or an upcoming retirement. Such letters may be formal or informal, depending on the relationship between the writer and the person addressed.

c. Letters to business associates within or outside the company on purely social matters.

1395 Social-business correspondence differs from ordinary business correspondence in three ways:

a. The inside address is typed at the bottom of the letter, aligned at the left margin and starting on the fifth line below the writer's signature or title (whichever comes last).

b. The salutation is followed by a comma rather than a colon.

c. Reference initials and notations pertaining to enclosures, copies, and mailing are typically omitted.

(Continued on page 304.)

AVON ADVISORY COUNCIL

192 West Main Street   Avon, Connecticut 06001

September 26, 1989
↓5

Dear Annie, ↓2

You and I have worked together on the Advisory Council for nearly six years, and in that time we have gotten to know each other pretty well. So you'll understand why I was deeply pained to hear that you and your husband have sold your house and are plan-ning to move to the Northwest next month. ↓2

We have not always seen eye to eye (I still think you were dead wrong to vote against the parking lot expansion), but there is no one who has given as much thought and imagination and caring service to this town as you have. ↓2

All of us on the Advisory Council are going to miss you very much, both as a forceful participant and as a warm and generous friend, but we wish you and George the best of luck as you make new lives for yourselves. We envy your new neighbors, for they will be the beneficiaries of what we in Avon have so long enjoyed—your vital presence. ↓2

We won't forget you, Annie. ↓2

                    Sincerely, ↓4

                    Harlan

                    Harlan W. Estabrook
                    Chairman ↓5

Mrs. Anne G. Wheatley
14 Tower Lane
Avon, Connecticut 06001

NOTE: Social-business correspondence also differs by being either *more* formal or *less* formal than ordinary business correspondence. For example, correspondence to high-level officials and dignitaries is customarily more formal. As a result, the word style for numbers and one of the special salutations in Section 17 should be used. However, in letters to business associates who are also close friends, the salutation and the complimentary closing may be very informal, and the writer's typewritten signature and title—and even the inside address—may be omitted. Moreover, when such letters are purely personal in nature, the writer may use plain stationery and omit the return address.

POSTCARDS

1396 When typing the message on a standard-size postcard (5½ by 3½ inches):

a. Leave minimum side margins of ½ inch. Since the 5½-inch width provides a total of 55 *pica* spaces, an allowance of ½ inch (5 spaces) on either side will yield a measure of 45 spaces for typing the message. If elite type is used, the 5½-inch width will provide 66 *elite* spaces; a ½-inch margin (6 elite spaces) on either side will yield a measure of 54 spaces.

b. Type the date on the third line from the top of the card, beginning at the center.

NOTE: Since the card has a depth of 3½ inches (21 lines), you must plan to end the typing on line 18 in order to leave a bottom margin of ½ inch (3 lines).

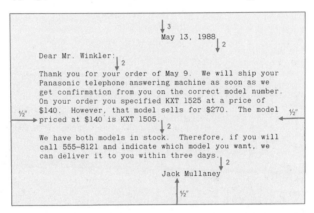

c. Omit the name and address of the person to whom the card is being sent.

d. Type the salutation (for example, *Dear Mrs. Davis:*) on the second line below the date, beginning at the left margin. If space is tight, you can omit the salutation.

e. Begin typing the message, using single spacing, on the second line below the salutation. To save space, do not indent paragraphs.

f. Type the closing lines starting on the second line below the last line of the message; begin each line at the center. In order to leave a bottom margin of ½ inch, omit the following elements if necessary: the complimentary closing (for example, *Sincerely*), the handwritten signature, the writer's title, and reference initials.

1397 On the front side of the card, type a return address and the mailing address just as you would on a No. 6¾ envelope. (See ¶¶1389–1390 and the illustration on page 294.)

Reports and Manuscripts

REPORTS

MANUSCRIPTS

REPORTS

Reports serve all kinds of purposes. Some simply communicate information—such as monthly sales figures or survey results—without any attempt to analyze or interpret the data. Others offer extensive analyses and make detailed recommendations for further action. As a result, reports come in all sizes and shapes. Some are done informally as memos or letters (depending on whether they are to be distributed inside or outside the organization). Some consist simply of fill-ins on preprinted forms. Many, however, are done in a more formal style. As you might expect, there is a wide variation to be found in what is acceptable from one authority to another and from one organization to another. Regardless of which guidelines you follow, be prepared to modify them to fit a specific situation.

CHOOSING A FORMAT

1401 Always try to get some guidelines from the person who requests the report on such matters as format, length, amount of detail desired, and distribution. Check the files for copies of similar reports done in the past. If guidelines or models are not provided or if you are doing the report on your own initiative, consider the following factors in choosing a format.

a. For whom are you writing the report? (If intended for your boss or a colleague on staff, the report could be done simply as a memo. If intended for top management or the board of directors, the report will often require a more formal approach. By the same token, an academic term paper will require a simpler format than a thesis for an advanced degree.)

b. What outcome do you hope to achieve? (If you are merely providing information without attempting to win someone over to your point of view, the simplest and clearest presentation of the information will suffice. If you are trying to persuade the reader to adopt your viewpoint and accept your recommendations, you will probably need to make a detailed argument and devise a more complex structure for your report.)

c. What is the existing mind-set of your reader? (If you will have to argue long and hard to win your reader over, you may need to develop a number of chapters, grouped by part. If you need to demonstrate that your argument is supported by much detailed research, you may have to quote from published sources and provide an elaborate set of data in the form of tables and charts. If you know that your intended reader already supports your argument or simply wants your judgment on a certain matter, a shorter and simpler document will usually suffice.)

PARTS OF A FORMAL REPORT

1402 A *formal* report typically has three parts: front matter, body, and back matter. Each of these parts, in turn, typically contains some (if not all) of the following elements.

a. Front Matter

TITLE PAGE — In a *business* report: gives the full title, the subtitle (if any), the writer's name, title, and department, and the date of submission; may also indicate for whom the report was written. In an *academic* report: gives the name of the writer, the instructor, and the course, along with the date of submission. (See ¶1414.)

LETTER OR MEMO OF TRANSMITTAL — May be done as a letter (for distribution outside the company) or as a memo (for inside distribution); may be clipped to the front of the report (or to the binder in which the report is inserted); may be inserted in the report itself as the page preceding the title page. (See ¶1415.)

TABLE OF CONTENTS — A list of all chapters (by number and title), along with the opening page number of each chapter. If chapters are grouped by part, the titles of the parts also appear in the table of contents. Sometimes main headings within the chapters are also given under each chapter title. (See ¶1416.)

LISTS OF TABLES AND ILLUSTRATIONS — Separate lists of tables and illustrations are included if they are numerous and likely to be frequently referred to by the reader. (See ¶1417.)

FOREWORD OR PREFACE — Indicates for whom the report is written, the objectives and the scope of the report, and the methods used to assemble the material in the report (see ¶1418). Acknowledgments of help received on the report are usually included here at the end, but if special emphasis is desired, the acknowledgments can be treated as a separate element of the front matter, immediately following the foreword.

SUMMARY — A one-page document (two pages at most) designed to save the reader's time by presenting conclusions and recommendations right at the outset of the report. If a foreword is not provided, the summary also includes some of the material that would have gone there. (See ¶1419.)

b. Body

INTRODUCTION — Sets forth (in greater detail than the foreword) the objectives, the scope, and the methods, along with any other relevant background information. In a report with several chapters, this may precede Chapter 1 of the text or be labeled as Chapter 1. (See ¶1421.)

MAIN DISCUSSION — Sets forth all the pertinent data, evidence, analyses, and interpretations needed to fulfill the purpose of the report. May consist of one long chapter that opens with an introduction and closes with conclusions and recommendations. May consist of several chapters; these may be grouped into *parts*, with a part-title page inserted to introduce each sequence of chapters. May use different levels of headings throughout the text to indicate what the discussion covers and how it is organized. (See ¶¶1422–1426.)

CONCLUSIONS — Presents the key points and the recommendations that the writer hopes the reader will be persuaded to accept. In a report with several chapters, this material represents the final chapter or the final part.

c. Back Matter

APPENDIXES	A collection of tables, charts, or other data too specific to be included in the body of the report but provided here as supporting detail for the interested reader. (See ¶1428.)
ENDNOTES	A collection—all in one place at the end of the report—of what would otherwise appear as footnotes at the bottom of various pages in the report. A device that simplifies the preparation of the report. (See ¶¶1501–1502, 1504–1505.)
BIBLIOGRAPHY	A list of all sources (1) that were consulted in the preparation of the report and (2) from which material was derived or directly quoted. (See ¶¶1532–1536.)
GLOSSARY	A list of terms (with definitions) that may not be readily understood by some of the intended readers. (See ¶1430.)

PARTS OF AN INFORMAL REPORT

1403 **a.** An *informal* report has no front matter. The information that would go on a separate title page appears at the top of the first page and is immediately followed by the body of the report. (See ¶¶1411–1413 for typing instructions.)

b. An informal report typically contains no back matter except possibly a list of *endnotes* (in place of separate footnotes throughout) and a *bibliography*.

PAPER, RIBBON, AND COPIES

1404 Use a good-quality bond paper and a black carbon ribbon for the best results. (Cloth ribbons may also be used.) Use only one side of the paper. If you have a word processing system, print the report on a letter-quality printer.

1405 Always make one photocopy or carbon copy for your files in case the original is lost or mislaid. Prepare additional copies as necessary for distribution.

MARGINS

1406 Side Margins

a. Line Length. Type all reports on a 6-inch line.

b. Margins for Unbound Reports. If a report is to remain unbound or will simply be stapled in the upper left corner, follow these guidelines:

	Spaces	Centering Point	Margins	Centering Point*	Margins
Pica	60	50	20–80	42	12–72
Elite	70	50	15–85	51	16–86

*These centering points will result if you align the left edge of your paper at zero on the carriage-position scale. (See also ¶1305b.)

c. Margins for Bound Reports. If a report is to be inserted in a binder or will be stapled in several places along the left edge of the paper, the left margin needs to be increased by 3 spaces. If your machine is already set up for an *unbound* report, the easiest way to adjust your side margins for a *bound* report is to insert your paper so that the left edge is 3 spaces to the left of zero on the carriage-position scale. If you prefer or if you are using a word processor, you can set new margins as follows:

	Spaces	Centering Point	Margins	Centering Point	Margins
Pica	60	53	23–83	45	15–75
Elite	70	53	18–88	54	19–89

1407 Top and Bottom Margins of Opening Pages

The following guidelines apply to (1) the first page of each chapter, (2) the first page of each distinct element in the front matter and back matter, and (3) the first page of an informal report that consists of only one chapter (without any separate title page or other front matter).

a. On these opening pages, leave a top margin of 12 lines (2 inches) and a bottom margin of 6 lines (1 inch). Since a standard page is 66 lines deep, the area for typing falls between line 13 and line 60. (On the title page and on part-title pages, where the copy is centered as a whole on the page, the top and bottom margins should each be a minimum of 6 lines.)

b. Ordinarily, no copy—not even a page number—is typed in the space that represents the top margin. However, in informal academic reports, it is customary to type certain information in the upper right corner. (See ¶1413.)

c. On these opening pages, the first line of typing—typically a heading—starts on line 13. On a full page of copy, the last line of text typically falls on line 57 and the page number on line 60. (See ¶1409 for exceptions to this standard.)

```
line 13                 CHAPTER 2.   ADMINISTRATIVE SERVICES
                                                           ↓ 3

            As part of a broad-based investigation into ways of increasing

    productivity and improving operating efficiency, the managers of all
```

```
        will entail a substantial investment in the various technologies that
      ┌ line 57
      └→characterize "the office of the future" and will require training
                                                                      ↓ 3

    line 60                              14
```

1408 Top and Bottom Margins of Other Pages

a. Leave 6 blank lines at both the top and bottom of other pages in a report.

b. In the *body* and *back matter* of a report, type the page number on line 7 at the right margin (see ¶1426) and continue the text from the preceding page on line 10. The last line of copy on a full page of text should fall on line 60.

```
        line 7                                                    23
                                                                      ↓ 3
      ┌─line 10
      └→ Both sides are motivated to forge a new partnership.   Industry

          has seen its technological base erode in the face of foreign
```

```
              Meanwhile, the universities are caught in a financial
      ┌─line 60
      └→ squeeze that is being intensified by dwindling enrollments
```

c. In the *front matter* of a report, the page number always goes at the foot of the page. Therefore, begin typing the text on line 7. On a full page of text, type the last line of text on line 57 and center the page number on line 60.

```
line 7 Part Three will explore alternative recommendations for

improving relations between factory personnel and first-line
```

```
        Part Six will analyze the pros and cons of attempting to
┌─line 57
└→ introduce quality circles and the costs that are likely to be
                                                              ↓ 3

line 60                          vii
```

1409 Page-Ending Considerations

As indicated in ¶¶1407–1408, if you want to maintain a consistent bottom margin of 6 blank lines, then strictly speaking, the last typing on a page should appear on line 60. In most cases this should be easy to achieve. However, in a few situations you may have to end the page one line long or several lines short.

a. On full pages of text where the page number must be typed at the bottom (see ¶¶1407 and 1408c), your goal is to type the last line of text on line 57 and the page number on line 60.

STANDARD PAGE-ENDING ARRANGEMENT

```
line 53     xxxxxxxxxxxxx.

line 55            Xxxxxxxxxxxxxxxxxxxxx

line 57     xxxxxxxxxxxxxxxxxxxxxxxxxxx
                                    ↓ 3

line 60                   47
```

However, if you are typing double-spaced text on even-numbered lines, it will be impossible for you to end the text on line 57. In such a case try to end the text on line 56 and keep the page number on line 60. In order to avoid a bad page break, you can end the text on line 58 and center the page number on line 61.

❏ *For examples of bad page breaks, see ¶1409c–h.*

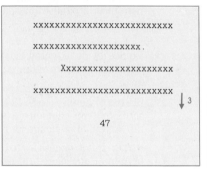

	PREFERABLE VARIATION		ACCEPTABLE VARIATION
line 52	xxxxxxxxxxxxxx .		xxxxxxxxxxxxxxxxxxxxxxxxx
line 54	Xxxxxxxxxxxxxxxxxxxxxx		xxxxxxxxxxxxxxxxxxx .
line 56	xxxxxxxxxxxxxxxxxxxxxxxxx ↓ 4		Xxxxxxxxxxxxxxxxxxxxx
line 58			xxxxxxxxxxxxxxxxxxxxxxxxx ↓ 3
line 60	47		
line 61			47

b. On full pages of text where the page number goes in the upper right corner on line 7, try to type the last line of text on line 60.

STANDARD PAGE-ENDING ARRANGEMENT

line 56	xxxxxxxxxxxxxx .
line 58	Xxxxxxxxxxxxxxxxxxxxxxxxx
line 60	xxxxxxxxxxxxxxxxxxxxxxxxxxxx

However, if you are typing double-spaced copy on odd-numbered lines, aim for line 59 but continue on to line 61 if necessary to avoid a bad break.

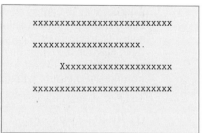

	PREFERABLE VARIATION		ACCEPTABLE VARIATION
line 55	xxxxxxxxxxxxxx .		xxxxxxxxxxxxxxxxxxxxxxxxx
line 57	Xxxxxxxxxxxxxxxxxxxxxx		xxxxxxxxxxxxxxxxxxx .
line 59	xxxxxxxxxxxxxxxxxxxxxxxxx		Xxxxxxxxxxxxxxxxxxxxx
line 61			xxxxxxxxxxxxxxxxxxxxxxxxx

c. In breaking a paragraph at the bottom of a page, always leave at least two lines at the bottom of the page and carry at least two lines to the top of the next.

NOTE: Three-line paragraphs pose a special problem. You must either fit all three lines at the bottom of one page or carry all three lines over to the top of the next page.

d. Do not type a *centered heading* or a *side heading* near the bottom of a page unless you can fit at least the first two lines of copy after the heading.

NOTE: A *run-in heading* (in the first line of a paragraph) can fall near the bottom of a page if one additional line of the paragraph will also fit there.

❏ *For a discussion of centered, side, and run-in headings, see ¶1425.*

e. Do not divide a quoted extract (see ¶1424*d*) unless you can leave at least two lines at the bottom of one page and carry over at least two lines to the top of the next.

f. If a list of items (see ¶1424*e*) has to be broken at the bottom of a page, break *between* items (not within an item). Moreover, try to leave at least two items at the bottom of one page and carry over at least two items to the top of the next.

NOTE: If it is necessary to break *within* an item, leave at least two lines at the bottom of one page and carry over at least two lines to the top of the next.

g. If it is not possible to start typing a table at the desired point of reference and have it all fit on the same page, then insert a parenthetical note at the appropriate point in the text (referring the reader to the next page) and continue with the text to the bottom of the page. Then at the top of the next page, type the complete table, leave 1 to 3 blank lines, and resume typing the text. (See Section 16 for guidelines on the typing of tables.)

NOTE: If a table is so long that it will not fit on one page even when typed single-spaced, then look for a sensible division point in the body of the table and end the first page there. At the top of the next page, repeat the complete title of the table (with *Continued* or *Cont.* inserted in parentheses at the end) and also repeat any column heads before continuing with the rest of the table. If there is any possibility that a reader could mistake the first part of the divided table as the complete table, then type a continuation line in parentheses or brackets. (See ¶1638 for details.)

h. If a footnote is so long that it cannot all fit on the page where the text reference occurs, continue it at the bottom of the following page. (See ¶1503*f*.)

1410 Controlling Margins

a. To control the bottom margin of each page when using a typewriter, draw a pencil mark 6 lines above the point where the last line is to be typed. (Make the mark before inserting the paper into the machine; then erase it later on.)

b. Another way to control the bottom margin is to prepare a page line guide as follows: Simply type a column of numbers—from 1 to 66—down the right edge of a fresh sheet of paper. Insert this sheet behind the paper on which you type; position it so that the column of numbers appears beyond the right edge of the top sheet. Then as you type and advance the paper, the column of numbers at the right will tell you how close you are to line 60.

c. To keep all margins uniform on all pages, prepare a *backing sheet* as follows:

    (1) Insert a blank sheet of paper in the typewriter, and set the left and right margins as indicated in ¶1406.

    (2) Space down to the seventh line from the top, and type a full row of Xs—60 for pica, 70 for elite.

    (3) Space down to line 54, and type another full row of Xs. (This will represent an early warning signal that the bottom of the page is near.)

    (4) Space down 6 lines to line 60, and type another full row of Xs. (This will represent the last line on which typing should occur.)

    (5) Draw a rectangle with heavy black lines to enclose the top and bottom rows of Xs and mark off the left and right margins.

NOTE: If you are using a word processor, you can set and adjust margins before printing the report.

TYPING INFORMAL BUSINESS REPORTS

These guidelines apply to business reports that typically consist of only one chapter and have no separate title page or other front matter.

1411 If the first page is typed on a *blank sheet of paper* (as in the illustration below):

a. Leave a top margin of 12 lines (2 inches).

b. On line 13 type the title of the report centered in all-capital letters. If a subtitle is used, type it centered in capital and small letters on the second line below the main title. (If the title or subtitle is long, break it into sensible phrases and arrange them on two or more single-spaced lines.)

c. Type *By* and the writer's name centered in capital and small letters on the second line below the title or subtitle.

d. Type the date on which the report is to be submitted on the second line, centered, below the writer's name.

NOTE: Additional details that appear on a title page (such as the writer's title and affiliation or the name and affiliation of the person or group for whom the report has been prepared) are omitted when the title starts on the same page as the body. If these elements need to be provided, you will have to prepare a separate title page. (See ¶1414.)

e. On the third line below the date, start the body of the report. (See ¶¶1424–1426 for details on spacing, indentions, headings, and page numbering.)

NOTE: On the first page of an informal business report, no page number should appear. Therefore, the text can continue to line 60 (or line 61 to avoid a bad page break). However, count this page as page 1.

line 13   ↓13   CHANGES IN DISCOUNT POLICY ↓2

line 15   An Analysis of the Impact of Suggested Revisions
line 16   on Sales Revenues and Net Operating Income ↓2

line 18   By Catherine R. Hemphill ↓2

line 20   September 20, 19— ↓3

line 23 In a memo dated August 13, the Marketing Managers Committee asked again that certain discounts in our pricing schedule be increased at the beginning of next year in order to stimulate larger orders from customers and to permit larger and more profitable production runs. At the request of the Executive Committee, I have prepared the following analysis, working on the basis of projections supplied by a number

line 59 If we were to increase our v discount from 33 1/3 percent to
line 61 40 percent, it is estimated that the immediate increase in sales

f. If the report requires more than one page, then on each continuation page leave 6 blank lines at the top, type the page number on line 7 (see also ¶1426), and resume the text on line 10.

↓ 7

2

↓ 3

are expected to produce sales increases of over 20 percent in the first

quarter of next year, 18 percent in the second quarter, 15 percent in

the third quarter, and 13 percent in the fourth.

g. If the report requires one or more elements of back matter—for example, endnotes or a bibliography—follow the style established for a formal report. (See ¶¶1501–1502, 1504–1505, 1532–1536.)

1412 If the first page of a report is typed on a *printed memo form* (as in the illustration below):

a. Give the report title (and subtitle, if any) as the *subject* of the memo. Supply all the other elements called for in the heading of the memo in the usual way. (See ¶1392.)

b. Then begin typing the body of the report on the third line below the last fill-in line in the heading. (See ¶¶1424–1425 for details on spacing, indentions, and headings.)

c. If the report requires more than one page, then type each continuation page on a blank sheet of paper. Beginning on line 7, use the same kind of continuation heading called for in any long memo (see also ¶1392o), and resume the text on the third line below the last line of the continuation heading. (See the two illustrations at the top of page 315.)

Interoffice Memorandum

To:	Executive Committee	From:	Catherine R. Hemphill
Dept.:		Dept.:	Profit Planning
Subject:	Changes in Discount Policy—An Analysis of the Impact of Suggested Revisions on Sales Revenues and Net Operating Income	Date:	September 20, 19—

↓ 3

In a memo dated August 13, the Marketing Managers Committee asked again that certain discounts in our pricing schedule be increased at the beginning of next year in order to stimulate larger orders from customers and to permit larger and more profitable production runs. At the request

↓ 7

Executive Committee   2   September 20, 19—— ↓ 3

OR:

↓ 7

Executive Committee
Page 2
September 20, 19—— ↓ 3

TYPING INFORMAL ACADEMIC REPORTS

1413 An academic report that consists of only one chapter and has no separate title page or other front matter is typed exactly like an informal business report (see ¶¶1411–1412) except for the opening of the first page.

a. Type some of the key information in a block in the upper right corner of the first page. Type the writer's name on line 7, the instructor's name on line 8, the course title on line 9, and the date on line 10—all aligned at the left, with the longest line ending at the right margin.

b. Starting on line 13, type the title and subtitle (if any) just as in an informal business report. (See ¶1411*b*.)

c. Start typing the body of the report on the third line below the preceding copy (title or subtitle).

↓ 7

Blake Trudeau
Mrs. Trenton
History 315
March 8, 19—— ↓ 3

ECONOMIC FACTORS CONTRIBUTING TO
THE WAR OF 1812 ↓ 3

INTRODUCTION ↓ 2

    While much emphasis has been placed on the political factors that

led to the start of the War of 1812, there has not been sufficient

attention given to the economic factors that led to the declaration of

TYPING THE FRONT MATTER OF FORMAL REPORTS

The following guidelines deal with the preparation of a title page, a letter or memo of transmittal, a table of contents, a list of tables, a list of illustrations, a foreword or preface, and a summary. For a formal report, only a separate title page is essential; all the other elements are optional.

1414 Title Page

There is no one correct arrangement for the elements on a title page. Here are two acceptable formats.

a. Three-Block Arrangement. Group the material into three blocks of type, and leave equal space (at least 3 blank lines) above and below the middle block. Position the material as a whole so that it appears centered horizontally and vertically on the page.

BUSINESS REPORT

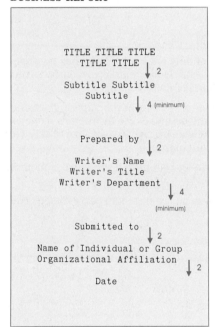

ACADEMIC REPORT

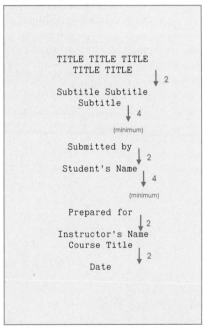

b. Two-Block Arrangement. Group the material into two blocks of type, and leave at least 6 blank lines between blocks. Position the material as a whole so that it appears centered horizontally and vertically on the page.

NOTE: The two-block arrangement works well when the title page does not attempt to show *to whom* the report is being submitted.

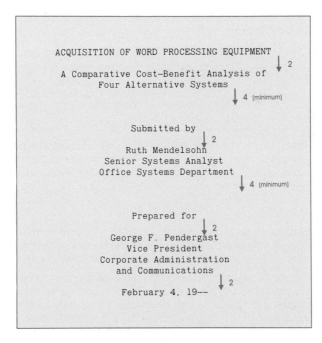

```
        TITLE TITLE TITLE
          TITLE TITLE
                        ↓ 2
        Subtitle Subtitle
           Subtitle
                        ↓ 7 (minimum)




            Prepared by
                        ↓ 2
           Writer's Name
           Writer's Title
        Writer's Department
                        ↓ 2
              Date
```

c. **Margins.** Regardless of which arrangement you use, leave a minimum margin of 6 lines (1 inch) at the top and bottom of the title page. Also leave minimum side margins equivalent to those used for the body of the report. (See ¶1406.)

d. **Title.** Type the title in all-capital letters. If the title is long, type it on two or more lines, single-spaced; try to break the title into meaningful phrases.

```
   ACQUISITION OF WORD PROCESSING EQUIPMENT
                                           ↓ 2
   A Comparative Cost-Benefit Analysis of
          Four Alternative Systems
                                    ↓ 4 (minimum)


              Submitted by
                           ↓ 2
            Ruth Mendelsohn
          Senior Systems Analyst
        Office Systems Department
                                    ↓ 4 (minimum)


              Prepared for
                           ↓ 2
          George F. Pendergast
             Vice President
        Corporate Administration
           and Communications
                           ↓ 2
           February 4, 19--
```

e. **Subtitle.** Type the subtitle, if any, in capital and small letters. If the subtitle requires more than one line, type it single-spaced. Leave 1 blank line between the main title and the subtitle. (See the illustration above.)

f. **Writer's Identification.** Leave a minimum of 3 blank lines before typing the writer's identification block. The writer's name may be preceded by the word *By* on the same line or by a phrase such as *Prepared by* or *Submitted by* (or simply *By*) typed 2 lines above. If appropriate, the writer's name may be followed by a title on the next line and by an organizational affiliation on the following line.

```
↓ 4 (minimum)
  By Patricia C. Shea
Manager, Accounts Payable
Financial Services Department
```

```
       ↓ 4 (minimum)
        Prepared by
                   ↓ 2
        Floyd Welliman
        Acting Director
   Marketing Research Unit
```

g. **Reader's Identification.** It is common (but not essential) to identify the individual or group for whom the report has been prepared. Leave a minimum of 3 blank lines before typing *Submitted to* or *Prepared for* or a similar phrase. Then on the second line below, type the name of the individual or the group. On succeeding lines, supply a title, an organizational affiliation, or both.

```
     ↓ 4 (minimum)
      Submitted to
                 ↓ 2
     Robert G. Paterno
      General Manager
   Corporate Graphic Arts
```

```
      ↓ 4 (minimum)
       Prepared for
                  ↓ 2
   The Finance Committee
   Davenport, Pierson,
      and Associates
```

NOTE: As an alternative, the reader's identification may be provided in the form of a subtitle.

```
AN ANALYSIS OF COMPUTERIZED GRAPHICS EQUIPMENT
                                            ↓ 2
        A Report to Robert G. Paterno
   General Manager, Corporate Graphic Arts
```

h. **Date.** Supply the date (month, day, and year) on which the report is being submitted. Type it on the second line below the reader's identification block (or, if none is given, on the second line below the writer's identification).

1415 Letter or Memo of Transmittal

a. A formal report is often accompanied by a letter or memo of transmittal. If the report is to be sent to people outside the company, use the letter format; if the report is to be sent only to people within the company, use a memo.

b. The message typically covers the following points: (1) a brief description of what is being transmitted; (2) a brief reference to the circumstances that prompted the report; (3) if necessary, a brief indication of why the report is being sent to the addressee; and (4) a statement about what action the addressee is expected to take. (See the illustration on page 319.)

c. The letter or memo of transmittal is typically clipped to the front of the report. If the report is in a binder, the transmittal document may be clipped to the front of the binder or inserted in the binder preceding the title page.

ATLANTIC ENTERPRISES INCORPORATED
44 Exchange Street / Portland, Maine 04107 / 207-555-5166

February 5, 19— ↓ 5

Mr. Frank M. Eggleston
Back Meadow Road
Damariscotta, Maine 04543 ↓ 2

Dear Frank: ↓ 2

I am enclosing a copy of a report entitled "Acquisition of
Word Processing Equipment," which I just completed for George
Pendergast. Because of your expertise in this area, George
has suggested that I send you the report with the hope that
you might have time to read it and give us your comments and
suggestions. ↓ 2

Because we need to make a decision by April 1 on what equipment
to buy, it would help us greatly if we could hear from you by
March 15. I know that given your busy schedule, you may not
be able to get back to us in writing that quickly. If you would
let George and me take you to lunch, we could talk about the
report then and spare you the need to put your thoughts in
writing. ↓ 2

I'll call you early next week so that we can decide what would
be the best way to proceed. ↓ 2

Sincerely, ↓ 4

(Ms.) Ruth Mendelsohn

Ruth Mendelsohn
Senior Systems Analyst
Office Systems Department ↓ 2

ctl
Enclosure

1416 Table of Contents

a. On a fresh page type *CONTENTS* (or *TABLE OF CONTENTS*) in all-capital letters, centered on line 13. On the third line below, begin typing the table double-spaced. Use the same side and bottom margins as for the text pages in the body of the report. (See ¶¶1406–1409.)

b. In typing the body of the table of contents, list every separate element that *follows* the table of contents in sequence—whether in the front matter, the body of the report, or the back matter. In the illustration on page 320, note the following aspects of the format:

(1) Individual entries pertaining to *chapters* begin with a chapter number (roman or arabic), followed by a period, 2 spaces, and then the chapter title typed in capital and small letters or in all-capital letters. Align the chapter numbers at the right, with the longest number positioned flush with the left margin. After each chapter title leave 1 blank space and type a solid row of leaders to guide the eye to the column of page numbers at the right. Leave 1 blank space between the final leader and the widest page number; all other page numbers should align at the right.

NOTE: If any chapter title should require more than one line, type the turnover line single-spaced and align it with the first letter of the chapter title in the line above.

(2) Individual entries pertaining to *front matter* and *back matter* begin at the left margin, with the title typed in capital and small letters or in all-capital letters, followed by a row of leaders and a page number (roman for front

↓ 13

CONTENTS ↓ 3

matter and arabic for back matter). Leave 2 blank lines *after* the front matter entries and 2 blank lines *before* the back matter entries.

(3) Individual entries pertaining to *part titles* are typed in all-capital letters and centered. The part numbers that precede the titles may be in arabic or roman numerals or (for formality) may be spelled out. Leave 2 blank lines before each part title and 1 blank line after.

c. If desired, the *main headings* within each chapter may be included in the table of contents. One acceptable arrangement is to indent each heading 2 spaces from the start of the chapter title and type it in capital and small letters. The list of headings for each chapter should be typed as a single-spaced block, with 1 blank line above and below it. Page numbers may be provided with the headings if desired.

1417 List of Tables or Illustrations

a. Start each list on a fresh page. Type the heading—*TABLES* (or *LIST OF TABLES*) or *ILLUSTRATIONS* (or *LIST OF ILLUSTRATIONS*)—in all-capital letters, centered on line 13.

b. On the third line below, begin typing the first entry in the list. Use the same format as for chapter titles in a table of contents. (See ¶1416*b*.)

NOTE: The tables or illustrations may be numbered consecutively throughout the report or consecutively within each chapter. The latter technique (which is recommended whenever last-minute additions and deletions are likely) uses the chapter number as a prefix in the numbering scheme.

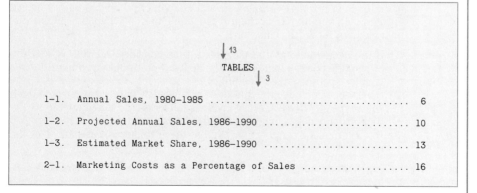

```
                              ↓ 13
                            TABLES
                              ↓ 3
1-1.  Annual Sales, 1980-1985 ................................... 6

1-2.  Projected Annual Sales, 1986-1990 ........................ 10

1-3.  Estimated Market Share, 1986-1990 ....................... 13

2-1.  Marketing Costs as a Percentage of Sales ................ 16
```

1418 Foreword or Preface

a. If a foreword or preface is to be provided, then on a fresh page type the appropriate title in all-capital letters, centered on line 13. Note that the correct spelling is *FOREWORD* (**NOT** FORWARD)!

b. On the third line below, begin typing the actual text. Use the same side and bottom margins as for the text pages in the body of the report (see ¶¶1406–1409). Also follow the same guidelines for spacing, indentions, and headings as given for the body of the report (see ¶¶1424–1425).

c. The foreword or preface should cover the following points: (1) *audience* (for whom the report is being written), (2) *stimulus* (what prompted the writing of the report), (3) *objectives* (what the writer hopes the report will accomplish), (4) *scope* (what the report covers and what it consciously does not try to deal with), (5) *methodology* (how the data and the conclusions were arrived at), and (6) *acknowledgments* (names of individuals and organizations that need to be thanked for their help). Other points may be included as appropriate.

NOTE: The acknowledgments may be treated as a separate element in the front matter, following the foreword in sequence and using the same format.

1419 Summary

a. If a summary (frequently called an *executive summary*) is to be provided, follow the format guidelines provided for a foreword in ¶1418*a–b* above.

b. Since this element is intended to be a time-saver, keep it short—ideally one page, at most two pages. The summary may be handled as a series of ordinary text paragraphs or as a series of numbered paragraphs typed with hanging indention (see ¶1424*e*).

1420 Numbering Front Matter Pages

a. On all pages of front matter except the title page, type a page number centered on line 60, the seventh line from the bottom of the page. Type the page number in small roman numerals (for example, *ii, iii, iv*).

NOTE: If necessary, the page number may fall on line 61. (See ¶1409*a*.)

b. Count the title page as page i, even though no number is typed on that page.

c. Leave 2 blank lines above the page number, more if the text above runs short.

TYPING THE BODY

1421 Introduction

a. If the body of a report contains several chapters and begins with a formal introduction, you may treat the introduction either as Chapter 1 or as a distinct element preceding Chapter 1.

(1) If you decide to treat it as Chapter 1, then consider *INTRODUCTION* to be the title of this chapter and handle it as you would any other title on a chapter-opening page. (See ¶1423.)

(2) If you decide to have the introduction precede Chapter 1, then on a fresh sheet type *INTRODUCTION* in all-capital letters, centered on line 13. On the third line below, begin typing the actual text.

(3) In either case treat the first page of the introduction as page 1 of the report. (See ¶1426.)

❑ *For guidelines on margins, see ¶¶1406–1409; for guidelines on spacing, indentions, and headings, see ¶¶1424–1425.*

b. If a report contains only one chapter and begins with an introductory section, treat the title *INTRODUCTION* as a first-level head (see ¶1425) and type it on the third line below the block of copy (title, etc.) at the top of the page. (See the illustration at the bottom of page 315.)

1422 Part-Title Pages

a. If the report contains several chapters organized in parts, insert a separate part-title page directly in front of the chapter that begins each part.

NOTE: If the body of the report begins with a formal introduction (see ¶1421*a*), then the part-title page for Part 1 should *follow* the introduction. (**REASON:** The introduction embraces the whole work and not simply Part 1.)

b. Type the word *PART* and the part number on one line. Underneath type the part title on one or more lines as appropriate. Use all-capital letters for emphasis, and space out the copy for maximum display effect. Center the copy as a whole horizontally and vertically.

```
                      PART 3

                   STRATEGIES FOR

               REGAINING MARKET SHARE
```

1423 Chapter-Opening Pages

a. Leave 12 blank lines (2 inches) at the top of each chapter-opening page.

b. Type the chapter number and title in all-capital letters, centered on line 13.

```
     ↓ 13
     CHAPTER II.   THE COMPUTER REVOLUTION
                                         ↓ 3
```

c. If the title is long, break it into sensible phrases and arrange them on two or more single-spaced lines. If the chapter number goes on a line by itself, leave 1 blank line before starting the chapter title.

```
                  ↓ 13
                CHAPTER 1 ↓ 2
       FACTORS CURRENTLY RESTRICTING OPPORTUNITIES
              FOR INCREASED PRODUCTIVITY
                                      ↓ 3
```

d. Begin typing the first line of copy (whether text matter or a heading) on the third line below the title.

1424 Text Spacing and Indentions

a. Running Text. Ordinarily, double-space all text matter. However, use single spacing or 1½-line spacing in business reports when the costs of paper, reproduction, file space, and mailing are important considerations. (When single-spacing the text, leave 1 blank line between text paragraphs.)

> ❏ *For guidelines on dividing words and word groups at the ends of lines and between one page and the next, see ¶¶901–920; for guidelines on the use of footnotes, endnotes, or textnotes, see Section 15.*

b. **Drafts.** Always double-space drafts to be submitted for editing or evaluation.

c. **Paragraphs.** Indent text paragraphs 5 spaces. At the bottom of a page, do not divide a paragraph with only two or three lines; always leave at least two lines of the paragraph at the bottom of one page and carry over at least two lines to the top of the next page.

d. **Quoted Material.** If a quotation will make four or more typewritten lines, type it as a single-spaced extract. Indent the extract 5 spaces from each side margin, and leave 1 blank line above and below the extract. If the quoted matter represents the start of a paragraph in the original, indent the first word an additional 5 spaces. (See ¶265*a*; for an illustration, see page 264.)

e. **Items in a List.** Type the list single-spaced with 1 blank line above and below the list as a whole. Either type the list on the full width of the 6-inch line, or indent the list 5 spaces from each side margin. If any item in the list requires more than one line, leave a blank line between all items in the list. If an item continues on to a second line, align the turnover with the first word in the line above.

12

```
The market analysis conducted by Witherspoon Associates has yielded some
surprising results.  For example, over 50 percent of our sales are made
in low-growth markets.  On that basis we need to ask: ↓ 2

    Will this heavy investment in low-growth markets permit us to
    meet our long-range profit goals?

    How can we most effectively increase our sales in high-growth
    markets?

    To what extent will domestic and international competition
    stymie our attempt to penetrate high-growth markets? ↓ 2
```

NOTE: If the items each begin with a number or letter, type a period after the number or letter and leave 2 spaces before typing the text that follows. Align the numbers or letters on the period. If an item continues on to a second line, align the turnover with the first word in the line above.

6

```
In evaluating various companies as candidates for acquisition, we must
address three basic questions:

    1.  What will be our criteria for identifying the desirable candidates
        for acquisition?

    2.  How much should we be prepared to pay?

    3.  How will each acquisition affect our overall financial performance?

Naturally, broad questions like these lead to a great number of other
questions.  I believe that we lack the internal resources to deal with
```

f. Tables. Tables may be typed with single, double, or 1½-line spacing. However, establish one style of spacing for all tables within a given report. (See Section 16 for a full discussion on how to plan and execute tables and for numerous illustrations.)

1425 Text Headings

Headings (or heads) are the key technique for letting readers see at a glance the scope of the writer's discussion and the way in which it is organized. Therefore, it is important that heads be used throughout the report to reflect the coverage and the structure of the material. It is also essential that the heads be typed in a way that clearly indicates different levels of importance or subordination. Here are several techniques for achieving these objectives.

a. Try to limit yourself to three levels of text heads (not counting the chapter title). If you use more than three, it will be difficult for the reader to grasp the typographical distinction between one level and another.

   NOTE: If you feel you need more than three levels, you are probably trying to cram too much into one chapter. Consider a different organization of the material to solve this problem.

b. Before typing the final draft of the report, make an outline of the heading structure as it then stands and analyze it for:

   (1) *Comprehensiveness.* Does it cover all aspects of the discussion, or are some topics not properly represented?

   (2) *Balance.* Is one section loaded with heads while a comparable section has only one or two?

   (3) *Parallel structure.* Are the heads all worded in a similar way, or are some complete sentences and others simply phrases?

c. Headings come in three styles:

   (1) A *centered head* is one centered on a line by itself, with 2 blank lines above and 1 blank line below. Either type it in all-capital letters, or type it in capital and small letters that are underscored. If the head is too long to fit on one line, center the turnover on the following line.

   (2) A *side head* starts flush with the left margin, on a line by itself. Ordinarily, it should have 2 blank lines above and 1 blank line below. However, if a side head comes directly below a centered head (without any intervening text), leave only 1 blank line above the side head. A side head may be typed either in all-capital letters or in capital and small letters that are underscored. If the head is too long to fit on one line, type the turnover flush left on the following line.

   (3) A *run-in head* (also called a *paragraph heading*) is one that begins a paragraph and is immediately followed by text matter on the same line. Like all new paragraphs, a paragraph that begins with a run-in heading should be preceded by 1 blank line (whether the text is typed with single, double, or 1½-line spacing). A run-in head should begin 5 spaces in from the left margin. It should be typed in capital and small letters, underscored, and followed by a period (unless some other mark of punctuation, such as a question mark, is required). The text then begins 2 spaces after the mark of punctuation.

❏ *For capitalization in headings, see ¶360.*

d. In a report that calls for only *one* level of heading, choose a side heading and type it in either of the styles shown below.

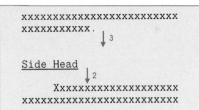

e. In a report that calls for *two* levels of headings, choose one of the styles shown below.

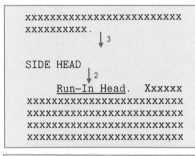

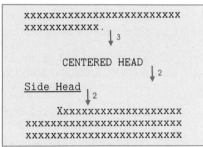

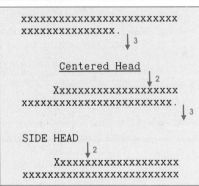

f. In a report with *three* levels of headings, choose one of the following styles.

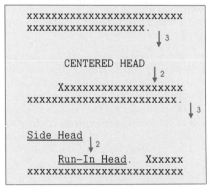

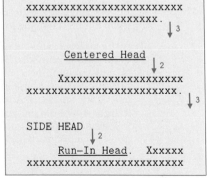

1426 Numbering Text Pages

a. When the first page contains the title of the report and the body starts on the third line below, count this as page 1, but do not type the number on the page.

b. When the report begins with a formal title page and one or more additional pages of front matter, give these pages a separate numbering sequence, using small *roman* numerals. (See ¶1420.)

c. In a formal report, consider the first page *following* the front matter as page 1 in the *arabic* numbering sequence.

d. If part-title pages are included in the report (see ¶1422), consider them in the numbering sequence for the body of the report, but do not type a number on these pages. (Thus if the first page following the front matter is the part-title page for Part I, it will count as page 1, but no number will appear.)

e. On the first page of each new element in the body or back matter of the report, on which a chapter title or some other title starts on line 13 near the top of the page, the page number should appear at the bottom of the page, as follows:

(1) Type the last line of the text on line 57 (the tenth line from the bottom of the page).

(2) Leave 2 blank lines, and then type the page number (without the word *Page*), centered on line 60 (the seventh line from the bottom).

❑ *For guidelines on ending a page, see ¶¶1407–1409.*

f. On all other pages in the body or back matter of the report, type the page number on the seventh line from the top. Place the number at the right margin. The word *Page* may precede the number. After typing the page number, begin the first line of text on the third line below (line 10). To save space, type the page number on line 4 (instead of line 7) and the first line of text on line 6. As an alternative arrangement, type these page numbers at the bottom of the page just as is done on opening pages (see ¶1426e above). In this case begin the text on line 7 (instead of line 10).

g. In a long report with several chapters written by different authors under a tight deadline, it may be necessary to type the chapters out of order. In such cases, you may use a separate sequence of page numbers for each chapter, with the chapter number serving as a prefix. Thus, for example, the pages in Chapter 1 would be numbered 1-1, 1-2, 1-3, . . .; those in Chapter 2 would be numbered 2-1, 2-2, 2-3, . . .; and so on.

TYPING THE BACK MATTER

1427 Following the last page of the body of the report are those elements of back matter that may be needed: appendixes, endnotes, bibliography, and glossary. Begin each of these elements on a fresh page. Use the same margins as for other pages in the report (see ¶¶1406–1409), and treat the numbering of these pages as discussed in ¶1426e–f.

1428 Appendixes

a. If more than one appendix is to be included, number or letter each in sequence. (See the illustration of the table of contents on page 320 for an example.)

b. Type the word *APPENDIX* (plus a number or letter, if appropriate) and the appendix title in all-capital letters, centered on line 13. If the title is long, type it in two or more centered lines, single-spaced.

c. Leave 2 blank lines before typing the body of the appendix. Since this material may be a table, a chart, a list, or straight text, choose the format that displays this copy to best effect.

1429 Endnotes and Bibliography

See ¶¶1501–1502, 1504–1505, 1532–1536.

1430 Glossary

If this element is to be provided, then on a fresh sheet type *GLOSSARY* or some other heading in all-capital letters, centered on line 13. Leave 2 blank lines, and begin the text on line 16. There are a variety of ways to set up a glossary.

a. **Two Columns.** Type the terms in alphabetic order in the left column and the corresponding definitions in the right column. Begin the right column at least 2 spaces to the right of the longest term in the left column. Single-space each definition, and align turnover lines flush with the left margin of this column. Leave 1 blank line between entries.

```
Elliptical expression   A condensed expression from which key words
                        are omitted.
                                    ↓ 2
Essential elements      Words, phrases, or clauses that are necessary
                        to the completeness of the structure or the
                        meaning of a sentence.
```

b. **Hanging Indention.** Begin each term at the left margin, underscore it, and follow with a colon, a dash, or some other device and then the definition. Type the definition single-spaced, and indent turnover lines 5 spaces from the left margin so that the term in the first line will stand out. Leave 1 blank line between entries.

```
elliptical expression:  a condensed expression from which key words
     are omitted
                       ↓ 2
essential elements:  words, phrases, or clauses that are necessary
     to the completeness of the structure or the meaning of a
     sentence
```

c. **Paragraph Style.** Indent each term 5 spaces from the left margin, underscore it, and follow with a colon, a dash, or some other device and then the definition. Type the definition single-spaced, with turnover lines flush with the left margin. Leave 1 blank line between entries.

```
     Elliptical expression--a condensed expression from which key
words are omitted.
                       ↓ 2
     Essential elements--words, phrases, or clauses that are necessary
to the completeness of the structure or the meaning of a sentence.
```

NOTE: Regardless of the format selected, the terms may be typed with initial caps or all in small letters (except for proper nouns and adjectives). The definitions may also be styled either way; however, if they are written in sentence form, it is best to use initial caps for both the term and the definition. The use of periods at the end of definitions is optional unless, of course, the definitions are written as complete sentences.

MANUSCRIPTS

The preparation of manuscripts is subject to virtually the same considerations that apply to the preparation of reports (¶¶1401–1430). However, manuscripts differ from reports in one fundamental way: they are written with the idea of publication in mind—whether as a self-contained book, as an article in a magazine or some other printed periodical, or as an item to be included in a bulletin or newsletter prepared on a typewriter or word processor. As a result, manuscripts require some special considerations concerning format.

PREPARING MANUSCRIPT FOR AN ARTICLE

1431 If you have been invited to write an article for a specific publication, ask the editor for concrete guidelines on line length, spacing, paragraph indention, heading style, preferences in capitalization and punctuation, overall length of the article, and so on.

1432 If you are writing an article only with the hope that it may be accepted by a certain publication, you will enhance your chances of favorable consideration by imitating all aspects of the publication's format and style. In particular, try to type your manuscript on a line length that equals an average line of copy in the finished publication. A manuscript prepared in this way will make it easy for the editor to determine how much space your article will fill in the publication.

a. If the manuscript is intended for a publication that uses typewriter spacing (for example, a company bulletin or an organizational newsletter), insert a previous issue in your typewriter and set your margins to the width of a single column. If you are using a word processor, measure the line, determine whether the type is elite or pica, and set your margins accordingly. If the publication is typed in elite (12 characters to the inch) and your machine has pica type (10 characters to the inch), or vice versa, follow the guidelines in *b* below.

b. If the manuscript is intended for a publication that uses proportional spacing (for example, a newspaper, a magazine, or a professional journal), you can determine the appropriate line length by copying 10 to 20 lines—on a line-for-line basis—from a representative article. Observe at what point most lines end, and set your margin stops accordingly.

c. Even if the publication puts two or more columns on a page, type only one column on a manuscript page, and try to center it on the page to provide space for editing.

d. Even if the publication uses single spacing, type your manuscript double-spaced—again, to allow room for editing.

e. Consistently type 25 lines of copy on a manuscript page (counting blank space above and below free-standing heads as lines of copy). In this way you and the editor can quickly calculate the total number of lines of copy.

NOTE: Be sure to keep the overall length of your manuscript within the range of the materials typically used by the intended publication. There is little point in submitting a 2000-line manuscript to a publication that carries articles of no more than 500 lines.

f. In trying to simulate the character count of a printed line on your typewriter or word processor, you may have to adjust some of the normal standards for typewritten material—for example, by using only 1 space after periods, question marks, exclamation points, and colons (instead of the customary 2 spaces) or by using only 2 or 3 spaces for paragraph indentions (instead of the usual 5 spaces).

PREPARING MANUSCRIPT FOR A BOOK

If you are writing a book or assisting someone who is, consider the following guidelines.

1433 If your manuscript will consist essentially of straight text matter (with perhaps a few tables and illustrations), then in establishing a format for your manuscript, you can follow the standard guidelines for a formal report with respect to margins, spacing, headings, page numbering, and other aspects involved in typing the front matter, the body, and the back matter. Indeed, if the manuscript is typed on a 70-character line, with 26 lines on a page (starting the text on line 10 and ending the text on line 60), then as a rule of thumb, three manuscript pages will convert to two typeset pages in a standard 6- by 9-inch book.

1434 If you think your manuscript, when set in type, will require a special format—for example, a larger-than-usual page size to accommodate extremely wide tables or to permit notes and small illustrations to run alongside the text or to allow for a two-column arrangement of the printed text—then the easiest way to establish a *typewritten* format for your manuscript page is to select a published work that has the kind of format you have in mind. On your typewriter or word processor, copy a full page of representative printed text—on a line-for-line basis, if possible—to determine the manuscript equivalent of a printed page. (If a printed line is too long to fit on one typewritten line and still leave a minimum margin of 1 inch on either side, choose some other typewritten format that you can readily execute.) The important thing is to determine how many pages of manuscript equal a page of printed text. Then, as you develop the manuscript, you can exercise some real control over the length of your material.

PRECAUTIONS FOR ALL MANUSCRIPTS

1435 When sending material to a publisher, always retain a duplicate copy in case the material goes astray in the mail.

1436 Your unpublished manuscript is automatically protected by the copyright law as soon as it is written, without your putting a copyright notice on it or registering it with the U.S. Copyright Office. If you are concerned that someone may copy your material without giving you appropriate credit or compensation, you may place a copyright notice on the first page (*Copyright © [current year] by [your name]*) to call attention to your ownership of the material. Since the copyright law only protects the written expression of your ideas and not the ideas themselves, you should obtain the help of a lawyer if you have an original publishing idea which you are concerned may be misappropriated.

Notes and Bibliographies

FOOTNOTES, ENDNOTES, AND TEXTNOTES

Date of Publication (¶1528)
Page Numbers (¶1529)
Subsequent References (¶¶1530–1531)

BIBLIOGRAPHIES (¶¶1532–1536)

FOOTNOTES, ENDNOTES, AND TEXTNOTES

FUNCTIONS OF NOTES

1501 **a.** In a report or manuscript, *notes* serve two functions: (1) they provide *comments* on the main text, conveying subordinate ideas that the writer feels might be distracting if incorporated within the main text; and (2) they serve as *bibliographic references*, identifying the source of a statement quoted or cited in the text.

Comment

    1.   The actual date on which Governor Galloway made this statement is uncertain, but there is no doubt that the statement is his.

Bibliographic Reference

    2.   David S. Broder, *Changing of the Guard,* Simon and Schuster, New York, 1980, p. 68.

❑ *For a discussion of whether to type the note number on the line (as shown above) or raised slightly above the line, see ¶1523b.*

b. When notes appear at the foot of a page, they are called *footnotes.* (See ¶1503.)

```
The incorrect grouping of sounds into words--technically called

metanalysis--has been referred to as the "Guylum Bardo syndrome."¹
                                       ↓2                             ↓1

        1.   William Safire, On Language, Times Books, New York, 1980,
p. 168.
```

c. When notes appear all together at the end of a complete report or manuscript (or sometimes at the end of each chapter), they are called *endnotes.* (See ¶¶1504–1505.)

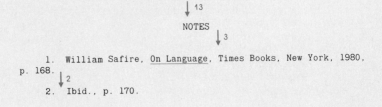

```
                              ↓13
                             NOTES
                                ↓3

        1.   William Safire, On Language, Times Books, New York, 1980,
p. 168.
              ↓2
        2.   Ibid., p. 170.
```

d. When bibliographic references appear parenthetically within the main text, they may be referred to as *textnotes*. (See ¶¶1506–1507.)

```
                                                          5

are sometimes run together.  The incorrect grouping of sounds into words--

technically called metanalysis--has been referred to as the "Guylum Bardo

syndrome."  (William Safire, On Language, Times Books, New York, 1980,

p. 168.)  "Notar Republic" and "Pullet Surprise" are two other examples
```

---

e. Footnotes or endnotes are ordinarily keyed by number to a word, phrase, or sentence in the text. Textnotes (which appear parenthetically at the desired point of reference right in the text itself) do not have to be keyed this way.

f. Endnotes are growing in popularity because (1) they are easier to type and (2) they leave the text pages looking less cluttered and less complicated. They do present one drawback, however: the reader does not know in each instance whether the endnote will contain a comment of substance (which is typically worth reading) or simply a bibliographic reference (which is usually of interest only in special cases).

g. Textnotes are also growing in popularity for the same reasons: ease of typing and lack of clutter. While it is possible to provide in a textnote all the information that a bibliographic reference typically contains, writers more often use this device to provide an abbreviated reference in the text, with the understanding that the reader who wants complete information will be able to consult a bibliography at the back of the report or manuscript. (See ¶1507 for examples of these abbreviated references.)

h. To take advantage of the benefits and avoid the drawbacks of these three types of notes, some writers use a hybrid system: they treat *comments* as footnotes and *bibliographic references* as endnotes or textnotes. In this way comments of substance are conveniently at hand, whereas all or most of the bibliographic detail is tucked out of sight but accessible whenever needed. (See ¶1502*g*.)

TEXT REFERENCES TO FOOTNOTES OR ENDNOTES

1502   **a.** To indicate the presence of a comment or a bibliographic reference at the bottom of the page or in a special section at the end, insert a *superior* (raised) figure following the appropriate word, phrase, or sentence in the text. (See ¶1502*c* for an example.)

NOTE: To type a superior figure, turn the cylinder back slightly with one hand and type the figure with the other hand.

❏ *For an alternative to the use of superior figures, see ¶1502h.*

b. Do not leave any space between the superior figure and the preceding word. If a punctuation mark follows the word, place the superior figure immediately after the punctuation mark. (**EXCEPTION:** The superior figure should precede, not follow, a dash.)

c. While the superior figure should come as close as possible to the appropriate word or phrase, it is often better to place the superior figure at the end of the sentence (if this will cause no misunderstanding) so as to avoid distracting the reader in the midst of the sentence.

ACCEPTABLE: Her latest article, "Automating the Small Legal Office,"[1] was published about three months ago.

PREFERABLE: Her latest article, "Automating the Small Legal Office," was published about three months ago.[1]

d. When a paragraph calls for two or more footnotes or endnotes, try to combine all the necessary information within one note if this can be done without any risk of confusing the reader. This approach will reduce the sense of irritation that a large number of footnotes or endnotes tend to produce.

NOTE: When this approach is used, the superior figure is typically placed after the last word in the sentence or paragraph, depending on how the text references are dispersed.

AVOID: The following analysis draws heavily on recent studies undertaken by Andrew Bowen,[1] Frances Kaplan,[2] and Minetta Coleman.[3]

1.   Andrew Bowen, . . .

2.   Frances Kaplan, . . .

3.   Minetta Coleman, . . .

PREFERABLE: The following analysis draws heavily on recent studies undertaken by Andrew Bowen, Frances Kaplan, and Minetta Coleman.[1]

1.   Andrew Bowen, . . .; Frances Kaplan, . . .; and Minetta Coleman, . . .

e. The numbering of footnotes or endnotes may (1) run consecutively throughout, (2) begin again with each new chapter, or (3) begin again with each new page. The third method should not be used for materials to be set in type, since the pagination will differ.

f. Footnotes are sometimes keyed by symbol rather than by number. This often occurs in tables with figures and in technical material with many formulas, where a raised figure—though intended to refer to a footnote or endnote— could be mistaken for a part of the tabular matter or the formula. When the use of symbols is appropriate, choose one of the following sequences: *, **, ***, etc. (these can be done on the typewriter); or *, †, ‡, §, ¶ (these must be inserted by hand and are preferred in a manuscript that will be set in type).

g. If you wish to treat *comments* as footnotes and *bibliographic references* as endnotes or textnotes (as suggested in ¶1501*h*), use *symbols* for the notes containing comments and use *figures* for the notes containing bibliographic references.

h. While the use of *superior* figures is the style still most commonly seen in business and academic reports, manuscripts, and published materials, some business writers are now using an "on-the-line" style for one of two reasons: (1) they dislike having to break their typing pace in order to adjust the cylinder each time they want to type a superior figure, or (2) they are using electronic equipment that cannot readily execute superior figures. If you wish to use this "on-the-line" style, follow the guidelines at the top of page 335.

(1) Enclose the figure in brackets (if your equipment has bracket keys); otherwise, enclose it in parentheses.

(2) Try to position the figure so that it *follows* the end of a sentence or, better yet, the end of a paragraph. Leave 1 space before the opening bracket or parenthesis; leave 2 spaces after the closing bracket or parenthesis if a new sentence begins on the same line.

```
. . . called "the age of instability." [1]   He goes on . . .
```

(3) If the figure has to go *within* a sentence, leave 1 space before the opening bracket or parenthesis and 1 space after the closing bracket or parenthesis. Try to place the enclosed figure so that it is not next to any other mark of sentence punctuation; otherwise, a cluttered and possibly confusing situation could result. Do not use a figure enclosed in parentheses within a sentence where it could be mistaken for part of an enumeration.

TYPING FOOTNOTES

1503   When notes are to be placed at the foot of a page:

a. Type an underscore 2 inches long (20 pica strokes, 24 elite strokes) to separate footnote material from the main text above. Type the underscore 1 line below the last line of text, starting at the left margin.

NOTE: If the text runs short on a page (say, the last page of a chapter), any footnotes related to that text must still be positioned at the *foot* of the page. In that case estimate the number of lines the footnote will occupy, and determine on which line the footnote material should begin in order to end at the foot of the page. Then type the underscore on the second line above the line on which the footnote material should begin.

b. Start the first footnote on the second line below the underscore.

❏ *For guidelines on how to construct bibliographic reference footnotes, see ¶¶1508–1531.*

c. Ordinarily, single-space each footnote, but in a manuscript to be set in type, use double spacing to allow room for editing. In either case leave 1 blank line between footnotes.

d. Indent the first line of each footnote 5 spaces. Type the footnote number on the line or as a superior figure (see ¶1523*b*). Type any additional lines within the footnote starting at the left margin.

```
in the coming decade.¹  According to one authoritative source, we

need to create a broad bipartisan consensus before we can develop

effective policies "to solve the problems of weakness in trade,

energy, and productivity."²  However, there has been no apparent
                                                              ↓1
    ──────────────────────────
                            ↓2
    1. This view is not universally shared.  For a summary of the
conflicting positions held by key members of Congress, see the dis-
cussion in Chapter 4, pp. 42–51.
                              ↓2
    2. Richard Bolling and John Bowles, America's Competitive
Edge:  How to Get Our Country Moving Again, McGraw–Hill, New York,
1982, p. 63.
```

e. As a rule, allow three to four lines for each bibliographic reference footnote; this estimate allows for space above and below each footnote. Footnotes that contain comments may run longer. Remember that on pages with a page number in the upper right corner, the last line of typing should fall on line 60 or (to avoid a bad page ending) on line 61; on pages where the page number falls at the bottom of the page, the last line of text or footnote should come no farther down than line 57 or (to avoid a bad break) line 58. (See ¶1409a and h for additional details on page-ending considerations.)

f. Ideally, the *complete* footnote should appear on the same page as the superior figure or symbol that refers to it. Occasionally, however, a footnote may be so long that it will not all fit on the page, even if it begins immediately following the line of text in which the superior figure or symbol occurs. In such a case follow this procedure:

(1) Once you have completed the line of text in which the footnote reference occurs, type a 2-inch underscore on the following line (see ¶1503a).

(2) If the long footnote is the only footnote on the page, start typing it on the second line below the underscore (as directed in ¶1503b–e). If other footnotes come before this long one on the page, begin typing the long one on the second line below the preceding footnote.

(3) Type as much of the footnote as will fit on the page. Try to end at a point that is obviously incomplete so that the reader will realize the footnote continues on to the next page. If that is not possible, you may need to insert a continuation line—for example, *Footnote continued on next page*—typed within parentheses or brackets and positioned at the right margin on the line directly below the last line of the footnote.

(4) On the next page, resume typing the text (along with any needed text references to further footnotes), but plan to end the text at a point that leaves enough space to (*a*) finish the footnote carried over from the preceding page and (*b*) insert any new footnotes called for in the text above.

STARTING A LONG FOOTNOTE

```
an outfit that would be appropriate to wear to any job interview.²
                                                                    ↓ 1
    ———————————————— ↓ 2
     1.  John T. Molloy, Dress for Success, Warner, New York, 1978,
p. 45. ↓ 2
     2.  Judith Martin (in Miss Manners' Guide to Excruciatingly Correct
Behavior, Atheneum, New York, 1982, p. 393) offers the following sug-
gestion to a person who asks how to dress for a formal interview with
an airline: "You do not say whether you are applying for a job as a
mechanic, a pilot, a stewardess, or an executive at this airline, but
the general rule about dressing for job interviews is to look like
```

CONTINUING A FOOTNOTE ON THE NEXT PAGE

```
may not think that it matters but it does.
                                           ↓ 1
    ———————————————— ↓ 2
someone who already has the job.  Thus, you would either wear dark
coveralls, a blue suit with a white shirt, a red-white-and-blue
dress with matching jacket, or a dark three-piece suit."
                                                          ↓ 2
     3.  Molloy, p. 52.
```

NOTE: If you expect to encounter a number of long notes that may not easily fit on the page where they are first referred to, you have an excellent reason for abandoning the footnote format and using endnotes instead.

❏ *For the treatment of footnotes that pertain to a table, see ¶¶1634–1636.*

TYPING ENDNOTES

1504 When notes are to appear all together as part of the back matter of a report or manuscript:

a. On a fresh page type *NOTES* in all-capital letters, centered on line 13.

b. On the third line below, begin typing the first endnote.

c. Ordinarily, single-space each endnote, but in a manuscript to be set in type, use double spacing to allow room for editing. In either case leave 1 blank line between endnotes.

d. Indent the first line of each endnote 5 spaces, and type any additional lines within the same endnote starting at the left margin.

e. Type the identifying number for each endnote on the line, not as a superior figure. (See also ¶1523*b*.)

```
                              ↓ 13
                            NOTES
                              ↓ 3

     1.   "The Socialist Vision of a High-Tech France," Business Week,
January 10, 1983, p. 47.
                          ↓ 2
     2.   Ibid., p. 51.
```

f. Use the same margins as for other pages in the body of the report or manuscript (see ¶¶1406–1409), and treat the numbering of these pages as shown in ¶1426*e–f*.

❏ *For guidelines on how to construct bibliographic reference endnotes, see ¶¶1508–1531.*

g. If the numbering of endnotes starts again with each new chapter or on each new page, insert an appropriate heading—*Chapter 1, Chapter 2*, etc., or *Page 1, Page 2*, etc.—over each sequence of endnotes in this section. Type the heading at the left margin in capital and small letters, underscored—or in all-capital letters without underscoring—and leave 2 blank lines above and 1 blank line below.

NOTE: If the numbering of endnotes is consecutive throughout, no headings are needed.

h. Insert this special section of endnotes in the back matter following any appendixes. If no appendix is given, the endnotes begin the back matter. (See also ¶1427.)

1505 When individual chapters of a report or a manuscript are prepared by different writers, it may be advantageous to have the endnotes that each author prepares inserted at the end of the respective chapter (instead of retyping all the endnotes as one continuous section in the back matter). The disadvantage of this approach is that the reader will have a bit more difficulty locating each set of notes than is true when all the endnotes are presented in one section at the very end.

NOTE: If this approach is used, the guidelines presented in ¶1504 will also apply here. However, the main heading on line 13 will have to be expanded in each case to read *NOTES TO CHAPTER 1*, *NOTES TO CHAPTER 2*, and so on.

TYPING TEXTNOTES

1506 In a report or manuscript with only a few bibliographic references and no bibliography at the end, it is acceptable to insert the data in parentheses within the main text.

↓ 7
1–3
↓ 3

If we decide to offer our employees free counseling on estate planning, we can hold down our expenses by asking employees to read about the seven plans most commonly used and then to tentatively select in advance the plan that seems best suited to their needs. (Arnold D. Kahn, Family Security Through Estate Planning, 2d ed., McGraw–Hill, New York, 1983, pp. 62–63.)

❏ *For guidelines on how to construct these bibliographic reference textnotes, see ¶¶1508–1531.*

NOTE: If some of the data called for in a bibliographic reference is already provided in the main text, there is no need to repeat it in the textnote.

↓ 7
1–3
↓ 3

If we decide to offer our employees free counseling on estate planning, we can hold down our expenses, according to legal expert Arnold D. Kahn, by asking employees to read about the seven plans most commonly used and then to tentatively select in advance the plan that seems best suited to their needs. (Family Security Through Estate Planning, 2d ed., McGraw–Hill, New York, 1983, pp. 62–63.)

1507 In a report or manuscript that contains a number of bibliographic references *and* a complete bibliography, textnotes may be used as follows:

a. At the appropriate point in the main text, supply the author's last name and the appropriate page number in parentheses. The reader who wants more complete information can consult the full entry in the bibliography.

The risk is excessive, according to one expert on bonds (Darst, p. 226); however, . . .

NOTE: Some authorities omit the abbreviations *p.* and *pp.* in this type of textnote.

b. If the author's name already appears in the main text, give only the page number in parentheses.

According to Darst (p. 226), the risk is excessive; however, . . .

c. If the bibliography lists more than one publication by the same author, then in the textnote use an abbreviated title or the year of publication to indicate which publication is being referred to.

. . . is excessive (Darst, *Handbook*, p. 226); however, . . .

OR: . . . is excessive (Darst, 1981, p. 226); however, . . .

d. If the bibliography lists publications by two or more authors with the same surname, use each author's first name or initial along with the surname.

. . . is excessive (David Darst, *Handbook,* p. 226); however, . . .

e. If the entries in the bibliography are numbered in sequence (see ¶1535*c*), then the textnote can simply list the appropriate "entry number" along with the page reference. Underscore the entry number to distinguish it from the page number, especially if the abbreviation *p.* or *pp.* is omitted.

. . . is excessive (22, p. 226); however, . . .

PATTERNS FOR CONSTRUCTING BIBLIOGRAPHIC REFERENCE NOTES

The following guidelines for constructing bibliographic reference notes deal with the situations that most commonly occur—whether in the form of footnotes, endnotes, or the type of textnote discussed in ¶1506. There is no clear-cut agreement among authorities as to how these notes should be constructed; rather, there are several schools of thought on the subject, and within each school there are slightly different variations between one reference manual and another.

Out of all the well-established conventions and variations, the style best suited for business use—and the one presented here—is a style that employs the simplest punctuation and the most straightforward presentation of the necessary data without any sacrifice in clarity or completeness. However, certain professional organizations—for example, the American Psychological Association, the American Medical Association, and the American Chemical Society—have each established a distinctive style, the use of which sometimes shows up in other fields. Moreover, slightly different patterns are often used in academic materials, such as those featured in the *MLA [Modern Language Association] Handbook*. If you are one of the many full-time business workers who are simultaneously taking one or more academic courses or one of the many full-time academic students who are concurrently holding down part- or full-time office jobs, you may need to familiarize yourself with more than one style. Note that along with the basic pattern for citing book titles (see ¶1508), you will find an "academic" variation that you may need to use from time to time. However, unless you are specifically directed to follow a particular style, the following "all-purpose" patterns—

based on well-established conventions—should meet your needs in virtually every type of situation you encounter.

NOTE: For detailed information about specific elements within these patterns, see the following paragraphs:

❏ *Note number: see ¶1523.*
❏ *Names of authors: see ¶1524.*
❏ *Title of the work: see ¶1525.*
❏ *Publisher's name: see ¶1526.*

❏ *Place of publication: see ¶1527.*
❏ *Date of publication: see ¶1528.*
❏ *Page numbers: see ¶1529.*
❏ *Subsequent references: see ¶¶1530–1531.*

1508 Book Title: Basic Pattern

a. Business Style

1. Author, <u>book title</u>, publisher, place of publication, year of publication, page number [if reference is being made to a specific page].

```
    1.  John Kenneth Galbraith, The Affluent Society,
Houghton Mifflin, Boston, 1958, p. 101.
```

NOTE: If any of these elements have already been identified in the text (for example, the author's name and the book title), they need not be repeated in the note. Moreover, if reference is made to the book as a whole rather than to a particular page, omit the page number.

```
According to Professor J. K. Galbraith, in his widely ac-
claimed book The Affluent Society, "It falls within the
power of the modern large corporation to mitigate or
eliminate (with one exception) every important risk to
which business enterprises have anciently been subject."¹
```

```
    1.  Houghton Mifflin, Boston, 1958, p. 101.
```

b. Academic Style

1. Author, <u>book title</u> (place of publication: publisher, year of publication), page number [if reference is being made to a specific page].

```
    1.  John Kenneth Galbraith, The Affluent Society (Boston:
Houghton Mifflin, 1958), p. 101.  (In endnotes, the note number is typed
```
on the line; in academic-style footnotes, the note number is typically typed above the line. See ¶ 1523*b*.)

NOTE: The key distinction between these two styles lies in a slightly different sequence of elements and a slightly different form of punctuation:

BUSINESS STYLE: . . . publisher, place of publication, year of publication . . .

ACADEMIC STYLE: . . . (place of publication: publisher, year of publication) . . .

The following patterns for books (in ¶¶1509–1516) show only the business style. However, you can readily convert them to academic style by simply changing the treatment of these three elements.

❏ *For the academic style for entries in bibliographies, see ¶1534c.*

1509 Book Title: With Edition Number

1. Author, <u>book title</u>, edition number [if not the first edition], publisher, place, year, page number.

```
    1.  Elbert S. Maloney, Dutton's Navigation & Piloting,
13th ed., Naval Institute Press, Annapolis, 1978, p. 375.
```

NOTE: Use an edition number only when the book is not in the first edition. If included, the edition number follows the main title and any related elements, such as the subtitle or the volume number and title. (For examples, see ¶¶1510–1511.) The following abbreviated forms are commonly used: *2d ed., 3d ed., 4th ed.,* and *rev. ed.* (for "revised edition").

1510   Book Title: With Subtitle

      1. Author, <u>book title: subtitle</u>, edition number [if not the first edition], publisher, place, year, page number.

      `1. Norman N. Barish and Seymour Kaplan,` <u>`Economic`</u> <u>`Analysis: For Engineering and Managerial Decision Making`</u>`, 2d ed., McGraw-Hill, New York, 1978, p. 277.`

NOTE: Do not give the subtitle of a book unless it is significant in identifying the book or in explaining its basic nature. If a subtitle is to be shown, separate it from the main title with a colon (unless the title page shows some other mark such as a dash). Type an underscore (without a break) from the start of the main title to the end of the subtitle. Capitalize the first word of the subtitle, even if it is a short preposition like *for* or a short conjunction like *or.* (See ¶360.)

      `1. Roy Blount, Jr.,` <u>`One Fell Soup: Or I'm Just a Bug on`</u> <u>`the Windshield of Life`</u>`, Little, Brown, Boston, 1983, p. 84.`

1511   Book Title: With Volume Number and Volume Title

      1. Author, <u>book title</u>, volume number, <u>volume title</u>, edition number [if not the first edition], publisher, place, year, page number.

      `1. E. Lipson,` <u>`The Economic History of England`</u>`, Vol. 1,` <u>`The Middle Ages`</u>`, 12th ed., Adam & Charles Black, London, 1959, pp. 511-594.`

NOTE: As a rule, do not show the volume title in a note unless it is significant in identifying the book. When the volume title is included, both the volume number and the volume title follow the book title (and subtitle, if any) but precede the edition number. The volume number is usually preceded by the abbreviation *Vol.* or by the word *Book* or *Part* (depending on the actual designation). The volume number may be arabic or roman, depending on the style used in the actual book.

❏ *See also ¶1512.*

1512   Book Title: With Volume Number Alone

      1. Author, <u>book title</u>, edition number [if not the first edition], publisher, place, year, volume number, page number.

      `1. Robert E. Spiller et al. (eds.),` <u>`Literary History`</u> <u>`of the United States`</u>`, Macmillan, New York, 1948, Vol. II, pp. 639-651. (OR: . . . II, 639-651.)`

NOTE: When the volume number is shown without the volume title, it follows the date of publication. When the volume number and page number occur one after the other, they may be styled as follows:

Style for Roman Volume Number	**Style for Arabic Volume Number**
Vol. III, p. 197 **OR** III, 197	Vol. 5, pp. 681–684 **OR** 5:681–684

Do not use the latter forms (with figures alone) if there is a chance your reader will not understand them.

1513 Book Title: With Chapter Reference

> 1. Author, <u>book title</u>, publisher, place, year, chapter number, "chapter title" [if significant], page number.

> 1. Will Durant and Ariel Durant, <u>The Age of Napoleon</u>, Simon and Schuster, New York, 1975, Chap. XII, "Napoleon and the Arts," pp. 278–285.

NOTE: When a note refers primarily to the title of a book, a chapter number and a chapter title are not usually included. If considered significant, however, these details can be inserted just before the page numbers. The word *chapter* is usually abbreviated as *Chap.*, the chapter number is arabic or roman (depending on the original), and the chapter title is enclosed in quotation marks.

1514 Selection From Collected Works of One Author

> 1. Author, "title of selection," <u>book title</u>, publisher, place, year, page number.

> 1. Sylvia Plath, "The Courage of Shutting Up," <u>Winter Trees</u>, Harper & Row, New York, 1972, pp. 8–9.

1515 Selection in Anthology

> 1. Author of selection, "title of selection," **in** editor of anthology **(ed.)**, <u>book title</u>, publisher, place, year, page number.

> 1. W. W. Rostow, "A New Economic Agenda," in C. Stewart Sheppard and Donald C. Carroll (eds.), <u>Working in the Twenty-First Century</u>, Wiley, New York, 1980, pp. 22–23.

> 2. Joseph Romano, "Operations Strategy," in Kenneth J. Albert (ed.), <u>The Strategic Management Handbook</u>, McGraw-Hill, New York, 1983, p. 136.

1516 Article in Reference Work

> 1. Author [if known], "article title," <u>name of reference work</u>, edition number [if not the first edition], publisher [usually omitted], place [usually omitted], year, page number [may be omitted].

> 1. Ware Myers, "Software Engineering," <u>McGraw-Hill Encyclopedia of Science and Technology</u>, 5th ed., 1982.

> 2. "Business Cycles," <u>Encyclopaedia Brittanica: Macropaedia</u>, 15th ed., 1980.

> 3. "Babbage, Charles," <u>Encyclopedia of Computer Science and Engineering</u>, 2d ed., Van Nostrand Reinhold, New York, 1983.

NOTE: It is not necessary to give the name of the publisher or the place of publication unless there is some possibility of confusion or the reference is not well known.

> 4. <u>Webster's New Collegiate Dictionary</u>, Merriam, Springfield, Mass., 1981, pp. 25a–29a.

> 5. <u>Webster's New World Dictionary of the American Language</u>, 2d concise ed., Collins, Cleveland, 1979.

> 6. Hugh Rawson, "Job Action," <u>A Dictionary of Euphemisms & Other Doubletalk</u>, Crown, New York, 1981.

Moreover, if you are making reference to an article or an entry that appears in alphabetic order in the main portion of the work, even the page number may be omitted. If the reference work carries the name of an editor rather than an author, the editor's name is also usually omitted.

1517   Article in Newspaper

1. Author [if known], "article title," name of newspaper, date, page number, column number.

1. Roger Lowenstein, "Alaska Proposing Japanese Connection," The Wall Street Journal, January 17, 1983, p. 26, cols. 2–4.

2. Jaye Scholl, "The Year's Action in the Dow: Wow!" Barron's, January 3, 1983, p. 20, col. 5.

❏ *See ¶1518, note.*

NOTE: If a particular issue of a newspaper is published in several sections and the page numbering begins anew with each section, include the section letter or number before the page number.

3. Georgia Dullea, "New Marital Stress: The Computer Complex," The New York Times, January 10, 1983, Sec. A, p. 17, cols. 2–6. (**OR:** . . . January 10, 1983, p. A17, . . .)

1518   Article in Magazine

1. Author [if known], "article title," name of magazine, date, page number.

1. "How to Judge Money–Market Funds," Consumer Reports, January 1983, pp. 30–34.

2. Thomas P. Murphy, "A Petunia in the Onion Patch," Forbes, January 3, 1983, p. 294.

3. Stephen J. Solarz, "America & Japan: A Search for Balance," Foreign Policy, Winter 1982–83, p. 84.

NOTE: Omit the comma between the article title and the name of the periodical if the article title ends with a question mark or an exclamation point.

4. "Can Mitterand Remake France's Economy?" Business Week, January 10, 1983, p. 44.

❏ *See also the second example in ¶1517.*

1519   Article in Professional Journal

1. Author, "article title," title of journal [often abbreviated], series number [if given], volume number, issue number [if given], date, page number.

1. Elizabeth E. Bailey and Ann F. Friedlaender, "Market Structure and Multiproduct Industries," The Journal of Economic Literature [**OR** JEL], Vol. XX, No. 3, September 1982, p. 1024.

NOTE: Titles of journals are often abbreviated in notes whenever these abbreviations are likely to be familiar to the intended readership or are clearly identified in a bibliography at the end.

1520 Bulletin, Pamphlet, or Monograph

> 1. Author [if given], "article title" [if appropriate], <u>title of bulletin</u>, series title and series number [if appropriate], volume number and issue number [if appropriate], sponsoring organization, place, date, page number.

> 1. "Telecommunications," <u>Washington Newsletter</u>, Vol. 34, No. 9, American Library Association, Washington, August 16, 1982, p. 4.

> 2. Jack Shuman, "Strategic Planning and Information Systems," <u>Bulletin of the American Society for Information Science</u>, Vol. 8, No. 5, June 1982, p. 23. (The name of the sponsoring organization is incorporated in the title of the bulletin.)

NOTE: Because the pertinent data used to identify bulletins, pamphlets, and monographs may vary widely, adapt the pattern shown above as necessary to fit each particular situation.

1521 Unpublished Dissertation or Thesis

> 1. Author, "title of thesis," **doctoral dissertation OR master's thesis** [identifying phrase to be inserted], name of academic institution, place, date, page number.

> 1. David Harry Weaver, "An Experimental Study of the Relative Impact of Controllable Factors of Difficulty in Typewriting Practice Material," doctoral dissertation, Syracuse University, Syracuse, N.Y., 1966, p. 121.

1522 Quotation From a Secondary Source

> 1. Author, <u>book title</u>, publisher, place, date, page number, **quoted by** author, <u>book title</u>, publisher, place, date, page number.

> 1. Herbert Marcuse, <u>One Dimensional Man</u>, Beacon, Boston, 1964, p. 7, quoted by William J. McGill, <u>The Year of the Monkey: Revolt on Campus, 1968–69</u>, McGraw–Hill, New York, 1982, p. 49.

NOTE: While it is always preferable to take the wording of a quotation from the original source, it is sometimes necessary to draw the wording from a secondary source. In such cases construct the note in two parts: in the first part, give as much information as possible about the *original* source (derived, of course, from the bibliographic reference note in the secondary source); in the second part, give the necessary information about the *secondary* source (which is at hand). Bridge the two parts of the note with a phrase such as *quoted by* or *cited by*. The pattern shown above assumes that the quotation originally appeared in a book and that the secondary source for the quoted matter was also a book. Naturally, if the original source or the secondary source is a work other than a book, use the pattern appropriate for that work in place of the "book" pattern shown above.

ELEMENTS OF BIBLIOGRAPHIC REFERENCE NOTES

1523 Note Number

a. Make sure that the number at the start of a footnote or an endnote corresponds to the appropriate reference number in the text.

b. Indent the note number 5 spaces, and type it (1) on the line (like an ordinary number), followed by a period and 2 spaces, or (2) as a superior (raised) figure without any space following it. Although the second style has traditionally been the one more commonly used (and is still preferred in academic work), the on-the-line style is now increasingly seen in business material because it is easier to type. Moreover, the on-the-line style must be used when typing endnotes. (See ¶1504.)

> 1. Nicholas Faith, Safety in Numbers, Viking, New York, 1982, pp. 45 ff.

OR:

> ¹Nicholas Faith, Safety in Numbers, Viking, New York, 1982, pp. 45 ff.

❑ *See ¶1502e on numbering notes consecutively; ¶1502f–g on the use of symbols in place of figures.*

1524 Names of Authors

a. Type an author's name (first name first) exactly as it appears on the title page of a book or in the heading of an article. (See ¶1508*a*, note.)

> 1. Arthur M. Schlesinger, Jr., A Thousand Days, Houghton Mifflin, Boston, 1965, p. 31.

> 2. T. S. Eliot, "The Dry Salvages," Four Quartets, Harcourt, Brace & World, New York, 1943, pp. 19–28.

> 3. Richard E. Peterson and Associates, Lifelong Learning in America, Jossey–Bass, San Francisco, 1979.

b. When two authors share a common surname, show the surname with each author's listing.

> 4. John W. Wyatt and Madie B. Wyatt, Business Law, 7th ed., McGraw–Hill, New York, 1985, pp. 98 ff.

c. When there are three or more authors, list only the first author's name followed by *et al.* (meaning "and others"). Do not underscore *et al.*

> 5. Eduardo B. Fernandez et al., Database Security and Integrity, Addison–Wesley, Reading, Mass., 1981, p. 133.

NOTE: If desired, the names of all the authors may be given. This style, if adopted for a given manuscript, should be used consistently throughout.

d. When an organization (rather than an individual) is the author of the material, show the organization's name in the author's position.

> 6. Commission on the Humanities, The Humanities in American Life, Univ. of California Press, Berkeley, 1980, p. 163.

However, if the organization is both the author and the publisher, show the organization's name only once—as the publisher.

> 7. Patterson's American Education, 1986, Educational Directories, Mount Prospect, Ill., 1985, Vol. LXXXII.

e. When a work such as an anthology carries an editor's name rather than an author's name, list the editor's name in the author's position, followed by the abbreviation *ed.* in parentheses. (If the names of two or more editors are listed, use the abbreviation *eds.* in parentheses.)

> 8. Leonard Michaels and Christopher Ricks (eds.), The State of the Language, Univ. of California Press, Berkeley, 1980.

NOTE: If a reference work carries the name of an editor rather than an author, the editor's name is usually omitted. (See ¶1516.)

f. If the author of a work is unknown, begin the note with the title of the work. Do not use *Anonymous* in place of the author's name.

1525 Title of the Work

a. In giving the title of the work, follow the title page of a book or the main heading of an article for wording, spelling, and punctuation. However, adjust the capitalization as necessary so that all titles cited in the notes conform to a standard style. (See ¶¶360–361, 363.)

b. If a title and a subtitle are shown on separate lines in the original work without any intervening punctuation, use a colon to separate them in the bibliographic reference note. (See ¶1510 for an example.)

c. In general, use underscoring for titles of *complete* published works and quotation marks for titles that refer to *parts* of complete published works.

❏ *For the use of underscoring with titles, see ¶289; for the use of quotation marks with titles, see ¶¶242–243.*

1526 Publisher's Name

a. List the publisher's name as it appears on the title page (for example, *McGraw-Hill Book Company*) or in a shortened form that is clearly recognizable *(McGraw-Hill);* use one form consistently throughout. If a division of the publishing company is also listed on the title page, it is not necessary to include this information in the footnote. Publishers, however, often do so in references to their own materials.

NOTE: The following brief list of examples will suggest acceptable patterns for abbreviating publishers' names. If in doubt, do not abbreviate.

Full Name	Acceptable Short Form
Alfred A. Knopf	Knopf
Charles Scribner's Sons	Scribner's
Simon and Schuster	—
Farrar Straus Giroux	—
Doubleday & Company, Inc.	Doubleday
Macmillan Publishing Co., Inc.	Macmillan
Little, Brown & Co.	Little, Brown
Harper & Row, Publishers	Harper & Row
McGraw-Hill Book Company	McGraw-Hill
The Viking Press	Viking
The Brookings Institution	Brookings
Basic Books	—
Yale University Press	Yale Univ. Press

b. Omit the publisher's name from references to magazines, newspapers, journals, and well-known reference works (for example, dictionaries and encyclopedias).

1527 Place of Publication

a. As a rule, list only the city of publication (for example, *New York, Cleveland, Washington, Toronto*). If the city is not well known or is likely to be confused with another city of the same name, add the state or the country (for example, *Cambridge, Mass.; Cambridge, England*). If the title page lists several cities in which the publisher has offices, use only the first city named.

b. Omit the place of publication from references to magazines, journals, and well-known reference works.

c. Incorporate the city name in the name of a newspaper that might otherwise be unrecognized. For example, *The Star-Ledger* (published in Newark, New Jersey) should be referred to in a note as *The Newark (N.J.) Star-Ledger*.

1528   Date of Publication

a. For books, show the year of publication. (If this date does not appear on the title page, use the most recent year shown in the copyright notice.)

b. For monthly periodicals, show both the month and the year. (See ¶1518 for an example.)

c. For weekly or daily periodicals, show the month, day, and year. (See ¶¶1517–1518 for examples.)

1529   Page Numbers

a. Page references in notes occur in the following forms:

p. 3	p. v	pp. 301 f. (meaning "page 301 and the following page")
pp. 3–4	pp. v–vi	pp. 301 ff. (meaning "page 301 and the following pages")

NOTE: Whenever possible, avoid using the indefinite abbreviations *f.* and *ff.*, and supply a specific range of page numbers instead.

b. In a range of page numbers the second number is sometimes abbreviated; for example, *pp. 981–983* may be expressed as *pp. 981–83*. (See ¶460.)

c. There is a trend toward dropping the abbreviations *p.* and *pp.* when there is no risk of mistaking the numbers for anything but page numbers.

SUBSEQUENT REFERENCES

1530   **a.** When a note refers to a work that was fully identified in the note *immediately preceding*, it may be shortened by use of the abbreviation *ibid.* (meaning "in the same place"). *Ibid.* replaces all those elements that would otherwise be carried over intact from the previous note. Do not underscore *ibid.*

      1.   Freeman Dyson, <u>Disturbing the Universe</u>, Harper & Row, New York, 1979, pp. 115–117.

      2.   Ibid., p. 63. *(Ibid. represents all the elements in the previous note except the page number.)*

      3.   Ibid. *(Referring to page 63 in the same work. Here ibid. represents everything in the preceding note, including the page number.)*

b. If you plan to use *ibid.* in a *footnote*, make sure that the footnote "immediately preceding" is no more than a few pages back. Otherwise, the interested reader will be put to the irritating task of having to riff back through the pages in order to find the "immediately preceding" footnote. To spare your reader this inconvenience, use the form suggested in ¶1531.

c. Do not use *ibid.* in a *textnote* unless the one "immediately preceding" is on the same page and easy to spot; otherwise, your reader will have to search through lines and lines of text to find it. To spare your reader, construct these "subsequent reference" textnotes along the same lines as "first reference" textnotes. (See ¶1507*a–e*.)

(Continued on page 348.)

NOTE: If you are using *endnotes,* the use of *ibid.* will cause no inconvenience, since it refers to the note typed directly above.

1531 **a.** When a note refers to a work fully identified in an earlier note but *not the one immediately preceding*, it may be shortened as follows:

    1. Author's surname, page number.

    8.   Dyson, p. 79. (Referring to the work fully identified before; see note 1 in ¶1530*a.*)

NOTE: When this short form is used for a subsequent reference, it is desirable to provide a complete bibliography as well, so that the interested reader can quickly find the complete reference in an alphabetic listing.

  b. When previous reference has been made to different authors with the same surname, the use of a surname alone in a subsequent reference would be confusing. Therefore, the basic pattern in ¶1531*a* must be modified in the following way:

    1. Author's initial(s) plus surname, page number.
OR: 2. Author's full name, page number.

    1. Benjamin Newman, <u>Forms Manual for the CPA</u>, Wiley, New York, 1980, pp. 252–255.

    2. Maurice S. Newman, <u>Accounting Estimates by Computer Sampling</u>, Wiley, New York, 1982, p. 42.

    3. B. Newman, p. 375.

    4. M. S. Newman, p. 55.

  c. If previous reference has been made to different works by the same author, any subsequent reference should contain the title of the specific work now being referred to. This title may be shortened to a key word or phrase; the word or phrase should be sufficiently clear, however, so that the full title can be readily identified in the bibliography or in an earlier note.

    1. Author's surname, <u>book title</u> [shortened if feasible], page number.

    1. Russell L. Ackoff, <u>The Art of Problem Solving</u>, Wiley, New York, 1978, p. 91.

    2. Russell L. Ackoff, <u>Creating the Corporate Future</u>, Wiley, New York, 1981, p. 117.

    3. Ackoff, <u>Problem Solving</u>, p. 113.

If referring to an article in a periodical, refer to the periodical title rather than the article title.

    2. Author's surname, <u>periodical title</u> [shortened if feasible], page number.

    4. George F. Kennan, "America's Unstable Soviet Policy," <u>The Atlantic</u>, November 1982, p. 71.

    5. Tracy Kidder, . . .

    6. Kennan, <u>Atlantic</u>, p. 79. (Referring to the work identified in note 4 above.)

d. A more formal style in subsequent references uses the abbreviations *loc. cit.* ("in the place cited") and *op. cit.* ("in the work cited").

    1.   Author's surname, **loc. cit.** (This pattern is used when reference is made to the *very same page* in the work previously identified.)

    2.   Author's surname, **op. cit.,** page number. (This pattern is used when reference is made to a *different page* in the work previously identified.)

    1.   `Erich A. Helfert,` <u>`Techniques of Financial Analysis,`</u> `5th ed., Irwin, Homewood, Ill., 1982, p. 187.`

    2.   `George Foster,` <u>`Financial Statement Analysis,`</u> `Prentice-Hall, Englewood Cliffs, N.J., 1978, p. 101.`

    3.   `Helfert, op. cit., p. 194.` (Referring to a different page in *Techniques of Financial Analysis.*)

    4.   `Foster, loc. cit.` (Referring to the same page in *Financial Statement Analysis.*)

    5.   `Ibid.` (Referring to exactly the same page as shown in note 4. *Ibid.* may be used only to refer to the note immediately preceding. See ¶1530.)

NOTE: Do not underscore *loc. cit.* or *op. cit.*

BIBLIOGRAPHIES

1532 A bibliography at the end of a manuscript or a report typically lists all the works *consulted* in the preparation of the material as well as all the works that were actually *cited* in the notes. The format of a bibliography is also used for any list of titles, such as a list of recommended readings or a list of new publications.

1533 **a.** On a new page type *BIBLIOGRAPHY* (or some other appropriate title) in all-capital letters, centered on line 13. Leave 2 blank lines, and begin typing the first entry on line 16. (See the illustration on page 351.)

    b. Use the same margins as for other pages in the body of the report or manuscript (see ¶¶1406–1409), and treat the numbering of these pages as shown in ¶1426*e–f.*

    c. Begin each entry at the left margin. Ordinarily, type the entries single-spaced, but use double spacing if the material is to be set in type.

    d. Indent turnover lines 5 spaces so that the first word in each entry will stand out.

    e. Leave 1 blank line between entries (whether single- or double-spaced).

1534 Entries in bibliographies contain the same elements and follow the same style as bibliographic reference notes except for two key differences.

    a. Begin each entry with the name of the author listed in inverted order (last name first). When an entry includes two or more authors' names, invert only the first author's name. When an organization is listed as the author, do not invert the name.

`Albert, Kenneth J. (ed.),` <u>`The Strategic Management Handbook,`</u> `McGraw-Hill, New York, 1983.`

(Continued on page 350.)

America, Richard F., and Bernard E. Anderson, <u>Moving Ahead: Black Managers in American Business</u>, McGraw-Hill, New York, 1978.

The Business Week Team, <u>The Reindustrialization of America</u>, McGraw-Hill, New York, 1982.

❑ *For additional examples, see the illustration on page 351.*

b. Include page numbers in bibliographic entries only when the material being cited is part of a larger work. In such cases show the range of pages (for example, *pp. 215–232*) on which the material appears.

Steingold, Fred S., "Competing With Your Former Employer," <u>Inc.</u>, January 1983, pp. 91–92.

c. In academic material, bibliographic entries typically follow a slightly different style. In the examples below, note that a period follows the three main parts of the entry (author's name, the title, and the publishing information). Also note that the parentheses that normally enclose the publishing information in an academic-style footnote or endnote (see ¶1508*b*) are omitted in the bibliographic entry.

Albert, Kenneth J. (ed.). <u>The Strategic Management Handbook</u>. New York: McGraw-Hill, 1983.

Steingold, Fred S. "Competing With Your Former Employer." <u>Inc.</u>, January 1983, pp. 91–92. (Note that the magazine title—in this case <u>Inc.</u>—is considered part of the publishing information. Thus a period follows the article title here to mark the end of the title information in the entry.)

1535 **a.** List the entries in a bibliography alphabetically by author's last name.

b. Entries lacking an author are alphabetized by title. Disregard the word *The* or *A* at the beginning of a title in determining alphabetic sequence. (For an example, see the next-to-last entry in the illustration on page 351. Note that this entry is alphabetized on the basis of *Guide*, following *Galbraith*.)

c. There is no need to number the alphabetized entries in a bibliography unless you plan to use the style of textnotes described in ¶1507*e*. In that case begin each entry of the bibliography with a number typed at the left margin, followed by a period and 2 spaces. Then type the rest of the entry in the customary way, but indent any turnover so that it begins under the first word in the line above. (In the parenthetical textnotes, you can then make reference to different works by their bibliographic "entry number" instead of by author.)

1. Blake, Robert R., and Jane Srygley Mouton, <u>Consultation: A Handbook for Individual and Organizational Development</u>, 2d ed., Addison-Wesley, Reading, Mass., 1983.

2. Drucker, Peter F., <u>Managing in Turbulent Times</u>, Harper & Row, New York, 1980.

1536 When a bibliography contains more than one work by the same author, replace the author's name with a long dash (six hyphens) in all the entries after the first. List the works alphabetically by title. (For examples, see the fifth, sixth, and seventh entries in the illustration on page 351. Note that these titles are alphabetized on the key words *Age*, *Budget*, and *New*. The eighth entry involves a coauthor and therefore follows the works written by the first author alone.)

NOTE: As an alternative, multiple entries pertaining to the same author may be listed in chronological sequence according to the date of each publication.

↓ 13
BIBLIOGRAPHY
↓ 3

Bain, David, <u>The Productivity Prescription</u>, McGraw-Hill, New York, 1982.
↓ 2

Chandler, Alfred D., Jr., and Herman Daems, <u>Managerial Hierarchies</u>, Harvard Univ. Press, Cambridge, Mass., 1980.

Christenson, Christina, et al., <u>Supervising</u>, Addison-Wesley, Reading, Mass., 1982.

Doktar, R., et al. (eds.), <u>The Implementation of Management Science</u>, Elsevier, New York, 1979.

Galbraith, John Kenneth, <u>The Age of Uncertainty</u>, Houghton Mifflin, Boston, 1977.

——, "The Budget and the Bust," <u>The New Republic</u>, March 17, 1982, pp. 9-13.

——, <u>The New Industrial State</u>, 3d rev. ed., Houghton Mifflin, Boston, 1978.

—— and Nicole Salinger, <u>Almost Everyone's Guide to Economics</u>, Houghton Mifflin, Boston, 1978.

<u>A Guide to Money, Power, and Politics</u>, Common Cause, Washington, 1981.

Harvard Business Review, <u>On Human Relations</u>, Harper & Row, New York, 1979.

Tables

You can fit a good deal of material into a compact space when you present it in the form of a table—with items arranged in *rows* (to be read horizontally) and in *columns* (to be read vertically). However, in designing a table, you should aim for more than compactness. Your reader should be able to locate specific information faster—and detect significant patterns or trends in the data more quickly—than if the same information were presented in the running text.

The following section presents guidelines on setting up and executing well-designed tables. Modify these guidelines as necessary in specific situations to achieve results that are easy to understand, attractive to look at, and as simple as possible to execute.

TYPES OF TABLES

1601 a. **Table Text Only.** A table may simply consist of two columns of data with as few as two rows in each column.

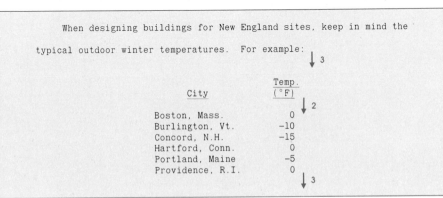

```
                                                                 4

        Our analysis of the latest reports indicates that sales are up by
    at least 10 percent in all regions:
                                       ↓ 2
              Eastern Region              16.2%
              North Central Region        11.0%
              Southern Region             18.4%
              Western Region              13.9% ↓ 2
        The primary reason for this upsurge, according to the managers of
    these regions, is the rebuilding of inventories, which were allowed to
```

NOTE: When a single-spaced table is inserted in the midst of single-spaced running text, leave 1 blank line above and below the table (as shown above). If the table is typed with double or 1½-line spacing or is inserted in the midst of running text typed with double or 1½-line spacing, leave 2 blank lines above and below. (See also ¶1604c.)

b. **Open (Unruled) Table.** An open table may consist of nothing more than two columns of data, each labeled with a column head. The table is called *open* because no horizontal rules are used in the table design.

```
    When designing buildings for New England sites, keep in mind the

    typical outdoor winter temperatures.  For example:
                                                       ↓ 3

                                   Temp.
                   City           ( °F)
                                          ↓ 2
              Boston, Mass.          0
              Burlington, Vt.      -10
              Concord, N.H.        -15
              Hartford, Conn.        0
              Portland, Maine       -5
              Providence, R.I.       0
                                          ↓ 3
```

NOTE: When a table begins with unruled column heads, leave 2 blank lines above and below the table as a whole. (See also ¶1604c.)

c. **Ruled Table.** A ruled table is so called because it has three horizontal rules: one above the column heads, one below the column heads, and one below the last line of the table text.

```
                                                                    12

with prefixes indicating multiples or fractions of a unit.  There are
seven base units in the SI metric system:
                                        ↓ 2
     _____        ↓ 2
                                                                 ↓ 1
          Quantity            Unit         Symbol
     _____        ↓ 2

       Length ................ meter         m
       Mass .................. kilogram      kg
       Time .................. second        s
       Electric current ...... ampere        A
       Thermodynamic
          temperature ........ kelvin        K
       Amount of substance .... mole         mol
       Luminous intensity ..... candela      cd  ↓ 1
     _____
                                                            ↓ 3

In addition, there are two supplementary units, the radian and the
steradian.
```

NOTE: When a table begins with ruled column heads, leave 2 blank lines above and below the table as a whole. (Type the first underscore on the second line beneath the running text to create the appearance of 2 blank lines.)

❏ *For the use of leaders between columns, see ¶1631d, note.*

d. **Boxed Table.** This is a ruled table to which vertical rules have been added.

```
                                                                    12

with prefixes indicating multiples or fractions of a unit.  There are
seven base units in the SI metric system:
                                        ↓ 2
     _____        ↓ 2
                  |              |                                ↓ 1
          Quantity |    Unit      |   Symbol
     _____|_____|_____       ↓ 2
                  |              |
       Length ....|... meter     |   m
       Mass ......|... kilogram   |   kg
       Time ......|... second     |   s
       Electric current ... ampere |   A
       Thermodynamic        |     |
          temperature ...... kelvin |   K
       Amount of substance ... mole |   mol
       Luminous intensity .... candela |  cd  ↓ 1
     _____|_____|_____
                                                            ↓ 3

In addition, there are two supplementary units, the radian and the
steradian.
```

❑ *For the use of leaders in a boxed table, see ¶1631e.*

e. Tables With Other Elements. The four types of tables identified in ¶1601*a–d* frequently carry additional elements, such as a table number, a table title, a subtitle, and notes. Moreover, *leaders* (rows of periods) may be used to lead the eye from items in the first column to corresponding items in the second column.

TABLE WITH TITLE

```
        ↓ 4

      ESTIMATED NUMBER OF EMPLOYEES IN
        MAJOR INDUSTRY GROUPS IN 1980
                                    ↓ 3


  Machinery (excluding electric) ... 2,410,800
  Electric and electronic
    equipment ...................... 1,963,200
  Transportation equipment ........ 1,771,000
  Fabricated metal products ....... 1,616,800
  Food and kindred products ....... 1,537,400
                                          ↓ 4
```

❑ *For the use of leaders between columns, see ¶1631d, note.*

TABLE WITH NUMBER, TITLE, AND SUBTITLE

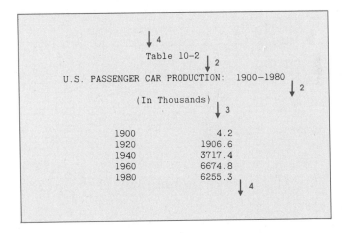

```
                 ↓ 4
               Table 10-2
                         ↓ 2
    U.S. PASSENGER CAR PRODUCTION:  1900–1980
                                            ↓ 2
             (In Thousands)
                           ↓ 3

        1900            4.2
        1920         1906.6
        1940         3717.4
        1960         6674.8
        1980         6255.3
                            ↓ 4
```

NOTE: When a table begins with a title or a table number, leave 3 blank lines above and below the table as a whole.

(Continued on page 356.)

OPEN TABLE WITH NUMBER, TITLE, SUBTITLE, COLUMN HEADS, AND NOTES

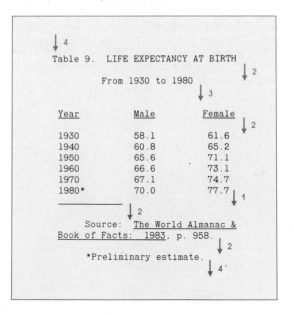

Table 9.   LIFE EXPECTANCY AT BIRTH

From 1930 to 1980

Year	Male	Female
1930	58.1	61.6
1940	60.8	65.2
1950	65.6	71.1
1960	66.6	73.1
1970	67.1	74.7
1980*	70.0	77.7

Source: The World Almanac & Book of Facts: 1983, p. 958.

*Preliminary estimate.

RULED TABLE WITH NUMBER, TITLE, SUBTITLE, COLUMN HEADS, AND NOTE

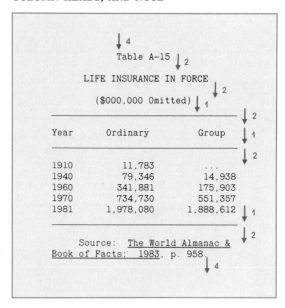

Table A-15

LIFE INSURANCE IN FORCE

($000,000 Omitted)

Year	Ordinary	Group
1910	11,783	...
1940	79,346	14,938
1960	341,881	175,903
1970	734,730	551,357
1981	1,978,080	1,888,612

Source: The World Almanac & Book of Facts: 1983, p. 958.

LOCATING TABLES WITHIN RUNNING TEXT

1602   **a.** Tables should be easy to refer to. Therefore, try to locate each table on the same page where the subject of the table is introduced in the running text. In this way the reader will have ready access to the table while reading the text commentary that may precede and follow.

b. Ideally, every table should fall immediately after the point in the running text where it is first mentioned. However, if placing the table within a paragraph is likely to disrupt the reader's grasp of the material, then locate the table at the end of the paragraph or at the top or bottom of the page. (See ¶1604c, note.)

1603 Avoid breaking a table at the bottom of a page. If starting a table at the ideal point means that it will not all fit in the space remaining on the page, then place the complete table at the top of the next page. (At the point in the text where the table is first mentioned, insert an appropriate cross-reference in parentheses. See ¶1608.)

NOTE: If you have to fit a number of relatively short tables (half a page or less) in a given report, memo, or letter, single-spacing the table text may maximize your chances of locating each table in the ideal place. (See ¶1624 on the issue of single vs. double spacing of tables. See ¶1637 for other techniques to limit the length of tables.)

1604 If a table is to appear on a page that also carries running text:

a. It should be centered horizontally within the established margins. (See ¶1609 for guidance on centering a table within these margins.)

b. Try to indent the table at least 5 spaces from each side margin. In any case, the width of the table should not exceed the width of the running text. (See ¶¶1640–1644 for ways to deal with an extrawide table.)

c. The table should be set off by 1 to 3 blank lines from the running text above and below, as follows:

Kind of Table	Spacing in Table Text	Blank Lines Above and Below Table	Illustration
Without column heads or table title	Single	1	¶1601a
Without column heads or table title	Double or 1½-line	2	—
With column heads (but no table title)	Single, double, or 1½-line	2	¶1601b, c, d
With table title	Single, double, or 1½-line	3	¶1601e

NOTE: Placing a table in the middle of a page (with running text above and below) requires you to leave up to 3 blank lines both above and below the table. If space is tight, place the table at the top or bottom of the page. In that way you can eliminate one set of blank lines and improve your chances of fitting the table on the desired page.

d. Before typing the table, count the number of lines it will require. Be sure to include in your count the blank lines within the table as well as above and below. (See the illustrations in ¶1601 for a quick guide to the allowance for blank lines.) On the basis of this count and an evaluation of the adjacent text material and the space available, you can decide on the best location for the table.

LOCATING TABLES ON SEPARATE PAGES

1605 When a table occupies more than two-thirds of a page, it can often be difficult to fit on the same page with running text. In such cases type the table on a separate page and place it immediately after the text page on which the table is first referred to.

1606 If a given document contains a number of tables, most of which will each require a separate page, then all the tables (short as well as long) may be executed as an appendix at the back of a report or as an attachment to a memo or letter. This arrangement—which permits the reader to keep the full set of tables alongside the running text (except in the case of bound reports)—can be very convenient, especially if some of the tables are repeatedly cited throughout the running text. (This arrangement also eliminates the problem of trying to fit long tables within the running text.)

1607 When a table is to appear on a page by itself, it should be centered horizontally and vertically within the established margins of the page. (See ¶¶1609–1611 for guidelines on centering horizontally and vertically.)

NOTE: If no margins have been established, leave a minimum margin of 1 inch (25 mm) on all four sides of the table.

1608 When a table is not located on the same page on which it is referred to, provide a cross-reference in parentheses to the appropriate page. For example:

(See Table 4 on page 18.) **OR** (See Table 2-2 on page 31.)

NOTE: These parenthetical cross-references may be treated as a separate sentence (as shown above) or as part of another sentence (see ¶220).

❑ *For the advisability of numbering tables to simplify the matter of cross-references, see ¶1613.*

CENTERING TABLES HORIZONTALLY

1609 To center a table horizontally in typewritten material and determine the starting point for each column within the table, use this procedure:

a. Establish a *key line* as follows:

(1) Select the longest item in each column, whether it occurs in the column head or the column text.

(2) Determine the number of spaces to be left between columns. Normally, leave 6 spaces; however, you may use any number of spaces that produces an attractive and readable table. Do not leave less than 2 spaces.

NOTE: In financial statements 2 blank spaces are customarily used between adjacent columns listing amounts of money.

(3) This combination of the longest item from each column plus an allowance for the space between each pair of columns makes up the key line. Here, for example, is the key line used to plan Table 16-1 (illustrated on page 363):

```
Year     5 Years       49,897      154,299      219,760
  123456         123456       123456       123456
```

b. Determine the centering point on the page. If the left and right margins have been established in advance, the centering point will fall halfway between these margins. If the left and right margins have not been established and are to be equal, use the exact center of the page as the centering point.

c. Clear all tab stops and the margin stops on the typewriter.

d. From the centering point, backspace once for each pair of strokes in the key line. Do not backspace for an odd stroke left over at the end.

e. At the point at which you stop backspacing, set the left margin stop. This will represent the left margin of the table and of the first column.

NOTE: If the process of backspacing carries you beyond the left margin of the running text, you will know that the table is too wide as it currently stands. (If a left margin has not been established and you backspace to a point that leaves a left margin of less than 1 inch, you will also know that the table is too wide.) As a first step, try reducing the space between columns to as little as 2 spaces; repeat steps *d* and *e* to see if this approach produces an acceptable left margin. (If the table is still too wide, see ¶¶1640–1644 for other solutions.)

f. From the left margin of the table, space forward once for each stroke in the longest item in the first column. Then space forward again for each blank space to be left between the first and second columns. At the point where you stop, set a tab stop. This will represent the start of the second column.

g. Repeat step *f* until you have set tab stops for each of the remaining columns.

NOTE: Some word processing systems can center a table automatically after it is keyboarded. You will still have to plan the tab stops.

CENTERING TABLES VERTICALLY

1610 To center a table vertically on a full 8½- by 11-inch sheet:

a. Count the number of lines in the table (including the blank lines).

NOTE: There is a total of 66 lines on a standard sheet of paper. In order to maintain a minimum margin of 1 inch (6 lines) at the top and bottom of the page, your count for the table should not exceed 54 lines. Moreover, if you are doing a report and must allow for a page number at the top or bottom of the page, your count for the table should not exceed 51 lines. If it appears that the table is running beyond these limits, consider the various alternatives for reducing the length of the table (see ¶1637). If none of these solve the problem, you will have to continue the table on to a second page (see ¶1638).

b. Find the difference between the total number of lines in the table (including blank lines) and 66, the total number of lines available on the page. (If a table will occupy a total of 39 lines, then the difference between 39 and 66 is 27.)

c. Divide the difference by 2 to find the line number on which to start the table. (Dividing 27 by 2 yields an answer of 13½.) If your answer has a fraction, ignore it. (In this case, then, you would start typing on line 13.)

1611 To center a table vertically on a full sheet of A4 paper (210 by 297 mm), use the same procedure described in ¶1610. However, there are 70 lines on an A4 sheet.

TABLE IDENTIFICATION

1612 Tables should be identified by *title* unless they are not very numerous and the significance of the tabular material is clear without some descriptive label.

1613 Tables should also be identified by *number* unless they are quite short, not very numerous, and typically referred to only on the page on which they fall. The use of table numbers simplifies the matter of cross-references, an important consideration if you expect that a number of tables will not fit on the page where they are first mentioned or if you know that certain tables will be referred to repeatedly throughout the running text.

NOTE: Tables may be numbered consecutively throughout a given document or consecutively within each chapter and each appendix (if the document is broken down in this way). With the latter technique, the chapter number (or the appendix number or letter) is used as a prefix in the numbering scheme. For example, Table 3-2 would be the second table in Chapter 3, and Table A-5 would be the fifth table in Appendix A.

1614　The table title may be followed by a *subtitle,* which provides additional information about the significance of the table, the period of time it covers, or the manner in which the information is organized or presented. Since a subtitle should be held to one line if possible (two at the most), a lengthy comment on any of these points should be handled as a note to the table rather than as a subtitle (see ¶¶1634–1636).

1615　Type the elements of table identification as follows:

a. **Table Title.** Type in all-capital letters and center. (See *d* below.)

b. **Table Number.** Type the word *Table* in capital and small letters, followed by the appropriate number. To give the table number special emphasis, center it on the second line above the table title. To hold down the length of the table, type the table number on the same line with the table title; in this case insert a period after the table number and leave 2 spaces before typing the table title.

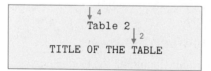
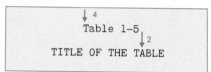

OR　　　　　　　　　　　　　　　　　　**OR**

NOTE: Within a given document treat all table numbers the same way.

c. **Table Subtitle.** Type in capital and small letters, centered on the second line below the title. The subtitle is usually enclosed in parentheses when it simply comments on the listing of data in some special order (for example, *In Descending Order by Sales Revenue*) or on the omission of zeros from figures given in the table (for example, *In Millions* or *000 Omitted*).

NOTE: If either the title or the subtitle requires more than one line, break it into sensible phrases and single-space any turnover lines. If possible, try to hold the title or the subtitle to two lines each.

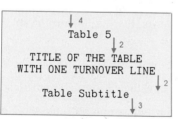
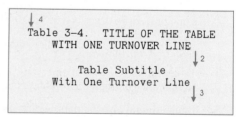

d. To center each line in the table identification, first determine the centering point for the table (see ¶1609*b*). Then from the centering point, backspace once for each pair of strokes in the line. (Do not backspace for an odd stroke left over at the end.) The point at which you stop backspacing is the point at which to begin typing the line in order to center it. Many word processors can center each line for you.

e. When a table falls on a page with running text above it, leave 3 blank lines above the first line of table identification. Leave 2 blank lines below the last line of table identification, whether the following copy consists of column heads or the table text.

COLUMN HEADS

1616   **a.** Unless a table is very simple and the significance of the material is clear without heads, provide a heading for each column. (A heading may be omitted over the first column, also known as the *stub*. See, for example, the illustration at the top of page 372.)

b. Whenever possible, use singular forms in the column heads. Thus, for example, over a column listing a number of cities, use the heading *City* (rather than *Cities*).

c. In order to hold down the length of column heads, use abbreviations and symbols as necessary. For example:

Acct. No.	Account number
% of Total	Percent of total
FY1986	Fiscal year 1986 (used to indicate that a company's *fiscal* year does not coincide with the *calendar* year)
1Q/1987	First quarter of 1987 (used with 2Q, 3Q, and 4Q to signify the four quarters of the year)
1988A	Actual results in 1988
1989B	Budgeted results in 1989
1989E	Estimated results in 1989
1990F	Forecast of results in 1990
Sales ($)	Sales results expressed as a dollar amount (in other words, sales revenues)
Sales (U)	Sales results expressed in terms of the number of units sold
Sales YTD ($)	Cumulative sales revenues so far this year (that is, year to date)
% O/(U) Last Year	Percentage by which this year's results are over (or under) last year's results

NOTE: If your reader may not understand some of the abbreviations and symbols you use, explain the unfamiliar ones in a footnote to the table. (See ¶¶1634–1636 and illustrations in ¶¶1622–1623.)

d. Long column heads may be broken into as many as five lines, single-spaced and centered on the column width. (See ¶¶1617–1618 on procedures for centering column heads.)

NOTE: In extreme situations, where the column heads are unusually long, it is permissible to type them vertically (reading up). However, because of the awkwardness for the reader and the complications for the typist, consider any alternative that will help you avoid this situation. (See ¶¶1640–1644.)

❑ *For illustrations of different types of column heads, see ¶¶1620–1623.*

1617   When a column head is *narrower* than the column text, center the column head over the text as follows:

a. Identify the longest line in the column head and the column text.

COLUMN HEAD: In–Service
                  12345678901234567
COLUMN TEXT: Computer literacy

b. Find the difference in the number of strokes between the longest line in the column head and the longest line in the column text. (In the example above, the difference is 7.)

c. Divide the difference by 2 (and ignore any fraction in the answer) to find how many spaces to indent the longest line in the column head. (Dividing 7 by 2 yields an answer of 3½, so the longest line in the column head should be indented 3 spaces.)

```
###In-Service####   ←—Note that when this method of centering is
Computer literacy      used, if a short line cannot be perfectly cen-
                       tered over the long line, the extra space al-
                       ways falls at the right.
```

d. To center the other lines in the column head in relation to the longest line, follow the same procedure described in *c* above. For example, if the longest line in the column head (*In-Service*) is 10 and another line (*Program*) is 7, divide the difference (3) and discard any fraction in the answer (1½). The resulting figure (1) indicates that the line in question should be indented 1 space.

```
In-Service
#Training#
#Program##
```

NOTE: The following illustration will provide a simple visual check on the correct alignment of lines in a column head.

```
123456#        #12345#        #1234##        ##123##        ##12###
1234567        1234567        1234567        1234567        1234567
```

1618 When a column head is *wider* than any item in the column text, center the column text under the column head as follows:

a. Type the longest line in the column head, starting at the left margin of the column. (Recall that in this case it is the longest line in the column head that determines the total width of the column.)

```
123456789
Household
```

b. Center any other lines in the column head in relation to the longest line. (See the examples in ¶1617*d*, note, as a visual check on your results.)

```
123456789
#Median##
#Income##
###per###
Household
```

c. Find the difference in the number of strokes between the longest line in the column head and the longest line in the column text. In this example, the longest line in the column head is 9, the longest line in the column text (*$19,074*) is 7, and the difference is 2.

d. Divide the difference by 2 (and discard any fraction) to find the number of spaces to indent the longest line in the column text. In this case dividing 2 by 2 gives an answer of 1, so indent the longest text line 1 space.

```
#Median##
#Income##
###per###
Household

#$19,074#
```

NOTE: Once the wide column head has been typed, you can reset the tab stop for this column to establish the starting point for most lines in the column text. In this example the column text will consist almost entirely of five-digit numbers; the dollar sign will appear only in the first entry and in the total line at the bottom of the column. Therefore, it makes sense to set the tab stop at the point at which the five-digit numbers will begin. (You will have to remember to space forward or back for any line that is shorter or longer.)

⌐Tab stop for
| column text
↓
$19,074
17,341
15,640
13,242
9,903

❑ *For guidelines on how to align items in column text, see ¶¶1625–1629. The alignment will depend on whether the items are all words, all figures (with or without decimal points), or some combination of words and figures.*

1619 In drafts and in informal reports, memos, and letters—where the occasion does not justify the time and effort that goes into centering column heads over column text—every line in the column head may start at the left margin of the column. For example:

In-Service	Average	Cumulative	1st-Year
Training	Annual	Compound	Sales
Program	Expenditures	Growth	Estimates

1620 Open (Unruled) Column Heads

a. Type column heads in capital and small letters, underscored and centered on the column width. (See ¶¶1617–1619 for guidance on centering.)

b. If the column heads in a table do not all take the same number of lines, align the column heads at the bottom.

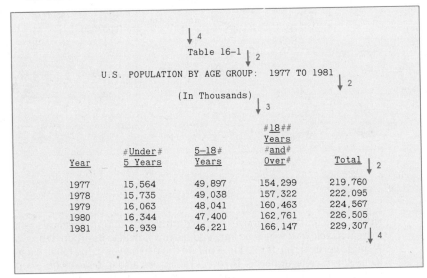

↓ 4
Table 16–1 | 2

U.S. POPULATION BY AGE GROUP: 1977 TO 1981 ↓ 2

(In Thousands) ↓ 3

Year	#Under# 5 Years	5–18# Years	#18## Years #and# Over#	Total
1977	15,564	49,897	154,299	219,760
1978	15,735	49,038	157,322	222,095
1979	16,063	48,041	160,463	224,567
1980	16,344	47,400	162,761	226,505
1981	16,939	46,221	166,147	229,307

↓ 4

KEY LINE:
| Year | 5 Years | 49,897 | 154,299 | 219,760 |
| 123456 | 123456 | 123456 | 123456 |

c. Leave 2 blank lines between the final line of the title or subtitle (whichever comes last) and the first line of the tallest column head.

d. Leave 1 blank line between the column heads and the table text.

1621 Ruled Column Heads

a. When column heads are preceded and followed by horizontal rules running the full width of the table, they are called *ruled* column heads. (If vertical rules are also used between each pair of columns, the heads are referred to as *boxed* column heads.)

b. Insert the first horizontal rule on the line directly below the final line of the title or subtitle (whichever comes last). Extend the underscore the full width of the table.

c. On the second line below the underscore, start the column head with the most lines. All the column heads should align at the bottom.

d. Type the column heads in capital and small letters, single-spaced and centered. (For guidance on centering, see ¶¶1617–1619.) Do not underscore the column heads when they are ruled or boxed.

e. On the line directly below the last line of the column heads, insert another horizontal rule the full width of the table. (When both horizontal rules are inserted, the column heads should appear to be centered between them, with 1 blank line above and below the column heads.)

f. On the second line below the second rule, start typing the table text.

Table A–14 ↓ 4
↓ 2
U.S. FIRE LOSSES FROM 1974 TO 1981 ↓ 1

Year	Total (000,000 Omitted)	Per Capita	Year	Total (000,000 Omitted)	Per Capita
1974	$3190	$15.09	1978	$4008	$18.05
1975	3560	16.52	1979	4851	21.60
1976	3558	16.59	1980	5579	24.56
1977	3764	17.13	1981	5625	24.53

NOTE: The illustration above of a table with ruled column heads also shows how to treat a table that would be long and narrow if held to its original three columns. A single vertical rule is used to separate the two halves of the table, each with the same set of column heads. If vertical rules are also to be used between the columns, use a double vertical rule to separate the two halves of the table.

1622 Braced Column Heads

a. Some complex tables contain *braced* column heads, that is, heads that "embrace" two or more columns.

b. Type braced column heads in capital and small letters. Single-space any turnover lines, and align braced heads of varying length at the bottom.

c. Center a braced heading over the columns to which it pertains. To do so, follow this procedure:

    (1) First plan the arrangement and type the column heads that are to go below the braced head, centering each over its own column text. Leave room, however, for the braced head.

    (2) Count the strokes in the longest items in the columns to be braced, and add in the number of blank spaces between the braced columns.

    (3) Count the strokes in the longest line in the braced column head, and subtract it from the figure calculated in step 2 above.

    (4) Divide your answer by 2 (and ignore any fraction) to find how many spaces to indent the longest line in the braced head.

    (5) Center any other lines in the braced head in relation to the placement of the longest line.

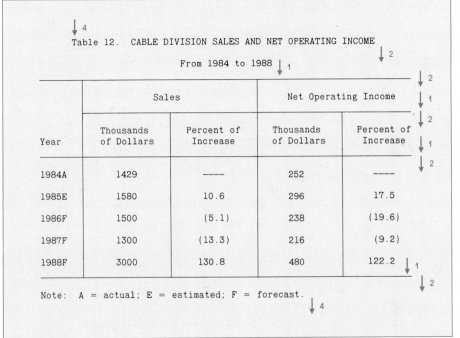

Table 12.   CABLE DIVISION SALES AND NET OPERATING INCOME

From 1984 to 1988

Year	Sales		Net Operating Income	
	Thousands of Dollars	Percent of Increase	Thousands of Dollars	Percent of Increase
1984A	1429	-----	252	-----
1985E	1580	10.6	296	17.5
1986F	1500	(5.1)	238	(19.6)
1987F	1300	(13.3)	216	(9.2)
1988F	3000	130.8	480	122.2

Note: A = actual; E = estimated; F = forecast.

NOTE: In the illustration above there is a total of 26 strokes to be braced in each case:

```
of Dollars      Percent of        of Dollars      Percent of
1234567890123456789012 3456        1234567890123456789012 3456
Sales                              Net Operating Income
```

To center the first braced head, subtract the strokes in *Sales* (5) from 26. Dividing the difference (21) by 2 yields an answer of 10½. Ignore the fraction, and indent *Sales* 10 spaces from the start of the first column to be braced. The second braced head, *Net Operating Income*, has 20 strokes. Subtracting 20 from 26 yields a difference of 6. Dividing 6 by 2 indicates that the braced head should be indented 3 spaces.

1623 Crossheads

a. Sometimes the data in the body of a table has to be separated into different categories. This separation can be accomplished by the use of *crossheads*, as shown in the illustration on page 366.

b. The first crosshead falls immediately below the column heads across the top of the table; the other crossheads occur within the body of the table at appropriate intervals.

c. Type each crosshead in capital and small letters, centered on the full width of the table. Backspace from the centering point to determine where to begin typing each crosshead.

d. Each crosshead should be preceded and followed by a horizontal rule running the full width of the table. For proper spacing above and below each crosshead, see the illustration below.

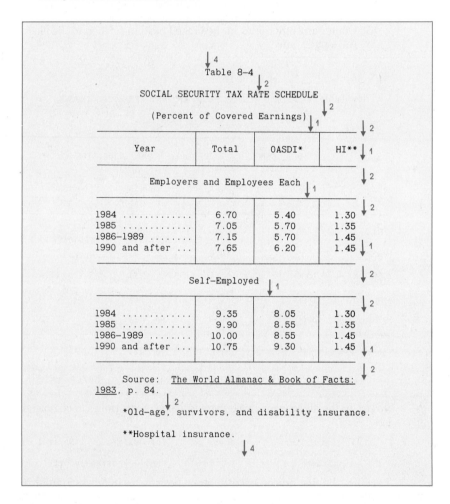

```
                              ↓ 4
                         Table 8-4
                              ↓ 2
               SOCIAL SECURITY TAX RATE SCHEDULE
                                              ↓ 2
                 (Percent of Covered Earnings) ↓ 1
                                                     ↓ 2
                                                  ↓ 1
        Year          Total      OASDI*      HI**
                                                     ↓ 2
              Employers and Employees Each ↓ 1
                                                     ↓ 2
1984 ............    6.70        5.40        1.30
1985 ............    7.05        5.70        1.35
1986-1989 .......    7.15        5.70        1.45
1990 and after ...   7.65        6.20        1.45 ↓ 1
                                                     ↓ 2
                  Self-Employed ↓ 1
                                                     ↓ 2
1984 ............    9.35        8.05        1.30
1985 ............    9.90        8.55        1.35
1986-1989 .......   10.00        8.55        1.45
1990 and after ...  10.75        9.30        1.45 ↓ 1
                                                     ↓ 2
    Source:   The World Almanac & Book of Facts:
1983, p. 84. ↓ 2
    *Old-age, survivors, and disability insurance.

    **Hospital insurance. ↓ 4
```

NOTE: The vertical rules in the table above should not intrude into the space set aside for the crossheads.

TABLE TEXT

1624 Spacing

a. The table text may be typed with single spacing, double spacing, or 1½-line spacing. However, within the same document try to treat all tables alike.

b. Double-space tables for better readability. However, if overall length must be held down and you wish to maximize your chances of locating each table on the page where it is first mentioned, use single spacing. (See also ¶1603.)

NOTE: If a single-spaced table runs quite long, you can break up the solid mass of table text by inserting a blank line or a horizontal rule at regular intervals or at points that serve to group the rows in a meaningful way.

c. If you would like to enhance readability *and* control overall length *and* fit each table in the ideal location, 1½-line spacing may be a good compromise.

d. As a rule, the table text is typed with the same spacing (or less) used for the running text. Thus when the running text is *single-spaced*, then all the tables are also single-spaced. When the running text is typed in *1½-line spacing*, all the tables may be typed in either 1½-line or single spacing. When the running text is *double-spaced*, then all the tables may be typed with double, single, or 1½-line spacing.

e. The following guide indicates where to begin typing the table text.

If the Table Text Is Preceded by:	Start Typing the Table Text on:
Running text with single spacing	Second line below
Running text with double or 1½-line spacing	Third line below
Column heads—open	Second line below
Column heads—ruled or boxed	Second line below underscore
Table title	Third line below
Table subtitle	Third line below

❑ *For examples of proper spacing, see the illustrations in ¶1601.*

1625 Items Consisting of Words

If the table text consists of items expressed entirely in words:

a. Capitalize only the first word of each item in the table text plus any proper nouns and proper adjectives.

NOTE: In special cases, where it may be important to show whether terms are capitalized or written with small letters, the first word in each item need not be consistently capitalized. (See, for example, the second and third columns of the table in ¶1601c.)

b. Use abbreviations and symbols as necessary to hold down the length of individual items. (See ¶1616c for examples.)

c. Align each item at the left margin of the column. If any item requires more than one line, indent the turnover line 2 spaces. However, if a column contains both main entries and subentries, begin the main entry at the left margin of the column text, indent the first line of subentries 2 spaces, and indent all turnover lines 4 spaces.

```
Photographs, prints,        Total weekly
   and illustrations ...        broadcast
Scientific or tech-            hours ......
   nical drawings ......     General
Commercial prints .....        programs ...
Reproductions of            Instructional
   works of art ........        programs ...
```

❑ *For guidelines on the use of leaders (rows of periods), see ¶1631.*

d. If an item in the first column requires more than one line and all the other items in the same row require only one line, align all the items in that row on the bottom.

```
Chemicals and allied products .... 151      201
Petroleum refining and related
    products ..................... 69       73   ←── Aligned at
Paper and allied products ........ 391      364       the bottom
```

e. If two or more items in a row each require more than one line, align all entries in that row at the top.

```
Employee benefits report      Prepared      Data based on    ←── Aligned at
                              quarterly     administra-           the top
                                            tive records
```

f. Do not use a period as terminal punctuation at the end of any item except in a column where all entries are in sentence form.

1626 Items Consisting of Figures

If the table text consists of items expressed entirely in figures:

a. Align columns of whole numbers at the right.

b. Align columns of decimal amounts on the decimal point.

c. In a column that contains both whole numbers and decimals, add a decimal point and zeros to the whole numbers to maintain a consistent appearance.

d. Omit commas in four-digit whole numbers unless they appear in the same column with larger numbers containing commas. Never insert commas in the decimal part of a number.

```
    325           465.2137
      1          1250.0004
152,657             1.0000
  1,489            37.9898
```

❑ *For the way to handle a total line in a column of figures, see ¶1628c.*

1627 Items Consisting of Figures and Words

Align a mixture of words and figures in the same column at the left.

Type of Food	Average Serving	Calorie Count
Bacon	2 strips	97
Beef, roast	4 oz	300
Broccoli	1 cup	44
Tomato, raw	Medium size	30

a. In a column containing dollar amounts, insert a dollar sign only before the first amount at the head of the column and before the total amount. The dollar signs should align in the first space to the left of the longest amount in the column.

```
$   45.50        $      165        $ 423.75
  2406.05          3,450             584.45
   783.25         98,932            1228.00
$3234.80        $102,547           $2236.20
```

b. Do not insert commas to set off thousands in four-digit numbers unless they appear in the same column with larger numbers. (See the examples above.) Moreover, if all the amounts in a column are whole dollar amounts, omit the decimal and zeros (as in the second example above). However, if any amount in a column includes cents, use a decimal and zeros with any whole dollar amount in the same column (as in the third example above).

c. If the table text ends with a *total* line:

(1) In an *open* table (one with no rules between columns of figures), simply type a row of underscores directly under the last amount. Make the underscore as wide as the longest entry in the column. In a single-spaced table, type the total amount on the line directly below the underscore. (To give the total amount greater emphasis, type it on the second line below the underscore.) In a double-spaced table, the amount must be typed on the second line below the underscore.

```
$1115.59 ↓ 1       $   529,310 ↓ 1      $21,348.75 ↓ 2
  803.61            1,114,310
 1027.64            1,227,620 ↓ 2          2,294.35
  528.66
$3475.50 ↓ 1       $2,871,240               688.50 ↓ 2

                                        $24,331.60
```

(2) In a *ruled* table (one with horizontal rules only), either treat the underscore as shown above or type a continuous underscore the full width of the table (as shown below) or extend it only across the full width of all the figure columns.

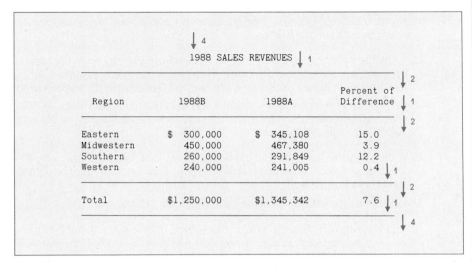

		↓ 4	
		1988 SALES REVENUES ↓ 1	
Region	1988B	1988A	Percent of Difference ↓ 1
Eastern	$ 300,000	$ 345,108	15.0
Midwestern	450,000	467,380	3.9
Southern	260,000	291,849	12.2
Western	240,000	241,005	0.4
Total	$1,250,000	$1,345,342	7.6

(3) In a *boxed* table (one with horizontal and vertical rules), either type a continuous underscore the full width of the table (as shown on page 369) or extend the underscore the full distance between verticals in any column that contains a total.

d. When a *total* line is being typed, the word *Total* in the first column may be typed with an initial cap only or (for emphasis) in all-capital letters. Start the word at the left margin of the column or (again, for emphasis) indent it 5 spaces—so long as the word does not intrude into the area established for the second column.

1629 Percentages

a. If all the figures in a column represent percentages, type a percent sign (%) directly after each figure unless the column heading clearly indicates that these are percentages.

b. Percentages involving decimals should align on the decimal point. If necessary, add zeros after the decimal part of the number so that each figure will align at the right. If any percentage is less than 1 percent, add one zero to the left of the decimal point.

Increase	Percent of Increase	Increase (%)
55.48%	11.63	24
0.80%	4.00	37
2.09%	25.60	120
13.00%	0.40	8

1630 Special Treatment of Figures in Tables

a. Columns of long figures can be reduced in width by omitting the digits representing thousands, millions, or billions and indicating this fact in parentheses. For example:

(000 Omitted)	**OR**	(In Thousands)
(000,000 Omitted)		(In Millions)
(000,000,000 Omitted)		(In Billions)

NOTE: The word forms on the right are easier to grasp and are usually shorter than the forms on the left.

b. If the parenthetical comment applies to all columns of figures in the table, it can be given as a subtitle to the table. However, if the comment applies only to one column of figures, insert the parenthetical comment in the column head.

NOTE: Sometimes because of space limitations a comment such as *(000 Omitted)* is reduced to *(000)*. The latter form is permissible if you are sure your reader will understand it.

c. If the parenthetical comment applies to columns of dollar amounts, this fact can also be noted within parentheses and the dollar sign can then be omitted from the column text.

($000 Omitted)   **OR**   (In Thousands of Dollars)   **OR**   ($000)

d. When omitting thousands, millions, or billions from a wide column of figures, you may use rounding or a shortened decimal (or both) to reflect the portion of the number that is being omitted.

Complete Version	Shortened Versions		
Sales Revenues	Sales Revenues ($000 Omitted)	Sales Revenues (In Millions)	Sales Revenues ($000,000)
$ 5,878,044	5,878	$ 5.9	6
29,023,994	29,024	29.0	29
14,229,683	14,230	14.2	14
$49,131,721	49,132	$49.1	49

e. A negative figure in a column may be designated by enclosing the figure in parentheses or by inserting a minus sign (represented by a hyphen) positioned directly to the left of the negative figure.

$1642.38	28.2%	Sales in 1985 ...	$264,238
−82.41	(14.5)%	Sales in 1986 ...	262,305
$1559.97	6.1%	Gain/(loss)	$ (1,933)

1631 Leaders

a. If the items in the first column vary greatly in length, you may use leaders (rows of periods) to lead the eye across to the adjacent item in the next column. The shortest line of leaders should have at least three periods.

b. Solid leaders (....) are preferred to open leaders (. . . .) because they are faster and simpler to type. Open leaders must be aligned vertically.

c. Leave 1 blank space before the start of a row of leaders and before the start of the second column.

d. In a table without vertical rules, you can easily determine in advance where the leaders should end. Simply backspace twice from the start of the second column, and at that point type a period to mark where the leaders are to stop.

NOTE: If you are planning to leave 6 spaces between columns, then between the longest item in the first column and the start of the adjacent item in the second column there should be 1 space followed by four periods and then another space. See, for example, the table in ¶1601c. The key line for this table would appear thus:

```
Amount of substance .... kilogram     Symbol
            123456            123456
```

However, in a table with only two columns, the space between columns (and thus the number of periods) can be adjusted to create the table width you want. In the first table in ¶1601e, the minimum number of periods (three) has been used. Therefore, the key line for this table would read:

```
Machinery (excluding electric) ... 2,410,800
                                12345
```

e. If you are planning to use leaders in the first column of a boxed table (one with vertical as well as horizontal rules), proceed as follows:

(1) Determine the space to be left between columns. (Assume the standard 6 spaces. Since the vertical rules will be centered between columns, there will be 3 blank spaces on either side of each vertical rule.)

(2) In planning a key line, take the longest line in the first column and to it add a space, three periods, plus another space. **REASON:** The shortest row of leaders must have three periods (see *a* above), and there must be 1 blank space before and after (see *c* above). In short, add five strokes to the longest line in the first column to arrive at the first vertical rule.

(3) Then add three strokes to allow space between the first vertical rule and the start of the second column. (These three strokes will balance the 3 spaces that occur between the end of the second column and the next vertical rule.)

↓ 4

Table 3.   NATIONAL INCOME BY SELECTED INDUSTRIES

(In Billions of Dollars) ↓ 1   ↓ 2

	1960	1970	1981
Agriculture, forestry, and fisheries	17.5	24.5	68.7
Contract construction	21.0	43.8	113.4
Finance, insurance, and real estate	48.6	92.7	324.2
Government enterprises ...	52.7	127.4	336.0
Manufacturing	125.4	215.4	580.8
Services	44.6	103.3	349.4

KEY LINE:

Government enterprises#...# 125.4   215.4   580.8

|123   123456   123456

1632   Accounting for Omitted Items

When there is no entry to be typed in a given row, it is permissible simply to leave a blank at that point. However, if doing so may raise a question in the mind of your reader, consider these alternatives:

a. Type the abbreviation *NA* (meaning "not available" or "not applicable") either flush left or centered on the column width (whichever looks better).

b. Type a row of periods or hyphens. Use as few as three (centered on the column width), or type the row to the full width of the column.

23,804	23,804	23,804	23.8
16,345	16,345	16,345	16.3
......	----	NA	NA
38,442	38,442	38,442	38.4

☐ *See ¶1622 for another illustration.*

TABLE RULES

1633   If a table requires rules, use any of the following methods to insert them:

a. Insert all rules on the typewriter, using the underscore. Place a horizontal rule above and below the column heads and at the bottom of the table; do not underscore the column heads. These rules should extend to the full width of the table. As shown in the illustrations in ¶¶1621–1623, type each rule on the line immediately following the preceding copy. This creates the appearance of a blank line above the underscore. Leave 1 blank line between an internal rule and any table copy that follows; leave 2 or 3 blank lines (see ¶1604c) between the bottom rule and any running text that follows. If vertical rules are to be used to separate the columns, insert the page sideways after you have finished typing the table text and type the vertical rules, using the underscore. Do not type rules at the left and right sides of the table; the sides should remain open.

b. Insert all rules with a ballpoint pen and a ruler after the typing has been completed. Be sure to leave space for these rules when typing the table.

c. Insert all horizontal rules on the typewriter, as described in *a* above. Insert all vertical rules with a ballpoint pen.

NOTE: In a table that is to contain vertical rules, leave a minimum of 2 spaces between columns.

d. Type both horizontal and vertical rules if you are using a word processing system with this capability.

TABLE NOTES

1634 **a.** If a table requires any explanatory notes or an identification of the source from which the table text was derived, place such material at the foot of the individual table. (Do not treat it as part of a sequence of notes to the running text.)

b. Separate the table text from the table notes by a row of underscores. In a ruled or boxed table, the full row of underscores at the bottom of the table text will provide the necessary separation. In a table without full-width horizontal rules, provide the separation by typing a 1-inch row of underscores (10 strokes in pica type, 12 in elite) on the line directly below the last line of table text.

c. Begin the first table note on the second line below the row of underscores.

d. If all the notes occupy no more than one full line each, begin each note at the left margin of the table (for the sake of appearance) and type the notes single-spaced. However, if any of the notes turn over onto a second line, indent the first line of each note 5 spaces, type all turnover lines starting at the left margin of the table, and leave 1 blank line between each pair of notes.

NOTE: Try to keep each line of the note from extending more than 1 or 2 spaces beyond the right edge of the table. (See, for example, the illustration in ¶1623.)

1635 If the material in the table has been derived from another source, indicate this fact as follows:

a. Type the word *Source* with only an initial cap or in all-capital letters, followed by a colon, 2 spaces, and the identifying data. (See ¶¶1508–1522 for appropriate models to follow in presenting this bibliographic data.)

b. A source note, if given, should precede any other table note.

```
    1983      84,019,214      18.39%
    1984      90,222,578*     24.16%


    Source:  Time, July 22, 1985, p. 88.
    *Estimated for the full year.
```

❏ *For illustrations of indented table notes, see ¶¶1601e (page 356), 1623.*

1636 **a.** If you use abbreviations or symbols that the reader may not understand, explain them at the bottom of the table. This explanation should follow the source note (if any) and precede any other table note. If more than one abbreviation or symbol needs decoding, the explanation can be handled as a series of separate notes (each preceded by a raised symbol or letter), or it may be done all in one note. For examples of both styles, see the illustrations in ¶¶1622–1623.

b. Every other table note should begin with a raised symbol or letter that keys the note to the appropriate word or figure in the table text (or title or subtitle) above. The corresponding symbol or letter should be typed immediately after the appropriate word or figure above, without any intervening space.

c. Ordinarily, use the following sequence of symbols: *, **, ***   **OR**   *, †, ‡, §, ¶. The latter set may have to be inserted by hand. (See also ¶1502f.)

d. Use raised lowercase letters (^{a}, ^{b}, ^{c}, etc.) in place of symbols when the notes are numerous and some are keyed to figures in the table text.

NOTE: Avoid the use of raised *figures* to identify table notes. They could be confusing if used in conjunction with figures in the table text. Moreover, if raised figures are already used for notes pertaining to the main text, it is wiser to use letters or symbols so as to distinguish notes that pertain to a specific table.

e. In assigning symbols or letters in sequence, go in order by row (horizontally), not by column (vertically).

DEALING WITH LONG TABLES

1637 To keep a table from extending beyond the page on which it starts, consider these techniques:

a. Put the table number (if any) on the same line as the table title rather than on the second line above. (See also ¶1615b.)

b. Use single spacing for the table text. (See also ¶1624.)

c. Shorten the wording of the table title, subtitle, column heads, and items in the table text to reduce turnover lines. Use abbreviations and symbols toward this end. (See also ¶1616c.) If necessary, provide a brief explanation in the table notes of any abbreviations and symbols that your reader may not immediately understand. (See also ¶1636.)

d. When the table text entails a long item that is out of proportion to all the other items (or is to be entered in several places in the table text), try to convert the item into a table note, keyed by a symbol or letter appropriately placed in the table above.

e. If a table is both narrow and long, you can save space by repeating the same sequence of column heads on both the left and right sides of the table. The first half of the table text appears on the left side of the table, and the remaining table text appears on the right. (See the illustration in ¶1621.)

NOTE: In order to achieve consistent treatment of tables throughout a given document, decide on the spacing, the placement of the table number, and the use of abbreviations and symbols before you start typing or printing out the document.

1638 If a table must continue on to one or more pages, follow this procedure:

a. At the bottom of the page where the table breaks, type a continuation line— for example, *Table continued on page 14*—unless it is quite obvious that the table runs on to the next page. If used, the continuation line should be typed in parentheses or brackets and positioned at the right margin, on the line directly below the point at which the table breaks.

NOTE: If you are breaking a table with ruled or boxed column heads, do not type a full-width underscore at the bottom of the page where the table text breaks off. This underscore should appear only at the very end of the table text.

b. At the top of the page on which the table continues, repeat the table number (if any) and the table title, followed by the word *Continued* or *Cont.* in parentheses. Also repeat the column heads before resuming the table text.

c. Ordinarily, all table notes should appear only on the page on which the table ends. However, to avoid inconveniencing a reader, place the appropriate notes at the bottom of each page, even if this means that some notes will have to be repeated on two or more pages. Insert a 1-inch row of underscores before such notes (as described in ¶1634).

1639 Do not start a table at the bottom of one page and continue it on to the top of the next page if the entire table will fit on one page (either by itself or with running text). In such a case start the table at the top of the next page and insert a cross-reference in the text. (See ¶1608.)

DEALING WITH WIDE TABLES

1640 To keep a wide table from extending beyond the margins established for the page, first consider these techniques:

a. Reduce the space between columns to as little as 2 spaces. (To preserve the clarity of the table, you can insert vertical rules.)

b. Use abbreviations and symbols to hold down the length of lines in the column heads and the column text. (In extreme cases the column heads can be typed vertically.)

c. If only a few entries are disproportionately wide or are repeated in the table and make it difficult to fit the table in the space available, consider the possibility of converting these items to table footnotes. (See also ¶1637*d.*)

1641 Making a Reduced Copy

If the suggestions in ¶1640 do not resolve the problem, consider this approach:

a. If you have access to a photocopier with the capability of producing copies in reduced size, type the extrawide table across the 11-inch dimension of a separate sheet. Reduce the space between columns to as little as 2 spaces in order to limit the overall width of the table.

b. Then make a reduced photocopy of the table that brings the table width down to the desired size. (A reduction of as much as 50 percent will still yield readable copy. Naturally, the less you reduce the copy, the better.)

c. With rubber cement, mount the reduced version of the table horizontally in the desired location (either on a page with running text or on a separate page).

d. Then make a fresh copy of the pasted-up page so that you wind up with a sheet with all the material on the same surface.

NOTE: In some situations the inclusion of a photocopied page along with typed originals may not be acceptable, and you will have to consider still other alternatives (see ¶¶1643–1644). However, if the use of a reduced photocopy will permit you to insert an extrawide table horizontally at the desired point of reference, the overall convenience to your reader should more than compensate for any sacrifice in appearance.

1642 Turning the Table

a. Whenever possible, a table should read horizontally, just like the running text. However, when other alternatives do not work or cannot be used, you may turn the table so that it runs vertically on a page by itself. In such a case the left margin of the table will fall toward the bottom of the page and the right margin toward the top.

b. In planning the layout of a turned table, be sure that the overall dimensions of the table will fit within the established margins for the normal pages in the given document. If no margins have been established, leave a minimum margin of 1 inch (25 mm) on all sides of the turned table.

1643 Spreading the Table Over Two Pages

An extrawide table may be spread horizontally over two pages. Each page is typed separately, and then the two pages are taped together to look like one continuous piece of work.

a. Select the best place to split the table between columns. Try to break as close to the middle of the table as possible.

b. Also find a good break between words in the title and the subtitle (if any) so that in the finished product these elements will appear to run without any noticeable break across the two pages.

c. If the table also carries a number (for example, *Table 8*), place it on the same line with the table title rather than on a line by itself. In that way you can avoid having to position the phrase off center (with *Table* on the left page and 8 on the right).

d. Establish a key line for each half of the table, and determine on which line the typing should begin.

e. To execute the left half of the table:

  (1) Backspace the left half of the title, starting from the right edge of the paper. At the point at which you stop backspacing, begin typing the first half of the title. Repeat this process for the first half of the subtitle (if any).
  (2) Next backspace the key line for the left half of the table, starting from the right edge of the paper, and set the left margin stop and the tab stops.
  (3) Then type the column heads and the table text.
  (4) If the table involves any horizontal rules, type them to the very edge of the right side of the page.

f. To execute the right half of the table:

  (1) Take a fresh sheet of paper and continue typing the title, starting from the left edge of the paper. Make sure that the continuation of the title (and the subtitle, if any) are perfectly aligned with the corresponding copy on the first page. When the two pages are taped together, the title and subtitle should appear to flow without a break. Also be sure that at the point at which the title and subtitle break, there will appear to be only 1 blank space between words when the two pages are taped together.
  (2) Use the key line for the right half of the table to establish appropriate tab stops and a right margin.
  (3) If the table involves horizontal rules, make sure that they begin at the very edge of the left side of the paper. When the two pages are taped together, the rules should appear to flow continuously across the entire table.

NOTE: On many word processors you can establish a format for the left side of the table and use it for the right side, revising it as necessary.

Left-Hand Page

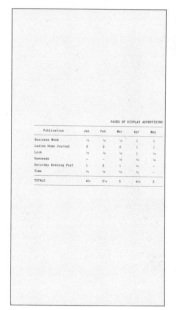

PAGES OF DISPLAY ADVERTISING

Publication	Jan	Feb	Mar	Apr	May
Business Week	½	½	½	1	1
Ladies Home Journal	2	2	2	1	1
Look	½	½	½	1	½
Newsweek	–	–	½	½	½
Saturday Evening Post	1	2	1	½	–
Time	½	½	½	½	–
TOTALS	4½	5½	5	4½	3

Right-Hand Page

IN THE PAST TWELVE MONTHS

Jun	Jul	Aug	Sep	Oct	Nov	Dec	Total
1	1	1	1	1	1	½	10
1	1	–	1	1	2	2	16
½	½	1	1	1	2	½	9½
½	½	½	½	1	1	½	6
–	–	–	½	1	2	–	8
½	–	–	½	½	1	–	4½
3½	3	2½	4½	5½	9	3½	54

g. Tape the two pages together, applying the tape on the underside of the sheets. Then fold vertically along the common edge so that the double page can be inserted in sequence with the other pages of the document. The taped fold should appear at the right so that the reader may unfold the table to the right.

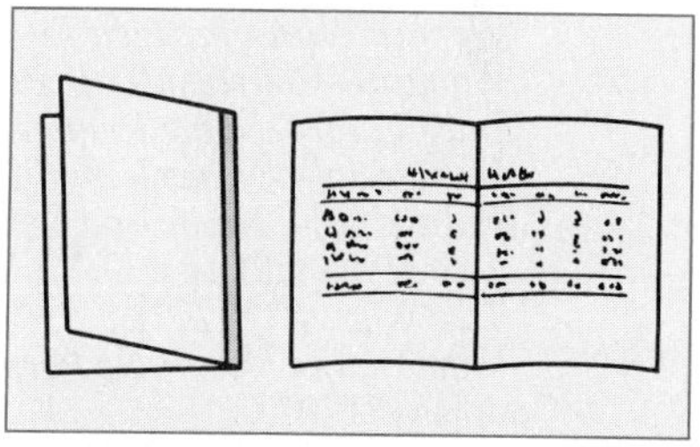

If the sheet could become caught in any binding or stapling along the left edge, fold the top sheet halfway back toward the right. This should keep the top page from getting snagged.

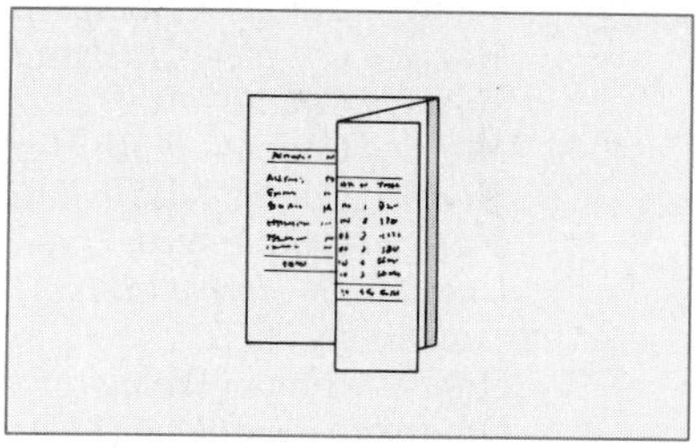

1644 Turning and Spreading the Table

Sometimes a table that is extrawide and extralong will fit only if it is turned vertically on a page and the individual rows of the table text are spread over two pages taped together. In such a case break the first half of the table at a point where the last line of text comes within one line from the bottom edge of the turned sheet. Then on a fresh sheet of paper, resume typing the table on a line as close to the top edge of the paper as possible. When the two pages are taped together, the spacing between lines at this point should look as normal as you can make it.

NOTE: When a turned table is spread over two pages, the column heads do not have to be repeated, since the lower half of the table will appear to be a simple extension of the top half, without any break.

Forms of Address

Government Officials (¶1706)
  President of the United States (¶1706a)
  Former President of the United States (¶1706b)
  Vice President of the United States (¶1706c)
  Cabinet Member (¶1706d)
  United States Senator (¶1706e)
  United States Representative (¶1706f)
  Chief Justice of the U.S. Supreme Court (¶1706g)
  Associate Justice of the U.S. Supreme Court (¶1706h)
  Judge of Federal, State, or Local Court (¶1706i)
  Governor (¶1706j)
  State Senator (¶1706k)
  State Representative or Assembly Member (¶1706l)
  Mayor (¶1706m)
Diplomats (¶1707)
  Secretary General of the United Nations (¶1707a)
  Ambassador to the United States (¶1707b)
  Minister to the United States (¶1707c)
  American Ambassador (¶1707d)
Members of the Armed Services (¶1708)
  Army, Air Force, and Marine Corps Officers (¶1708a)
  Navy and Coast Guard Officers (¶1708b)
  Enlisted Personnel (¶1708c)
Roman Catholic Dignitaries (¶1709)
  Pope (¶1709a)
  Cardinal (¶1709b)
  Archbishop and Bishop (¶1709c)
  Monsignor (¶1709d)
  Priest (¶1709e)
  Mother Superior (¶1709f)
  Sister (¶1709g)
  Brother (¶1709h)
Protestant Dignitaries (¶1710)
  Protestant Episcopal Bishop (¶1710a)
  Protestant Episcopal Dean (¶1710b)
  Methodist Bishop (¶1710c)
  Minister With Doctor's Degree (¶1710d)
  Minister Without Doctor's Degree (¶1710e)
Jewish Dignitaries (¶1711)
  Rabbi With Doctor's Degree (¶1711a)
  Rabbi Without Doctor's Degree (¶1711b)

The following forms are correct for addressing letters to individuals, couples, organizations, professional people, education officials, government officials, diplomats, military personnel, and religious dignitaries.

IMPORTANT NOTE: In the salutations that follow the forms of address, the most formal one is listed first. Unless otherwise indicated, the ellipsis marks in the salutation stand for the surname alone.

❏ *For a detailed discussion of how to construct inside addresses, see ¶¶1317–1344; for further information on salutations, see ¶¶1346–1351; for details on how to handle addresses on envelopes, see ¶¶1389–1390.*

For the sake of simplicity, only the masculine forms of address have been given in most illustrations. When an office or position is held by a woman, make the following substitutions:

For *Sir,* use *Madam.*

For *Mr.* followed by a name (for example, *Mr. Wyatt*), use *Miss, Mrs.,* or *Ms.,* whichever is appropriate.

For *His,* use *Her.*

For *Mr.* followed by a title (for example, *Mr. President, Mr. Secretary, Mr. Mayor*), use *Madam.*

1701 Individuals

a. Man With Courtesy Title

Mr. . . . . *(full name)*
Address

Dear Mr. . . . :

b. Woman With Courtesy Title

Ms. (**OR** Miss **OR** Mrs.) . . . *(full name)*
Address

Dear Ms. (**OR** Miss **OR** Mrs.) . . . :

NOTE: If a woman prefers one of these titles, respect her preference.

c. Woman—Courtesy Title Preference Unknown

Ms. . . . *(full name)*
Address

Dear Ms. . . . :
OR:
. . . *(full name with no title)*
Address

Dear . . . *(first name and surname)*:

d. Individual—Name Known, Gender Unknown

. . . *(full name with no title)*
Address

Dear . . . *(first name or initials plus surname)*:

e. Individual—Name Unknown, Gender Known

. . . *(title of individual)*
. . . *(name of organization)*
Address

Sir:
Dear Sir:
OR:
Madam:
Dear Madam:

f. Individual—Name and Gender Unknown

. . . *(title of individual)*
. . . *(name of organization)*
Address

Sir or Madam:
Dear Sir or Madam:
OR:
Madam or Sir:
Dear Madam or Sir:

g. Two Men

Mr. . . . *(full name)*
Mr. . . . *(full name)*
Address

Gentlemen:
Dear Messrs. . . . and . . . :
Dear Mr. . . . and Mr. . . . :

h. Two Women

Ms. . . . *(full name)*
Ms. . . . *(full name)*
Address

Dear Mses. (**OR** Mss.) . . . and . . . :
Dear Ms. . . . and Ms. . . . :
OR:
Mrs. . . . *(full name)*
Mrs. . . . *(full name)*
Address

Dear Mesdames . . . and . . . :
Dear Mrs. . . . and Mrs. . . . :
OR:
Miss . . . *(full name)*
Miss . . . *(full name)*
Address

Dear Misses . . . and . . . :
Dear Miss . . . and Miss . . . :
OR:
Ms. . . . *(full name)*
Mrs. . . . *(full name)*
Address

Dear Ms. . . . and Mrs. . . . :
OR:
Miss . . . *(full name)*
Ms. . . . *(full name)*
Address

Dear Miss . . . and Ms. . . . :
OR:
Mrs. . . . *(full name)*
Miss . . . *(full name)*
Address

Dear Mrs. . . . and Miss . . . :

i. Woman and Man—No Personal Relationship

Ms. (**OR** Mrs. **OR** Miss) . . . *(full name)*
Mr. . . . *(full name)*
Address

Dear Ms. (**OR** Mrs. **OR** Miss) . . .
and Mr. . . . :

OR:

Mr. . . . *(full name)*
Miss (**OR** Mrs. **OR** Ms.) . . . *(full name)*
Address

Dear Mr. . . . and Miss (**OR** Mrs.
OR Ms.) . . . :

1702 Couples

a. Married Couple—No Special Titles

Mr. and Mrs. . . . *(husband's full name)*
Address

Dear Mr. and Mrs. . . . *(husband's surname)*:

b. Married Couple—Husband Has Special Title

Dr. and Mrs. . . . *(husband's full name)*
Address

Dear Dr. and Mrs. . . . *(husband's surname)*:*

c. Married Couple—Wife Has Special Title

Senator . . . *(wife's full name)*
Mr. . . . *(husband's full name)*
Address

Dear Senator and Mr. . . . *(husband's surname)*:*

d. Married Couple—Both Have Special Titles

Captain . . . *(husband's full name)*
Professor . . . *(wife's full name)*
Address

Dear Captain and Professor . . . *(husband's surname)*:*

Dr. . . . *(wife's full name)*
Dr. . . . *(husband's full name)*
Address

Dear Drs. . . . *(husband's surname)*:

*In situations where the title of either spouse is irrelevant, simply address the couple as *Mr. and Mrs.* (See also ¶1323*d*.)

e. Married Couple—Wife Retains Maiden Name

Mr. . . . *(husband's full name)*
Ms. (**OR** Miss) . . . *(wife's full name)*
Address

Dear Mr. . . . *(husband's surname)* and Ms. (**OR** Miss) . . . *(wife's maiden name)*:

f. Married Couple With Hyphenated Name

Mr. and Mrs. . . . *(husband's first name and middle initial, plus wife's maiden name followed by hyphen and husband's surname)*
Address

Dear Mr. and Mrs. . . . *(wife's maiden name followed by hyphen and husband's surname)*:

g. Unmarried Couple Living Together

Mr. . . . *(full name)*
Ms. (**OR** Miss) . . . *(full name)*
Address

Dear Mr. . . . and Ms. (**OR** Miss) . . . :

1703 Organizations

a. Organization of Women

. . . *(name of organization)*
Address

Mesdames:
Ladies:

b. Organization of Men

. . . *(name of organization)*
Address

Gentlemen:

c. Organization of Women and Men

. . . *(name of organization)*
Address

Ladies and Gentlemen:
Gentlemen and Ladies:
Gentlemen: (see ¶1350)
Dear . . . *(name of organization)*: (see ¶1350*c*)

OR:

Mr. . . . *(name of organization head)*
President *(or other appropriate title)*
. . . *(name of organization)*
Address

Dear Mr. . . . :

(Continued on page 382.)

OR:
> Chief Executive Officer (*or other appropriate title*)
> . . . (*name of organization*)
> Address

> Sir or Madam:
> Dear Sir or Madam:

OR:
> Madam or Sir:
> Dear Madam or Sir:

1704 Professionals

a. Lawyers

> Mr. . . . (*full name*)
> Attorney-at-Law
> Address

OR:
> . . . (*full name*), Esq.*
> Address

> Dear Mr. . . . :

b. Physicians and Others With Doctoral Degrees

> Dr. . . . (*full name*)
> Address

OR:
> . . . (*full name*), M.D.*
> Address

> Dear Dr. . . . :

1705 Education Officials

a. President of College or University

> . . . (*full name, followed by comma and highest degree*)
> President, . . . (*name of college*)
> Address

OR:
> Dr. . . . (*full name*)
> President, . . . (*name of college*)
> Address

OR:
> President . . . (*full name*)
> . . . (*name of college*)
> Address

> Dear President . . . :
> Dear Dr. . . . :

*When an abbreviation such as *Esq., M.D.,* or *Ph.D.* follows a name, do not use a courtesy title such as *Mr.* or *Dr.* before it. (See also ¶¶518c, 519c.)

b. Dean of College or University

> . . . (*full name, followed by comma and highest degree*)
> Dean, . . . (*name of school or division*)
> . . . (*name of college*)
> Address

OR:
> Dr. . . . (*full name*)
> Dean, . . . (*name of school or division*)
> . . . (*name of college*)
> Address

OR:
> Dean . . . (*full name*)
> . . . (*name of school or division*)
> . . . (*name of college*)
> Address

> Dear Dean . . . :
> Dear Dr. . . . :

c. Professor

> Professor . . . (*full name*)
> Department of . . . (*subject*)
> . . . (*name of college*)
> Address

OR:
> . . . (*full name, followed by comma and highest degree*)
> Department of (**OR** Professor of) . . . (*subject*)
> . . . (*name of college*)
> Address

OR:
> Dr. . . . (*full name*)
> Department of (**OR** Professor of) . . . (*subject*)
> . . . (*name of college*)
> Address

> Dear Professor (**OR** Dr.) . . . :
> Dear Mr. . . . :

d. Superintendent of Schools

> Mr. (**OR** Dr.) . . . (*full name*)
> Superintendent of . . . Schools
> Address

> Dear Mr. (**OR** Dr.) . . . :

e. Member of Board of Education

> Mr. . . . (*full name*)
> Member, . . . (*name of city*)
> Board of Education
> Address

> Dear Mr. . . . :

f. Principal

> Mr. (**OR** Dr.) . . . (*full name*)
> Principal, . . . (*name of school*)
> Address

> Dear Mr. (**OR** Dr.) . . . :

g. Teacher

Mr. (**OR** Dr.) . . . (*full name*)
. . . (*name of school*)
Address

Dear Mr. (**OR** Dr.) . . .:

1706 Government Officials

a. President of the United States

The President
The White House
Washington, DC 20500

Mr. President:
Dear Mr. President:

b. Former President of the United States

The Honorable . . . (*full name*)
Local address

Dear Mr. . . .:

c. Vice President of the United States

The Vice President
United States Senate
Washington, DC 20510
OR:
The Honorable . . . (*full name*)
Vice President of the United States
Washington, DC 20510

Sir:
Dear Mr. Vice President:

d. Cabinet Member

The Honorable . . . (*full name*)
Secretary of . . . (*department*)
Washington, DC   ZIP Code
OR:
The Secretary of . . . (*department*)
Washington, DC   ZIP Code

Sir:
Dear Mr. Secretary:

e. United States Senator

The Honorable . . . (*full name*)
United States Senate
Washington, DC 20510
OR:
The Honorable . . . (*full name*)
United States Senator
Local address

Sir:
Dear Senator . . .:

f. United States Representative

The Honorable . . . (*full name*)
House of Representatives
Washington, DC 20515
OR:
The Honorable . . . (*full name*)
Representative in Congress
Local address

Sir:
Dear Representative . . .:
Dear Mr. . . .:

g. Chief Justice of the U.S. Supreme Court

The Chief Justice of the
    United States
Washington, DC 20543
OR:
The Chief Justice
The Supreme Court
Washington, DC 20543

Sir:
Dear Mr. Chief Justice:

h. Associate Justice of the U.S. Supreme Court

Mr. Justice . . . (*last name only*)
The Supreme Court
Washington, DC 20543

Sir:
Dear Mr. Justice:

i. Judge of Federal, State, or Local Court

The Honorable . . . (*full name*)
Judge of the . . . (*name of court*)
Address

Dear Judge . . .:

j. Governor

The Honorable . . . (*full name*)
Governor of . . . (*state*)
State Capital, State   ZIP Code

Sir:
Dear Governor . . .:

k. State Senator

The Honorable . . . (*full name*)
The State Senate
State Capital, State   ZIP Code

Sir:
Dear Senator . . .:

l. State Representative or Assembly Member

The Honorable . . . *(full name)*
House of Representatives
  (**OR** The State Assembly)
State Capital, State ZIP Code

Sir:
Dear Mr. . . . :

m. Mayor

The Honorable . . . *(full name)*
Mayor of . . . *(city)*
City, State ZIP Code
OR:
The Mayor of the City of . . .
City, State ZIP Code

Sir:
Dear Mr. Mayor:
Dear Mayor . . . :

1707 Diplomats

a. Secretary General of the United Nations

His Excellency . . . *(full name)*
Secretary General of the United Nations
United Nations Plaza
New York, NY 10017

Excellency:
Dear Mr. Secretary General:
Dear Mr. . . . :

b. Ambassador to the United States

His Excellency . . . *(full name)*
Ambassador of . . . *(country)*
Address

Excellency:
Dear Mr. Ambassador:

c. Minister to the United States

The Honorable . . . *(full name)*
Minister of . . . *(department)*
Address

Sir:
Dear Mr. Minister:

d. American Ambassador

The Honorable . . . *(full name)*
American Ambassador (**OR** The Ambassador of the United States of America)
Foreign address of U.S. embassy

Sir:
Dear Mr. Ambassador:

1708 Members of the Armed Services

The addresses of both officers and enlisted personnel in the armed services should include title or rank and full name followed by a comma and the initials USA, USN, USAF, USMC, or USCG. Below are some specific examples with appropriate salutations.

a. Army, Air Force, and Marine Corps Officers

Lieutenant General . . . *(full name)*,
  USA (**OR** USAF **OR** USMC)
Address

Sir:
Dear General . . . :*
(**NOT:** Dear Lieutenant General . . . :)

b. Navy and Coast Guard Officers

Rear Admiral . . . *(full name)*, USN (**OR** USCG)
Address

Sir:
Dear Admiral . . . :*

For officers below the rank of commander, use:

Dear Mr. . . . :

c. Enlisted Personnel

Sergeant . . . *(full name)*, USA
Address

Seaman . . . *(full name)*, USN
Address

Dear Sergeant (**OR** Seaman) . . . :

1709 Roman Catholic Dignitaries

a. Pope

His Holiness the Pope
OR:
His Holiness Pope . . . *(given name)*
Vatican City
00187 Rome
ITALY

Your Holiness:
Most Holy Father:

*Use the salutation *Dear General* . . . whether the officer is a full general or only a lieutenant general, a major general, or a brigadier general. Similarly, use *Dear Colonel* . . . for either a full colonel or a lieutenant colonel and *Dear Lieutenant* . . . for either a first or second lieutenant. Also use *Dear Admiral* . . . for a full admiral, a vice admiral, or a rear admiral.

b. Cardinal

His Eminence . . . *(given name)*
    Cardinal . . . *(surname)*
Archbishop of . . . *(place)*
Address

Your Eminence:
Dear Cardinal . . . :

c. Archbishop and Bishop

The Most Reverend . . . *(full name)*
Archbishop (**OR** Bishop) of
    . . . *(place)*
Address

Your Excellency:
Dear Archbishop (**OR** Bishop) . . . :

d. Monsignor

The Reverend Monsignor
    . . . *(full name)*
Address

Reverend Monsignor:
Dear Monsignor . . . :

e. Priest

The Reverend . . . *(full name, followed by comma and initials of order)*
Address

Reverend Father:
Dear Father . . . :
Dear Father:

f. Mother Superior

The Reverend Mother Superior
Address
OR:
Reverend Mother . . . *(name, followed by comma and initials of order)*
Address

Reverend Mother:
Dear Reverend Mother:
Dear Mother . . . :

g. Sister

Sister . . . *(name, followed by comma and initials of order)*
Address

Dear Sister . . . :
Dear Sister:

h. Brother

Brother . . . *(name, followed by comma and initials of order)*
Address

Dear Brother . . . :
Dear Brother:

1710   Protestant Dignitaries

a. Protestant Episcopal Bishop

The Right Reverend . . . *(full name)*
Bishop of . . . *(place)*
Address

Right Reverend Sir:
Dear Bishop . . . :

b. Protestant Episcopal Dean

The Very Reverend . . . *(full name)*
Dean of . . . *(place)*
Address

Very Reverend Sir:
Dear Dean . . . :

c. Methodist Bishop

The Reverend . . . *(full name)*
Bishop of . . . *(place)*
Address
OR:
Bishop . . . *(full name)*
Address

Reverend Sir:
Dear Bishop . . . :

d. Minister With Doctor's Degree

The Reverend Dr. . . . *(full name)*
Address
OR:
The Reverend . . . *(full name)*, D.D.
Address

Reverend Sir:
Dear Dr. . . . :

e. Minister Without Doctor's Degree

The Reverend . . . *(full name)*
Address

Reverend Sir:
Dear Mr. . . . :

1711   Jewish Dignitaries

a. Rabbi With Doctor's Degree

Rabbi . . . *(full name)*, D.D.
Address
OR:
Dr. . . . *(full name)*
Address

Dear Rabbi (**OR** Dr.) . . . :

b. Rabbi Without Doctor's Degree

Rabbi . . . *(full name)*
Address

Dear Rabbi . . . :

Glossary of Grammatical Terms

Adjective
Adverb
Adverbial Conjunctive (*or* Connective)
Antecedent
Appositive
Article
Case
  Nominative Case
  Objective Case
  Possessive Case
Clause
  Adjective Clause
  Adverbial Clause
  Coordinate Clauses
  Elliptical Clause
  Essential (or *Restrictive*) *Clause*
  Nonessential (or *Nonrestrictive*) *Clause*
  Noun Clause
Comparison
  Positive
  Comparative
  Superlative
Complement
  Object
  Predicate Noun or Pronoun
  Predicate Adjective

Conjunction
  Coordinating Conjunction
  Correlative Conjunctions
  Subordinating Conjunction
Connective
Consonants
Contraction
Dangling Modifier
Direct Address
Elliptical Expressions
Essential Elements
Gender
Gerund
  Dangling Gerund
Infinitive
Interjection
Modifier
Mood (Mode)
  Indicative
  Imperative
  Subjunctive
Nonessential Elements
Noun
  Abstract Noun
  Collective Noun
  Common Noun
  Proper Noun
Number

Object
  Direct Object
  Indirect Object
Ordinal Number
Parenthetical Elements
Participle
  Present Participle
  Past Participle
  Perfect Participle
  Dangling Participle
Parts of Speech
Person
Phrase
  Adjective Phrase
  Adverbial Phrase
  Essential (or *Restrictive*) *Phrase*
  Gerund Phrase
  Infinitive Phrase
  Nonessential (or *Nonrestrictive*)
    Phrase
  Noun Phrase
  Participial Phrase
  Prepositional Phrase
  Prepositional-Gerund Phrase
Predicate
  Complete Predicate
  Simple Predicate
  Compound Predicate
Prefix
Preposition
Principal Parts
Pronoun
Punctuation
  Terminal (or *End*) *Punctuation*
  Internal Punctuation

Question
  Direct Question
  Indirect Question
  Independent Question
Quotation
  Direct Quotation
  Indirect Quotation
Sentence
  Simple Sentence
  Compound Sentence
  Complex Sentence
  Compound-Complex Sentence
  Declarative Sentence
  Elliptical Sentence
  Exclamatory Sentence
  Imperative Sentence
  Interrogative Sentence
  Sentence Fragment
  Statement
Subject
  Compound Subject
Suffix
Syllable
Tense
Transitional Expressions
Verb
  Auxiliary (*Helping*) *Verb*
  Intransitive Verb
  Linking Verb
  Transitive Verb
Verbal
Voice
  Active Voice
  Passive Voice
Vowels

1801 This glossary provides brief definitions of common grammatical terms.

Adjective. A word that answers the question *what kind* (*excellent* results), *how many* (*four* songs), or *which one* (the *latest* data). An adjective may be a single word (a *wealthy* man), a phrase (a man *of great wealth*), or a clause (a man *who possesses great wealth*). An adjective modifies the meaning of a noun (fresh *fish*) or a pronoun (unlucky *me, I* was wrong).

Adjective, predicate. See *Complement.*

Adverb. A word that answers the question *when, where, why, in what manner,* or *to what extent.* An adverb may be a single word (speak *clearly*), a phrase (speak *in a clear voice*), or a clause (speak *as clearly as you can*). An adverb modifies the meaning of a verb, an adjective, or another adverb.

> We closed the deal *quickly.* (Modifies the verb *closed.*)
>
> Caroline seemed *genuinely* pleased. (Modifies the adjective *pleased.*)
>
> My presentation went *surprisingly* well. (Modifies the adverb *well.*)

Adverbial conjunctive (or **connective**). An adverb that connects the main clauses of a compound sentence; for example, *however, therefore, nevertheless, hence, moreover, otherwise, consequently.* (See also ¶178.)

Antecedent. A noun or a noun phrase to which a pronoun refers.

She is the *person who* wrote the letter. (*Person* is the antecedent of *who.*)

Owning a home has *its* advantages. (*Owning a home* is the antecedent of *its.*)

Appositive. A noun or a noun phrase that identifies another noun or pronoun that immediately precedes it. (See ¶¶148–150.)

Mr. Mancuso, *our purchasing agent,* would like to meet you.

Article. Classed as an adjective. The *definite* article is *the;* the *indefinite, a* or *an.* (See *A–an* in ¶1101.)

Case. The form of a noun or of a pronoun that indicates its relation to other words in the sentence. There are three cases: nominative, objective, and possessive. *Nouns* have the same form in the nominative and objective cases but a special ending for the possessive. The forms for *pronouns* are:

Nominative	Objective	Possessive
I	me	my, mine
you	you	your, yours
he, she, it	him, her, it	his, hers, its
we	us	our, ours
they	them	their, theirs
who	whom	whose

Nominative case. Used for the subject or the complement of a verb.

She sings well. (Subject.)   It is *I.* (Complement.)

Objective case. Used for (1) the object of a verb, (2) the object of a preposition, (3) the subject of an infinitive, (4) the object of an infinitive, or (5) the complement of the infinitive *to be.*

Can you deliver our *order* by Monday? (Object of the verb *can deliver.*)

Brenda has not written to *me.* (Object of the preposition *to.*)

The president encouraged *her* to run for office. (Subject of the infinitive *to run.*)

You ought to see *him* today. (Object of the infinitive *to see.*)

They believed me to be *her.* (Complement of the infinitive *to be.*)

Possessive case. Used to show ownership. (See ¶¶627–651.)

Clause. A group of related words that contains a subject and a predicate. An *independent* clause (also known as a *main clause* or *principal clause*) expresses a complete thought and can stand alone as a sentence. A *dependent* clause (also known as a *subordinate clause*) does not express a complete thought and cannot stand alone as a sentence.

I will go (independent clause) if I am invited (dependent clause).

Adjective clause. A dependent clause that modifies a noun or a pronoun in the main clause. Adjective clauses are joined to the main clause by relative pronouns (*which, that, who, whose, whom*).

The charge, *which includes servicing,* seems reasonable. (Modifies *charge.*)

Adverbial clause. A dependent clause that functions as an adverb in its relation to the main clause. Adverbial clauses indicate time, place, manner, cause, purpose, condition, result, reason, or contrast.

These orders can be filled *as soon as stock is received.* (Time.)

I was advised to live *where the climate is dry.* (Place.)

She worked *as though her life depended on it.* (Manner.)

Please write me at once *if you have any suggestions.* (Condition.)

Because our plant is closed in August, we cannot fill your order now. (Reason.)

Coordinate clauses. Clauses of the same rank. They may be independent or dependent clauses.

Carl will oversee the day-to-day operations, and Sheila will be responsible for the finances. (Coordinate independent clauses.)

When you have read the chapter and *you can answer all the questions correctly,* you ought to try these special problems. (Coordinate dependent clauses.)

Elliptical clause. A clause from which key words have been omitted. (See ¶¶102, 111, 119, 130*b*, 1082*d*.)

Now, for the next topic.   *Really?*   *If possible,* arrive at one.

Essential (or **restrictive**) **clause.** A dependent clause that cannot be omitted without changing the meaning of the main clause. Essential clauses are *not* set off by commas.

The magazine *that came yesterday* contains an evaluation of computer software.

Nonessential (or **nonrestrictive**) **clause.** A dependent clause that adds descriptive information but could be omitted without changing the meaning of the main clause. Such clauses are separated or set off from the main clause by commas.

Her latest book, *which deals with corporate financial analysis,* has sold quite well.

Noun clause. A dependent clause that functions as a noun in the main clause.

Whether the proposal will be accepted remains to be seen. (Noun clause as subject.)

They thought *that the plan was a failure.* (Noun clause as object.)

Comparison. The forms of an adjective or adverb that indicate degrees in quality, quantity, or manner. There are three degrees: positive, comparative, and superlative. (See ¶1071.)

Positive. The simple form; for example, *old, beautiful* (adjectives); *soon, quietly* (adverbs).

Comparative. Indicates a higher or lower degree of quality or manner than is expressed by the positive degree. It is used when two things are compared. It is regularly formed by adding *er* to the positive degree (*older, sooner*). In longer words it is formed by adding *more* or *less* to the positive (*more beautiful, less beautiful; more quietly, less quietly*).

Superlative. Denotes the highest or lowest degree of quality or manner and is used when more than two things are compared. It is regularly formed by adding *est* to the positive degree (*oldest, soonest*). In longer words it is formed by adding *most* or *least* (*most beautiful, least beautiful; most quietly, least quietly*).

Complement. A word or phrase that completes the sense of the verb. It may be an object, a predicate noun, a predicate pronoun, or a predicate adjective.

Object. Follows a transitive verb. (See *Verb.*)

I have already mailed the *letter.*

Predicate noun or pronoun. Follows a linking verb. It explains the subject and is identical with it. (Also called a *predicate complement, subject complement,* and *predicate nominative.*)

Miss Kwong is our *accountant.* (*Accountant* refers to *Miss Kwong.*)

The person responsible for the divestiture decision was *I.* (The pronoun *I* refers to *person.*)

(Continued on page 390.)

Predicate adjective. Completes the sense of a linking verb. (Also called a *predicate complement.*)

The charge is *excessive.* (The adjective *excessive* refers to *charge.*)

NOTE: In this manual, *complement* is used to refer only to a predicate noun, pronoun, or adjective following a linking verb. The term *object* is used to denote the complement of a transitive verb.

Conjunction. A word or phrase that connects words, phrases, or clauses.

Coordinating conjunction. Connects words, phrases, or clauses of equal rank. The coordinating conjunctions are *and, but, or,* and *nor.*

Correlative conjunctions. Coordinating conjunctions used in pairs; for example, *both . . . and, not only . . . but (also), either . . . or, neither . . . nor.*

Subordinating conjunction. Used to join subordinate clauses to main clauses. A few common ones are *when, where, after, before, if.* (See ¶132.)

Connective. A word that joins words, phrases, or clauses. The chief types of connectives are conjunctions, adverbial conjunctives, prepositions, and relative pronouns.

Consonants. The letters *b, c, d, f, g, h, j, k, l, m, n, p, q, r, s, t, v, w, x, y, z.* The letters *w* and *y* sometimes serve as vowels (as in *saw* and *rhyme*).

Contraction. A shortened form of a word or phrase in which an apostrophe indicates the omitted letters or words; for example, *don't* for *do not.* (See ¶505.)

Dangling modifier. A modifier that is attached either to no word in a sentence or to the wrong word. (See ¶1082.)

Direct address. A construction in which a speaker or a writer addresses another person directly. For example, "What do you think, Sylvia?"

Elliptical expressions. Condensed expressions from which key words have been omitted. (See also *Clause; Sentence.*)

Essential elements. Words, phrases, or clauses needed to complete the structure or meaning of a sentence. (See also *Clause; Phrase.*)

Gender. The characteristic of nouns and pronouns that indicates whether the thing named is *masculine (man, boy, stallion, he), feminine (woman, girl, mare, she),* or *neuter (book, concept, it).* Nouns that refer to either males or females have *common* gender *(person, child, horse).*

Gerund. A verb form ending in *ing* and used as a *noun.*

Selling requires special skills. (Subject.)   I enjoy *selling.* (Direct object of *enjoy.*)
She is experienced in *selling.* (Object of preposition *in.*)

Dangling gerund. A prepositional-gerund phrase that is attached either to no word in a sentence or to the wrong word. (See ¶1082c.)

Imperative. See *Mood.*

Indicative. See *Mood.*

Infinitive. The form of the verb usually introduced by *to* (see ¶¶1044–1046). An infinitive may be used as a noun, an adjective, or an adverb.

NOUN: *To do her a favor* is a pleasure. (Subject.)

                  She asked *to see the book.* (Object.)

ADJECTIVE: I still have two more contracts *to draft.* (Modifies *contracts.*)

ADVERB: He resigned *to take another position.* (Modifies *resigned.*)

Interjection. A word that shows emotion; usually without grammatical connection to other parts of a sentence.

Oh, so that's what he meant.   *Wow!* What a weekend!

Modifier. A word, phrase, or clause that qualifies, limits, or restricts the meaning of a word. (See *Adjective; Adverb; Dangling modifier.*)

Mood (mode). The form of the verb that shows the manner of the action. There are three moods: indicative, imperative, and subjunctive.

    Indicative. States a fact or asks a question.

    The lease has expired.   When does the lease expire?

    Imperative. Expresses a command or makes a request.

    Call me next week.   Please send me a catalog.

    Subjunctive. Used following clauses of necessity, demand, or wishing (see ¶¶1038–1039); also used in *if, as if,* and *as though* clauses that state conditions which are improbable, doubtful, or contrary to fact (see ¶¶1040–1043).

    It is imperative that he *be* notified.   I demand that we *be* heard.
    If he *were* appointed head of the   We urge that she *be* elected.
      department, I would quit.   I wish I *were* going.

Nonessential elements. Words, phrases, or clauses that are not needed to complete the structure or meaning of a sentence. (See also *Clause; Phrase.*)

Noun. The name of a person, place, object, idea, quality, or activity.

    Abstract noun. The name of a quality or a general idea; for example, *courage, freedom.*

    Collective noun. A noun that represents a group of persons, animals, or things; for example, *audience, company, flock.* (See ¶1019.)

    Common noun. The name of a class of persons, places, or things; for example, *child, house.* (See ¶¶307–310.)

    Predicate noun. See *Complement.*

    Proper noun. The official name of a particular person, place, or thing; for example, *Ellen, San Diego, Wednesday.* Proper nouns are capitalized. (See ¶¶303–306.)

Number. The characteristic of a noun, pronoun, or verb that indicates whether one person or thing (singular) or more than one (plural) is meant.

    NOUN: girl, girls   **PRONOUN:** she, they   **VERB:** he *works,* they *work*

Object. The person or thing that receives the action of the verb. An object may be a word, a phrase, or a clause.

    I bought a *microcomputer.* (Word.)
    She likes *to sculpt.* (Infinitive phrase.)
    I did not realize *that it was so late.* (Clause.)

    Direct object. The person or thing that is directly affected by the action of the verb. (The object in each of the three sentences above is a *direct* object.)

    Indirect object. The person or thing indirectly affected by the action of the verb. The indirect object can be made the object of the preposition *to* or *for.*

    He gave (to) *me* the book.

Ordinal number. The form of a number that indicates order or succession; for example, *first, second, twelfth.* (See ¶¶424–426.)

Parenthetical elements. Words, phrases, or clauses that are not necessary to the completeness of the structure or the meaning of a sentence.

Participle. A word that may stand alone as an adjective or may be combined with helping verbs to form different tenses (see ¶¶1033–1034). There are three forms: present, past, and perfect.

Present participle. Ends in *ing;* for example, *making, advertising.*

Past participle. Regularly ends in *ed* (as in *asked* or *filed*) but may be irregularly formed (as in *lost, seen,* and *sung*). (See ¶1030*a*–*b*.)

Perfect participle. Consists of *having* plus the past participle; for example, *having asked, having lost.*

When a participle functions as an *adjective*, it modifies a noun or a pronoun.

A *leaking* pipe caused all the trouble. (Modifies *pipe*.)

Having retired last year, I now do volunteer work. (Modifies *I*.)

Because a participle has many of the characteristics of a verb, it may take an object and be modified by an adverb. The participle and its object and modifiers make up a *participial phrase*.

Waving his hand, he drove quickly away. (Object is *hand*.)

Speaking quickly, she described the project in detail. (*Quickly* modifies *speaking*.)

Dangling participle. A participial phrase attached either to no word in a sentence or to the wrong word. (See ¶1082*a*.)

Parts of speech. The eight classes into which words are grouped according to their uses in a sentence: verb, noun, pronoun, adjective, adverb, conjunction, preposition, and interjection.

Person. The characteristic of a word that indicates whether a person is speaking (*first person*), is spoken to (*second person*), or is spoken about (*third person*). Only personal pronouns and verbs change their forms to show person. All nouns are considered third person.

	Singular	**Plural**
FIRST PERSON:	*I* liked this book.	*We* liked this book.
SECOND PERSON:	*You* liked this book.	*You* liked this book.
THIRD PERSON:	*She* liked this book.	*They* liked this book.

Phrase. A group of two or more words not having a subject and a predicate, used as a noun, an adjective, or an adverb.

Adjective phrase. A phrase that functions as an adjective (such as an infinitive phrase, a participial phrase, or a prepositional phrase).

Adverbial phrase. A phrase that functions as an adverb (such as an infinitive phrase or a prepositional phrase).

Essential (or **restrictive**) **phrase.** A phrase that limits, defines, or identifies; cannot be omitted without changing the meaning of the main clause.

The chapter *explaining that law* appears at the end of the book.

Gerund phrase. A gerund plus its object and modifiers; used as a noun.

Running your own business requires a wide range of skills.

Infinitive phrase. An infinitive plus its object and modifiers; may be used as a noun, an adjective, or an adverb. An infinitive phrase that is attached to either no word in a sentence or to the wrong word is called a *dangling* infinitive (see ¶1082*b*).

To get TF's okay on this purchase order took some doing. (As a noun; serves as subject of the verb *took*.)

The decision *to close the Morrisville plant* was not made easily. (As an adjective; tells what kind of decision.)

Janice resigned *to open her own business*. (As an adverb; tells why Janice resigned.)

NOTE: An infinitive phrase, unlike other phrases, may sometimes have a subject. This subject precedes the infinitive and is in the objective case.

I have asked *her to review this draft for accuracy*. (*Her* is the subject of *to review*.)

Nonessential (or **nonrestrictive**) **phrase.** A phrase that can be omitted without changing the meaning of the sentence.

The Stanforth-Palmer Company, *one of the country's largest financial services organizations*, is expanding into satellite communications.

Noun phrase. A phrase that functions as a noun (such as a gerund phrase, an infinitive phrase, or a prepositional phrase).

Participial phrase. A participle and its object and modifiers; used as an adjective.

The committee *considering your proposal* should come to a decision this week.

I prefer the cover sample *printed in blue and yellow*.

Prepositional phrase. A preposition and its object and modifiers; may be used as a noun, an adjective, or an adverb.

From Boston to Tulsa is about 1550 miles. (As a noun; serves as subject of the verb *is*.)

Profits *in the automobile industry* are up sharply this quarter. (As an adjective; indicates which type of profits.)

You handled Dr. Waterman's objections *with great skill*. (As an adverb; indicates the manner in which the objections were handled.)

Prepositional-gerund phrase. A phrase that begins with a preposition and has a gerund as the object. (See ¶1082c.)

By rechecking the material before it is set in type, you avoid expensive corrections later on. (*By* is the preposition; *rechecking*, a gerund, is the object of *by*.)

NOTE: The term *verb phrase* is often used to indicate the individual words that make up the verb in a sentence. Sometimes the verb phrase includes an adverb. A verb phrase can function only as a verb.

You *should work together* with Nora on the report. (The verb phrase consists of the verb form *should work* plus the adverb *together*.)

Positive degree. See *Comparison*.

Predicate. That part of a sentence which tells what the subject does or what is done to the subject or what state of being the subject is in.

Complete predicate. The complete predicate consists of a verb and its complement along with any modifiers.

Barbara *has handled the job well*.

Simple predicate. The simple predicate is the verb alone, without regard for any complement or modifiers that may accompany it.

Barbara *has handled* the job well.

Compound predicate. Two or more predicates in the same sentence.

Barbara *has handled the job well* and *deserves a good deal of praise*.

Prefix. A letter, syllable, or word added to the beginning of a word to change its meaning; for example, *a*float, *re*upholster, *under*nourished.

Preposition. A connective that shows the relation of a noun or pronoun to some other word in the sentence. The noun or pronoun following a preposition is in the objective case. (See ¶¶1077–1080.)

Martin's work was reviewed *by Hedley and me.*

Principal parts. The forms of a verb from which all other forms are derived: the *present*, the *past*, the *past participle*, and the *present participle*. (See ¶¶1030–1035.)

Pronoun. A word used in place of a noun. (See ¶¶1049–1064.)

DEMONSTRATIVE: *this, that, these, those*

INDEFINITE: *each, either, any, anyone, someone, everyone, few, all,* etc.

INTENSIVE: *myself, yourself,* etc.

INTERROGATIVE: *who, which, what,* etc.

PERSONAL: *I, you, he, she, it, we, they*

RELATIVE: *who, whose, whom, which, that,* and compounds with *ever* (such as *whoever*)

Punctuation. Marks used to indicate relationships between words, phrases, and clauses.

Terminal (or **end**) **punctuation.** The period, the question mark, and the exclamation point—the three marks that may indicate the end of a sentence.

NOTE: When a sentence breaks off abruptly, a dash may be used to mark the end of the sentence (see ¶207). When a sentence trails off without really ending, ellipsis marks (three periods) are used to mark the end of the sentence (see ¶291*b*).

Internal punctuation. The comma, the semicolon, the colon, the dash, parentheses, quotation marks, the underscore, the apostrophe, ellipsis marks, the asterisk, the diagonal, and brackets.

Question, direct. A question in its original form, as spoken or written.

He then asked me, "What is your opinion?"

Indirect question. A statement of the substance of a question without the use of the exact words of the speaker.

He then asked me what my opinion was.

Independent question. A question that represents a complete sentence but is incorporated in a larger sentence.

The main question is, Who will translate this idea into a clear plan of action?

Quotation, direct. A quotation of words exactly as spoken or written.

I myself heard Ed say, "I will arrive in Santa Fe on Tuesday."

Indirect quotation. A statement of the substance of a quotation without using the exact words.

I myself heard Ed say that he would arrive in Santa Fe on Tuesday.

Sentence. A group of words representing a complete thought and containing a subject and a verb (predicate) along with any complements and modifiers.

Simple sentence. A sentence consisting of one independent clause.

I have no recollection of the meeting.

Compound sentence. A sentence consisting of two or more independent clauses.

Our Boston office will be closed, and our Dallas office will be relocated.

Complex sentence. A sentence consisting of one independent clause and one or more dependent clauses.

We will make an exception to the policy if circumstances warrant.

Compound-complex sentence. A sentence consisting of two independent clauses and one or more dependent clauses.

I tried to handle the monthly report alone, but when I began to analyze the data, I realized that I needed your help.

Declarative sentence. A sentence that makes a statement.

All the newspapers were sold.

Elliptical sentence. A word or phrase treated as a complete sentence, even though the subject and verb are understood but not expressed.

Enough on that subject.   Why not?

Exclamatory sentence. A sentence that expresses strong feeling.

Don't even think of smoking here!

Imperative sentence. A sentence that expresses a command or a request. (The subject *you* is understood if it is not expressed.)

Send a check at once.   Please close the door.

Interrogative sentence. A sentence that asks a question.

When does the conference begin?

Sentence fragment. A phrase or clause that is incorrectly treated as a sentence. (See ¶102, note.)

Statement. A sentence that asserts a fact. (See also *Sentence, declarative.*)

Subject. A word, phrase, or clause that names the person, place, or thing about which something is said.

The law firm with the best reputation in town is Barringer and Doyle.

Whoever applies for the job from within the department will get special consideration.

Compound subject. A subject consisting of two or more simple subjects joined by conjunctions.

My wife and my three sons are off on a white-water rafting trip.

Subjunctive. See *Mood.*

Suffix. A letter, syllable, or word added to the end of a word to modify its meaning; for example, trend*y*, friend*ly*, count*less*, receiver*ship*, lone*some*.

Superlative degree. See *Comparison.*

Syllable. A single letter or a group of letters that form one sound.

Tense. The property of a verb that expresses *time*. (See ¶¶1031–1035.) The three *primary* tenses correspond to the three time divisions:

PRESENT:	they think
PAST:	they thought
FUTURE:	they will think

There are three *perfect* tenses, corresponding to the primary tenses:

PRESENT PERFECT:	they have thought
PAST PERFECT:	they had thought
FUTURE PERFECT:	they will have thought

There are six *progressive* tenses, corresponding to each of the primary and perfect tenses:

PRESENT PROGRESSIVE:	they are thinking
PAST PROGRESSIVE:	they were thinking
FUTURE PROGRESSIVE:	they will be thinking
PRESENT PERFECT PROGRESSIVE:	they have been thinking
PAST PERFECT PROGRESSIVE:	they had been thinking
FUTURE PERFECT PROGRESSIVE:	they will have been thinking

There are two *emphatic* tenses:

PRESENT EMPHATIC:	they do think
PAST EMPHATIC:	they did think

Transitional expressions. Expressions that link independent clauses or sentences; for example, *as a result, therefore, on the other hand, nevertheless.* (See also ¶138*a*.)

Verb. A word used to express action or state of being. (See also *Mood.*)

Enniston *has boosted* its sales goals for the year. (Action.)

My son-in-law *was* originally a lawyer, but he *has* now *become* a computer-game designer. (State of being.)

Auxiliary (helping) verb. A verb that helps in the formation of another verb. The chief auxiliaries are *be, can, could, do, have, may, might, must, ought, shall, should, will, would.*

Intransitive verb. A verb that does not require an object to complete its meaning.

As the plane *circled* for a landing and the island *emerged* in full view, our excitement *increased* and our expectations *rose.*

Linking verb. A verb that connects a subject with a predicate adjective, noun, or pronoun. The various forms of *to be* are the most commonly used linking verbs. *Become, look, seem, appear,* and *grow* are often used as linking verbs. (See ¶1067.)

Laura *seemed* willing to compromise, but Frank *became* obstinate in his demands. Was he afraid that any concession might make him *appear* a fool?

Principal parts of verbs. See *Principal parts.*

Transitive verb. A verb that requires an object to complete its meaning. (See also *Object.*)

Fusilli *has rejected* all offers to purchase his business.

Verbal. A word that partakes of the nature of a verb but functions in some other way. (See *Gerund; Infinitive; Participle.*)

Voice. The property of a verb that indicates whether the subject acts or is acted upon.

Active voice. A verb is in the active voice when its subject is the doer of the act.

About a dozen people *reviewed* the report in draft form.

Passive voice. A verb is in the passive voice when its subject is acted upon.

The report *was reviewed* in draft form by about a dozen people.

Vowels. The letters *a, e, i, o,* and *u.* The letters *w* and *y* sometimes act like vowels (as in *awl* or in *cry*). (See also *Consonants.*)

Glossary of Word Processing Terms

Access
   Random Access
   Serial Access
Access Time
Adjust
ADP
Alphanumeric
Applications Software
Archive
Author
Automatic Carrier Return
Automatic Centering
Automatic Decimal Tab
Automatic File Select
Automatic File Sort
Automatic Footnote Tie-In
Automatic Hyphenation
Automatic Line or Paragraph
  Numbering
Automatic Line Spacing
Automatic Page Numbering
Automatic Pagination
Automatic Underlining
Background Printing
Backup
Batch Processing
Baud
Binary
Bit
Bits per Second

Block Copy
Block Move
Boilerplate
Boldface Printing
Boot
Buffer Memory
Byte
Cassette
Cathode-Ray Tube
Central Processing Unit
Character
Character Set
Character Size Control
Character String
Characters per Second
Chip
Clear
Code
Code Key
Column Move or Delete
Command
Compatibility
Computer
Configuration
Control Character
Control Code Display
cps
CPU
Crossfooting
CRT

Cursor
Cursor Positioning
Daisy Wheel
Data Base
Data Processing
Default Format Statement
Delete
Dictionary
Disk
Disk Drive
Diskette
   Dual-Density Diskette
Display Screen
Distributed Logic System
Document
Document Assembly
Dot Matrix
Downtime
Dual Column
Dual Display
Dual Pitch
Dual Sheet Feeder
Duplexing
Editing
EDP
Electronic Mail
Electronic Typewriter
Elite
Ergonomics
Execute
Field
Floppy Disk
Font
Footer
Footnote Drag
Format
Forms Mode
Full-Page Display
Global
Graphics
Hard Copy
Hard Disk
Hardware
Hardwired
Header
Home
Hot Zone
Hyphen Drop
Indexing
Information Processing
Input
Insert
Integrated Circuit
Interface
Internal Processor
Interword Spacing
I/O

Justification
K
Keyboard
Keyboarding
Keystroke
Kilobyte
Linear Display
List Processing
Local Area Network (LAN)
Mag
Magnetic Card
Magnetic Medium
Magnetic Tape
Mask
Memory
   Random-Access Memory
   Read-Only Memory
Menu
Merge
Microcomputer
Microprocessor
Mnemonics
Modem
Mouse
Off-Line
On-Line
Optical Character Reader
Originator
Orphan Adjust
Outlining
Output
Overwriting
Page Break
Paragraph Numbering
Partial-Page Display
Password
Peripheral
Permanent Memory
Personal Computer
Pica
Pitch
Playback
Playout
Principal
Printers
   Impact Printers
   Nonimpact Printers
   Character Printers
   Line Printers
   Letter-Quality Printers
   Dot Matrix Printers
   Twin-Track Printers
   Bidirectional Printers
Printout
Printout Queuing
Printwheel
Program

Prompt
Protocol
RAM
Read
Read In
Read Out
Reconstruction
Record
Records Processing
Response Time
ROM
Scanning
Screen Load
Scroll
Search and Replace
Shadow Printing
Shared Logic System
Shared Resource System
Sheet Feeder
Simultaneous Input/Output
Soft Copy
Software
Split Screen
Stand-Alone Unit
Stop Code
Storage
   External Storage
   Internal Storage
Storage Medium

Store
Subscript
Superscript
Switch Code
Tab Grid
Telecommunication Lines
Temporary Memory
Terminal
Text
Text Editor
Text Entry
Turnaround Time
User-Friendly
Variable
Video Display Terminal (VDT)
Widow Adjust
Windowing
Word Processing
   Centralized Word Processing
   Decentralized Word Processing
Word Processing System
Word Processor
   Blind Word Processor
   Communicating Word Processor
   Dedicated Word Processor
Workstation
   Dumb Workstation
   Intelligent Workstation
Wraparound

1901   As the world of the office continues to undergo a series of rapid technological changes, a whole new vocabulary has begun to emerge—a vocabulary that often seems more dazzling or bewildering than the actual changes themselves. The following glossary provides brief and simple definitions of the key terms and concepts that are part of this new vocabulary.

NOTE: When boldface type is used to highlight a word or phrase within a definition, it signifies that the highlighted word or phrase is defined elsewhere in this glossary.

Access. To call up information out of **storage;** also, to transfer newly **keyboarded** information into storage.

   Random access. A technique that permits stored **text** to be directly retrieved, regardless of its location on the **storage medium.**

   Serial access. A technique for retrieving stored information that requires a sequential search through one item after another on the **storage medium.** (Serial access is needed, for example, to locate information stored on **magnetic tape.**)

Access time. The amount of time it takes a **word processing system** to locate previously stored information; also, the time needed to transfer newly **keyboarded** information into **storage.**

Adjust. A **command** that automatically changes the length of **keyboarded** lines to make them fit within new margin settings. (See also *Wraparound.*)

ADP. Automatic **data processing.**

Alphanumeric. Consisting of letters and numbers.

Applications software. **Programs** designed to perform **data processing** or **word processing** tasks for a specific type of business or activity.

Archive. **Storage** of duplicate **text** on **disks** or **diskettes.** Usually refers to data that is infrequently used or stored as **backup** material.

Author. The creator of a **document** that passes through a **word processing system;** also called *principal* or *originator.*

Automatic carrier return. The ability of a **word processor** to advance automatically to the beginning of the next line during **keyboarding** without requiring the operator to touch the Return key. (See also *Wraparound.*)

Automatic centering. The ability of a **word processor** to center **text** between margins, tab settings, or other designated points.

Automatic decimal tab. The ability of a **word processor** to automatically align columns of figures on the decimal point as they are **keyboarded.** Columns of whole numbers are automatically aligned on the last digit.

Automatic file select. The ability of a **word processor** to pick out certain items from a collection of information on the basis of the **characters** that appear in certain positions. (For example, the word processor can examine a list of subscribers and choose only those whose subscriptions expire in a certain month.)

Automatic file sort. The ability of a **word processor** to rearrange a collection of information into alphabetic or numeric order on the basis of the **characters** that appear in certain positions. (For example, the word processor can arrange a randomly typed list of names and addresses into numeric order by ZIP Code and then alphabetically by name within each ZIP Code.)

Automatic footnote tie-in. The ability of a **word processor** to automatically position footnotes on the same page as the **text** they refer to. If the text is moved to another page, any related footnotes will also be transferred to that page. Also known as *footnote drag.*

Automatic hyphenation. The ability of a **word processor** to automatically hyphenate and divide words that do not fit at the end of a line. If the **text** is later revised so that the divided word no longer begins at the right margin, the hyphen is automatically removed and the word prints solid. (See also *Hyphen drop.*)

Automatic line or paragraph numbering. The ability of a **word processor** to automatically number each line or paragraph sequentially in the rough-draft copy of a **document.** The line or paragraph numbers are automatically deleted during final **printout.**

Automatic line spacing. The ability of a **word processor** to automatically change vertical line spacing during **printout** (for example, from double to single to double again) on the basis of **commands** given at the time of **text entry.**

Automatic page numbering. The ability of a **word processor** to automatically print sequential page numbers on the pages that make up an entire **document.** If the document is revised, with a gain or loss in the total number of pages, the page numbering is automatically adjusted in the next **printout.**

Automatic pagination. The ability of a **word processor** to take a continuous piece of **text** and automatically divide it into pages with a specified number of lines per page. If the text is changed because of the addition, deletion, or rearrangement of copy, the word processor will automatically repage the material to maintain the proper page length.

Automatic underlining. The ability of a **word processor** to automatically underscore **text** without requiring the operator to touch the underscore key once for each underlined **character.** The underscoring is done on the basis of a **command** (at the time of **text entry**) that indicates how much text to underline.

Background printing. The ability of a **word processor** to print a **document** while other work is being done on the **keyboard** and the **display screen** at the same time.

Backup. Storage of duplicate text on **disks** or **diskettes** as a safety measure in the event the original medium is damaged or lost.

Batch processing. Performing a single operation on a group of items at the same time rather than processing each item completely as it comes up.

Baud. See *Bits per second (bps).*

Binary. A numbering system in which all numbers are represented by various combinations of the digits 0 and 1.

Bit. Binary digit. The smallest unit of information that can be recognized by a **computer.** Bits are combined to represent **characters.** (See also *Byte.*)

Bits per second (bps). A measurement used to describe the speed of transmission between two pieces of equipment. Also known as *baud.*

Block copy. A **command** to reproduce a segment of **text** in another place without erasing it from its original position.

Block move. A **command** to reproduce a segment of **text** in another place and at the same time erase it from its original position.

Boilerplate. Standard wording (for example, sentences or paragraphs in form letters or clauses in legal documents) that is held in **storage.** When needed, it can be used as is, with minor modification, or in combination with new material to produce tailor-made **documents.** Also known as *repetitive text.*

Boldface printing. A method of printing in which certain **characters** appear darker than the surrounding **text.** (See also *Shadow printing.*)

Boot. (Short for *bootstrap.*) A **program** that instructs a **word processor** to store its operating system and prepare to **execute** an applications program. (See also *Applications software.*)

Buffer memory. See *Memory, random-access.*

Byte. The sequence of **bits** that represents a **character.** Eight bits are the number required in each byte.

Cassette. A cartridge holding **magnetic tape.** (See also *Magnetic medium.*)

Cathode-ray tube (CRT). See *Display screen.*

Central processing unit (CPU). The brains of a **word processing system;** controls the interpretation and execution of instructions. (See also *Internal processor.*)

Character. A single letter, figure, or symbol produced by a **keystroke** on a **word processor.**

Character set. The complete set of characters displayable on a **word processor.** These characters can be alphabetic (in capital or small letters), numeric, or symbolic.

Character size control. The ability of a **word processor** to display a full page of **text** at regular size or one half-page at double size. Some systems also will display extrawide text at half size.

Character string. A specified sequence of typed characters, usually representing a word or phrase. A character string is often used to locate a particular word or phrase wherever it appears in a **document** so that it can be automatically replaced with another word or phrase. Thus if a person's name has been consistently misspelled or a date has been given incorrectly in several places, the error can be easily corrected. (See also *Search and replace*.)

Characters per second (cps). The number of characters printed in one second; a measurement frequently used to describe the speed of a **printer.**

Chip. An **integrated circuit** used in **computers** and **word processors.**

Clear. A **command** to erase material from **storage.**

Code. The language used to translate **bytes** into recognizable **characters.** Also, the pattern or system of signals recorded on media which stand for alphabetic or numeric characters or machine functions.

Code key. A special key on the **keyboard** used to **command** a **word processor** to perform a function. (See also *Mnemonics*.)

Column move or delete. A **command** that permits a **word processor** to move or delete vertical blocks of **characters** with a minimum number of steps. In unsophisticated systems, where columns must be moved or deleted one line at a time, the operator must go through a time-consuming process.

Command. An instruction, given through a special **keystroke** or series of keystrokes, that causes a **word processor** to perform a function.

Compatibility. The ability of one type of **word processor** or **computer** to share **storage media** or to communicate with another.

Computer. An electronic device that is capable of (1) accepting, storing, and logically manipulating data or **text** that is **input** and (2) processing and producing **output** (results or decisions) on the basis of stored **programs** of instructions. (See also *Word processor*.)

Configuration. The components that make up a **word processor.** Most systems include a **keyboard** for **text entry,** a **central processing unit,** one or more **disk drives,** and a **printer.** Most systems also have a **display screen.**

Control character. A special **character** which is never printed but causes a visible result during printing. For example, spacing, tabulation, and carrier return are all achieved by means of control characters.

Control code display. The ability of a **word processor** to display instructions, **commands,** or **control characters** on the screen or a **printout.**

cps. See *Characters per second.*

CPU. See *Central processing unit.*

Crossfooting. The ability of a **word processor** to total numeric amounts arranged in rows and columns. The answers are then placed at the end of each row or at the bottom of each column.

CRT. Cathode-ray tube. (See *Display screen.*)

Cursor. A special **character** (usually a blinking underscore, dot, arrow, or box) that indicates where the next typed character will appear on the **display screen.**

Cursor positioning. The movement of the **cursor** on the **display screen.** Most **word processors** have four keys to signify *up, down, left,* and *right* movement. Some require the use of a **code key** plus another key to move the cursor.

Daisy wheel. A printing element made of plastic or metal and used on certain impact **printers.** Each **character** is engraved at the end of a spoke, so that the entire element resembles a daisy. Daisy wheels come in many type styles.

Data base. A stored collection of information.

Data processing. The mathematical or other logical manipulation of numbers or symbols, based on a stored **program** of instructions. Also known as *electronic data processing (EDP)*. (See also *Word processing.*)

Default format statement. A previously programmed instruction on **format** that will be followed by a **word processor** unless the operator gives specific format directions. (A 6-inch line is a common default format.)

Delete. A **command** to erase something held in **storage**—from as little as a single **character** to as much as a page or more of **text.**

Dictionary. A **program** used to check the spelling of each word entered in the **word processor.** If the **keyboarded** word does not agree with the corresponding item in the dictionary or does not appear in the dictionary, it is highlighted on the **display screen** as a possible misspelling. The operator must then either make the necessary correction or confirm that the word is correct as keyboarded.

Disk. A random-**access,** magnetically coated storage medium, shaped like a phonograph record, with high storage capacity (up to 500-plus pages). May be hard or flexible. (See also *Diskette.*)

Disk drive. The component of a **word processor** or a **microcomputer** into which a **diskette** is inserted so that it can be read or written on.

Diskette. A small, nonrigid disk with limited storage capacity (normally 30 to 200 pages). Also known as a *floppy disk.*

> **Dual-density diskette.** A floppy disk with twice the normal storage capacity. Also known as a *double-density diskette.*

Display screen. A device similar to a television screen and used on a **word processor** to display **text** and **graphics.** Also called a *cathode-ray tube (CRT)* or a *video display terminal (VDT).*

Distributed logic system. A system in which several **word processors** share **storage** and an **internal processor,** but each individual word processor retains some internal processing capability. (See also *Shared logic system.*)

Document. Any printed business communication—for example, a letter, memo, report, statistical table, or form. (Some authorities use the term to refer only to larger or more complex material such as reports and tables.)

Document assembly. The creation of a new **document** by combining pieces of previously stored **text** and sometimes newly typed material. (See also *List processing; Boilerplate; Merge.*)

Dot matrix. The use of closely spaced dots to form **characters** on some **display screens** and **printers.** (See also *Printers, dot matrix.*)

Downtime. The period when equipment is unusable because of a malfunction.

Dual column. The ability of a **word processor** to take **text** stored in one column and print it in two columns.

Dual display. The capability of a **word processor** to show two or more video images simultaneously either on the same screen or on two different screens. See also *Split screen.*

Dual pitch. The ability of a typewriter or **printer** to print either 10 or 12 characters to the inch. (See also *Pitch.*)

Dual sheet feeder. A device that can insert two different types of paper automatically into a **printer.**

Duplexing. Printing on both sides of the paper.

Editing. The process of changing **text** by inserting, deleting, replacing, rearranging, and reformatting.

EDP. Electronic **data processing.**

Electronic mail. The transfer of **documents** through telecommunication channels without the physical movement of paper.

Electronic typewriter. A **word processor** with limited functions; typically has no **display screen.** (See also *Word processor, blind.*)

Elite. Any typeface that allows the printing of 12 characters to the inch. Also known as *12 pitch.* (See also *Pica.*)

Ergonomics. The science of adapting working conditions and equipment to meet the physical needs of workers.

Execute. To perform an action specified by the operator or the **program.**

Field. A group of related **characters** treated as a unit (such as a name).

Floppy disk. See *Diskette.*

Font. An assortment or set of type of one size or style. Includes all letters of the alphabet, arabic numerals, and punctuation marks. (See also *Character set.*)

Footer. Repetitive information which appears at the bottom (the foot) of every page of a **document.** A page number is a common footer. (See also *Header.*)

Footnote drag. See *Automatic footnote tie-in.*

Format. The physical specifications that affect the appearance and arrangement of a **document**—for example, margins, spacing, **pitch.**

Forms mode. The ability of a **word processor** to store the **format** of a blank **document** or form so that it can later be displayed on the screen and completed by the operator. Once a fill-in has been entered, the **cursor** automatically advances to the beginning of the next area to be filled in. (See also *Mask.*)

Full-page display. The ability of a **word processor** to show the equivalent of an 8½- by 11-inch page of **text** on the **display screen.** (See also *Partial-page display.*)

Global. Describing any function that can be performed on an entire **document** without requiring individual **commands** for each use.

Graphics. Pictures displayed or printed by means of horizontal, vertical, diagonal, and curved lines.

Hard copy. **Text** printed on paper. (See also *Soft copy.*)

Hard disk. A rigid **magnetic** storage **medium** with the capacity to store large amounts of **text.**

Hardware. The physical equipment itself: the **central processing unit,** the **display screen,** the **keyboard,** the **disk drive,** and the **printer.** (See also *Software.*)

Hardwired. Describing a **word processor** that has its **programs** built into the circuitry of the machine. These programs cannot be changed.

Header. Repetitive information which appears at the top (the head) of every page of a **document.** A page number is a common header. (See also *Footer.*)

Home. The upper left corner of the **display screen;** the starting position of a page or **document.**

Hot zone. The area before the right margin, usually seven to ten characters wide. Words in this area may have to be divided or moved to the next line.

Hyphen drop. The ability of a **word processor** to automatically delete a hyphen previously inserted to divide a word at the end of a line if the **text** is later revised and the word reappears in the middle of a line.

Indexing. The ability of a **word processor** to accumulate a list of words or phrases that appear in a **document,** along with their corresponding page numbers, and to print out or display the list in alphabetic order.

Information processing. The coordination of people, equipment, and procedures to handle information, including **word processing** and **data processing** and the distribution, **storage,** and retrieval of information.

Input. Information entered into the system for processing. *Inputting* information means **keyboarding** it on a **word processor** or **microcomputer.**

Insert. To add **text** to a **document.**

Integrated circuit. A tiny complex of electronic components produced as a solid unit. May be used as circuitry for logic or as storage modules.

Interface. The electrical connection that links two pieces of equipment together so that they can communicate with each other.

Internal processor. The component of a **word processor** that contains the operating instructions and acts as the "brains" or "logic" of the unit. (See also *Central processing unit.*)

Interword spacing. Inserting extra space between words so as to make each line of **text** end at the same point. (See also *Justification.*)

I/O. Input/output. (See also *Simultaneous input/output.*)

Justification. A method of printing in which additional space is inserted between words or **characters** to force each line to the same length.

K. The abbreviation for *kilo,* meaning "1000." In word processing, K stands for *kilobyte* (1024 **bytes**). K is often used to describe a **word processor's** storage capacity. Thus, for example, 256K means 256 kilobytes of storage.

Keyboard. The device for entering **input** into a **word processor.**

Keyboarding. Entering **characters** into the **memory** of a **word processor.**

Keystroke. The depression of one key on a **keyboard.**

Kilobyte. See *K.*

Linear display. The ability of a **word processor** to allow the operator to view **characters** in a single line of type on the **display screen.**

List processing. The ability of a **word processor** to maintain lists of information that can be easily updated and rearranged in alphabetic or numeric order. A list can also be combined with other stored **text** to create new **documents.**

Local area network (LAN). A system that uses cable or other means to permit high-speed communication between various kinds of electronic equipment within a small area.

Mag. Short for *magnetic;* used in expressions like *mag card* and *mag tape.*

Magnetic card. A card coated with magnetic material that can store one or two pages of information typed on a **word processor.** Also called a *mag card.*

Magnetic medium. Any device coated with a magnetic material that can be used to store information entered in a **word processor**—for example, **magnetic cards, magnetic tapes, disks,** and **diskettes.**

Magnetic tape. Tape coated with a magnetic material on which information may be stored.

Mask. A **document** or form that is stored in a **word processor** and displayed on the **display screen** with blank areas that must be filled in by the operator. A form letter that requires the operator to enter a name, an address, and a salutation is one example of a mask. (See also *Forms mode.*)

Memory. The part of a **word processor** that stores information. (See also *Storage.*)

> **Random-access memory (RAM).** The temporary memory that allows information to be stored randomly and accessed quickly and directly (without the need to go through intervening data). Also known as the *buffer memory.*

> **Read-only memory (ROM).** The permanent memory of a **word processor;** a set of instructions that has been built into the word processor by the manufacturer and cannot be **accessed** or changed by the operator.

Menu. A list of choices or questions programmed into a **word processor** to guide the operator through a function. For example, a "printing" menu would ask about the desired paper size, the **pitch** to be used, and so on.

Merge. A **command** to create one **document** by combining **text** that is stored in two different locations. For example, a **word processor** can merge the standard text of a form letter with a mailing list to produce a batch of letters with a different name, address, and salutation on each letter. (See also *Document assembly; List processing.*)

Microcomputer. A small and relatively inexpensive computer system commonly consisting of a **display screen,** a **keyboard,** a **central processing unit,** one or more **disk drives,** and a **printer,** with limited **storage** based upon a **microprocessor.**

Microprocessor. The electronic component of a **microcomputer** consisting of **integrated circuits** contained on a silicon **chip.**

Mnemonics. A **word processor's** system of **commands,** structured to assist the operator's memory. Often, the commands are abbreviations of the functions they perform (for example, *C* for *center,* *U* for *underline*).

Modem. Abbreviation for "*mo*dulator/*dem*odulator." A device that converts electrical signals into tones for transmission over telephone lines or converts the tones back into electrical signals at the receiving end.

Mouse. A hand-operated electronic device used to move the **cursor** around on the **display screen.** Mostly used with **microcomputers.**

Off-line. Refers to an operation performed by electronic equipment not tied into a centralized **word processing system.**

On-line. Refers to an operation performed by electronic equipment controlled by a remote **central processing unit.**

Optical character reader (OCR). A device that can read **text** and enter it automatically into a **word processor** for **storage** or **editing.** Also called an *optical scanner.*

Originator. See *Author.*

Orphan adjust. The ability of a **word processor** to prevent the first line of a paragraph from being printed as the last line on a page. (See also *Widow adjust.*)

Outlining. The ability of a **word processor** to automatically number and letter items typed with an indented format. If **text** is added or deleted, the numbering sequence may be automatically corrected. Also known as *paragraph numbering.*

Output. The results of a **word processing** operation.

Overwriting. Recording and storing information in a specific location to destroy whatever had been stored there previously.

Page break. A **command** that tells the **printer** where to end one page and begin the next.

Paragraph numbering. See *Outlining.*

Partial-page display. The ability of a **word processor** to show up to three-quarters of an 8½- by 11-inch page of **text** on the **display screen.** (See also *Full-page display.*)

Password. An identification code required to **access** stored material. A device intended to prevent **documents** from being viewed, **edited,** or printed by unauthorized persons.

Peripheral. Any device that extends the capabilities of a **word processing system** but is not necessary for its operation (for example, an **optical character reader).**

Permanent memory. See *Memory, read-only.*

Personal computer. A **microcomputer** for personal and office use.

Pica. Any typeface that allows the printing of 10 characters to the inch. Also known as *10 pitch.* (See also *Elite.*)

Pitch. Measurement for the number of characters in a horizontal inch. For example, *12 pitch* means that 12 characters will be printed in 1 inch; *10 pitch* means that 10 characters will be printed in 1 inch. (See also *Dual pitch.*)

Playback. The process of displaying or printing **text** after it has been entered.

Playout. The process of printing **keyboarded** copy. (See also *Printout.*)

Principal. See *Author.*

Printers. Devices of various types that produce copy on paper.

Impact printers. Devices that produce **characters** on paper by striking a printing element against a ribbon.

Nonimpact printers. Devices that produce characters on paper without striking a ribbon or the paper. *Ink-jet printers* form characters by spraying tiny, electrically charged ink droplets on paper. *Laser printers* use a narrow beam of pure red light to burn characters onto light-sensitive paper.

Character printers. These print one character at a time.

Line printers. These print an entire line at a time and thus produce work more quickly than character printers.

Letter-quality printers. These printers produce high-quality work that looks as if it had been done on a carbon-ribbon typewriter.

Dot matrix printers. Substantially cheaper than letter-quality printers, these use needles or bristles to produce characters made up of small dots. The work they produce, while legible, is usually considered acceptable only for personal or in-house use; for documents being sent outside or even to top-level management, letter-quality printing is normally required.

Twin-track printers. Devices capable of producing two different type styles within the same **document** without requiring the operator to change the printing element. Also known as *dual-head printers*.

Bidirectional printers. Devices that can print from left to right and from right to left. Because they eliminate unnecessary carriage returns, they speed up the printing process.

Printout. The paper copy of a **document** produced on a **word processor;** also, the process of printing the copy.

Printout queuing. A procedure that allows the **printer** to line up a number of **documents** for printing. Having given the **command** to print, the operator is free to go on to other jobs while all the documents are being printed.

Printwheel. See *Daisy wheel.*

Program. An established sequence of instructions that tells a **word processor** or a **computer** what to do. (See also *Software.*)

Prompt. A message given on the **display screen** to (1) indicate the status of a function (for example, "Command Incomplete"), (2) help the operator complete a function, or (3) indicate that an attempted function cannot be performed.

Protocol. A formal set of rules that governs the transmission of information from one piece of equipment to another.

RAM. See *Memory, random-access.*

Read. To transfer information from an external storage medium into internal storage. (See also *Storage, external* and *internal.*)

Read in. To store data in a specific location.

Read out. To copy information held in internal storage and transfer it to some form of external storage. (See also *Storage, external* and *internal.*)

Reconstruction. The ability of a **word processor** to salvage information stored on a damaged **disk** or **diskette** and transfer it to an undamaged one.

Record (n.). All the information pertaining to a particular subject. Records are often typed in a list format so that the information can be easily manipulated and combined with other **text** to create new **documents.** (See also *Document assembly; List processing.*)

Record (v.). To store the **keystrokes** entered into a **word processor** or the sounds spoken into a dictation device.

Records processing. See *Document assembly; List processing.*

Response time. The time a **word processor** takes to execute a **command.**

ROM. See *Memory, read-only.*

Scanning. Examining **text** on the **display screen** for **editing** purposes.

Screen load. The amount of **text** that can be displayed on a screen at once.

Scroll. The capability to display a large body of **text** by rolling it past the **display screen** either horizontally or vertically. As text disappears off one edge of the screen, new text appears at the opposite edge of the screen.

Search and replace. A **command** that directs the **word processor** to locate a **character string** wherever it occurs in a **document** and replace it with a different character string. ◆

Shadow printing. A method of printing darker **characters.** The **printer** strikes each character twice; because the second image is not exactly on top of the first character, it creates a shadow and makes the character appear darker than the surrounding characters. (See also *Boldface printing.*)

Shared logic system. A system in which a number of **word processors** share the processing and **storage** capabilities of one **central processing unit.** If the central processor malfunctions, each word processor is affected.

Shared resource system. A clustered word processing system in which **workstations** have their own **internal processors** but share resources, such as **printers** and central **storage.** Each **word processor** can function independently. (See also *Word processing system, clustered.*)

Sheet feeder. A device that inserts sheets of paper into a **printer.**

Simultaneous input/output (I/O). The ability of a **word processor** to allow the **text** of one **document** to be entered or edited while a different document is being printed. (See also *Background printing.*)

Soft copy. **Text** displayed on the **display screen.** (See also *Hard copy.*)

Software. The operating instructions or programming of a **word processor** or **computer.** (See also *Hardware.*)

Split screen. The capability of some **word processors** to display two or more different video images on the screen at the same time. A type of *dual display.* (See also *Windowing.*)

Stand-alone unit. A self-contained **word processing** unit that functions independently, without the aid of other equipment or a central **computer.**

Stop code. A **command** that causes the **printer** to halt during printing; used to allow the operator to change the **font** or paper on the printer.

Storage. The **memory** of a **word processor.**

   External storage. **Magnetic cards, magnetic tapes, disks,** and **diskettes** used to store information; can be removed from the word processor.

   Internal storage. An integral component of a word processor, used to store information.

Storage medium. See *Magnetic medium.*

Store. To place information in **memory** for later use.

Subscript. A **command,** given at the time of **text entry,** that instructs the **printer** to print one or more **characters** slightly below the regular line of type, usually by a half or quarter of a line. Often used in scientific notations (for example, H_2CO_3). (See also *Superscript.*)

Superscript. A **command,** given at the time of **text entry,** that instructs the **printer** to print one or more **characters** slightly above the regular line of type, usually by a half or quarter of a line. (See also *Subscript.*)

Switch code. A **command,** given at the time of **text entry,** that tells the **word processor** to go from one storage station to another to find text for insertion in the **document** being prepared.

Tab grid. A series of indentions (usually 5 spaces apart) that are preset in a **word processor.**

Telecommunication lines. Telephone and other communication lines used to transmit information from one location to another.

Temporary memory. See *Memory, random-access.*

Terminal. Any device that can transmit or receive electronic information.

Text. The written material to be displayed on a screen or printed on paper.

Text editor. A word processing typewriter.

Text entry. The initial act of **keystroking** that places **text** in **storage.**

Turnaround time. The time it takes for a **document** to be entered, edited, proofread, corrected, printed, and returned to the person who created it.

User-friendly. Describes electronic equipment and **applications software** that are easy to learn how to use.

Variable. Information in a standard **document** that changes each time the document is produced (for example, the name and address in a form letter).

Video display terminal (VDT). See *Display screen*.

Widow adjust. The ability of a **word processor** to avoid printing the last line of a paragraph as the first line on a page. (See also *Orphan adjust*.)

Windowing. The ability of a **word processor** to split its **display screen** into two or more segments so that the operator can view several different **documents** or perform several different functions simultaneously. (See also *Split screen*.)

Word processing. A system of personnel, procedures, and automated equipment designed to handle communications efficiently and economically. *Word processing* also refers to the electronic manipulation of alphabetic and numeric characters to serve various communication purposes.

    Centralized word processing. A system that locates all word processing activities within a single area in an organization.

    Decentralized word processing. A system that locates separate word processing facilities in different departments of an organization. The separate facilities are often called *satellite word processing centers*.

Word processing system. A specific combination of personnel, procedures, and automated equipment designed to handle the production of communications.

Word processor. The components that make up an **information processing** system. Most systems include a CPU (**central processing unit**), a **keyboard**, a **display screen**, a form of magnetic **storage**, and a **printer**.

    Blind word processor. A **word processor** without a **display screen**.

    Communicating word processor. A **word processor** that can transmit **text** and **graphics** to and receive them from a computer or another word processor via telephone lines or other electronic transmission links.

    Dedicated word processor. Electronic equipment designed specifically to perform text **editing** functions. (See also *Microcomputer*.)

Workstation. The basic components of a **word processor** (**keyboard, display screen,** and **printer**). *Workstation* also refers to a work area for an individual worker.

    Dumb workstation. A word processor in a **shared logic system,** which is entirely dependent on a remote **central processing unit** for operating instructions and **storage.** (Often called a *dumb terminal*.)

    Intelligent workstation. A word processor equipped with its own **central processing unit** and **storage.**

Wraparound. The ability of a **word processor** to automatically move words from one line to the next (*word wraparound*) or from one page to the next (*page wraparound*) as a result of insertions, deletions, or margin adjustments.

INDEX

This index contains many entries for individual words. If you are looking for a specific word that is not listed, refer to ¶719, which contains a 13-page guide to words that are frequently confused because they sound alike or look alike (for example, *capital–capitol–Capitol* or *stationary–stationery*).

NOTE: The **boldface** numbers in this index refer to paragraph numbers; the lightface numbers refer to page numbers.